THE

INNOCENTS ABROAD

THE OXFORD MARK TWAIN
Shelley Fisher Fishkin, Editor

The Celebrated Jumping Frog of Calaveras County, and Other Sketches
  Introduction: Roy Blount Jr.
  Afterword: Richard Bucci

The Innocents Abroad
  Introduction: Mordecai Richler
  Afterword: David E. E. Sloane

Roughing It
  Introduction: George Plimpton
  Afterword: Henry B. Wonham

The Gilded Age
  Introduction: Ward Just
  Afterword: Gregg Camfield

Sketches, New and Old
  Introduction: Lee Smith
  Afterword: Sherwood Cummings

The Adventures of Tom Sawyer
  Introduction: E. L. Doctorow
  Afterword: Albert E. Stone

A Tramp Abroad
  Introduction: Russell Banks
  Afterword: James S. Leonard

The Prince and the Pauper
>Introduction: Judith Martin
>Afterword: Everett Emerson

Life on the Mississippi
>Introduction: Willie Morris
>Afterword: Lawrence Howe

Adventures of Huckleberry Finn
>Introduction: Toni Morrison
>Afterword: Victor A. Doyno

A Connecticut Yankee in King Arthur's Court
>Introduction: Kurt Vonnegut, Jr.
>Afterword: Louis J. Budd

Merry Tales
>Introduction: Anne Bernays
>Afterword: Forrest G. Robinson

The American Claimant
>Introduction: Bobbie Ann Mason
>Afterword: Peter Messent

The £1,000,000 Bank-Note and Other New Stories
>Introduction: Malcolm Bradbury
>Afterword: James D. Wilson

Tom Sawyer Abroad
>Introduction: Nat Hentoff
>Afterword: M. Thomas Inge

The Tragedy of Pudd'nhead Wilson and the Comedy
Those Extraordinary Twins
>Introduction: Sherley Anne Williams
>Afterword: David Lionel Smith

Personal Recollections of Joan of Arc
  Introduction: Justin Kaplan
  Afterword: Susan K. Harris

The Stolen White Elephant and Other Detective Stories
  Introduction: Walter Mosley
  Afterword: Lillian S. Robinson

How to Tell a Story and Other Essays
  Introduction: David Bradley
  Afterword: Pascal Covici, Jr.

Following the Equator and Anti-imperialist Essays
  Introduction: Gore Vidal
  Afterword: Fred Kaplan

The Man That Corrupted Hadleyburg and Other Stories and Essays
  Introduction: Cynthia Ozick
  Afterword: Jeffrey Rubin-Dorsky

The Diaries of Adam and Eve
  Introduction: Ursula K. Le Guin
  Afterword: Laura E. Skandera-Trombley

What Is Man?
  Introduction: Charles Johnson
  Afterword: Linda Wagner-Martin

The $30,000 Bequest and Other Stories
  Introduction: Frederick Busch
  Afterword: Judith Yaross Lee

Christian Science
  Introduction: Garry Wills
  Afterword: Hamlin Hill

Chapters from My Autobiography
  Introduction: Arthur Miller
  Afterword: Michael J. Kiskis

1601, and Is Shakespeare Dead?
  Introduction: Erica Jong
  Afterword: Leslie A. Fiedler

Extract from Captain Stormfield's Visit to Heaven
  Introduction: Frederik Pohl
  Afterword: James A. Miller

Speeches
  Introduction: Hal Holbrook
  Afterword: David Barrow

The
Innocents Abroad

Mark Twain

FOREWORD

SHELLEY FISHER FISHKIN

INTRODUCTION

MORDECAI RICHLER

AFTERWORD

DAVID E. E. SLOANE

New York   Oxford

OXFORD UNIVERSI'

1996

OXFORD UNIVERSITY PRESS

Oxford   New York

Athens, Auckland, Bangkok, Bogotá, Bombay

Buenos Aires, Calcutta, Cape Town, Dar es Salaam

Delhi, Florence, Hong Kong, Istanbul, Karachi

Kuala Lumpur, Madras, Madrid, Melbourne

Mexico City, Nairobi, Paris, Singapore

Taipei, Tokyo, Toronto

and associated companies in

Berlin, Ibadan

Published by

Oxford University Press, Inc.

198 Madison Avenue, New York,

New York 10016

Library of Congress

Cataloging-in-Publication Data

Twain, Mark, 1835–1910.

The innocents abroad, or, The new Pilgrims'

progress / by Mark Twain; with an introduction

by Mordecai Richler; and an afterword by

David E. E. Sloane.

p. cm. — (The Oxford Mark Twain)

Includes bibliographical references.

1. Middle East—Description and travel.

2. Europe—Description and travel. I. Title.

II. Series Twain, Mark, 1835-1910. Works. 1996.

813'.403—dc20

[B]

96-12306

CIP

ISBN 0-19-510132-4 (trade ed.)

ISBN 0-19-511402-7 (lib. ed.)

ISBN 0-19-509088-8 (trade ed. set)

ISBN 0-19-511345-4 (lib. ed. set)

9 8 7 6 5 4 3 2 1

Printed in the United States of America

on acid-free paper

FRONTISPIECE

Samuel L. Clemens is seen here in 1869, the year
The Innocents Abroad was published. (From the
Mark Twain Collection of The James S. Copley
Library, La Jolla, California)

CONTENTS

Editor's Note, x

Foreword SHELLEY FISHER FISHKIN, xi

Introduction MORDECAI RICHLER, xxxi

The Innocents Abroad, or The New Pilgrims' Progress, follows xlv

Afterword DAVID E. E. SLOANE, 1

For Further Reading DAVID E. E. SLOANE, 19

Illustrators and Illustrations in Mark Twain's First
American Editions BEVERLY R. DAVID & RAY SAPIRSTEIN, 23

Reading the Illustrations in *The Innocents Abroad*
BEVERLY R. DAVID & RAY SAPIRSTEIN, 27

A Note on the Text ROBERT H. HIRST, 33

Contributors, 37

Acknowledgments, 39

EDITOR'S NOTE

The Oxford Mark Twain consists of twenty-nine volumes of facsimiles of the first American editions of Mark Twain's works, with an editor's foreword, new introductions, afterwords, notes on the texts, and essays on the illustrations in volumes with artwork. The facsimiles have been reproduced from the originals unaltered, except that blank pages in the front and back of the books have been omitted, and any seriously damaged or missing pages have been replaced by pages from other first editions (as indicated in the notes on the texts).

In the foreword, introduction, afterword, and essays on the illustrations, the titles of Mark Twain's works have been capitalized according to modern conventions, as have the names of characters (except where otherwise indicated). In the case of discrepancies between the title of a short story, essay, or sketch as it appears in the original table of contents and as it appears on its own title page, the title page has been followed. The parenthetical numbers in the introduction, afterwords, and illustration essays are page references to the facsimiles.

FOREWORD

Shelley Fisher Fishkin

Samuel Clemens entered the world and left it with Halley's Comet, little dreaming that generations hence Halley's Comet would be less famous than Mark Twain. He has been called the American Cervantes, our Homer, our Tolstoy, our Shakespeare, our Rabelais. Ernest Hemingway maintained that "all modern American literature comes from one book by Mark Twain called *Huckleberry Finn*." President Franklin Delano Roosevelt got the phrase "New Deal" from *A Connecticut Yankee in King Arthur's Court*. *The Gilded Age* gave an entire era its name. "The future historian of America," wrote George Bernard Shaw to Samuel Clemens, "will find your works as indispensable to him as a French historian finds the political tracts of Voltaire."[1]

There is a Mark Twain Bank in St. Louis, a Mark Twain Diner in Jackson Heights, New York, a Mark Twain Smoke Shop in Lakeland, Florida. There are Mark Twain Elementary Schools in Albuquerque, Dayton, Seattle, and Sioux Falls. Mark Twain's image peers at us from advertisements for Bass Ale (his drink of choice was Scotch), for a gas company in Tennessee, a hotel in the nation's capital, a cemetery in California.

Ubiquitous though his name and image may be, Mark Twain is in no danger of becoming a petrified icon. On the contrary: Mark Twain lives. *Huckleberry Finn* is "the most taught novel, most taught long work, and most taught piece of American literature" in American schools from junior high to the graduate level.[2] Hundreds of Twain impersonators appear in theaters, trade shows, and shopping centers in every region of the country.[3] Scholars publish hundreds of articles as well as books about Twain every year, and he is the subject of daily exchanges on the Internet. A journalist somewhere in the world finds a reason to quote Twain just about every day. Television series such as *Bonanza, Star Trek: The Next Generation*, and *Cheers* broadcast episodes that feature Mark Twain as a character. Hollywood screenwriters regularly produce movies inspired by his works, and writers of mysteries and science fiction continue to weave him into their plots.[4]

A century after the American Revolution sent shock waves throughout Europe, it took Mark Twain to explain to Europeans and to his countrymen alike what that revolution had wrought. He probed the significance of this new land and its new citizens, and identified what it was in the Old World that America abolished and rejected. The founding fathers had thought through the political dimensions of making a new society; Mark Twain took on the challenge of interpreting the social and cultural life of the United States for those outside its borders as well as for those who were living the changes he discerned.

Americans may have constructed a new society in the eighteenth century, but they articulated what they had done in voices that were largely interchangeable with those of Englishmen until well into the nineteenth century. Mark Twain became the voice of the new land, the leading translator of what and who the "American" was — and, to a large extent, is. Frances Trollope's *Domestic Manners of the Americans,* a best-seller in England, Hector St. John de Crèvecoeur's *Letters from an American Farmer,* and Tocqueville's *Democracy in America* all tried to explain America to Europeans. But Twain did more than that: he allowed European readers to *experience* this strange "new world." And he gave his countrymen the tools to do two things they had not quite had the confidence to do before. He helped them stand before the cultural icons of the Old World unembarrassed, unashamed of America's lack of palaces and shrines, proud of its brash practicality and bold inventiveness, unafraid to reject European models of "civilization" as tainted or corrupt. And he also helped them recognize their own insularity, boorishness, arrogance, or ignorance, and laugh at it — the first step toward transcending it and becoming more "civilized," in the best European sense of the word.

Twain often strikes us as more a creature of our time than of his. He appreciated the importance and the complexity of mass tourism and public relations, fields that would come into their own in the twentieth century but were only fledgling enterprises in the nineteenth. He explored the liberating potential of humor and the dynamics of friendship, parenting, and marriage. He narrowed the gap between "popular" and "high" culture, and he meditated on the enigmas of personal and national identity. Indeed, it would be difficult to find an issue on the horizon today that Twain did not touch on somewhere in his work. Heredity versus environment? Animal rights? The boundaries of gender? The place of black voices in the cultural heritage of the United States? Twain was there.

With startling prescience and characteristic grace and wit, he zeroed in on many of the key challenges — political, social, and technological — that would face his country and the world for the next hundred years: the challenge of race relations in a society founded on both chattel slavery and ideals of equality, and the intractable problem of racism in American life; the potential of new technologies to transform our lives in ways that can be both exhilarating and terrifying — as well as unpredictable; the problem of imperialism and the difficulties entailed in getting rid of it. But he never lost sight of the most basic challenge of all: each man or woman's struggle for integrity in the face of the seductions of power, status, and material things.

Mark Twain's unerring sense of the right word and not its second cousin taught people to pay attention when he spoke, in person or in print. He said things that were smart and things that were wise, and he said them incomparably well. He defined the rhythms of our prose and the contours of our moral map. He saw our best and our worst, our extravagant promise and our stunning failures, our comic foibles and our tragic flaws. Throughout the world he is viewed as the most distinctively American of American authors — and as one of the most universal. He is assigned in classrooms in Naples, Riyadh, Belfast, and Beijing, and has been a major influence on twentieth-century writers from Argentina to Nigeria to Japan. The Oxford Mark Twain celebrates the versatility and vitality of this remarkable writer.

The Oxford Mark Twain reproduces the first American editions of Mark Twain's books published during his lifetime.[5] By encountering Twain's works in their original format — typography, layout, order of contents, and illustrations — readers today can come a few steps closer to the literary artifacts that entranced and excited readers when the books first appeared. Twain approved of and to a greater or lesser degree supervised the publication of all of this material.[6] The Mark Twain House in Hartford, Connecticut, generously loaned us its originals.[7] When more than one copy of a first American edition was available, Robert H. Hirst, general editor of the Mark Twain Project, in cooperation with Marianne Curling, curator of the Mark Twain House (and Jeffrey Kaimowitz, head of Rare Books for the Watkinson Library of Trinity College, Hartford, where the Mark Twain House collection is kept), guided our decision about which one to use.[8] As a set, the volumes also contain more than eighty essays commissioned especially for The Oxford Mark Twain, in which distinguished contributors reassess Twain's achievement as a writer and his place in the cultural conversation that he did so much to shape.

Each volume of The Oxford Mark Twain is introduced by a leading American, Canadian, or British writer who responds to Twain — often in a very personal way — as a fellow writer. Novelists, journalists, humorists, columnists, fabulists, poets, playwrights — these writers tell us what Twain taught them and what in his work continues to speak to them. Reading Twain's books, both famous and obscure, they reflect on the genesis of his art and the characteristics of his style, the themes he illuminated, and the aesthetic strategies he pioneered. Individually and collectively their contributions testify to the place Mark Twain holds in the hearts of readers of all kinds and temperaments.

Scholars whose work has shaped our view of Twain in the academy today have written afterwords to each volume, with suggestions for further reading. Their essays give us a sense of what was going on in Twain's life when he wrote the book at hand, and of how that book fits into his career. They explore how each book reflects and refracts contemporary events, and they show Twain responding to literary and social currents of the day, variously accepting, amplifying, modifying, and challenging prevailing paradigms. Sometimes they argue that works previously dismissed as quirky or eccentric departures actually address themes at the heart of Twain's work from the start. And as they bring new perspectives to Twain's composition strategies in familiar texts, several scholars see experiments in form where others saw only form-lessness, method where prior critics saw only madness. In addition to eluci-dating the work's historical and cultural context, the afterwords provide an overview of responses to each book from its first appearance to the present.

Most of Mark Twain's books involved more than Mark Twain's words: unique illustrations. The parodic visual send-ups of "high culture" that Twain himself drew for *A Tramp Abroad*, the sketch of financial manipulator Jay Gould as a greedy and sadistic "Slave Driver" in *A Connecticut Yankee in King Arthur's Court*, and the memorable drawings of Eve in *Eve's Diary* all helped Twain's books to be sold, read, discussed, and preserved. In their es-says for each volume that contains artwork, Beverly R. David and Ray Sapirstein highlight the significance of the sketches, engravings, and pho-tographs in the first American editions of Mark Twain's works, and tell us what is known about the public response to them.

The Oxford Mark Twain invites us to read some relatively neglected works by Twain in the company of some of the most engaging literary figures of our time. Roy Blount Jr., for example, riffs in a deliciously Twain-like manner on "An Item Which the Editor Himself Could Not Understand," which may well rank as one of the least-known pieces Twain ever published. Bobbie Ann Mason celebrates the "mad energy" of Twain's most obscure comic novel, *The American Claimant*, in which the humor "hurtles beyond tall tale into simon-pure absurdity."[9] Garry Wills finds that *Christian Science* "gets us very close to the heart of American culture." Lee Smith reads "Political Economy" as a sharp and funny essay on language. Walter Mosley sees "The Stolen White Elephant," a story "reduced to a series of ridiculous telegrams related by an untrustworthy narrator caught up in an adventure that is as impossible as it is ludicrous," as a stunningly compact and economical satire of a world we still recognize as our own. Anne Bernays returns to "The Private History of a Campaign That Failed" and finds "an antiwar manifesto that is also confession, dramatic monologue, a plea for understanding and absolution, and a romp that gradually turns into atrocity even as we watch." After revisiting Captain Stormfield's heaven, Frederik Pohl finds that there "is no imaginable place more pleasant to spend eternity." Indeed, Pohl writes, "one would almost be willing to die to enter it."

While less familiar works receive fresh attention in The Oxford Mark Twain, new light is cast on the best-known works as well. Judith Martin ("Miss Manners") points out that it is by reading a court etiquette book that Twain's pauper learns how to behave as a proper prince. As important as etiquette may be in the palace, Martin notes, it is even more important in the slums.

> That etiquette is a sorer point with the ruffians in the street than with the proud dignitaries of the prince's court may surprise some readers. As in our own streets, etiquette is always a more volatile subject among those who cannot count on being treated with respect than among those who have the power to command deference.

And taking a fresh look at *Adventures of Huckleberry Finn,* Toni Morrison writes,

> much of the novel's genius lies in its quiescence, the silences that pervade it and give it a porous quality that is by turns brooding and soothing. It lies in . . . the subdued images in which the repetition of a simple word, such as "lonesome," tolls like an evening bell; the moments when nothing is said, when scenes and incidents swell the heart unbearably precisely because unarticulated, and force an act of imagination almost against the will.

Engaging Mark Twain as one writer to another, several contributors to The Oxford Mark Twain offer new insights into the processes by which his books came to be. Russell Banks, for example, reads *A Tramp Abroad* as "an important revision of Twain's incomplete first draft of *Huckleberry Finn,* a second draft, if you will, which in turn made possible the third and final draft." Erica Jong suggests that *1601,* a freewheeling parody of Elizabethan manners and mores, written during the same summer Twain began *Huckleberry Finn*, served as "a warm-up for his creative process" and "primed the pump for other sorts of freedom of expression." And Justin Kaplan suggests that "one of the transcendent figures standing behind and shaping" *Joan of Arc* was Ulysses S. Grant, whose memoirs Twain had recently published, and who, like Joan, had risen unpredictably "from humble and obscure origins" to become a "military genius" endowed with "the gift of command, a natural eloquence, and an equally natural reserve."

As a number of contributors note, Twain was a man ahead of his times. *The Gilded Age* was the first "Washington novel," Ward Just tells us, because "Twain was the first to see the possibilities that had eluded so many others." Commenting on *The Tragedy of Pudd'nhead Wilson,* Sherley Anne Williams observes that "Twain's argument about the power of environment in shaping character runs directly counter to prevailing sentiment where the negro was concerned." Twain's fictional technology, wildly fanciful by the standards of his day, predicts developments we take for granted in ours. DNA cloning, fax machines, and photocopiers are all prefigured, Bobbie Ann Mason tells us, in *The American Claimant.* Cynthia Ozick points out that the "telelectrophonoscope" we meet in "From the 'London Times' of 1904" is suspiciously like what we know as "television." And Malcolm Bradbury suggests that in the "phrenophones" of "Mental Telegraphy" "the Internet was born."

Twain turns out to have been remarkably prescient about political affairs as well. Kurt Vonnegut sees in *A Connecticut Yankee* a chilling foreshadowing (or perhaps a projection from the Civil War) of "all the high-tech atrocities which followed, and which follow still." Cynthia Ozick suggests that "The Man That Corrupted Hadleyburg," along with some of the other pieces collected under that title — many of them written when Twain lived in a Vienna ruled by Karl Lueger, a demagogue Adolf Hitler would later idolize — shoot up moral flares that shed an eerie light on the insidious corruption, prejudice, and hatred that reached bitter fruition under the Third Reich. And Twain's portrait in this book of "the dissolving Austria-Hungary of the 1890s," in Ozick's view, presages not only the Sarajevo that would erupt in 1914 but also "the disintegrated components of the former Yugoslavia" and "the *fin-de-siècle* Sarajevo of our own moment."

Despite their admiration for Twain's ambitious reach and scope, contributors to The Oxford Mark Twain also recognize his limitations. Mordecai Richler, for example, thinks that "the early pages of *Innocents Abroad* suffer from being a tad broad, proffering more burlesque than inspired satire," perhaps because Twain was "trying too hard for knee-slappers." Charles Johnson notes that the Young Man in Twain's philosophical dialogue about free will and determinism (*What Is Man?*) "caves in far too soon," failing to challenge what through late-twentieth-century eyes looks like "pseudoscience" and suspect essentialism in the Old Man's arguments.

Some contributors revisit their first encounters with Twain's works, recalling what surprised or intrigued them. When David Bradley came across "Fenimore Cooper's Literary Offences" in his college library, he "did not at first realize that Twain was being his usual ironic self with all this business about the 'nineteen rules governing literary art in the domain of romantic fiction,' but by the time I figured out there was no such list outside Twain's own head, I had decided that the rules made *sense*. . . . It seemed to me they were a pretty good blueprint for writing — Negro writing included." Sherley Anne Williams remembers that part of what attracted her to *Pudd'nhead Wilson* when she first read it thirty years ago was "that Twain, writing at the end of the nineteenth century, could imagine negroes as characters, albeit white ones, who actually thought for and of themselves, whose actions were the product of their thinking rather than the spontaneous ephemera of physical instincts that stereotype assigned to blacks." Frederik Pohl recalls his first reading of *Huckleberry Finn* as "a watershed event" in his life, the first book he read as a child in which "bad people" ceased to exercise a monopoly on doing "bad things." In *Huckleberry Finn* "some seriously bad things — things like the possession and mistreatment of black slaves, like stealing and lying, even like killing other people in duels — were quite often done by people who not only thought of themselves as exemplarily moral but, by any other standards I knew how to apply, actually *were* admirable citizens." The world that

Tom and Huck lived in, Pohl writes, "was filled with complexities and contradictions," and resembled "the world I appeared to be living in myself."

Other contributors explore their more recent encounters with Twain, explaining why they have revised their initial responses to his work. For Toni Morrison, parts of *Huckleberry Finn* that she "once took to be deliberate evasions, stumbles even, or a writer's impatience with his or her material," now strike her "as otherwise: as entrances, crevices, gaps, seductive invitations flashing the possibility of meaning. Unarticulated eddies that encourage diving into the novel's undertow — the real place where writer captures reader." One such "eddy" is the imprisonment of Jim on the Phelps farm. Instead of dismissing this portion of the book as authorial bungling, as she once did, Morrison now reads it as Twain's commentary on the 1880s, a period that "saw the collapse of civil rights for blacks," a time when "the nation, as well as Tom Sawyer, was deferring Jim's freedom in agonizing play." Morrison believes that Americans in the 1880s were attempting "to bury the combustible issues Twain raised in his novel," and that those who try to kick Huck Finn out of school in the 1990s are doing the same: "The cyclical attempts to remove the novel from classrooms extend Jim's captivity on into each generation of readers."

Although imitation-Hemingway and imitation-Faulkner writing contests draw hundreds of entries annually, no one has ever tried to mount a faux-Twain competition. Why? Perhaps because Mark Twain's voice is too much a part of who we are and how we speak even today. Roy Blount Jr. suggests that it is impossible, "at least for an American writer, to parody Mark Twain. It would be like doing an impression of your father or mother: he or she is already there in your voice."

Twain's style is examined and celebrated in The Oxford Mark Twain by fellow writers who themselves have struggled with the nuances of words, the structure of sentences, the subtleties of point of view, and the trickiness of opening lines. Bobbie Ann Mason observes, for example, that "Twain loved the sound of words and he knew how to string them by sound, like different shades of one color: 'The earl's barbaric eye,' 'the Usurping Earl,' 'a double-dyed humbug.'" Twain "relied on the punch of plain words" to show writers how to move beyond the "wordy romantic rubbish" so prevalent in nineteenth-century fiction, Mason says; he "was one of the first writers in America to deflower literary language." Lee Smith believes that "American writers have benefited as much from the way Mark Twain opened up the possibilities of first-person narration as we have from his use of vernacular language." (She feels that "the ghost of Mark Twain was hovering someplace in the background" when she decided to write her novel *Oral History* from the standpoint of multiple first-person narrators.) Frederick Busch maintains that "A Dog's Tale" "boasts one of the great opening sentences" of all time: "My father was a St. Bernard, my mother was a collie, but I am a Presbyterian." And Ursula Le Guin marvels at the ingenuity of the following sentence that she encounters in *Extracts from Adam's Diary*.

> . . . This made her sorry for the creatures which live in there, which she calls fish, for she continues to fasten names on to things that don't need them and don't come when they are called by them, which is a matter of no consequence to her, as she is such a numskull anyway; so she got a lot of them out and brought them in last night and put them in my bed to keep warm, but I have noticed them now and then all day, and I don't see that they are any happier there than they were before, only quieter.[10]

Le Guin responds,

> Now, that is a pure Mark-Twain-tour-de-force sentence, covering an immense amount of territory in an effortless, aimless ramble that seems to be heading nowhere in particular and ends up with breathtaking accuracy at the gold mine. Any sensible child would find that funny, perhaps not following all its divagations but delighted by the swing of it, by the word "numskull," by the idea of putting fish in the bed; and as that child grew older and reread it, its reward would only grow; and if that grown-up child had to write an essay on the piece and therefore earnestly studied and pored over this sentence, she would end up in unmitigated admiration of its vocabulary, syntax, pacing, sense, and rhythm, above all the beautiful

timing of the last two words; and she would, and she does, still find it funny.

The fish surface again in a passage that Gore Vidal calls to our attention, from *Following the Equator*: "'The Whites always mean well when they take human fish out of the ocean and try to make them dry and warm and happy and comfortable in a chicken coop,' which is how, through civilization, they did away with many of the original inhabitants. Lack of empathy is a principal theme in Twain's meditations on race and empire."

Indeed, empathy — and its lack — is a principal theme in virtually all of Twain's work, as contributors frequently note. Nat Hentoff quotes the following thoughts from Huck in *Tom Sawyer Abroad*:

I see a bird setting on a dead limb of a high tree, singing with its head tilted back and its mouth open, and before I thought I fired, and his song stopped and he fell straight down from the limb, all limp like a rag, and I run and picked him up and he was dead, and his body was warm in my hand, and his head rolled about this way and that, like his neck was broke, and there was a little white skin over his eyes, and one little drop of blood on the side of his head; and laws! I could n't see nothing more for the tears; and I hain't never murdered no creature since that war n't doing me no harm, and I ain't going to.[11]

"The Humane Society," Hentoff writes, "has yet to say anything as powerful — and lasting."

Readers of The Oxford Mark Twain will have the pleasure of revisiting Twain's Mississippi landmarks alongside Willie Morris, whose own lower Mississippi Valley boyhood gives him a special sense of connection to Twain. Morris knows firsthand the mosquitoes described in *Life on the Mississippi* — so colossal that "two of them could whip a dog" and "four of them could hold a man down"; in Morris's own hometown they were so large during the flood season that "local wags said they wore wristwatches." Morris's Yazoo City and Twain's Hannibal shared a "rough-hewn democracy ... complicated by all the visible textures of caste and class, ... harmless boyhood fun and mischief right along with . . . rank hypocrisies, churchgoing sanctimonies, racial hatred, entrenched and unrepentant greed."

For the West of Mark Twain's *Roughing It*, readers will have George Plimpton as their guide. "What a group these newspapermen were!" Plimpton writes about Twain and his friends Dan De Quille and Joe Goodman in Virginia City, Nevada. "Their roisterous carryings-on bring to mind the kind of frat-house enthusiasm one associates with college humor magazines like the *Harvard Lampoon*." Malcolm Bradbury examines Twain as "a living example of what made the American so different from the European." And Hal Holbrook, who has interpreted Mark Twain on stage for some forty years, describes how Twain "played" during the civil rights movement, during the Vietnam War, during the Gulf War, and in Prague on the eve of the demise of Communism.

Why do we continue to read Mark Twain? What draws us to him? His wit? His compassion? His humor? His bravura? His humility? His understanding of who and what we are in those parts of our being that we rarely open to view? Our sense that he knows we can do better than we do? Our sense that he knows we can't? E. L. Doctorow tells us that children are attracted to *Tom Sawyer* because in this book "the young reader confirms his own hope that no matter how troubled his relations with his elders may be, beneath all their disapproval is their underlying love for him, constant and steadfast." Readers in general, Arthur Miller writes, value Twain's "insights into America's always uncertain moral life and its shifting but everlasting hypocrisies"; we appreciate the fact that he "is not using his alienation from the public illusions of his hour in order to reject the country implicitly as though he could live without it, but manifestly in order to correct it." Perhaps we keep reading Mark Twain because, in Miller's words, he "wrote much more like a father than a son. He doesn't seem to be sitting in class taunting the teacher but standing at the head of it challenging his students to acknowledge their own humanity, that is, their immemorial attraction to the untrue."

Mark Twain entered the public eye at a time when many of his countrymen considered "American culture" an oxymoron; he died four years before a world conflagration that would lead many to question whether the contradiction in terms was not "European civilization" instead. In between he worked in journalism, printing, steamboating, mining, lecturing, publishing, and editing, in virtually every region of the country. He tried his hand at humorous sketches, social satire, historical novels, children's books, poetry, drama, science fiction, mysteries, romance, philosophy, travelogue, memoir, polemic, and several genres no one had ever seen before or has ever seen since. He invented a self-pasting scrapbook, a history game, a vest strap, and a gizmo for keeping bed sheets tucked in; he invested in machines and processes designed to revolutionize typesetting and engraving, and in a food supplement called "Plasmon." Along the way he cheerfully impersonated himself and prior versions of himself for doting publics on five continents while playing out a charming rags-to-riches story followed by a devastating riches-to-rags story followed by yet another great American comeback. He had a long-running real-life engagement in a sumptuous comedy of manners, and then in a real-life tragedy not of his own design: during the last fourteen years of his life almost everyone he ever loved was taken from him by disease and death.

Mark Twain has indelibly shaped our views of who and what the United States is as a nation and of who and what we might become. He understood the nostalgia for a "simpler" past that increased as that past receded — and he saw through the nostalgia to a past that was just as complex as the present. He recognized better than we did ourselves our potential for greatness and our potential for disaster. His fictions brilliantly illuminated the world in which he lived, changing it — and us — in the process. He knew that our feet often danced to tunes that had somehow remained beyond our hearing; with perfect pitch he played them back to us.

My mother read *Tom Sawyer* to me as a bedtime story when I was eleven. I thought Huck and Tom could be a lot of fun, but I dismissed Becky Thatcher as a bore. When I was twelve I invested a nickel at a local garage sale in a book that contained short pieces by Mark Twain. That was where I met Twain's Eve. Now, *that's* more like it, I decided, pleased to meet a female character I could identify *with* instead of against. Eve had spunk. Even if she got a lot wrong, you had to give her credit for trying. "The Man That Corrupted

Hadleyburg" left me giddy with satisfaction: none of my adolescent reveries of getting even with my enemies were half as neat as the plot of the man who got back at that town. "How I Edited an Agricultural Paper" set me off in uncontrollable giggles.

People sometimes told me that I looked like Huck Finn. "It's the freckles," they'd explain — not explaining anything at all. I didn't read *Huckleberry Finn* until junior year in high school in my English class. It was the fall of 1965. I was living in a small town in Connecticut. I expected a sequel to *Tom Sawyer*. So when the teacher handed out the books and announced our assignment, my jaw dropped: "Write a paper on how Mark Twain used irony to attack racism in *Huckleberry Finn*."

The year before, the bodies of three young men who had gone to Mississippi to help blacks register to vote — James Chaney, Andrew Goodman, and Michael Schwerner — had been found in a shallow grave; a group of white segregationists (the county sheriff among them) had been arrested in connection with the murders. America's inner cities were simmering with pent-up rage that began to explode in the summer of 1965, when riots in Watts left thirty-four people dead. None of this made any sense to me. I was confused, angry, certain that there was something missing from the news stories I read each day: the why. Then I met Pap Finn. And the Phelpses.

Pap Finn, Huck tells us, "had been drunk over in town" and "was just all mud." He erupts into a drunken tirade about "a free nigger . . . from Ohio — a mulatter, most as white as a white man," with "the whitest shirt on you ever see, too, and the shiniest hat; and there ain't a man in town that's got as fine clothes as what he had."

> . . . they said he was a p'fessor in a college, and could talk all kinds of languages, and knowed everything. And that ain't the wust. They said he could *vote*, when he was at home. Well, that let me out. Thinks I, what is the country a-coming to? It was 'lection day, and I was just about to go and vote, myself, if I warn't too drunk to get there; but when they told me there was a State in this country where they'd let that nigger vote, I drawed out. I says I'll never vote agin. Them's the very words I said. . . . And to see the

cool way of that nigger — why, he wouldn't a give me the road if I hadn't shoved him out o' the way.[12]

Later on in the novel, when the runaway slave Jim gives up his freedom to nurse a wounded Tom Sawyer, a white doctor testifies to the stunning altruism of his actions. The Phelpses and their neighbors, all fine, upstanding, well-meaning, churchgoing folk,

> agreed that Jim had acted very well, and was deserving to have some notice took of it, and reward. So every one of them promised, right out and hearty, that they wouldn't curse him no more.
>
> Then they come out and locked him up. I hoped they was going to say he could have one or two of the chains took off, because they was rotten heavy, or could have meat and greens with his bread and water, but they didn't think of it.[13]

Why did the behavior of these people tell me more about why Watts burned than anything I had read in the daily paper? And why did a drunk Pap Finn railing against a black college professor from Ohio whose vote was as good as his own tell me more about white anxiety over black political power than anything I had seen on the evening news?

Mark Twain knew that there was nothing, absolutely *nothing*, a black man could do — including selflessly sacrificing his freedom, the only thing of value he had — that would make white society see beyond the color of his skin. And Mark Twain knew that depicting racists with chilling accuracy would expose the viciousness of their world view like nothing else could. It was an insight echoed some eighty years after Mark Twain penned Pap Finn's rantings about the black professor, when Malcolm X famously asked, "Do you know what white racists call black Ph.D.'s?" and answered, " '*Nigger!*' "[14]

Mark Twain taught me things I needed to know. He taught me to understand the raw racism that lay behind what I saw on the evening news. He taught me that the most well-meaning people can be hurtful and myopic. He taught me to recognize the supreme irony of a country founded in freedom that continued to deny freedom to so many of its citizens. Every time I hear of another effort to kick Huck Finn out of school somewhere, I recall everything that Mark Twain taught *this* high school junior, and I find myself jumping into the fray.[15] I remember the black high school student who called CNN during the phone-in portion of a 1985 debate between Dr. John Wallace, a black educator spearheading efforts to ban the book, and myself. She accused Dr. Wallace of insulting her and all black high school students by suggesting they weren't smart enough to understand Mark Twain's irony. And I recall the black cameraman on the *CBS Morning News* who came up to me after he finished shooting another debate between Dr. Wallace and myself. He said he had never read the book by Mark Twain that we had been arguing about — but now he really wanted to. One thing that puzzled him, though, was why a white woman was defending it and a black man was attacking it, because as far as he could see from what we'd been saying, the book made whites look pretty bad.

As I came to understand *Huckleberry Finn* and *Pudd'nhead Wilson* as commentaries on the era now known as the nadir of American race relations, those books pointed me toward the world recorded in nineteenth-century black newspapers and periodicals and in fiction by Mark Twain's black contemporaries. My investigation of the role black voices and traditions played in shaping Mark Twain's art helped make me aware of their role in shaping all of American culture.[16] My research underlined for me the importance of changing the stories we tell about who we are to reflect the realities of what we've been.[17]

Ever since our encounter in high school English, Mark Twain has shown me the potential of American literature and American history to illuminate each other. Rarely have I found a contradiction or complexity we grapple with as a nation that Mark Twain had not puzzled over as well. He insisted on taking America seriously. And he insisted on *not* taking America seriously: "I think that there is but a single specialty with us, only one thing that can be called by the wide name 'American,'" he once wrote. "That is the national devotion to ice-water."[18]

Mark Twain threw back at us our dreams and our denial of those dreams, our greed, our goodness, our ambition, and our laziness, all rattling around together in that vast echo chamber of our talk — that sharp, spunky American talk that Mark Twain figured out how to write down without robbing it of its energy and immediacy. Talk shaped by voices that the official arbiters of "culture" deemed of no importance — voices of children, voices of slaves, voices of servants, voices of ordinary people. Mark Twain listened. And he made us listen. To the stories he told us, and to the truths they conveyed. He still has a lot to say that we need to hear.

Mark Twain lives — in our libraries, classrooms, homes, theaters, movie houses, streets, and most of all in our speech. His optimism energizes us, his despair sobers us, and his willingness to keep wrestling with the hilarious and horrendous complexities of it all keeps us coming back for more. As the twenty-first century approaches, may he continue to goad us, chasten us, delight us, berate us, and cause us to erupt in unrestrained laughter in unexpected places.

NOTES

1. Ernest Hemingway, *Green Hills of Africa* (New York: Charles Scribner's Sons, 1935), 22. George Bernard Shaw to Samuel L. Clemens, July 3, 1907, quoted in Albert Bigelow Paine, *Mark Twain: A Biography* (New York: Harper and Brothers, 1912), 3:1398.

2. Allen Carey-Webb, "Racism and *Huckleberry Finn*: Censorship, Dialogue and Change," *English Journal* 82, no. 7 (November 1993):22.

3. See Louis J. Budd, "Impersonators," in J. R. LeMaster and James D. Wilson, eds., *The Mark Twain Encyclopedia* (New York: Garland Publishing Company, 1993), 389–91.

4. See Shelley Fisher Fishkin, "Ripples and Reverberations," part 3 of *Lighting Out for the Territory: Reflections on Mark Twain and American Culture* (New York: Oxford University Press, 1996).

5. There are two exceptions. Twain published chapters from his autobiography in the *North American Review* in 1906 and 1907, but this material was not published in book form in Twain's lifetime; our volume reproduces the material as it appeared in the *North American Review*. The other exception is our final volume, *Mark Twain's Speeches*, which appeared two months after Twain's death in 1910.

An unauthorized handful of copies of *1601* was privately printed by an Alexander Gunn of Cleveland at the instigation of Twain's friend John Hay in 1880. The first American edition authorized by Mark Twain, however, was printed at the United States Military Academy at West Point in 1882; that is the edition reproduced here.

It should further be noted that four volumes — *The Stolen White Elephant and Other Detective Stories, Following the Equator and Anti-imperialist Essays, The Diaries of Adam and Eve, and 1601, and Is Shakespeare Dead?* — bind together material originally published separately. In each case the first American edition of the material is the version that has been reproduced, always in its entirety. Because Twain constantly recycled and repackaged previously published works in his collections of short pieces, a certain amount of duplication is unavoidable. We have selected volumes with an eye toward keeping this duplication to a minimum.

Even the twenty-nine-volume Oxford Mark Twain has had to leave much out. No edition of Twain can ever claim to be "complete," for the man was too prolix, and the file drawers of both ephemera and as yet unpublished texts are deep.

6. With the possible exception of *Mark Twain's Speeches*. Some scholars suspect Twain knew about this book and may have helped shape it, although no hard evidence to that effect has yet surfaced. Twain's involvement in the production process varied greatly from book to book. For a fuller sense of authorial intention, scholars will continue to rely on the superb definitive editions of Twain's works produced by the Mark Twain Project at the University of California at Berkeley as they become available. Dense with annotation documenting textual emendation and related issues, these editions add immeasurably to our understanding of Mark Twain and the genesis of his works.

7. Except for a few titles that were not in its collection. The American Antiquarian Society in Worcester, Massachusetts, provided the first edition of *King Leopold's Soliloquy*; the Elmer Holmes Bobst Library of New York University furnished the 1906–7 volumes of the *North American Review* in which *Chapters from My Autobiography* first appeared; the Harry Ransom Humanities Research Center at the University of Texas at Austin made their copy of the West Point edition of *1601* available; and the Mark Twain Project provided the first edition of *Extract from Captain Stormfield's Visit to Heaven*.

8. The specific copy photographed for Oxford's facsimile edition is indicated in a note on the text at the end of each volume.

9. All quotations from contemporary writers in this essay are taken from their introductions to the volumes of The Oxford Mark Twain, and the quotations from Mark Twain's works are taken from the texts reproduced in The Oxford Mark Twain.

10. *The Diaries of Adam and Eve*, The Oxford Mark Twain [hereafter OMT] (New York: Oxford University Press, 1996), p. 33.

11. *Tom Sawyer Abroad*, OMT, p. 74.

12. *Adventures of Huckleberry Finn*, OMT, p. 49–50.

13. Ibid., p. 358.

14. Malcolm X, *The Autobiography of Malcolm X*, with the assistance of Alex Haley (New York: Grove Press, 1965), p. 284.

15. I do not mean to minimize the challenge of teaching this difficult novel, a challenge for which all teachers may not feel themselves prepared. Elsewhere I have developed some concrete strategies for approaching the book in the classroom, including teaching it in the context of the history of American race relations and alongside books by black writers. See Shelley Fisher Fishkin, "Teaching *Huckleberry Finn*," in James S. Leonard, ed., *Making Mark Twain Work in the Classroom* (Durham: Duke University Press, forthcoming). See also Shelley Fisher Fishkin, *Was Huck Black? Mark Twain and African-American Voices* (New York: Oxford University Press, 1993), pp. 106–8, and a curriculum kit in preparation at the Mark Twain House in Hartford, containing teaching suggestions from myself, David Bradley, Jocelyn Chadwick-Joshua, James Miller, and David E. E. Sloane.

16. See Fishkin, *Was Huck Black?* See also Fishkin, "Interrogating 'Whiteness,' Complicating 'Blackness': Remapping American Culture," in Henry Wonham, ed., *Criticism and the Color Line: Desegregating American Literary Studies* (New Brunswick: Rutgers UP, 1996, pp. 251–90 and in shortened form in *American Quarterly* 47, no. 3 (September 1995):428–66.

17. I explore the roots of my interest in Mark Twain and race at greater length in an essay entitled "Changing the Story," in Jeffrey Rubin-Dorsky and Shelley Fisher Fishkin, eds., *People of the Book: Thirty Scholars Reflect on Their Jewish Identity* (Madison: U of Wisconsin Press, 1996), pp. 47–63.

18. "What Paul Bourget Thinks of Us," *How to Tell a Story and Other Essays*, OMT, p. 197.

INTRODUCTION

Mordecai Richler

The business of getting from here to there has become increasingly frustrating, even infuriating, and I speak as someone who once adored traveling, the slaphappy sensation of traipsing down the twisting streets of a foreign city for the first time, your jaded senses heightened by what Gerard Manley Hopkins celebrated as "all things counter, original, spare, strange."

Nowadays, disembark in Moscow, Barcelona, or Tel Aviv, set out for the main boulevard, and you are bound to be deflated by the familiar: a McDonald's, a Giorgio Armani boutique, a Gucci, a pizza bar, and a shop called Wyatt Urp or Doge City specializing in designer jeans and hand-tooled Western boots made by prisoners in China. Overpriced restaurants will welcome American Express, Visa, and Mastercharge. CNN will be available on your hotel TV, and you can count on the indigenous channel to be showing reruns of *Dallas* or *Cheers*, dubbed in Russian, Spanish, or Hebrew. Mind you, these latter variations on the familiar can be inadvertently amusing.

Item: In 1951, drifting down the Ramblas in Barcelona, somewhat footsore, I slipped into a cinema to catch a Joel McCrea Western dubbed in Spanish, and lo and behold, good old reliable Joel moseyed up to a saloon bar in Tombstone and demanded, *"Uno cognac, por favor."*

I first crossed the Atlantic, at the age of nineteen, in 1950, on board the *Franconia*, outward bound from Quebec City to Liverpool. In those days everybody in tourist class on an ocean liner or propeller-driven airplane was equal, paying the same fare. But nowadays, after you have probably forked out something like a thousand bucks for your jumbo jet "hospitality" (that is to say, cattle-class) round-trip ticket to Paris, Rome, or wherever, the odds are that the three-hundred-pound behemoth shoehorned into the seat beside you, having promised to fly on a rainy Wednesday while wearing his track suit with the Day-Glo stripes, has acquired his ticket for $49.95, payable in twelve installments. Furthermore, that price includes four nights in a two-star hotel, a clutch of theater tickets, and coupons that will yield magnums of Dom Perignon in any number of restaurants. And if that isn't enough to put you in yippee mood, it turns out that fatso, once he has stowed away a ton of "carry-on" luggage under his seat *and* yours, is a compulsive nose picker or a master of the silent fart, earning *you* dirty looks from everyone in the rows ahead and behind. And naturally he is a talker who wants to know how the world is treating you and where do you hail from?

"Montreal," I once said, on an Air France flight out of New York.

"Gosh. That's my favorite city in the United States."

Freeze out your seatmate, and he retaliates by fishing into one of his bulging flight bags and surfacing with the latest Garfield paperback, which has him quaking with laughter for the next four hours of flight time. The rest of the jet, it goes without saying, is usually filled with shrieking babes, kids playing tag, teenagers jerking their heads in time to the rock beat leaking out of the Walkman clamped to their ears, middle-aged wits who feel entitled to flirt with the stewardesses ("I've got the time, if you've got the place?"), and battalions of Japanese tourists laden with state-of-the-art camcorders, shooting videos of cloud formations, of flight attendants propelling drink trolleys, and of each other standing up, sitting down, and performing other astonishing feats.

Then, after bouncing about at 35,000 feet for seven hours, snug as a sardine in a tin, you land, ears throbbing with pain, and line up in an overheated hall to pass through immigration. This will take an hour, maybe more, because either you have arrived just after a flight from Colombia, every passenger a suspected drug smuggler, or there's an obviously troubled African immediately ahead of you in line, who claims to be a citizen of Finland and is armed with an inch-thick passport that opens like an accordion and calls for a half-hour examination by the suspicious immigration officer.

Finally, you reach your hotel — smelly, eyes bloodshot — only to be welcomed by the news that they have no record of your reservation or that your room, overlooking a parking lot, won't be ready for another four hours. Never mind. The bar is open, and there you can contemplate the ordeals that lie ahead: all those museums and churches and castles you will be obliged to visit and, in the most exclusive restaurants, the snotty waiters you will have to tolerate. Because you are a North American, they will unfailingly check you out to make sure you are wearing shoes, and treat you as if you were about to sample your first glass of wine.

Ah, but it was utterly different, still an amazing, even daring adventure, when the incomparable Mark Twain, né Samuel Langhorne Clemens in 1835, set out on an "EXCURSION TO THE HOLY LAND, EGYPT, THE CRIMEA, GREECE, AND INTERMEDIATE POINTS OF INTEREST" on the *Quaker City*, a paddle steamer, sailing out of New York on June 8, 1867. In Twain's time the world had not yet become a village to be avoided. Escape was still possible and novelty was the happy rule.

"The proprietors of the *Daily Alta California*," Twain recalled in his autobiography, "engaged me to write an account of the trip for that paper — fifty letters of a column and a half each, which would be about 2,000 words per letter, and the pay to be twenty dollars per letter."

Twain, thirty-one years old at the time, set sail as just another freelance hack, and returned as the first true master of the American idiom. This he accomplished at a time when, as Stephen Leacock wrote in his biography of Twain, "of American literature there was much doubt in Europe; of American honesty, much more; of American manners, more still." But I knew nothing of that when I first came across the writings of Mark Twain, introduced to them, like most boys of my generation, through *The Adventures of Tom Sawyer*, a gift from an uncle.

I would like to claim that reading Twain for the first time made for an epiphany, but it wasn't the case. I was far more taken with *Scaramouche*, *The Three Musketeers*, *The Count of Monte Cristo*, and *Robin Hood*. Settling into bed for the night, I dreamed of humiliating the dastardly Sheriff of Nottingham with my dazzling swordplay, or galloping off with D'Artagnan and his chums, all for one, one for all. Titled ladies were my heart's desire. My problem was I knew kids like Tom Sawyer, who might try to con me into painting their fence. It was familiar and therefore couldn't count as literature, like, say, Shelley's "Ode to the West Wind," which I had to copy out ten times after my class master caught me ogling a copy of *Sunbathing* in his Highroads to Reading class.

I was a slow learner. And so only later, after I had read *Huckleberry Finn* for a second time, did I grasp that I was in the presence of a great writer, somebody who could convey more about the white American's prejudice against blacks in one seemingly effortless colloquial exchange than many a polemicist could manage in ten fulminating, fact-bound pages.

Huck tells Aunt Sally, "It warn't the grounding [of the steamer] — that didn't keep us back but a little. We blowed out a cylinder-head."

"Good gracious! Anybody hurt?"

"No'm. Killed a nigger."

"Well, it's lucky; because sometimes people do get hurt."

The advertisement for the sailing of the *Quaker City* claimed there would be cabins sufficient to accommodate "a select company" of 150 on a "first-class steamer" provided "with every necessary comfort, including library and musical instruments," as well as "an experienced physician . . . on board" (20). The price, on what was actually America's first venture into mass tourism, a harbinger of the heavy traffic to come, was $1,250 for each adult passenger, who was advised that $5 per day, in gold, would be sufficient to handle any needs on shore.

Anticipating many an overpromoted tour in later years, the promised shipboard celebrities were notable by their absence. Urgent duties, a bemused Twain noted, obliged the Reverend Henry Ward Beecher to give up the idea, and the Indian wars compelled Lieutenant General Sherman's presence on the plains. "A popular actress has entered her name on the ship's books, but something interfered, and *she* couldn't go. The 'Drummer Boy of the Potomac' deserted, and lo, we had never a celebrity left!"

As with so many of today's "love boats," advertised by decks adorned with sexy, bikini-clad young women, what the *Quaker City* did in fact deliver was a plethora of what my daughter calls cotton-tops, or as Twain had it, venerable people, among them "three ministers of the gospel, eight doctors, sixteen or eighteen ladies, several military and naval chieftains with sounding titles, an ample crop of 'Professors' of various kinds, and a gentleman who had 'COMMISSIONER OF THE UNITED STATES OF AMERICA TO EUROPE, ASIA, AND AFRICA' thundering under his name in one awful blast!" And none of them, I'm sure, suspected that they would be the victims of a rollicking satire that still reads freshly more than a century after its first publication.

In Twain's belowdecks cabin, which he was to share with a young gentleman, there was room to turn around in but not to swing a cat. Happily, however, the saloon bar, which the unregenerated dubbed the "Synagogue," was a good fifty or sixty feet long, and the ship's company boasted not one, not two, but five captains.

Having crossed the Atlantic several times myself on modern liners equipped with stabilizers, still a sick-making ordeal in heavy seas, I can only marvel at what Twain and his companions must have endured on their little paddle steamer. But Twain makes reference to only one Atlantic gale, wherein the *Quaker City* "climbed aloft as if she would climb to heaven — then paused an instant that seemed a century, and plunged headlong down again, as from a precipice" (62).

First port of call was in the Azores, and it becomes instantly clear that the freewheeling Twain, bless him, is not going to be shackled by political correctness. Oh dear oh dear. Given today's touchy political climate, I suspect there is sufficient kindling in *The Innocents Abroad* to light a fire of protest under Portuguese, Italians, Moslems, Catholics, Turks, Greeks, feminists, Arabs, American Indians, and other sensitive types. I have no doubt that

Innocents Abroad, released today, would be banned in schools, the author condemned as a racist, and possibly, just possibly, finding himself the subject of a *fatwa*.

The Portuguese people of the Azores, wrote Twain, lie, and cheat the stranger, and are "slow, poor, shiftless, sleepy, and lazy." He didn't fancy the women of Tangier.

> I have caught a glimpse of the faces of several Moorish women, (for they are only human, and will expose their faces for the admiration of a Christian dog when no male Moor is by,) and I am full of veneration for the wisdom that leads them to cover up such atrocious ugliness. (85)

Unaware of what would become modish everywhere today, he added, "They carry their children at their backs, in a sack, like other savages the world over." But Twain did allow that "weak, stupid, ignorant" Abdul Aziz, sultan of Turkey, lord of the Ottoman Empire, was a true representative of the people, which is to say, he was "by nature and training filthy, brutish, ignorant, un-progressive, superstitious." Twain was not enchanted by Civitavecchia, which he adjudged "the finest nest of dirt, vermin and ignorance we have found yet, except that African perdition they call Tangier, which is just like it."

Poor Twain was born too soon to appreciate that a "dwarf" is actually a "vertically challenged" person and that "cripple" has been displaced by "physically disadvantaged."

> If you want dwarfs — I mean just a few dwarfs for a curiosity — go to Genoa. If you wish to buy them by the gross, for retail, go to Milan.... But if you want to see the very heart and home of cripples and human monsters, both, go straight to Constantinople. (361)

A writer who usually got his priorities right, he was perturbed by the scarcity of whiskey in Constantinople, and didn't much care for the Greeks, Turks, or Armenians in town.

> [Their] morals consist only in attending church regularly on the appoint-ed Sabbaths, and in breaking the ten commandments all the balance of the

week. It comes natural to them to lie and cheat in the first place, and then go on and improve on nature until they arrive at perfection. (369)

Twain was appalled by "the usual assemblage of squalid humanity" that waited outside the pilgrim's camp on the outskirts of Damascus.

They sat in silence, and with tireless patience watched our every motion with that vile, uncomplaining impoliteness which is so truly Indian, and which makes a white man so nervous and uncomfortable and savage that he wants to exterminate the whole tribe.

These people about us had other peculiarities, which I have noticed in the noble red man, too: they were infested with vermin, and the dirt caked on them till it amounted to bark. (473)

He pronounced Magdala thoroughly Syrian, that is to say, "thoroughly ugly, and cramped, squalid, uncomfortable, and filthy." In Jerusalem, a city of a mere fourteen thousand souls when Twain visited, he inveighed against Moslem rule.

Rags, wretchedness, poverty and dirt, those signs and symbols that indicate the presence of Moslem rule more surely than the crescent-flag itself, abound. Lepers, cripples, the blind, and the idiotic, assail you on every hand, and they know but one word of but one language apparently — the eternal "bucksheesh." (559)

Twain couldn't know that something like a hundred and twenty-five years after the right-wing editor of the *Jerusalem Post*, David Bar-Illan, would brandish his condemnation of Moslem rule as a license for Israel's sole possession of the city.

The majesty of the Sphinx impressed Twain, but not the "corrugated, unsightly mountain of stone" that formed the Great Pyramid of Cheops. In Cairo, of course, he was immediately surrounded by the usual rabble demanding bucksheesh. But he wasn't nearly as naughty about Cairo as an earlier distinguished visitor, the twenty-seven-year-old Gustave Flaubert, who was there in 1849, and wrote in *Flaubert in Egypt: A Sensibility on Tour* that on his first day he was immediately surrounded: "The girls were making imitation fart sounds with their hands. The boy was excellent — short, ugly, stocky: 'If you will give me five paras I'll bring you my mother to fuck. I wish you all kinds of prosperity, especially a long prick.'"

I didn't get to Egypt myself until 1992, but not much had changed since Mark Twain came and went. Approaching the Great Pyramid on foot, my wife and I were instantly besieged by vendors and supplicants, old men and boys, offering T-shirts, posters, sun hats, bottles of mineral water, camel or horseback rides, a helping hand to enter the pyramid — everybody after bucksheesh, the grease that turns the Egyptian wheel. Furthermore, our guide, whose license advertised that he spoke English, had to be a direct descendant of one Twain had endured. He was contemptuous of the smaller, sometimes crumbling pyramids at Giza: "They was for nobbels or womens and womens not equals mens."

Leading us to the Sphinx, he asked, "Why is it the Sphinx has it head man's and body of lions? It is to show intelligence of mens and muskels of beast togethered."

One hundred and twenty-seven years after it was first published, *Innocents Abroad* can be read not only for its literary delights, and the pleasures of reading a major writer when he was young and just beginning to flex his muscles, but also as an enduring, no-nonsense guide for the first-time traveler to Europe and the Holy Land.

The grandchildren of the mendacious guides Twain suffered here, there, and everywhere will still inveigle travelers "into shirt stores, boot stores, tailor shops" where they are entitled to a commission on sales. Perdition catch all guides, wrote Twain, after an experience in Italy with a guide who claimed to be "the most gifted linguist in Genoa, as far as English was concerned, and that only two persons in the city beside himself could talk the language at all." In a memorable exchange, Twain and his chum, the doctor, do manage to get the better of this particular guide, whom they have dubbed Ferguson.

"Come wis me, genteelmen! — come! I show you ze letter writing by

Christopher Colombo! — write it himself! — write it wis his own hand! Come!"

He took us to the municipal palace. After much impressive fumbling of keys and opening of locks, the stained and aged document was spread before us. . . .

"What I tell you, genteelmen! Is it no so? See! handwriting Christopher Colombo! — write it himself!"

We looked indifferent — unconcerned. The doctor examined the document deliberately, during a painful pause. — Then he said, without any show of interest:

"Ah — Ferguson — what — what did you say was the name of the party who wrote this?"

"Christopher Colombo! ze great Christopher Colombo!"

Another deliberate examination.

"Ah — did he write it himself, or — or how?"

"He write it himself! — Christopher Colombo! he's own hand-writing, write by himself!"

"Why, I have seen boys in America only fourteen years old that could write better than that."

"But zis is ze great Christo -- "

"I don't care who it is! It's the worst writing I ever saw. Now you mustn't think you can impose on us because we are strangers. We are not fools, by a good deal. If you have got any specimens of penmanship of real merit, trot them out! — and if you haven't, drive on!" (290–92)

Shocks of recognition abound in *Innocents Abroad*. I am willing to swear, for instance, that the Fergusons Twain suffered in Milan and elsewhere were the progenitors of that babbler of statistics who drove my wife and me to Masada on our extended tour of Israel in 1992. "Their tongues are never still," wrote Twain. "They talk forever and forever. . . . they interrupt every dream, every pleasant train of thought, with their tiresome cackling."

Only last year, arriving at a hotel in Paris, I stood by, a helpless victim, as the doorman removed our bags from a taxi, deposited them at the front door, and extended his hand for a tip. Then another man carried our bags as far as the registration desk, and extended his hand. Finally, a third man lugged the bags to our room, and held out his hand for the obligatory *pourboire*. So I clapped hands at Twain's description of the avarice he witnessed at Vesuvius.

> . . . they seize a lady's shawl from a chair and hand it to her and charge a penny; they open a carriage door, and charge for it — shut it when you get out, and charge for it; . . . brush your clothes and make them worse than they were before — two cents; smile upon you — two cents; bow, with lick-spittle smirk, hat in hand — two cents. (309)

Like Twain, I have visited the Haram al-Sharif (the Noble Sanctuary) in the Old City of Jerusalem, and descended the steps of the Dome of the Rock to gawk at the fabled Stone of Foundation, where, it is claimed, Adam was molded from dust. This is amply demonstrated, wrote Twain, "by the fact that in six thousand years no man has ever been able to prove that the dirt was *not* procured here whereof he was made." It was on this busiest of rocks, according to legend, that Cain killed Abel, and Abraham, put to the test by Jehovah, prepared to sacrifice Isaac. Jesus is said to have preached here. And this is exactly where Mohammed stopped on his *isra*, his celebrated nocturnal flight to heaven, traveling from Mecca to Jerusalem and ascending to heaven on his horse. "Where Mahomet stood," wrote Twain, "he left his foot-prints in the solid stone. I should judge he wore about eighteens" (579).

In his autobiography, Twain said that he "did not lean heavily on the *Alta* letters" in composing *Innocents Abroad*. "I found they were newspaper matter, not book matter." He used several of the letters, ten or twelve perhaps, and claims to have churned out the rest, some two hundred thousand words, in sixty days. On one level, surely, *Innocents Abroad* was meant as an antidote to the insufferably romantic, cliché-ridden travel books of the period, written by intimidated colonials genuflecting to European culture and exaggerating the charms of the Holy Land. Giving them the raspberry, Twain wrote:

> If any man has a right to feel proud of himself, and satisfied, surely it is I.

For I have written about the Coliseum, and the gladiators, the martyrs, and the lions, and yet have never once used the phrase "butchered to make a Roman holyday." I am the only free white man of mature age, who has accomplished this since Byron originated the expression.

Twain was especially scornful of one "Wm. C. Grimes," actually William C. Prime, a hack much given to florid descriptions, and Charles Wyllys Elliott, identified only as "C. W. E.," author of *Life in the Holy Land*, who easily outdid today's most gushing travel brochure in his celebration of the Sea of Galilee, pronouncing it a "terrestrial paradise." The truth of the matter, wrote Twain, is that the Sea of Galilee, stripped for inspection, "proves to be only an unobtrusive basin of water, some mountainous desolation, and one tree."

Familiar as he was with the grandeur, and incredible variety, of the yet untamed American continent, Twain was far from enchanted with Palestine, venturing that it was a hopeless, dreary, heartbroken land. "The hills are barren," he wrote, "they are dull of color, they are unpicturesque in shape." But Twain was alert to beauty whenever he stumbled on it, as he did once in Smyrna, where he observed a passing camel train.

They stride along these streets, in single file, a dozen in a train, with heavy loads on their backs, and a fancy-looking negro in Turkish costume, or an Arab, preceding them on a little donkey and completely overshadowed and rendered insignificant by the huge beasts. To see a camel train laden with the spices of Arabia and the rare fabrics of Persia come marching through the narrow alleys of the bazaar, among porters with their burdens, money-changers, lamp-merchants, Alnaschars in the glassware business, portly cross-legged Turks smoking the famous narghili, and the crowds drifting to and fro in fanciful costumes of the East, is a genuine revelation of the Orient. The picture lacks nothing. (410–11)

Mark Twain set sail on the *Quaker City*, a largely unknown young journalist enjoying a freebie passage, at a time when America's most celebrated humorists were Petroleum Vesuvius Nasby and Orpheus C. Kerr, long since forgotten, as well as Artemus Ward. Possibly trying too hard for knee-slappers, the early pages of *Innocents Abroad* suffer from being a tad broad, proffering more burlesque than inspired satire. But as the voyage proceeds, Twain's voice starts to emerge, gathering assurance and force. The book begins to soar. The comic genius who will go on to write *Life on the Mississippi* and *Huckleberry Finn* declares himself, staking out a territory.

One of the joys of reading *Innocents Abroad* is the opportunity it affords us of watching the young Twain liberate himself, and American writing, from the yoke of the European tradition, doing a necessary demolition job on it, and on the pilgrims that revere often second-rate pictures, proclaiming them masterpieces.

> "O, wonderful!"
> "Such faultless drawing!"
> "Such feeling!"

Leonardo's *Last Supper* was seriously flawed for Twain because he couldn't tell whether the disciples were Hebrews or Italians.

> The Italian artists painted Italian Virgins, the Dutch painted Dutch Virgins, the Virgins of the French painters were Frenchwomen — none of them ever put into the face of the Madonna that indescribable something which proclaims the Jewess, whether you find her in New York, in Constantinople, in Paris, Jerusalem, or in the Empire of Morocco. (195)

With the best of intentions, Jean-Paul Sartre once wrote a foolish polemic denying that there was any such thing as a "Jewish face," but Twain, poor man, didn't realize that identifying "that indescribable something" which proclaims it would one day be adjudged politically incorrect. Mind you, even the most exacting prejudice-sniffer employed by B'nai B'rith's Anti-Defamation League would have his work cut out trying to label Twain an anti-Semite. If anything, he was a Judeophile. In *Innocents Abroad*, he contrasts the plight of Jews confined to European and Near Eastern ghettos with their fulfillment in America, where, he wrote, they were treated just like human beings instead of dogs.

They can work at any business they please; they can sell brand new goods if they want to. . . . they can practice medicine among Christians; . . . they can associate with them, just the same as one human being does with another human being; they don't have to stay shut up in one corner of the towns; they can live in any part of town they like best. . . . they never have had to run races naked through the public streets, against jackasses, to please the people in carnival time; [in America] they never have been driven by the soldiers into a church every Sunday for hundreds of years to hear themselves and their religion especially and particularly cursed; at this very day, in that curious country, a Jew is allowed to vote, hold office, yea, get up on a rostrum in the public street and express his opinion of the government if the government doesn't suit him! Ah, it is wonderful. (269–70)

Trading on his satirist's license, overstating his case, Twain extols the pristine quality of Lake Tahoe over one as inconsequential as Lake Como, and the grandeur of his cherished Mississippi as opposed to such piddling bodies of water as the Tiber or the Arno, failing to acknowledge the splendor of the bridges over the latter river, or the incomparable beauty of the city it divides. The dull waters of Lake Como, he wrote, could not compare with the wonderful transparence of Lake Tahoe, "where one can count the scales on a trout at a depth of a hundred and eighty feet." Those dark and bloody Florentines, he remarked, call the Arno a river, and "they even help out the delusion by building bridges over it. I do not see why they are too good to wade." And the Tiber, he complained, "is not so long, nor yet so wide, as the American Mississippi — nor yet the Ohio, nor even the Hudson."

I must also grudgingly acknowledge that those cultural ruffians who have now taken so vociferously against what they denounce as Eurocentricism do, alas, sometimes make a valid point. Celebrating Columbus in the *Pinta*'s shrouds, Twain wrote, "he swung his hat above a fabled sea and gazed abroad upon *an unknown world*" (emphasis mine). A world unknown to Europeans, whose pretensions Twain punctures with such abandon in *Innocents Abroad*, but not to the Indians rooted there since time immemorial.

Twain, a writer with an enduring affection for chicanery and those who can get away with it, takes obvious delight in the Church of Rome's humbug, coming back to it again and again. He first encounters the holiest of Christian relics in the Azores.

> We visited a Jesuit cathedral nearly two hundred years old, and found in it a piece of the veritable cross upon which our Saviour was crucified. It was polished and hard, and in an excellent state of preservation as if the dread tragedy on Calvary had occurred yesterday instead of eighteen centuries ago. (57)

Then, lo and behold, in the Cathedral of Notre Dame, he is shown "some nails of the true cross, a fragment of the cross itself, a part of the crown of thorns." And in the chapel of St. John the Baptist, in Genoa, there are the relics again.

> We find a piece of the true cross in every old church we go into, and some of the nails that held it together. I would not like to be positive, but I think we have seen as much as a keg of those nails. (165)

But when he finally gets to the Church of the Holy Sepulcher, in Jerusalem, he discovers that the piece of the true cross no longer rests in the niche where they used to preserve it.

> The Latin priests say it was stolen away, long ago, by priests of another sect. That seems like a hard statement to make, but we know very well that it *was* stolen, because we have seen it ourselves in several of the cathedrals of Italy and France. (562)

The vandalism of the *Quaker City*'s pilgrims, a harbinger of offenses to come, was a recurring embarrassment to Twain. They break off fragments of Noah's tomb, and in Damascus, the tomb of Nimrod the Hunter. Servicing their insatiable appetite for souvenirs, they are at it again in Jerusalem, "hacking and chipping away at those arches that Jesus looked upon in the flesh." In Nazareth, coming upon a chapel rising out of a huge boulder, the pilgrims "would have liked very well to get out their lampblack and stencil-plates and paint their names on that rock, together with the names of the villages they hail from in America, but the priests permit nothing of that kind" (529). In Egypt, however, the indefatigable pilgrims are at it once more, actually hacking away at the Sphinx.

Were Twain alive today I imagine he would be relieved to know that the Japanese have displaced Americans as Europe's most acquisitive and objectionable tourists. Only last week in the Louvre my wife was unable even to glimpse the *Mona Lisa* in passing. It was surrounded by throngs of Japanese, none of them the least bit interested in looking at the painting, all of them posing to have their pictures taken in turn before it. They were, however, unable to chip away at it, the *Mona Lisa* now being sheltered by a glass guard.

A major innovator's work is never done.

In March 1995, speaking at the British Council's English 2000 project, Prince Charles warned against the threat to "proper English" from the spread of the American vernacular, which he pronounced very corrupting. Because of American influence, he said, "people tend to invent all sorts of nouns and verbs, and make words that shouldn't be. I think we have to be a bit careful, otherwise the whole thing can get rather a mess."

Obviously Prince Charles has never read Mark Twain, or Mencken on the American language, or Twain's successors (say, Hemingway, Bellow, Toni Morrison, and Raymond Carver, among others), and is unaware of how they have enriched a living language that is constantly evolving. He should be sent immediately a copy of *Innocents Abroad*, the American coming-of-cultural-age book, the first major offering of a great writer, which belongs on a small shelf of Twain classics, alongside *Life on the Mississippi*, *Huckleberry Finn*, and *A Connecticut Yankee in King Arthur's Court*.

THE

INNOCENTS ABROAD,

OR

THE NEW

PILGRIMS' PROGRESS

THE
INNOCENTS ABROAD
OR THE NEW
PILGRIM'S PROGRESS.

MARK TWAIN

THE QUAKER CITY IN A STORM.   (Page 62)

THE PILGRIM'S VISION.

THE

INNOCENTS ABROAD,

OR

THE NEW PILGRIMS' PROGRESS;

BEING SOME ACCOUNT OF THE STEAMSHIP QUAKER CITY'S PLEASURE
EXCURSION TO EUROPE AND THE HOLY LAND; WITH
DESCRIPTIONS OF COUNTRIES, NATIONS,
INCIDENTS AND ADVENTURES,
AS THEY APPEARED
TO THE

AUTHOR.

WITH TWO HUNDRED AND THIRTY-FOUR ILLUSTRATIONS.

BY

MARK TWAIN,

(SAMUEL L. CLEMENS.)

HARTFORD, CONN.:

AMERICAN PUBLISHING COMPANY.

BLISS & CO., NEWARK, N. J.; R. W. BLISS & CO., TOLEDO, OHIO.
F. G. GILMAN & CO., CHICAGO, ILL.; NETTLETON & CO., CINCINNATI, OHIO.
F. A. HUTCHINSON & CO., ST. LOUIS, MO.

H. H. BANCROFT AND COMPANY, SAN FRANCISCO, CAL.

1869.

To

My Most Patient Reader

and

Most Charitable Critic,

MY AGED MOTHER,

This Volume is Affectionately

Inscribed.

PREFACE.

THIS book is a record of a pleasure-trip. If it were a record of a solemn scientific expedition, it would have about it that gravity, that profundity, and that impressive incomprehensibility which are so proper to works of that kind, and withal so attractive. Yet notwithstanding it is only a record of a pic-nic, it has a purpose, which is, to suggest to the reader how *he* would be likely to see Europe and the East if he looked at them with his own eyes instead of the eyes of those who travelled in those countries before him. I make small pretence of showing any one how he *ought* to look at objects of interest beyond the sea—other books do that, and therefore, even if I were competent to do it, there is no need.

I offer no apologies for any departures from the usual style of travel-writing that may be charged against me—for I think I have seen with impartial eyes, and I am sure I have written at least honestly, whether wisely or not.

In this volume I have used portions of letters which I wrote for the *Daily Alta California*, of San Francisco, the proprietors of that journal having waived their rights and given me the necessary permission. I have also inserted portions of several letters written for the New York *Tribune* and the New York *Herald*.

THE AUTHOR.

SAN FRANCISCO, 1869.

LIST OF ILLUSTRATIONS.

PAGE

1. THE QUAKER CITY IN A STORM........................ ... .FRONTISPIECE.... —
2. ILLUMINATED TITLE-PAGE—THE PILGRIM'S VISION.............................. .... —
3. "I 'LL PAY YOU IN PARIS"... 28
4. THE START............... 30
5. "GOOD MORNING, SIR"....……..... 34
6. THE OLD PIRATE..... 36
7. DANCING UNDER DIFFICULTIES... 42
8. THE MOCK TRIAL 44
9. "LAND, HO!" 49
10. THE CAPOTE 52
11. RUIN AND DESOLATION 53
12. PORT OF HORTA, FAYAL (FULL PAGE), FACE PAGE 56
13. "SEKKI-YAH!".. 59
14. BEAUTIFUL STRANGER 64
15. ROCK OF GIBRALTAR (FULL PAGE), FACE PAGE........................ 65
16. "QUEEN'S CHAIR".. 67
17. THE ORACLE.. 70
18. THE INTERROGATION POINT.. 71
19. GARRISON AT MALABAT.. 72
20. ENTERTAINING AN ANGEL.. 74
21. VIEW OF A STREET IN TANGIER 77
22. CHANGE FOR A NAPOLEON.. 81
23. THE CONSUL'S FAMILY. 88
24. "POET LARIAT" 91
25. FIRST SUPPER IN FRANCE.. 95
26. PAINTING.. 96
27. RINGING FOR SOAP 99
28. "WINE, SIR!"........ 100
29. THE PILGRIM 101
30. THE PRISONER 103
31. HOMELESS FRANCE (FULL PAGE), FACE PAGE..... 106
32. RAILROAD OFFICIAL IN FRANCE........... 108
33. "FIVE MINUTES FOR REFRESHMENTS." AMERICA...... 109

PAGE

84. "THIRTY MINUTES FOR DINNER." FRANCE 110
85. THE OLD TRAVELLER.. 111
86. A DECIDED SHAVE. 115
87. A GAS-TLY SUBSTITUTE 117
88. THE THREE GUIDES.. 119
89. "ZE SILK MAGAZIN"... 122
40. RETURN IN WAR PAINT 124
41. NAPOLEON III... 126
42. ABDUL AZIZ... 126
43. THE MORGUE... 132
44. WE TOOK A WALK.. 135
45. THE CAN-CAN... 136
46. GRAVES OF ABELARD AND HELOISE.. 141
47. A PAIR OF CANONS OF 13TH CENTURY... 142
48. THE PRIVATE MARRIAGE.. 144
49. AMERICAN DRINKS... 148
50. ROYAL HONORS TO A YANKEE.. 150
51. THE GRISETTE... 151
52. FOUNTAIN AT VERSAILLES... 154
53. WOMEN OF GENOA.. 161
54. PETRIFIED LACKEY.. 163
55. PRIEST AND FRIAR.. 164
56. STATUE OF COLUMBUS 168
57. GRAVES OF SIXTY THOUSAND... 169
58. ROOF AND SPIRES OF CATHEDRAL AT MILAN (FULL PAGE), FACE PAGE............... 172
59. CENTRAL DOOR OF CATHEDRAL AT MILAN... 173
60. INTERIOR OF CATHEDRAL AT MILAN.. 174
61. BOYHOOD'S EXPERIENCE.. 176
62. TREASURES OF THE CATHEDRAL... 179
63. CATHEDRAL AT MILAN 181
64. LA SCALA THEATRE 184
65. COPYING FROM OLD MASTERS 191
66. FACIAL EXPRESSION... 194
67. THE ECHO.. 196
68. NOTE BOOK 197
69. A KISS FOR A FRANC.. 198
70. THE FUMIGATION... 200
71. LAKE COMO... 202
72. GARDEN, LAKE COMO (FULL PAGE), FACE PAGE 204
73. SOCIAL DRIVER.. 207
74. WAYSIDE SHRINE 208
75. PEACE AND HAPPINESS.. 209
76. CASTLE OF COUNT LUIGI.. 210
77. THE WICKED BROTHER... 216
78. DISGUSTED GONDOLIER.. 220
79. CATHEDRAL OF ST. MARK... 226
80. THE PEG 229
81. "GOOD-BY ".. 230
82. M'SIEUR GOR-R-DONG... 234
83. MONUMENT TO THE DOGE.. 236
84. ST. MARK. BY THE OLD MASTERS.. 238
85. ST. MATTHEW. BY THE OLD MASTERS.. 238
86. ST. JEROME. BY THE OLD MASTERS 238
87. ST. SEBASTIAN. BY THE OLD MASTERS.. 239
88. ST. UNKNOWN. BY THE OLD MASTERS 239

PAGE

89. RIALTO BRIDGE....... 241
90. BRIDGE OF SIGHS 241
91. FLORENCE... 245
92. THE PENSIONER 246
93. "I WANT TO GO HOME"... 248
94. THE LEANING TOWER... 250
95. THE CONTRAST 258
96. ITALIAN PASTIMES 263
97. INCENDIARY DOCUMENT 264
98. A ROMAN OF 1869.. 267
99. MAMERTINE PRISON............... 276
100. OLD ROMAN 278
101. COLISEUM OF ANCIENT ROME............... 281
102. DID NOT COMPLAIN 285
103. HUMBOLDT HOUSE 286
104. DAN... 288
105. BRONZE STATUE 289
106. PENMANSHIP.. 291
107. ON A BUST.... 293
108. VAULTS OF THE CONVENT 299
109. DRIED CONVENT FRUITS.. 302
110. AT THE STORE... 303
111. AT HOME.. 304
112. SOOTHING THE PILGRIMS 309
113. ASCENT OF MT. VESUVIUS.. 313
114. BAY OF NAPLES... 316
115. THE MUSTANG... 319
116. ISLAND OF CAPRI.... 320
117. BLUE GROTTO... 321
118. VESUVIUS AND BAY OF NAPLES (FULL PAGE), FACE PAGE.......................... 323
119. THE DESCENT. 325
120. RUINS, POMPEII.. 327
121. FORUM OF JUSTICE, POMPEII. 330
122. HOUSE, POMPEII 335
123. STROMBOLI... 338
124. VIEW OF THE ACROPOLIS, LOOKING WEST.. 341
125. "HO!"... 343
126. THE ASSAULT... 344
127. THE CARYATIDES............................... 346
128. THE PARTHENON (FULL PAGE), FACE PAGE 348
129. WE SIDLED, NOT RAN... 350
130. ANCIENT ACROPOLIS.. 352
131. TAIL PIECE, RUINS............ 353
132. QUEEN OF GREECE... 355
133. PALACE AT ATHENS... 356
134. STREET SCENE IN CONSTANTINOPLE (FULL PAGE) FACE PAGE................... 359
135. GOOSE RANCHER............ 360
136. MOSQUE OF ST. SOPHIA.... 363
137. TURKISH MAUSOLEUM..... 365
138. SLANDERED DOGS... 371
139. THE CENSOR ON DUTY.. 374
140. TURKISH BATH.. 378
141. FAR-AWAY-MOSES... 382
142. A FRAGMENT... 385
143. TAIL-PIECE—A MEMENTO.. 386

PAGE

144. YALTA FROM THE EMPEROR'S PALACE.................................. 392
145. EMPEROR OF RUSSIA.. 393
146. TINSEL KING.. 399
147. SHIP EMPEROR.. 404
148. THE RECEPTION... 405
149. STREET SCENE IN SMYRNA.. 411
150. SMYRNA... 413
151. AN APPARENT SUCCESS.. 416
152. DRIFTING TO STARBOARD... 419
153. A SPOILED NAP... 420
154. ANCIENT AMPHITHEATRE AT EPHESUS.............................. 422
155. MODERN AMPHITHEATRE AT EPHESUS.............................. 423
156. RUINS OF EPHESUS.. 424
157. THE JOURNEY... 425
158. GRAVES OF THE SEVEN SLEEPERS................................. 429
159. THE SELECTION.. 434
160. CAMPING OUT.. 436
161. TAIL PIECE—ARABS' TENTS...................................... 437
162. A GOOD FEEDER.. 439
163. INTERESTING FÊTE.. 440
164. SUNDAY SCHOOL GRAPES... 442
165. AN OLD FOGY.. 445
166. RACE WITH A CAMEL.. 446
167. TEMPLE OF THE SUN... 447
168. RUINS OF BAALBEC... 449
169. HEWN STONES IN QUARRY.. 450
170. MERCY... 452
171. PATRON SAINT... 453
172. WATER CARRIER.. 455
173. VIEW OF DAMASCUS, (FULL PAGE) FACE PAGE 456
174. STREET CARS OF DAMASCUS...................................... 460
175. FULL DRESSED TOURIST... 466
176. IMPROMPTU HOSPITAL... 474
177. THE HORSE "BAALBEC".. 476
178. OAK OF BASHAN.. 479
179. DANGEROUS ARAB.. 482
180. GRIMES ON THE WAR-PATH....................................... 483
181. TAIL-PIECE—BEDOUIN CAMP...................................... 487
182. HOME OF ANCIENT POMP... 489
183. JACK.. 490
184. A DISAPPOINTED AUDIENCE...................................... 491
185. FIG-TREE.. 495
186. "FARE TOO HIGH".. 497
187. SYRIAN HOUSE... 504
188. TIBERIAS AND SEA OF GALILEE.................................. 506
189. THE GUARD.. 516
190. MOUNT TABOR.. 521
191. TAIL-PIECE—GATHERING FUEL.................................... 524
192. FOUNTAIN OF THE VIRGIN....................................... 530
193. "MADONNA-LIKE BEAUTY".. 531
194. PUTNAM OUTDONE... 533
195. THE BASTINADO.. 535
196. "I WEPT"... 536
197. WANT OF DIGNITY.. 539
198. AN ORIENTAL WELL... 544

PAGE

199. Arabs Saluting.. 545
200. Free Sons of the Desert 546
201. Shechem 552
202. Tail Piece—Gate of Jerusalem.. 556
203. Beggars in Jerusalem.. 559
204. Church of the Holy Sepulchre.. 564
205. Grave of Adam.. 566
206. View of Jerusalem (Full Page), face page..................... 574
207. The Wandering Jew.. 577
208. Mosque of Omar 581
209. An Epidemic 589
210. Charge on Bedouins... 590
211. Dead Sea.. 594
212. Grotto of the Nativity (Full Page), face page.......... 601
213. Jaffa (Full Page), face page........ 606
214. Rear Elevation of Jack........ 610
215. Street in Alexandria 611
216. Viceroy of Egypt... 612
217. Eastern Monarch... 614
218. Moses S. Beach.. 615
219. Room No. 15.... 617
220. The Nilometer............................. 620
221. Ascent of the Pyramids.. 622
222. High Hopes Frustrated.. 625
223. King's Chamber in the Pyramid, (Full Page), face page 626
224. A Powerful Argument... 627
225. Pyramids and Sphynx, (Full Page), face page........ 629
226. The Relic Hunter... 630
227. The Mameluke's Leap... 631
228. Would not be Comforted.. 633
229. Tail Piece, The Traveler... 634
230. Homeward Bound... 635
231. Bad Coffee...... 639
232. Our Friends the Bermudians... 640
233. Captain Duncan.. 641
234. Tail Piece, Finis.. 651

CONTENTS.

CHAPTER I.

PAGE

Popular Talk of the Excursion—Programme of the Trip—Duly Ticketed for the Excursion—Defection of the Celebrities............................ 19

CHAPTER II.

Grand Preparations—An Imposing Dignitary—The European Exodus—Mr. Blucher's Opinion—Stateroom No. 10—The Assembling of the Clans—At Sea at last 26

CHAPTER III.

"Averaging" the Passengers—"Far, far at Sea"—Tribulation among the Patriarchs—Seeking Amusement under Difficulties—Five Captains in the Ship 32

CHAPTER IV.

The Pilgrims Becoming Domesticated—Pilgrim Life at Sea—"Horse-Billiards" —The "Synagogue"—The Writing School—Jack's "Journal"—The "Q. C. Club"—The Magic Lantern—State Ball on Deck—Mock Trials— Charades—Pilgrim Solemnity—Slow Music—The Executive Officer Delivers an Opinion 38

CHAPTER V.

Summer in Mid-Atlantic—An Eccentric Moon—Mr. Blucher Loses Confidence —The Mystery of "Ship Time"—The Denizens of the Deep—"Land-Ho!"—The First Landing on a Foreign Shore—Sensation among the Natives—Something about the Azores Islands--Blucher's Disastrous Dinner—The Happy Result 47

CHAPTER VI.

Solid Information—A Fossil Community—Curious Ways and Customs—Jesuit Humbuggery—Fantastic Pilgrimizing—Origin of the Russ Pavement— Squaring Accounts with the Fossils—At Sea Again................... 55

CHAPTER VII.

A Tempest at Night—Spain and Africa on Exhibition—Greeting a Majestic Stranger—The Pillars of Hercules—The Rock of Gibraltar—Tiresome Repetition—"The Queen's Chair"—Serenity Conquered—Curiosities of the Secret Caverns—Personnel of Gibraltar—Some Odd Characters—A Private Frolic in Africa—Bearding a Moorish Garrison (without loss of life)—Vanity Rebuked—Disembarking in the Empire of Morocco....... 62

CHAPTER VIII.

PAGE

The Ancient City of Tangier, Morocco—Strange Sights—A Cradle of Antiquity—We become Wealthy—How they Rob the Mail in Africa—The Danger of being Opulent in Morocco.............................. 76

CHAPTER IX.

A Pilgrim in Deadly Peril—How they Mended the Clock—Moorish Punishments for Crime—Marriage Customs—Looking Several ways for Sunday—Shrewd Practice of Mohammedan Pilgrims—Reverence for Cats—Bliss of being a Consul-General... 83

CHAPTER X.

Fourth of July at Sea—Mediterranean Sunset—The " Oracle " is Delivered of an Opinion—Celebration Ceremonies—The Captain's Speech—France in Sight—The Ignorant Native—In Marseilles—Another Blunder—Lost in the Great City—Found Again—A Frenchy Scene 90

CHAPTER XI.

Getting "Used to it "—No Soap—Bill of Fare, Table d'hôte—"An American Sir!"—A Curious Discovery—The "Pilgrim" Bird—Strange Companionship—A Grave of the Living—A Long Captivity—Some of Dumas' Heroes—Dungeon of the Famous "Iron Mask."........................ 98

CHAPTER XII.

A Holiday Flight through France—Summer Garb of the Landscape—Abroad on the Great Plains—Peculiarities of French Cars—French Politeness—American Railway Officials—" Twenty Mnutes to Dinner !"—Why there are no Accidents—The " Old Travellers"—Still on the Wing—Paris at Last—French Order and Quiet—Place of the Bastile—Seeing the Sights —A Barbarous Atrocity—Absurd Billiards....................... 105

CHAPTER XIII.

More Trouble—Monsieur Billfinger—Re-Christening the Frenchman—In the Clutches of a Paris Guide—The International Exposition—Fine Military Review—Glimpse of the Emperor Napoleon and the Sultan of Turkey.... 118

CHAPTER XIV.

The Venerable Cathedral of Notre-Dame—Jean Sanspeur's Addition—Treasures and Sacred Relics—The Legend of the Cross—The Morgue—The Outrageous *Can- Can*—Blondin Aflame—The Louvre Palace—The Great Park—Showy Pageantry—Preservation of Noted Things............. 130

CHAPTER XV.

French National Burying-Ground—Among the Great Dead—The Shrine of Disappointed Love—The Story of Abelard and Heloise—" English Spoken Here "—" American Drinks Compounded Here "—Imperial Honors to an American—The Over-estimated Grisette—Departure from Paris—A Deliberate Opinion Concerning the Comeliness of American Women....... 139

CHAPTER XVI.

Versailles—Paradise Regained—A Wonderful Park—Paradise Lost—Napoleonic Strategy.. 153

CHAPTER XVII.

War—The American Forces Victorious—" Home Again "—Italy in Sight—
The " City of Palaces "—Beauty of the Genoese Women—The " Stub-
Hunters "—Among the Palaces—Gifted Guide—Church Magnificence—
" Women not Admitted "—How the Genoese Live—Massive Architecture
—A Scrap of Ancient History—Graves for 60,000................... 159

CHAPTER XVIII.

Flying Through Italy—Marengo—First Glimpse of the Famous Cathedral—
Description of some of its Wonders—A Horror Carved in Stone—An
Unpleasant Adventure—A Good Man—A Sermon from the Tomb—
Tons of Gold and Silver—Some More Holy Relics—Solomon's Temple
Rivalled.. 171

CHAPTER XIX.

"Do You Wis zo Haut can be ? "—La Scala—Petrarch and Laura—Lucrezia
Borgia—Ingenious Frescoes—Ancient Roman Amphitheatre—A Clever
Delusion—Distressing Billiards—The Chief Charm of European Life—An
Italian Bath—Wanted: Soap—Crippled French—Mutilated English—The
Most Celebrated Painting in the World—Amateur Raptures—Uninspired
Critics—Anecdote—A Wonderful Echo—A Kiss for a Franc 183

CHAPTER XX.

Rural Italy by Rail—Fumigated, According to Law—The Sorrowing Englishman—Night by the Lake of Como—The Famous Lake—Its Scenery—
Como compared with Tahoe—Meeting a Shipmate.................... 199

CHAPTER XXI.

The Pretty Lago di Lecco—A Carriage Drive in the Country—Astonishing
Sociability in a Coachman—A Sleepy Land—Bloody Shrines—The Heart
and Home of Priestcraft—A Thrilling Mediæval Romance—The Birthplace
of Harlequin—Approaching Venice 207

CHAPTER XXII.

Night in Venice—The " Gay Gondolier "—The Grand Fête by Moonlight—The
Notable Sights of Venice—The Mother of the Republics Desolate 217

CHAPTER XXIII.

The Famous Gondola—The Gondola in an Unromantic Aspect—The Great
Square of St. Mark and the Winged Lion—Snobs, at Home and Abroad—
Sepulchres of the Great Dead—A Tilt at the " Old Masters "—A Contra-
band Guide—The Conspiracy—Moving Again........................ 228

CHAPTER XXIV.

Down Through Italy by Rail—Idling in Florence—Dante and Galileo—An
Ungrateful City—Dazzling Generosity—Wonderful Mosaics—The Histori-
cal Arno—Lost Again—Found Again, but no Fatted Calf Ready—The
Leaning Tower of Pisa—The Ancient Duomo—The Old Original First
Pendulum that Ever Swung—An Enchanting Echo—A New Holy
Sepulchre—A Relic of Antiquity—A Fallen Republic—At Leghorn—At
Home Again, and Satisfied, on Board the Ship—Our Vessel an Object of
Grave Suspicion—Gen. Garibaldi Visited—Threats of Quarantine 244

CHAPTER XXV.

PAGE

The Works of Bankruptcy—Railway Grandeur—How to Fill an Empty Treasury—The Sumptuousness of Mother Church—Ecclesiastical Splendor—Magnificence and Misery—General Execration—More Magnificence —A Good Word for the Priests—Civita Vecchia the Dismal—Off for Rome 255

CHAPTER XXVI.

The Modern Roman on His Travels—The Grandeur of St. Peter's—Holy Relics —Grand View from the Dome—The Holy Inquisition—Interesting Old Monkish Frauds—The Ruined Coliseum—The Coliseum in the Days of its Prime—Ancient Play-bill of a Coliseum Performance—A Roman Newspaper Criticism 1700 Years Old............................. 266

CHAPTER XXVII.

"Butchered to Make a Roman Holiday"—The Man who Never Complained —An Exasperating Subject—Asinine Guides—The Roman Catacombs— The Saint Whose Fervor Burst his Ribs—The Miracle of the Bleeding Heart—The Legend of Ara Cœli................................. 284

CHAPTER XXVIII.

Picturesque Horrors—The Legend of Brother Thomas—Sorrow Scientifically Analyzed—A Festive Company of the Dead—The Great Vatican Museum —Artist Sins of Omission—The Rape of the Sabines—Papal Protection of Art—High Price of "Old Masters"—Improved Scripture—Scale of Rank of the Holy Personages in Rome—Scale of Honors Accorded Them—Fossilizing—Away for Naples 298

CHAPTER XXIX.

Naples—In Quarantine at Last—Annunciation—Ascent of Mount Vesuvius —A Two-Cent Community—The Black Side of Neapolitan Character— Monkish Miracles—Ascent of Mount Vesuvius Continued—The Stranger and the Hackman—Night View of Naples from the Mountain-side— Ascent of Vesuvius Continued.................................. 308

CHAPTER XXX.

Ascent of Vesuvius Continued—Beautiful View at Dawn—Less Beautiful View in the Back Streets—Ascent of Vesuvius Continued—Dwellings a Hundred Feet High—A Motley Procession—Bill of Fare for a Pedler's Breakfast—Princely Salaries—Ascent of Vesuvius Continued—An Average of Prices—The Wonderful "Blue Grotto"—Visit to Celebrated Localities in the Bay of Naples—The Poisoned "Grotto of the Dog"—A Petrified Sea of Lava—The Ascent Continued—The Summit Reached— Description of the Crater—Descent of Vesuvius..................... 315

CHAPTER XXXI.

The Buried City of Pompeii—How Dwellings Appear that have been Unoccupied for Eighteen Hundred Years—The Judgment Seat—Desolation—The Footprints of the Departed—"No Women Admitted"—Theatres, Bakeshops, Schools, etc.—Skeletons Preserved by the Ashes and Cinders—The Brave Martyr to Duty—Rip Van Winkle—The Perishable Nature of Fame 327

Contents.

CHAPTER XXXII.

PAGE

At Sea Once More—The Pilgrims all Well—Superb Stromboli—Sicily by Moonlight—Scylla and Charybdis—The " Oracle " at Fault—Skirting the Isles of Greece—Ancient Athens—Blockaded by Quarantine and Refused Permission to Enter—Running the Blockade—A Bloodless Midnight Adventure—Turning Robbers from Necessity—Attempt to Carry the Acropolis by Storm—We Fail—Among the Glories of the Past—A World of Ruined Sculpture—A Fairy Vision—Famous Localities—Retreating in Good Order—Captured by the Guards—Travelling in Military State—Safe on Board Again 337

CHAPTER XXXIII.

Modern Greece—Fallen Greatness—Sailing Through the Archipelago and the Dardanelles—Footprints of History—The First Shoddy Contractor of whom History gives any Account—Anchored Before Constantinople—Fantastic Fashions—The Ingenious Goose-Rancher—Marvellous Cripples —The Great Mosque—The Thousand and One Columns—The Grand Bazaar of Stamboul 354

CHAPTER XXXIV.

Scarcity of Morals and Whiskey—Slave-Girl Market Report—Commercial Morality at a Discount—The Slandered Dogs of Constantinople—Questionable Delights of Newspaperdom in Turkey—Ingenious Italian Journalism—No More Turkish Lunches Desired—The Turkish Bath Fraud—The Narghileh Fraud—Jackplaned by a Native—The Turkish Coffee Fraud 368

CHAPTER XXXV.

Sailing Through the Bosporus and the Black Sea—" Far-Away Moses "—Melancholy Sebastopol—Hospitably Received in Russia—Pleasant English People—Desperate Fighting—Relic Hunting—How Travellers Form " Cabinets " 381

CHAPTER XXXVI.

Nine Thousand Miles East—Imitation American Town in Russia—Gratitude that Came Too Late—To Visit the Autocrat of All the Russias 387

CHAPTER XXXVII.

Summer Home of Royalty—Practising for the Dread Ordeal—Committee on Imperial Address—Reception by the Emperor and Family—Dresses of the Imperial Party—Concentrated Power—Counting the Spoons—At the Grand Duke's—A Charming Villa—A Knightly Figure—The Grand Duchess—A Grand Ducal Breakfast—Baker's Boy, the Famine-Breeder—Theatrical Monarchs a Fraud—Saved as by Fire—The Governor-General's Visit to the Ship—Official "Style "—Aristocratic Visitors—" Munchausenizing " with Them—Closing Ceremonies...................... 390

CHAPTER XXXVIII.

Return to Constantinople—We Sail for Asia—The Sailors Burlesque the Imperial Visitors—Ancient Smyrna—The " Oriental Splendor " Fraud—The " Biblical Crown of Life "—Pilgrim Prophecy-Savans—Sociable Armenian Girls—A Sweet Reminiscence—"The Camels are Coming, Ha-ha! " 403

CHAPTER XXXIX.

Smyrna's Lions—The Martyr Polycarp—The "Seven Churches"—Remains of the Six Smyrnas—Mysterious Oyster Mine—Oysters Seeking Scenery—A Millerite Tradition—A Railroad Out of its Sphere............ 412

CHAPTER XL.

Journeying Toward Ancient Ephesus—Ancient Ayassalook—The Villanous Donkey—A Fantastic Procession—Bygone Magnificence—Fragments of History—The Legend of the Seven Sleepers....................... 418

CHAPTER XLI.

Vandalism Prohibited—Angry Pilgrims—Approaching Holy Land!—The "Shrill Note of Preparation—Distress About Dragomans and Transportation—The "Long Route" Adopted—In Syria—Something about Beirout —A Choice Specimen of a Greek "Ferguson"—Outfits—Hideous Horseflesh—Pilgrim "Style"—What of Aladdin's Lamp? 430

CHAPTER XLII.

"Jacksonville," in the Mountains of Lebanon—Breakfasting above a Grand Panorama—The Vanished City—The Peculiar Steed, "Jericho"—The Pilgrim's Progress—Bible Scenes—Mount Hermon, Joshua's Battle-Fields, etc.—The Tomb of Noah—A Most Unfortunate People........ 438

CHAPTER XLIII.

Patriarchal Customs—Magnificent Baalbec—Description of the Ruins—Scribbling Smiths and Joneses—Pilgrim Fidelity to the Letter of the Law—The Revered Fountain of Baalam's Ass.............................. 445

CHAPTER XLIV.

Extracts from Note-Book—Mahomet's Paradise and the Bible's—Beautiful Damascus, the Oldest City on Earth—Oriental Scenes within the Curious Old City—Damascus Street Car—The Story of St. Paul—The "Street called Straight"—Mahomet's Tomb and St. George's—The Christian Massacre—Mohammedan Dread of Pollution—The House of Naaman—The Horrors of Leprosy... 454

CHAPTER XLV.

The Cholera by way of Variety—Hot—Another Outlandish Procession—Pen-and-Ink Photograph of "Jonesborough," Syria—Tomb of Nimrod, the Mighty Hunter—The Stateliest Ruin of All—Stepping over the Borders of Holy Land—Bathing in the Sources of Jordan—More "Specimen"-Hunting—Ruins of Cesarea-Philippi—"On This Rock Will I Build my Church"—The People the Disciples Knew—The Noble Steed "Baalbec" —Sentimental Horse Idolatry of the Arabs....................... 465

CHAPTER XLVI.

Dan—Bashan—Genessaret—A Notable Panorama—Smallness of Palestine—Scraps of History—Character of the Country—Bedouin Shepherds—Glimpses of the Hoary Past—Mr. Grimes's Bedouins—A Battle-Ground of Joshua—That Soldier's Manner of Fighting—Barak's Battle—The Necessity of Unlearning Some Things—Desolation.................. 478

CHAPTER XLVII.

PAGE

Jack's Adventure—Joseph's Pit—The Story of Joseph—Joseph's Magnanim-
ity and Esau's—The Sacred Lake of Genessaret—Enthusiasm of the Pilgrims—Why We did not Sail on Galilee—About Capernaum—Concerning
the Saviour's Brothers and Sisters—Journeying toward Magdala 488

CHAPTER XLVIII.

Curious Specimens of Art and Architecture—Public Reception of the Pilgrims
—Mary Magdalen's House—Tiberias and its Queer Inhabitants—The Sacred Sea of Galilee—Galilee by Night................................ 503

CHAPTER XLIX.

The Ancient Baths—Ye Apparition—A Distinguished Panorama—The Last
Battle of the Crusades—The Story of the Lord of Kerak—Mount Tabor—
What one Sees from its Top—A Memory of a Wonderful Garden—The
House of Deborah the Prophetess.................................. 514

CHAPTER L.

Toward Nazareth—Bitten By a Camel—Grotto of the Annunciation, Nazareth
—Noted Grottoes in General—Joseph's Workshop—A Sacred Bowlder—
The Fountain of the Virgin—Questionable Female Beauty—Literary Cu-
riosities. 525

CHAPTER LI.

The Boyhood of the Saviour—Unseemly Antics of Sober Pilgrims—Home of
the Witch of Endor—Nain—Profanation—A Popular Oriental Picture—
Biblical Metaphors Becoming steadily More Intelligible—The Shunem
Miracle—The "Free Son of The Desert"—Ancient Jezreel—Jehu's
Achievements—Samaria and its Famous Siege...................... 537

CHAPTER LII.

A Curious Remnant of the Past—Shechem—The Oldest "First Family" on
Earth—The Oldest Manuscript Extant—The Genuine Tomb of Joseph—
Jacob's Well—Shiloh—Camping with the Arabs—Jacob's Ladder—More
Desolation—Ramah, Beroth, the Tomb of Samuel, the Fountain of Beira
—Impatience—Approaching Jerusalem—The Holy City in Sight—Noting
its Prominent Features—Domiciled Within the Sacred Walls.......... 551

CHAPTER LIII.

"The Joy of the Whole Earth"—Description of Jerusalem—Church of the
Holy Sepulchre—The Stone of Unction—The Grave of Jesus—Graves
of Nicodemus and Joseph of Arimathea—Places of the Apparition—The
Finding of the Three Crosses—The Legend—Monkish Impostures—The
Pillar of Flagellation—The Place of a Relic—Godfrey's Sword—"The
Bonds of Christ"—"The Center of the Earth"—Place whence the Dust
was taken of which Adam was Made—Grave of Adam—The Martyred
Soldier—The Copper Plate that was On the Cross—The Good St. Helena
—Place of the Division of the Garments—St. Dimas, the Penitent Thief—
The Late Emperor Maximilian's Contribution—Grotto wherein the Crosses
were Found, and the Nails, and the Crown of Thorns—Chapel of the
Mocking—Tomb of Melchizedek—Graves of Two Renowned Crusaders
—The Place of the Crucifixion 558

CHAPTER LIV.

PAGE

The "Sorrowful Way"—The Legend of St. Veronica's Handkerchief—An Illustrious Stone—House of the Wandering Jew—The Tradition of the Wanderer—Solomon's Temple—Mosque of Omar—Moslem Traditions—"Women not Admitted"—The Fate of a Gossip—Turkish Sacred Relics—Judgment Seat of David and Saul—Genuine Precious Remains of Solomon's Temple—Surfeited with Sights—The Pool of Siloam—The Garden of Gethsemane and Other Sacred Localities....................... 574

CHAPTER LV.

Rebellion in the Camp—Charms of Nomadic Life—Dismal Rumors—En Route for Jericho and The Dead Sea—Pilgrim Strategy—Bethany and the Dwelling of Lazarus—"Bedouins!"—Ancient Jericho—Misery—The Night March—The Dead Sea—An Idea of What a "Wilderness" in Palestine is—The Holy Hermits of Mars Saba—Good St. Saba—Women not Admitted—Buried from the World for all Time—Unselfish Catholic Benevolence—Gazelles—The Plain of the Shepherds—Birthplace of the Saviour, Bethlehem—Church of the Nativity—Its Hundred Holy Places—The Famous "Milk" Grotto—Tradition—Return to Jerusalem—Exhausted.... 586

CHAPTER LVI.

Departure from Jerusalem—Samson—The Plain of Sharon—Arrival at Joppa—House of Simon the Tanner—The Long Pilgrimage Ended—Character of Palestine Scenery—The Curse........   604

CHAPTER LVII.

The Happiness of being at Sea once more—"Home" as it is in a Pleasure-Ship—"Shaking Hands" with the Vessel—Jack in Costume—His Father's Parting Advice—Approaching Egypt—Ashore in Alexandria—A Deserved Compliment for the Donkeys—Invasion of the Lost Tribes of America—End of the Celebrated "Jaffa Colony"—Scenes in Grand Cairo—Shepheard's Hotel Contrasted with a Certain American Hotel—Preparing for the Pyramids.. 609

CHAPTER LVIII.

"Recherché" Donkeys—A Wild Ride—Specimens of Egyptian Modesty—Moses in the Bulrushes—Place where the Holy Family Sojourned—Distant view of the Pyramids—A Nearer View—The Ascent—Superb View from the top of the Pyramid—"Backsheesh! Backsheesh!"—An Arab Exploit—In the Bowels of the Pyramid—Strategy—Reminiscence of "Holiday's Hill"—Boyish Exploit—The Majestic Sphynx—Things the Author will not Tell—Grand Old Egypt............................ 618

CHAPTER LIX.

Going Home—A Demoralized Note-Book—A Boy's Diary—Mere Mention of Old Spain—Departure from Cadiz—A Deserved Rebuke—The Beautiful Madeiras—Tabooed—In the Delightful Bermudas—An English Welcome—Good-by to "Our Friends the Bermudians"—Packing Trunks for Home—Our First Accident—The Long Cruise Drawing to a Close—At Home—Amen.. 635

CHAPTER LX.

Thankless Devotion—A Newspaper Valedictory—Conclusion.............. 638

CHAPTER I.

FOR months the great Pleasure Excursion to Europe and the Holy Land was chatted about in the newspapers every where in America, and discussed at countless firesides. It was a novelty in the way of Excursions—its like had not been thought of before, and it compelled that interest which attractive novelties always command. It was to be a picnic on a gigantic scale. The participants in it, instead of freighting an ungainly steam ferry-boat with youth and beauty and pies and doughnuts, and paddling up some obscure creek to disembark upon a grassy lawn and wear themselves out with a long summer day's laborious frolicking under the impression that it was fun, were to sail away in a great steamship with flags flying and cannon pealing, and take a royal holiday beyond the broad ocean, in many a strange clime and in many a land renowned in history! They were to sail for months over the breezy Atlantic and the sunny Mediterranean; they were to scamper about the decks by day, filling the ship with shouts and laughter—or read novels and poetry in the shade of the smoke-stacks, or watch for the jelly-fish and the nautilus, over the side, and the shark, the whale, and other strange monsters of the deep; and at night they were to dance in the open air, on the upper deck, in the midst of a ball-room that stretched from horizon to horizon, and was domed by the bending heavens and lighted by no meaner lamps than the stars and the magnificent moon—dance, and promenade, and smoke, and sing, and make love, and search the skies for constellations that never associate with the "Big Dipper" they were so tired of; and they were to see the ships of twenty navies—the customs and costumes of twenty curious peoples —the great cities of half a world—they were to hob-nob with nobility and hold friendly converse with kings and princes, Grand Moguls, and the anointed lords of mighty empires!

It was a brave conception; it was the offspring of a most ingenious brain. It was well advertised, but it hardly needed it: the bold originality, the extraordinary character, the seductive nature, and the vastness of the enterprise provoked comment every where and advertised it in every household in the land. Who could read the programme of the excursion without longing to make one of the party? I will insert it here. It is almost as good as a map. As a text for this book, nothing could be better:

EXCURSION TO THE HOLY LAND, EGYPT, THE CRIMEA, GREECE, AND INTERMEDIATE POINTS OF INTEREST.

BROOKLYN, *February 1st*, 1867.

The undersigned will make an excursion as above during the coming season, and begs to submit to you the following programme:

A first-class steamer, to be under his own command, and capable of accommodating at least one hundred and fifty cabin passengers, will be selected, in which will be taken a select company, numbering not more than three-fourths of the ship's capacity. There is good reason to believe that this company can be easily made up in this immediate vicinity, of mutual friends and acquaintances.

The steamer will be provided with every necessary comfort, including library and musical instruments.

An experienced physician will be on board.

Leaving New York about June 1st, a middle and pleasant route will be taken across the Atlantic, and passing through the group of Azores, St. Michael will be reached in about ten days. A day or two will be spent here, enjoying the fruit and wild scenery of these islands, and the voyage continued, and Gibraltar reached in three or four days.

A day or two will be spent here in looking over the wonderful subterraneous fortifications, permission to visit these galleries being readily obtained.

From Gibraltar, running along the coasts of Spain and France, Marseilles will be reached in three days. Here ample time will be given not only to look over the city, which was founded six hundred years before the Christian era, and its artificial port, the finest of the kind in the Mediterranean, but to visit Paris during the Great Exhibition; and the beautiful city of Lyons, lying intermediate, from the heights of which, on a clear day, Mont Blanc and the Alps can be distinctly seen. Passengers who may wish to extend the time at Paris can do so, and, passing down through Switzerland, rejoin the steamer at Genoa.

From Marseilles to Genoa is a run of one night. The excursionists will have an opportunity to look over this, the "magnificent city of palaces," and visit the birthplace of Columbus, twelve miles off, over a beautiful road built by Napoleon I. From this point, excursions may be made to Milan, Lakes Como and Maggiore, or to Milan, Verona, (famous for its extraordinary fortifications,) Padua, and Venice. Or, if passengers desire to visit Parma (famous for Correggio's frescoes,) and Bologna, they can by rail go on to Florence, and rejoin the steamer at Leghorn, thus spending about three weeks amid the cities most famous for art in Italy.

From Genoa the run to Leghorn will be made along the coast in one night, and time appropriated to this point in which to visit Florence, its palaces and galleries; Pisa, its Cathedral and "Leaning Tower," and Lucca and its baths, and Roman amphitheatre; Florence, the most remote, being distant by rail about sixty miles.

From Leghorn to Naples, (calling at Civita Vecchia to land any who may prefer to go to Rome from that point,) the distance will be made in about thirty-six hours; the route will lay along the coast of Italy, close by Caprera, Elba, and Corsica. Arrangements have been made to take on board at Leghorn a pilot for Caprera, and, if practicable, a call will be made there to visit the home of Garibaldi.

Rome, [by rail] Herculaneum, Pompeii, Vesuvius, Virgil's tomb, and possibly, the ruins of Pæstum, can be visited, as well as the beautiful surroundings of Naples and its charming bay.

The next point of interest will be Palermo, the most beautiful city of Sicily, which will be reached in one night from Naples. A day will be spent here, and leaving in the evening, the course will be taken towards Athens.

Skirting along the north coast of Sicily, passing through the group of Æolian Isles, in sight of Stromboli and Vulcania, both active volcanoes, through the Straits of Messina, with "Scylla" on the one hand and "Charybdis" on the other, along the east coast of Sicily, and in sight of Mount Ætna, along the south coast of Italy, the west and south coast of Greece, in sight of ancient Crete, up Athens Gulf, and into the Piræus, Athens will be reached in two and a half or three days. After tarrying here awhile, the Bay of Salamis will be crossed, and a day given to Corinth, whence the voyage will be continued to Constantinople, passing on the way through the Grecian Archipelago, the Dardanelles, the Sea of Marmora, and the mouth of the Golden Horn, and arriving in about forty-eight hours from Athens.

After leaving Constantinople, the way will be taken out through the beautiful Bosphorus, across the Black Sea to Sebastopol and Balaklava, a run of about twenty-four hours. Here it is proposed to remain two days, visiting the harbors, fortifications, and battle-fields of the Crimea; thence back through the Bosphorus, touching at Constantinople to take in any who may have preferred to remain there; down through the Sea of Marmora and the Dardanelles, along the coasts of ancient Troy and Lydia in Asia, to Smyrna, which will be reached in two or two and a half days from Constantinople. A sufficient stay will be made here to give opportunity of visiting Ephesus, fifty miles distant by rail.

From Smyrna towards the Holy Land the course will lay through the Grecian

Archipelago, close by the Isle of Patmos, along the coast of Asia, ancient Pamphylia, and the Isle of Cyprus. Beirout will be reached in three days. At Beirout time will be given to visit Damascus; after which the steamer will proceed to Joppa.

From Joppa, Jerusalem, the River Jordan, the Sea of Tiberias, Nazareth, Bethany, Bethlehem, and other points of interest in the Holy Land can be visited, and here those who may have preferred to make the journey from Bierout *through* the country, passing through Damascus, Galilee, Capernaum, Samaria, and by the River Jordan and Sea of Tiberias, can rejoin the steamer.

Leaving Joppa, the next point of interest to visit will be Alexandria, which will be reached in twenty-four hours. The ruins of Cæsar's Palace, Pompey's Pillar, Cleopatra's Needle, the Catacombs, and ruins of ancient Alexandria, will be found worth the visit. The journey to Cairo, one hundred and thirty miles by rail, can be made in a few hours, and from which can be visited the site of ancient Memphis, Joseph's Granaries, and the Pyramids.

From Alexandria the route will be taken homeward, calling at Malta, Cagliari (in Sardinia,) and Parma (in Majorca,) all magnificent harbors, with charming scenery, and abounding in fruits.

A day or two will be spent at each place, and leaving Parma in the evening, Valencia in Spain will be reached the next morning. A few days will be spent in this, the finest city of Spain.

From Valencia, the homeward course will be continued, skirting along the coast of Spain. Alicant, Carthagena, Palos, and Malaga, will be passed but a mile or two distant, and Gibraltar reached in about twenty-four hours.

A stay of one day will be made here, and the voyage continued to Madeira, which will be reached in about three days. Captain Marryatt writes : "I do not know a spot on the globe which so much astonishes and delights upon first arrival as Madeira." A stay of one or two days will be made here, which, if time permits, may be extended, and passing on through the islands, and probably in sight of the Peak of Teneriffe, a southern track will be taken, and the Atlantic crossed within the latitudes of the Northeast trade winds, where mild and pleasant weather, and a smooth sea, can always be expected.

A call will be made at Bermuda, which lies directly in this route homeward, and will be reached in about ten days from Madeira, and after spending a short time with our friends the Bermudians, the final departure will be made for home, which will be reached in about three days.

Already, applications have been received from parties in Europe wishing to join the Excursion there.

The ship will at all times be a home, where the excursionists, if sick, will be surrounded by kind friends, and have all possible comfort and sympathy.

Should contagious sickness exist in any of the ports named in the programme, such ports will be passed, and others of interest substituted.

The price of passage is fixed at $1,250, currency, for each adult passenger. Choice of rooms and of seats at the tables apportioned in the order in which passages are engaged, and no passage considered engaged until ten per cent. of the passage money is deposited with the treasurer.

Passengers can remain on board of the steamer, at all ports, if they desire, without additional expense, and all boating at the expense of the ship.

All passages must be paid for when taken, in order that the most perfect arrangements be made for starting at the appointed time.

Applications for passage must be approved by the committee before tickets are issued, and can be made to the undersigned.

Articles of interest or curiosity, procured by the passengers during the voyage, may be brought home in the steamer free of charge.

Five dollars per day, in gold, it is believed, will be a fair calculation to make for *all* traveling expenses on shore, and at the various points where passengers may wish to leave the steamer for days at a time.

The trip can be extended, and the route changed, by *unanimous* vote of the passengers.

CHAS. C. DUNCAN,

117 WALL STREET, NEW YORK.

R. R. G******, Treasurer.

COMMITTEE ON APPLICATIONS.

J. T. H*****, ESQ., R. R. G*****, ESQ., C. C. DUNCAN.

COMMITTEE ON SELECTING STEAMER.

CAPT. W. W. S****. *Surveyor for Board of Underwriters.*
C. W. C*******, *Consulting Engineer for U. S. and Canada.*
J. T. H*****, ESQ.
C. C. DUNCAN.

P. S.—The very beautiful and substantial side wheel steamship "*Quaker City*" has been chartered for the occasion, and will leave New York, June 8th. Letters have been issued by the government commending the party to courtesies abroad.

What was there lacking about that programme, to make it perfectly irresistible? Nothing, that any finite mind could discover. Paris, England, Scotland, Switzerland, Italy—Garibaldi! The Grecian archipelago! Vesuvius! Constantinople! Smyrna! The Holy Land! Egypt and "our friends the Bermudians!" People in Europe desiring to join the Excursion—contagious sickness to be avoided—boating at the expense of the ship—physician on board—the circuit of the globe to be made if the passengers unanimously desired it—the company to be rigidly selected by a pitiless "Committee on Applications"—the vessel to be as rigidly selected by as pitiless a "Committee on Selecting Steamer." Human nature could not withstand these bewildering temptations. I hurried to the Treasurer's office and deposited my ten per cent. I rejoiced to know that a few vacant state-rooms were still left. I *did* avoid a critical personal examination into my character, by that bowelless committee, but I referred to all the people of high standing I could think of in the community who would be least likely to know any thing about me.

Shortly a supplementary programme was issued which set forth that the Plymouth Collection of Hymns would be used on board the ship. I then paid the balance of my passage money.

I was provided with a receipt, and duly and officially accepted as an excursionist. There was happiness in that, but it was tame compared to the novelty of being "select."

This supplementary programme also instructed the excursionists to provide themselves with light musical instruments for amusement in the ship; with saddles for Syrian travel; green spectacles and umbrellas; veils for Egypt; and substantial clothing to use in rough pilgrimizing in the Holy Land. Furthermore, it was suggested that although the ship's library would afford a fair amount of reading matter, it would still be well if each passenger would provide himself with a few guide-books, a Bible and some standard works of travel. A list was appended, which consisted chiefly of books relating to the Holy Land, since the Holy Land was part of the excursion and seemed to be its main feature.

Rev. Henry Ward Beecher was to have accompanied the expedition, but urgent duties obliged him to give up the idea. There were other passengers who could have been spared better, and would have been spared more willingly. Lieut. Gen. Sherman was to have been of the party, also, but the Indian war compelled his presence on the plains. A popular actress had entered her name on the ship's books, but something interfered, and *she* couldn't go. The "Drummer Boy of the Potomac" deserted, and lo, we had never a celebrity left!

However, we were to have a "battery of guns" from the Navy Department, (as per advertisement,) to be used in

answering royal salutes; and the document furnished by the
Secretary of the Navy, which was to make "Gen. Sherman
and party" welcome guests in the courts and camps of the
old world, was still left to us, though both document and battery, I think, were shorn of somewhat of their original august
proportions. However, had not we the seductive programme,
still, with its Paris, its Constantinople, Smyrna, Jerusalem,
Jericho, and "our friends the Bermudians?" What did we
care?

CHAPTER II.

OCCASIONALLY, during the following month, I dropped in at 117 Wall-street to inquire how the repairing and refurnishing of the vessel was coming on; how additions to the passenger list were averaging; how many people the committee were decreeing not "select," every day, and banishing in sorrow and tribulation. I was glad to know that we were to have a little printing-press on board and issue a daily newspaper of our own. I was glad to learn that our piano, our parlor organ and our melodeon were to be the best instruments of the kind that could be had in the market. I was proud to observe that among our excursionists were three ministers of the gospel, eight doctors, sixteen or eighteen ladies, several military and naval chieftains with sounding titles, an ample crop of "Professors" of various kinds, and a gentleman who had "COMMISSIONER OF THE UNITED STATES OF AMERICA TO EUROPE, ASIA, AND AFRICA" thundering after his name in one awful blast! I had carefully prepared myself to take rather a back seat in that ship, because of the uncommonly select material that would alone be permitted to pass through the camel's eye of that committee on credentials; I had schooled myself to expect an imposing array of military and naval heroes, and to have to set that back seat still further back in consequence of it, may be; but I state frankly that I was all unprepared for *this* crusher.

I fell under that titular avalanche a torn and blighted thing. I said that if that potentate *must* go over in our ship, why, I supposed he must—but that to my thinking, when the United

States considered it necessary to send a dignitary of that tonnage across the ocean, it would be in better taste, and safer, to take him apart and cart him over in sections, in several ships.

Ah, if I had only known, then, that he was only a common mortal, and that his mission had nothing more overpowering about it than the collecting of seeds, and uncommon yams and extraordinary cabbages and peculiar bullfrogs for that poor, useless, innocent, mildewed old fossil, the Smithsonian Institute, I would have felt *so* much relieved.

During that memorable month I basked in the happiness of being for once in my life drifting with the tide of a great popular movement. Every body was going to Europe—I, too, was going to Europe. Every body was going to the famous Paris Exposition—I, too, was going to the Paris Exposition. The steamship lines were carrying Americans out of the various ports of the country at the rate of four or five thousand a week, in the aggregate. If I met a dozen individuals, during that month, who were not going to Europe shortly, I have no distinct remembrance of it now. I walked about the city a good deal with a young Mr. Blucher, who was booked for the excursion. He was confiding, good-natured, unsophisticated, companionable; but he was not a man to set the river on fire. He had the most extraordinary notions about this European exodus, and came at last to consider the whole nation as packing up for emigration to France. We stepped into a store in Broadway, one day, where he bought a handkerchief, and when the man could not make change, Mr. B. said:

"Never mind, I'll hand it to you in Paris."

"But I am not going to Paris."

"How is—what did I understand you to say?"

"I said I am not going to Paris."

"Not going to *Paris!* Not g—well then, where in the nation *are* you going to?"

"Nowhere at all."

"Not any where whatsoever?—not any place on earth but this?"

"Not any place at all but just this—stay here all summer."

My comrade took his purchase and walked out of the store without a word—walked out with an injured look upon his countenance. Up the street apiece he broke silence and said impressively: "It was a lie—that is my opinion of it!"

"I'LL PAY YOU IN PARIS."

In the fullness of time the ship was ready to receive her passengers. I was introduced to the young gentleman who was to be my room mate, and found him to be intelligent, cheerful of spirit, unselfish, full of generous impulses, patient, considerate, and wonderfully good-natured. Not any passenger that sailed in the *Quaker City* will withhold his indorsement of what I have just said. We selected a state-room forward of the wheel, on the starboard side, "below decks." It had two berths in it, a dismal dead-light, a sink with a wash-bowl in it, and a long, sumptuously cushioned locker, which was to do service as a sofa—partly, and partly as a hiding-place for our things. Notwithstanding all this furniture, there was still room to turn around in, but not to swing a cat in, at least with entire security to the cat. However, the room was large, for a ship's state-room, and was in every way satisfactory.

The vessel was appointed to sail on a certain Saturday early in June.

A little after noon, on that distinguished Saturday, I reached the ship and went on board. All was bustle and confusion. [I have seen that remark before, somewhere.] The pier was crowded with carriages and men; passengers were arriving and hurrying on board; the vessel's decks were encumbered with trunks and valises; groups of excursionists, arrayed in unattractive traveling costumes, were moping about in a drizzling rain and looking as droopy and woe-begone as so many molting chickens. The gallant flag was up, but it was under the spell, too, and hung limp and disheartened by the mast. Altogether, it was the bluest, bluest spectacle! It was a pleasure excursion—there was no gainsaying that, because the programme said so—it was so nominated in the bond—but it surely hadn't the general aspect of one.

Finally, above the banging, and rumbling, and shouting and hissing of steam, rang the order to "cast off!"—a sudden rush to the gangways—a scampering ashore of visitors—a revolution of the wheels, and we were off—the pic-nic was begun! Two very mild cheers went up from the dripping crowd on the pier; we answered them gently from the slippery decks; the flag made an effort to wave, and failed; the "battery of guns" spake not—the ammunition was out.

We steamed down to the foot of the harbor and came to anchor. It was still raining. And not only raining, but storming. "Outside" we could see, ourselves, that there was a tremendous sea on. We must lie still, in the calm harbor, till the storm should abate. Our passengers hailed from fifteen

THE START.

States; only a few of them had ever been to sea before; manifestly it would not do to pit them against a full-blown tempest until they had got their sea-legs on.   Toward evening the two steam-tugs that had accompanied us with a rollicking champagne-party of young New Yorkers on board who wished to bid farewell to one of our number in due and ancient form, departed, and we were alone on the deep. On deep five fathoms, and anchored fast to the bottom. And out in the solemn rain, at that. This was pleasuring with a vengeance.

It was an appropriate relief when the gong sounded for prayer meeting. The first Saturday night of any other pleasure excursion might have been devoted to whist and dancing; but I submit it to the unprejudiced mind if it would have been in good taste for *us* to engage in such frivolities, considering what we had gone through and the frame of mind we were in. We would have shone at a wake, but not at any thing more festive.

However, there is always a cheering influence about the sea; and in my berth, that night, rocked by the measured swell of the waves, and lulled by the murmur of the distant surf, I soon passed tranquilly out of all consciousness of the dreary experiences of the day and damaging premonitions of the future.

CHAPTER III.

ALL day Sunday at anchor. The storm had gone down a
great deal, but the sea had not. It was still piling its
frothy hills high in air " outside," as we could plainly see with
the glasses. We could not properly begin a pleasure excursion on Sunday; we could not offer untried stomachs to so
pitiless a sea as that. We must lie still till Monday. And
we did. But we had repetitions of church and prayer-meet-
ings; and so, of course, we were just as eligibly situated as we
could have been any where.

I was up early that Sabbath morning, and was early to
breakfast. I felt a perfectly natural desire to have a good,
long, unprejudiced look at the passengers, at a time when they
should be free from self-consciousness—which is at breakfast,
when such a moment occurs in the lives of human beings at
all.

I was greatly surprised to see so many elderly people—I
might almost say, so many venerable people. A glance at the
long lines of heads was apt to make one think it was *all* gray.
But it was not. There was a tolerably fair sprinkling of
young folks, and another fair sprinkling of gentlemen and
ladies who were non-committal as to age, being neither actually old or absolutely young.

The next morning, we weighed anchor and went to sea. It
was a great happiness to get away, after this dragging,
dispiriting delay. I thought there never was such gladness in
the air before, such brightness in the sun, such beauty in the

sea. I was satisfied with the picnic, then, and with all its belongings. All my malicious instincts were dead within me; and as America faded out of sight, I think a spirit of charity rose up in their place that was as boundless, for the time being, as the broad ocean that was heaving its billows about us. I wished to express my feelings—I wished to lift up my voice and sing; but I did not know any thing to sing, and so I was obliged to give up the idea. It was no loss to the ship though, perhaps.

It was breezy and pleasant, but the sea was still very rough. One could not promenade without risking his neck; at one moment the bowsprit was taking a deadly aim at the sun in mid-heaven, and at the next it was trying to harpoon a shark in the bottom of the ocean. What a weird sensation it is to feel the stern of a ship sinking swiftly from under you and see the bow climbing high away among the clouds! One's safest course, that day, was to clasp a railing and hang on; walking was too precarious a pastime.

By some happy fortune I was not seasick.—That was a thing to be proud of. I had not always escaped before. If there is one thing in the world that will make a man peculiarly and insufferably self-conceited, it is to have his stomach behave itself, the first day at sea, when nearly all his comrades are seasick. Soon, a venerable fossil, shawled to the chin and bandaged like a mummy, appeared at the door of the after deck-house, and the next lurch of the ship shot him into my arms. I said:

"Good-morning, Sir. It is a fine day."

He put his hand on his stomach and said, " *Oh*, my!" and then staggered away and fell over the coop of a sky-light.

Presently another old gentleman was projected from the same door, with great violence. I said:

"Calm yourself, Sir—There is no hurry. It is a fine day, Sir."

He, also, put his hand on his stomach and said " *Oh*, my!" and reeled away.

3

In a little while another veteran was discharged abruptly
from the same door, clawing at the air for a saving support.
I said:

"Good-morning, Sir.   It is a fine day for pleasuring.   You
were about to say—"

"GOOD MORNING, SIR."

"*Oh*, my!"

I thought so.   I anticipated *him*, any how.   I staid there
and was bombarded with old gentlemen for an hour perhaps;
and all I got out of any of them was "*Oh*, my!"

I went away, then, in a thoughtful mood.   I said, this is a
good pleasure excursion.   I like it.   The passengers are not
garrulous, but still they are sociable.   I like those old people,

but somehow they all seem to have the " Oh, my " rather bad.

I knew what was the matter with them. They were seasick. And I was glad of it. We all like to see people seasick when we are not, ourselves. Playing whist by the cabin lamps when it is storming outside, is pleasant; walking the quarter-deck in the moonlight, is pleasant; smoking in the breezy foretop is pleasant, when one is not afraid to go up there; but these are all feeble and commonplace compared with the joy of seeing people suffering the miseries of seasickness.

I picked up a good deal of information during the afternoon. At one time I was climbing up the quarter-deck when the vessel's stern was in the sky; I was smoking a cigar and feeling passably comfortable. Somebody ejaculated:

" Come, now, *that* won't answer. Read the sign up there— No SMOKING ABAFT THE WHEEL!"

It was Capt. Duncan, chief of the expedition. I went forward, of course. I saw a long spy-glass lying on a desk in one of the upper-deck state-rooms back of the pilot-house, and reached after it—there was a ship in the distance:

" Ah, ah—hands off! Come out of that!"

I came out of that. I said to a deck-sweep—but in a low voice:

" Who is that overgrown pirate with the whiskers and the discordant voice?"

" It's Capt. Bursley—executive officer—sailing-master."

I loitered about awhile, and then, for want of something better to do, fell to carving a railing with my knife. Somebody said, in an insinuating, admonitory voice:

" Now *say*—my friend—don't you know any better than to be whittling the ship all to pieces that way? *You* ought to know better than that."

I went back and found the deck-sweep:

" Who is that smooth-faced animated outrage yonder in the fine clothes?"

" That's Capt. L****, the owner of the ship—he's one of the main bosses."

In the course of time I brought up on the starboard side of the pilot-house, and found a sextant lying on a bench. Now, I said, they "take the sun" through this thing; I should think I might see that vessel through it. I had hardly got it to my eye when some one touched me on the shoulder and said, deprecatingly:

"I'll have to get you to give that to me, Sir. If there's any

THE OLD PIRATE.

thing you'd like to know about taking the sun, I'd as soon tell you as not—but I don't like to trust any body with that instrument. If you want any figuring done— Aye-aye, Sir!"

He was gone, to answer a call from the other side. I sought the deck-sweep:

"Who is that spider-legged gorilla yonder with the sancti-monious countenance?"

"It's Capt. Jones, Sir—the chief mate."

"Well. This goes clear away ahead of any thing I ever heard of before. Do you—now I ask you as a man and a brother—*do* you think I could venture to throw a rock here in any given direction without hitting a captain of this ship?"

"Well, Sir, I don't know—I think likely you'd fetch the captain of the watch, may be, because he's a-standing right yonder in the way."

I went below—meditating, and a little down-hearted. I thought, if five cooks can spoil a broth, what may not five captains do with a pleasure excursion.

CHAPTER IV.

WE plowed along bravely for a week or more, and without any conflict of jurisdiction among the captains worth mentioning. The passengers soon learned to accommodate themselves to their new circumstances, and life in the ship became nearly as systematically monotonous as the routine of a barrack. I do not mean that it was dull, for it was not entirely so by any means—but there was a good deal of sameness about it. As is always the fashion at sea, the passengers shortly began to pick up sailor terms—a sign that they were beginning to feel at home. Half-past six was no longer half-past six to these pilgrims from New England, the South, and the Mississippi Valley, it was "seven bells;" eight, twelve and four o'clock were "eight bells;" the captain did not take the longitude at nine o'clock, but at "two bells." They spoke glibly of the "after cabin," the "for'rard cabin," "port and starboard" and the "fo'castle."

At seven bells the first gong rang; at eight there was breakfast, for such as were not too seasick to eat it. After that all the well people walked arm-in-arm up and down the long promenade deck, enjoying the fine summer mornings, and the seasick ones crawled out and propped themselves up in the lee of the paddle-boxes and ate their dismal tea and toast, and looked wretched. From eleven o'clock until luncheon, and from luncheon until dinner at six in the evening, the employments and amusements were various. Some reading was done; and much smoking and sewing, though not by the same parties; there were the monsters of the deep to be looked after and wondered at; strange ships had to be scrutinized through opera-glasses, and sage decisions arrived at concerning them; and more than that, every body took a personal interest in seeing that the flag was run up and politely dipped three times in response to the salutes of those strangers; in the smoking-room there were always parties of gentlemen playing euchre, draughts and dominoes, especially dominoes, that delightfully harmless game; and down on the main deck, "for'rard"— for'rard of the chicken-coops and the cattle—we had what was called "horse-billiards." Horse-billiards is a fine game. It affords good, active exercise, hilarity, and consuming excitement. It is a mixture of "hop-scotch" and shuffle-board played with a crutch. A large hop-scotch diagram is marked out on the deck with chalk, and each compartment numbered. You stand off three or four steps, with some broad wooden disks before you on the deck, and these you send forward with a vigorous thrust of a long crutch. If a disk stops on a chalk line, it does not count any thing. If it stops in division No. 7, it counts 7 ; in 5, it counts 5, and so on. The game is 100, and four can play at a time. That game would be very simple, played on a stationary floor, but with us, to play it well required science. We had to allow for the reeling of the ship to the right or the left. Very often one made calculations for a heel to the right and the ship did not go that way. The consequence was that that disk missed the whole hop-scotch plan a yard or two, and then there was humiliation on one side and laughter on the other.

When it rained, the passengers had to stay in the house, of course—or at least the cabins—and amuse themselves with games, reading, looking out of the windows at the very familiar billows, and talking gossip.

By 7 o'clock in the evening, dinner was about over; an hour's promenade on the upper deck followed; then the gong sounded and a large majority of the party repaired to the after cabin (upper) a handsome saloon fifty or sixty feet long, for prayers. The unregenerated called this saloon the "Synagogue." The devotions consisted only of two hymns from the "Plymouth Collection," and a short prayer, and seldom occupied more than fifteen minutes. The hymns were accompanied by parlor organ music when the sea was smooth enough to allow a performer to sit at the instrument without being lashed to his chair.

After prayers the Synagogue shortly took the semblance of a writing-school. The like of that picture was never seen in a ship before. Behind the long dining-tables on either side of the saloon, and scattered from one end to the other of the latter, some twenty or thirty gentlemen and ladies sat them down under the swaying lamps, and for two or three hours wrote diligently in their journals. Alas! that journals so voluminously begun should come to so lame and impotent a conclusion as most of them did! I doubt if there is a single pilgrim of all that host but can show a hundred fair pages of journal concerning the first twenty days' voyaging in the Quaker City; and I am morally certain that not ten of the party can show twenty pages of journal for the succeeding twenty thousand miles of voyaging! At certain periods it becomes the dearest ambition of a man to keep a faithful record of his performances in a book; and he dashes at this work with an enthusiasm that imposes on him the notion that keeping a journal is the veriest pastime in the world, and the pleasantest. But if he only lives twenty-one days, he will find out that only those rare natures that are made up of pluck, endurance, devotion to duty for duty's sake, and invincible determination, may hope to venture upon so tremendous an enterprise as the keeping of a journal and not sustain a shameful defeat.

One of our favorite youths, Jack, a splendid young fellow with a head full of good sense, and a pair of legs that were a wonder to look upon in the way of length, and straightness, and slimness, used to report progress every morning in the most glowing and spirited way, and say:

"Oh, I'm coming along bully!" (he was a little given to slang, in his happier moods,) "I wrote ten pages in my journal last night—and you know I wrote nine the night before, and twelve the night before that. Why it's only fun!"

"What do you find to put in it, Jack?"

" Oh, every thing. Latitude and longitude, noon every day; and how many miles we made last twenty-four hours; and all the domino-games I beat, and horse-billiards; and whales and sharks and porpoises; and the text of the sermon, Sundays; (because that'll tell at home, you know,) and the ships we saluted and what nation they were; and which way the wind was, and whether there was a heavy sea, and what sail we carried, though we don't ever carry *any*, principally, going against a head wind always—wonder what is the reason of that?—and how many lies Moult has told—Oh, every thing! I've got every thing down. My father told me to keep that journal. Father wouldn't take a thousand dollars for it when I get it done."

" No, Jack; it will be worth more than a thousand dollars— when you get it done."

" Do you?—no, but do you think it will, though?"

" Yes, it will be worth at least as much as a thousand dollars—when you get it done. May be, more."

" Well, I about half think so, myself. It ain't no slouch of a journal."

But it shortly became a most lamentable " slouch of a journal." One night in Paris, after a hard day's toil in sight-seeing, I said:

" Now I'll go and stroll around the cafés awhile, Jack, and give you a chance to write up your journal, old fellow."

His countenance lost its fire. He said:

" Well, no, you needn't mind. I think I won't run that journal any more. It is awful tedious. Do you know—I reckon I'm as much as four thousand pages behind hand. I haven't got any France in it at all. First I thought I'd leave France out and start fresh. But that wouldn't do, *would* it? The governor would say, ' Hello, here—didn't see any thing in France?' *That* cat wouldn't fight, you know. First I thought I'd copy France out of the guide-book, like old Badger in the for'rard cabin who's writing a book, but there's more than three hundred pages of it. Oh, *I* don't think a journal's any use— do you? They're only a bother, *ain't* they?"

"Yes, a journal that is incomplete isn't of much use, but a journal properly kept, is worth a thousand dollars,—when you've got it done."

"A thousand!—well I should think so. *I* wouldn't finish it for a million."

His experience was only the experience of the majority of

DANCING UNDER DIFFICULTIES.

that industrious night-school in the cabin. If you wish to inflict a heartless and malignant punishment upon a young person, pledge him to keep a journal a year.

A good many expedients were resorted to to keep the excursionists amused and satisfied. A club was formed, of all the passengers, which met in the writing-school after prayers and read aloud about the countries we were approaching, and discussed the information so obtained.

Several times the photographer of the expedition brought out his transparent pictures and gave us a handsome magic lantern exhibition. His views were nearly all of foreign scenes, but there were one or two home pictures among them. He advertised that he would "open his performance in the after cabin at 'two bells,' (9, p. m.,) and show the passengers where they shall eventually arrive "—which was all very well, but by a funny accident the first picture that flamed out upon the canvas was a view of Greenwood Cemetery!

On several starlight nights we danced on the upper deck, under the awnings, and made something of a ball-room display of brilliancy by hanging a number of ship's lanterns to the stanchions. Our music consisted of the well-mixed strains of a melodeon which was a little asthmatic and apt to catch its breath where it ought to come out strong; a clarinet which was a little unreliable on the high keys and rather melancholy on the low ones; and a disreputable accordion that had a leak somewhere and breathed louder than it squawked—a more elegant term does not occur to me just now. However, the dancing was infinitely worse than the music. When the ship rolled to starboard the whole platoon of dancers came charging down to starboard with it, and brought up in mass at the rail; and when it rolled to port, they went floundering down to port with the same unanimity of sentiment. Waltzers spun around precariously for a matter of fifteen seconds and then went skurrying down to the rail as if they meant to go overboard. The Virginia reel, as performed on board the *Quaker City*, had more genuine reel about it than any reel I ever saw before, and was as full of interest to the spectator as it was full of desperate chances and hairbreadth escapes to the participant. We gave up dancing, finally.

We celebrated a lady's birthday anniversary, with toasts, speeches, a poem, and so forth. We also had a mock trial. No ship ever went to sea that hadn't a mock trial on board. The purser was accused of stealing an overcoat from state-room

No. 10. A judge was appointed; also clerks, a crier of the court, constables, sheriffs; counsel for the State and for the defendant; witnesses were subpœnaed, and a jury empaneled after much challenging. The witnesses were stupid, and unreliable and contradictory, as witnesses always are. The counsel were eloquent, argumentative and vindictively abusive of each other, as was characteristic and proper. The case was

MOCK TRIAL.

at last submitted, and duly finished by the judge with an absurd decision and a ridiculous sentence.

The acting of charades was tried, on several evenings, by the young gentlemen and ladies, in the cabins, and proved the most distinguished success of all the amusement experiments.

An attempt was made to organize a debating club, but it was a failure. There was no oratorical talent in the ship.

We all enjoyed ourselves—I think I can safely say that, but

it was in a rather quiet way. We very, very seldom played the piano; we played the flute and the clarinet together, and made good music, too, what there was of it, but we always played the same old tune; it was a very pretty tune—how well I remember it—I wonder when I shall ever get rid of it. We never played either the melodeon or the organ, except at devotions—but I am too fast: young Albert *did* know part of a tune—something about "O Something-Or-Other How Sweet it is to Know that he's his What's-his-Name," (I do not remember the exact title of it, but it was very plaintive, and full of sentiment;) Albert played that pretty much all the time, until we contracted with him to restrain himself. But nobody ever sang by moonlight on the upper deck, and the congregational singing at church and prayers was not of a superior order of architecture. I put up with it as long as I could, and then joined in and tried to improve it, but this encouraged young George to join in too, and that made a failure of it; because George's voice was just "turning," and when he was singing a dismal sort of base, it was apt to fly off the handle and startle every body with a most discordant cackle on the upper notes. George didn't know the tunes, either, which was also a drawback to his performances. I said:

"Come, now, George, *don't* improvise. It looks too egotistical. It will provoke remark. Just stick to 'Coronation,' like the others. It is a good tune—*you* can't improve it any, just off-hand, in this way."

"Why I'm not trying to improve it—and I *am* singing like the others—just as it is in the notes."

And he honestly thought he was, too; and so he had no one to blame but himself when his voice caught on the centre occasionally, and gave him the lockjaw.

There were those among the unregenerated who attributed the unceasing head-winds to our distressing choir-music. There were those who said openly that it was taking chances enough to have such ghastly music going on, even when it was at its best; and that to exaggerate the crime by letting George help, was simply flying in the face of Providence. These said that the choir would keep up their lacerating attempts at melody until they would bring down a storm some day that would sink the ship.

There were even grumblers at the prayers. The executive officer said the Pilgrims had no charity:

"There they are, down there every night at eight bells, praying for fair winds—when they know as well as I do that this is the only ship going east this time of the year, but there's a thousand coming west—what's a fair wind for us is a *head* wind to them—the Almighty's blowing a fair wind for a thousand vessels, and this tribe wants him to turn it clear around so as to accommodate *one*,—and she a steamship at that! It ain't good sense, it ain't good reason, it ain't good Christianity, it ain't common human charity. Avast with such nonsense!"

CHAPTER V.

TAKING it "by and large," as the sailors say, we had a pleasant ten days' run from New York to the Azores islands—not a fast run, for the distance is only twenty-four hundred miles—but a right pleasant one, in the main. True, we had head-winds *all* the time, and several stormy experiences which sent fifty per cent. of the passengers to bed, sick, and made the ship look dismal and deserted—stormy experiences that all will remember who weathered them on the tumbling deck, and caught the vast sheets of spray that every now and then sprang high in air from the weather bow and swept the ship like a thunder-shower; but for the most part we had balmy summer weather, and nights that were even finer than the days. We had the phenomenon of a full moon located just in the same spot in the heavens at the same hour every night. The reason of this singular conduct on the part of the moon did not occur to us at first, but it did afterward when we reflected that we were gaining about twenty minutes every day, because we were going east so fast —we gained just about enough every day to keep along with the moon. It was becoming an old moon to the friends we had left behind us, but to us Joshuas it stood still in the same place, and remained always the same.

Young Mr. Blucher, who is from the Far West, and is on his first voyage, was a good deal worried by the constantly changing "ship-time." He was proud of his new watch at first, and used to drag it out promptly when eight bells struck at noon, but he came to look after a while as if he were losing

confidence in it.   Seven days out from New York he came on
deck, and said with great decision:

"This thing's a swindle !"

"What's a swindle ?"

"Why, this watch.   I bought her out in Illinois—gave $150
for her—and I thought she was good.   And, by George, she *is*
good on shore, but somehow she don't keep up her lick here
on the water—gets seasick, may be.   She skips; she runs along
regular enough till half-past eleven, and then, all of a sudden,
she lets down.   I've set that old regulator up faster and faster,
till I've shoved it clear around; but it don't do any good; she
just distances every watch in the ship, and clatters along in a
way that's astonishing till it is noon, but them eight bells always gets in about ten minutes ahead of her any way.   I don't
know what to do with her now.   She's doing all she can—
she's going her best gait, but it won't save her.   Now, don't
you know, there ain't a watch in the ship that's making better
time than she is: but what does it signify ?   When you hear
them eight bells you'll find her just about ten minutes short of
her score, sure."

The ship was gaining a full hour every three days, and this
fellow was trying to make his watch go fast enough to keep up
to her.   But, as he had said, he had pushed the regulator up
as far as it would go, and the watch was "on its best gait,"
and so nothing was left him but to fold his hands and see the
ship beat the race.   We sent him to the captain, and he explained to him the mystery of "ship-time," and set his troubled
mind at rest.   This young man asked a great many questions
about seasickness before we left, and wanted to know what its
characteristics were, and how he was to tell when he had it.
He found out.

We saw the usual sharks, blackfish, porpoises, &c., of course,
and by and by large schools of Portuguese men-of-war were
added to the regular list of sea wonders.   Some of them were
white and some of a brilliant carmine color.   The nautilus is
nothing but a transparent web of jelly, that spreads itself to
catch the wind, and has fleshy-looking strings a foot or two

long dangling from it to keep it steady in the water. It is an
accomplished sailor, and has good sailor judgment. It reefs its
sail when a storm threatens or the wind blows pretty hard, and
furls it entirely and goes down when a gale blows. Ordinarily
it keeps its sail wet and in good sailing order by turning over
and dipping it in the water for a moment. Seamen say the
nautilus is only found in these waters between the 35th and
45th parallels of latitude.

"LAND, HO!"

At three o'clock on the morning of the 21st of June, we
were awakened and notified that the Azores islands were in
sight. I said I did not take any interest in islands at three
o'clock in the morning. But another persecutor came, and
then another and another, and finally believing that the general
enthusiasm would permit no one to slumber in peace, I got up
and went sleepily on deck. It was five and a half o'clock now,
and a raw, blustering morning. The passengers were huddled
about the smoke-stacks and fortified behind ventilators, and all
were wrapped in wintry costumes, and looking sleepy and unhappy in the pitiless gale and the drenching spray.

4

The island in sight was Flores. It seemed only a mountain of mud standing up out of the dull mists of the sea. But as we bore down upon it, the sun came out and made it a beautiful picture—a mass of green farms and meadows that swelled up to a height of fifteen hundred feet, and mingled its upper outlines with the clouds. It was ribbed with sharp, steep ridges, and cloven with narrow canons, and here and there on the heights, rocky upheavals shaped themselves into mimic battlements and castles; and out of rifted clouds came broad shafts of sunlight, that painted summit, and slope, and glen, with bands of fire, and left belts of sombre shade between. It was the aurora borealis of the frozen pole exiled to a summer land!

We skirted around two-thirds of the island, four miles from shore, and all the opera-glasses in the ship were called into requisition to settle disputes as to whether mossy spots on the uplands were groves of trees or groves of weeds, or whether the white villages down by the sea were really villages or only the clustering tombstones of cemeteries. Finally, we stood to sea and bore away for San Miguel, and Flores shortly became a dome of mud again, and sank down among the mists and disappeared. But to many a seasick passenger it was good to see the green hills again, and all were more cheerful after this episode than any body could have expected them to be, considering how sinfully early they had gotten up.

But we had to change our purpose about San Miguel, for a storm came up about noon that so tossed and pitched the vessel that common sense dictated a run for shelter. Therefore we steered for the nearest island of the group—Fayal, (the people there pronounce it Fy-all, and put the accent on the first syllable.) We anchored in the open roadstead of Horta, half a mile from the shore. The town has eight thousand to ten thousand inhabitants. Its snow-white houses nestle cosily in a sea of fresh green vegetation, and no village could look prettier or more attractive. It sits in the lap of an amphitheatre of hills which are three hundred to seven hundred feet high, and carefully cultivated clear to their summits—not a foot of soil left idle. Every farm and every acre is cut up into little square

inclosures by stone walls, whose duty it is to protect the growing products from the destructive gales that blow there. These
hundreds of green squares, marked by their black lava walls,
make the hills look like vast checker-boards.

The islands belong to Portugal, and every thing in Fayal has
Portuguese characteristics about it. But more of that anon.
A swarm of swarthy, noisy, lying, shoulder-shrugging, gesticulating Portuguese boatmen, with brass rings in their ears, and
fraud in their hearts, climbed the ship's sides, and various parties of us contracted with them to take us ashore at so much a
head, silver coin of any country. We landed under the walls
of a little fort, armed with batteries of twelve and thirty-two
pounders, which Horta considered a most formidable institution, but if we were ever to get after it with one of our turreted monitors, they would have to move it out in the country
if they wanted it where they could go and find it again when
they needed it. The group on the pier was a rusty one—men
and women, and boys and girls, all ragged, and barefoot, uncombed and unclean, and by instinct, education, and profession,
beggars. They trooped after us, and never more, while we
tarried in Fayal, did we get rid of them. We walked up the
middle of the principal street, and these vermin surrounded us
on all sides, and glared upon us; and every moment excited
couples shot ahead of the procession to get a good look back,
just as village boys do when they accompany the elephant on
his advertising trip from street to street. It was very flattering
to me to be part of the material for such a sensation. Here
and there in the doorways we saw women, with fashionable
Portuguese hoods on. This hood is of thick blue cloth,
attached to a cloak of the same stuff, and is a marvel of ugliness. It stands up high, and spreads far abroad, and is unfath-
omably deep. It fits like a circus tent, and a woman's head is
hidden away in it like the man's who prompts the singers from
his tin shed in the stage of an opera. There is no particle of
trimming about this monstrous *capote*, as they call it—it is just
a plain, ugly dead-blue mass of sail, and a woman can't go
within eight points of the wind with one of them on; she has

to go before the wind or not at all. The general style of the capote is the same in all the islands, and will remain so for the next ten thousand years, but each island shapes its capotes just enough differently from the others to enable an observer to tell at a glance what particular island a lady hails from.

CAPOTE.

The Portuguese pennies or *reis* (pronounced rays) are prodigious. It takes one thousand reis to make a dollar, and all financial estimates are made in reis. We did not know this until after we had found it out through Blucher. Blucher said he was so happy and so grateful to be on solid land once more, that he wanted to give a feast—said he had heard it was a cheap land, and he was bound to have a grand banquet. He invited nine of us, and we ate an excellent dinner at the principal hotel. In the midst of the jollity produced by good cigars, good wine, and passable anecdotes, the landlord presented his bill. Blucher glanced at it and his countenance fell. He took another look to assure himself that his senses had not deceived him, and then read the items aloud, in a faltering voice, while the roses in his cheeks turned to ashes:

"'Ten dinners, at 600 reis, 6,000 reis!' Ruin and desolation!"

"'Twenty-five cigars, at 100 reis, 2,500 reis!' Oh, my sainted mother!"

"'Eleven bottles of wine, at 1,200 reis, 13,200 reis!' Be with us all!"

"'TOTAL, TWENTY-ONE THOUSAND SEVEN HUNDRED REIS!' The suffering Moses!—there ain't money enough in the ship to pay that bill! Go—leave me to my misery, boys, I am a ruined community."

I think it was the blankest looking party I ever saw. No body could say a word. It was as if every soul had been stricken dumb. Wine-glasses descended slowly to the table, their contents untasted. Cigars dropped unnoticed from nerveless fingers. Each man sought his neighbor's eye, but found in it no ray of hope, no encouragement. At last the fearful silence was broken. The shadow of a desperate resolve settled

"RUIN AND DESOLATION!"

upon Blucher's countenance like a cloud, and he rose up and said :

"Landlord, this is a low, mean swindle, and I'll never, never stand it. Here's a hundred and fifty dollars, Sir, and it's all you'll get—I'll swim in blood, before I'll pay a cent more."

Our spirits rose and the landlord's fell—at least we thought so ; he was confused at any rate, notwithstanding he had not understood a word that had been said. He glanced from the little pile of gold pieces to Blucher several times, and then went out. He must have visited an American, for, when he returned, he brought back his bill translated into a language that a Christian could understand—thus :

```
10 dinners, 6,000 reis, or....................................$6.00
25 cigars, 2,500 reis, or.....................................  2.50
11 bottles wine, 13,200 reis, or..............................13.20
                                                             ─────
    Total 21,700 reis, or.............................$21.70
```

Happiness reigned once more in Blucher's dinner party. More refreshments were ordered.

CHAPTER VI.

I THINK the Azores must be very little known in America.
Out of our whole ship's company there was not a solitary
individual who knew any thing whatever about them. Some
of the party, well read concerning most other lands, had no
other information about the Azores than that they were a group
of nine or ten small islands far out in the Atlantic, something
more than half way between New York and Gibraltar. That
was all. These considerations move me to put in a paragraph
of dry facts just here.

The community is eminently Portuguese—that is to say, it
is slow, poor, shiftless, sleepy, and lazy. There is a civil governor, appointed by the King of Portugal; and also a military
governor, who can assume supreme control and suspend the
civil government at his pleasure. The islands contain a population of about 200,000, almost entirely Portuguese. Every
thing is staid and settled, for the country was one hundred
years old when Columbus discovered America. The principal
crop is corn, and they raise it and grind it just as their great-
great-great-grandfathers did. They plow with a board slightly
shod with iron; their trifling little harrows are drawn by men
and women; small windmills grind the corn, ten bushels a
day, and there is one assistant superintendent to feed the mill
and a general superintendent to stand by and keep him from
going to sleep. When the wind changes they hitch on some
donkeys, and actually turn the whole upper half of the mill
around until the sails are in proper position, instead of fixing
the concern so that the sails could be moved instead of the

mill. Oxen tread the wheat from the ear, after the fashion prevalent in the time of Methuselah. There is not a wheel-barrow in the land—they carry every thing on their heads, or on donkeys, or in a wicker-bodied cart, whose wheels are solid blocks of wood and whose axles turn with the wheel. There is not a modern plow in the islands, or a threshing-machine. All attempts to introduce them have failed. The good Cath-olic Portuguese crossed himself and prayed God to shield him from all blasphemous desire to know more than his father did before him. The climate is mild; they never have snow or ice, and I saw no chimneys in the town. The donkeys and the men, women and children of a family, all eat and sleep in the same room, and are unclean, are ravaged by vermin, and are truly happy. The people lie, and cheat the stranger, and are desperately ignorant, and have hardly any reverence for their dead. The latter trait shows how little better they are than the donkeys they eat and sleep with. The only well-dressed Portuguese in the camp are the half a dozen well-to-do families, the Jesuit priests and the soldiers of the little garri-son. The wages of a laborer are twenty to twenty-four cents a day, and those of a good mechanic about twice as much. They count it in reis at a thousand to the dollar, and this makes them rich and contented. Fine grapes used to grow in the islands, and an excellent wine was made and exported. But a disease killed all the vines fifteen years ago, and since that time no wine has been made. The islands being wholly of volcanic origin, the soil is necessarily very rich. Nearly every foot of ground is under cultivation, and two or three crops a year of each article are produced, but nothing is exported save a few oranges—chiefly to England. Nobody comes here, and nobody goes away. News is a thing unknown in Fayal. A thirst for it is a passion equally unknown. A Portuguese of average intelligence inquired if our civil war was over? because, he said, somebody had told him it was—or at least it ran in his mind that somebody had told him some-thing like that! And when a passenger gave an officer of the garrison copies of the *Tribune*, the *Herald*, and *Times*, he was

PORT OF HORTA, FAYAL.

surprised to find later news in them from Lisbon than he had just received by the little monthly steamer. He was told that it came by cable. He said he knew they had tried to lay a cable ten years ago, but it had been in his mind, somehow, that they hadn't succeeded!

It is in communities like this that Jesuit humbuggery flourishes. We visited a Jesuit cathedral nearly two hundred years old, and found in it a piece of the veritable cross upon which our Saviour was crucified. It was polished and hard, and in as excellent a state of preservation as if the dread tragedy on Calvary had occurred yesterday instead of eighteen centuries ago. But these confiding people believe in that piece of wood unhesitatingly.

In a chapel of the cathedral is an altar with facings of solid silver—at least they call it so, and I think myself it would go a couple of hundred to the ton (to speak after the fashion of the silver miners,) and before it is kept forever burning a small lamp. A devout lady who died, left money and contracted for unlimited masses for the repose of her soul, and also stipulated that this lamp should be kept lighted always, day and night. She did all this before she died, you understand. It is a very small lamp, and a very dim one, and it could not work her much damage, I think, if it went out altogether.

The great altar of the cathedral, and also three or four minor ones, are a perfect mass of gilt gimcracks and gingerbread. And they have a swarm of rusty, dusty, battered apostles standing around the filagree work, some on one leg and some with one eye out but a gamey look in the other, and some with two or three fingers gone, and some with not enough nose left to blow—all of them crippled and discouraged, and fitter subjects for the hospital than the cathedral.

The walls of the chancel are of porcelain, all pictured over with figures of almost life size, very elegantly wrought, and dressed in the fanciful costumes of two centuries ago. The design was a history of something or somebody, but none of us were learned enough to read the story. The old father, reposing under a stone close by, dated 1686, might have told us if he could have risen. But he didn't.

As we came down through the town, we encountered a squad of little donkeys ready saddled for use. The saddles were peculiar, to say the least. They consisted of a sort of saw-buck, with a small mattress on it, and this furniture covered about half the donkey. There were no stirrups, but really such supports were not needed—to use such a saddle was the next thing to riding a dinner table—there was ample support clear out to one's knee joints. A pack of ragged Portuguese muleteers crowded around us, offering their beasts at half a dollar an hour—more rascality to the stranger, for the market price is sixteen cents. Half a dozen of us mounted the ungainly affairs, and submitted to the indignity of making a ridiculous spectacle of ourselves through the principal streets of a town of 10,000 inhabitants.

We started. It was not a trot, a gallop, or a canter, but a stampede, and made up of all possible or conceivable gaits. No spurs were necessary. There was a muleteer to every donkey and a dozen volunteers beside, and they banged the donkeys with their goad-sticks, and pricked them with their spikes, and shouted something that sounded like " *Sekki-yah !*" and kept up a din and a racket that was worse than Bedlam itself. These rascals were all on foot, but no matter, they were always up to time—they can outrun and outlast a donkey. Altogether ours was a lively and a picturesque procession, and drew crowded audiences to the balconies wherever we went.

Blucher could do nothing at all with his donkey. The beast scampered zigzag across the road and the others ran into him ; he scraped Blucher against carts and the corners of houses ; the road was fenced in with high stone walls, and the donkey gave him a polishing first on one side and then on the other, but never once took the middle ; he finally came to the house he was born in and darted into the parlor, scraping Blucher off at the doorway. After remounting, Blucher said to the muleteer, " Now, that's enough, you know ; you go slow here-

after." But the fellow knew no English and did not understand, so he simply said, "*Sekki-yah!*" and the donkey was
off again like a shot. He turned a corner suddenly, and
Blucher went over his head. And, to speak truly, every mule
stumbled over the two, and the whole cavalcade was piled up

"SEKKI-YAH!"

in a heap. No harm done. A fall from one of those donkeys
is of little more consequence than rolling off a sofa. The
donkeys all stood still after the catastrophe, and waited for
their dismembered saddles to be patched up and put on by the
noisy muleteers. Blucher was pretty angry, and wanted to
swear, but every time he opened his mouth his animal did so

also, and let off a series of brays that drowned all other
sounds.

It was fun, skurrying around the breezy hills and through
the beautiful canons. There was that rare thing, novelty,
about it; it was a fresh, new, exhilarating sensation, this
donkey riding, and worth a hundred worn and threadbare
home pleasures.

The roads were a wonder, and well they might be. Here
was an island with only a handful of people in it—25,000—
and yet such fine roads do not exist in the United States outside of Central Park. Every where you go, in any direction,
you find either a hard, smooth, level thoroughfare, just
sprinkled with black lava sand, and bordered with little gutters
neatly paved with small smooth pebbles, or compactly paved
ones like Broadway. They talk much of the Russ pavement
in New York, and call it a new invention—yet here they
have been using it in this remote little isle of the sea for two
hundred years! Every street in Horta is handsomely paved
with the heavy Russ blocks, and the surface is neat and true
as a floor—not marred by holes like Broadway. And every
road is fenced in by tall, solid lava walls, which will last a
thousand years in this land where frost is unknown. They are
very thick, and are often plastered and whitewashed, and
capped with projecting slabs of cut stone. Trees from gardens
above hang their swaying tendrils down, and contrast their
bright green with the whitewash or the black lava of the
walls, and make them beautiful. The trees and vines stretch
across these narrow roadways sometimes, and so shut out the
sun that you seem to be riding through a tunnel. The pavements, the roads, and the bridges are all government work.

The bridges are of a single span—a single arch—of cut
stone, without a support, and paved on top with flags of lava
and ornamental pebble work. Every where are walls, walls,
walls,—and all of them tasteful and handsome—and eternally substantial; and every where are those marvelous pavements, so neat, so smooth, and so indestructible. And if ever
roads and streets, and the outsides of houses, were perfectly

free from any sign or semblance of dirt, or dust, or mud, or uncleanliness of any kind, it is Horta, it is Fayal. The lower classes of the people, in their persons and their domicils, are not clean—but there it stops—the town and the island are miracles of cleanliness.

We arrived home again finally, after a ten-mile excursion, and the irrepressible muleteers scampered at our heels through the main street, goading the donkeys, shouting the everlasting "*Sekki-yah*," and singing "John Brown's Body" in ruinous English.

When we were dismounted and it came to settling, the shouting and jawing, and swearing and quarreling among the muleteers and with us, was nearly deafening. One fellow would demand a dollar an hour for the use of his donkey; another claimed half a dollar for pricking him up, another a quarter for helping in that service, and about fourteen guides presented bills for showing us the way through the town and its environs; and every vagrant of them was more vociferous, and more vehement, and more frantic in gesture than his neighbor. We paid one guide, and paid for one muleteer to each donkey.

The mountains on some of the islands are very high. We sailed along the shore of the Island of Pico, under a stately green pyramid that rose up with one unbroken sweep from our very feet to an altitude of 7,613 feet, and thrust its summit above the white clouds like an island adrift in a fog!

We got plenty of fresh oranges, lemons, figs, apricots, etc. in these Azores, of course. But I will desist. I am not here to write Patent-Office reports.

We are on our way to Gibraltar, and shall reach there five or six days out from the Azores.

CHAPTER VII.

A WEEK of buffeting a tempestuous and relentless sea; a week of seasickness and deserted cabins; of lonely quarter-decks drenched with spray—spray so ambitious that it even coated the smoke-stacks thick with a white crust of salt to their very tops; a week of shivering in the shelter of the life-boats and deck-houses by day, and blowing suffocating "clouds" and boisterously performing at dominoes in the smoking room at night.

And the last night of the seven was the stormiest of all. There was no thunder, no noise but the pounding bows of the ship, the keen whistling of the gale through the cordage, and the rush of the seething waters. But the vessel climbed aloft as if she would climb to heaven—then paused an instant that seemed a century, and plunged headlong down again, as from a precipice. The sheeted sprays drenched the decks like rain. The blackness of darkness was every where. At long intervals a flash of lightning clove it with a quivering line of fire, that revealed a heaving world of water where was nothing before, kindled the dusky cordage to glittering silver, and lit up the faces of the men with a ghastly lustre!

Fear drove many on deck that were used to avoiding the night-winds and the spray. Some thought the vessel could not live through the night, and it seemed less dreadful to stand out in the midst of the wild tempest and *see* the peril that threatened than to be shut up in the sepulchral cabins, under the dim lamps and imagine the horrors that were abroad on the ocean. And once out—once where they could see the ship struggling in the strong grasp of the storm—once where they could hear the shriek of the winds, and face the driving spray and look out upon the majestic picture the lightnings disclosed, they were prisoners to a fierce fascination they could not resist, and so remained. It was a wild night—and a very, very long one.

Every body was sent scampering to the deck at seven o'clock this lovely morning of the 30th of June with the glad news that land was in sight! It was a rare thing and a joyful, to see *all* the ship's family abroad once more, albeit the happiness that sat upon every countenance could only partly conceal the ravages which that long siege of storms had wrought there. But dull eyes soon sparkled with pleasure, pallid cheeks flushed again, and frames weakened by sickness gathered new life from the quickening influences of the bright, fresh morning. Yea, and from a still more potent influence: the worn casta-ways were to see the blessed land again!—and to see it was to bring back that mother-land that was in all their thoughts.

Within the hour we were fairly within the Straits of Gib-raltar, the tall yellow-splotched hills of Africa on our right, with their bases veiled in a blue haze and their summits swathed in clouds—the same being according to Scripture, which says that "clouds and darkness are over the land." The words were spoken of this particular portion of Africa, I be-lieve. On our left were the granite-ribbed domes of old Spain. The Strait is only thirteen miles wide in its narrowest part.

At short intervals, along the Spanish shore, were quaint-looking old stone towers—Moorish, we thought—but learned better afterwards. In former times the Morocco rascals used to coast along the Spanish Main in their boats till a safe oppor-tunity seemed to present itself, and then dart in and capture a Spanish village, and carry off all the pretty women they could find. It was a pleasant business, and was very popular. The Spaniards built these watchtowers on the hills to enable them to keep a sharper lookout on the Moroccan speculators.

The picture on the other hand was very beautiful to eyes weary of the changeless sea, and bye and bye the ship's company grew wonderfully cheerful. But while we stood admiring the cloud-capped peaks and the lowlands robed in misty gloom, a finer picture burst upon us and chained every eye like a magnet—a stately ship, with canvas piled on canvas till

BEAUTIFUL STRANGER.

she was one towering mass of bellying sail! She came speeding over the sea like a great bird. Africa and Spain were forgotten. All homage was for the beautiful stranger. While every body gazed, she swept superbly by and flung the Stars and Stripes to the breeze! Quicker than thought, hats and handkerchiefs flashed in the air, and a cheer went up! She was beautiful before—she was radiant now. Many a one on our decks knew then for the first time how tame a sight his country's flag is at home compared to what it is in a foreign land. To see it is to see a vision of home itself and all its idols, and feel a thrill that would stir a very river of sluggish blood!

We were approaching the famed Pillars of Hercules, and already the African one, "Ape's Hill," a grand old mountain with summit streaked with granite ledges, was in sight. The other, the great Rock of Gibraltar, was yet to come. The ancients considered the Pillars of Hercules the head of navigation and the end of the world. The information the ancients didn't have was very voluminous. Even the prophets wrote book after book and epistle after epistle, yet never once hinted at the existence of a great continent on our side of the water; yet they must have known it was there, I should think.

In a few moments a lonely and enormous mass of rock,

ROCK OF GIBRALTER.

standing seemingly in the centre of the wide strait and apparently washed on all sides by the sea, swung magnificently into view, and we needed no tedious traveled parrot to tell us it was Gibraltar. There could not be two rocks like that in one kingdom.

The Rock of Gibraltar is about a mile and a half long, I should say, by 1,400 to 1,500 feet high, and a quarter of a mile wide at its base. One side and one end of it come about as straight up out of the sea as the side of a house, the other end is irregular and the other side is a steep slant which an army would find very difficult to climb. At the foot of this slant is the walled town of Gibraltar—or rather the town occupies part of the slant. Every where—on hillside, in the precipice, by the sea, on the heights,—every where you choose to look, Gibraltar is clad with masonry and bristling with guns. It makes a striking and lively picture, from whatsoever point you contemplate it. It is pushed out into the sea on the end of a flat, narrow strip of land, and is suggestive of a "gob" of mud on the end of a shingle. A few hundred yards of this flat ground at its base belongs to the English, and then, extending across the strip from the Atlantic to the Mediterranean, a distance of a quarter of a mile, comes the "Neutral Ground," a space two or three hundred yards wide, which is free to both parties.

"Are you going through Spain to Paris?" That question was bandied about the ship day and night from Fayal to Gibraltar, and I thought I never could get so tired of hearing any one combination of words again, or more tired of answering, "I don't know." At the last moment six or seven had sufficient decision of character to make up their minds to go, and did go, and I felt a sense of relief at once—it was forever too late, now, and I could make up my mind at my leisure, not to go. I must have a prodigious quantity of mind; it takes me as much as a week, sometimes, to make it up.

But behold how annoyances repeat themselves. We had no sooner gotten rid of the Spain distress than the Gibraltar guides started another—a tiresome repetition of a legend that

5

had nothing very astonishing about it, even in the first place :
" That high hill yonder is called the Queen's Chair; it is
because one of the Queens of Spain placed her chair there
when the French and Spanish troops were besieging Gibraltar,
and said she would never move from the spot till the English
flag was lowered from the fortresses. If the English hadn't
been gallant enough to lower the flag for a few hours one day,
she'd have had to break her oath or die up there."

We rode on asses and mules up the steep, narrow streets
and entered the subterranean galleries the English have blasted
out in the rock. These galleries are like spacious railway
tunnels, and at short intervals in them great guns frown out
upon sea and town through port-holes five or six hundred feet
above the ocean. There is a mile or so of this subterranean
work, and it must have cost a vast deal of money and labor.
The gallery guns command the peninsula and the harbors of
both oceans, but they might as well not be there, I should
think, for an army could hardly climb the perpendicular wall
of the rock any how. Those lofty port-holes afford superb
views of the sea, though. At one place, where a jutting crag
was hollowed out into a great chamber whose furniture was
huge cannon and whose windows were port-holes, a glimpse
was caught of a hill not far away, and a soldier said :

" That high hill yonder is called the Queen's Chair; it is
because a queen of Spain placed her chair there, once, when
the French and Spanish troops were besieging Gibraltar, and
said she would never move from the spot till the English
flag was lowered from the fortresses. If the English hadn't
been gallant enough to lower the flag for a few hours, one day,
she'd have had to break her oath or die up there."

On the topmost pinnacle of Gibraltar we halted a good
while, and no doubt the mules were tired. They had a right
to be. The military road was good, but rather steep, and
there was a good deal of it. The view from the narrow ledge
was magnificent; from it vessels seeming like the tiniest little
toy-boats, were turned into noble ships by the telescopes; and
other vessels that were fifty miles away, and even sixty, they

said, and invisible to the naked eye, could be clearly distinguished through those same telescopes. Below, on one side,
we looked down upon an endless mass of batteries, and on the
other straight down to the sea.

While I was resting ever so comfortably on a rampart, and
cooling my baking head in the delicious breeze, an officious
guide belonging to another party came up and said :

"Senor, that high hill yonder is called the Queen's Chair"—

"QUEEN'S CHAIR."

"Sir, I am a helpless orphan
in a foreign land. Have pity
on me. Don't—now *don't* inflict
that most in-FERNAL old legend on me any more to-day !"

There—I had used strong language, after promising I would
never do so again ; but the provocation was more than human
nature could bear. If you had been bored so, when you had
the noble panorama of Spain and Africa and the blue Medi-

terranean, spread abroad at your feet, and wanted to gaze, and enjoy, and surfeit yourself with its beauty in silence, you might have even burst into stronger language than I did.

Gibraltar has stood several protracted sieges, one of them of nearly four years duration (it failed,) and the English only captured it by stratagem. The wonder is that any body should ever dream of trying so impossible a project as the taking it by assault—and yet it has been tried more than once.

The Moors held the place twelve hundred years ago, and a stanch old castle of theirs of that date still frowns from the middle of the town, with moss-grown battlements and sides well scarred by shots fired in battles and sieges that are forgotten now. A secret chamber, in the rock behind it, was discovered some time ago, which contained a sword of exquisite workmanship, and some quaint old armor of a fashion that antiquaries are not acquainted with, though it is supposed to be Roman. Roman armor and Roman relics, of various kinds, have been found in a cave in the sea extremity of Gibraltar; history says Rome held this part of the country about the Christian era, and these things seem to confirm the statement.

In that cave, also, are found human bones, crusted with a very thick, stony coating, and wise men have ventured to say that those men not only lived before the flood, but as much as ten thousand years before it. It may be true—it looks reasonable enough—but as long as those parties can't vote any more, the matter can be of no great public interest. In this cave, likewise, are found skeletons and fossils of animals that exist in every part of Africa, yet within memory and tradition have never existed in any portion of Spain save this lone peak of Gibraltar! So the theory is that the channel between Gibraltar and Africa was once dry land, and that the low, neutral neck between Gibraltar and the Spanish hills behind it was once ocean, and of course that these African animals, being over at Gibraltar (after rock, perhaps—there is plenty there,) got closed out when the great change occurred. The hills in

Africa, across the channel, are full of apes, and there are now, and always have been, apes on the rock of Gibraltar —but not elsewhere in Spain! The subject is an interesting one.

There is an English garrison at Gibraltar of 6,000 or 7,000 men, and so uniforms of flaming red are plenty; and red and blue, and undress costumes of snowy white, and also the queer uniform of the bare-kneed Highlander; and one sees soft-eyed Spanish girls from San Roque, and veiled Moorish beauties (I suppose they are beauties) from Tarifa, and turbaned, sashed and trowsered Moorish merchants from Fez, and long-robed, bare-legged, ragged Mohammedan vagabonds from Tetouan and Tangier, some brown, some yellow and some as black as virgin ink—and Jews from all around, in gaberdine, skull-cap and slippers, just as they are in pictures and theatres, and just as they were three thousand years ago, no doubt. You can easily understand that a tribe (somehow our pilgrims suggest that expression, because they march in a straggling procession through these foreign places with such an Indian-like air of complacency and independence about them,) like ours, made up from fifteen or sixteen States of the Union, found enough to stare at in this shifting panorama of fashion to-day.

Speaking of our pilgrims reminds me that we have one or two people among us who are sometimes an annoyance. However, I do not count the Oracle in that list. I will explain that the Oracle is an innocent old ass who eats for four and looks wiser than the whole Academy of France would have any right to look, and never uses a one-syllable word when he can think of a longer one, and never by any possible chance knows the meaning of any long word he uses, or ever gets it in the right place: yet he will serenely venture an opinion on the most abstruse subject, and back it up complacently with quotations from authors who never existed, and finally when cornered will slide to the other side of the question, say he has been there all the time, and come back at you with your own spoken arguments, only with the big words all tangled, and play them in your very teeth as original with himself. He reads a chapter in the guide-books, mixes the facts all up, with his bad memory, and then goes off to inflict the whole mess on somebody as wisdom which has been festering in his brain for years, and which he gathered in college from erudite authors who are dead, now, and out of print. This morning at breakfast he pointed out of the window, and said :

"Do you see that there hill out there on that African coast? —It's one of them Pillows of Herkewls, I should say—and there's the ultimate one alongside of it."

"The ultimate one—that is a good word—but the Pillars are not both on the same side of the strait." (I saw he had been deceived by a carelessly written sentence in the Guide Book.)

"Well, it ain't for you to say, nor for me. Some authors states it that way, and some states it different. Old Gibbons don't say nothing about it, —just shirks it complete — Gibbons always done that when he got stuck— but there is Rolampton, what does *he* say? Why, he says

THE ORACLE.

that they was both on the same side, and Trinculian, and Sobaster, and Syraccus, and Langomarganbl—"

"Oh, that will do—that's enough. If you have got your hand in for inventing authors and testimony, I have nothing more to say—let them *be* on the same side."

We don't mind the Oracle. We rather like him. We can tolerate the Oracle very easily; but we have a poet and a good-natured enterprising idiot on board, and they *do* distress the company. The one gives copies of his verses to Consuls, commanders, hotel keepers, Arabs, Dutch,—to any body, in fact, who will submit to a grievous infliction most kindly meant. His poetry is all very well on shipboard, notwithstanding when he wrote an "Ode to the Ocean in a Storm" in one half-hour, and an "Apostrophe to the Rooster in the Waist of the Ship" in the next, the transition was considered to be rather abrupt; but when he sends an invoice of rhymes to the Governor of Fayal and another to the commander-in-chief and other dignitaries in Gibraltar, with the compliments of the Laureate of the Ship, it is not popular with the passengers.

The other personage I have mentioned is young and green, and not bright, not learned and not wise. He will be, though, some day, if he recollects the answers to all his questions. He is known about the ship as the "Interrogation Point," and this by constant use has become shortened to "Interrogation." He has distinguished himself twice already. In Fayal they pointed out a hill and told him it was eight hundred feet high and eleven hundred feet long. And they told him there was a tunnel two thousand feet long and one thousand feet high running through the hill, from end to end.

"INTERROGATION POINT."

He believed it. He repeated it to every body, discussed it, and read it from his notes. Finally, he took a useful hint from this remark which a thoughtful old pilgrim made:

"Well, yes, it *is* a little remarkable—singular tunnel altogether—stands up out of the top of the hill about two hundred feet, and one end of it sticks out of the hill about nine hundred!"

Here in Gibraltar he corners these educated British officers and badgers them with braggadocio about America and the wonders she can perform. He told one of them a couple of our gunboats could come here and knock Gibraltar into the Mediterranean Sea!

At this present moment, half a dozen of us are taking a private pleasure excursion of our own devising. We form rather more than half the list of white passengers on board a small steamer bound for the venerable Moorish town of Tangier, Africa. Nothing could be more absolutety certain than that we are enjoying ourselves. One can not do otherwise who speeds over these sparkling waters, and breathes the soft atmosphere of this sunny land. Care can not assail us here. We are out of its jurisdiction.

We even steamed recklessly by the frowning fortress of Malabat, (a stronghold of the Emperor of Morocco,) without a

GARRISON AT MALABAT.

twinge of fear. The whole garrison turned out under arms, and assumed a threatening attitude—yet still we did not fear. The entire garrison marched and countermarched, within the rampart, in full view—yet notwithstanding even this, we never flinched.

I suppose we really do not know what fear is. I inquired the name of the garrison of the fortress of Malabat, and they said it was Mehemet Ali Ben Sancom. I said it would be a good idea to get some more garrisons to help him; but they said no; he had nothing to do but hold the place, and he was competent to do that; had done it two years already. That was evidence which one could not well refute. There is nothing like reputation.

Every now and then, my glove purchase in Gibraltar last night intrudes itself upon me. Dan and the ship's surgeon and I had been up to the great square, listening to the music of the fine military bands, and contemplating English and Spanish female loveliness and fashion, and, at 9 o'clock, were on our way to the theatre, when we met the General, the Judge, the Commodore, the Colonel, and the Commissioner of the United States of America to Europe, Asia, and Africa, who had been to the Club House, to register their several titles and impoverish the bill of fare; and they told us to go over to the little variety store, near the Hall of Justice, and buy some kid gloves. They said they were elegant, and very moderate in price. It seemed a stylish thing to go to the theatre in kid gloves, and we acted upon the hint. A very handsome young lady in the store offered me a pair of blue gloves. I did not want blue, but she said they would look very pretty on a hand like mine. The remark touched me tenderly. I glanced furtively at my hand, and somehow it did seem rather a comely member. I tried a glove on my left, and blushed a little. Manifestly the size was too small for me. But I felt gratified when she said:

"Oh, it is just right!"—yet I knew it was no such thing.

I tugged at it diligently, but it was discouraging work. She said:

"Ah! I see *you* are accustomed to wearing kid gloves—but some gentlemen are *so* awkward about putting them on."

It was the last compliment I had expected. I only understand putting on the buckskin article perfectly. I made another effort, and tore the glove from the base of the thumb

into the palm of the hand—and tried to hide the rent. She
kept up her compliments, and I kept up my determination to
deserve them or die:

"Ah, you have had experience!" [A rip down the back
of the hand.] "They are just right for you—your hand is
very small—if they
tear you need not
pay for them." [A
rent across the
middle.] "I can
always tell when a
gentleman under-
stands putting on
kid gloves. There
is a grace about it
that only comes
with long practice.
[The whole after-
guard of the glove
"fetched away," as
the sailors say, the

ENTERTAINING AN ANGEL.

fabric parted across the knuckles, and nothing was left but a
melancholy ruin.]

I was too much flattered to make an exposure, and throw
the merchandise on the angel's hands. I was hot, vexed, confused, but still happy; but I hated the other boys for taking
such an absorbing interest in the proceedings. I wished they
were in Jericho. I felt exquisitely mean when I said cheerfully,—

"This one does very well; it fits elegantly. I like a glove
that fits. No, never mind, ma'am, never mind; I'll put the
other on in the street. It is warm here."

It *was* warm. It was the warmest place I ever was in. I
paid the bill, and as I passed out with a fascinating bow, I
thought I detected a light in the woman's eye that was gently
ironical; and when I looked back from the street, and she was
laughing all to herself about something or other, I said to my-

self, with withering sarcasm, " Oh, certainly ; *you* know how to put on kid gloves, don't you ?—a self-complacent ass, ready to be flattered out of your senses by every petticoat that chooses to take the trouble to do it!"

The silence of the boys annoyed me. Finally, Dan said, musingly :

" Some gentlemen don't know how to put on kid gloves at all ; but some do."

And the doctor said (to the moon, I thought,)

" But it is always easy to tell when a gentleman is used to putting on kid gloves."

Dan solilopuized, after a pause :

" Ah, yes ; there is a grace about it that only comes with long, very long practice."

" Yes, indeed, I've noticed that when a man hauls on a kid glove like he was dragging a cat out of an ash-hole by the tail, *he* understands putting on kid gloves ; *he's* had ex—"

" Boys, enough of a thing 's enough ! You think you are very smart, I suppose, but I don't. And if you go and tell any of those old gossips in the ship about this thing, I'll never forgive you for it ; that 's all."

They let me alone then, for the time being. We always let each other alone in time to prevent ill feeling from spoiling a joke. But they had bought gloves, too, as I did. We threw all the purchases away together this morning. They were coarse, unsubstantial, freckled all over with broad yellow splotches, and could neither stand wear nor public exhibition. We had entertained an angel unawares, but we did not take her in. She did that for us.

Tangier ! A tribe of stalwart Moors are wading into the sea to carry us ashore on their backs from the small boats.

CHAPTER VIII.

THIS is royal! Let those who went up through Spain make the best of it—these dominions of the Emperor of Morocco suit our little party well enough. We have had enough of Spain at Gibraltar for the present. Tangier is the spot we have been longing for all the time. Elsewhere we have found foreign-looking things and foreign-looking people, but always with things and people intermixed that we were familiar with before, and so the novelty of the situation lost a deal of its force. We wanted something thoroughly and un-compromisingly foreign—foreign from top to bottom—foreign from centre to circumference—foreign inside and outside and all around—nothing any where about it to dilute its foreign-ness—nothing to remind us of any other people or any other land under the sun. And lo! in Tangier we have found it. Here is not the slightest thing that ever we have seen save in pictures—and we always mistrusted the pictures before. We can not any more. The pictures used to seem exaggerations —they seemed too weird and fanciful for reality. But behold, they were not wild enough—they were not fanciful enough— they have not told half the story. Tangier is a foreign land if ever there was one; and the true spirit of it can never be found in any book save the Arabian Nights. Here are no white men visible, yet swarms of humanity are all about us. Here is a packed and jammed city inclosed in a massive stone wall which is more than a thousand years old. All the houses nearly are one and two-story; made of thick walls of stone; plastered outside; square as a dry-goods box; flat as a floor on

top; no cornices; whitewashed all over—a crowded city of
snowy tombs! And the doors are arched with the peculiar
arch we see in Moorish pictures; the floors are laid in vari-
colored diamond-flags; in tesselated many-colored porcelain
squares wrought in the furnaces of Fez; in red tiles and broad
bricks that time can not wear; there is no furniture in the

VIEW OF A STREET IN TANGIER.

rooms (of Jewish dwellings) save divans—what there is in
Moorish ones no man may know; within their sacred walls no
Christian dog can enter. And the streets are oriental—some
of them three feet wide, some six, but only two that are over
a dozen; a man can blockade the most of them by extending
his body across them. Isn't it an oriental picture?

There are stalwart Bedouins of the desert here, and stately
Moors, proud of a history that goes back to the night of time;
and Jews, whose fathers fled hither centuries upon centuries
ago; and swarthy Riffians from the mountains—born cut-

throats—and original, genuine negroes, as black as Moses; and howling dervishes, and a hundred breeds of Arabs—all sorts and descriptions of people that are foreign and curious to look upon.

And their dresses are strange beyond all description. Here is a bronzed Moor in a prodigious white turban, curiously embroidered jacket, gold and crimson sash, of many folds, wrapped round and round his waist, trowsers that only come a little below his knee, and yet have twenty yards of stuff in them, ornamented scimetar, bare shins, stockingless feet, yellow slippers, and gun of preposterous length—a mere soldier!—I thought he was the Emperor at least. And here are aged Moors with flowing white beards, and long white robes with vast cowls; and Bedouins with long, cowled, striped cloaks, and negroes and Riffians with heads clean-shaven, except a kinky scalp-lock back of the ear, or rather up on the after corner of the skull, and all sorts of barbarians in all sorts of weird costumes, and all more or less ragged. And here are Moorish women who are enveloped from head to foot in coarse white robes and whose sex can only be determined by the fact that they only leave one eye visible, and never look at men of their own race, or are looked at by them in public. Here are five thousand Jews in blue gaberdines, sashes about their waists, slippers upon their feet, little skull-caps upon the backs of their heads, hair combed down on the forehead, and cut straight across the middle of it from side to side—the self-same fashion their Tangier ancestors have worn for I don't know how many bewildering centuries. Their feet and ankles are bare. Their noses are all hooked, and hooked alike. They all resemble each other so much that one could almost believe they were of one family. Their women are plump and pretty, and do smile upon a Christian in a way which is in the last degree comforting.

What a funny old town it is! It seems like profanation to laugh, and jest, and bandy the frivolous chat of our day amid its hoary relics. Only the stately phraseology and the measured speech of the sons of the Prophet are suited to a venerable antiquity like this. Here is a crumbling wall that was old when Columbus discovered America; was old when Peter the Hermit roused the knightly men of the Middle Ages to arm for the first Crusade; was old when Charlemagne and his paladins beleaguered enchanted castles and battled with giants and genii in the fabled days of the olden time; was old when Christ and his disciples walked the earth; stood where it stands to-day when the lips of Memnon were vocal, and men bought and sold in the streets of ancient Thebes!

The Phœnicians, the Carthagenians, the English, Moors, Romans, all have battled for Tangier—all have won it and lost it. Here is a ragged, oriental-looking negro from some desert place in interior Africa, filling his goat-skin with water from a stained and battered fountain built by the Romans twelve hundred years ago. Yonder is a ruined arch of a bridge built by Julius Cæsar nineteen hundred years ago. Men who had seen the infant Saviour in the Virgin's arms, have stood upon it, may be.

Near it are the ruins of a dock-yard where Cæsar repaired his ships and loaded them with grain when he invaded Britain, fifty years before the Christian era.

Here, under the quiet stars, these old streets seem thronged with the phantoms of forgotten ages. My eyes are resting upon a spot where stood a monument which was seen and described by Roman historians less than two thousand years ago, whereon was inscribed:

"WE ARE THE CANAANITES. WE ARE THEY THAT HAVE BEEN DRIVEN OUT OF THE LAND OF CANAAN BY THE JEWISH ROBBER, JOSHUA."

Joshua drove them out, and they came here. Not many leagues from here is a tribe of Jews whose ancestors fled thither after an unsuccessful revolt against King David, and these their descendants are still under a ban and keep to themselves.

Tangier has been mentioned in history for three thousand years. And it was a town, though a queer one, when Hercules, clad in his lion-skin, landed here, four thousand years ago. In these streets he met Anitus, the king of the country, and brained him with his club, which was the fashion among gentlemen in those days. The people of Tangier (called Tingis, then,) lived in the rudest possible huts, and dressed in skins and carried clubs, and were as savage as the wild beasts they were constantly obliged to war with. But they were a gentlemanly race, and did no work. They lived on the natural products of the land. Their king's country residence was at the famous Garden of Hesperides, seventy miles down the coast from here. The garden, with its golden apples, (oranges,) is gone now—no vestige of it remains. Antiquarians concede that such a personage as Hercules did exist in ancient times, and agree that he was an enterprising and energetic man, but decline to believe him a good, bona fide god, because that would be unconstitutional.

Down here at Cape Spartel is the celebrated cave of Hercules, where that hero took refuge when he was vanquished and driven out of the Tangier country. It is full of inscriptions in the dead languages, which fact makes me think Hercules could not have traveled much, else he would not have kept a journal.

Five days' journey from here—say two hundred miles—are the ruins of an ancient city, of whose history there is neither record nor tradition. And yet its arches, its columns, and its statues, proclaim it to have been built by an enlightened race.

The general size of a store in Tangier is about that of an ordinary shower-bath in a civilized land. The Mohammedan merchant, tinman, shoemaker, or vendor of trifles, sits cross-legged on the floor, and reaches after any article you may want to buy. You can rent a whole block of these pigeon-holes for fifty dollars a month. The market people crowd the market-place with their baskets of figs, dates, melons, apricots, etc., and among them file trains of laden asses, not much larger, if any, than a Newfoundland dog. The scene is lively, is pic-turesque, and smells like a police court. The Jewish money-changers have their dens close at hand; and all day long are counting bronze coins and transferring them from one bushel basket to another. They don't coin much money now-a-days, I think. I saw none but what was dated four or five hundred years back, and was badly worn and battered. These coins are not very valuable. Jack went out to get a Napoleon changed, so as to have money suited to the general cheapness of things, and came back and said he had "swamped the bank; had bought eleven quarts of coin, and the head of the firm had gone

CHANGE FOR A NAPOLEON.

on the street to negotiate for the balance of the change." I bought nearly half a pint of their money for a shilling myself. I am not proud on account of having so much money, though. I care nothing for wealth.

The Moors have some small silver coins, and also some silver slugs worth a dollar each. The latter are exceedingly scarce—so much so that when poor ragged Arabs see one they beg to be allowed to kiss it.

They have also a small gold coin worth two dollars. And that reminds me of something. When Morocco is in a state of war, Arab couriers carry letters through the country, and charge a liberal postage. Every now and then they fall into the hands of marauding bands and get robbed. Therefore, warned by experience, as soon as they have collected two dollars' worth of money they exchange it for one of those little gold pieces, and when robbers come upon them, swallow it. The stratagem was good while it was unsuspected, but after that the marauders simply gave the sagacious United States mail an emetic and sat down to wait.

6

The Emperor of Morocco is a soulless despot, and the great officers under him are despots on a smaller scale. There is no regular system of taxation, but when the Emperor or the Bashaw want money, they levy on some rich man, and he has to furnish the cash or go to prison. Therefore, few men in Morocco dare to be rich. It is too dangerous a luxury. Vanity occasionally leads a man to display wealth, but sooner or later the Emperor trumps up a charge against him-—any sort of one will do—and confiscates his property. Of course, there are many rich men in the empire, but their money is buried, and they dress in rags and counterfeit poverty. Every now and then the Emperor imprisons a man who is suspected of the crime of being rich, and makes things so uncomfortable for him that he is forced to discover where he has hidden his money.

Moors and Jews sometimes place themselves under the protection of the foreign consuls, and then they can flout their riches in the Emperor's face with impunity.

CHAPTER IX.

ABOUT the first adventure we had yesterday afternoon, after landing here, came near finishing that heedless Blucher. We had just mounted some mules and asses, and started out under the guardianship of the stately, the princely, the magnificent Hadji Mohammed Lamarty, (may his tribe increase!) when we came upon a fine Moorish mosque, with tall tower, rich with checker-work of many-colored porcelain, and every part and portion of the edifice adorned with the quaint architecture of the Alhambra, and Blucher started to ride into the open door-way. A startling "Hi-hi!" from our camp-followers, and a loud "Halt!" from an English gentleman in the party checked the adventurer, and then we were informed that so dire a profanation is it for a Christian dog to set foot upon the sacred threshold of a Moorish mosque, that no amount of purification can ever make it fit for the faithful to pray in again. Had Blucher succeeded in entering the place, he would no doubt have been chased through the town and stoned; and the time has been, and not many years ago either, when a Christian would have been most ruthlessly slaughtered, if captured in a mosque. We caught a glimpse of the handsome tesselated pavements within, and of the devotees performing their ablutions at the fountains; but even that we took that glimpse was a thing not relished by the Moorish bystanders.

Some years ago the clock in the tower of the mosque got out of order. The Moors of Tangier have so degenerated that it has been long since there was an artificer among them capable of curing so delicate a patient as a debilitated clock. The great men of the city met in solemn conclave to consider how the difficulty was to be met. They discussed the matter thoroughly but arrived at no solution. Finally, a patriarch arose and said:

"Oh, children of the Prophet, it is known unto you that a Portuguee dog of a Christian clock-mender pollutes the city of Tangier with his presence. Ye know, also, that when mosques are builded, asses bear the stones and the cement, and cross the sacred threshold. Now, therefore, send the Christian dog on all fours, and barefoot, into the holy place to mend the clock, and let him go as an ass!"

And in that way it was done. Therefore, if Blucher ever sees the inside of a mosque, he will have to cast aside his humanity and go in his natural character. We visited the jail, and found Moorish prisoners making mats and baskets. (This thing of utilizing crime savors of civilization.) Murder is punished with death. A short time ago, three murderers were taken beyond the city walls and shot. Moorish guns are not good, and neither are Moorish marksmen. In this instance, they set up the poor criminals at long range, like so many targets, and practiced on them—kept them hopping about and dodging bullets for half an hour before they managed to drive the centre.

When a man steals cattle, they cut off his right hand and left leg, and nail them up in the market-place as a warning to every body. Their surgery is not artistic. They slice around the bone a little; then break off the limb. Sometimes the patient gets well; but, as a general thing, he don't. However, the Moorish heart is stout. The Moors were always brave. These criminals undergo the fearful operation without a wince, without a tremor of any kind, without a groan! No amount of suffering can bring down the pride of a Moor, or make him shame his dignity with a cry.

Here, marriage is contracted by the parents of the parties to it. There are no valentines, no stolen interviews, no riding out, no courting in dim parlors, no lovers' quarrels and recon-

ciliations—no nothing that is proper to approaching matri
mony. The young man takes the girl his father selects for
him, marries her, and after that she is unveiled, and he sees
her for the first time. If, after due acquaintance, she suits
him, he retains her; but if he suspects her purity, he bundles
her back to her father; if he finds her diseased, the same;
or if, after just and reasonable time is allowed her, she neglects to bear children, back she goes to the home of her childhood.

Mohammedans here, who can afford it, keep a good many
wives on hand. They are called wives, though I believe the
Koran only allows four genuine wives—the rest are concubines. The Emperor of Morocco don't know how many
wives he has, but thinks he has five hundred. However, that
is near enough—a dozen or so, one way or the other, don't
matter.

Even the Jews in the interior have a plurality of wives.

I have caught a glimpse of the faces of several Moorish
women, (for they are only human, and will expose their faces
for the admiration of a Christian dog when no male Moor
is by,) and J am full of veneration for the wisdom that leads
them to cover up such atrocious ugliness.

They carry their children at their backs, in a sack, like
other savages the world over.

Many of the negroes are held in slavery by the Moors. But
the moment a female slave becomes her master's concubine
her bonds are broken, and as soon as a male slave can read the
first chapter of the Koran (which contains the creed,) he can
no longer be held in bondage.

They have three Sundays a week in Tangier. The Mohammedan's comes on Friday, the Jew's on Saturday, and that of
the Christian Consuls on Sunday. The Jews are the most
radical. The Moor goes to his mosque about noon on his
Sabbath, as on any other day, removes his shoes at the door,
performs his ablutions, makes his salaams, pressing his forehead to the pavement time and again, says his prayers, and
goes back to his work.

But the Jew shuts up shop; will not touch copper or bronze money at all; soils his fingers with nothing meaner than silver and gold; attends the synagogue devoutly; will not cook or have any thing to do with fire; and religiously refrains from embarking in any enterprise.

The Moor who has made a pilgrimage to Mecca is entitled to high distinction. Men call him Hadji, and he is thenceforward a great personage. Hundreds of Moors come to Tangier every year, and embark for Mecca. They go part of the way in English steamers; and the ten or twelve dollars they pay for passage is about all the trip costs. They take with them a quantity of food, and when the commissary department fails they "skirmish," as Jack terms it in his sinful, slangy way. From the time they leave till they get home again, they never wash, either on land or sea. They are usually gone from five to seven months, and as they do not change their clothes during all that time, they are totally unfit for the drawing-room when they get back.

Many of them have to rake and scrape a long time to gather together the ten dollars their steamer passage costs; and when one of them gets back he is a bankrupt forever after. Few Moors can ever build up their fortunes again in one short lifetime, after so reckless an outlay. In order to confine the dignity of Hadji to gentlemen of patrician blood and possessions, the Emperor decreed that no man should make the pilgrimage save bloated aristocrats who were worth a hundred dollars in specie. But behold how iniquity can circumvent the law! For a consideration, the Jewish money-changer lends the pilgrim one hundred dollars long enough for him to swear himself through, and then receives it back before the ship sails out of the harbor!

Spain is the only nation the Moors fear. The reason is, that Spain sends her heaviest ships of war and her loudest guns to astonish these Moslems; while America, and other nations, send only a little contemptible tub of a gun-boat occasionally. The Moors, like other savages, learn by what they see; not what they hear or read. We have great fleets in the

Mediterranean, but they seldom touch at African ports. The Moors have a small opinion of England, France, and America, and put their representatives to a deal of red tape circumlocution before they grant them their common rights, let alone a favor. But the moment the Spanish Minister makes a demand, it is acceded to at once, whether it be just or not.

Spain chastised the Moors five or six years ago, about a disputed piece of property opposite Gibraltar, and captured the city of Tetouan. She compromised on an augmentation of her territory; twenty million dollars indemnity in money; and peace. And then she gave up the city. But she never gave it up until the Spanish soldiers had eaten up all the cats. They would not compromise as long as the cats held out. Spaniards are very fond of cats. On the contrary, the Moors reverence cats as something sacred. So the Spaniards touched them on a tender point that time. Their unfeline conduct in eating up all the Tetouan cats aroused a hatred toward them in the breasts of the Moors, to which even the driving them out of Spain was tame and passionless. Moors and Spaniards are foes forever now. France had a Minister here once who embittered the nation against him in the most innocent way. He killed a couple of battalions of cats (Tangier is full of them,) and made a parlor carpet out of their hides. He made his carpet in circles—first a circle of old gray tom-cats, with their tails all pointing towards the centre; then a circle of yellow cats; next a circle of black cats and a circle of white ones; then a circle of all sorts of cats; and, finally, a centrepiece of assorted kittens. It was very beautiful; but the Moors curse his memory to this day.

When we went to call on our American Consul-General, to-day, I noticed that all possible games for parlor amusement seemed to be represented on his centre-tables. I thought that hinted at lonesomeness. The idea was correct. His is the only American family in Tangier. There are many foreign Consuls in this place; but much visiting is not indulged in. Tangier is clear out of the world; and what is the use of

visiting when people have nothing on earth to talk about?
There is none.   So each Consul's family stays at home
chiefly, and amuses itself as best it can.   Tangier is full of
interest for one day, but after that it is a weary prison.   The
Consul-General has been here five years, and has got enough
of it to do him for a century, and is going home shortly.   His
family seize upon their letters and papers when the mail
arrives, read them over and over again for two days or three,
talk them over and over again for two or three more, till they
wear them out, and after that, for days together, they eat and
drink and sleep, and ride out over the same old road, and see
the same old tiresome things that even decades of centuries have scarcely changed, and say never a single word!

THE CONSULS' FAMILY.

They have literally nothing whatever to talk about.   The ar-
rival of an American man-of-war is a god-send to them.
" Oh, Solitude, where are the charms which sages have seen in
thy face?"   It is the completest exile that I can conceive of.
I would seriously recommend to the Government of the
United States that when a man commits a crime so heinous

that the law provides no adequate punishment for it, they make him Consul-General to Tangier.

I am glad to have seen Tangier—the second oldest town in the world. But I am ready to bid it good bye, I believe.

We shall go hence to Gibraltar this evening or in the morning; and doubtless the Quaker City will sail from that port within the next forty-eight hours.

CHAPTER X.

WE passed the Fourth of July on board the Quaker City, in mid-ocean. It was in all respects a characteristic Mediterranean day—faultlessly beautiful. A cloudless sky; a refreshing summer wind; a radiant sunshine that glinted cheerily from dancing wavelets instead of crested mountains of water; a sea beneath us that was so wonderfully blue, so richly, brilliantly blue, that it overcame the dullest sensibilities with the spell of its fascination.

They even have fine sunsets on the Mediterranean—a thing that is certainly rare in most quarters of the globe. The evening we sailed away from Gibraltar, that hard-featured rock was swimming in a creamy mist so rich, so soft, so enchantingly vague and dreamy, that even the Oracle, that serene, that inspired, that overpowering humbug, scorned the dinner-gong and tarried to worship!

He said: "Well, that's gorgis, ain't it! They don't have none of them things in our parts, *do* they? I consider that them effects is on account of the superior refragability, as you may say, of the sun's diramic combination with the lymphatic forces of the perihelion of Jubiter. What should you think?"

"Oh, *go* to bed!" Dan said that, and went away.

"Oh, yes, it's all very well to say go to bed when a man makes an argument which another man can't answer. Dan don't never stand any chance in an argument with me. And he knows it, too. What should you say, Jack?"

"Now doctor, don't you come bothering around me with that dictionary bosh. I don't do you any harm, do I? Then you let *me* alone."

"He's gone, too.   Well, them fellows have all tackled the old Oracle, as they say, but the old man's most too many for 'em. May be the Poet Lariat ain't satisfied with them deductions?"

The poet replied with a barbarous rhyme, and went below.

"'Pears that *he* can't qualify, neither.   Well, I didn't expect nothing out of *him*.   I never see one of them poets yet that knowed any thing. He'll go down, now, and grind out about four reams of the awfullest slush about that old rock, and give it to a consul, or a pilot, or a nigger, or any body he comes across first which he can impose on.   Pity

"POET LARIAT."

but somebody'd take that poor old lunatic and dig all that poetry rubbage out of him.   Why can't a man put his intellect onto things that's some value?   Gibbons, and Hippocratus, and Sarcophagus, and all them old ancient philosophers was down on poets—"

"Doctor," I said, "you are going to invent authorities, now, and I'll leave you, too.   I always enjoy your conversation, notwithstanding the luxuriance of your syllables, when the philosophy you offer rests on your own responsibility; but when you begin to soar—when you begin to support it with the evidence of authorities who are the creations of your own fancy, I lose confidence."

That was the way to flatter the doctor.   He considered it a sort of acknowledgment on my part of a fear to argue with him.   He was always persecuting the passengers with abstruse propositions framed in language that no man could understand, and they endured the exquisite torture a minute or two and then abandoned the field.   A triumph like this, over half a dozen antagonists was sufficient for one day; from that time forward he would patrol the decks beaming blandly upon all comers, and so tranquilly, blissfully happy!

But I digress. The thunder of our two brave cannon announced the Fourth of July, at daylight, to all who were awake. But many of us got our information at a later hour, from the almanac. All the flags were sent aloft, except half a dozen that were needed to decorate portions of the ship below, and in a short time the vessel assumed a holiday appearance. During the morning, meetings were held and all manner of committees set to work on the celebration ceremonies. In the afternoon the ship's company assembled aft, on deck, under the awnings; the flute, the asthmatic melodeon, and the consumptive clarinet crippled the Star Spangled Banner, the choir chased it to cover, and George came in with a peculiarly lacerating screech on the final note and slaughtered it. Nobody mourned.

We carried out the corpse on three cheers (that joke was not intentional and I do not indorse it,) and then the President, throned behind a cable-locker with a national flag spread over it, announced the "Reader," who rose up and read that same old Declaration of Independence which we have all listened to so often without paying any attention to what it said; and after that the President piped the Orator of the Day to quarters and he made that same old speech about our national greatness which we so religiously believe and so fervently applaud. Now came the choir into court again, with the complaining instruments, and assaulted Hail Columbia; and when victory hung wavering in the scale, George returned with his dreadful wild-goose stop turned on and the choir won of course. A minister pronounced the benediction, and the patriotic little gathering disbanded. The Fourth of July was safe, as far as the Mediterranean was concerned.

At dinner in the evening, a well-written original poem was recited with spirit by one of the ship's captains, and thirteen regular toasts were washed down with several baskets of champagne. The speeches were bad—execrable, almost without exception. In fact, without *any* exception, but one. Capt. Duncan made a good speech; he made the only good speech of the evening. He said:

"LADIES AND GENTLEMEN:—May we all live to a green old age, and be prosperous and happy. Steward, bring up another basket of champagne."

It was regarded as a very able effort.

The festivities, so to speak, closed with another of those miraculous balls on the promenade deck. We were not used to dancing on an even keel, though, and it was only a questionable success. But take it altogether, it was a bright, cheerful, pleasant Fourth.

Toward nightfall, the next evening, we steamed into the great artificial harbor of this noble city of Marseilles, and saw the dying sunlight gild its clustering spires and ramparts, and flood its leagues of environing verdure with a mellow radiance that touched with an added charm the white villas that flecked the landscape far and near. [Copyright secured according to law.]

There were no stages out, and we could not get on the pier from the ship. It was annoying. We were full of enthusiasm—we wanted to see France! Just at nightfall our party of three contracted with a waterman for the privilege of using his boat as a bridge—its stern was at our companion ladder and its bow touched the pier. We got in and the fellow backed out into the harbor. I told him in French that all we wanted was to walk over his thwarts and step ashore, and asked him what he went away out there for? He said he could not understand me. I repeated. Still, he could not understand. He appeared to be very ignorant of French. The doctor tried him, but he could not understand the doctor. I asked this boatman to explain his conduct, which he did; and then I couldn't understand *him*. Dan said:

"Oh, go to the pier, you old fool—that's where we want to go!"

We reasoned calmly with Dan that it was useless to speak to this foreigner in English—that he had better let us conduct this business in the French language and not let the stranger see how uncultivated he was.

"Well, go on, go on," he said, "don't mind me. I don't wish to interfere. Only, if you go on telling him in your kind of French he never will find out where we want to go to. That is what I think about it."

We rebuked him severely for this remark, and said we never knew an ignorant person yet but was prejudiced. The Frenchman spoke again, and the doctor said:

"There, now, Dan, he says he is going to *allez* to the *douain*. Means he is going to the hotel. Oh, certainly—*we* don't know the French language."

This was à crusher, as Jack would say. It silenced further criticism from the disaffected member. We coasted past the sharp bows of a navy of great steamships, and stopped at last at a government building on a stone pier. It was easy to remember then, that the *douain* was the custom-house, and not the hotel. We did not mention it, however. With winning French politeness, the officers merely opened and closed our satchels, declined to examine our passports, and sent us on our way. We stopped at the first café we came to, and entered. An old woman seated us at a table and waited for orders. The doctor said:

"Avez vous du vin?"

The dame looked perplexed. The doctor said again, with elaborate distinctness of articulation:

"Avez-vous du—vin!"

The dame looked more perplexed than before. I said:

"Doctor, there is a flaw in your pronunciation somewhere. Let me try her. Madame, avez-vous du vin? It isn't any use, doctor—take the witness."

"Madame, avez-vous du vin—ou fromage—pain—pickled pigs' feet—beurre—des œfs—du beuf—horse-radish, sour-crout, hog and hominy—any thing, *any thing* in the world that can stay a Christian stomach!"

She said:

"Bless you, why didn't you speak English before?—I don't know any thing about your plagued French!"

The humiliating taunts of the disaffected member spoiled

the supper, and we dispatched it in angry silence and got away as soon as we could. Here we were in beautiful France—in a vast stone house of quaint architecture—surrounded by all

FIRST SUPPER IN FRANCE.

manner of curiously worded French signs—stared at by strangely-habited, bearded French people—every thing gradually and surely forcing upon us the coveted consciousness that at last, and beyond all question we *were* in beautiful France and absorbing its nature to the forgetfulness of every thing else, and coming to feel the happy romance of the thing in all its enchanting delightfulness—and to think of this skinny veteran intruding with her vile English, at such a moment, to blow the fair vision to the winds! It was exasperating.

We set out to find the centre of the city, inquiring the direction every now and then. We never did succeed in making any body understand just exactly what we wanted, and neither did we ever succeed in comprehending just exactly what they said in reply—but then they always pointed—they always did that, and we bowed politely and said "Merci, Monsieur," and so it was a blighting triumph over the disaffected member, any way. He was restive under these victories and often asked:

POINTING.

"What did that pirate say?"

"Why, he told us which way to go, to find the Grand Casino."

"Yes, but what did he *say?*"

"Oh, it don't matter what he said—*we* understood him. These are educated people—not like that absurd boatman."

"Well, I wish they were educated enough to tell a man a direction that goes *some* where—for we've been going around in a circle for an hour—I've passed this same old drug store seven times."

We said it was a low, disreputable falsehood, (but we knew it was not.) It was plain that it would not do to pass that drug store again, though—we might go on asking directions, but we must cease from following finger-pointings if we hoped to check the suspicions of the disaffected member.

A long walk through smooth, asphaltum-paved streets bordered by blocks of vast new mercantile houses of cream-colored stone,—every house and every block precisely like all the other houses and all the other blocks for a mile, and all brilliantly lighted,—brought us at last to the principal thoroughfare. On every hand were bright colors, flashing constellations of gas-burners, gaily dressed men and women thronging the side-walks—hurry, life, activity, cheerfulness, conversation and laughter every where! We found the Grand Hotel du Louvre et de la Paix, and wrote down who we were, where we were born, what our occupations were, the place we came from last, whether we were married or single, how we liked it, how old we were, where we were bound for and when we expected to

get there, and a great deal of information of similar importance—all for the benefit of the landlord and the secret police.
We hired a guide and began the business of sight-seeing immediately. That first night on French soil was a stirring one.
I can not think of half the places we went to, or what we particularly saw; we had no disposition to examine carefully into
any thing at all—we only wanted to glance and go—to move,
keep moving! The spirit of the country was upon us. We
sat down, finally, at a late hour, in the great Casino, and called
for unstinted champagne. It is so easy to be bloated aristocrats
where it costs nothing of consequence! There were about five
hundred people in that dazzling place, I suppose, though the
walls being papered entirely with mirrors, so to speak, one could
not really tell but that there were a hundred thousand.
Young, daintily dressed exquisites and young, stylishly dressed
women, and also old gentlemen and old ladies, sat in couples
and groups about innumerable marble-topped tables, and ate
fancy suppers, drank wine and kept up a chattering din of conversation that was dazing to the senses. There was a stage
at the far end, and a large orchestra; and every now and then
actors and actresses in preposterous comic dresses came out
and sang the most extravagantly funny songs, to judge by
their absurd actions; but that audience merely suspended its
chatter, stared cynically, and never once smiled, never once
applauded! I had always thought that Frenchmen were ready
to laugh at any thing.

7

CHAPTER XI.

WE are getting foreignized rapidly, and with facility. We are getting reconciled to halls and bed-chambers with unhomelike stone floors, and no carpets—floors that ring to the tread of one's heels with a sharpness that is death to sentimental musing. We are getting used to tidy, noiseless waiters, who glide hither and thither, and hover about your back and your elbows like butterflies, quick to comprehend orders, quick to fill them; thankful for a gratuity without regard to the amount; and always polite—never otherwise than polite. That is the strangest curiosity yet—a really polite hotel waiter who isn't an idiot. We are getting used to driving right into the central court of the hotel, in the midst of a fragrant circle of vines and flowers, and in the midst, also, of parties of gentlemen sitting quietly reading the paper and smoking. We are getting used to ice frozen by artificial process in ordinary bottles—the only kind of ice they have here. We are getting used to all these things; but we are *not* getting used to carrying our own soap. We are sufficiently civilized to carry our own combs and tooth-brushes; but this thing of having to ring for soap every time we wash is new to us, and not pleasant at all. We think of it just after we get our heads and faces thoroughly wet, or just when we think we have been in the bath-tub long enough, and then, of course, an annoying delay follows. These Marseillaise make Marseillaise hymns, and Marseilles vests, and Marseilles soap for all the world; but they never sing their hymns, or wear their vests, or wash with their soap themselves.

We have learned to go through the lingering routine of the table d'hote with patience, with serenity, with satisfaction.

We take soup; then wait a few minutes for the fish; a few minutes more and the plates are chang- ed, and the roast beef comes; another change and we take peas; change again and take lentils; change and take snail patties (I pre- fer grasshoppers;) change and take roast chicken and sal- ad; then strawberry pie and ice cream; then green figs, pears, oranges, green almonds, &c.; finally coffee. Wine with

RINGING FOR SOAP.

every course, of course, being in France. With such a cargo on board, digestion is a slow process, and we must sit long in the cool chambers and smoke—and read French newspapers, which have a strange fashion of telling a perfectly straight story till you get to the "nub" of it, and then a word drops in that no man can translate, and that story is ruined. An em- bankment fell on some Frenchmen yesterday, and the papers are full of it to-day—but whether those sufferers were killed, or crippled, or bruised, or only scared, is more than I can pos- sibly make out, and yet I would just give any thing to know.

We were troubled a little at dinner to-day, by the conduct of an American, who talked very loudly and coarsely, and laughed boisterously where all others were so quiet and well- behaved. He ordered wine with a royal flourish, and said:

" I never dine without wine, sir," (which was a pitiful false-hood,) and looked around upon the company to bask in the admiration he expected to find in their faces. All these airs

WINE, SIR!

in a land where they would as soon expect to leave the soup out of the bill of fare as the wine!—in a land where wine is nearly as common among all ranks as water! This fellow said : " I am a free-born sovereign, sir, an Ameri-can, sir, and I want every body to know it!" He did not mention that he was a lineal descendant of Balaam's ass ; but every body knew that without his telling it.

We have driven in the Prado—that superb avenue bordered with patrician mansions and noble shade-trees—and have visited the Chateau Boarely and its curious museum. They showed us a miniature cemetery there—a copy of the first graveyard that was ever in Marseilles, no doubt. The delicate little skeletons were lying in broken vaults, and had their household gods and kitchen utensils with them. · The original of this cemetery was dug up in the principal street of the city a few years ago. It had remained there, only twelve feet under ground, for a matter of twenty-five hundred years, or thereabouts. Romulus was here before he built Rome, and thought something of founding a city on this spot, but gave up the idea. He may have been personally acquainted with some of these Phœnicians whose skeletons we have been ex-amining.

In the great Zoölogical Gardens, we found specimens of all the animals the world produces, I think, including a drome-dary, a monkey ornamented with tufts of brilliant blue and carmine hair—a very gorgeous monkey he was—a hippopotamus from the Nile, and a sort of tall, long-legged bird with a beak like a powder-horn, and close-fitting wings like the tails of a dress coat. This fellow stood up with his eyes shut and his shoulders stooped forward a little, and looked as if he had his hands under his coat tails. Such tranquil stupidity, such supernatural gravity, such self-righteousness, and such ineffable self-complacency as were in the countenance and attitude of that gray-bodied, dark-winged, bald-headed, and preposterously uncomely bird! He was so ungainly, so pimply about the head, so scaly about the legs; yet so serene, so unspeakably satisfied! He was the most comical looking creature that can be imagined. It was good to hear Dan and the doctor laugh—such natural and such enjoyable laughter had not been heard among our excursionists since our ship sailed away from America. This bird was a god-send to us, and I should be an ingrate if I forgot to make honorable mention of him in these pages. Ours was a pleasure excursion; therefore we stayed with that bird an hour, and made the most of him. We stirred him up occasionally, but he only unclosed an eye and slowly closed it again, abating no jot of his stately piety of demeanor or his tremendous

THE PILGRIM.

seriousness. He only seemed to say, " Defile not Heaven's anointed with unsanctified hands." We did not know his name, and so we called him " The Pilgrim." Dan said:

" All he wants now is a Plymouth Collection."

The boon companion of the colossal elephant was a common cat! This cat had a fashion of climbing up the elephant's hind legs, and roosting on his back. She would sit up there, with her paws curved under her breast, and sleep in the sun half the afternoon. It used to annoy the elephant at first, and he would reach up and take her down, but she would go aft and climb up again. She persisted until she finally conquered the elephant's prejudices, and now they are inseparable friends. The cat plays about her comrade's forefeet or his trunk often, until dogs approach, and then she goes aloft out of danger. The elephant has annihilated several dogs lately, that pressed his companion too closely.

We hired a sail-boat and a guide and made an excursion to one of the small islands in the harbor to visit the Castle d'If. This ancient fortress has a melancholy history. It has been used as a prison for political offenders for two or three hundred years, and its dungeon walls are scarred with the rudely carved names of many and many a captive who fretted his life away here, and left no record of himself but these sad epitaphs wrought with his own hands. How thick the names were! And their long-departed owners seemed to throng the gloomy cells and corridors with their phantom shapes. We loitered through dungeon after dungeon, away down into the living rock below the level of the sea, it seemed. Names every where!—some plebeian, some noble, some even princely. Plebeian, prince, and noble, had one solicitude in common—they would not be forgotten! They could suffer solitude, inactivity, and the horrors of a silence that no sound ever disturbed; but they could not bear the thought of being utterly forgotten by the world. Hence the carved names. In one cell, where a little light penetrated, a man had lived twenty-seven years without seeing the face of a human being—lived in filth and wretchedness, with no companionship but his own thoughts, and they were sorrowful enough, and hopeless enough, no doubt. Whatever his jailers considered that he needed was conveyed to his cell by night, through a wicket.

This man carved the walls of his prison-house from floor to
roof with all manner of figures of men and animals, grouped

THE PRISONER.

in intricate designs. He had
toiled there year after year, at
his self-appointed task, while
infants grew to boyhood—to vigorous youth—idled through
school and college—acquired a profession—claimed man's mature estate—married and looked back to infancy as to a thing

of some vague, ancient time, almost.   But who shall tell how
many ages it seemed to this prisoner?   With the one, time
flew sometimes; with the other, never—it crawled always.
To the one, nights spent in dancing had seemed made of
minutes instead of hours; to the other, those self-same nights
had been like all other nights of dungeon life, and seemed
made of slow, dragging weeks, instead of hours and minutes.

One prisoner of fifteen years had scratched verses upon his
walls, and brief prose sentences—brief, but full of pathos. These
spoke not of himself and his hard estate; but only of the shrine
where his spirit fled the prison to worship—of home and the
idols that were templed there.   He never lived to see them.

The walls of these dungeons are as thick as some bed-chambers at home are wide—fifteen feet.   We saw the damp, dismal cells in which two of Dumas' heroes passed their confine-
ment—heroes of "Monte Christo."   It was here that the
brave Abbé wrote a book with his own blood; with a pen
made of a piece of iron hoop, and by the light of a lamp made
out of shreds of cloth soaked in grease obtained from his food;
and then dug through the thick wall with some trifling instrument which he wrought himself out of a stray piece of iron or
table cutlery, and freed Dantés from his chains.   It was a pity
that so many weeks of dreary labor should have come to
naught at last.

They showed us the noisome cell where the celebrated
" Iron Mask "—that ill-starred brother of a hard-hearted king
of France—was confined for a season, before he was sent to
hide the strange mystery of his life from the curious in the
dungeons of St. Marguerite.   The place had a far greater
interest for us than it could have had if we had known beyond all question who the Iron Mask was, and what his history had been, and why this most unusual punishment had been
meted out to him.   Mystery!   That was the charm.   That
speechless tongue, those prisoned features, that heart so
freighted with unspoken troubles, and that breast so oppressed
with its piteous secret, had been here.   These dank walls had
known the man whose dolorous story is a sealed book forever!
There was fascination in the spot.

CHAPTER XII.

WE have come five hundred miles by rail through the heart of France. What a bewitching land it is!— What a garden! Surely the leagues of bright green lawns are swept and brushed and watered every day and their grasses trimmed by the barber. Surely the hedges are shaped and measured and their symmetry preserved by the most architectural of gardeners. Surely the long straight rows of stately poplars that divide the beautiful landscape like the squares of a checker-board are set with line and plummet, and their uniform height determined with a spirit level. Surely the straight, smooth, pure white turnpikes are jack-planed and sandpapered every day. How else are these marvels of symmetry, cleanliness and order attained? It is wonderful. There are no unsightly stone walls, and never a fence of any kind. There is no dirt, no decay, no rubbish any where—nothing that even hints at untidiness—nothing that ever suggests neglect. All is orderly and beautiful—every thing is charming to the eye.

We had such glimpses of the Rhone gliding along between its grassy banks; of cosy cottages buried in flowers and shrubbery; of quaint old red-tiled villages with mossy mediæval cathedrals looming out of their midst; of wooded hills with ivy-grown towers and turrets of feudal castles projecting above the foliage; such glimpses of Paradise, it seemed to us, such visions of fabled fairy-land!

We knew, then, what the poet meant, when he sang of—

> "—thy cornfields green, and sunny vines,
> O pleasant land of France!"

And it *is* a pleasant land. No word describes it so felici-
tously as that one. They say there is no word for "home" in
the French language. Well, considering that they have the
article itself in such an attractive aspect, they ought to manage
to get along without the word. Let us not waste too much
pity on "homeless" France. I have observed that Frenchmen abroad seldom wholly give up the idea of going back to
France some time or other. I am not surprised at it now.

We are not infatuated with these French railway cars,
though. We took first class passage, not because we wished
to attract attention by doing a thing which is uncommon in
Europe, but because we could make our journey quicker by so
doing. It is hard to make railroading pleasant, in any country.
It is too tedious. Stage-coaching is infinitely more delightful.
Once I crossed the plains and deserts and mountains of the
West, in a stage-coach, from the Missouri line to California,
and since then all my pleasure trips must be measured to that
rare holiday frolic. Two thousand miles of ceaseless rush and
rattle and clatter, by night and by day, and never a weary
moment, never a lapse of interest! The first seven hundred
miles a level continent, its grassy carpet greener and softer
and smoother than any sea, and figured with designs fitted to
its magnitude—the shadows of the clouds. Here were no
scenes but summer scenes, and no disposition inspired by them
but to lie at full length on the mail sacks, in the grateful
breeze, and dreamily smoke the pipe of peace—what other,
where all was repose and contentment? In cool mornings,
before the sun was fairly up, it was worth a lifetime of city
toiling and moiling, to perch in the foretop with the driver
and see the six mustangs scamper under the sharp snapping
of a whip that never touched them; to scan the blue distances
of a world that knew no lords but us; to cleave the wind with
uncovered head and feel the sluggish pulses rousing to the spirit
of a speed that pretended to the resistless rush of a typhoon!
Then thirteen hundred miles of desert solitudes; of limitless
panoramas of bewildering perspective; of mimic cities, of pinnacled cathedrals, of massive fortresses, counterfeited in the

HOMELESS FRANCE.

eternal rocks and splendid with the crimson and gold of the setting sun ; of dizzy altitudes among fog-wreathed peaks and never-melting snows, where thunders and lightnings and tempests warred magnificently at our feet and the storm-clouds above swung their shredded banners in our very faces !

But I forgot. I am in elegant France, now, and not skurrying through the great South Pass and the Wind River Mountains, among antelopes and buffaloes, and painted Indians on the war path. It is not meet that I should make too disparaging comparisons between hum-drum travel on a railway and that royal summer flight across a continent in a stage-coach. I meant in the beginning, to say that railway journeying is tedious and tiresome, and so it is—though at the time, I was thinking particularly of a dismal fifty-hour pilgrimage between New York and St. Louis. Of course our trip through France was not really tedious, because all its scenes and experiences were new and strange ; but as Dan says, it had its "discrepancies."

The cars are built in compartments that hold eight persons each. Each compartment is partially subdivided, and so there are two tolerably distinct parties of four in it. Four face the other four. The seats and backs are thickly padded and cushioned and are very comfortable ; you can smoke, if you wish ; there are no bothersome peddlers ; you are saved the infliction of a multitude of disagreeable fellow-passengers. So far, so well. But then the conductor locks you in when the train starts ; there is no water to drink, in the car ; there is no heating apparatus for night travel ; if a drunken rowdy should get in, you could not remove a matter of twenty seats from him, or enter another car ; but above all, if you are worn out and must sleep, you must sit up and do it in naps, with cramped legs and in a torturing misery that leaves you withered and lifeless the next day—for behold they have not that culmination of all charity and human kindness, a sleeping car, in all France. I prefer the American system. It has not so many grievous "discrepancies."

In France, all is clockwork, all is order. They make no

mistakes. Every third man wears a uniform, and whether he
be a Marshal of the Empire or a brakeman, he is ready and
perfectly willing to answer all your questions with tireless
politeness, ready to tell you which car to take, yea, and ready
to go and put you into it to make sure that you shall not
go astray. You can not pass into the waiting-room of the
depot till you have secured your ticket, and you can not pass
from its only exit till the train is at its threshold to receive

RAILROAD OFFICIAL IN FRANCE.

you. Once on board, the train will not start till your ticket
has been examined—till every passenger's ticket has been
inspected. This is chiefly for your own good. If by any
possibility you have managed to take the wrong train, you
will be handed over to a polite official who will take you
whither you belong, and bestow you with many an affable
bow. Your ticket will be inspected every now and then along
the route, and when it is time to change cars you will know it.
You are in the hands of officials who zealously study your
welfare and your interest, instead of turning their talents to
the invention of new methods of discommoding and snubbing
you, as is very often the main employment of that exceedingly
self-satisfied monarch, the railroad conductor of America.

But the happiest regulation in French railway government,

is—thirty minutes to dinner! No five-minute boltings of
flabby rolls, muddy coffee, questionable eggs, gutta-percha
beef, and pies whose conception and execution are a dark and
bloody mystery to all save the cook that created them! No;
we sat calmly down—it was in old Dijon, which is so easy to
spell and so impossible to pronounce, except when you civilize
it and call it Demijohn—and poured out rich Burgundian
wines and munched calmly through a long table d'hote bill of
fare, snail-patties, delicious fruits and all, then paid the trifle
it cost and stepped happily aboard the train again, without

"FIVE MINUTES FOR REFRESHMENTS."—AMERICA.

once cursing the railroad company. A rare experience, and
one to be treasured forever.

They say they do not have accidents on these French roads,
and I think it must be true. If I remember rightly, we passed
high above wagon roads, or through tunnels under them, but
never crossed them on their own level. About every quarter
of a mile, it seemed to me, a man came out and held up a club
till the train went by, to signify that every thing was safe
ahead. Switches were changed a mile in advance, by pulling
a wire rope that passed along the ground by the rail, from

station to station. Signals for the day and signals for the night
gave constant and timely notice of the position of switches.

No, they have no railroad accidents to speak of in France.
But why? Because when one occurs, *somebody* has to hang for
it!* Not hang, may be, but be punished at least with such
vigor of emphasis as to make negligence a thing to be shud-
dered at by railroad officials for many a day thereafter. "No
blame attached to the officers"—that lying and disaster-breed-
ing verdict so common to our soft-hearted juries, is seldom

"THIRTY MINUTES FOR DINNER!"—FRANCE.

rendered in France. If the trouble occurred in the conduct-
or's department, that officer must suffer if his subordinate
can not be proven guilty; if in the engineer's department, and
the case be similar, the engineer must answer.

The Old Travelers—those delightful parrots who have
"been here before," and know more about the country than
Louis Napoleon knows now or ever will know,—tell us these
things, and we believe them because they are pleasant things
to believe, and because they are plausible and savor of the

* They go on the principle that it is better that one innocent man should suffer
than five hundred.

rigid subjection to law and order which we behold about us every where.

But we love the Old Travelers. We love to hear them prate, and drivel and lie. We can tell them the moment we see them. They always throw out a few feelers; they never cast themselves adrift till they have sounded every individual and know that he has not traveled. Then they open their throttle-valves, and how they do brag, and sneer, and swell, and soar, and blaspheme the sacred name of Truth! Their central idea, their grand aim, is to subjugate you, keep you down, make you feel insignificant and humble in the blaze of their cosmopolitan glory! They

THE OLD TRAVELER.

will not let you know any thing. They sneer at your most inoffensive suggestions; they laugh unfeelingly at your treasured dreams of foreign lands; they brand the statements of your traveled aunts and uncles as the stupidest absurdities; they deride your most trusted authors and demolish the fair images they have set up for your willing worship with the pitiless ferocity of the fanatic iconoclast! But still I love the Old Travelers. I love them for their witless platitudes; for their supernatural ability to bore; for their delightful asinine vanity; for their luxuriant fertility of imagination; for their startling, their brilliant, their overwhelming mendacity!

By Lyons and the Saone (where we saw the lady of Lyons and thought little of her comeliness;) by Villa Franca, Tonnere, venerable Sens, Melun, Fontainebleau, and scores of other beautiful cities, we swept, always noting the absence of hog-wallows, broken fences, cowlots, unpainted houses and mud, and always noting, as well, the presence of cleanliness, grace, taste in adorning and beautifying, even to the disposition of a tree or the turning of a hedge, the marvel of roads in perfect repair, void of ruts and guiltless of even an inequality of surface—we bowled along, hour after hour, that brilliant summer day, and as nightfall approached we entered a wilderness of odorous flowers and shrubbery, sped through it, and then, excited, delighted, and half persuaded that we were only the sport of a beautiful dream, lo, we stood in magnificent Paris!

What excellent order they kept about that vast depot! There was no frantic crowding and jostling, no shouting and swearing, and no swaggering intrusion of services by rowdy hackmen. These latter gentry stood outside—stood quietly by their long line of vehicles and said never a word. A kind of hackman-general seemed to have the whole matter of transportation in his hands. He politely received the passengers and ushered them to the kind of conveyance they wanted, and told the driver where to deliver them. There was no "talking back," no dissatisfaction about overcharging, no grumbling about any thing. In a little while we were speeding through the streets of Paris, and delightfully recognizing certain names and places with which books had long ago made us familiar. It was like meeting an old friend when we read "*Rue de Rivoli*" on the street corner; we knew the genuine vast palace of the Louvre as well as we knew its picture; when we passed by the Column of July we needed no one to tell us what it was, or to remind us that on its site once stood the grim Bastile, that grave of human hopes and happiness, that dismal prison-house within whose dungeons so many young faces put on the wrinkles of age, so many proud spirits grew humble, so many brave hearts broke.

We secured rooms at the hotel, or rather, we had three beds put into one room, so that we might be together, and then we went out to a restaurant, just after lamp-lighting, and ate a comfortable, satisfactory, lingering dinner. It was a pleasure to eat where every thing was so tidy, the food so well cooked, the waiters so polite, and the coming and departing company so moustached, so frisky, so affable, so fearfully and wonderfully Frenchy! All the surroundings were gay and enlivening. Two hundred people sat at little tables on the sidewalk, sipping wine and coffee ; the streets were thronged with light vehicles and with joyous pleasure seekers; there was music in the air, life and action all about us, and a conflagration of gaslight every where!

After dinner we felt like seeing such Parisian specialties as we might see without distressing exertion, and so we sauntered through the brilliant streets and looked at the dainty trifles in variety stores and jewelry shops. Occasionally, merely for the pleasure of being cruel, we put unoffending Frenchmen on the rack with questions framed in the incomprehensible jargon of their native language, and while they writhed, we impaled them, we peppered them, we scarified them, with their own vile verbs and participles.

We noticed that in the jewelry stores they had some of the articles marked "gold," and some labeled "imitation." We wondered at this extravagance of honesty, and inquired into the matter. We were informed that inasmuch as most people are not able to tell false gold from the genuine article, the government compels jewelers to have their gold work assayed and stamped officially according to its fineness, and their imitation work duly labeled with the sign of its falsity. They told us the jewelers would not dare to violate this law, and that whatever a stranger bought in one of their stores might be depended upon as being strictly what it was represented to be.—Verily, a wonderful land is France!

Then we hunted for a barber-shop. From earliest infancy it had been a cherished ambition of mine to be shaved some day in a palatial barber-shop of Paris. I wished to recline at full length in a cushioned invalid chair, with pictures about me, and sumptuous furniture; with frescoed walls and gilded arches above me, and vistas of Corinthian columns stretching far before me; with perfumes of Araby to intoxicate my senses, and the slumbrous drone of distant noises to soothe me to sleep. At the end of an hour I would wake up regretfully and find my face as smooth and as soft as an infant's. Departing, I would lift my hands above that barber's head and say, " Heaven bless you, my son !"

So we searched high and low, for a matter of two hours, but never a barber-shop could we see. We saw only wig-making establishments, with shocks of dead and repulsive hair bound upon the heads of painted waxen brigands who stared out from glass boxes upon the passer-by, with their stony eyes, and scared him with the ghostly white of their countenances. We shunned these signs for a time, but finally we concluded that the wig-makers must of necessity be the barbers as well, since we could find no single legitimate representative of the fraternity. We entered and asked, and found that it was even so.

I said I wanted to be shaved. The barber inquired where my room was. I said, never mind where my room was, I wanted to be shaved—there, on the spot. The doctor said he would be shaved also. Then there was an excitement among those two barbers ! There was a wild consultation, and afterwards a hurrying to and fro and a feverish gathering up of razors from obscure places and a ransacking for soap. Next they took us into a little mean, shabby back room ; they got two ordinary sitting-room chairs and placed us in them, with our coats on. My old, old dream of bliss vanished into thin air !

I sat bolt upright, silent, sad, and solemn. One of the wig-making villains lathered my face for ten terrible minutes and finished by plastering a mass of suds into my mouth. I expelled the nasty stuff with a strong English expletive and said, " Foreigner, beware !" Then this outlaw strapped his razor on his boot, hovered over me ominously for six fearful seconds, and then swooped down upon me like the genius of destruction. The first rake of his razor loosened the very hide from my face and lifted me out of the chair. I stormed and raved, and the other boys enjoyed it. Their beards are not strong and thick. Let us draw the curtain over this harrowing scene.

Suffice it that I submitted, and went through with the cruel infliction of a shave by a French barber; tears of exquisite agony coursed down my cheeks, now and then, but I survived. Then the incipient assassin held a basin of water under my chin and slopped its contents over my face, and into my bosom, and down the back of my neck, with a mean pretense of washing away the soap and blood. He dried my features

A DECIDED SHAVE.

with a towel, and was going to comb my hair; but I asked to be excused. I said, with withering irony, that it was sufficient to be skinned—I declined to be scalped.

I went away from there with my handkerchief about my face, and never, never, never desired to dream of palatial Parisian barber-shops any more. The truth is, as I believe I have since found out, that they have no barber shops worthy of the name, in Paris—and no barbers, either, for that matter. The impostor who does duty as a barber, brings his pans and napkins and implements of torture to your residence and deliberately skins you in your private apartments. Ah, I have suffered, suffered, suffered, here in Paris, but never mind —the time is coming when I shall have a dark and bloody revenge. Some day a Parisian barber will come to my room to skin me, and from that day forth, that barber will never be heard of more.

At eleven o'clock we alighted upon a sign which manifestly referred to billiards. Joy! We had played billiards in the Azores with balls that were not round, and on an ancient table that was very little smoother than a brick pavement— one of those wretched old things with dead cushions, and with patches in the faded cloth and invisible obstructions that made the balls describe the most astonishing and unsuspected angles and perform feats in the way of unlooked-for and almost impossible "scratches," that were perfectly bewildering. We had played at Gibraltar with balls the size of a walnut, on a table like a public square—and in both instances we achieved far more aggravation than amusement. We expected to fare better here, but we were mistaken. The cushions were a good deal higher than the balls, and as the balls had a fashion of always stopping under the cushions, we accomplished very little in the way of caroms. The cushions were hard and unelastic, and the cues were so crooked that in making a shot you had to allow for the curve or you would infallibly put the "English" on the wrong side of the ball. Dan was to mark while the doctor and I played. At the end of an hour neither of us had made a count, and so Dan was tired of keeping tally with nothing to tally, and we were heated and angry and disgusted. We paid the heavy bill—about six cents—and said we would call around some time when we had a week to spend, and finish the game.

We adjourned to one of those pretty cafés and took supper and tested the wines of the country, as we had been instructed to do, and found them harmless and unexciting. They might have been exciting, however, if we had chosen to drink a sufficiency of them.

To close our first day in Paris cheerfully and pleasantly, we now sought our grand room in the Grand Hotel du Louvre and climbed into our sumptuous bed, to read and smoke—but alas!

> It was pitiful,
> In a whole city-full,
> Gas we had none.

No gas to read by—nothing but dismal candles. It was a shame. We tried to map out excursions for the morrow; we puzzled over French "Guides to Paris;" we talked disjointedly, in a vain endeavor to make head or tail of the wild chaos of

A GAS-TLY SUBSTITUTE

the day's sights and experiences; we subsided to indolent smoking; we gaped and yawned, and stretched—then feebly wondered if we were really and truly in renowned Paris, and drifted drowsily away into that vast mysterious void which men call sleep.

* Joke by the Doctor.

CHAPTER XIII.

THE next morning we were up and dressed at ten o'clock. We went to the *commissionaire* of the hotel—I don't know what a *commissionaire* is, but that is the man we went to —and told him we wanted a guide. He said the great International Exposition had drawn such multitudes of Englishmen and Americans to Paris that it would be next to impossible to find a good guide unemployed. He said he usually kept a dozen or two on hand, but he only had three now. He called them. One looked so like a very pirate that we let him go at once. The next one spoke with a simpering precision of pronunciation that was irritating, and said:

"If ze zhentlemans will to me make ze grande honneur to me rattain in hees serveece, I shall show to him every sing zat is magnifique to look upon in ze beautiful Parree. I speaky ze Angleesh pairfaitemaw."

He would have done well to have stopped there, because he had that much by heart and said it right off without making a mistake. But his self-complacency seduced him into attempting a flight into regions of unexplored English, and the reckless experiment was his ruin. Within ten seconds he was so tangled up in a maze of mutilated verbs and torn and bleeding forms of speech that no human ingenuity could ever have gotten him out of it with credit. It was plain enough that he could not "speaky" the English quite as "pairfaitemaw" as he had pretended he could.

The third man captured us. He was plainly dressed, but he had a noticeable air of neatness about him. He wore a high silk hat which was a little old, but had been carefully brushed. He wore second-hand kid gloves, in good repair,

THE THREE GUIDES.

and carried a small rattan cane with a curved handle—a female leg, of ivory. He stepped as gently and as daintily as a cat crossing a muddy street; and oh, he was urbanity; he was quiet, unobtrusive self-possession; he was deference itself! He spoke softly and guardedly; and when he was about to make a statement on his sole responsibility, or offer a suggestion, he weighed it by drachms and scruples first, with the crook of his little stick placed meditatively to his teeth. His opening speech was perfect. It was perfect in construction, in phraseology, in grammar, in emphasis, in pronunciation— every thing. He spoke little and guardedly, after that. We were charmed. We were more than charmed—we were overjoyed. We hired him at once. We never even asked him his price. This man—our lackey, our servant, our unquestioning slave though he was, was still a gentleman—we could see that —while of the other two one was coarse and awkward, and the other was a born pirate. We asked our man Friday's name. He drew from his pocket-book a snowy little card, and passed it to us with a profound bow:

A. BILLFINGER,

Guide to Paris, France, Germany,
Spain, &c., &c.,

Grande Hotel du Louvre.

"Billfinger!   Oh, carry me home to die!"

That was an "aside" from Dan.   The atrocious name grated harshly on my ear, too.   The most of us can learn to forgive, and even to like, a countenance that strikes us unpleasantly at first, but few of us, I fancy, become reconciled to a jarring name so easily.   I was almost sorry we had hired this man, his name was so unbearable.   However, no matter.   We were impatient to start.   Billfinger stepped to the door to call a carriage, and then the doctor said:

"Well, the guide goes with the barber-shop, with the billiard-table, with the gasless room, and may be with many another pretty romance of Paris.   I expected to have a guide named Henri de Montmorency, or Armand de la Chartreuse, or something that would sound grand in letters to the villagers at home; but to think of a Frenchman by the name of Billfinger!   Oh! this is absurd, you know.   This will never do. We can't say Billfinger; it is nauseating.   Name him over again: what had we better call him?   Alexis du Caulaincourt?"

"Alphonse Henri Gustave de Hauteville," I suggested.

"Call him Ferguson," said Dan.

That was practical, unromantic good sense.   Without debate, we expunged Billfinger as Billfinger, and called him Ferguson.

The carriage—an open barouche—was ready.   Ferguson mounted beside the driver, and we whirled away to breakfast. As was proper, Mr. Ferguson stood by to transmit our orders and answer questions.   Bye and bye, he mentioned casually— the artful adventurer—that he would go and get his breakfast as soon as we had finished ours.   He knew we could not get along without him, and that we would not want to loiter about and wait for him.   We asked him to sit down and eat with us.   He begged, with many a bow, to be excused.   It was not proper, he said; he would sit at another table.   We ordered him peremptorily to sit down with us.

Here endeth the first lesson.   It was a mistake.

As long as we had that fellow after that, he was always

hungry; he was always thirsty. He came early; he stayed late; he could not pass a restaurant; he looked with a lecherous eye upon every wine shop. Suggestions to stop, excuses to eat and to drink were forever on his lips. We tried all we could to fill him so full that he would have no room to spare for a fortnight; but it was a failure. He did not hold enough to smother the cravings of his superhuman appetite.

He had another "discrepancy" about him. He was always wanting us to buy things. On the shallowest pretenses, he would inveigle us into shirt stores, boot stores, tailor shops, glove shops—any where under the broad sweep of the heavens that there seemed a chance of our buying any thing. Any one could have guessed that the shopkeepers paid him a per centage on the sales; but in our blessed innocence we didn't, until this feature of his conduct grew unbearably prominent. One day, Dan happened to mention that he thought of buying three or four silk dress patterns for presents. Ferguson's hungry eye was upon him in an instant. In the course of twenty minutes, the carriage stopped.

"What's this?"

"Zis is ze finest silk magazin in Paris—ze most celebrate."

"What did you come here for? We told you to take us to the palace of the Louvre."

"I suppose ze gentleman say he wish to buy some silk."

"You are not required to 'suppose' things for the party, Ferguson. We do not wish to tax your energies too much. We will bear some of the burden and heat of the day ourselves. We will endeavor to do such 'supposing' as is really necessary to be done. Drive on." So spake the doctor.

Within fifteen minutes the carriage halted again, and before another silk store. The doctor said:

"Ah, the palace of the Louvre: beautiful, beautiful edifice! Does the Emperor Napoleon live here now, Ferguson?"

"Ah, doctor! you do jest; zis is not ze palace; we come there directly. But since we pass right by zis store, where is such beautiful silk—"

"Ah! I see, I see. I meant to have told you that we did not wish to purchase any silks to-day; but in my absent-mindedness I forgot it. I also meant to tell you we wished to go directly to the Louvre; but I forgot that also. However, we will go there now. Pardon my seeming carelessness, Ferguson. Drive on."

Within the half hour, we stopped again—in front of another silk store. We were angry; but the doctor was always serene, always smooth-voiced. He said:

"At last! How imposing the Louvre is, and yet how small! how exquisitely fashioned! how charmingly situated! —Venerable, venerable pile—"

"Pairdon, doctor, zis is not ze Louvre—it is—"

"*What* is it?"

"I have ze idea—it come to me in a moment—zat ze silk in zis magazin—"

"ZE SILK MAGAZIN."

"Ferguson, how heedless I am. I fully intended to tell you

that we did not wish to buy any silks to-day, and I also intended to tell you that we yearned to go immediately to the palace of the Louvre, but enjoying the happiness of seeing you devour four breakfasts this morning has so filled me with pleasurable emotions that I neglect the commonest interests of the time. However, we will proceed now to the Louvre, Ferguson."

"But doctor," (excitedly,) "it will take not a minute—not but one small minute! Ze gentleman need not to buy if he not wish to—but only *look* at ze silk—*look* at ze beautiful fabric." [Then pleadingly.] "*Sair*—just only one *leetle* moment!"

Dan said, "Confound the idiot! I don't want to see any silks to-day, and I *won't* look at them. Drive on."

And the doctor: "We need no silks now, Ferguson. Our hearts yearn for the Louvre. Let us journey on—let us journey on."

"But *doctor!* it is only one moment—one leetle moment. And ze time will be save—entirely save! Because zere is nothing to see, now—it is too late. It want ten minute to four and ze Louvre close at four—*only* one leetle moment, doctor!"

The treacherous miscreant! After four breakfasts and a gallon of champagne, to serve us such a scurvy trick. We got no sight of the countless treasures of art in the Louvre galleries that day, and our only poor little satisfaction was in the reflection that Ferguson sold not a solitary silk dress pattern.

I am writing this chapter partly for the satisfaction of abusing that accomplished knave, Billfinger, and partly to show whosoever shall read this how Americans fare at the hands of the Paris guides, and what sort of people Paris guides are. It need not be supposed that we were a stupider or an easier prey than our countrymen generally are, for we were not. The guides deceive and defraud every American who goes to Paris for the first time and sees its sights alone or in company with others as little experienced as himself. I shall visit

Paris again some day, and then let the guides beware! I shall go in my war-paint—I shall carry my tomahawk along.

I think we have lost but little time in Paris. We have

RETURN IN WAR-PAINT.

gone to bed every night tired out. Of course we visited the renowned International Exposition. All the world did that. We went there on our third day in Paris—and we stayed there *nearly two hours.* That was our first and last visit. To tell the truth, we saw at a glance that one would have to spend weeks—yea, even months —in that monstrous establishment, to get an intelligible idea of it. It was a wonderful show, but the moving masses of people of all nations we saw there were a still more wonderful show. I discovered that if I were to stay there a month, I should still find myself looking at the people instead of the inanimate objects on exhibition. I got a little interested in some curious old tapestries of the thirteenth century, but a party of Arabs came by, and their dusky faces and quaint costumes called my attention away at once. I watched a silver swan, which had a living grace about his movements, and a living intelligence in his eyes—watched him swimming about as comfortably and as unconcernedly as if he had been born in a morass instead of a jeweller's shop—watched him seize a silver fish from under the water and hold up his head and go through all the customary and elaborate motions of swallowing it—but the moment it disappeared down his throat some tattooed South Sea Islanders approached and I yielded to their attractions.

Presently I found a revolving pistol several hundred years old which looked strangely like a modern Colt, but just then I heard that the Empress of the French was in another part of the building, and hastened away to see what she might look like. We heard martial music—we saw an unusual number of soldiers walking hurriedly about—there was a general movement among the people. We inquired what it was all about, and learned that the Emperor of the French and the Sultan of Turkey were about to review twenty-five thousand troops at the *Arc de l'Etoile.* We immediately departed. I had a greater anxiety to see these men than I could have had to see twenty Expositions.

We drove away and took up a position in an open space opposite the American Minister's house. A speculator bridged a couple of barrels with a board and we hired standing-places on it. Presently there was a sound of distant music; in another minute a pillar of dust came moving slowly toward us; a moment more, and then, with colors flying and a grand crash of military music, a gallant array of cavalrymen emerged from the dust and came down the street on a gentle trot. After them came a long line of artillery; then more cavalry, in splendid uniforms; and then their Imperial Majesties Napoleon III. and Abdul Aziz. The vast concourse of people swung their hats and shouted—the windows and house-tops in the wide vicinity burst into a snow-storm of waving handkerchiefs, and the wavers of the same mingled their cheers with those of the masses below. It was a stirring spectacle.

But the two central figures claimed all my attention. Was ever such a contrast set up before a multitude till then ? Napoleon, in military uniform—a long-bodied, short-legged man, fiercely moustached, old, wrinkled, with eyes half closed, and *such* a deep, crafty, scheming expression about them!—Napoleon, bowing ever so gently to the loud plaudits, and watching every thing and every body with his cat-eyes from under his depressed hat-brim, as if to discover any sign that those cheers were not heartfelt and cordial.

Abdul Aziz, absolute lord of the Ottoman Empire,—

NAPOLEON III.

clad in dark green European clothes, almost without ornament or insignia of rank; a red Turkish fez on his head—a short, stout, dark man, black-bearded, black-eyed, stupid, unprepossessing—a man whose whole appearance somehow suggested that if he only had a cleaver in his hand and a white apron on, one would not be at all surprised to hear him say: " A mutton-roast to-day, or will you have a nice porter-house steak?"

ABDUL AZIZ.

Napoleon III., the representative of the highest modern civilization, progress, and refinement; Abdul-Aziz, the representative of a people by nature and training filthy, brutish, ignorant, unprogressive, superstitious—and a government whose Three Graces are Tyranny, Rapacity, Blood. Here in brilliant Paris, under this majestic Arch of Triumph, the First Century greets the Nineteenth!

NAPOLEON III., Emperor of France! Surrounded by shouting thousands, by military pomp, by the splendors of his capital city, and companioned by kings and princes—this is the man who was sneered at, and reviled, and called Bastard —yet who was dreaming of a crown and an Empire all the while; who was driven into exile—but carried his dreams with him; who associated with the common herd in America, and ran foot-races for a wager—but still sat upon a throne, in fancy; who braved every danger to go to his dying mother— and grieved that she could not be spared to see him cast aside his plebeian vestments for the purple of royalty; who kept his faithful watch and walked his weary beat a common policeman of London—but dreamed the while of a coming night when he should tread the long-drawn corridors of the Tuileries; who made the miserable *fiasco* of Strasbourg; saw his poor, shabby eagle, forgetful of its lesson, refuse to perch upon his shoulder; delivered his carefully-prepared, sententious burst of eloquence, unto unsympathetic ears; found himself a prisoner, the butt of small wits, a mark for the pitiless ridicule of all the world—yet went on dreaming of coronations and splendid pageants, as before; who lay a forgotten captive in the dungeons of Ham—and still schemed and planned and pondered over future glory and future power; President of France at last! a *coup d'etat*, and surrounded by applauding armies, welcomed by the thunders of cannon, he mounts a throne and waves before an astounded world the sceptre of a mighty Empire! Who talks of the marvels of fiction? Who speaks of the wonders of romance? Who prates of the tame achievements of Aladdin and the Magii of Arabia?

ABDUL-AZIZ, Sultan of Turkey, Lord of the Ottoman Empire! Born to a throne; weak, stupid, ignorant, almost, as his meanest slave; chief of a vast royalty, yet the puppet of his Premier and the obedient child of a tyrannical mother; a man who sits upon a throne—the beck of whose finger moves navies and armies—who holds in his hands the power of life and death over millions—yet who sleeps, sleeps, eats, eats, idles with his eight hundred concubines, and when he is surfeited with eating and sleeping and idling, and would rouse up and take the reins of government and threaten to *be* a Sultan, is charmed from his purpose by wary Fuad Pacha with a pretty plan for a new palace or a new ship—charmed away with a new toy, like any other restless child; a man who sees his people robbed and oppressed by soulless tax-gatherers, but speaks no word to save them; who believes in gnomes, and genii and the wild fables of the Arabian Nights, but has small regard for the mighty magicians of to-day, and is nervous in the presence of their mysterious railroads and steamboats and telegraphs; who would see undone in Egypt all that great Mehemet Ali achieved, and would prefer rather to forget than emulate him; a man who found his great Empire a blot upon the earth—a degraded, poverty-stricken, miserable, infamous agglomeration of ignorance, crime, and brutality, and will idle away the allotted days of his trivial life, and then pass to the dust and the worms and leave it so!

Napoleon has augmented the commercial prosperity of France, in ten years, to such a degree that figures can hardly compute it. He has rebuilt Paris, and has partly rebuilt every city in the State. He condemns a whole street at a time, assesses the damages, pays them and rebuilds superbly. Then speculators buy up the ground and sell, but the original owner is given the first choice by the government at a stated price before the speculator is permitted to purchase. But above all things, he has taken the sole control of the Empire of France into his hands, and made it a tolerably free land—for people who will not attempt to go too far in medding with government affairs. No country offers greater security to life and property than France, and one has all the freedom he wants, but no license—no license to interfere with any body, or make any one uncomfortable.

As for the Sultan, one could set a trap any where and catch a dozen abler men in a night.

The bands struck up, and the brilliant adventurer, Napoleon III., the genius of Energy, Persistence, Enterprise; and the feeble Abdul-Aziz, the genius of Ignorance, Bigotry and Indolence, prepared for the Forward—March!

We saw the splendid review, we saw the white-moustached old Crimean soldier, Canrobert, Marshal of France, we saw—well, we saw every thing, and then we went home satisfied.

9

CHAPTER XIV.

WE went to see the Cathedral of Notre Dame.—We had heard of it before. It surprises me, sometimes, to think how much we *do* know, and how intelligent we are. We recognized the brown old Gothic pile in a moment; it was like the pictures. We stood at a little distance and changed from one point of observation to another, and gazed long at its lofty square towers and its rich front, clustered thick with stony, mutilated saints who had been looking calmly down from their perches for ages. The Patriarch of Jerusalem stood under them in the old days of chivalry and romance, and preached the third Crusade, more than six hundred years ago; and since that day they have stood there and looked quietly down upon the most thrilling scenes, the grandest pageants, the most extraordinary spectacles that have grieved or delighted Paris. These battered and broken-nosed old fellows saw many and many a cavalcade of mail-clad knights come marching home from Holy Land; they heard the bells above them toll the signal for the St. Bartholomew's Massacre, and they saw the slaughter that followed; later, they saw the Reign of Terror, the carnage of the Revolution, the overthrow of a king, the coronation of two Napoleons, the christening of the young prince that lords it over a regiment of servants in the Tuileries to-day—and they may possibly continue to stand there until they see the Napoleon dynasty swept away and the banners of a great Republic floating above its ruins. I wish these old parties could speak. They could tell a tale worth the listening to.

They say that a pagan temple stood where Notre Dame now

stands, in the old Roman days, eighteen or twenty centuries ago—remains of it are still preserved in Paris; and that a Christian church took its place about A. D. 300; another took the place of that in A. D. 500; and that the foundations of the present Cathedral were laid about A. D. 1100. The ground ought to be measurably sacred by this time, one would think. One portion of this noble old edifice is suggestive of the quaint fashions of ancient times. It was built by Jean Sans-Peur, Duke of Burgundy, to set his conscience at rest—he had assassinated the Duke of Orleans. Alas! those good old times are gone, when a murderer could wipe the stain from his name and soothe his troubles to sleep simply by getting out his bricks and mortar and building an addition to a church.

The portals of the great western front are bisected by square pillars. They took the central one away, in 1852, on the occasion of thanksgivings for the reinstitution of the Presidential power—but precious soon they had occasion to reconsider that motion and put it back again! And they did.

We loitered through the grand aisles for an hour or two, staring up at the rich stained glass windows embellished with blue and yellow and crimson saints and martyrs, and trying to admire the numberless great pictures in the chapels, and then we were admitted to the sacristy and shown the magnificent robes which the Pope wore when he crowned Napoleon I.; a wagon-load of solid gold and silver utensils used in the great public processions and ceremonies of the church; some nails of the true cross, a fragment of the cross itself, a part of the crown of thorns. We had already seen a large piece of the true cross in a church in the Azores, but no nails. They showed us likewise the bloody robe which that Archbishop of Paris wore who exposed his sacred person and braved the wrath of the insurgents of 1848, to mount the barricades and hold aloft the olive branch of peace in the hope of stopping the slaughter. His noble effort cost him his life. He was shot dead. They showed us a cast of his face, taken after death, the bullet that killed him, and the two vertebræ in which it lodged. These people have a somewhat singular taste in the matter of relics. Ferguson told us that the silver cross which the good Archbishop wore at his girdle was seized and thrown into the Seine, where it lay embedded in the mud for fifteen years, and then an angel appeared to a priest and told him where to dive for it; he *did* dive for it and got it, and now it is there on exhibition at Notre Dame, to be inspected by any body who feels an interest in inanimate objects of miraculous intervention.

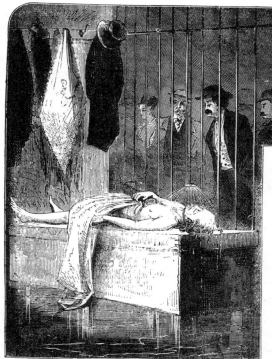

THE MORGUE.

Next we went to visit the Morgue, that horrible receptacle for the dead who die mysteriously and leave the manner of their taking off a dismal secret. We stood before a grating and looked through into a room which was hung all about with the clothing of dead men; coarse blouses, water-soaked; the delicate garments of women and children; patrician vestments, hacked and stabbed and stained with red; a hat that was crushed and bloody. On a slanting stone lay a drowned man, naked, swollen, purple; clasping the fragment of a broken bush with a grip which death had so petrified that human strength could not unloose it—mute witness of the last despairing effort to save the life that was doomed beyond all help. A stream of water trickled ceaselessly over the hideous face. We knew that the body and the clothing were there for identification by friends, but still we wondered if anybody could love that repulsive object or grieve for its loss. We grew meditative and wondered if, some forty years ago, when the mother of that ghastly thing was dandling it upon her knee, and kissing it and petting it and displaying it with satisfied pride to the passers-by, a prophetic vision of this dread ending ever flitted through her brain. I half feared that the mother, or the wife or a brother of the dead man might come while we stood there, but nothing of the kind occurred. Men and women came, and some looked eagerly in, and pressed their faces against the bars; others glanced carelessly at the body, and turned away with a disappointed look—people, I thought, who live upon strong excitements, and who attend the exhibitions of the Morgue regularly, just as other people go to see theatrical spectacles every night. When one of these looked in and passed on, I could not help thinking—

"Now this don't afford you any satisfaction—a party with his head shot off is what *you* need."

One night we went to the celebrated *Jardin Mabille*, but only staid a little while. We wanted to see some of this kind of Paris life, however, and therefore, the next night we went to a similar place of entertainment in a great garden in the suburb of Asniéres. We went to the railroad depot, toward evening, and Ferguson got tickets for a second-class carriage. Such a perfect jam of people I have not often seen—but there was no noise, no disorder, no rowdyism. Some of the women and young girls that entered the train we knew to be of the *demi-monde*, but others we were not at all sure about.

The girls and women in our carriage behaved themselves

modestly and becomingly, all the way out, except that they smoked. When we arrived at the garden in Asniéres, we paid a franc or two admission, and entered a place which had flower-beds in it, and grass plats, and long, curving rows of ornamental shrubbery, with here and there a secluded bower convenient for eating ice-cream in. We moved along the sinuous gravel walks, with the great concourse of girls and young men, and suddenly a domed and filagreed white temple, starred over and over and over again with brilliant gas-jets, burst upon us like a fallen sun. Near by was a large, handsome house with its ample front illuminated in the same way, and above its roof floated the Star Spangled Banner of America.

"Well!" I said. "How is this?" It nearly took my breath away.

Ferguson said an American—a New Yorker—kept the place, and was carrying on quite a stirring opposition to the *Jardin Mabille.*

Crowds, composed of both sexes and nearly all ages, were frisking about the garden or sitting in the open air in front of the flag-staff and the temple, drinking wine and coffee, or smoking. The dancing had not begun, yet. Ferguson said there was to be an exhibition. The famous Blondin was going to perform on a tight-rope in another part of the garden. We went thither. Here the light was dim, and the masses of people were pretty closely packed together. And now I made a mistake which any donkey might make, but a sensible man never. I committed an error which I find myself repeating every day of my life.—Standing right before a young lady, I said—

"Dan, just look at this girl, how beautiful she is!"

"I thank you more for the evident sincerity of the compliment, sir, than for the extraordinary publicity you have given to it!" This in good, pure English.

We took a walk, but my spirits were very, very sadly dampened. I did not feel right comfortable for some time afterward. Why *will* people be so stupid as to suppose themselves the only foreigners among a crowd of ten thousand persons?

But Blondin came out shortly. He appeared on a stretched cable, far away above the sea of tossing hats and handkerchiefs, and in the glare of the hundreds of rockets that whizzed heavenward by him he looked like a wee insect. He balanced

WE TOOK A WALK.

his pole and walked the length of his rope—two or three hundred feet; he came back and got a man and carried him across; he returned to the centre and danced a jig; next he performed some gymnastic and balancing feats too perilous to afford a pleasant spectacle; and he finished by fastening to his person a thousand Roman candles, Catherine wheels, serpents and rockets of all manner of brilliant colors, setting them on fire all at once and walking and waltzing across his rope again in a blinding blaze of glory that lit up the garden and the people's faces like a great conflagration at midnight.

The dance had begun, and we adjourned to the temple. Within it was a drinking saloon; and all around it was a broad circular platform for the dancers. I backed up against the wall of the temple, and waited. Twenty sets formed, the music struck up, and then—I placed my hands before my face for very shame. But I looked through my fingers. They were dancing the renowned " *Can-can.*" A handsome girl in the set before me tripped forward lightly to meet the opposite gentleman—tripped back again, grasped her dresses vigorously on both sides with her hands, raised them pretty high, danced an extraordinary jig that had more activity and exposure about it than any jig I ever saw before, and then, drawing her clothes still higher, she advanced gaily to the centre and launched a vicious kick full at her *vis-a-vis* that must infallibly have removed his nose if he had been seven feet high. It was a mercy he was only six.

CAN-CAN.

That is the *can-can.* The idea of it is to dance as wildly, as noisily, as furiously as you can; expose yourself as much as possible if you are a woman; and kick as high as you can, no matter which sex you belong to. There is no word of exaggeration in this. Any of the staid, respectable, aged people who were there that night can testify to the truth of that statement. There were a good many such people present. I suppose French morality is not of that straight-laced description which is shocked at trifles.

I moved aside and took a general view of the *can-can.* Shouts, laughter, furious music, a bewildering chaos of darting and intermingling forms, stormy jerking and snatching of gay dresses, bobbing heads, flying arms, lightning-flashes of white stockinged calves and dainty slippers in the air, and then a grand final rush, riot, a terrific hubbub and a wild stampede! Heavens! Nothing like it has been seen on earth since trembling Tam O'Shanter saw the devil and the witches at their orgies that stormy night in "Alloway's auld haunted kirk."

We visited the Louvre, at a time when we had no silk purchases in view, and looked at its miles of paintings by the old masters. Some of them were beautiful, but at the same time they carried such evidences about them of the cringing spirit of those great men that we found small pleasure in examining them. Their nauseous adulation of princely patrons was more prominent to me and chained my attention more surely than the charms of color and expression which are claimed to be in the pictures. Gratitude for kindnesses is well, but it seems to me that some of those artists carried it so far that it ceased to be gratitude, and became worship. If there is a plausible excuse for the worship of men, then by all means let us forgive Rubens and his brethren.

But I will drop the subject, lest I say something about the old masters that might as well be left unsaid.

Of course we drove in the *Bois de Boulogne*, that limitless park, with its forests, its lakes, its cascades, and its broad avenues. There were thousands upon thousands of vehicles abroad, and the scene was full of life and gayety. There were very common hacks, with father and mother and all the children in them; conspicuous little open carriages with celebrated ladies of questionable reputation in them; there were Dukes and Duchesses abroad, with gorgeous footmen perched behind, and equally gorgeous outriders perched on each of the six horses; there were blue and silver, and green and gold, and pink and black, and all sorts and descriptions of stunning and startling liveries out, and I almost yearned to be a flunkey myself, for the sake of the fine clothes.

But presently the Emperor came along and he out-shone them all. He was preceded by a body guard of gentlemen on horseback in showy uniforms, his carriage-horses (there ap peared to be somewhere in the remote neighborhood of a thousand of them,) were bestridden by gallant looking fellows, also in stylish uniforms, and after the carriage followed another detachment of body-guards. Every body got out of the way; every body bowed to the Emperor and his friend the Sultan, and they went by on a swinging trot and disappeared.

I will not describe the *Bois de Boulogne*. I can not do it. It is simply a beautiful, cultivated, endless, wonderful wilderness. It is an enchanting place. It is in Paris, now, one may say, but a crumbling old cross in one portion of it reminds one that it was not always so. The cross marks the spot where a celebrated troubadour was waylaid and murdered in the fourteenth century. It was in this park that that fellow with an unpronounceable name made the attempt upon the Russian Czar's life last spring with a pistol. The bullet struck a tree. Ferguson showed us the place. Now in America that interesting tree would be chopped down or forgotten within the next five years, but it will be treasured here. The guides will point it out to visitors for the next eight hundred years, and when it decays and falls down they will put up another there and go on with the same old story just the same.

CHAPTER XV.

ONE of our pleasantest visits was to Père la Chaise, the national burying-ground of France, the honored resting-place of some of her greatest and best children, the last home of scores of illustrious men and women who were born to no titles, but achieved fame by their own energy and their own genius. It is a solemn city of winding streets, and of miniature marble temples and mansions of the dead gleaming white from out a wilderness of foliage and fresh flowers. Not every city is so well peopled as this, or has so ample an area within its walls. Few palaces exist in any city, that are so exquisite in design, so rich in art, so costly in material, so graceful, so beautiful.

We had stood in the ancient church of St. Denis, where the marble effigies of thirty generations of kings and queens lay stretched at length upon the tombs, and the sensations invoked were startling and novel; the curious armor, the obsolete costumes, the placid faces, the hands placed palm to palm in eloquent supplication—it was a vision of gray antiquity. It seemed curious enough to be standing face to face, as it were, with old Dagobert I., and Clovis and Charlemagne, those vague, colossal heroes, those shadows, those myths of a thousand years ago! I touched their dust-covered faces with my finger, but Dagobert was deader than the sixteen centuries that have passed over him, Clovis slept well after his labor for Christ, and old Charlemagne went on dreaming of his paladins, of bloody Roncesvalles, and gave no heed to me.

The great names of Père la Chaise impress one, too, but differently. There the suggestion brought constantly to his mind is, that this place is sacred to a nobler royalty—the royalty of heart and brain. Every faculty of mind, every noble trait of human nature, every high occupation which men engage in seems represented by a famous name. The effect is a curious medley. Davoust and Massena, who wrought in many a battle-tragedy, are here, and so also is Rachel, of equal renown in mimic tragedy on the stage. The Abbé Sicard sleeps here—the first great teacher of the deaf and dumb—a man whose heart went out to every unfortunate, and whose life was given to kindly offices in their service; and not far off, in repose and peace at last, lies Marshal Ney, whose stormy spirit knew no music like the bugle call to arms. The man who originated public gas-lighting, and that other benefactor who introduced the cultivation of the potato and thus blessed millions of his starving countrymen, lie with the Prince of Masserano, and with exiled queens and princes of Further India. Gay-Lussac the chemist, Laplace the astronomer, Larrey the surgeon, de Séze the advocate, are here, and with them are Talma, Bellini, Rubini; de Balzac, Beaumarchais, Beranger; Molière and Lafontaine, and scores of other men whose names and whose worthy labors are as familiar in the remote by-places of civilization as are the historic deeds of the kings and princes that sleep in the marble vaults of St. Denis.

But among the thousands and thousands of tombs in Père la Chaise, there is one that no man, no woman, no youth of either sex, ever passes by without stopping to examine. Every visitor has a sort of indistinct idea of the history of its dead, and comprehends that homage is due there, but not one in twenty thousand clearly remembers the story of that tomb and its romantic occupants. This is the grave of Abelard and Heloise—a grave which has been more revered, more widely known, more written and sung about and wept over, for seven hundred years, than any other in Christendom, save only that of the Saviour. All visitors linger pensively about

it; all young people capture and carry away keepsakes and
mementoes of it; all Parisian youths and maidens who are
disappointed in love come there to bail out when they are full
of tears; yea, many stricken lovers make pilgrimages to this
shrine from distant provinces to weep and wail and "grit"
their teeth over their heavy sorrows, and to purchase the sympathies of the chastened spirits of that tomb with offerings of
immortelles and budding flowers.

Go when you will, you find somebody snuffling over that
tomb. Go when you will, you find it furnished with those

GRAVE OF ABELARD AND HELOISE.

bouquets and immortelles.   Go when you will, you find a
gravel-train from Marseilles arriving to supply the deficiencies
caused by memento-cabbaging vandals whose affections have
miscarried.

Yet who really knows the story of Abelard and Heloise?
Precious few people.   The names are perfectly familiar to
every body, and that is about all.   With infinite pains I have
acquired a knowledge of that history, and I propose to narrate
it here, partly for the honest information of the public and
partly to show that public that they have been wasting a good
deal of marketable sentiment very unnecessarily.

STORY OF ABELARD AND HELOISE.

Heloise was born seven hundred and sixty-six years ago.

She may have had parents. There is no telling. She lived with her uncle Fulbert, a canon of the cathedral of Paris. I do not know what a canon of a cathedral is, but that is what he was. He was nothing more than a sort of a mountain howitzer, likely, because they had no heavy artillery in those days. Suffice it, then, that Heloise lived with her uncle the howitzer, and was happy.—She spent the most of her childhood in the convent of Argenteuil—never heard of Argenteuil before, but suppose there was really such a place. She then returned to her uncle, the old gun, or son of a gun, as the case may be, and he taught her to write and speak Latin, which was the

A PAIR OF CANONS, 13TH CENTURY.

language of literature and polite society at that period.

Just at this time, Pierre Abelard, who had already made himself widely famous as a rhetorician, came to found a school of rhetoric in Paris. The originality of his principles, his eloquence, and his great physical strength and beauty created a profound sensation. He saw Heloise, and was captivated by her blooming youth, her beauty and her charming disposition. He wrote to her; she answered. He wrote again, she answered again. He was now in love. He longed to know her—to speak to her face to face.

His school was near Fulbert's house. He asked Fulbert to allow him to call. The good old swivel saw here a rare opportunity: his niece, whom he so much loved, would absorb knowledge from this man, and it would not cost him a cent. Such was Fulbert—penurious.

Fulbert's first name is not mentioned by any author, which

is unfortunate. However, George W. Fulbert will answer for him as well as any other. We will let him go at that. He asked Abelard to teach her.

Abelard was glad enough of the opportunity. He came often and staid long. A letter of his shows in its very first sentence that he came under that friendly roof like a cold-hearted villain as he was, with the deliberate intention of debauching a confiding, innocent girl. This is the letter:

"I can not cease to be astonished at the simplicity of Fulbert; I was as much surprised as if he had placed a lamb in the power of a hungry wolf. Heloise and I, under pretext of study, gave ourselves up wholly to love, and the solitude that love seeks our studies procured for us. Books were open before us, but we spoke oftener of love than philosophy, and kisses came more readily from our lips than words."

And so, exulting over an honorable confidence which to his degraded instinct was a ludicrous "simplicity," this unmanly Abelard seduced the niece of the man whose guest he was. Paris found it out. Fulbert was told of it—told often—but refused to believe it. He could not comprehend how a man could be so depraved as to use the sacred protection and security of hospitality as a means for the commission of such a crime as that. But when he heard the rowdies in the streets singing the love-songs of Abelard to Heloise, the case was too plain—love-songs come not properly within the teachings of rhetoric and philosophy.

He drove Abelard from his house. Abelard returned secretly and carried Heloise away to Palais, in Brittany, his native country. Here, shortly afterward, she bore a son, who, from his rare beauty, was surnamed Astrolabe—William G. The girl's flight enraged Fulbert, and he longed for vengeance, but feared to strike lest retaliation visit Heloise—for he still loved her tenderly. At length Abelard offered to marry Heloise—but on a shameful condition: that the marriage should be kept secret from the world, to the end that (while her good name remained a wreck, as before,) his priestly reputation might be kept untarnished. It was like that miscreant. Fulbert saw his opportunity and consented. He would see

the parties married, and then violate the confidence of the
man who had taught him that trick; he would divulge the
secret and so remove somewhat of the obloquy that attached
to his niece's fame. But the niece suspected his scheme. She
refused the marriage, at first; she said Fulbert would betray
the secret to save her, and besides, she did not wish to drag
down a lover who was so gifted, so honored by the world, and
who had such a splendid career before him. It was noble,
self-sacrificing love, and characteristic of the pure-souled
Heloise, but it was not good sense.

But she was overruled, and the private marriage took place.
Now for Fulbert! The heart so wounded should be healed at

THE PRIVATE MARRIAGE.

last; the proud spirit so tortured should find rest again; the
humbled head should be lifted up once more. He proclaimed the marriage in the high places of the city, and rejoiced that dishonor had departed from his house. But lo!
Abelard denied the marriage! Heloise denied it! The
people, knowing the former circumstances, might have believed Fulbert, had only Abelard denied it, but when the person chiefly interested—the girl herself—denied it, they laughed
despairing Fulbert to scorn.

The poor canon of the cathedral of Paris was spiked again. The last hope of repairing the wrong that had been done his house was gone. What next? Human nature suggested revenge. He compassed it. The historian says:

"Ruffians, hired by Fulbert, fell upon Abelard by night, and inflicted upon him a terrible and nameless mutilation."

I am seeking the last resting-place of those "ruffians." When I find it I shall shed some tears on it, and stack up some bouquets and immortelles, and cart away from it some gravel whereby to remember that howsoever blotted by crime their lives may have been, these ruffians did one just deed, at any rate, albeit it was not warranted by the strict letter of the law.

Heloise entered a convent and gave good-bye to the world and its pleasures for all time. For twelve years she never heard of Abelard—never even heard his name mentioned. She had become prioress of Argenteuil, and led a life of complete seclusion. She happened one day to see a letter written by him, in which he narrated his own history. She cried over it, and wrote him. He answered, addressing her as his "sister in Christ." They continued to correspond, she in the unweighed language of unwavering affection, he in the chilly phraseology of the polished rhetorician. She poured out her heart in passionate, disjointed sentences; he replied with finished essays, divided deliberately into heads and sub-heads, premises and argument. She showered upon him the tenderest epithets that love could devise, he addressed her from the North Pole of his frozen heart as the "Spouse of Christ!" The abandoned villain!

On account of her too easy government of her nuns, some disreputable irregularities were discovered among them, and the Abbot of St. Denis broke up her establishment. Abelard was the official head of the monastery of St. Gildas de Ruys, at that time, and when he heard of her homeless condition a sentiment of pity was aroused in his breast (it is a wonder the unfamiliar emotion did not blow his head off,) and he placed

10

her and her troop in the little oratory of the Paraclete, a religious establishment which he had founded. She had many privations and sufferings to undergo at first, but her worth and her gentle disposition won influential friends for her, and she built up a wealthy and flourishing nunnery. She became a great favorite with the heads of the church, and also the people, though she seldom appeared in public. She rapidly advanced in esteem, in good report and in usefulness, and Abelard as rapidly lost ground. The Pope so honored her that he made her the head of her order. Abelard, a man of splendid talents, and ranking as the first debater of his time, became timid, irresolute, and distrustful of his powers. He only needed a great misfortune to topple him from the high position he held in the world of intellectual excellence, and it came. Urged by kings and princes to meet the subtle St. Bernard in debate and crush him, he stood up in the presence of a royal and illustrious assemblage, and when his antagonist had finished he looked about him, and stammered a commencement; but his courage failed him, the cunning of his tongue was gone: with his speech unspoken, he trembled and sat down, a disgraced and vanquished champion.

He died a nobody, and was buried at Cluny, A. D., 1144. They removed his body to the Paraclete afterward, and when Heloise died, twenty years later, they buried her with him, in accordance with her last wish. He died at the ripe age of 64, and she at 63. After the bodies had remained entombed three hundred years, they were removed once more. They were removed again in 1800, and finally, seventeen years afterward, they were taken up and transferred to Père la Chaise, where they will remain in peace and quiet until it comes time for them to get up and move again.

History is silent concerning the last acts of the mountain howitzer. Let the world say what it will about him, *I*, at least, shall always respect the memory and sorrow for the abused trust, and the broken heart, and the troubled spirit of the old smooth-bore. Rest and repose be his!

Such is the story of Abelard and Heloise. Such is the history that Lamartine has shed such cataracts of tears over. But that man never could come within the influence of a subject in the least pathetic without overflowing his banks. He ought to be dammed—or leveed, I should more properly say. Such is the history—not as it is usually told, but as it is when stripped of the nauseous sentimentality that would enshrine for our loving worship a dastardly seducer like Pierre Abelard. I have not a word to say against the misused, faithful girl, and would not withhold from her grave a single one of those simple tributes which blighted youths and maidens offer to her memory, but I am sorry enough that I have not time and opportunity to write four or five volumes of my opinion of her friend the founder of the Parachute, or the Paraclete, or whatever it was.

The tons of sentiment I have wasted on that unprincipled humbug, in my ignorance! I shall throttle down my emotions hereafter, about this sort of people, until I have read them up and know whether they are entitled to any tearful attentions or not. I wish I had my immortelles back, now, and that bunch of radishes.

In Paris we often saw in shop windows the sign, "*English Spoken Here*," just as one sees in the windows at home the sign, "*Ici on parle francaise.*" We always invaded these places at once—and invariably received the information, framed in faultless French, that the clerk who did the English for the establishment had just gone to dinner and would be back in an hour—would Monsieur buy something? We wondered why those parties happened to take their dinners at such erratic and extraordinary hours, for we never called at a time when an exemplary Christian would be in the least likely to be abroad on such an errand. The truth was, it was a base fraud—a snare to trap the unwary—chaff to catch fledglings with. They had no English-murdering clerk. They trusted to the sign to inveigle foreigners into their lairs, and trusted to their own blandishments to keep them there till they bought something.

We ferreted out another French imposition—a frequent

sign to this effect: "ALL MANNER OF AMERICAN DRINKS
ARTISTICALLY PREPARED HERE." We procured the services
of a gentleman experienced in the nomenclature of the American bar, and moved upon the works of one of these impos-
tors. A bowing, aproned Frenchman skipped forward and
said:

"Que voulez les messieurs?" I do not know what Que
voulez les messieurs means, but such was his remark.

Our General said, "We will take a whisky-straight."

[A stare from the Frenchman.]

AMERICAN DRINKS.

"Well, if you don't know what that is, give us a champagne cock-tail."

[A stare and a shrug.]

"Well, then, give us a sherry cobbler."

The Frenchman was checkmated. This was all Greek to him.

"Give us a brandy smash!"

The Frenchman began to back away, suspicious of the ominous vigor of the last order—began to back away, shrugging his shoulders and spreading his hands apologetically.

The General followed him up and gained a complete victory. The uneducated foreigner could not even furnish a Santa Cruz Punch, an Eye-Opener, a Stone-Fence, or an Earthquake. It was plain that he was a wicked impostor.

An acquaintance of mine said, the other day, that he was doubtless the only American visitor to the Exposition who had had the high honor of being escorted by the Emperor's body guard. I said with unobtrusive frankness that I was astonished that such a long-legged, lantern-jawed, unprepossessing looking spectre as he should be singled out for a distinction like that, and asked how it came about. He said he had attended a great military review in the *Champ de Mars*, some time ago, and while the multitude about him was growing thicker and thicker every moment, he observed an open space inside the railing. He left his carriage and went into it. He was the only person there, and so he had plenty of room, and the situation being central, he could see all the preparations going on about the field. By and by there was a sound of music, and soon the Emperor of the French and the Emperor of Austria, escorted by the famous *Cent Gardes*, entered the inclosure. They seemed not to observe him, but directly, in response to a sign from the commander of the Guard, a young lieutenant came toward him with a file of his men following, halted, raised his hand and gave the military salute, and then said in a low voice that he was sorry to have to disturb a stranger and a gentleman, but the place was sacred to royalty. Then this New Jersey phantom rose up and bowed and begged pardon, then with the officer beside him, the file of men marching behind him, and with every mark of respect, he was escorted to his carriage by the imperial *Cent*

Gardes! The officer saluted again and fell back, the New Jersey sprite bowed in return and had presence of mind enough to pretend that he had simply called on a matter of private business with those emperors, and so waved them an adieu, and drove from the field!

ROYAL HONORS TO A YANKEE.

Imagine a poor Frenchman ignorantly intruding upon a public rostrum sacred to some six-penny dignitary in America. The police would scare him to death, first, with a storm of their elegant blasphemy, and then pull him to pieces getting him away from there. We are measurably superior to the French in some things, but they are immeasurably our betters in others.

Enough of Paris for the present. We have done our whole duty by it. We have seen the Tuileries, the Napoleon Column, the Madeleine, that wonder of wonders the tomb of Napoleon, all the great churches and museums, libraries, imperial palaces, and sculpture and picture galleries, the Pantheon, *Jardin des Plantes*, the opera, the circus, the Legislative Body, the billiard-rooms, the barbers, the *grisettes*—

Ah, the *grisettes!* I had almost forgotten. They are another romantic fraud. They were (if you let the books of travel tell it,) always so beautiful—so neat and trim, so graceful—so naive and trusting—so gentle, so winning—so faithful to their shop duties, so irresistible to buyers in their prattling importunity—so devoted to their poverty-stricken students of the Latin Quarter—so light hearted and happy on their Sunday picnics in the suburbs—and oh, so charmingly, so delightfully immoral!

Stuff! For three or four days I was constantly saying:

"Quick, Ferguson! is that a *grisette?*"

And he always said "No."

He comprehended, at last, that I wanted to see a grisette. Then he showed me dozens of them. They were like nearly all the Frenchwomen I ever saw—homely. They had large hands, large feet, large mouths; they had pug noses as a general thing, and mustaches that not even good breeding could overlook; they combed their hair straight back without parting; they were ill-shaped, they were not winning, they were not graceful; I knew by their looks that they ate garlic and onions; and lastly and finally, to my thinking it would be base flattery to call them immoral.

Aroint thee, wench! I sorrow for the vagabond student of the Latin Quarter now, even more than formerly I envied him. Thus topples to earth another idol of my infancy.

We have seen everything, and to-morrow we go to Versailles. We shall see Paris only for a little while as we come back to

GRISETTE

take up our line of march for the ship, and so I may as well bid the beautiful city a regretful farewell. We shall travel many thousands of miles after we leave here, and visit many great cities, but we shall find none so enchanting as this.

Some of our party have gone to England, intending to take a roundabout course and rejoin the vessel at Leghorn or Naples, several weeks hence. We came near going to Geneva, but have concluded to return to Marseilles and go up through Italy from Genoa.

I will conclude this chapter with a remark that I am sincerely proud to be able to make—and glad, as well, that my comrades cordially indorse it, to wit: by far the handsomest women we have seen in France were born and reared in America.

I feel, now, like a man who has redeemed a failing reputation and shed lustre upon a dimmed escutcheon, by a single just deed done at the eleventh hour.

Let the curtain fall, to slow music.

CHAPTER XVI.

VERSAILLES! It is wonderfully beautiful! You gaze, and stare, and try to understand that it is real, that it is on the earth, that it is not the Garden of Eden—but your brain grows giddy, stupefied by the world of beauty around you, and you half believe you are the dupe of an exquisite dream. The scene thrills one like military music! A noble palace, stretching its ornamented front block upon block away, till it seemed that it would never end; a grand promenade before it, whereon the armies of an empire might parade; all about it rainbows of flowers, and colossal statues that were almost numberless, and yet seemed only scattered over the ample space; broad flights of stone steps leading down from the promenade to lower grounds of the park—stairways that whole regiments might stand to arms upon and have room to spare; vast fountains whose great bronze effigies discharged rivers of sparkling water into the air and mingled a hundred curving jets together in forms of matchless beauty; wide grass-carpeted avenues that branched hither and thither in every direction and wandered to seemingly interminable distances, walled all the way on either side with compact ranks of leafy trees whose branches met above and formed arches as faultless and as symmetrical as ever were carved in stone; and here and there were glimpses of sylvan lakes with miniature ships glassed in their surfaces. And every where—on the palace steps, and the great promenade, around the fountains, among the trees, and far under the arches of the endless avenues, hundreds and hundreds of people in gay costumes walked or ran or danced, and gave to the fairy picture the life and animation which was all of perfection it could have lacked.

It was worth a pilgrimage to see. Every thing is on so gigantic a scale. Nothing is small—nothing is cheap. The statues are all large; the palace is grand; the park covers a fair-sized county; the avenues are interminable. All the distances and all the dimensions about Versailles are vast. I

FOUNTAIN AT VERSAILLES.

used to think the pictures exaggerated these distances and these dimensions beyond all reason, and that they made Versailles more beautiful than it was possible for any place in the world to be. I know now that the pictures never came up to the subject in any respect, and that no painter could represent Versailles on canvas as beautiful as it is in reality. I used to abuse Louis XIV. for spending two hundred millions of dollars in creating this marvelous park, when bread was so scarce with some of his subjects; but I have forgiven him now. He took a tract of land sixty miles in circumference and set to work to make this park and build this palace and a road to it from Paris. He kept 36,000 men employed daily on it, and the labor was so unhealthy that they used to die and be hauled off by cart-loads every night. The wife of a nobleman of the time speaks of this as an "*inconvenience*," but naively remarks that "it does not seem worthy of attention in the happy state of tranquillity we now enjoy."

I always thought ill of people at home, who trimmed their shrubbery into pyramids, and squares, and spires, and all manner of unnatural shapes, and when I saw the same thing being practiced in this great park I began to feel dissatisfied. But I soon saw the idea of the thing and the wisdom of it. They seek the *general* effect. We distort a dozen sickly trees into unaccustomed shapes in a little yard no bigger than a dining-room, and then surely they look absurd enough. But here they take two hundred thousand tall forest trees and set them in a double row; allow no sign of leaf or branch to grow on the trunk lower down than six feet above the ground; from that point the boughs begin to project, and very gradually they extend outward further and further till they meet overhead, and a faultless tunnel of foliage is formed. The arch is mathematically precise. The effect is then very fine. They make trees take fifty different shapes, and so these quaint effects are infinitely varied and picturesque. The trees in no two avenues are shaped alike, and consequently the eye is not fatigued with any thing in the nature of monotonous uniformity. I will drop this subject now, leaving it to others to determine how these people manage to make endless ranks of lofty forest trees grow to just a certain thickness of trunk (say a foot and two-thirds;) how they make them spring to precisely the same height for miles; how they make them grow so close together; how they compel one huge limb to spring from the same identical spot on each tree and form the main sweep of the arch; and how all these things are kept exactly in the same condition, and in the same exquisite shapeliness and symmetry month after month and year after year—for I have tried to reason out the problem, and have failed.

We walked through the great hall of sculpture and the one hundred and fifty galleries of paintings in the palace of Versailles, and felt that to be in such a place was useless unless one had a whole year at his disposal. These pictures are all battle-scenes, and only one solitary little canvas among them all treats of anything but great French victories. We wandered, also, through the Grand Trianon and the Petit Trianon, those monuments of royal prodigality, and with histories so mournful—filled, as it is, with souvenirs of Napoleon the First, and three dead Kings and as many Queens. In one sumptuous bed they had all slept in succession, but no one occupies it now. In a large dining-room stood the table at which Louis XIV. and his mistress, Madame Maintenon, and after them Louis XV., and Pompadour, had sat at their meals naked and unattended—for the table stood upon a trap-door, which descended with it to regions below when it was necessary to replenish its dishes. In a room of the Petit Trianon stood the furniture, just as poor Marie Antoinette left it when the mob came and dragged her and the King to Paris, never to return. Near at hand, in the stables, were prodigious carriages that showed no color but gold—carriages used by former Kings of France on state occasions, and never used now save when a kingly head is to be crowned, or an imperial infant christened. And with them were some curious sleighs, whose bodies were shaped like lions, swans, tigers, etc.—vehicles that had once been handsome with pictured designs and fine workmanship, but were dusty and decaying now. They had their history. When Louis XIV. had finished the Grand Trianon, he told Maintenon he had created a Paradise for her, and asked if she could think of any thing now to wish for. He said he wished the Trianon to be perfection—nothing less. She said she could think of but one thing—it was summer, and it was balmy France—yet she would like well to sleigh-ride in the leafy avenues of Versailles! The next morning found miles and miles of grassy avenues spread thick with snowy salt and sugar, and a procession of those quaint sleighs waiting to receive the chief concubine of the gayest and most unprincipled court that France has ever seen !

From sumptuous Versailles, with its palaces, its statues, its gardens and its fountains, we journeyed back to Paris and sought its antipodes—the Faubourg St. Antoine. Little, narrow streets; dirty children blockading them; greasy, slovenly women capturing and spanking them; filthy dens on first floors, with rag stores in them (the heaviest business in the Faubourg is the chiffonier's;) other filthy dens where whole suits of second and third-hand clothing are sold at prices that would ruin any proprietor who did not steal his stock; still other filthy dens where they sold groceries—sold them by the half-pennyworth—five dollars would buy the man out, good-will and all. Up these little crooked streets they will murder a man for seven dollars and dump the body in the Seine. And up some other of these streets—most of them, I should say—live lorettes.

All through this Faubourg St. Antoine, misery, poverty, vice and crime go hand in hand, and the evidences of it stare one in the face from every side. Here the people live who begin the revolutions. Whenever there is any thing of that kind to be done, they are always ready. They take as much genuine pleasure in building a barricade as they do in cutting a throat or shoving a friend into the Seine. It is these savage-looking ruffians who storm the splendid halls of the Tuileries, occasionally, and swarm into Versailles when a King is to be called to account.

But they will build no more barricades, they will break no more soldiers' heads with paving-stones. Louis Napoleon has taken care of all that. He is annihilating the crooked streets, and building in their stead noble boulevards as straight as an arrow—avenues which a cannon ball could traverse from end to end without meeting an obstruction more irresistible than the flesh and bones of men—boulevards whose stately edifices will never afford refuges and plotting-places for starving, discontented revolution-breeders. Five of these great thorough-

fares radiate·from one ample centre—a centre which is exceedingly well adapted to the accommodation of heavy artillery.
The mobs used to riot there, but they must seek another rally-
ing-place in future.   And this ingenious Napoleon paves the
streets of his great cities with a smooth, compact composition
of asphaltum and sand.   No more barricades of flag-stones—
no more assaulting his Majesty's troops with cobbles.   I can
not feel friendly toward my quondam fellow-American, Napoleon III., especially at this time,* when in fancy I see his
credulous victim, Maximilian, lying stark and stiff in Mexico,
and his maniac widow watching eagerly from her French
asylum for the form that will never come—but I do admire
his nerve, his calm self-reliance, his shrewd good sense.

* July, 1867.

CHAPTER XVII.

WE had a pleasant journey of it seaward again. We found that for the three past nights our ship had been in a state of war. The first night the sailors of a British ship, being happy with grog, came down on the pier and challenged our sailors to a free fight. They accepted with alacrity, repaired to the pier and gained—their share of a drawn battle. Several bruised and bloody members of both parties were carried off by the police, and imprisoned until the following morning. The next night the British boys came again to renew the fight, but our men had had strict orders to remain on board and out of sight. They did so, and the besieging party grew noisy, and more and more abusive as the fact became apparent (to them,) that our men were afraid to come out. They went away, finally, with a closing burst of ridicule and offensive epithets. The third night they came again, and were more obstreperous than ever. They swaggered up and down the almost deserted pier, and hurled curses, obscenity and stinging sarcasms at our crew. It was more than human nature could bear. The executive officer ordered our men ashore—with instructions not to fight. They charged the British and gained a brilliant victory. I probably would not have mentioned this war had it ended differently. But I travel to learn, and I still remember that they picture no French defeats in the battle-galleries of Versailles.

It was like home to us to step on board the comfortable ship again, and smoke and lounge about her breezy decks. And yet it was not altogether like home, either, because so many members of the family were away. We missed some pleasant faces which we would rather have found at dinner, and at night there were gaps in the euchre-parties which could not be satisfactorily filled. "Moult." was in England, Jack in Switzerland, Charley in Spain. Blucher was gone, none could tell where. But we were at sea again, and we had the stars and the ocean to look at, and plenty of room to meditate in.

In due time the shores of Italy were sighted, and as we stood gazing from the decks early in the bright summer morning, the stately city of Genoa rose up out of the sea and flung back the sunlight from her hundred palaces.

Here we rest, for the present—or rather, here we have been trying to rest, for some little time, but we run about too much to accomplish a great deal in that line.

I would like to remain here. I had rather not go any further. There may be prettier women in Europe, but I doubt it. The population of Genoa is 120,000; two-thirds of these are women, I think, and at least two-thirds of the women are beautiful. They are as dressy, and as tasteful and as graceful as they could possibly be without being angels. However, angels' are not very dressy, I believe. At least the angels in pictures are not—they wear nothing but wings. But these Genoese women do look so charming. Most of the young demoiselles are robed in a cloud of white from head to foot, though many trick themselves out more elaborately. Nine-tenths of them wear nothing on their heads but a filmy sort of veil, which falls down their backs like a white mist. They are very fair, and many of them have blue eyes, but black and dreamy dark brown ones are met with oftenest.

The ladies and gentlemen of Genoa have a pleasant fashion of promenading in a large park on the top of a hill in the centre of the city, from six till nine in the evening, and then eating ices in a neighboring garden an hour or two longer. We went to the park on Sunday evening. Two thousand persons were present, chiefly young ladies and gentlemen. The gentlemen were dressed in the very latest Paris fashions, and the robes of the ladies glinted among the trees like so many snow-flakes. The multitude moved round and round the park in a great procession. The bands played, and so did the fountains; the moon and the gas lamps lit up the scene, and altogether it was a brilliant and an animated picture. I scanned every female face that passed, and it seemed to me that all were handsome. I never saw such a freshet of loveliness before. I do not see how a man of only ordinary decision of character

WOMEN OF GENOA.

could marry here, because, before he could get his mind made up he would fall in love with somebody else.

Never smoke any Italian tobacco. Never do it on any account. It makes me shudder to think what it must be made of. You can not throw an old cigar "stub" down any where, but some vagabond will pounce upon it on the instant. I like to smoke a good deal, but it wounds my sensibilities to see one of these stub-hunters watching me out of the corners of his hungry eyes and calculating how long my cigar will be likely to last. It reminded me too painfully of that San Francisco undertaker who used to go to sick-beds with his watch in his hand and time the corpse. One of these stub-hunters followed us all over the park last night, and we never had a smoke that was worth any thing. We were always moved to appease him with the stub before the cigar was half gone, because he looked so viciously anxious. He regarded us as his own legitimate prey, by right of discovery, I think, because he drove off several other professionals who wanted to take stock in us.

Now, they surely must chew up those old stubs, and dry and sell them for smoking-tobacco. Therefore, give your custom to other than Italian brands of the article.

" The Superb " and the " City of Palaces " are names which Genoa has held for centuries. She is full of palaces, certainly, and the palaces are sumptuous inside, but they are very rusty without, and make no pretensions to architectural magnificence. " Genoa, the Superb," would be a felicitous title if it referred to the women.

We have visited several of the palaces—immense thick-walled piles, with great stone staircases, tesselated marble pavements on the floors, (sometimes they make a mosaic work, of intricate designs, wrought in pebbles, or little fragments of marble laid in cement,) and grand *salons* hung with pictures by Rubens, Guido, Titian, Paul Veronese, and so on, and portraits of heads of the family, in plumed helmets and gallant coats of mail, and patrician ladies, in stunning costumes of centuries ago. But, of course, the folks were all out in the country for the summer, and might not have known enough to ask us to dinner if they had been at home, and so all the grand empty *salons*, with their resounding pavements, their grim pictures of dead ancestors, and tattered banners with the dust of bygone centuries upon them, seemed to brood solemnly of death and the grave, and our spirits ebbed away, and our cheerfulness passed from us. We never went up to the eleventh story. We always began to suspect ghosts. There was always an undertaker-looking servant along, too, who handed us a programme, pointed to the picture that began the list of the *salon* he was in, and then stood stiff and stark and unsmiling in his petrified livery till we were ready to move on to the next chamber, whereupon he marched sadly ahead and took up another malignantly respectful position as before. I wasted so much time praying that the roof would fall in on these

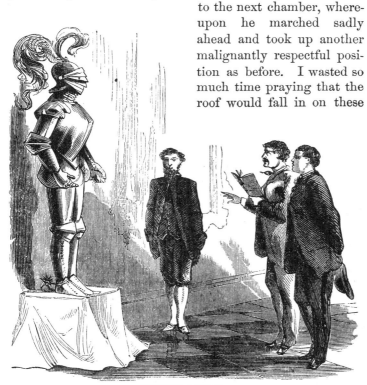

PETRIFIED LACKEY.

dispiriting flunkeys that I had but little left to bestow upon palace and pictures.

And besides, as in Paris, we had a guide. Perdition catch all the guides. This one said he was the most gifted linguist in Genoa, as far as English was concerned, and that only two persons in the city beside himself could talk the language at all. He showed us the birthplace of Christopher Columbus, and after we had reflected in silent awe before it for fifteen minutes, he said it was not the birthplace of Columbus, but of Columbus's grandmother! When we demanded an explanation of his conduct he only shrugged his shoulders and answered in barbarous Italian. I shall speak further of this guide in a future chapter. All the information we got out of him we shall be able to carry along with us, I think.

I have not been to church so often in a long time as I have

PRIEST AND FRIAR.

in the last few weeks. The people in these old lands seem to make churches their specialty. Especially does this seem to be the case with the citizens of Genoa. I think there is a church every three or four hundred yards all over town. The streets are sprinkled from end to end with shovel-hatted, long-robed, well-fed priests, and the church bells by dozens are pealing all the day long, nearly. Every now and then one comes across a friar of orders gray, with shaven head, long, coarse robe, rope girdle and beads, and with feet cased in sandals or entirely bare. These worthies suffer in the flesh, and do penance all their lives, I suppose, but they look like consummate famine-breeders. They are all fat and serene.

The old Cathedral of San Lorenzo is about as notable a building as we have found in Genoa. It is vast, and has colonnades of noble pillars, and a great organ, and the customary pomp of gilded moldings, pictures, frescoed ceilings, and so forth. I can not describe it, of course—it would require a good many pages to do that. But it is a curious place. They said that half of it—from the front door half way down to the altar—was a Jewish Synagogue before the Saviour was born, and that no alteration had been made in it since that time. We doubted the statement, but did it reluctantly. We would much rather have believed it. The place looked in too perfect repair to be so ancient.

The main point of interest about the Cathedral is the little Chapel of St. John the Baptist. They only allow women to enter it on one day in the year, on account of the animosity they still cherish against the sex because of the murder of the Saint to gratify a caprice of Herodias. In this Chapel is a marble chest, in which, they told us, were the ashes of St. John; and around it was wound a chain, which, they said, had confined him when he was in prison. We did not desire to disbelieve these statements, and yet we could not feel certain that they were correct—partly because we could have broken that chain, and so could St. John, and partly because we had seen St. John's ashes before, in another Church. We could not bring ourselves to think St. John had two sets of ashes.

They also showed us a portrait of the Madonna which was painted by St. Luke, and it did not look half as old and smoky as some of the pictures by Rubens. We could not help admiring the Apostle's modesty in never once mentioning in his writings that he could paint.

But isn't this relic matter a little overdone? We find a piece of the true cross in every old church we go into, and some of the nails that held it together. I would not like to be positive, but I think we have seen as much as a keg of these nails. Then there is the crown of thorns; they have part of one in Sainte Chapelle, in Paris, and part of one, also, in Notre Dame. And as for bones of St. Denis, I feel certain we have seen enough of them to duplicate him, if necessary.

I only meant to write about the churches, but I keep wandering from the subject. I could say that the Church of the Annunciation is a wilderness of beautiful columns, of statues,

gilded moldings, and pictures almost countless, but that
would give no one an entirely perfect idea of the thing, and
so where is the use ?   One family built the whole edifice, and
have got money left.   There is where the mystery lies.   We
had an idea at first that only a mint could have survived the
expense.

These people here live in the heaviest, highest, broadest,
darkest, solidest houses one can imagine.   Each one might
" laugh a siege to scorn."   A hundred feet front and a hundred high is about the style, and you go up three flights of
stairs before you begin to come upon signs of occupancy.
Every thing is stone, and stone of the heaviest—floors, stairways, mantels, benches—every thing.   The walls are four to
five feet thick.   The streets generally are four or five to eight
feet wide and as crooked as a corkscrew.   You go along one
of these gloomy cracks, and look up and behold the sky like a
mere ribbon of light, far above your head, where the tops of
the tall houses on either side of the street bend almost
together.   You feel as if you were at the bottom of some tremendous abyss, with all the world far above you.   You wind
in and out and here and there, in the most mysterious way,
and have no more idea of the points of the compass than if you
were a blind man.   You can never persuade yourself that
these are actually streets, and the frowning, dingy, monstrous
houses dwellings, till you see one of these beautiful, prettily
dressed women emerge from them—see her emerge from a
dark, dreary-looking den that looks dungeon all over, from the
ground away half-way up to heaven.   And then you wonder
that such a charming moth could come from such a forbidding
shell as that.   The streets are wisely made narrow and the
houses heavy and thick and stony, in order that the people
may be cool in this roasting climate.   And they are cool, and
stay so.   And while I think of it—the men wear hats and
have very dark complexions, but the women wear no head-
gear but a flimsy veil like a gossamer's web, and yet are
exceedingly fair as a general thing.   Singular, isn't it ?

The huge palaces of Genoa are each supposed to be occupied

by one family, but they could accommodate a hundred, I should think. They are relics of the grandeur of Genoa's palmy days —the days when she was a great commercial and maritime power several centuries ago. These houses, solid marble palaces though they be, are in many cases of a dull pinkish color, outside, and from pavement to eaves are pictured with Genoese battle-scenes, with monstrous Jupiters and Cupids and with familiar illustrations from Grecian mythology. Where the paint has yielded to age and exposure and is peeling off in flakes and patches, the effect is not happy. A noseless Cupid, or a Jupiter with an eye out, or a Venus with a fly-blister on her breast, are not attractive features in a picture. Some of these painted walls reminded me somewhat of the tall van, plastered with fanciful bills and posters, that follows the band-wagon of a circus about a country village. I have not read or heard that the outsides of the houses of any other European city are frescoed in this way.

I can not conceive of such a thing as Genoa in ruins. Such massive arches, such ponderous substructions as support these towering broad-winged edifices, we have seldom seen before; and surely the great blocks of stone of which these edifices are built can never decay; walls that are as thick as an ordinary American doorway is high, can not crumble.

The Republics of Genoa and Pisa were very powerful in the middle ages. Their ships filled the Mediterranean, and they carried on an extensive commerce with Constantinople and Syria. Their warehouses were the great distributing depots from whence the costly merchandise of the East was sent abroad over Europe. They were warlike little nations, and defied, in those days, governments that overshadow them now as mountains overshadow molehills. The Saracens captured and pillaged Genoa nine hundred years ago, but during the following century Genoa and Pisa entered into an offensive and defensive alliance and besieged the Saracen colonies in Sardinia and the Balearic Isles with an obstinacy that maintained its pristine vigor and held to its purpose for forty long years. They were victorious at last, and divided their conquests equably among their great patrician families. Descendants of some of those proud families still inhabit the palaces of Genoa, and trace in their own features a resemblance to the grim knights whose portraits hang in their stately halls, and to pictured beauties with pouting lips and merry eyes whose originals have been dust and ashes for many a dead and forgotten century.

The hotel we live in belonged to one of those great orders of knights of the Cross in the times of the Crusades, and its mailed sentinels once kept watch and ward in its massive turrets and woke the echoes of these halls and corridors with their iron heels.

STATUE OF COLUMBUS.

But Genoa's greatness has degenerated into an unostentatious commerce in velvets and silver filagree work. They say that each European town has its specialty. These filagree things are Genoa's specialty. Her smiths take silver ingots and work them up into all manner of graceful and beautiful forms. They make bunches of flowers, from flakes and wires of silver, that counterfeit the delicate creations the frost weaves upon a window pane; and we were shown a miniature silver temple whose fluted columns, whose Corinthian capitals and rich entablatures, whose spire, statues, bells, and ornate lavishness of sculpture were wrought in polished silver, and with such matchless art that every detail was a fascinating study, and the finished edifice a wonder of beauty.

We are ready to move again, though we are not really tired, yet, of the narrow passages of this old marble cave. Cave is a good word—when speaking of Genoa under the stars. When we have been prowling at midnight through the gloomy crevices they call streets, where no foot falls but ours were echoing, where only ourselves were abroad, and lights appeared only at long intervals and at a distance, and mysteriously disappeared

GRAVES OF SIXTY THOUSAND.

again, and the houses at our elbows seemed to stretch upward farther than ever toward the heavens, the memory of a cave I used to know at home was always in my mind, with its lofty passages, its silence and solitude, its shrouding gloom, its sepulchral echoes, its flitting lights, and more than all, its sudden revelations of branching crevices and corridors where we least expected them.

We are not tired of the endless processions of cheerful, chattering gossipers that throng these courts and streets all day long, either; nor of the coarse-robed monks; nor of the "Asti" wines, which that old doctor (whom we call the Oracle,) with customary felicity in the matter of getting every thing wrong, misterms " nasty." But we must go, nevertheless.

Our last sight was the cemetery, (a burial-place intended to accommodate 60,000 bodies,) and we shall continue to remember it after we shall have forgotten the palaces. It is a vast marble collonaded corridor extending around a great unoccupied square of ground; its broad floor is marble, and on every slab is an inscription—for every slab covers a corpse. On either side, as one walks down the middle of the passage, are monuments, tombs, and sculptured figures that are exquisitely wrought and are full of grace and beauty. They are new, and snowy; every outline is perfect, every feature guiltless of mutilation, flaw or blemish; and therefore, to us these far-reaching ranks of bewitching forms are a hundred fold more lovely than the damaged and dingy statuary they have saved from the wreck of ancient art and set up in the galleries of Paris for the worship of the world.

Well provided with cigars and other necessaries of life, we are now ready to take the cars for Milan.

CHAPTER XVIII.

ALL day long we sped through a mountainous country whose peaks were bright with sunshine, whose hillsides were dotted with pretty villas sitting in the midst of gardens and shrubbery, and whose deep ravines were cool and shady, and looked ever so inviting from where we and the birds were winging our flight through the sultry upper air.

We had plenty of chilly tunnels wherein to check our perspiration, though. We timed one of them. We were twenty minutes passing through it, going at the rate of thirty to thirty-five miles an hour.

Beyond Alessandria we passed the battle-field of Marengo.

Toward dusk we drew near Milan, and caught glimpses of the city and the blue mountain peaks beyond. But we were not caring for these things—they did not interest us in the least. We were in a fever of impatience; we were dying to see the renowned Cathedral! We watched—in this direction and that—all around—every where. We needed no one to point it out—we did not wish any one to point it out—we would recognize it, even in the desert of the great Sahara.

At last, a forest of graceful needles, shimmering in the amber sunlight, rose slowly above the pigmy house-tops, as one sometimes sees, in the far horizon, a gilded and pinnacled mass of cloud lift itself above the waste of waves, at sea,—the Cathedral! We knew it in a moment.

Half of that night, and all of the next day, this architectural autocrat was our sole object of interest.

What a wonder it is! So grand, so solemn, so vast! And

yet so delicate, so airy, so graceful! A very world of solid weight, and yet it seems in the soft moonlight only a fairy delusion of frost-work that might vanish with a breath! How sharply its pinnacled angles and its wilderness of spires were cut against the sky, and how richly their shadows fell upon its snowy roof! It was a vision!—a miracle!—an anthem sung in stone, a poem wrought in marble!

Howsoever you look at the great Cathedral, it is noble, it is beautiful! Wherever you stand in Milan, or within seven miles of Milan, it is visible—and when it is visible, no other object can chain your whole attention. Leave your eyes unfettered by your will but a single instant and they will surely turn to seek it. It is the first thing you look for when you rise in the morning, and the last your lingering gaze rests upon at night. Surely, it must be the princeliest creation that ever brain of man conceived.

At nine o'clock in the morning we went and stood before this marble colossus. The central one of its five great doors is bordered with a bas-relief of birds and fruits and beasts and insects, which have been so ingeniously carved out of the marble that they seem like living creatures—and the figures are so numerous and the design so complex, that one might study it a week without exhausting its interest. On the great steeple—surmounting the myriad of spires—inside of the spires—over the doors, the windows—in nooks and corners—every where that a niche or a perch can be found about the enormous building, from summit to base, there is a marble statue, and every statue is a study in itself! Raphael, Angelo, Canova—giants like these gave birth to the designs, and their own pupils carved them. Every face is eloquent with expression, and every attitude is full of grace. Away above, on the lofty roof, rank on rank of carved and fretted spires spring high in the air, and through their rich tracery one sees the sky beyond. In their midst the central steeple towers proudly up like the mainmast of some great Indiaman among a fleet of coasters.

We wished to go aloft. The sacristan showed us a marble

ROOFS AND SPIRES OF CATHEDRAL AT MILAN.

stairway (of course it was marble, and of the purest and whitest
—there is no other stone, no brick, no wood, among its build-

CENTRAL DOOR OF CATHEDRAL AT MILAN.

ing materials,) and told us to go up one hundred and eighty-
two steps and stop till he came. It was not necessary to say
stop—we should have done that any how. We were tired by
the time we got there. This was the roof. Here, springing
from its broad marble flagstones, were the long files of spires,
looking very tall close at hand, but diminishing in the distance like the pipes of an organ. We could see, now, that
the statue on the top of each was the size of a large man,
though they all looked like dolls from the street. We could

see, also, that from the inside of each and every one of these hollow spires, from sixteen to thirty-one beautiful marble statues looked out upon the world below.

From the eaves to the comb of the roof stretched in endless succession great curved marble beams, like the fore-and-aft braces of a steamboat, and along each beam from end to end stood up a row of richly carved flowers and fruits—each separate and distinct in kind, and over 15,000 species represented. At a little distance these rows seem to close together like the ties of a railroad track, and then the mingling together of the

INTERIOR OF THE CATHEDRAL AT MILAN.

buds and blossoms of this marble garden forms a picture that is very charming to the eye.

We descended and entered. Within the church, long rows of fluted columns, like huge monuments, divided the building into broad aisles, and on the figured pavement fell many a soft blush from the painted windows above. I knew the church was very large, but I could not fully appreciate its great size until I noticed that the men standing far down by the altar looked like boys, and seemed to glide, rather than walk. We loitered about gazing aloft at the monster windows all aglow with brilliantly colored scenes in the lives of the Saviour and his followers. Some of these pictures are mosaics, and so artistically are their thousand particles of tinted glass or stone put together that the work has all the smoothness and finish of a painting. We counted sixty panes of glass in one window, and each pane was adorned with one of these master achievements of genius and patience.

The guide showed us a coffee-colored piece of sculpture which he said was considered to have come from the hand of Phidias, since it was not possible that any other artist, of any epoch, could have copied nature with such faultless accuracy. The figure was that of a man without a skin; with every vein, artery, muscle, every fibre and tendon and tissue of the human frame, represented in minute detail. It looked natural, because somehow it looked as if it were in pain. A skinned man would be likely to look that way, unless his attention were occupied with some other matter. It was a hideous thing, and yet there was a fascination about it some where. I am very sorry I saw it, because I shall always see it, now. I shall dream of it, sometimes. I shall dream that it is resting its corded arms on the bed's head and looking down on me with its dead eyes; I shall dream that it is stretched between the sheets with me and touching me with its exposed muscles and its stringy cold legs.

It is hard to forget repulsive things. I remember yet how I ran off from school once, when I was a boy, and then, pretty late at night, concluded to climb into the window of my father's office and sleep on a lounge, because I had a delicacy about going home and getting thrashed. As I lay on the lounge and my eyes grew accustomed to the darkness, I fancied I could see a long, dusky, shapeless thing stretched

upon the floor. A cold shiver went through me. I turned
my face to the wall. That did not answer. I was afraid that
that thing would creep over and seize me in the dark. I
turned back and stared at it for minutes and minutes—they
seemed hours. It appeared to me that the lagging moonlight
never, never would get to it. I turned to the wall and
counted twenty, to pass the feverish time away. I looked—
the pale square was nearer. I turned again and counted fifty
—it was almost touching it. With desperate will I turned
again and counted one hundred, and faced about, all in a
tremble. A white human hand lay in the moonlight! Such

BOYHOOD EXPERIENCE.

an awful sinking at the heart—such a sudden gasp for breath!
I felt—I can not tell *what* I felt. When I recovered strength
enough, I faced the wall again. But no boy could have
remained so, with that mysterious hand behind him. I
counted again, and looked—the most of a naked arm was

exposed. I put my hands over my eyes and counted till I could stand it no longer, and then—the pallid face of a man was there, with the corners of the mouth drawn down, and the eyes fixed and glassy in death! I raised to a sitting posture and glowered on that corpse till the light crept down the bare breast,—line by line—inch by inch—past the nipple,— and then it disclosed a ghastly stab!

I went away from there. I do not say that I went away in any sort of a hurry, but I simply went—that is sufficient. I went out at the window, and I carried the sash along with me. I did not need the sash, but it was handier to take it than it was to leave it, and so I took it.—I was not scared, but I was considerably agitated.

When I reached home, they whipped me, but I enjoyed it. It seemed perfectly delightful. That man had been stabbed near the office that afternoon, and they carried him in there to doctor him, but he only lived an hour. I have slept in the same room with him often, since then—in my dreams.

Now we will descend into the crypt, under the grand altar of Milan Cathedral, and receive an impressive sermon from lips that have been silent and hands that have been gestureless for three hundred years.

The priest stopped in a small dungeon and held up his candle. This was the last resting-place of a good man, a warm-hearted, unselfish man; a man whose whole life was given to succoring the poor, encouraging the faint-hearted, visiting the sick; in relieving distress, whenever and wherever he found it. His heart, his hand and his purse were always open. With his story in one's mind he can almost see his benignant countenance moving calmly among the haggard faces of Milan in the days when the plague swept the city, brave where all others were cowards, full of compassion where pity had been crushed out of all other breasts by the instinct of self-preservation gone mad with terror, cheering all, praying with all, helping all, with hand and brain and purse, at a time when parents forsook their children, the friend deserted

12

the friend, and the brother turned away from the sister while her pleadings were still wailing in his ears.

This was good St. Charles Borroméo, Bishop of Milan. The people idolized him; princes lavished* uncounted treasures upon him. We stood in his tomb. Near by was the sarcophagus, lighted by the dripping candles. The walls were faced with bas-reliefs representing scenes in his life done in massive silver. The priest put on a short white lace garment over his black robe, crossed himself, bowed reverently, and began to turn a windlass slowly. The sarcophagus separated in two parts, lengthwise, and the lower part sank down and disclosed a coffin of rock crystal as clear as the atmosphere. Within lay the body, robed in costly habiliments covered with gold embroidery and starred with scintillating gems. The decaying head was black with age, the dry skin was drawn tight to the bones, the eyes were gone, there was a hole in the temple and another in the cheek, and the skinny lips were parted as in a ghastly smile! Over this dreadful face, its dust and decay, and its mocking grin, hung a crown sown thick with flashing brilliants; and upon the breast lay crosses and croziers of solid gold that were splendid with emeralds and diamonds.

How poor, and cheap, and trivial these gew-gaws seemed in presence of the solemnity, the grandeur, the awful majesty of Death! Think of Milton, Shakspeare, Washington, standing before a reverent world tricked out in the glass beads, the brass ear-rings and tin trumpery of the savages of the plains!

Dead Bartoloméo preached his pregnant sermon, and its burden was: You that worship the vanities of earth—you that long for worldly honor, worldly wealth, worldly fame—behold their worth!

To us it seemed that so good a man, so kind a heart, so simple a nature, deserved rest and peace in a grave sacred from the intrusion of prying eyes, and believed that he himself would have preferred to have it so, but peradventure our wisdom was at fault in this regard.

As we came out upon the floor of the church again, another priest volunteered to show us the treasures of the church.

What, more? The furniture of the narrow chamber of death
we had just visited, weighed six millions of francs in ounces
and carats alone, without a penny thrown into the account for
the costly workmanship bestowed upon them! But we followed into a large room filled with tall wooden presses like
wardrobes. He threw them open, and behold, the cargoes of
"crude bullion" of the assay offices of Nevada faded out of
my memory. There were Virgins and bishops there, above
their natural size, made of solid silver, each worth, by weight,

TREASURES OF THE CATHEDRAL.

from eight hundred thousand to two millions of francs, and
bearing gemmed books in their hands worth eighty thousand;
there were bas-reliefs that weighed six hundred pounds, carved
in solid silver; croziers and crosses, and candlesticks six and
eight feet high, all of virgin gold, and brilliant with precious
stones; and beside these were all manner of cups and vases,
and such things, rich in proportion. It was an Aladdin's

palace. The treasures here, by simple weight, without counting workmanship, were valued at fifty millions of francs! If I could get the custody of them for a while, I fear me the market price of silver bishops would advance shortly, on account of their exceeding scarcity in the Cathedral of Milan.

The priests showed us two of St. Paul's fingers, and one of St. Peter's; a bone of Judas Iscariot, (it was black.) and also bones of all the other disciples; a handkerchief in which the Saviour had left the impression of his face. Among the most precious of the relics were a stone from the Holy Sepulchre, part of the crown of thorns, (they have a whole one at Notre Dame,) a fragment of the purple robe worn by the Saviour, a nail from the Cross, and a picture of the Virgin and Child painted by the veritable hand of St. Luke. This is the second of St. Luke's Virgins we have seen. Once a year all these holy relics are carried in procession through the streets of Milan.

I like to revel in the dryest details of the great cathedral. The building is five hundred feet long by one hundred and eighty wide, and the principal steeple is in the neighborhood of four hundred feet high. It has 7,148 marble statues, and will have upwards of three thousand more when it is finished. In addition, it has one thousand five hundred bas-reliefs. It has one hundred and thirty-six spires—twenty-one more are to be added. Each spire is surmounted by a statue six and a half feet high. Every thing about the church is marble, and all from the same quarry; it was bequeathed to the Archbishopric for this purpose centuries ago. So nothing but the mere workmanship costs; still that is expensive—the bill foots up six hundred and eighty-four millions of francs, thus far (considerably over a hundred millions of dollars,) and it is estimated that it will take a hundred and twenty years yet to finish the cathedral. It looks complete, but is far from being so. We saw a new statue put in its niche yesterday, alongside of one which had been standing these four hundred years, they said. There are four staircases leading up to the main steeple, each of which cost a hundred thousand dollars,

with the four hundred and eight statues which adorn them.
Marco Compioni was the architect who designed the wonderful
structure more than five hundred years ago, and it took him
forty-six years to work out the plan and get it ready to hand

CATHEDRAL AT MILAN.

over to the builders. He is dead now. The building was
begun a little less than five hundred years ago, and the third
generation hence will not see it completed.

The building looks best by moonlight, because the older
portions of it being stained with age, contrast unpleasantly

with the newer and whiter portions. It seems somewhat too broad for its height, but may be familiarity with it might dissipate this impression.

They say that the Cathedral of Milan is second only to St. Peter's at Rome. I can not understand how it can be second to any thing made by human hands.

We bid it good-bye, now—possibly for all time. How surely, in some future day, when the memory of it shall have lost its vividness, shall we half believe we have seen it in a wonderful dream, but never with waking eyes!

CHAPTER XIX.

"Do you wis zo haut can be?"

That was what the guide asked, when we were looking up at the bronze horses on the Arch of Peace. It meant, do you wish to go up there? I give it as a specimen of guide-English. These are the people that make life a burthen to the tourist. Their tongues are never still. They talk forever and forever, and that is the kind of billingsgate they use. Inspiration itself could hardly comprehend them. If they would only show you a masterpiece of art, or a venerable tomb, or a prison-house, or a battle-field, hallowed by touching memories or historical reminiscences, or grand traditions, and then step aside and hold still for ten minutes and let you think, it would not be so bad. But they interrupt every dream, every pleasant train of thought, with their tiresome cackling. Sometimes when I have been standing before some cherished old idol of mine that I remembered years and years ago in pictures in the geography at school, I have thought I would give a whole world if the human parrot at my side would suddenly perish where he stood and leave me to gaze, and ponder, and worship.

No, we did not "wis zo haut can be." We wished to go to La Scala, the largest theatre in the world, I think they call it. We did so. It was a large place. Seven separate and distinct masses of humanity—six great circles and a monster parquette.

We wished to go to the Ambrosian Library, and we did that also. We saw a manuscript of Virgil, with annotations in the handwriting of Petrarch, the gentleman who loved another man's Laura, and lavished upon her all through life a love which was a clear waste of the raw material. It was sound sentiment, but bad judgment. It brought both parties fame,

LA SCALA THEATRE.

and created a fountain of commiseration for them in sentimental breasts that is running yet. But who says a word in behalf of poor Mr. Laura? (I do not know his other name.) Who glorifies him? Who bedews him with tears? Who writes poetry about him? Nobody. How do you suppose *he* liked the state of things that has given the world so much pleasure? How did he enjoy having another man following his wife every where and making her name a familiar word in every garlic-exterminating mouth in Italy with his sonnets to her pre-empted eyebrows? *They* got fame and sympathy—he got neither. This is a peculiarly felicitous instance of what is called poetical justice. It is all very fine; but it does not chime with my notions of right. It is too one-sided—too ungenerous. Let the world go on fretting about Laura and Petrarch if it will; but as for me, my tears and my lamentations shall be lavished upon the unsung defendant.

We saw also an autograph letter of Lucrezia Borgia, a lady for whom I have always entertained the highest respect, on account of her rare histrionic capabilities, her opulence in solid gold goblets made of gilded wood, her high distinction as an operatic screamer, and the facility with which she could order a sextuple funeral and get the corpses ready for it. We saw one single coarse yellow hair from Lucrezia's head, likewise. It awoke emotions, but we still live. In this same library we saw some drawings by Michael Angelo (these Italians call him Mickel Angelo,) and Leonardo da Vinci. (They spell it Vinci and pronounce it Vinchy; foreigners always spell better than they pronounce.) We reserve our opinion of these sketches.

In another building they showed us a fresco representing some lions and other beasts drawing chariots; and they seemed to project so far from the wall that we took them to be sculptures. The artist had shrewdly heightened the delusion by painting dust on the creatures' backs, as if it had fallen there naturally and properly. Smart fellow—if it be smart to deceive strangers.

Elsewhere we saw a huge Roman amphitheatre, with its stone seats still in good preservation. Modernized, it is now the scene of more peaceful recreations than the exhibition of a party of wild beasts with Christians for dinner. Part of the time, the Milanese use it for a race track, and at other seasons they flood it with water and have spirited yachting regattas there. The guide told us these things, and he would hardly try so hazardous an experiment as the telling of a falsehood, when it is all he can do to speak the truth in English without getting the lock-jaw.

In another place we were shown a sort of summer arbor, with a fence before it. We said that was nothing. We looked again, and saw, through the arbor, an endless stretch of garden, and shrubbery, and grassy lawn. We were perfectly willing to go in there and rest, but it could not be done. It was only another delusion—a painting by some ingenious artist with little charity in his heart for tired folk. The deception was perfect. No one could have imagined the park was not real. We even thought we smelled the flowers at first.

We got a carriage at twilight and drove in the shaded avenues with the other nobility, and after dinner we took wine and ices in a fine garden with the great public. The music was excellent, the flowers and shrubbery were pleasant to the eye, the scene was vivacious, every body was genteel and well-behaved, and the ladies were slightly moustached, and handsomely dressed, but very homely.

We adjourned to a café and played billiards an hour, and I made six or seven points by the doctor pocketing his ball, and he made as many by my pocketing my ball. We came near making a carom sometimes, but not the one we were trying to make. The table was of the usual European style—cushions dead and twice as high as the balls; the cues in bad repair. The natives play only a sort of pool on them. We have never seen any body playing the French three-ball game yet, and I doubt if there is any such game known in France, or that there lives any man mad enough to try to play it on one of these European tables. We had to stop playing, finally, because Dan got to sleeping fifteen minutes between the counts and paying no attention to his marking.

Afterward we walked up and down one of the most popular streets for some time, enjoying other people's comfort and wishing we could export some of it to our restless, driving, vitality-consuming marts at home. Just in this one matter lies the main charm of life in Europe—comfort. In America, we hurry—which is well; but when the day's work is done, we go on thinking of losses and gains, we plan for the morrow, we even carry our business cares to bed with us, and toss and worry over them when we ought to be restoring our racked bodies and brains with sleep. We burn up our energies with these excitements, and either die early or drop into a lean and mean old age at a time of life which they call a man's prime in Europe. When an acre of ground has produced long and

well, we let it lie fallow and rest for a season; we take no man
clear across the continent in the same coach he started in—the
coach is stabled somewhere on the plains and its heated machinery allowed to cool for a few days; when a razor has seen
long service and refuses to hold an edge, the barber lays it
away for a few weeks, and the edge comes back of its own
accord. We bestow thoughtful care upon inanimate objects,
but none upon ourselves. What a robust people, what a nation of thinkers we might be, if we would only lay ourselves
on the shelf occasionally and renew our edges!

I do envy these Europeans the comfort they take. When
the work of the day is done, they forget it. Some of them go,
with wife and children, to a beer hall, and sit quietly and gen-
teelly drinking a mug or two of ale and listening to music;
others walk the streets, others drive in the avenues; others
assemble in the great ornamental squares in the early evening
to enjoy the sight and the fragrance of flowers and to hear the
military bands play—no European city being without its fine
military music at eventide; and yet others of the populace sit
in the open air in front of the refreshment houses and eat ices
and drink mild beverages that could not harm a child. They
go to bed moderately early, and sleep well. They are always
quiet, always orderly, always cheerful, comfortable, and appre-
ciative of life and its manifold blessings. One never sees a
drunken man among them. The change that has come over
our little party is surprising. Day by day we lose some of our
restlessness and absorb some of the spirit of quietude and ease
that is in the tranquil atmosphere about us and in the demeanor of the people. We grow wise apace. We begin to
comprehend what life is for.

We have had a bath in Milan, in a public bath-house. They
were going to put all three of us in one bath-tub, but we ob-
jected. Each of us had an Italian farm on his back. We
could have felt affluent if we had been officially surveyed and
fenced in. We chose to have three bath-tubs, and large ones
—tubs suited to the dignity of aristocrats who had real estate,
and brought it with them. After we were stripped and had

taken the first chilly dash, we discovered that haunting atrocity
that has embittered our lives in so many cities and villages of
Italy and France—there was no soap. I called. A woman
answered, and I barely had time to throw myself against the
door—she would have been in, in another second. I said:

"Beware, woman! Go away from here—go away, now, or
it will be the worse for you. I am an unprotected male, but I
will preserve my honor at the peril of my life!"

These words must have frightened her, for she skurried away
very fast.

Dan's voice rose on the air:

"Oh, bring some soap, why don't you!"

The reply was Italian. Dan resumed:

"Soap, you know—soap. That is what I want—soap.
S-o-a-p, soap; s-o-p-e, soap; s-o-u-p, soap. Hurry up! I don't
know how you Irish spell it, but I want it. Spell it to suit
yourself, but fetch it. I'm freezing."

I heard the doctor say, impressively:

"Dan, how often have we told you that these foreigners can
not understand English? Why will you not depend upon us?
Why will you not tell *us* what you want, and let us ask for it
in the language of the country? It would save us a great deal
of the humiliation your reprehensible ignorance causes us. I
will address this person in his mother tongue: 'Here, cospetto!
corpo di Bacco! Sacramento! Solferino!—Soap, you son of a
gun!' Dan, if you would let *us* talk for you, you would never
expose your ignorant vulgarity."

Even this fluent discharge of Italian did not bring the soap
at once, but there was a good reason for it. There was not
such an article about the establishment. It is my belief that
there never had been. They had to send far up town, and to
several different places before they finally got it, so they said.
We had to wait twenty or thirty minutes. The same thing
had occurred the evening before, at the hotel. I think I have
divined the reason for this state of things at last. The English know how to travel comfortably, and they carry soap with
them; other foreigners do not use the article.

At every hotel we stop at we always have to send out for soap, at the last moment, when we are grooming ourselves for dinner, and they put it in the bill along with the candles and other nonsense. In Marseilles they make half the fancy toilet soap we consume in America, but the Marseillaise only have a vague theoretical idea of its use, which they have obtained from books of travel, just as they have acquired an uncertain notion of clean shirts, and the peculiarities of the gorilla, and other curious matters. This reminds me of poor Blucher's note to the landlord in Paris:

"PARIS, le 7 Juillet.

"*Monsieur le Landlord*—Sir: *Pourquoi* don't you *mettez* some *savon* in your bedchambers? *Est-ce que vous pensez* I will steal it? *La nuit passée* you charged me *pour deux chandelles* when I only had one; *hier vous avez* charged me *avec glace* when I had none at all; *tout les jours* you are coming some fresh game or other on me, *mais vous ne pouvez pas* play this *savon* dodge on me twice. *Savon* is a necessary *de la vie* to any body but a Frenchman, *et je l'aurai hors de cet hôtel* or make trouble. You hear *me*. *Allons*.

BLUCHER."

I remonstrated against the sending of this note, because it was so mixed up that the landlord would never be able to make head or tail of it; but Blucher said he guessed the old man could read the French of it and average the rest.

Blucher's French is bad enough, but it is not much worse than the English one finds in advertisements all over Italy every day. For instance, observe the printed card of the hotel we shall probably stop at on the shores of Lake Como:

"NOTISH."
"This hotel which the best it is in Italy and most superb, is handsome locate on the best situation of the lake, with the most splendid view near the Villas Melzy, to the King of Belgian, and Serbelloni. This hotel have recently enlarge, do offer all commodities on moderate price, at the strangers gentlemen who whish spend the seasons on the Lake Come."

How is that, for a specimen? In the hotel is a handsome little chapel where an English clergyman is employed to preach to such of the guests of the house as hail from England and

America, and this fact is also set forth in barbarous English in the same advertisement. Wouldn't you have supposed that the adventurous linguist who framed the card would have known enough to submit it to that clergyman before he sent it to the printer?

Here, in Milan, in an ancient tumble-down ruin of a church, is the mournful wreck of the most celebrated painting in the world—"The Last Supper," by Leonardo da Vinci. We are not infallible judges of pictures, but of course we went there to see this wonderful painting, once so beautiful, always so worshipped by masters in art, and forever to be famous in song and story. And the first thing that occurred was the infliction on us of a placard fairly reeking with wretched English. Take a morsel of it:

"Bartholomew (that is the first figure on the left hand side at the spectator,) uncertain and doubtful about what he thinks to have heard, and upon which he wants to be assured by himself at Christ and by no others."

Good, isn't it? And then Peter is described as " argumenting in a threatening and angrily condition at Judas Iscariot."

This paragraph recalls the picture. "The Last Supper" is painted on the dilapidated wall of what was a little chapel attached to the main church in ancient times, I suppose. It is battered and scarred in every direction, and stained and discolored by time, and Napoleon's horses kicked the legs off most the disciples when they (the horses, not the disciples,) were stabled there more than half a century ago.

I recognized the old picture in a moment—the Saviour with bowed head seated at the centre of a long, rough table with scattering fruits and dishes upon it, and six disciples on either side in their long robes, talking to each other—the picture from which all engravings and all copies have been made for three centuries. Perhaps no living man has ever known an attempt to paint the Lord's Supper differently. The world seems to have become settled in the belief, long ago, that it is not possible for human genius to outdo this creation of Da Vinci's. I suppose painters will go on copying it as long as any of the original is left visible to the eye. There were a dozen easels in the room, and as many artists transferring the great picture to their canvases. Fifty proofs of steel engravings and lithographs were scattered around, too. And as usual, I could not help noticing how superior the copies were to the original, that is, to my inexperienced eye. Wherever you find a Raphael, a Rubens, a Michael Angelo, a Caracci, or a Da Vinci (and we see them every day,) you find artists copying them, and the copies are always the handsomest. May be the originals were handsome when they were new, but they are not now.

COPYING FROM OLD MASTERS.

This picture is about thirty feet long, and ten or twelve high, I should think, and the figures are at least life size. It is one of the largest paintings in Europe. The colors are dimmed with age; the countenances are scaled and marred, and nearly all expression is gone from them; the hair is a dead blur upon the wall, and there is no life in the eyes. Only the attitudes are certain.

People come here from all parts of the world, and glorify this masterpiece. They stand entranced before it with bated breath and parted lips, and when they speak, it is only in the catchy ejaculations of rapture:

" O, wonderful !"

" Such expression !"

" Such grace of attitude !"

" Such dignity !"

" Such faultless drawing !"

" Such matchless coloring !"

" Such feeling !"

" What delicacy of touch !"

" What sublimity of conception !"

" A vision ! a vision !"

I only envy these people ; I envy them their honest admiration, if it be honest—their delight, if they feel delight. I harbor no animosity toward any of them. But at the same time the thought *will* intrude itself upon me, How can they see what is not visible ? What would you think of a man who looked at some decayed, blind, toothless, pock-marked Cleopatra, and said: " What matchless beauty ! What soul ! What expression !" What would you think of a man who gazed upon a dingy, foggy sunset, and said: " What sublimity ! what feeling ! what richness of coloring !" What would you think of a man who stared in ecstacy upon a desert of stumps and said : " Oh, my soul, my beating heart, what a noble forest is here !"

You would think that those men had an astonishing talent for seeing things that had already passed away. It was what I thought when I stood before the Last Supper and heard men apostrophizing wonders, and beauties and perfections which had faded out of the picture and gone, a hundred years before they were born. We can imagine the beauty that was once in an aged face; we can imagine the forest if we see the stumps;

but we can not absolutely *see* these things when they are not there. I am willing to believe that the eye of the practiced artist can rest upon the Last Supper and renew a lustre where only a hint of it is left, supply a tint that has faded away, restore an expression that is gone; patch, and color, and add, to the dull canvas until at last its figures shall stand before him aglow with the life, the feeling, the freshness, yea, with all the noble beauty that was theirs when first they came from the hand of the master. But *I* can not work this miracle. Can those other uninspired visitors do it, or do they only happily imagine they do?

After reading so much about it, I am satisfied that the Last Supper was a very miracle of art once. But it was three hundred years ago.

It vexes me to hear people talk so glibly of " feeling," " expression," " tone," and those other easily acquired and inexpensive technicalities of art that make such a fine show in conversations concerning pictures. There is not one man in seventy-five hundred that can tell *what* a pictured face is intended to express. There is not one man in five hundred that can go into a court-room and be sure that he will not mistake some harmless innocent of a juryman for the black-hearted assassin on trial. Yet such people talk of " character " and presume to interpret " expression " in pictures. There is an old story that Matthews, the actor, was once lauding the ability of the human face to express the passions and emotions hidden in the breast. He said the countenance could disclose what was passing in the heart plainer than the tongue could.

" Now," he said, " observe my face—what does it express?"

" Despair !"

" Bah, it expresses peaceful resignation ! What does *this* express?"

" Rage !"

" Stuff ! it means terror ! *This !*"

" Imbecility !"

" Fool ! It is smothered ferocity ! Now *this !*"

" Joy !"

"Oh, perdition! *Any* ass can see it means insanity!"

Expression! People coolly pretend to read it who would think themselves presumptuous if they pretended to interpret the hieroglyphics on the obelisks of Luxor—yet they are fully as competent to do the one thing as the other. . I have heard

FACIAL EXPRESSION.

two very intelligent critics speak of Murillo's Immaculate Conception (now in the museum at Seville,) within the past few days. One said :

"Oh, the Virgin's face is full of the ecstasy of a joy that is complete—that leaves nothing more to be desired on earth!"

The other said :

"Ah, that wonderful face is so humble, so pleading—it says as plainly as words could say it : ' I fear; I tremble; I am unworthy.. But Thy will be done ; sustain Thou Thy servant !' "

The reader can see the picture in any drawing-room ; it can be easily recognized : the Virgin (the only young and really beautiful Virgin that was ever painted by one of the old masters, some of us think,) stands in the crescent of the new moon, with a multitude of cherubs hovering about her, and more coming ; her hands are crossed upon her breast, and upon her uplifted countenance falls a glory out of the heavens. The reader may amuse himself, if he chooses, in trying to determine which of these gentlemen read the Virgin's "expression" aright, or if either of them did it.

Any one who is acquainted with the old masters will comprehend how much the Last Supper is damaged when I say that the spectator can not really tell, now, whether the disciples are Hebrews or Italians. These ancient painters never succeeded in denationalizing themselves. The Italian artists painted Italian Virgins, the Dutch painted Dutch Virgins, the Virgins of the French painters were Frenchwomen—none of them ever put into the face of the Madonna that indescribable something which proclaims the Jewess, whether you find her in New York, in Constantinople, in Paris, Jerusalem, or in the Empire of Morocco. I saw in the Sandwich Islands, once, a picture, copied by a talented German artist from an engraving in one of the American illustrated papers. It was an allegory, representing Mr. Davis in the act of signing a secession act or some such document. Over him hovered the ghost of Washington in warning attitude, and in the background a troop of shadowy soldiers in Continental uniform were limping with shoeless, bandaged feet through a driving snow-storm. Valley Forge was suggested, of course. The copy seemed accurate, and yet there was a discrepancy somewhere. After a long examination I discovered what it was—the shadowy soldiers were all Germans! Jeff. Davis was a German! even the hovering ghost was a German ghost! The artist had unconsciously worked his nationality into the picture. To tell the truth, I am getting a little perplexed about John the Baptist and his portraits. In France I finally grew reconciled to him as a Frenchman; here he is unquestionably an Italian. What next? Can it be possible that the painters make John the Baptist a Spaniard in Madrid and an Irishman in Dublin?

We took an open barouche and drove two miles out of Milan to "see ze echo," as the guide expressed it. The road was smooth, it was bordered by trees, fields, and grassy meadows, and the soft air was filled with the odor of flowers. Troops of picturesque peasant girls, coming from work, hooted at us, shouted at us, made all manner of game of us, and entirely delighted me. My long-cherished judgment was confirmed. I always did think those frowsy, romantic, unwashed peasant girls I had read so much about in poetry were a glaring fraud.

We enjoyed our jaunt. It was an exhilarating relief from tiresome sight-seeing.

We distressed ourselves very little about the astonishing

echo the guide talked so much about. We were growing accustomed to encomiums on wonders that too often proved no wonders at all. And so we were most happily disappointed to find in the sequel that the guide had even failed to rise to the magnitude of his subject.

We arrived at a tumble-down old rookery called the Palazzo Simonetti—a massive hewn-stone affair occupied by a family

THE ECHO.

of ragged Italians. A good-looking young girl conducted us to a window on the second floor which looked out on a court walled on three sides by tall buildings. She put her head out at the window and shouted. The echo answered more times than we could count. She took a speaking trumpet and through it she shouted, sharp and quick, a single

"Ha!" The echo answered:

"Ha!———ha!——ha!—ha!—ha!—ha! ha! h-a-a-a-a-a!"

and finally went off into a rollicking convulsion of the jolliest laughter that could be imagined. It was so joyful—so long continued—so perfectly cordial and hearty, that every body was forced to join in. There was no resisting it.

Then the girl took a gun and fired it. We stood ready to count the astonishing clatter of reverberations. We could not say one, two, three, fast enough, but we could dot our note-books with our pencil points almost rapidly enough to take down a sort of short-hand report of the result. My page revealed the following account. I could not keep up, but I did as well as I could:

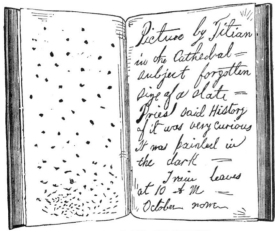

FIFTY-TWO DISTINCT REPETITIONS.

I set down fifty-two distinct repetitions, and then the echo got the advantage of me. The doctor set down sixty-four, and thenceforth the echo moved too fast for him, also. After the separate concussions could no longer be noted, the reverberations dwindled to a wild, long-sustained clatter of sounds such as a watchman's rattle produces. It is likely that this is the most remarkable echo in the world.

The doctor, in jest, offered to kiss the young girl, and was taken a little aback when she said he might for a franc! The commonest gallantry compelled him to stand by his offer, and so he paid the franc and took the kiss. She was a philosopher. She said a franc was a good thing to have, and she did not care any thing for one paltry kiss, because she had a million left. Then our comrade, always a shrewd business man, offered to take the whole cargo at thirty days, but that little

A KISS FOR A FRANC.

financial scheme was a failure.

CHAPTER XX.

WE left Milan by rail. The Cathedral six or seven miles behind us—vast, dreamy, blueish snow-clad mountains twenty miles in front of us,—these were the accented points in the scenery. The more immediate scenery consisted of fields and farm-houses outside the car and a monster-headed dwarf and a moustached woman inside it. These latter were not show-people. Alas, deformity and female beards are too common in Italy to attract attention.

We passed through a range of wild, picturesque hills, steep, wooded, cone-shaped, with rugged crags projecting here and there, and with dwellings and ruinous castles perched away up toward the drifting clouds. We lunched at the curious old town of Como, at the foot of the lake, and then took the small steamer and had an afternoon's pleasure excursion to this place,—Bellaggio.

When we walked ashore, a party of policemen (people whose cocked hats and showy uniforms would shame the finest uni-form in the military service of the United States,) put us into a little stone cell and locked us in. We had the whole passen-ger list for company, but their room would have been prefer-able, for there was no light, there were no windows, no venti-lation. It was close and hot. We were much crowded. It was the Black Hole of Calcutta on a small scale. Presently a smoke rose about our feet—a smoke that smelt of all the dead things of earth, of all the putrefaction and corruption imaginable.

We were there five minutes, and when we got out it was hard to tell which of us carried the vilest fragrance.

These miserable outcasts called that "fumigating" us, and the term was a tame one indeed. They fumigated us to guard themselves against the cholera, though we hailed from no infected port. We had left the cholera far behind us all the time. However, they must keep epidemics away somehow or other, and fumigation is cheaper than soap. They must either wash themselves or fumigate other people. Some of the lower classes had rather die than wash, but the fumigation of stran-

THE FUMIGATION.

gers causes them no pangs. They need no fumigation themselves. Their habits make it unnecessary. They carry their preventive with them; they sweat and fumigate all the day long. I trust I am a humble and a consistent Christian. I try to do what is right. I know it is my duty to " pray for them that despitefully use me ;" and therefore, hard as it is, I shall still try to pray for these fumigating, maccaroni-stuffing organ grinders.

Our hotel sits at the water's edge—at least its front garden does—and we walk among the shrubbery and smoke at twilight; we look afar off at Switzerland and the Alps, and feel an indolent willingness to look no closer; we go down the steps and swim in the lake; we take a shapely little boat and sail abroad among the reflections of the stars; lie on the thwarts and listen to the distant laughter, the singing, the soft melody of flutes and guitars that comes floating across the water from pleasuring gondolas; we close the evening with exasperating billiards on one of those same old execrable tables. A midnight luncheon in our ample bed-chamber; a final smoke in its contracted veranda facing the water, the gardens and the mountains; a summing up of the day's events. Then to bed, with drowsy brains harassed with a mad panorama that mixes up pictures of France, of Italy, of the ship, of the ocean, of home, in grotesque and bewildering disorder. Then a melting away of familiar faces, of cities and of tossing waves, into a great calm of forgetfulness and peace.

After which, the nightmare.

Breakfast in the morning, and then the Lake.

I did not like it yesterday. I thought Lake Tahoe was *much* finer. I have to confess now, however, that my judgment erred somewhat, though not extravagantly. I always had an idea that Como was a vast basin of water, like Tahoe, shut in by great mountains. Well, the border of huge mountains is here, but the lake itself is not a basin. It is as crooked as any brook, and only from one-quarter to two-thirds as wide as the Mississippi. There is not a yard of low ground on either side of it—nothing but endless chains of mountains that spring abruptly from the water's edge, and tower to altitudes varying from a thousand to two thousand feet. Their craggy sides are clothed with vegetation, and white specks of houses peep out from the luxuriant foliage every where; they are even perched upon jutting and picturesque pinnacles a thousand feet above your head.

Again, for miles along the shores, handsome country seats, surrounded by gardens and groves, sit fairly in the water, some-

times in nooks carved by Nature out of the vine-hung precipices, and with no ingress or egress save by boats. Some have
great broad stone staircases leading down to the water, with
heavy stone balustrades ornamented with statuary and fanci-
fully adorned with creeping vines and bright-colored flowers—
for all the world like a drop-curtain in a theatre, and lacking
nothing but long-waisted, high-heeled women and plumed
gallants in silken tights coming down to go serenading in the
splendid gondola in waiting.

LAKE COMO.

A great feature of Como's attractiveness is the multitude of
pretty houses and gardens that cluster upon its shores and on
its mountain sides. They look so snug and so homelike, and
at eventide when every thing seems to slumber, and the music
of the vesper bells comes stealing over the water, one almost
believes that nowhere else than on the Lake of Como can there
be found such a paradise of tranquil repose.

From my window here in Bellaggio, I have a view of the other side of the lake now, which is as beautiful as a picture. A scarred and wrinkled precipice rises to a height of eighteen hundred feet; on a tiny bench half way up its vast wall, sits a little snow-flake of a church, no bigger than a martin-box, apparently; skirting the base of the cliff are a hundred orange groves and gardens, flecked with glimpses of the white dwellings that are buried in them; in front, three or four gondolas lie idle upon the water—and in the burnished mirror of the lake, mountain, chapel, houses, groves and boats are counterfeited so brightly and so clearly that one scarce knows where the reality leaves off and the reflection begins!

The surroundings of this picture are fine. A mile away, a grove-plumed promontory juts far into the lake and glasses its palace in the blue depths; in midstream a boat is cutting the shining surface and leaving a long track behind, like a ray of light; the mountains beyond are veiled in a dreamy purple haze; far in the opposite direction a tumbled mass of domes and verdant slopes and valleys bars the lake, and here indeed does distance lend enchantment to the view—for on this broad canvas, sun and clouds and the richest of atmospheres have blended a thousand tints together, and over its surface the filmy lights and shadows drift, hour after hour, and glorify it with a beauty that seems reflected out of Heaven itself. Beyond all question, this is the most voluptuous scene we have yet looked upon.

Last night the scenery was striking and picturesque. On the other side crags and trees and snowy houses were reflected in the lake with a wonderful distinctness, and streams of light from many a distant window shot far abroad over the still waters. On this side, near at hand, great mansions, white with moonlight, glared out from the midst of masses of foliage that lay black and shapeless in the shadows that fell from the cliff above—and down in the margin of the lake every feature of the weird vision was faithfully repeated.

To-day we have idled through a wonder of a garden attached to a ducal estate—but enough of description is enough, I judge.

I suspect that this was the same place the gardener's son deceived the Lady of Lyons with, but I do not know. You may
have heard of the passage somewhere:

> " A deep vale,
> Shut out by Alpine hills from the rude world,
> Near a clear lake margined by fruits of gold
> And whispering myrtles:
> Glassing softest skies, cloudless,
> Save with rare and roseate shadows;
> A palace, lifting to eternal heaven its marbled walls,
> From out a glossy bower of coolest foliage musical with birds."

That is all very well, except the " clear " part of the lake.
It certainly is clearer than a great many lakes, but how dull
its waters are compared with the wonderful transparence of
Lake Tahoe! I speak of the north shore of Tahoe, where one
can count the scales on a trout at a depth of a hundred and
eighty feet. I have tried to get this statement off at par here,
but with no success; so I have been obliged to negotiate it at
fifty per cent. discount. At this rate I find some takers; perhaps the reader will receive it on the same terms—ninety feet
instead of one hundred and eighty. But let it be remembered
that those are forced terms—Sheriff's sale prices. As far as I
am privately concerned, I abate not a jot of the original assertion that in those strangely magnifying waters one may count
the scales on a trout (a trout of the large kind,) at a depth of
a hundred and eighty feet—may see every pebble on the bottom—might even count a paper of dray-pins. People talk of
the transparent waters of the Mexican Bay of Acapulco, but in
my own experience I know they can not compare with those I am
speaking of. I have fished for trout, in Tahoe, and at a measured depth of eighty-four feet I have seen them put their noses to
the bait and I could see their gills open and shut. I could hardly
have seen the trout themselves at that distance in the open air.

As I go back in spirit and recall that noble sea, reposing
among the snow-peaks six thousand feet above the ocean, the
conviction comes strong upon me again that Como would only
seem a bedizened little courtier in that august presence.

GARDEN, LAKE COMO.

Sorrow and misfortune overtake the Legislature that still from year to year permits Tahoe to retain its unmusical cognomen! Tahoe! It suggests no crystal waters, no picturesque shores, no sublimity. Tahoe for a sea in the clouds: a sea that has character, and asserts it in solemn calms, at times, at times in savage storms; a sea, whose royal seclusion is guarded by a cordon of sentinel peaks that lift their frosty fronts nine thousand feet above the level world; a sea whose every aspect is impressive, whose belongings are all beautiful, whose lonely majesty types the Deity!

Tahoe means grasshoppers. It means grasshopper soup. It is Indian, and suggestive of Indians. They say it is Pi-ute—possibly it is Digger. I am satisfied it was named by the Diggers—those degraded savages who roast their dead relatives, then mix the human grease and ashes of bones with tar, and "gaum" it thick all over their heads and foreheads and ears, and go caterwauling about the hills and call it *mourning*. *These* are the gentry that named the Lake.

People say that Tahoe means "Silver Lake"—"Limpid Water"—"Falling Leaf." Bosh. It means grasshopper soup, the favorite dish of the Digger tribe—and of the Pi-utes as well. It isn't worth while, in these practical times, for people to talk about Indian poetry—there never was any in them—except in the Fennimore Cooper Indians. But *they* are an extinct tribe that never existed. I know the Noble Red Man. I have camped with the Indians; I have been on the war-path with them, taken part in the chase with them—for grasshoppers; helped them steal cattle; I have roamed with them, scalped them, had them for breakfast. I would gladly eat the whole race if I had a chance.

But I am growing unreliable. I will return to my comparison of the Lakes. Como is a little deeper than Tahoe, if people here tell the truth. They say it is eighteen hundred feet deep at this point, but it does not look a dead enough blue for that. Tahoe is one thousand five hundred and twenty-five feet deep in the centre, by the State Geologist's measurement. They say the great peak opposite this town is five thousand

feet high : but I feel sure that three thousand feet of that statement is a good honest lie. The lake is a mile wide, here, and
maintains about that width from this point to its northern extremity—which is distant sixteen miles : from here to its southern extremity—say fifteen miles—it is not over half a mile
wide in any place, I should think. Its snow-clad mountains
one hears so much about are only seen occasionally, and then
in the distance, the Alps. Tahoe is from ten to eighteen miles
wide, and its mountains shut it in like a wall. Their summits
are never free from snow the year round. One thing about it
is very strange : it never has even a skim of ice upon its surface, although lakes in the same range of mountains, lying in
a lower and warmer temperature, freeze over in winter.

It is cheerful to meet a shipmate in these out-of-the-way
places and compare notes with him. We have found one of
ours here—an old soldier of the war, who is seeking bloodless
adventures and rest from his campaigns, in these sunny lands.*

* Col. J. HERON FOSTER, editor of a Pittsburgh journal, and a most estimable
gentleman. As these sheets are being prepared for the press, I am pained to learn
of his decease shortly after his return home.—M. T.

CHAPTER XXI.

WE voyaged by steamer down the Lago di Lecco, through wild mountain scenery, and by hamlets and villas, and disembarked at the town of Lecco. They said it was two hours, by carriage to the ancient city of Bergamo, and that we would arrive there in good season for the railway train. We got an open barouche and a wild, boisterous driver, and set out. It was delightful. We had a fast team and a perfectly smooth road. There were towering cliffs on our left, and the pretty Lago di Lecco on our right, and every now and then it rained on us. Just before starting, the driver picked up, in the street, a stump of a cigar an inch long, and put it in his mouth. When he had carried it thus about an hour, I thought it would be only Christian charity to give him a light. I handed him my cigar, which I had just lit, and he put it in his mouth and returned his stump to his pocket! I never saw a more sociable man. At least I never saw a man who was more sociable on a short acquaintance.

SOCIAL DRIVER.

We saw interior Italy, now. The houses were of solid stone, and not often in good repair. The peasants and their children were idle, as a general thing, and the donkeys and chickens made themselves at home in drawing-room and bed-chamber and were not molested. The drivers of each and every one of the slow-moving market-carts we met were stretched in the sun upon their merchandise, sound asleep. Every three or four hundred yards, it seemed to me, we came upon the shrine of some saint or other—a rude picture of him built into a huge cross or a stone pillar by the road-side.—Some of the pictures of the Saviour were curiosities in their way. They represented him stretched upon the cross, his countenance distorted with agony. From the wounds of the crown of thorns; from the pierced side; from the mutilated hands and feet; from the scourged body —from every handbreadth of his person streams of blood were flowing! Such a gory, ghastly spectacle would frighten the children out of their senses, I should think. There were some unique auxiliaries to the painting which added to its spirited effect. These were genuine wooden and iron implements, and were prominently disposed round about the figure: a bundle of nails; the hammer to drive them; the sponge; the reed that supported it; the cup of vinegar; the ladder for the ascent of the cross; the spear that pierced the Saviour's side. The crown of thorns was made of real thorns, and was nailed to the sacred head. In some Italian church-paintings,

WAYSIDE SHRINE.

even by the old masters, the Saviour and the Virgin wear silver or gilded crowns that are fastened to the pictured head with nails.   The effect is as grotesque as it is incongruous.

Here and there, on the fronts of roadside inns, we found huge, coarse frescoes of suffering martyrs like those in the shrines.   It could not have diminished their sufferings any to be so uncouthly represented.   We were in the heart and home of priestcraft—of a happy, cheerful, contented ignorance, superstition, degradation, poverty, indolence, and everlasting unaspiring worthlessness.   And we said fervently, It suits these people precisely; let them enjoy it, along with the other animals, and Heaven forbid that they be molested.   *We* feel no malice toward these fumigators.

We passed through the strangest, funniest, undreampt-of old towns, wedded to the customs and steeped in the dreams of the elder ages, and perfectly unaware that the world turns round !   And perfectly indifferent, too, as to whether it turns around or stands still.   *They* have nothing to do but eat and sleep and sleep and eat, and toil a little when they can get a friend to stand by and keep them awake.   *They* are not paid for thinking—*they* are not paid to fret about the world's con-

cerns.   They were not respectable people—they were not worthy people—they were not learned and wise and brilliant people—but in their breasts, all their stupid lives long, resteth a peace that passeth understanding !   How can men, calling themselves men, consent to be so degraded and happy.

PEACE AND HAPPINESS.

We whisked by many a gray old medieval castle, clad thick with ivy that swung its green banners down from towers and turrets where once some old Crusader's flag had floated. The driver pointed to one of these ancient fortresses, and said, (I translate):

"Do you see that great iron hook that projects from the wall just under the highest window in the ruined tower?"

We said we could not see it at such a distance, but had no doubt it was there.

"Well," he said, "there is a legend connected with that

CASTLE OF COUNT LUIGI.

iron hook. Nearly seven hundred years ago, that castle was the property of the noble Count Luigi Gennaro Guido Alphonso di Genova—"

"What was his other name?" said Dan.

"He had no other name. The name I have spoken was all
the name he had. He was the son of—"

"Poor but honest parents—that is all right—never mind the
particulars—go on with the legend."

THE LEGEND.

Well, then, all the world, at that time, was in a wild excitement about the Holy Sepulchre. All the great feudal lords in
Europe were pledging their lands and pawning their plate to
fit out men-at-arms so that they might join the grand armies
of Christendom and win renown in the Holy Wars. The
Count Luigi raised money, like the rest, and one mild September morning, armed with battle-ax, portcullis and thundering
culverin, he rode through the greaves and bucklers of his
donjon-keep with as gallant a troop of Christian bandits as ever
stepped in Italy. He had his sword, Excalibur, with him.
His beautiful countess and her young daughter waved him a
tearful adieu from the battering-rams and buttresses of the
fortress, and he galloped away with a happy heart.

He made a raid on a neighboring baron and completed his
outfit with the booty secured. He then razed the castle to the
ground, massacred the family and moved on. They were
hardy fellows in the grand old days of chivalry. Alas! those
days will never come again.

Count Luigi grew high in fame in Holy Land. He plunged
into the carnage of a hundred battles, but his good Excalibur
always brought him out alive, albeit often sorely wounded.
His face became browned by exposure to the Syrian sun in
long marches; he suffered hunger and thirst; he pined in
prisons, he languished in loathsome plague-hospitals. And
many and many a time he thought of his loved ones at home,
and wondered if all was well with them. But his heart said,
Peace, is not thy brother watching over thy household?

  *   *   *   *   *   *   *

Forty-two years waxed and waned; the good fight was won;
Godfrey reigned in Jerusalem—the Christian hosts reared the
banner of the cross above the Holy Sepulchre!

Twilight was approaching. Fifty harlequins, in flowing robes, approached this castle wearily, for they were on foot, and the dust upon their garments betokened that they had traveled far. They overtook a peasant, and asked him if it were likely they could get food and a hospitable bed there, for love of Christian charity, and if perchance, a moral parlor entertainment might meet with generous countenance—" for," said they, " this exhibition hath no feature that could offend the most fastidious taste."

" Marry," quoth the peasant, " an' it please your worships, ye had better journey many a good rood hence with your juggling circus than trust your bones in yonder castle."

" How now, sirrah !" exclaimed the chief monk, " explain thy ribald speech, or by'r Lady it shall go hard with thee."

" Peace, good mountebank, I did but utter the truth that was in my heart. San Paolo be my witness that did ye but find the stout Count Leonardo in his cups, sheer from the castle's topmost battlements would he hurl ye all! Alack-a-day, the good Lord Luigi reigns not here in these sad times."

" The good Lord Luigi ?"

" Aye, none other, please your worship. In his day, the poor rejoiced in plenty and the rich he did oppress ; taxes were not known, the fathers of the church waxed fat upon his bounty ; travelers went and came, with none to interfere ; and whosoever would, might tarry in his halls in cordial welcome, and eat his bread and drink his wine, withal. But woe is me ! some two and forty years agone the good count rode hence to fight for Holy Cross, and many a year hath flown since word or token have we had of him. Men say his bones lie bleaching in the fields of Palestine."

" And now ?"

" *Now !* God 'a mercy, the cruel Leonardo lords it in the castle. He wrings taxes from the poor ; he robs all travelers that journey by his gates ; he spends his days in feuds and murders, and his nights in revel and debauch ; he roasts the fathers of the church upon his kitchen spits, and enjoyeth the same, calling it pastime. These thirty years Luigi's countess hath not been seen by any he in all this land, and many whisper that she pines in the dungeons of the castle for that she will not wed with Leonardo, saying her dear lord still liveth and that she will die ere she prove false to him. They whisper likewise that her daughter is a prisoner as well. Nay, good jugglers, seek ye refreshment other wheres. 'Twere better that ye perished in a Christian way than that ye plunged from off yon dizzy tower. Give ye good-day."

"God keep ye, gentle knave—farewell."

But heedless of the peasant's warning, the players moved straightway toward the castle.

Word was brought to Count Leonardo that a company of mountebanks besought his hospitality.

"'Tis well. Dispose of them in the customary manner. Yet stay! I have need of them. Let them come hither. Later, cast them from the battlements—or—how many priests have ye on hand?"

"The day's results are meagre, good my lord. An abbot and a dozen beggarly friars is all we have."

"Hell and furies! Is the estate going to seed? Send hither the mountebanks. Afterward, broil them with the priests."

The robed and close-cowled harlequins entered. The grim Leonardo sate in state at the head of his council board. Ranged up and down the hall on either hand stood near a hundred men-at-arms.

"Ha, villains!" quoth the count, "What can ye do to earn the hospitality ye crave."

"Dread lord and mighty, crowded audiences have greeted our humble efforts with rapturous applause. Among our body count we the versatile and talented Ugolino; the justly celebrated Rodolpho; the gifted and accomplished Roderigo; the management have spared neither pains nor expense—"

"S'death! what can ye *do?* Curb thy prating tongue."

"Good my lord, in acrobatic feats, in practice with the dumb-bells, in balancing and ground and lofty tumbling are we versed—and sith your highness asketh me, I venture here to publish that in the truly marvelous and entertaining Zampillaerostation—"

"Gag him! throttle him! Body of Bacchus! am I a dog that I am to be assailed with polysyllabled blasphemy like to this? But hold! Lucretia, Isabel, stand forth! Sirrah, behold this dame, this weeping wench. The first I marry, within the hour; the other shall dry her tears or feed the vultures. Thou and thy vagabonds shall crown the wedding with thy merry-makings. Fetch hither the priest!"

The dame sprang toward the chief player.

"O, save me!" she cried; "save me from a fate far worse than death! Behold these sad eyes, these sunken cheeks, this withered frame! See thou the wreck this fiend hath made, and let thy heart be moved with pity! Look upon this damosel; note her wasted form, her halting step, her bloomless cheeks where youth should blush and happiness exult in smiles! Hear us and have compassion. This monster was my husband's brother. He who should have been our shield against all harm, hath kept us shut within the noisome caverns of his donjon-keep for lo these thirty years. And for what crime? None other than that I would not belie my troth, root out my strong love for him who marches with the legions of the cross in Holy Land, (for O, he is not dead!) and wed with him! Save us, O, save thy persecuted suppliants!"

She flung herself at his feet and clasped his knees.

"Ha!-ha!-ha!" shouted the brutal Leonardo. "Priest, to thy work!" and he dragged the weeping dame from her refuge. "Say, once for all, *will* you be mine?—for by my halidome, that breath that uttereth thy refusal shall be thy last on earth!"

"NE-VER?"

"Then die!" and the sword leaped from its scabbard.

Quicker than thought, quicker than the lightning's flash, fifty monkish habits disappeared, and fifty knights in splendid armor stood revealed! fifty falchions gleamed in air above the men-at-arms, and brighter, fiercer than them all, flamed Excalibur aloft, and cleaving downward struck the brutal Leonardo's weapon from his grasp!

"A Luigi to the rescue! Whoop!"

"A Leonardo! tare an ouns!"

"Oh, God, Oh, God, my husband!"

"Oh, God, Oh, God, my wife!"

"My father!"

"My precious!" [Tableau.]

Count Luigi bound his usurping brother hand and foot.
The practiced knights from Palestine made holyday sport of carving the awkward men-at-arms into chops and steaks. The victory was complete. Happiness reigned. The knights all married the daughter. Joy! wassail! finis!

WICKED BROTHER.

"But what did they do with the wicked brother?"

"Oh nothing—only hanged him on that iron hook I was speaking of. By the chin."

"As how?"

"Passed it up through his gills into his mouth."

"Leave him there?"

"Couple of years."

"Ah—is—is he dead?"

"Six hundred and fifty years ago, or such a matter."

"Splendid legend—splendid lie—drive on."

We reached the quaint old fortified city of Bergamo, the renowned in history, some three-quarters of an hour before the train was ready to start. The place has thirty or forty thousand inhabitants and is remarkable for being the birthplace of harlequin. When we discovered that, that legend of our driver took to itself a new interest in our eyes.

Rested and refreshed, we took the rail happy and contented. I shall not tarry to speak of the handsome Lago di Gardi; its stately castle that holds in its stony bosom the secrets of an age so remote that even tradition goeth not back to it;

the imposing mountain scenery that ennobles the landscape thereabouts; nor yet of ancient Padua or haughty Verona; nor of their Montagues and Capulets, their famous balconies and tombs of Juliet and Romeo *et al.*, but hurry straight to the ancient city of the sea, the widowed bride of the Adriatic. It was a long, long ride. But toward evening, as we sat silent and hardly conscious of where we were—subdued into that meditative calm that comes so surely after a conversational storm—some one shouted—

"VENICE!"

And sure enough, afloat on the placid sea a league away, lay a great city, with its towers and domes and steeples drowsing in a golden mist of sunset.

CHAPTER XXII.

THIS Venice, which was a haughty, invincible, magnificent Republic for nearly fourteen hundred years; whose armies compelled the world's applause whenever and wherever they battled; whose navies well nigh held dominion of the seas, and whose merchant fleets whitened the remotest oceans with their sails and loaded these piers with the products of every clime, is fallen a prey to poverty, neglect and melancholy decay. Six hundred years ago, Venice was the Autocrat of Commerce; her mart was the great commercial centre, the distributing-house from whence the enormous trade of the Orient was spread abroad over the Western world. To-day her piers are deserted, her warehouses are empty, her merchant fleets are vanished, her armies and her navies are but memories. Her glory is departed, and with her crumbling grandeur of wharves and palaces about her she sits among her stagnant lagoons, forlorn and beggared, forgotten of the world. She that in her palmy days commanded the commerce of a hemisphere and made the weal or woe of nations with a beck of her puissant finger, is become the humblest among the peoples of the earth,—a peddler of glass beads for women, and trifling toys and trinkets for school-girls and children.

The venerable Mother of the Republics is scarce a fit subject for flippant speech or the idle gossiping of tourists. It seems a sort of sacrilege to disturb the glamour of old romance that pictures her to us softly from afar off as through a tinted mist, and curtains her ruin and her desolation from our view. One ought, indeed, to turn away from her rags, her poverty and her humiliation, and think of her only as she was when she sunk the fleets of Charlemagne; when she humbled Frederick Barbarossa or waved her victorious banners above the battlements of Constantinople.

We reached Venice at eight in the evening, and entered a hearse belonging to the Grand Hotel d'Europe. At any rate, it was more like a hearse than any thing else, though to speak by the card, it was a gondola. And this was the storied gondola of Venice!—the fairy boat in which the princely cavaliers of the olden time were wont to cleave the waters of the moonlit canals and look the eloquence of love into the soft eyes of patrician beauties, while the gay gondolier in silken doublet touched his guitar and sang as only gondoliers can sing! This the famed gondola and this the gorgeous gondolier!—the one an inky, rusty old canoe with a sable hearse-body clapped on to the middle of it, and the other a mangy, barefooted gutter-snipe with a portion of his raiment on exhibition which should have been sacred from public scrutiny. Presently, as he turned a corner and shot his hearse into a dismal ditch between two long rows of towering, untenanted buildings, the gay gondolier began to sing, true to the traditions of his race. I stood it a little while. Then I said:

"Now, here, Roderigo Gonzales Michael Angelo, I'm a pilgrim, and I'm a stranger, but I am not going to have my feelings lacerated by any such caterwauling as that. If that goes on, one of us has got to take water. It is enough that my cherished dreams of Venice have been blighted forever as to the romantic gondola and the gorgeous gondolier; this system of destruction shall go no farther; I will accept the hearse, under protest, and you may fly your flag of truce in peace, but here I register a dark and bloody oath that you shan't sing. Another yelp, and overboard you go."

I began to feel that the old Venice of song and story had departed forever. But I was too hasty. In a few minutes we swept gracefully out into the Grand Canal, and under the mellow moonlight the Venice of poetry and romance stood revealed. Right from the water's edge rose long lines of stately palaces of marble; gondolas were gliding swiftly hither and

thither and disappearing suddenly through unsuspected gates
and alleys; ponderous stone bridges threw their shadows
athwart the glittering waves.   There was life and motion everywhere, and yet everywhere there was a hush, a stealthy sort
of stillness, that was suggestive of secret enterprises of bravoes
and of lovers; and clad half in moonbeams and half in mysterious shadows, the grim old mansions of the Republic seemed
to have an expression about them of having an eye out for just
such enterprises as these at that same moment.   Music came
floating over the waters—Venice was complete.

It was a beautiful picture—very soft and dreamy and beautiful.   But what was this Venice to compare with the Venice
of midnight? Nothing.   There was a fête—a grand fête in
honor of some saint who had been instrumental in checking
the cholera three hundred years ago, and all Venice was abroad
on the water.   It was no common affair, for the Venetians did
not know how soon they might need the saint's services again,
now that the cholera was spreading every where.   So in one
vast space—say a third of a mile wide and two miles long—
were collected two thousand gondolas, and every one of them
had from two to ten, twenty and even thirty colored lanterns
suspended about it, and from four to a dozen occupants.   Just
as far as the eye could reach, these painted lights were massed
together—like a vast garden of many-colored flowers, except
that these blossoms were never still; they were ceaselessly gliding in and out, and mingling together, and seducing you into
bewildering attempts to follow their mazy evolutions.   Here
and there a strong red, green, or blue glare from a rocket that
was struggling to get away, splendidly illuminated all the boats
around it.   Every gondola that swam by us, with its crescents
and pyramids and circles of colored lamps hung aloft, and
lighting up the faces of the young and the sweet-scented and
lovely below, was a picture; and the reflections of those lights,
so long, so slender, so numberless, so many-colored and so distorted and wrinkled by the waves, was a picture likewise, and
one that was enchantingly beautiful.   Many and many a party
of young ladies and gentlemen had their state gondolas hand-

somely decorated, and ate supper on board, bringing their swallow-tailed, white-cravatted varlets to wait upon them, and having their tables tricked out as if for a bridal supper. They had brought along the costly globe lamps from their drawing-rooms, and the lace and silken curtains from the same places, I suppose. And they had also brought pianos and guitars, and they played and sang operas, while the plebeian paper-lanterned gondolas from the suburbs and the back alleys crowded around to stare and listen.

There was music every where—chorusses, string bands, brass bands, flutes, every thing. I was so surrounded, walled in, with music, magnificence and loveliness, that I became inspired with the spirit of the scene, and sang one tune myself. However, when I observed that the other gondolas had sailed away, and my gondolier was preparing to go overboard, I stopped.

DISGUSTED GONDOLIER.

The fête was magnificent. They kept it up the whole night long, and I never enjoyed myself better than I did while it lasted.

What a funny old city this Queen of the Adriatic is! Narrow streets, vast, gloomy marble palaces, black with the corroding damps of centuries, and all partly submerged; no dry land visible any where, and no sidewalks worth mentioning; if you want to go to church, to the theatre, or to the restaurant, you must call a gondola. It must be a paradise for cripples, for verily a man has no use for legs here.

For a day or two the place looked so like an overflowed Arkansas town, because of its currentless waters laving the very doorsteps of all the houses, and the cluster of boats made fast under the windows, or skimming in and out of the alleys and by-ways, that I could not get rid of the impression that there was nothing the matter here but a spring freshet, and that the river would fall in a few weeks and leave a dirty high-water mark on the houses, and the streets full of mud and rubbish.

In the glare of day, there is little poetry about Venice, but under the charitable moon her stained palaces are white again, their battered sculptures are hidden in shadows, and the old city seems crowned once more with the grandeur that was hers five hundred years ago. It is easy, then, in fancy, to people these silent canals with plumed gallants and fair ladies—with Shylocks in gaberdine and sandals, venturing loans upon the rich argosies of Venetian commerce—with Othellos and Desdemonas, with Iagos and Roderigos—with noble fleets and victorious legions returning from the wars. In the treacherous sunlight we see Venice decayed, forlorn, poverty-stricken, and commerceless—forgotten and utterly insignificant. But in the moonlight, her fourteen centuries of greatness fling their glories about her, and once more is she the princeliest among the nations of the earth.

> "There is a glorious city in the sea;
> The sea is in the broad, the narrow streets,
> Ebbing and flowing; and the salt-sea weed
> Clings to the marble of her palaces.
> No track of men, no footsteps to and fro,
> Lead to her gates! The path lies o'er the sea,
> Invisible: and from the land we went,
> As to a floating city—steering in,
> And gliding up her streets, as in a dream,
> So smoothly, silently—by many a dome,
> Mosque-like, and many a stately portico,
> The statues ranged along an azure sky;

By many a pile, in more than Eastern pride,
Of old the residence of merchant kings;
The fronts of some, tho' time had shatter'd them,
Still glowing with the richest hues of art,
As tho' the wealth within them had run o'er."

What would one naturally wish to see first in Venice? The Bridge of Sighs, of course—and next the Church and the Great Square of St. Mark, the Bronze Horses, and the famous Lion of St. Mark.

We intended to go to the Bridge of Sighs, but happened into the Ducal Palace first—a building which necessarily figures largely in Venetian poetry and tradition. In the Senate Chamber of the ancient Republic we wearied our eyes with staring at acres of historical paintings by Tintoretto and Paul Veronese, but nothing struck us forcibly except the one thing that strikes *all* strangers forcibly—a black square in the midst of a gallery of portraits. In one long row, around the great hall, were painted the portraits of the Doges of Venice (venerable fellows, with flowing white beards, for of the three hundred Senators eligible to the office, the oldest was usually chosen Doge,) and each had its complimentary inscription attached—till you came to the place that should have had Marino Faliero's picture in it, and that was blank and black—blank, except that it bore a terse inscription, saying that the conspirator had died for his crime. It seemed cruel to keep that pitiless inscription still staring from the walls after the unhappy wretch had been in his grave five hundred years.

At the head of the Giant's Staircase, where Marino Faliero was beheaded, and where the Doges were crowned in ancient times, two small slits in the stone wall were pointed out—two harmless, insignificant orifices that would never attract a stranger's attention—yet these were the terrible Lions' Mouths! The heads were gone (knocked off by the French during their occupation of Venice,) but these were the throats, down which went the anonymous accusation, thrust in secretly at dead of night by an enemy, that doomed many an innocent man to walk the Bridge of Sighs and descend into the dungeon which none entered and hoped to see the sun again. This was in the old days when the Patricians alone governed Venice—the common herd had no vote and no voice. There were one thousand five hundred Patricians; from these, three hundred Senators were chosen; from the Senators a Doge and a Council of Ten were selected, and by secret ballot the Ten chose from their own number a Council of Three. All these were Government spies, then, and every spy was under surveillance himself—men spoke in whispers in Venice, and no man trusted his neighbor—not always his own brother. No man knew who the Council of Three were—not even the Senate, not even the Doge; the members of that dread tribunal met at night in a chamber to themselves, masked, and robed from head to foot in scarlet cloaks, and did not even know each other, unless by voice. It was their duty to judge heinous political crimes, and from their sentence there was no appeal. A nod to the executioner was sufficient. The doomed man was marched down a hall and out at a door-way into the covered Bridge of Sighs, through it and into the dungeon and unto his death. At no time in his transit was he visible to any save his conductor. If a man had an enemy in those old days, the cleverest thing he could do was to slip a note for the Council of Three into the Lion's mouth, saying "This man is plotting against the Government." If the awful Three found no proof, ten to one they would drown him anyhow, because he was a deep rascal, since his plots were unsolvable. Masked judges and masked executioners, with unlimited power, and no appeal from their judgments, in that hard, cruel age, were not likely to be lenient with men they suspected yet could not convict.

We walked through the hall of the Council of Ten, and presently entered the infernal den of the Council of Three.

The table around which they had sat was there still, and likewise the stations where the masked inquisitors and executioners formerly stood, frozen, upright and silent, till they received a bloody order, and then, without a word, moved off, like the inexorable machines they were, to carry it out. The frescoes on the walls were startlingly suited to the place. In all the other saloons, the halls, the great state chambers of the palace, the walls and ceilings were bright with gilding, rich with elaborate carving, and resplendent with gallant pictures of Venetian victories in war, and Venetian display in foreign courts, and hallowed with portraits of the Virgin, the Saviour of men, and the holy saints that preached the Gospel of Peace upon earth—but here, in dismal contrast, were none but pictures of death and dreadful suffering!—not a living figure but was writhing in torture, not a dead one but was smeared with blood, gashed with wounds, and distorted with the agonies that had taken away its life!

From the palace to the gloomy prison is but a step—one might almost jump across the narrow canal that intervenes. The ponderous stone Bridge of Sighs crosses it at the second story—a bridge that is a covered tunnel—you can not be seen when you walk in it. It is partitioned lengthwise, and through one compartment walked such as bore light sentences in ancient times, and through the other marched sadly the wretches whom the Three had doomed to lingering misery and utter oblivion in the dungeons, or to sudden and mysterious death. Down below the level of the water, by the light of smoking torches, we were shown the damp, thick-walled cells where many a proud patrician's life was eaten away by the long-drawn miseries of solitary imprisonment—without light, air, books; naked, unshaven, uncombed, covered with vermin; his useless tongue forgetting its office, with none to speak to; the days and nights of his life no longer marked, but merged into one eternal eventless night; far away from all cheerful sounds, buried in the silence of a tomb; forgotten by his helpless friends, and his fate a dark mystery to them forever; losing his own memory at last, and knowing no more who he was or how he came there; devouring the loaf of bread and drinking the water that were thrust into the cell by unseen hands, and troubling his worn spirit no more with hopes and fears and doubts and longings to be free; ceasing to scratch vain prayers and complainings on walls where none, not even himself, could see them, and resigning himself to hopeless apathy, driveling childishness, lunacy! Many and many a sorrowful story like this these stony walls could tell if they could but speak.

In a little narrow corridor, near by, they showed us where many a prisoner, after lying in the dungeons until he was forgotten by all save his persecutors, was brought by masked executioners and garroted, or sewed up in a sack, passed through a little window to a boat, at dead of night, and taken to some remote spot and drowned.

They used to show to visitors the implements of torture wherewith the Three were wont to worm secrets out of the accused—villainous machines for crushing thumbs; the stocks where a prisoner sat immovable while water fell drop by drop upon his head till the torture was more than humanity could bear; and a devilish contrivance of steel, which inclosed a prisoner's head like a shell, and crushed it slowly by means of a screw. It bore the stains of blood that had trickled through its joints long ago, and on one side it had a projection whereon the torturer rested his elbow comfortably and bent down his ear to catch the moanings of the sufferer perishing within.

Of course we went to see the venerable relic of the ancient glory of Venice, with its pavements worn and broken by the passing feet of a thousand years of plebeians and patricians—The Cathedral of St. Mark. It is built entirely of precious marbles, brought from the Orient—nothing in its composition is domestic. Its hoary traditions make it an object of absorbing interest to even the most careless stranger, and thus far it had interest for me; but no further. I could not go into ecstacies over its coarse mosaics, its unlovely Byzantine architecture, or its five hundred curious interior columns from as many distant quarries. Every thing was worn out—every block of stone was smooth and almost shapeless with the polishing hands and shoulders of loungers who devoutly idled here in by-gone centuries and have died and gone to the dev—no, simply died, I mean.

Under the altar repose the ashes of St. Mark—and Matthew, Luke and John, too, for all I know. Venice reveres those relics above all things earthly. For fourteen hundred years St. Mark has been her patron saint. Every thing about the city

15

seems to be named after him or so named as to refer to him in some way—so named, or some purchase rigged in some way to scrape a sort of hurrahing acquaintance with him. That seems to be the idea. To be on good terms with St. Mark, seems to be the very summit of Venetian ambition. They say St. Mark had a tame lion, and used to travel with him—and every where

THE CATHEDRAL OF ST. MARK'S.

that St. Mark went, the lion was sure to go. It was his protector, his friend, his librarian. And so the Winged Lion of St. Mark, with the open Bible under his paw, is a favorite emblem in the grand old city. It casts its shadow from the most ancient pillar in Venice, in the Grand Square of St. Mark, upon the throngs of free citizens below, and has so done for many a long century. The winged lion is found every where—and doubtless here, where the winged lion is, no harm can come.

St. Mark died at Alexandria, in Egypt. He was martyred, I think. However, that has nothing to do with my legend. About the founding of the city of Venice—say four hundred and fifty years after Christ—(for Venice is much younger than any other Italian city,) a priest dreamed that an angel told him that until the remains of St. Mark were brought to Venice, the city could never rise to high distinction among the nations; that the body must be captured, brought to the city, and a magnificent church built over it; and that if ever the Venetians allowed the Saint to be removed from his new resting-place, in that day Venice would perish from off the face of the the earth. The priest proclaimed his dream, and forthwith Venice set about procuring the corpse of St. Mark. One expedition after another tried and failed, but the project was never abandoned during four hundred years. At last it was secured by stratagem, in the year eight hundred and something. The commander of a Venetian expedition disguised himself, stole the bones, separated them, and packed them in vessels filled with lard. The religion of Mahomet causes its devotees to abhor anything that is in the nature of pork, and so when the Christian was stopped by the officers at the gates of the city, they only glanced once into his precious baskets, then turned up their noses at the unholy lard, and let him go. The bones were buried in the vaults of the grand cathedral, which had been waiting long years to receive them, and thus the safety and the greatness of Venice were secured. And to this day there be those in Venice who believe that if those holy ashes were stolen away, the ancient city would vanish like a dream, and its foundations be buried forever in the unremembering sea.

CHAPTER XXIII.

THE Venetian gondola is as free and graceful, in its gliding movement, as a serpent. It is twenty or thirty feet long, and is narrow and deep, like a canoe; its sharp bow and stern sweep upward from the water like the horns of a crescent with the abruptness of the curve slightly modified.

The bow is ornamented with a steel comb with a battle-ax attachment which threatens to cut passing boats in two occasionally, but never does. The gondola is painted black because in the zenith of Venetian magnificence the gondolas became too gorgeous altogether, and the Senate decreed that all such display must cease, and a solemn, unembellished black be substituted. If the truth were known, it would doubtless appear that rich plebeians grew too prominent in their affectation of patrician show on the Grand Canal, and required a wholesome snubbing. Reverence for the hallowed Past and its traditions keeps the dismal fashion in force now that the compulsion exists no longer. So let it remain. It is the color of mourning. Venice mourns. The stern of the boat is decked over and the gondolier stands there. He uses a single oar—a long blade, of course, for he stands nearly erect. A wooden peg, a foot and a half high, with two slight crooks or curves in one side of it and one in the other, projects above the starboard gunwale. Against that peg the gondolier takes a purchase with his oar, changing it at intervals to the other side of the peg or dropping it into another of the crooks, as the steering of the craft may demand—and how in the world

he can back and fill, shoot straight ahead, or flirt suddenly
around a corner, and make the oar stay in those insignificant
notches, is a problem to me and a never diminishing matter
of interest.   I am afraid I study the gondolier's marvelous skill more than I do the
sculptured palaces we glide among.   He
cuts a corner so closely, now and then, or
misses another gondola by such an imperceptible hair-breadth that I feel myself
"scrooching," as the children say, just as
one does when a buggy wheel grazes his
elbow.   But he makes all his calculations
with the nicest precision, and goes darting

PEG.

in and out among a Broadway confusion of busy craft with
the easy confidence of the educated hackman.   He never
makes a mistake.

Sometimes we go flying down the great canals at such a gait
that we can get only the merest glimpses into front doors, and
again, in obscure alleys in the suburbs, we put on a solemnity
suited to the silence, the mildew, the stagnant waters, the
clinging weeds, the deserted houses and the general lifeless-
ness of the place, and move to the spirit of grave meditation.

The gondolier *is* a picturesque rascal for all he wears no
satin harness, no plumed bonnet, no silken tights.   His attitude is stately ; he is lithe and supple ; all his movements are
full of grace.   When his long canoe, and his fine figure, towering from its high perch on the stern, are cut against the
evening sky, they make a picture that is very novel and striking to a foreign eye.

We sit in the cushioned carriage-body of a cabin, with the
curtains drawn, and smoke, or read, or look out upon the passing boats, the houses, the bridges, the people, and enjoy ourselves much more than we could in a buggy jolting over our
cobble-stone pavements at home.   This is the gentlest, pleasantest locomotion we have ever known.

But it seems queer—ever so queer—to see a boat doing

duty as a private carriage. We see business men come to the
front door, step into a gondola, instead of a street car, and go
off down town to the counting-room.

We see visiting young ladies stand on the stoop, and laugh,
and kiss good-bye, and flirt their fans and say "Come soon—

"GOOD-BYE."

now *do*—you've been just as mean as ever you can be—
mother's dying to see you—and we've moved into the new
house, O such a love of a place!—so convenient to the post-
office and the church, and the Young Men's Christian Association; and we do have such fishing, and such carrying on,

and *such* swimming-matches in the back yard—Oh, you *must* come—no distance at all, and if you go down through by St. Mark's and the Bridge of Sighs, and cut through the alley and come up by the church of Santa Maria dei Frari, and into the Grand Canal, there isn't a *bit* of current—now *do* come, Sally Maria—by-bye!" and then the little humbug trips down the steps, jumps into the gondola, says, under her breath, "Disagreeable old thing, I hope she *won't!*" goes skimming away, round the corner; and the other girl slams the street door and says, "Well, *that* infliction's over, any way,—but I suppose I've got to go and see her—tiresome stuck-up thing!" Human nature appears to be just the same, all over the world. We see the diffident young man, mild of moustache, affluent of hair, indigent of brain, elegant of costume, drive up to *her* father's mansion, tell his hackman to bail out and wait, start fearfully up the steps and meet " the old gentleman " right on the threshold!—hear him ask what street the new British Bank is in—as if *that* were what he came for—and then bounce into his boat and skurry away with his coward heart in his boots!—see him come sneaking around the corner again, directly, with a crack of the curtain open toward the old gentleman's disappearing gondola, and out scampers his Susan with a flock of little Italian endearments fluttering from her lips, and goes to drive with him in the watery avenues down toward the Rialto.

We see the ladies go out shopping, in the most natural way, and flit from street to street and from store to store, just in the good old fashion, except that they leave the gondola, instead of a private carriage, waiting at the curbstone a couple of hours for them,—waiting while they make the nice young clerks pull down tons and tons of silks and velvets and moire antiques and those things; and then they buy a paper of pins and go paddling away to confer the rest of their disastrous patronage on some other firm. And they always have their purchases sent home just in the good old way. Human nature is *very* much the same all over the world; and it is *so* like my dear native home to see a Venetian lady go into a store and buy ten cents' worth of blue ribbon and have it sent home in a scow. Ah, it is these little touches of nature that move one to tears in these far-off foreign lands.

We see little girls and boys go out in gondolas with their nurses, for an airing. We see staid families, with prayer-book and beads, enter the gondola dressed in their Sunday best, and float away to church. And at midnight we see the theatre break up and discharge its swarm of hilarious youth and beauty; we hear the cries of the hackman-gondoliers, and behold the struggling crowd jump aboard, and the black multitude of boats go skimming down the moonlit avenues; we see them separate here and there, and disappear up divergent streets; we hear the faint sounds of laughter and of shouted farewells floating up out of the distance; and then, the strange pageant being gone, we have lonely stretches of glittering water—of stately buildings—of blotting shadows—of weird stone faces creeping into the moonlight—of deserted bridges—of motionless boats at anchor. And over all broods that mysterious stillness, that stealthy quiet, that befits so well this old dreaming Venice.

We have been pretty much every where in our gondola. We have bought beads and photographs in the stores, and wax matches in the Great Square of St. Mark. The last remark suggests a digression. Every body goes to this vast square in the evening. The military bands play in the centre of it and countless couples of ladies and gentlemen promenade up and down on either side, and platoons of them are constantly drifting away toward the old Cathedral, and by the venerable column with the Winged Lion of St. Mark on its top, and out to where the boats lie moored; and other platoons are as constantly arriving from the gondolas and joining the great throng. Between the promenaders and the side-walks are seated hundreds and hundreds of people at small tables, smoking and taking *granita*, (a first cousin to ice-cream;) on the side-walks are more employing themselves in the same way. The shops in the first floor of the tall rows of buildings that wall in three sides of the square are brilliantly lighted, the air is filled with music and merry voices, and altogether the scene is as bright and spirited and full of cheerfulness as any man could desire. We enjoy it thoroughly. Very many of the young women are exceedingly pretty and dress with rare good taste. We are gradually and laboriously learning the ill-manners of staring them unflinchingly in the face—not because such conduct is agreeable to us, but because it is the custom of the country and they say the girls like it. We wish to learn all the curious, outlandish ways of all the different countries, so that we can "show off" and astonish people when we get home. We wish to excite the envy of our untraveled friends with our strange foreign fashions 'which we can't shake off. All our passengers are paying strict attention to this thing, with the end in view which I have mentioned. The gentle reader will never, never know what a consummate ass he can become, until he goes abroad. I speak now, of course, in the supposition that the gentle reader has not been abroad, and therefore is not already a consummate ass. If the case be otherwise, I beg his pardon and extend to him the cordial hand of fellowship and call him brother. I shall always delight to meet an ass after my own heart when I shall have finished my travels.

On this subject let me remark that there are Americans abroad in Italy who have actually forgotten their mother tongue in three months—forgot it in France. They can not even write their address in English in a hotel register. I append these evidences, which I copied *verbatim* from the register of a hotel in a certain Italian city:

"John P. Whitcomb, *Etats Unis.*

"Wm. L. Ainsworth, *travailleur* (he meant traveler, I suppose,) *Etats Unis.*

"George P. Morton *et fils, d'Amerique.*

"Lloyd B. Williams, *et trois amis, ville de* Boston, *Amerique.*

"J. Ellsworth Baker, *tout de suite de France, place de naissance Amerique, destination la Grand Bretagne.*"

I love this sort of people. A lady passenger of ours tells of a fellow-citizen of hers who spent eight weeks in Paris and then returned home and addressed his dearest old bosom friend Herbert as Mr. "Er-bare!" He apologized, though, and said, "'Pon my soul it is aggravating, but I cahn't help it —I have got so used to speaking nothing but French, my dear Erbare—damme there it goes again!—got so used to French pronunciation that I cahn't get rid of it—it is positively annoying, I assure you." This entertaining idiot, whose name was Gordon, allowed himself to be hailed three times in the street before he paid any attention, and then begged a thousand pardons and said he had grown so accustomed to hearing himself addressed as M'sieu Gor-r-*dong*," with a roll to the r,

that he had forgotten the legitimate sound of his name! He wore a rose in his button-hole; he gave the French salutation—two flips of the hand in front of the face; he called Paris *Pair-ree* in ordinary English conversation; he carried envelopes bearing foreign postmarks protruding from his breast-pocket; he cultivated a moustache and imperial, and did what else he could to suggest to the beholder his pet fancy that he resembled Louis Napoleon— and in a spirit of thankfulness which is entirely unaccountable, considering the slim foundation there was for it, he praised his Maker that he was *as* he

M'SIEU GOR-R-DONG.

was, and went on enjoying his little life just the same as if he really *had* been deliberately designed and erected by the great Architect of the Universe.

Think of our Whitcombs, and our Ainsworths and our Williamses writing themselves down in dilapidated French in foreign hotel registers! We laugh at Englishmen, when we are at home, for sticking so sturdily to their national ways and customs, but we look back upon it from abroad very forgivingly. It is not pleasant to see an American thrusting his nationality forward *obtrusively* in a foreign land, but Oh, it is pitiable to see him making of himself a thing that is neither male nor female, neither fish, flesh, nor fowl—a poor, miserable, hermaphrodite Frenchman!

Among a long list of churches, art galleries, and such things, visited by us in Venice, I shall mention only one—the church of Santa Maria dei Frari. It is about five hundred years old, I believe, and stands on twelve hundred thousand piles. In it lie the body of Canova and the heart of Titian, under magnificent monuments. Titian died at the age of almost one hundred years. A plague which swept away fifty thousand lives was raging at the time, and there is notable evidence of the reverence in which the great painter was held, in the fact that to him alone the state permitted a public funeral in all that season of terror and death.

In this church, also, is a monument to the doge Foscari, whose name a once resident of Venice, Lord Byron, has made permanently famous.

The monument to the doge Giovanni Pesaro, in this church, is a curiosity in the way of mortuary adornment. It is eighty feet high and is fronted like some fantastic pagan temple. Against it stand four colossal Nubians, as black as night, dressed in white marble garments. The black legs are bare, and through rents in sleeves and breeches, the skin, of shiny black marble, shows. The artist was as ingenious as his funeral designs were absurd. There are two bronze skeletons bearing scrolls, and two great dragons uphold the sarcophagus. On high, amid all this grotesqueness, sits the departed doge.

In the conventual buildings attached to this church are the state archives of Venice. We did not see them, but they are said to number millions of documents. "They are the records of centuries of the most watchful, observant and suspicious government that ever existed—in which every thing was written down and nothing spoken out." They fill nearly three hundred rooms. Among them are manuscripts from the archives of nearly two thousand families, monasteries and convents. The secret history of Venice for a thousand years is here—its plots, its hidden trials, its assassinations, its commissions of hireling spies and masked bravoes—food, ready to hand, for a world of dark and mysterious romances.

Yes, I think we have seen all of Venice. We have seen, in these old churches, a profusion of costly and elaborate

sepulchre ornamentation such as we never dreampt of before. We have stood in the dim religious light of these hoary sanctuaries, in the midst of long ranks of dusty monuments and effigies of the great dead of Venice, until we seemed drifting back, back, back, into the solemn past, and looking upon the scenes and mingling with the peoples of a remote antiquity. We have been in a half-waking sort of dream all the time. I do not know how else to describe the feeling. A part of our being has remained still in the nineteenth century, while another part of it has seemed in some unaccountable way walking among the phantoms of the tenth.

MONUMENT TO THE DOGE.

We have seen famous pictures until our eyes are weary with looking at them and refuse to find interest in them any longer. And what wonder, when there are twelve hundred pictures by Palma the Younger in Venice and fifteen hundred by Tintoretto? And behold there are Titians and the works of other artists in proportion. We have seen Titian's celebrated Cain and Abel, his David and Goliah, his Abraham's Sacrifice. We have seen Tintoretto's monster picture, which is seventy-four feet long and I do not know how many feet high, and thought it a very commodious picture. We have seen pictures of martyrs enough, and saints enough, to regenerate the world. I ought not to confess it, but still, since one has no opportunity in America to acquire a critical judgment in art, and since I could not hope to become educated in it in Europe in a few short weeks, I may therefore as well acknowledge with such apologies as may be due, that to me it seemed that when I had seen one of these martyrs I had seen them all. They all have a marked family resemblance to each other, they dress alike, in coarse monkish robes and sandals, they are all bald headed, they all stand in about the same attitude, and without exception they are gazing heavenward with countenances which the Ainsworths, the Mortons and the Williamses, *et fils*, inform me are full of "expression." To me there is nothing tangible about these imaginary portraits, nothing that I can grasp and take a living interest in. If great Titian had only been gifted with prophecy, and had skipped a martyr, and gone over to England and painted a portrait of Shakspeare, even as a youth, which we could all have confidence in now, the world down to the latest generations would have forgiven him the lost martyr in the rescued seer. I think posterity could have spared one more martyr for the sake of a great historical picture of Titian's time and painted by his brush—such as Columbus returning in chains from the discovery of a world, for instance. The old masters did paint some Venetian historical pictures, and these we did not tire of looking at, notwithstanding representations of the formal introduction of defunct doges to the Virgin Mary in regions beyond the clouds clashed rather harshly with the proprieties, it seemed to us.

But humble as we are, and unpretending, in the matter of art, our researches among the painted monks and martyrs have not been wholly in vain. We have striven hard to learn. We have had some success. We have mastered some things, possibly of trifling import in the eyes of the learned, but to us they give pleasure, and we take as much pride in our little acquirements as do others who have learned far more, and we love to display them full as well.

ST. MARK, BY THE OLD MASTERS.

ST. MATTHEW, BY THE OLD MASTERS.

ST. JEROME, BY THE OLD MASTERS.

When we see a monk going about with a lion and looking tranquilly up to heaven, we know that that is St. Mark. When we see a monk with a book and a pen, looking tranquilly up to heaven, trying to think of a word, we know that that is St. Matthew. When we see a monk sitting on a rock, looking tranquilly up to heaven, with a human skull beside him, and without other baggage, we know that that is St. Jerome. Because we know that he always went flying light in the matter of baggage. When we see a party looking tranquilly up to heaven, unconscious that his body is shot through and through with arrows, we know that that is St. Sebastian. When we see other monks looking tranquilly up to heaven, but having no trade-mark, we always ask who those parties are. We do this because we humbly wish to learn. We have seen thirteen thousand St. Jeromes, and twenty-two thousand St. Marks, and sixteen thousand St. Matthews, and sixty thousand St. Sebastians, and four millions of assorted monks, undesignated, and we feel encouraged to believe that when we have seen some more of these various pictures, and had a larger experience, we shall begin to take an absorbing interest in them like our cultivated countrymen from *Amerique.*

ST. SEBASTIAN, BY THE OLD MASTERS.

Now it does give me real pain to speak in this almost unappreciative way of the old masters and their martyrs, because good friends of mine in the ship—friends who do thoroughly and conscientiously appreciate them and are in every way competent to discriminate between good pictures and inferior ones—have urged me for my own sake not to make public the fact that I lack this appreciation and this critical discrimination myself. I believe that what I have written and may still write about pictures will give them pain, and I am honestly sorry for it. I even promised that I would hide my uncouth sentiments in my own breast. But alas! I never could keep a promise. I do not blame myself for this weakness, because the fault

ST. UNKNOWN, BY THE OLD MASTERS.

must lie in my physical organization. It is likely that such a very liberal amount of space was given to the organ which enables me to *make* promises, that the organ which should enable me to keep them was crowded out. But I grieve not. I like no half-way things. I had rather have one faculty nobly developed than two faculties of mere ordinary capacity. I certainly meant to keep that promise, but I find I can not do it. It is impossible to travel through Italy without speaking of pictures, and can I see them through others' eyes?

If I did not so delight in the grand pictures that are spread before me every day of my life by that monarch of all the old masters, Nature, I should come to believe, sometimes, that I had in me no appreciation of the beautiful, whatsoever.

It seems to me that whenever I glory to think that for once I have discovered an ancient painting that is beautiful and worthy of all praise, the pleasure it gives me is an infallible proof that it is *not* a beautiful picture and not in any wise worthy of commendation. This very thing has occurred more times than I can mention, in Venice. In every single instance the guide has crushed out my swelling enthusiasm with the remark:

"It is nothing—it is of the *Renaissance*."

I did not know what in the mischief the Renaissance was, and so always I had to simply say,

"Ah! so it is—I had not observed it before."

I could not bear to be ignorant before a cultivated negro, the offspring of a South Carolina slave. But it occurred too often for even my self-complacency, did that exasperating "It is nothing—it is of the *Renaissance*." I said at last:

"*Who* is this Renaissance? Where did he come from? Who gave him permission to cram the Republic with his execrable daubs?"

We learned, then, that Renaissance was not a man; that *renaissance* was a term used to signify what was at best but an imperfect rejuvenation of art. The guide said that after Titian's time and the time of the other great names we had grown so familiar with, high art declined; then it partially rose again—an inferior sort of painters sprang up, and these shabby pictures were the work of their hands. Then I said, in my heat, that I "wished to goodness high art had declined five hundred years sooner." The Renaissance pictures suit me very well, though sooth to say its school were too much given to painting real men and did not indulge enough in martyrs.

The guide I have spoken of is the only one we have had

yet who knew any thing. He was born in South Carolina, of slave parents. They came to Venice while he was an infant. He has grown up here. He is well educated. He reads, writes, and speaks English, Italian, Spanish, and French, with perfect facility; is a worshipper of art and thoroughly conversant with it; knows the history of Venice by heart and never tires of talking of her illustrious career. He dresses better than any of us, I think, and is daintily polite. Negroes are deemed as good as white people, in Venice, and so this man feels no

RIALTO BRIDGE

BRIDGE OF SIGHS

desire to go back to his native land. His judgment is correct.

I have had another shave. I was writing in our front room this afternoon and trying hard to keep my attention on my work and refrain from looking out upon the canal. I was resisting the soft influences of the climate as well as I could, and endeavoring to overcome the desire to be indolent and happy. The boys sent for a barber. They asked me if I would be shaved. I reminded them of my tortures in Genoa, Milan, Como; of my declaration that I would suffer no more on Italian soil. I said "Not any for me, if you please."

I wrote on. The barber began on the doctor. I heard him say:

"Dan, this is the easiest shave I have had since we left the ship."

He said again, presently:

"Why Dan, a man could go to sleep with this man shaving him."

Dan took the chair. Then he said:

"Why this is Titian. This is one of the old masters."

I wrote on. Directly Dan said:

"Doctor, it is perfect luxury. The ship's barber isn't any thing to him."

My rough beard was distressing me beyond measure. The barber was rolling up his apparatus. The temptation was too strong. I said:

"Hold on, please. Shave me also."

I sat down in the chair and closed my eyes. The barber soaped my face, and then took his razor and gave me a rake that well nigh threw me into convulsions. I jumped out of the chair: Dan and the doctor were both wiping blood off their faces and laughing.

I said it was a mean, disgraceful fraud.

They said that the misery of this shave had gone so far beyond any thing they had ever experienced before, that they could not bear the idea of losing such a chance of hearing a cordial opinion from me on the subject.

It was shameful. But there was no help for it. The skinning was begun and had to be finished. The tears flowed with every rake, and so did the fervent execrations. The barber grew confused, and brought blood every time. I think the boys enjoyed it better than any thing they have seen or heard since they left home.

We have seen the Campanile, and Byron's house and Balbi's the geographer, and the palaces of all the ancient dukes and doges of Venice, and we have seen their effeminate descendants airing their nobility in fashionable French attire in the Grand Square of St. Mark, and eating ices and drinking cheap wines, instead of wearing gallant coats of mail and destroying fleets and armies as their great ancestors did in the days of Venetian glory. We have seen no bravoes with poisoned stilettos, no masks, no wild carnival; but we have seen the ancient pride of Venice, the grim Bronze Horses that figure in a thousand legends. Venice may well cherish them, for they are the only horses she ever had. It is said there are hundreds of people in this curious city who never have seen a living horse in their lives. It is entirely true, no doubt.

And so, having satisfied ourselves, we depart to-morrow, and leave the venerable Queen of the Republics to summon her vanished ships, and marshal her shadowy armies, and know again in dreams the pride of her old renown.

CHAPTER XXIV.

SOME of the Quaker City's passengers had arrived in Venice from Switzerland and other lands before we left there, and others were expected every day. We heard of no casualties among them, and no sickness.

We were a little fatigued with sight seeing, and so we rattled through a good deal of country by rail without caring to stop. I took few notes. I find no mention of Bologna in my memorandum book, except that we arrived there in good season, but saw none of the sausages for which the place is so justly celebrated.

Pistoia awoke but a passing interest.

Florence pleased us for a while. I think we appreciated the great figure of David in the grand square, and the sculptured group they call the Rape of the Sabines. We wandered through the endless collections of paintings and statues of the Pitti and Ufizzi galleries, of course. I make that statement in self-defense; there let it stop. I could not rest under the imputation that I visited Florence and did not traverse its weary miles of picture galleries. We tried indolently to recollect something about the Guelphs and Ghibelines and the other historical cut-throats whose quarrels and assassinations make up so large a share of Florentine history, but the subject was not attractive. We had been robbed of all the fine mountain scenery on our little journey by a system of railroading that had three miles of tunnel to a hundred yards of daylight, and we were not inclined to be sociable with Florence. We had seen the spot, outside the city somewhere, where these people had allowed the bones of Galileo to rest in unconsecrated ground for an age because his great discovery that the world turned around was regarded as a damning heresy by the church; and we know that long after the world had accepted his theory and raised his name high in the list of its great men, they had still let him rot there. That we had lived to see his dust in honored sepulture in the church of Santa Croce we owed to a society of *literati*, and not to Florence or her rulers. We saw Danté's tomb in that church, also, but we were glad to know that his body was not in it; that the ungrateful city that had exiled him and persecuted him would give much to have it there, but need not hope to ever secure that high honor to herself. Medicis are good enough for Florence. Let her plant Medicis and build grand monuments over them to testify how gratefully she was wont to lick the hand that scourged her.

FLORENCE.

Magnanimous Florence! Her jewelry marts are filled with artists in mosaic. Florentine mosaics are the choicest in all the world. Florence loves to have that said. Florence is proud of it. Florence would foster this specialty of hers. She is grateful to the artists that bring to her this high credit and fill her coffers with foreign money, and so she encourages them with pensions. With pensions! Think of the lavish-

THE PENSIONER.

ness of it. She knows that people who piece together the beautiful trifles die early, because the labor is so confining, and so ex- hausting to hand and brain, and so she has decreed that all these people who reach the age of sixty shall have a pension after that! I have not heard that any of them have called for their dividends yet. One man did fight along till he was sixty, and started after his pension, but it appeared that there had been a mis- take of a year in his fam- ily record, and so he gave it up and died.

These artists will take particles of stone or glass no larger than a mustard seed, and piece them together on a sleeve but- ton or a shirt stud, so smoothly and with such nice adjust- ment of the delicate shades of color the pieces bear, as to form a pigmy rose with stem, thorn, leaves, petals complete, and all as softly and as truthfully tinted as though Nature had builded it herself. They will counterfeit a fly, or a high- toned bug, or the ruined Coliseum, within the cramped circle of a breastpin, and do it so deftly and so neatly that any man might think a master painted it.

I saw a little table in the great mosaic school in Florence— a little trifle of a centre table—whose top was made of some sort of precious polished stone, and in the stone was inlaid the figure of a flute, with bell-mouth and a mazy complication of keys. No painting in the world could have been softer or richer; no shading out of one tint into another could have been more perfect; no work of art of any kind could have been more faultless than this flute, and yet to count the multitude of little fragments of stone of which they swore it was formed would bankrupt any man's arithmetic! I do not think one could have seen where two particles joined each other with eyes of ordinary shrewdness. Certainly *we* could detect no such blemish. This table-top cost the labor of one man for ten long years, so they said, and it was for sale for thirty-five thousand dollars.

We went to the Church of Santa Croce, from time to time, in Florence, to weep over the tombs of Michael Angelo, Raphael and Machiavelli, (I suppose they are buried there, but it may be that they reside elsewhere and rent their tombs to other parties—such being the fashion in Italy,) and between times we used to go and stand on the bridges and admire the Arno. It is popular to admire the Arno. It is a great historical creek with four feet in the channel and some scows floating around. It would be a very plausible river if they would pump some water into it. They all call it a river, and they honestly think it *is* a river, do these dark and bloody Florentines. They even help out the delusion by building bridges over it. I do not see why they are too good to wade.

How the fatigues and annoyances of travel fill one with bitter prejudices sometimes! I might enter Florence under happier auspices a month hence and find it all beautiful, all attractive. But I do not care to think of it now, at all, nor of its roomy shops filled to the ceiling with snowy marble and alabaster copies of all the celebrated sculptures in Europe— copies so enchanting to the eye that I wonder how they can really be shaped like the dingy petrified nightmares they are the portraits of. I got lost in Florence at nine o'clock, one night, and staid lost in that labyrinth of narrow streets and long rows of vast buildings that look all alike, until toward

three o'clock in the morning. It was a pleasant night and at
first there were a good many people abroad, and there were
cheerful lights about.   Later, I grew accustomed to prowling
about mysterious drifts and tunnels and astonishing and interesting myself with coming around corners expecting to find
the hotel staring me in the face, and not finding it doing any
thing of the kind.   Later still, I felt tired.   I soon felt remarkably tired.   But there was no one abroad, now—not even
a policeman.   I walked till I was out of all patience, and very
hot and thirsty.   At last, somewhere after one o'clock, I
came unexpectedly to one of the city gates.   I knew then that
I was very far from the hotel.   The soldiers thought I wanted
to leave the city, and they sprang up and barred the way with
their muskets.   I said :

I WANT TO GO HOME.

" Hotel d'Europe !"
It was all the Italian I knew, and I was not certain whether
that was Italian or French.   The soldiers looked stupidly at

each other and at me, and shook their heads and took me into custody. I said I wanted to go home. They did not understand me. They took me into the guard-house and searched me, but they found no sedition on me. They found a small piece of soap (we carry soap with us, now,) and I made them a present of it, seeing that they regarded it as a curiosity. I continued to say Hotel d'Europe, and they continued to shake their heads, until at last a young soldier nodding in the corner roused up and said something. He said he knew where the hotel was, I suppose, for the officer of the guard sent him away with me. We walked a hundred or a hundred and fifty miles, it appeared to me, and then *he* got lost. He turned this way and that, and finally gave it up and signified that he was going to spend the remainder of the morning trying to find the city gate again. At that moment it struck me that there was something familiar about the house over the way. It was the hotel!

It was a happy thing for me that there happened to be a soldier there that knew even as much as he did; for they say that the policy of the government is to change the soldiery from one place to another constantly and from country to city, so that they can not become acquainted with the people and grow lax in their duties and enter into plots and conspiracies with friends. My experiences of Florence were chiefly unpleasant. I will change the subject.

At Pisa we climbed up to the top of the strangest structure the world has any knowledge of—the Leaning Tower. As every one knows, it is in the neighborhood of one hundred and eighty feet high—and I beg to observe that one hundred and eighty feet reach to about the hight of four ordinary three-story buildings piled one on top of the other, and is a very considerable altitude for a tower of uniform thickness to aspire to, even when it stands upright—yet this one leans more than thirteen feet out of the perpendicular. It is seven hundred years old, but neither history or tradition say whether it was built as it is, purposely, or whether one of its sides has settled. There is no record that it ever stood straight up. It is built of marble. It is an airy and a beautiful structure, and each of its eight stories is encircled by fluted columns, some of

LEANING TOWER.

marble and some of granite, with Corinthian capitals that were handsome when they were new. It is a bell tower, and in its top hangs a chime of ancient bells. The winding staircase within is dark, but one always knows which side of the tower he is on because of his naturally gravitating from one side to the other of the staircase with the rise or dip of the tower. Some of the stone steps are foot-worn only on one end; others only on the other end; others only in the middle. To look down into the tower from the top is like looking down into a tilted well. A rope that hangs from the centre of the top touches the wall before it reaches the bottom. Standing on the summit, one does not feel altogether comfortable when he looks down from the high side; but to crawl on your breast to the verge on the lower side and try to stretch your neck out far enough to see the base of the tower, makes your flesh creep, and convinces you for a single moment in spite of all your philosophy, that the building is falling. You handle yourself very carefully, all the time, under the silly impression that if it is *not* falling, your trifling weight will start it unless you are particular not to "bear down" on it.

The Duomo, close at hand, is one of the finest cathedrals in Europe. It is eight hundred years old. Its grandeur has outlived the high commercial prosperity and the political importance that made it a necessity, or rather a possibility. Surrounded by poverty, decay and ruin, it conveys to us a more tangible impression of the former greatness of Pisa than books could give us.

The Baptistery, which is a few years older than the Leaning Tower, is a stately rotunda, of huge dimensions, and was a costly structure. In it hangs the lamp whose measured swing suggested to Galileo the pendulum. It looked an insignificant thing to have conferred upon the world of science and mechanics such a mighty extension of their dominions as it has. Pondering, in its suggestive presence, I seemed to see a crazy universe of swinging disks, the toiling children of this sedate parent. He appeared to have an intelligent expression about him of knowing that he was not a lamp at all; that he was a Pendulum; a pendulum disguised, for prodigious and inscrutable purposes of his own deep devising, and not a common pendulum either, but the old original patriarchal Pendulum—the Abraham Pendulum of the world.

This Baptistery is endowed with the most pleasing echo of all the echoes we have read of. The guide sounded two sonorous notes, about half an octave apart; the echo answered with the most enchanting, the most melodious, the richest blending of sweet sounds that one can imagine. It was like a long-drawn chord of a church organ, infinitely softened by distance. I may be extravagant in this matter, but if this be the case my ear is to blame—not my pen. I am describing a memory—and one that will remain long with me.

The peculiar devotional spirit of the olden time, which placed a higher confidence in outward forms of worship than in the watchful guarding of the heart against sinful thoughts and the hands against sinful deeds, and which believed in the protecting virtues of inanimate objects made holy by contact with holy things, is illustrated in a striking manner in one of the cemeteries of Pisa. The tombs are set in soil brought in ships from the Holy Land ages ago. To be buried in such ground was regarded by the ancient Pisans as being more potent for salvation than many masses purchased of the church and the vowing of many candles to the Virgin.

Pisa is believed to be about three thousand years old. It was one of the twelve great cities of ancient Etruria, that commonwealth which has left so many monuments in testimony of its extraordinary advancement, and so little history of itself that is tangible and comprehensible. A Pisan antiquarian gave me an ancient tear-jug which he averred was full four thousand years old. It was found among the ruins of one of the oldest of the Etruscan cities. He said it came from a tomb, and was used by some bereaved family in that remote age when even the Pyramids of Egypt were young, Damascus a village, Abraham a prattling infant and ancient Troy not yet dreampt of, to receive the tears wept for some lost idol of a household. It spoke to us in a language of its own; and with a pathos more tender than any words might bring, its mute eloquence swept down the long roll of the centuries with its tale of a vacant chair, a familiar footstep missed from the threshold, a pleasant voice gone from the chorus, a vanished form!—a tale which is always so new to us, so startling, so terrible, so benumbing to the senses, and behold how threadbare and old it is! No shrewdly-worded history could have brought the myths and shadows of that old dreary age before us clothed with human flesh and warmed with human sympathies so vividly as did this poor little unsentient vessel of pottery.

Pisa was a republic in the middle ages, with a government of her own, armies and navies of her own and a great commerce.   She was a warlike power, and inscribed upon her banners many a brilliant fight with Genoese and Turks.   It is said that the city once numbered a population of four hundred thousand ; but her sceptre has passed from her grasp, now, her ships and her armies are gone, her commerce is dead. Her battle-flags bear the mold and the dust of centuries, her marts are deserted, she has shrunken far within her crumbling walls, and her great population has diminished to twenty thousand souls.   She has but one thing left to boast of, and that is not much, viz: she is the second city of Tuscany.

We reached Leghorn in time to see all we wished to see of it long before the city gates were closed for the evening, and then came on board the ship.

We felt as though we had been away from home an age.   We never entirely appreciated, before, what a very pleasant den our state-room is ; nor how jolly it is to sit at dinner in one's own seat in one's own cabin, and hold familiar conversation with friends in one's own language.   Oh, the rare happiness of comprehending every single word that is said, and knowing that every word one says in return will be understood as well! We would talk ourselves to death, now, only there are only about ten passengers out of the sixty-five to talk to.   The others are wandering, we hardly know where.   We shall not go ashore in Leghorn.   We are surfeited with Italian cities for the present, and much prefer to walk the familiar quarter-deck and view this one from a distance.

The stupid magnates of this Leghorn government can not understand that so large a steamer as ours could cross the broad Atlantic with no other purpose than to indulge a party of ladies and gentlemen in a pleasure excursion.   It looks too improbable.   It is suspicious, they think.   Something more important must be hidden behind it all.   They can not understand it, and they scorn the evidence of the ship's papers. They have decided at last that we are a battalion of incendiary, blood-thirsty Garibaldians in disguise! And in all seriousness they have set a gun-boat to watch the vessel night and day, with orders to close down on any revolutionary movement in a twinkling! Police boats are on patrol duty about us all the time, and it is as much as a sailor's liberty is worth to show himself in a red shirt. These policemen follow the executive officer's boat from shore to ship and from ship to shore and watch his dark maneuvres with a vigilant eye. They will arrest him yet unless he assumes an expression of countenance that shall have less of carnage, insurrection and sedition in it. A visit paid in a friendly way to General Garibaldi yesterday (by cordial invitation,) by some of our passengers, has gone far to confirm the dread suspicions the government harbors toward us. It is thought the friendly visit was only the cloak of a bloody conspiracy. These people draw near and watch us when we bathe in the sea from the ship's side. Do they think we are communing with a reserve force of rascals at the bottom?

It is said that we shall probably be quarantined at Naples. Two or three of us prefer not to run this risk. Therefore, when we are rested, we propose to go in a French steamer to Civita Vecchia, and from thence to Rome, and by rail to Naples. They do not quarantine the cars, no matter where they got their passengers from.

CHAPTER XXV.

THERE are a good many things about this Italy which I do not understand—and more especially I can not understand how a bankrupt Government can have such palatial railroad depots and such marvels of turnpikes. Why, these latter are as hard as adamant, as straight as a line, as smooth as a floor, and as white as snow. When it is too dark to see any other object, one can still see the white turnpikes of France and Italy; and they are clean enough to eat from, without a table-cloth. And yet no tolls are charged.

As for the railways—we have none like them. The cars slide as smoothly along as if they were on runners. The depots are vast palaces of cut marble, with stately colonnades of the same royal stone traversing them from end to end, and with ample walls and ceilings richly decorated with frescoes. The lofty gateways are graced with statues, and the broad floors are all laid in polished flags of marble.

These things win me more than Italy's hundred galleries of priceless art treasures, because I can understand the one and am not competent to appreciate the other. In the turnpikes, the railways, the depots, and the new boulevards of uniform houses in Florence and other cities here, I see the genius of Louis Napoleon, or rather, I see the works of that statesman imitated. But Louis has taken care that in France there shall be a foundation for these improvements—money. He has always the wherewithal to back up his projects; they strengthen France and never weaken her. Her material prosperity is genuine. But here the case is different. This country is bankrupt. There is no real foundation for these great works. The prosperity they would seem to indicate is a pretence. There is no money in the treasury, and so they enfeeble her instead of strengthening. Italy has achieved the dearest wish of her heart and become an independent State—and in so doing she has drawn an elephant in the political lottery. She has nothing to feed it on. Inexperienced in government, she plunged into all manner of useless expenditure, and swamped her treasury almost in a day. She squandered millions of francs on a navy which she did not need, and the first time she took her new toy into action she got it knocked higher than Gilderoy's kite—to use the language of the Pilgrims.

But it is an ill-wind that blows nobody good. A year ago, when Italy saw utter ruin staring her in the face and her greenbacks hardly worth the paper they were printed on, her Parliament ventured upon a *coup de main* that would have appalled the stoutest of her statesmen under less desperate circumstances. They, in a manner, confiscated the domains of the Church! This in priest-ridden Italy! This in a land which has groped in the midnight of priestly superstition for sixteen hundred years! It was a rare good fortune for Italy, the stress of weather that drove her to break from this prison-house.

They do not call it *confiscating* the church property. That would sound too harshly yet. But it amounts to that. There are thousands of churches in Italy, each with untold millions of treasures stored away in its closets, and each with its battalion of priests to be supported. And then there are the estates of the Church—league on league of the richest lands and the noblest forests in all Italy—all yielding immense revenues to the Church, and none paying a cent in taxes to the State. In some great districts the Church owns *all* the property—lands, watercourses, woods, mills and factories. They buy, they sell, they manufacture, and since they pay no taxes, who can hope to compete with them?

Well, the Government has seized all this in effect, and will yet seize it in rigid and unpoetical reality, no doubt. Something must be done to feed a starving treasury, and there is no other resource in all Italy—none but the riches of the Church. So the Government intends to take to itself a great portion of the revenues arising from priestly farms, factories, etc., and also intends to take possession of the churches and carry them on, after its own fashion and upon its own responsibility. In a few instances it will leave the establishments of great pet churches undisturbed, but in all others only a handful of priests will be retained to preach and pray, a few will be pensioned, and the balance turned adrift.

Pray glance at some of these churches and their embellishments, and see whether the Government is doing a righteous thing or not. In Venice, to-day, a city of a hundred thousand inhabitants, there are twelve hundred priests. Heaven only knows how many there were before the Parliament reduced their numbers. There was the great Jesuit Church. Under the old regime it required sixty priests to engineer it—the Government does it with five, now, and the others are discharged from service. All about that church wretchedness and poverty abound. At its door a dozen hats and bonnets were doffed to us, as many heads were humbly bowed, and as many hands extended, appealing for pennies—appealing with foreign words we could not understand, but appealing mutely, with sad eyes, and sunken cheeks, and ragged raiment, that no words were needed to translate. Then we passed within the great doors, and it seemed that the riches of the world were before us! Huge columns carved out of single masses of marble, and inlaid from top to bottom with a hundred intricate figures wrought in costly verde antique; pulpits of the same rich materials, whose draperies hung down in many a pictured fold, the stony fabric counterfeiting the delicate work of the loom; the grand altar brilliant with polished facings and balustrades of oriental agate, jasper, verde antique, and other precious stones, whose names, even, we seldom hear—and slabs of priceless lapis lazuli lavished every where as recklessly as if the church had owned a quarry of it. In the midst of all this magnificence, the solid gold and silver furniture of the altar seemed cheap and trivial. Even the floors and ceilings cost a princely fortune.

Now, where is the use of allowing all those riches to lie idle, while half of that community hardly know, from day to day, how they are going to keep body and soul together? And, where is the wisdom in permitting hundreds upon hundreds of millions of francs to be locked up in the useless trumpery of churches all over Italy, and the people ground to death with taxation to uphold a perishing Government?

As far as I can see, Italy, for fifteen hundred years, has turned all her energies, all her finances, and all her industry to the building up of a vast array of wonderful church edifices, and starving half her citizens to accomplish it. She is to-day one vast museum of magnificence and misery. All the churches in an ordinary American city put together could hardly buy the jeweled frippery in one of her hundred cathedrals. And for every beggar in America, Italy can show a

THE CONTRAST.

hundred—and rags and vermin to match. It is the wretchedest, princeliest land on earth.

Look at the grand Duomo of Florence—a vast pile that has

been sapping the purses of her citizens for five hundred years, and is not nearly finished yet. Like all other men, I fell down and worshipped it, but when the filthy beggars swarmed around me the contrast was too striking, too suggestive, and I said, " O, sons of classic Italy, *is* the spirit of enterprise, of self-reliance, of noble endeavor, utterly dead within ye ? Curse your indolent worthlessness, why don't you rob your church ?"

Three hundred happy, comfortable priests are employed in that Cathedral.

And now that my temper is up, I may as well go on and abuse every body I can think of. They have a grand mausoleum in Florence, which they built to bury our Lord and Saviour and the Medici family in. It sounds blasphemous, but it is true, and here they *act* blasphemy. The dead and damned Medicis who cruelly tyrannized over Florence and were her curse for over two hundred years, are salted away in a circle of costly vaults, and in their midst the Holy Sepulchre was to have been set up. The expedition sent to Jerusalem to seize it got into trouble and could not accomplish the burglary, and so the centre of the mausoleum is vacant now. They say the entire mausoleum was intended for the Holy Sepulchre, and was only turned into a family burying place after the Jerusalem expedition failed—but you will excuse me. Some of those Medicis would have smuggled themselves in sure.— What *they* had not the effrontery to do, was not worth doing. Why, they had their trivial, forgotten exploits on land and sea pictured out in grand frescoes (as did also the ancient Doges of Venice) with the Saviour and the Virgin throwing bouquets to them out of the clouds, and the Deity himself applauding from his throne in Heaven ! And who painted these things ? Why, Titian, Tintoretto, Paul Veronese, Raphael—none other than the world's idols, the " old masters."

Andrea del Sarto glorified his princes in pictures that must save them for ever from the oblivion they merited, and they let him starve. Served him right. Raphael pictured such infernal villains as Catherine and Marie de Medicis seated in heaven and conversing familiarly with the Virgin Mary and the angels, (to say nothing of higher personages,) and yet my friends abuse me because I am a little prejudiced against the old masters—because I fail sometimes to see the beauty that is in their productions. I can not help but see it, now and then, but I keep on protesting against the groveling spirit that could persuade those masters to prostitute their noble talents to the adulation of such monsters as the French, Venetian and Florentine Princes of two and three hundred years ago, all the same.

I am told that the old masters had to do these shameful things for bread, the princes and potentates being the only patrons of art. If a grandly gifted man may drag his pride and his manhood in the dirt for bread rather than starve with the nobility that is in him untainted, the excuse is a valid one. It would excuse theft in Washingtons and Wellingtons, and unchastity in women as well.

But somehow, I can not keep that Medici mausoleum out of my memory. It is as large as a church; its pavement is rich enough for the pavement of a King's palace; its great dome is gorgeous with frescoes; its walls are made of—what? Marble?—plaster?—wood?—paper? No. Red porphyry—verde antique—jasper—oriental agate—alabaster—mother-of-pearl—chalcedony—red coral—lapis lazuli! All the vast walls are made wholly of these precious stones, worked in, and in and in together in elaborate patterns and figures, and polished till they glow like great mirrors with the pictured splendors reflected from the dome overhead. And before a statue of one of those dead Medicis reposes a crown that blazes with diamonds and emeralds enough to buy a ship-of-the-line, almost. These are the things the Government has its evil eye upon, and a happy thing it will be for Italy when they melt away in the public treasury.

And now—. However, another beggar approaches. I will go out and destroy him, and then come back and write another chapter of vituperation.

Having eaten the friendless orphan—having driven away his

comrades—having grown calm and reflective at length—I now feel in a kindlier mood. I feel that after talking so freely about the priests and the churches, justice demands that if I know any thing good about either I ought to say it. I *have* heard of many things that redound to the credit of the priesthood, but the most notable matter that occurs to me now is the devotion one of the mendicant orders showed during the prevalence of the cholera last year. I speak of the Dominican friars—men who wear a coarse, heavy brown robe and a cowl, in this hot climate, and go barefoot. They live on alms altogether, I believe. They must unquestionably love their religion, to suffer so much for it. When the cholera was raging in Naples; when the people were dying by hundreds and hundreds every day; when every concern for the public welfare was swallowed up in selfish private interest, and every citizen made the taking care of himself his sole object, these men banded themselves together and went about nursing the sick and burying the dead. Their noble efforts cost many of them their lives. They laid them down cheerfully, and well they might. Creeds mathematically precise, and hair-splitting niceties of doctrine, are absolutely necessary for the salvation of some kinds of souls, but surely the charity, the purity, the unselfishness that are in the hearts of men like these would save their souls though they were bankrupt in the true religion —which is ours.

One of these fat bare-footed rascals came here to Civita Vecchia with us in the little French steamer. There were only half a dozen of us in the cabin. He belonged in the steerage. He was the life of the ship, the bloody-minded son of the Inquisition! He and the leader of the marine band of a French man-of-war played on the piano and sang opera turn about; they sang duets together; they rigged impromptu theatrical costumes and gave us extravagant farces and pantomimes. We got along first-rate with the friar, and were excessively conversational, albeit he could not understand what we said, and certainly he never uttered a word that we could guess the meaning of.

This Civita Vecchia is the finest nest of dirt, vermin and ignorance we have found yet, except that African perdition they call Tangier, which is just like it.   The people here live in alleys two yards wide, which have a smell about them which is peculiar but not entertaining.   It is well the alleys are not wider, because they hold as much smell now as a person can stand, and of course, if they were wider they would hold more, and then the people would die.   These alleys are paved with stone, and carpeted with deceased cats, and decayed rags, and decomposed vegetable-tops, and remnants of old boots, all soaked with dish-water, and the people sit around on stools and enjoy it.   They are indolent, as a general thing, and yet have few pastimes.   They work two or three hours at a time, but not hard, and then they knock off and catch flies.   This does not require any talent, because they only have to grab—if they do not get the one they are after, they get another.   It is all the same to them.   They have no partialities.   Whichever one they get is the one they want.

They have other kinds of insects, but it does not make them arrogant.   They are very quiet, unpretending people.   They have more of these kind of things than other communities, but they do not boast.

They are very uncleanly—these people—in face, in person and dress.   When they see any body with a clean shirt on, it arouses their scorn.   The women wash clothes, half the day, at the public tanks in the streets, but they are probably somebody else's.   Or may be they keep one set to wear and another to wash; because they never put on any that have ever been washed.   When they get done washing, they sit in the alleys and nurse their cubs.   They nurse one ash-cat at a time, and the others scratch their backs against the door-post and are happy.

All this country belongs to the Papal States.   They do not appear to have any schools here, and only one billiard table.   Their education is at a very low stage.   One portion of the men go into the military, another into the priesthood, and the rest into the shoe-making business.

They keep up the passport system here, but so they do in Turkey. This shows that the Papal States are as far advanced as Turkey. This fact will be alone sufficient to silence the

ITALIAN PASTIMES.

tongues of malignant calumniators. I had to get my passport *vised* for Rome in Florence, and then they would not let me come ashore here until a policeman had examined it on the wharf and sent me a permit. They did not even dare to let me take my passport in my hands for twelve hours, I looked so formidable. They judged it best to let me cool down. They thought I wanted to take the town, likely. Little did they know me. I wouldn't have it. They examined my baggage at the depot. They took one of my ablest jokes and read it over carefully twice and then read it backwards. But it was too deep for them. They passed it around, and every body speculated on it awhile, but it mastered them all.

It was no common joke. At length a veteran officer spelled it over deliberately and shook his head three or four times and said that in his opinion it was seditious. That was the first time I felt alarmed. I immediately said I would explain the document, and they crowded around. And so I explained and explained and explained, and they took notes of all I said, but the more I explained the more they could not understand it, and when they desisted at last, I could not even understand it myself.

INCENDIARY DOCUMENT.

They said they believed it was an incendiary document, leveled at the government. I declared solemnly that it was not, but they only shook their heads and would not be satisfied. Then they consulted a good while; and finally they confiscated it. I was very sorry for this, because I had worked a long time on that joke, and took a good deal of pride in it, and now I suppose I shall never see it any more. I suppose it will be sent up and filed away among the criminal archives of Rome, and will always be regarded as a mysterious infernal machine which would have blown up like a mine and scattered the good Pope all around, but for a miraculous providential interference. And I suppose that all the time I am in Rome the police will dog me about from place to place because they think I am a dangerous character.

It is fearfully hot in Civita Vecchia. The streets are made very narrow and the houses built very solid and heavy and high, as a protection against the heat. This is the first Italian town I have seen which does not appear to have a patron saint. I suppose no saint but the one that went up in the chariot of fire could stand the climate.

There is nothing here to see. They have not even a cathedral, with eleven tons of solid silver archbishops in the back room; and they do not show you any moldy buildings that are seven thousand years old; nor any smoke-dried old fire-screens which are *chef d'œuvres* of Reubens or Simpson, or Titian or Ferguson, or any of those parties; and they haven't any bottled fragments of saints, and not even a nail from the true cross. We are going to Rome. There is nothing to see here.

CHAPTER XXVI.

WHAT is it that confers the noblest delight? What is that which swells a man's breast with pride above that which any other experience can bring to him? Discovery! To know that you are walking where none others have walked; that you are beholding what human eye has not seen before; that you are breathing a virgin atmosphere. To give birth to an idea—to discover a great thought—an intellectual nugget, right under the dust of a field that many a brain-plow had gone over before. To find a new planet, to invent a new hinge, to find the way to make the lightnings carry your messages. To be the *first*—that is the idea. To do something, say something, see something, before *any body* else— these are the things that confer a pleasure compared with which other pleasures are tame and commonplace, other ecstasies cheap and trivial. Morse, with his first message, brought by his servant, the lightning; Fulton, in that long-drawn century of suspense, when he placed his hand upon the throttle-valve and lo, the steamboat moved; Jenner, when his patient with the cow's virus in his blood, walked through the small-pox hospitals unscathed; Howe, when the idea shot through his brain that for a hundred and twenty generations the eye had been bored through the wrong end of the needle; the nameless lord of art who laid down his chisel in some old age that is forgotten, now, and gloated upon the finished Laocoon; Daguerre, when he commanded the sun, riding in the zenith, to print the landscape upon his insignificant silvered plate, and he obeyed; Columbus, in the Pinta's shrouds, when he swung his hat above a fabled sea and gazed abroad upon an unknown world! These are the men who have really *lived*—who have actually comprehended what pleasure is—who have crowded long lifetimes of ecstasy into a single moment.

What is there in Rome for me to see that others have not seen before me? What is there for me to touch that others have not touched? What is there for me to feel, to learn, to hear, to know, that shall thrill me before it pass to others? What can I discover?—Nothing. Nothing whatsoever. One charm of travel dies here. But if I were only a Roman!—If, added to my own I could be gifted with modern Roman sloth, modern Roman superstition, and modern Roman boundlessness of ignorance, what bewildering worlds of unsuspected wonders I would discover! Ah, if I were only a habitant of the Campagna five and twenty miles from Rome! *Then* I would travel.

A ROMAN OF 1869.

I would go to America, and see, and learn, and return to the Campagna and stand before my countrymen an illustrious discoverer. I would say:

"I saw there a country which has no overshadowing Mother Church, and yet the people survive. I saw a government which never was protected by foreign soldiers at a cost greater than that required to carry on the government itself. I saw common men and common women who could read; I even saw small children of common country people reading from books; if I dared think you would believe it, I would say they could write, also. In the cities I saw people drinking a delicious beverage made of chalk and water, but never once saw goats driven through their Broadway or their Pennsylvania Avenue or their Montgomery street and milked at the doors of the houses. I saw real glass windows in the houses of even the commonest people. Some of the houses are not of stone, nor yet of bricks; I solemnly swear they are made of wood. Houses there will take fire and burn, sometimes—actually burn entirely down, and not leave a single vestige behind. I could state that for a truth, upon my death-bed. And as a proof that the circumstance is not rare, I aver that they have a thing which they call a fire-engine, which vomits forth great streams of water, and is kept always in readiness, by night and by day, to rush to houses that are burning. You would think one engine would be sufficient, but some great cities have a hundred; they keep men hired, and pay them by the month to do nothing but put out fires. For a certain sum of money other men will insure that your house shall not burn down; and if it burns they will pay you for it. There are hundreds and thousands of schools, and any body may go and learn to be wise, like a priest. In that singular country if a rich man dies a sinner, he is damned; he can not buy salvation with money for masses. There is really not much use in being rich, there. Not much use as far as the other world is concerned, but much, very much use, as concerns this; because there, if a man be rich, he is very greatly honored, and can become a legislator, a governor, a general, a senator, no matter how ignorant an ass he is— just as in our beloved Italy the nobles hold all the great places, even though sometimes they are born noble idiots. There, if a man be rich, they give him costly presents, they ask him to feasts, they invite him to drink complicated beverages; but if he be poor and in debt, they require him to do that which they term to "settle." The women put on a different dress almost every day; the dress is usually fine, but absurd in shape; the very shape and fashion of it changes twice in a hundred years; and did I but covet to be called an extravagant falsifier, I would say it changed even oftener. Hair does not grow upon the American women's heads; it is made for them by cunning workmen in the shops, and is curled and frizzled into scandalous and ungodly forms. Some persons wear eyes of glass which they see through with facility per-

haps, else they would not use them; and in the mouths of
some are teeth made by the sacrilegious hand of man. The
dress of the men is laughably grotesque. They carry no
musket in ordinary life, nor no long-pointed pole; they wear
no wide green-lined cloak; they wear no peaked black felt
hat, no leathern gaiters reaching to the knee, no goat-skin
breeches with the hair side out, no hob-nailed shoes, no prodigious spurs. They wear a conical hat termed a "nail-kag;"
a coat of saddest black; a shirt which shows dirt so easily that
it has to be changed every month, and is very troublesome;
things called pantaloons, which are held up by shoulder
straps, and on their feet they wear boots which are ridiculous
in pattern and can stand no wear. Yet dressed in this fantastic garb, these people laughed at *my* costume. In that
country, books are so common that it is really no curiosity to
see one. Newspapers also. They have a great machine which
prints such things by thousands every hour.

"I saw common men, there—men who were neither priests
nor princes—who yet absolutely owned the land they tilled.
It was not rented from the church, nor from the nobles. I am
ready to take my oath of this. In that country you might fall
from a third story window three several times, and not mash
either a soldier or a priest.—The scarcity of such people is
astonishing. In the cities you will see a dozen civilians for
every soldier, and as many for every priest or preacher. Jews,
there, are treated just like human beings, instead of dogs.
They can work at any business they please; they can sell
brand new goods if they want to; they can keep drug-stores;
they can practice medicine among Christians; they can even
shake hands with Christians if they choose; they can associate
with them, just the same as one human being does with
another human being; they don't have to stay shut up in one
corner of the towns; they can live in any part of a town they
like best; it is said they even have the privilege of buying
land and houses, and owning them themselves, though I doubt
that, myself; they never have had to run races naked through
the public streets, against jackasses, to please the people in

carnival time; there they never have been driven by the
soldiers into a church every Sunday for hundreds of years to
hear themselves and their religion especially and particularly
cursed; at this very day, in that curious country, a Jew is
allowed to vote, hold office, yea, get up on a rostrum in the
public street and express his opinion of the government if the
government don't suit him! Ah, it is wonderful. The common people there know a great deal; they even have the
effrontery to complain if they are not properly governed, and
to take hold and help conduct the government themselves; if
they had laws like ours, which give one dollar of every three a
crop produces to the government for taxes, they would have
that law altered: instead of paying thirty-three dollars in
taxes, out of every one hundred they receive, they complain if
they have to pay seven. They are curious people. They do
not know when they are well off. Mendicant priests do not
prowl among them with baskets begging for the church and
eating up their substance. One hardly ever sees a minister of
the gospel going around there in his bare feet, with a basket,
begging for subsistence. In that country the preachers are not
like our mendicant orders of friars—they have two or three
suits of clothing, and they wash sometimes. In that land are
mountains far higher than the Alban mountains; the vast
Roman Campagna, a hundred miles long and full forty broad,
is really small compared to the United States of America; the
Tiber, that celebrated river of ours, which stretches its mighty
course almost two hundred miles, and which a lad can scarcely
throw a stone across at Rome, is not so long, nor yet so wide, as
the American Mississippi—nor yet the Ohio, nor even the Hudson. In America the people are absolutely wiser and know much
more than their grandfathers did. *They* do not plow with a sharpened stick, nor yet with a three-cornered block of wood that
merely scratches the top of the ground. We do that because
our fathers did, three thousand years ago, I suppose. But
those people have no holy reverence for their ancestors. They
plow with a plow that is a sharp, curved blade of iron, and it
cuts into the earth full five inches. And this is not all. They

cut their grain with a horrid machine that mows down whole
fields in a day. If I dared, I would say that sometimes they
use a blasphemous plow that works by fire and vapor and
tears up an acre of ground in a single hour—but—but—I see
by your looks that you do not believe the things I am telling
you. Alas, my character is ruined, and I am a branded
speaker of untruths!"

Of course we have been to the monster Church of St. Peter,
frequently. I knew its dimensions. I knew it was a prodigious
structure. I knew it was just about the length of the capitol at
Washington—say seven hundred and thirty feet. I knew it was
three hundred and sixty-four feet wide, and consequently wider
than the capitol. I knew that the cross on the top of the dome
of the church was four hundred and thirty-eight feet above the
ground, and therefore about a hundred or may be a hundred and
twenty-five feet higher than the dome of the capitol.—Thus I had
one gauge. I wished to come as near forming a correct idea of
how it was going to look, as possible ; I had a curiosity to see
how much I would err. I erred considerably. St. Peter's did
not look nearly so large as the capitol, and certainly not a
twentieth part as beautiful, from the outside.

When we reached the door, and stood fairly within the
church, it was impossible to comprehend that it was a *very*
large building. I had to *cipher* a comprehension of it. I had
to ransack my memory for some more similes. St. Peter's is
bulky. Its height and size would represent two of the Washington capitol set one on top of the other—if the capitol were
wider ; or two blocks or two blocks and a half of ordinary buildings set one on top of the other. St. Peter's *was* that large, but
it could and would not look so. The trouble was that every thing
in it and about it was on such a scale of uniform vastness that
there were no contrasts to judge by—none but the people, and
I had not noticed them. They were insects. The statues of
children holding vases of holy water were immense, according
to the tables of figures, but so was every thing else around
them. The mosaic pictures in the dome were huge, and were
made of thousands and thousands of cubes of glass as large as

the end of my little finger, but those pictures looked smooth, and gaudy of color, and in good proportion to the dome. Evidently they would not answer to measure by. Away down toward the far end of the church (I thought it was really clear at the far end, but discovered afterward that it was in the centre, under the dome,) stood the thing they call the *baldacchino*—a great bronze pyramidal frame-work like that which upholds a mosquito bar. It only looked like a considerably magnified bedstead—nothing more. Yet I knew it was a good deal more than half as high as Niagara Falls. It was overshadowed by a dome so mighty that its own height was snubbed. The four great square piers or pillars that stand equidistant from each other in the church, and support the roof, I could not work up to their real dimensions by any method of comparison. I knew that the faces of each were about the width of a very large dwelling-house front, (fifty or sixty feet,) and that they were twice as high as an ordinary three-story dwelling, but still they looked small. I tried all the different ways I could think of to compel myself to understand how large St. Peter's was, but with small success. The mosaic portrait of an Apostle who was writing with a pen six feet long seemed only an ordinary Apostle.

But the people attracted my attention after a while. To stand in the door of St. Peter's and look at men down toward its further extremity, two blocks away, has a diminishing effect on them; surrounded by the prodigious pictures and statues, and lost in the vast spaces, they look very much smaller than they would if they stood two blocks away in the open air. I "averaged" a man as he passed me and watched him as he drifted far down by the *baldacchino* and beyond—watched him dwindle to an insignificant school-boy, and then, in the midst of the silent throng of human pigmies gliding about him, I lost him. The church had lately been decorated, on the occasion of a great ceremony in honor of St. Peter, and men were engaged, now, in removing the flowers and gilt paper from the walls and pillars. As no ladders could reach the great heights, the men swung themselves down from balustrades and the capitals of pilasters by ropes, to do this work. The upper gallery which encircles the inner sweep of the dome is two hundred and forty feet above the floor of the church—very few steeples in America could reach up to it. Visitors always go up there to look down into the church because one gets the best idea of some of the heights and distances from that point. While we stood on the floor one of the workmen swung loose from that gallery at the end of a long rope. I had not supposed, before, that a man *could* look so much like a spider. He was insignificant in size, and his rope seemed only a thread. Seeing that he took up so little space, I could believe the story, then, that ten thousand troops went to St. Peter's, once, to hear mass, and their commanding officer came afterward, and not finding them, supposed they had not yet arrived. But they were in the church, nevertheless—they were in one of the transepts. Nearly fifty thousand persons assembled in St. Peter's to hear the publishing of the dogma of the Immaculate Conception. It is estimated that the floor of the church affords standing room for—for a large number of people; I have forgotten the exact figures. But it is no matter—it is near enough.

They have twelve small pillars, in St. Peter's, which came from Solomon's Temple. They have, also—which was far more interesting to me—a piece of the true cross, and some nails, and a part of the crown of thorns.

Of course we ascended to the summit of the dome, and of course we also went up into the gilt copper ball which is above it.—There was room there for a dozen persons, with a little crowding, and it was as close and hot as an oven. Some of those people who are so fond of writing their names in prominent places had been there before us—a million or two, I should think. From the dome of St. Peter's one can see every notable object in Rome, from the Castle of St. Angelo to the Coliseum. He can discern the seven hills upon which Rome is built. He can see the Tiber, and the locality of the bridge which Horatius kept "in the brave days of old" when Lars Porsena attempted to cross it with his invading host. He can see the spot where the Horatii and the Curatii fought their famous battle. He can see the broad green Campagna, stretching away toward the mountains, with its scattered arches and broken aqueducts of the olden time, so picturesque in their gray ruin, and so daintily festooned with vines. He can see the Alban Mountains, the Appenines, the Sabine Hills, and the blue Mediterranean. He can see a panorama that is varied, extensive, beautiful to the eye, and more illustrious in history than any other in Europe.—About his feet is spread the remnant of a city that once had a population of four million souls; and among its massed edifices stand the ruins of temples, columns, and triumphal arches that knew the Cæsars, and the noonday of Roman splendor; and close by them, in unimpaired strength, is a drain of arched and heavy masonry that belonged to that older city which stood here before Romulus and Remus were born or Rome thought of. The Appian Way is here yet, and looking much as it did, perhaps, when the triumphal processions of the Emperors moved over it in other days bringing fettered princes from the confines of the earth. We can not see the long array of chariots and mail-clad men laden with the spoils of conquest, but we can imagine the pageant, after a fashion. We look out upon many objects of interest from the dome of St. Peter's; and last of all, almost at our feet, our eyes rest upon the building which was once the Inquisition. How times changed, between the older ages and the new! Some seventeen or eighteen centuries ago, the ignorant men of Rome were wont to put Christians in the arena of the Coliseum yonder, and turn the wild beasts in upon them for a show. It was for a lesson as well. It was to teach the people to abhor and fear the new doctrine the followers of Christ were teaching. The beasts tore the victims limb from limb and made poor mangled corpses of them in the twinkling of an eye. But when the Christians came into power, when the holy Mother Church became mistress of the barbarians, she taught them the error of their ways by no such means. No, she put them in this pleasant Inquisition and pointed to the Blessed Redeemer, who was so gentle

and so merciful toward all men, and they urged the barbarians
to love him; and they did all they could to persuade them to
love and honor him—first by twisting their thumbs out of
joint with a screw; then by nipping their flesh with pincers—
red-hot ones, because they are the most comfortable in cold
weather; then by skinning them alive a little, and finally by
roasting them in public. They always convinced those barbarians. The true religion, properly administered, as the good
Mother Church used to administer it, is very, very soothing. It
is wonderfully persuasive, also. There is a great difference
between feeding parties to wild beasts and stirring up their
finer feelings in an Inquisition. One is the system of degraded
barbarians, the other of enlightened, civilized people. It is a
great pity the playful Inquisition is no more.

I prefer not to describe St. Peter's. It has been done
before. The ashes of Peter, the disciple of the Saviour, repose
in a crypt under the *baldacchino*. We stood reverently in that
place; so did we also in the Mamertine Prison, where he was
confined, where he converted the soldiers, and where tradition
says he caused a spring of water to flow in order that he might
baptize them. But when they showed us the print of Peter's
face in the hard stone of the prison wall and said he made that
by falling up against it, we doubted. And when, also, the
monk at the church of San Sebastian showed us a paving-stone
with two great footprints in it and said that Peter's feet made
those, we lacked confidence again. Such things do not impress
one. The monk said that angels came and liberated Peter
from prison by night, and he started away from Rome by the
Appian Way. The Saviour met him and told him to go back,
which he did. Peter left those footprints in the stone upon
which he stood at the time. It was not stated how it was ever
discovered whose footprints they were, seeing the interview
occurred secretly and at night. The print of the face in the
prison was that of a man of common size; the footprints were
those of a man ten or twelve feet high. The discrepancy confirmed our unbelief.

We necessarily visited the Forum, where Cæsar was assassi-

nated, and also the Tarpeian Rock. We saw the Dying Gladiator at the Capitol, and I think that even we appreciated that
wonder of art; as much, perhaps, as we did that fearful story

THE MAMERTINE PRISON.

wrought in marble, in the
Vatican—the Laocoon. And
then the Coliseum.

Every body knows the pic-
ture of the Coliseum; every
body recognizes at once that
" looped and windowed " band-
box with a side bitten out.
Being rather isolated, it shows
to better advantage than any other of the monuments of ancient
Rome. Even the beautiful Pantheon, whose pagan altars uphold
the cross, now, and whose Venus, tricked out in consecrated
gimcracks, does reluctant duty as a Virgin Mary to-day, is built
about with shabby houses and its stateliness sadly marred.
But the monarch of all European ruins, the Coliseum, maintains that reserve and that royal seclusion which is proper to
majesty. Weeds and flowers spring from its massy arches and
its circling seats, and vines hang their fringes from its lofty

walls. An impressive silence broods over the monstrous structure where such multitudes of men and women were wont to
assemble in other days. The butterflies have taken the places
of the queens of fashion and beauty of eighteen centuries ago,
and the lizards sun themselves in the sacred seat of the Emperor. More vividly than all the written histories, the Coliseum
tells the story of Rome's grandeur and Rome's decay. It is
the worthiest type of both that exists. Moving about the
Rome of to-day, we might find it hard to believe in her old
magnificence and her millions of population; but with this
stubborn evidence before us that she was obliged to have a
theatre with sitting room for eighty thousand persons and
standing room for twenty thousand more, to accommodate such
of her citizens as required amusement, we find belief less difficult. The Coliseum is over one thousand six hundred feet
long, seven hundred and fifty wide, and one hundred and sixty-
five high. Its shape is oval.

In America we make convicts useful at the same time that
we punish them for their crimes. We farm them out and
compel them to earn money for the State by making barrels
and building roads. Thus we combine business with retribution, and all things are lovely. But in ancient Rome they
combined religious duty with pleasure. Since it was necessary
that the new sect called Christians should be exterminated, the
people judged it wise to make this work profitable to the State
at the same time, and entertaining to the public. In addition
to the gladiatorial combats and other shows, they sometimes
threw members of the hated sect into the arena of the Coliseum
and turned wild beasts in upon them. It is estimated that
seventy thousand Christians suffered martyrdom in this place.
This has made the Coliseum holy ground, in the eyes of the
followers of the Saviour. And well it might; for if the chain
that bound a saint, and the footprints a saint has left upon a
stone he chanced to stand upon, be holy, surely the spot where
a man gave up his life for his faith is holy.

Seventeen or eighteen centuries ago this Coliseum was *the*
theatre of Rome, and Rome was mistress of the world. Splen-

did pageants were exhibited here, in presence of the Emperor, the great ministers of State, the nobles, and vast audiences of citizens of smaller consequence. Gladiators fought with gladiators and at times with warrior prisoners from many a distant land. It was *the* theatre of Rome—of the world— and the man of fashion who could not let fall in a casual and unintentional manner something about "my private box at the Coliseum" could not move in the first circles. When the clothing-store merchant wished to consume the corner grocery man with envy, he bought secured seats in the front row and let the thing be known. When the irresistible dry goods clerk wished to blight and destroy, according to his native instinct, he got himself up regardless of expense and took some other fellow's young lady to the Coliseum, and then

OLD ROMAN.

accented the affront by cramming her with ice cream between the acts, or by approaching the cage and stirring up the martyrs with his whalebone cane for her edification. The Roman swell was in his true element only when he stood up against a pillar and fingered his moustache unconscious of the ladies; when he viewed the bloody combats through an opera-glass two inches long; when he excited the envy of provincials by criticisms which showed that he had been to the Coliseum many and many a time and was long ago over the novelty of it; when he turned away with a yawn at last and said, "*He* a star! handles his sword like an apprentice brigand! he'll do for the country, may be, but he don't answer for the metropolis!"

Glad was the contraband that had a seat in the pit at the Saturday matinee, and happy the Roman street-boy who ate his peanuts and guyed the gladiators from the dizzy gallery.

For me was reserved the high honor of discovering among the rubbish of the ruined Coliseum the only playbill of that establishment now extant. There was a suggestive smell of mint-drops about it still, a corner of it had evidently been chewed, and on the margin, in choice Latin, these words were written in a delicate female hand:

"*Meet me on the Tarpeian Rock to-morrow evening, dear, at sharp seven. Mother will be absent on a visit to her friends in the Sabine Hills.*

CLAUDIA."

Ah, where is that lucky youth to-day, and where the little hand that wrote those dainty lines? Dust and ashes these seventeen hundred years!

Thus reads the bill:

ROMAN COLISEUM.

UNPARALLELED ATTRACTION!

NEW PROPERTIES! NEW LIONS! NEW GLADIATORS!

Engagement of the renowned
MARCUS MARCELLUS VALERIAN!

FOR SIX NIGHTS ONLY!

The management beg leave to offer to the public an entertainment surpassing in magnificence any thing that has heretofore been attempted on any stage. No expense has been spared to make the opening season one which shall be worthy the generous patronage which the management feel sure will crown their efforts. The management beg leave to state that they have succeeded in securing the services of a

GALAXY OF TALENT!

such as has not been beheld in Rome before.

The performance will commence this evening with a

GRAND BROADSWORD COMBAT!

between two young and promising amateurs and a celebrated Parthian gladiator who has just arrived a prisoner from the Camp of Verus.

This will be followed by a grand moral

BATTLE-AX ENGAGEMENT!

between the renowned Valerian (with one hand tied behind him,) and two gigantic savages from Britain.

After which the renowned Valerian (if he survive,) will fight with the broadsword,

LEFT-HANDED !

against six Sophomores and a Freshman from the Gladiatorial College !

A long series of brilliant engagements will follow, in which the finest talent of the Empire will take part.

After which the celebrated Infant Prodigy known as

"THE YOUNG ACHILLES,"

will engage four tiger whelps in combat, armed with no other weapon than his little spear !

The whole to conclude with a chaste and elegant

GENERAL SLAUGHTER!

In which thirteen African Lions and twenty-two Barbarian Prisoners will war with each other until all are exterminated.

BOX OFFICE NOW OPEN.

Dress Circle One Dollar ; Children and Servants half price.

An efficient police force will be on hand to preserve order and keep the wild beasts from leaping the railings and discommoding the audience.

Doors open at 7 ; performance begins at 8.

POSITIVELY NO FREE LIST.

Diodorus Job Press.

It was as singular as it was gratifying that I was also so fortunate as to find among the rubbish of the arena, a stained and mutilated copy of the *Roman Daily Battle-Ax*, containing a critique upon this very performance. It comes to hand too late by many centuries to rank as news, and therefore I translate and publish it simply to show how very little the general style and phraseology of dramatic criticism has altered in the ages that have dragged their slow length along since the carriers laid this one damp and fresh before their Roman patrons:

"THE OPENING SEASON.—COLISEUM.—Notwithstanding the inclemency of the weather, quite a respectable number of the rank and fashion of the city assembled last night to witness the debut upon metropolitan boards of the young tragedian who has of late been winning such golden opinions in the amphitheatres of the provinces. Some sixty thousand persons were present, and but for the fact that the streets were almost impassable, it is fair to presume that the house would have been full. His august Majesty, the Emperor Aurelius, occupied the imperial box, and was the cynosure of all eyes. Many illustrious nobles and generals of the Empire graced the occasion with their presence, and not the least among them was the young patrician lieutenant whose laurels, won in the ranks of the "Thundering Legion," are still so green upon his brow. The cheer which greeted his entrance was heard beyond the Tiber!

"The late repairs and decorations add both to the comeliness and the comfort of the Coliseum. The new cushions are a great improvement upon the hard marble seats we have been so long accustomed to. The present management deserve well of the public. They have restored to the Coliseum the gilding, the rich upholstery

COLISEUM OF ANCIENT ROME.

and the uniform magnificence which old Coliseum frequenters tell us Rome was so proud of fifty years ago.

"The opening scene last night—the broadsword combat between two young amateurs and a famous Parthian gladiator who was sent here a prisoner—was very fine. The elder of the two young gentlemen handled his weapon with a grace that marked the possession of extraordinary talent. His feint of thrusting, followed instantly by a happily delivered blow which unhelmeted the Parthian, was received with hearty applause. He was not thoroughly up in the backhanded stroke, but it was very gratifying to his numerous friends to know that, in time, practice would have overcome this defect. However, he was killed. His sisters, who were present, expressed considerable regret. His mother left the Coliseum. The other youth maintained the contest with such spirit as to call forth enthusiastic bursts of applause. When at last he fell a corpse, his aged mother ran screaming, with hair disheveled and tears streaming from her eyes, and swooned away just as her hands were clutching at the railings of the arena. She was promptly removed by the police. Under the circumstances the woman's conduct was pardonable, perhaps, but we suggest that such exhibitions interfere with the decorum which should be preserved during the performances, and are highly improper in the presence of the Emperor. The Parthian prisoner fought bravely and well; and well he might, for he was fighting for both life and liberty. His wife and children were there to nerve his arm with their love, and to remind him of the old home he should see again if he conquered. When his second assailant fell, the woman clasped her children to her breast and wept for joy. But it was only a transient happiness. The captive staggered toward her and she saw that the liberty he had earned was earned too late. He was wounded unto death. Thus the first act closed in a manner which was entirely satisfactory. The manager was called before the curtain and returned his thanks for the honor done him, in a speech which was replete with wit and humor, and closed by hoping that his humble efforts to afford cheerful and instructive entertainment would continue to meet with the approbation of the Roman public.

"The star now appeared, and was received with vociferous applause and the simultaneous waving of sixty thousand handkerchiefs. Marcus Marcellus Valerian (stage name—his real name is Smith,) is a splendid specimen of physical development, and an artist of rare merit. His management of the battle-ax is wonderful. His gayety and his playfulness are irresistible, in his comic parts, and yet they are inferior to his sublime conceptions in the grave realm of tragedy. When his ax was describing fiery circles about the heads of the bewildered barbarians, in exact time with his springing body and his prancing legs, the audience gave way to uncontrollable bursts of laughter; but when the back of his weapon broke the skull of one and almost in the same instant its edge clove the other's body in twain, the howl of enthusiastic applause that shook the building, was the acknowledgment of a critical assemblage that he was a master of the noblest department of his profession. If he has a fault, (and we are sorry to even intimate that he has,) it is that of glancing at the audience, in the midst of the most exciting moments of the performance, as if seeking admiration. The pausing in a fight to bow when bouquets are thrown to him is also in bad taste. In the great left-handed combat he appeared to be looking at the audience half the time, instead of carving his adversaries; and when he had slain all the sophomores and was dallying with the freshman, he

ANCIENT ROMAN NEWSPAPER CRITIQUE.

stooped and snatched a bouquet as it fell, and offered it to his adversary at a time when a blow was descending which promised favorably to be his death-warrant. Such levity is proper enough in the provinces, we make no doubt, but it ill suits the dignity of the metropolis. We trust our young friend will take these remarks in good part, for we mean them solely for his benefit. All who know us are aware that although we are at times justly severe upon tigers and martyrs, we never intentionally offend gladiators.

"The Infant Prodigy performed wonders. He overcame his four tiger whelps with ease, and with no other hurt than the loss of a portion of his scalp. The General Slaughter was rendered with a faithfulness to details which reflects the highest credit upon the late participants in it.

"Upon the whole, last night's performances shed honor not only upon the management but upon the city that encourages and sustains such wholesome and instructive entertainments. We would simply suggest that the practice of vulgar young boys in the gallery of shying peanuts and paper pellets at the tigers, and saying "Hi-yi!" and manifesting approbation or dissatisfaction by such observations as "Bully for the lion!" "Go it, Gladdy!" "Boots!" "Speech!" "Take a walk round the block!" and so on, are extremely reprehensible, when the Emperor is present, and ought to be stopped by the police. Several times last night, when the supernumeraries entered the arena to drag out the bodies, the young ruffians in the gallery shouted, "Supe! supe!" and also, "Oh, what a coat!" and "Why don't you pad them shanks?" and made use of various other remarks expressive of derision. These things are very annoying to the audience.

"A matinee for the little folks is promised for this afternoon, on which occasion several martyrs will be eaten by the tigers. The regular performance will continue every night till further notice. Material change of programme every evening. Benefit of Valerian, Tuesday, 29th, if he lives."

I have been a dramatic critic myself, in my time, and I was often surprised to notice how much more I knew about Hamlet than Forrest did; and it gratifies me to observe, now, how much better my brethren of ancient times knew how a broadsword battle ought to be fought than the gladiators.

CHAPTER XXVII.

SO far, good. If any man has a right to feel proud of himself, and satisfied, surely it is I. For I have written about the Coliseum, and the gladiators, the martyrs, and the lions, and yet have never once used the phrase "butchered to make a Roman holyday." I am the only free white man of mature age, who has accomplished this since Byron originated the expression.

Butchered to make a Roman holyday sounds well for the first seventeen or eighteen hundred thousand times one sees it in print, but after that it begins to grow tiresome. I find it in all the books concerning Rome—and here latterly it reminds me of Judge Oliver. Oliver was a young lawyer, fresh from the schools, who had gone out to the deserts of Nevada to begin life. He found that country, and our ways of life, there, in those early days, different from life in New England or Paris. But he put on a woollen shirt and strapped a navy revolver to his person, took to the bacon and beans of the country, and determined to do in Nevada as Nevada did. Oliver accepted the situation so completely that although he must have sorrowed over many of his trials, he never complained—that is, he never complained but once. He, two others, and myself, started to the new silver mines in the Humboldt mountains—he to be Probate Judge of Humboldt county, and we to mine. The distance was two hundred miles. It was dead of winter. We bought a two-horse wagon and put eighteen hundred pounds of bacon, flour, beans, blasting-powder, picks and shovels in it; we bought two sorry-looking

Mexican "plugs," with the hair turned the wrong way and more corners on their bodies than there are on the mosque of Omar; we hitched up and started. It was a dreadful trip. But Oliver did not complain. The horses dragged the wagon two miles from town and then gave out. Then we three pushed the wagon seven miles, and Oliver moved ahead and pulled the horses after him by the bits. We complained, but

DID NOT COMPLAIN.

Oliver did not. The ground was frozen, and it froze our backs while we slept; the wind swept across our faces and froze our noses. Oliver did not complain. Five days of pushing the wagon by day and freezing by night brought us to the bad part of the journey—the Forty Mile Desert, or the Great American Desert, if you please. Still, this mildest-mannered man that ever was, had not complained. We started across at eight in the morning, pushing through sand that had no bottom; toiling all day long by the wrecks of a thousand wagons, the skeletons of ten thousand oxen; by wagon-tires enough to hoop the Washington Monument to the top, and ox-chains enough to girdle Long Island; by human graves; with our throats parched always, with thirst; lips bleeding from the alkali dust; hungry, perspiring, and very, very weary—so weary that when we dropped in the sand every fifty yards to rest the horses, we could hardly keep from going to sleep—no complaints from Oliver: none the next morning at three o'clock, when we got across, tired to death.

Awakened two or three nights afterward at midnight, in a narrow canon, by the snow falling on our faces, and appalled at the imminent danger of being "snowed in," we harnessed up and pushed on till eight in the morning, passed the "Divide" and knew we were saved. No complaints. Fifteen days of hardship and fatigue brought us to the end of the two hundred miles, and the Judge had not complained. We wondered if any thing *could* exasperate him. We built a Humboldt house. It is done in this way. You dig a square in the steep base of the mountain, and set up two uprights and top them with two joists. Then you stretch a great sheet of "cotton domestic" from the point where the joists join the hill-side down over the joists to the ground; this makes the roof and the front of

HUMBOLDT HOUSE.

the mansion; the sides and back are the dirt walls your digging has left. A chimney is easily made by turning up one corner of the roof. Oliver was sitting alone in this dismal den, one night, by a sage-brush fire, writing poetry; he was very fond of digging poetry out of himself—or blasting it out when it came hard. He heard an animal's footsteps close to the roof; a stone or two and some dirt came through and fell by him. He grew uneasy and said "Hi!—clear out from there, can't you!"—from time to time. But by and by he fell asleep where he sat, and pretty soon a mule fell down the chimney! The fire flew in every direction, and Oliver went over backwards. About ten nights after that, he recovered confidence enough to go to writing poetry again. Again he dozed off to sleep, and again a mule fell down the chimney. This time, about half of that side of the house came in with the mule. Struggling to get up, the mule kicked the candle out and smashed most of the kitchen furniture, and raised considerable dust. These violent awakenings must have been annoying to Oliver, but he never complained. He moved to a mansion on the opposite side of the canon, because he had noticed the mules did not go there. One night about eight o'clock he was endeavoring to finish his poem, when a stone rolled in—then a hoof appeared below the canvas—then part of a cow—the after part. He leaned back in dread, and shouted "Hooy! hooy! get out of this!" and the cow struggled manfully—lost ground steadily—dirt and dust streamed down, and before Oliver could get well away, the entire cow crashed through on to the table and made a shapeless wreck of every thing!

Then, for the first time in his life, I think, Oliver complained. He said,

"*This thing is growing monotonous!*"

Then he resigned his judgeship and left Humboldt county. "Butchered to make a Roman holyday" has grown monotonous to me.

In this connection I wish to say one word about Michael Angelo Buonarotti. I used to worship the mighty genius of Michael Angelo—that man who was great in poetry, painting, sculpture, architecture—great in every thing he undertook. But I do not want Michael Angelo for breakfast—for luncheon —for dinner—for tea—for supper—for between meals. I like a change, occasionally. In Genoa, he designed every thing; in Milan he or his pupils designed every thing; he designed the Lake of Como; in Padua, Verona, Venice, Bologna, who did we ever hear of, from guides, but Michael Angelo? In Florence, he painted every thing, designed every thing, nearly, and what he did not design he used to sit on a favorite stone and look at, and they showed us the stone. In Pisa he designed every thing but the old shot-tower, and they would have attributed that to him if it had not been so awfully out of the perpendicular. He designed the piers of Leghorn and the custom house regulations of Civita Vecchia. But, here—here it is frightful. He designed St. Peter's; he designed the Pope; he designed the Pantheon, the uniform of the Pope's soldiers, the Tiber, the Vatican, the Coliseum, the Capitol, the Tarpeian Rock, the Barberini Palace, St. John Lateran, the Campagna, the Appian Way, the Seven Hills, the Baths of Caracalla, the Claudian Aqueduct, the Cloaca Maxima—the eternal bore designed the Eternal City, and unless all men and books do lie, he painted every thing in it! Dan said the other day to the guide, " Enough, enough, enough! Say no more! Lump the whole thing! say that the Creator made Italy from designs by Michael Angelo!"

DAN.

I never felt so fervently thankful, so soothed, so tranquil, so filled with a blessed peace, as I did yesterday when I learned that Michael Angelo was dead.

But we have taken it out of this guide. He has marched us through miles of pictures and sculpture in the vast corridors of the Vatican; and through miles of pictures and sculpture in twenty other palaces; he has shown us the great picture in the Sistine Chapel, and frescoes enough to frescoe the heavens—pretty much all done by Michael Angelo. So with him we have played that game which has vanquished so many guides for us—imbecility and idiotic questions. These creatures never suspect—they have no idea of a sarcasm.

He shows us a figure and says: "Statoo brunzo." (Bronze statue.)

We look at it indifferently and the doctor asks: "By Michael Angelo?"

"No—not know who."

Then he shows us the ancient Roman Forum. The doctor asks: "Michael Angelo?"

A stare from the guide. "No—thousan' year before he is born."

Then an Egyptian obelisk. Again: "Michael Angelo?"

BRONZE STATUE.

"Oh, *mon dieu*, genteelmen! Zis is *two* thousan' year before he is born!"

He grows so tired of that unceasing question sometimes, that he dreads to show us any thing at all. The wretch has tried all the ways he can think of to make us comprehend that Michael Angelo is only responsible for the creation of a *part* of the world, but somehow he has not succeeded yet. Relief for overtasked eyes and brain from study and sight-seeing is necessary, or we shall become idiotic sure enough. Therefore this guide must continue to suffer. If he does not enjoy it, so much the worse for him. We do.

In this place I may as well jot down a chapter concerning those necessary nuisances, European guides. Many a man has wished in his heart he could do without his guide; but knowing he could not, has wished he could get some amusement out of him as a remuneration for the affliction of his society. We accomplished this latter matter, and if our experience can be made useful to others they are welcome to it.

Guides know about enough English to tangle every thing up so that a man can make neither head or tail of it. They know their story by heart—the history of every statue, painting, cathedral or other wonder they show you. They know it and tell it as a parrot would—and if you interrupt, and throw them off the track, they have to go back and begin over again. All their lives long, they are employed in showing strange things to foreigners and listening to their bursts of admiration. It is human nature to take delight in exciting admiration. It is what prompts children to say "smart" things, and do absurd ones, and in other ways "show off" when company is present. It is what makes gossips turn out in rain and storm to go and be the first to tell a startling bit of news. Think, then, what a passion it becomes with a guide, whose privilege it is, every day, to show to strangers wonders that throw them into perfect ecstasies of admiration! He gets so that he could not by any possibility live in a soberer atmosphere. After we discovered this, we *never* went into ecstacies any more—we never admired any thing—we never showed any but impassible faces and stupid indifference in the presence of the sublimest wonders a guide had to display. We had found their weak point. We have made good use of it ever since. We have made some of those people savage, at times, but we have never lost our own serenity.

The doctor asks the questions, generally, because he can keep his countenance, and look more like an inspired idiot, and throw more imbecility into the tone of his voice than any man that lives. It comes natural to him.

The guides in Genoa are delighted to secure an American party, because Americans so much wonder, and deal so much in sentiment and emotion before any relic of Columbus. Our guide there fidgeted about as if he had swallowed a spring mattrass. He was full of animation—full of impatience. He said:

"Come wis me, genteelmen!—come! I show you ze letter writing by Christopher Colombo!—write it himself!—write it wis his own hand!—come!"

He took us to the municipal palace. After much impressive fumbling of keys and opening of locks, the stained and aged document was spread before us. The guide's eyes sparkled. He danced about us and tapped the parchment with his finger:

"What I tell you, genteelmen! Is it not so? See! handwriting Christopher Colombo!—write it himself!"

We looked indifferent—unconcerned. The doctor examined the document very deliberately, during a painful pause.—Then he said, without any show of interest:

"Ah—Ferguson—what—what did you say was the name of the party who wrote this?"

"Christopher Colombo! ze great Christopher Colombo!"

Another deliberate examination.

"Ah—did he write it himself, or—or how?"

PENMANSHIP.

"He write it himself!—Christopher Colombo! he's own hand-writing, write by himself!"

Then the doctor laid the document down and said:

"Why, I have seen boys in America only fourteen years old that could write better than that."

"But zis is ze great Christo—"

"I don't care who it is! It's the worst writing I ever saw. Now you musn't think you can impose on us because we are strangers. We are not fools, by a good deal. If you have got any specimens of penmanship of real merit, trot them out! —and if you haven't, drive on!"

We drove on. The guide was considerably shaken up, but he made one more venture. He had something which he thought would overcome us. He said:

"Ah, genteelmen, you come wis me! I show you beautiful, O, magnificent bust Christopher Colombo!—splendid, grand, magnificent!"

He brought us before the beautiful bust—for it *was* beautiful—and sprang back and struck an attitude:

"Ah, look, genteelmen!—beautiful, grand,—bust Christopher Colombo!—beautiful bust, beautiful pedestal!"

The doctor put up his eye-glass—procured for such occasions:

"Ah—what did you say this gentleman's name was?"

"Christopher Colombo!—ze great Christopher Colombo!"

"Christopher Colombo—the great Christopher Colombo. Well, what did *he* do?"

"Discover America!—discover America, Oh, ze devil!"

"Discover America. No—that statement will hardly wash. We are just from America ourselves. We heard nothing about it. Christopher Colombo—pleasant name—is—is he dead?"

"Oh, corpo di Baccho!—three hundred year!"

"What did he die of?"

"I do not know!—I can not tell."

"Small-pox, think?"

"I do not know, genteelmen!—I do not know *what* he die of!"

"Measles, likely?"

"May be—may be—I do *not* know—I think he die of somethings."

"Parents living?"

"Im-posseeble!"

"Ah—which is the bust and which is the pedestal?"

"Santa Maria!—*zis* ze bust!—*zis* ze pedestal!"

"Ah, I see, I see—happy combination—very happy combination, indeed. Is—is this the first time this gentleman was ever on a bust?"

ON A BUST.

That joke was lost on the foreigner—guides can not master the subtleties of the American joke.

We have made it interesting for this Roman guide. Yesterday we spent three or four hours in the Vatican, again, that wonderful world of curiosities. We came very near expressing interest, sometimes—even admiration—it was very hard to keep from it. We succeeded though. Nobody else ever did, in the Vatican museums. The guide was bewildered—non-plussed. He walked his legs off, nearly, hunting up extraordinary things, and exhausted all his ingenuity on us, but it was a failure; we never showed any interest in any thing. He had reserved what he considered to be his greatest wonder till the last—a royal Egyptian mummy, the best preserved in the world, perhaps. He took us there. He felt so sure, this time, that some of his old enthusiasm came back to him:

"See, genteelmen!—Mummy! Mummy!"

The eye-glass came up as calmly, as deliberately as ever.

"Ah,—Ferguson—what did I understand you to say the gentleman's name was?"

"Name?—he got no name!—Mummy!—'Gyptian mummy!"

"Yes, yes. Born here?"

"No! *'Gyptian* mummy!"

"Ah, just so. Frenchman, I presume?"

"No!—*not* Frenchman, not Roman!—born in Egypta!"

"Born in Egypta. Never heard of Egypta before. Foreign locality, likely. Mummy—mummy. How calm he is—how self-possessed. Is, ah—is he dead?"

"Oh, *sacre bleu*, been dead three thousan' year!"

The doctor turned on him savagely:

"Here, now, what do you mean by such conduct as this! Playing us for Chinamen because we are strangers and trying to learn! Trying to impose your vile second-hand carcasses on *us!*—thunder and lightning, I've a notion to—to—if you've got a nice *fresh* corpse, fetch him out!—or by George we'll brain you!"

We make it exceedingly interesting for this Frenchman. However, he has paid us back, partly, without knowing it. He came to the hotel this morning to ask if we were up, and he endeavored as well as he could to describe us, so that the landlord would know which persons he meant. He finished with the casual remark that we were lunatics. The observation was so innocent and so honest that it amounted to a very good thing for a guide to say.

There is one remark (already mentioned,) which never yet has failed to disgust these guides. We use it always, when we can think of nothing else to say. After they have exhausted their enthusiasm pointing out to us and praising the beauties of some ancient bronze image or broken-legged statue, we look at it stupidly and in silence for five, ten, fifteen minutes—as long as we can hold out, in fact—and then ask:

"Is—is he dead?"

That conquers the serenest of them. It is not what they are looking for—especially a new guide. Our Roman Ferguson is the most patient, unsuspecting, long-suffering subject we have had yet. We shall be sorry to part with him. We have enjoyed his society very much. We trust he has enjoyed ours, but we are harassed with doubts.

We have been in the catacombs. It was like going down into a very deep cellar, only it was a cellar which had no end to it. The narrow passages are roughly hewn in the rock, and on each hand as you pass along, the hollowed shelves are carved out, from three to fourteen deep; each held a corpse once. There are names, and Christian symbols, and prayers, or sentences expressive of Christian hopes, carved upon nearly every sarcophagus. The dates belong away back in the dawn of the Christian era, of course. Here, in these holes in the ground, the first Christians sometimes burrowed to escape persecution. They crawled out at night to get food, but remained under cover in the day time. The priest told us that St. Sebastian lived under ground for some time while he was being hunted; he went out one day, and the soldiery discovered and shot him to death with arrows. Five or six of the early Popes—those who reigned about sixteen hundred years ago—held their papal courts and advised with their clergy in the bowels of the earth. During seventeen years—from A. D. 235 to A. D. 252—the Popes did not appear above ground. Four were raised to the great office during that period. Four years apiece, or thereabouts. It is very suggestive of the unhealthiness of underground graveyards as places of residence. One Pope afterward spent his entire pontificate in the catacombs—eight years. Another was discovered in them and murdered in the episcopal chair. There was no satisfaction in being a Pope in those days. There were too many annoy-ances. There are one hundred and sixty catacombs under Rome, each with its maze of narrow passages crossing and re-crossing each other and each passage walled to the top with scooped graves its entire length. A careful estimate makes the length of the passages of all the catacombs combined foot up nine hundred miles, and their graves number seven millions. We did not go through all the passages of all the catacombs. We were very anxious to do it, and made the necessary ar-rangements, but our too limited time obliged us to give up the idea. So we only groped through the dismal labyrinth of St. Callixtus, under the Church of St. Sebastian. In the various catacombs are small chapels rudely hewn in the stones, and here the early Christians often held their religious services by dim, ghostly lights. Think of mass and a sermon away down in those tangled caverns under ground !

In the catacombs were buried St. Cecilia, St. Agnes, and several other of the most celebrated of the saints. In the catacomb of St. Callixtus, St. Bridget used to remain long hours in holy contemplation, and St. Charles Borroméo was wont to spend whole nights in prayer there. It was also the scene of a very marvelous thing.

"Here the heart of St. Philip Neri was so inflamed with divine love as to burst his ribs."

I find that grave statement in a book published in New York in 1858, and written by "Rev. William H. Neligan, LL.D., M. A., Trinity College, Dublin ; Member of the Ar-chæological Society of Great Britain." Therefore, I believe it. Otherwise, I could not. Under other circumstances I should have felt a curiosity to know what Philip had for din-ner.

This author puts my credulity on its mettle every now and then. He tells of one St. Joseph Calasanctius whose house in Rome he visited ; he visited only the house—the priest has been dead two hundred years. He says the Virgin Mary ap-peared to this saint. Then he continues:

"His tongue and his heart, which were found after nearly a century to be whole, when the body was disinterred before his canonization, are still preserved in a glass case, and after two centuries the heart is still whole. When the French troops came to Rome, and when Pius VII. was carried away prisoner, blood dropped from it."

To read that in a book written by a monk far back in the Middle Ages, would surprise no one; it would sound natural and proper; but when it is seriously stated in the middle of the nineteenth century, by a man of finished education, an LL.D., M. A., and an Archæological magnate, it sounds strangely enough. Still, I would gladly change my unbelief for Neligan's faith, and let him make the conditions as hard as he pleased.

The old gentleman's undoubting, unquestioning simplicity has a rare freshness about it in these matter-of-fact railroading and telegraphing days. Hear him, concerning the church of Ara Cœli:

"In the roof of the church, directly above the high altar, is engraved, '*Regina Cœli laetare Alleluia*.'" In the sixth century Rome was visited by a fearful pestilence. Gregory the Great urged the people to do penance, and a general procession was formed. It was to proceed from Ara Cœli to St. Peter's. As it passed before the mole of Adrian, now the Castle of St. Angelo, the sound of heavenly voices was heard singing (it was Easter morn,) '*Regina Cœli, laetare! alleluia! quia quem meruisti portare, alleluia! resurrexit sicut dixit; alleluia!*' The Pontiff, carrying in his hands the portrait of the Virgin, (which is over the high altar and is said to have been painted by St. Luke,) answered, with the astonished people, '*Ora pro nobis Deum, alleluia!*' At the same time an angel was seen to put up a sword in a scabbard, and the pestilence ceased on the same day. There are four circumstances which *confirm** this miracle: the annual procession which takes place in the western church on the feast of St. Mark; the statue of St. Michael, placed on the mole of Adrian, which has since that time been called the Castle of St. Angelo; the antiphon Regina Cœli, which the Catholic church sings during paschal time; and the inscription in the church."

* The italics are mine.—M. T.

CHAPTER XXVIII.

FROM the sanguinary sports of the Holy Inquisition; the slaughter of the Coliseum; and the dismal tombs of the Catacombs, I naturally pass to the picturesque horrors of the Capuchin Convent. We stopped a moment in a small chapel in the church to admire a picture of St. Michael vanquishing Satan—a picture which is so beautiful that I can not but think it belongs to the reviled "*Renaissance*," notwithstanding I believe they told us one of the ancient old masters painted it—and then we descended into the vast vault underneath.

Here was a spectacle for sensitive nerves! Evidently the old masters had been at work in this place. There were six divisions in the apartment, and each division was ornamented with a style of decoration peculiar to itself—and these decorations were in every instance formed of human bones! There were shapely arches, built wholly of thigh bones; there were startling pyramids, built wholly of grinning skulls; there were quaint architectural structures of various kinds, built of shin bones and the bones of the arm; on the wall were elaborate frescoes, whose curving vines were made of knotted human vertebræ; whose delicate tendrils were made of sinews and tendons; whose flowers were formed of knee-caps and toe-nails. Every lasting portion of the human frame was represented in these intricate designs (they were by Michael Angelo, I think,) and there was a careful finish about the work, and an attention to details that betrayed the artist's love of his labors as well as his schooled ability. I asked the good-natured monk who accompanied us, who did this? And he said, "*We* did it"— meaning himself and his brethren up stairs. I could see that

the old friar took a high pride in his curious show. We made
him talkative by exhibiting an interest we never betrayed to
guides.

"Who were these people?"

"We—up stairs—Monks of the Capuchin order—my brethren."

VAULTS OF THE CONVENT.

"How many departed monks were required to upholster
these six parlors?"

"These are the bones of four thousand."

"It took a long time to get enough?"

"Many, many centuries."

"Their different parts are well separated—skulls in one room, legs in another, ribs in another—there would be stirring times here for a while if the last trump should blow. Some of the brethren might get hold of the wrong leg, in the confusion, and the wrong skull, and find themselves limping, and looking through eyes that were wider apart or closer together than they were used to. You can not tell any of these parties apart, I suppose?"

"Oh, yes, I know many of them."

He put his finger on a skull. "This was Brother Anselmo—dead three hundred years—a good man."

He touched another. "This was Brother Alexander—dead two hundred and eighty years. This was Brother Carlo—dead about as long."

Then he took a skull and held it in his hand, and looked reflectively upon it, after the manner of the grave-digger when he discourses of Yorick.

"This," he said, "was Brother Thomas. He was a young prince, the scion of a proud house that traced its lineage back to the grand old days of Rome well nigh two thousand years ago. He loved beneath his estate. His family persecuted him; persecuted the girl, as well. They drove her from Rome; he followed; he sought her far and wide; he found no trace of her. He came back and offered his broken heart at our altar and his weary life to the service of God. But look you. Shortly his father died, and likewise his mother. The girl returned, rejoicing. She sought every where for him whose eyes had used to look tenderly into hers out of this poor skull, but she could not find him. At last, in this coarse garb we wear, she recognized him in the street. He knew her. It was too late. He fell where he stood. They took him up and brought him here. He never spoke afterward. Within the week he died. You can see the color of his hair—faded, somewhat—by this thin shred that clings still to the temple. "This," [taking up a thigh bone,] "was his. The veins of this leaf in the decorations over your head, were his finger-joints, a hundred and fifty years ago."

This business-like way of illustrating a touching story of the heart by laying the several fragments of the lover before us and naming them, was as grotesque a performance, and as ghastly, as any I ever witnessed. I hardly knew whether to smile or shudder. There are nerves and muscles in our frames whose functions and whose methods of working it seems a sort of sacrilege to describe by cold physiological names and surgical technicalities, and the monk's talk suggested to me something of this kind. Fancy a surgeon, with his nippers lifting tendons, muscles and such things into view, out of the complex machinery of a corpse, and observing, "Now this little nerve quivers—the vibration is imparted to this muscle—from here it is passed to this fibrous substance; here its ingredients are separated by the chemical action of the blood—one part goes to the heart and thrills it with what is popularly termed emotion, another part follows this nerve to the brain and communicates intelligence of a startling character—the third part glides along this passage and touches the spring connected with the fluid receptacles that lie in the rear of the eye. Thus, by this simple and beautiful process, the party is informed that his mother is dead, and he weeps." Horrible!

I asked the monk if all the brethren up stairs expected to be put in this place when they died. He answered quietly:

"We must all lie here at last."

See what one can accustom himself to.—The reflection that he must some day be taken apart like an engine or a clock, or like a house whose owner is gone, and worked up into arches and pyramids and hideous frescoes, did not distress this monk' in the least. I thought he even looked as if he were thinking, with complacent vanity, that his own skull would look well on top of the heap and his own ribs add a charm to the frescoes which possibly they lacked at present.

Here and there, in ornamental alcoves, stretched upon beds of bones, lay dead and dried-up monks, with lank frames dressed in the black robes one sees ordinarily upon priests. We examined one closely. The skinny hands were clasped upon the breast; two lustreless tufts of hair stuck to the skull;

the skin was brown and sunken; it stretched tightly over the cheek bones and made them stand out sharply; the crisp dead eyes were deep in the sockets; the nostrils were painfully prominent, the end of the nose being gone; the lips had shriveled away from the yellow teeth: and brought down to us through the circling years, and petrified there, was a weird laugh a full century old!

DRIED CONVENT FRUIT.

It was the jolliest laugh, but yet the most dreadful, that one can imagine. Surely, I thought, it must have been a most extraordinary joke this veteran produced with his latest breath, that he has not got done laughing at it yet. At this moment I saw that the old instinct was strong upon the boys, and I said we had better hurry to St. Peter's. They were trying to keep from asking, "Is—is he dead?"

It makes me dizzy, to think of the Vatican—of its wilderness of statues, paintings, and curiosities of every description and every age. The "old masters" (especially in sculpture,) fairly swarm, there. I can not write about the Vatican. I think I shall never remember any thing I saw there distinctly but the mummies, and the Transfiguration, by Raphael, and some other things it is not necessary to mention now. I shall remember the Transfiguration partly because it was placed in a room almost by itself; partly because it is acknowledged by all to be the first oil painting in the world; and partly because it was wonderfully beautiful. The colors are fresh and rich, the "expression," I am told, is fine, the "feeling" is lively, the "tone" is good, the "depth" is profound, and the width is about four and a half feet, I should judge. It is a picture that really holds one's attention; its beauty is fascinating. It is fine enough to be a *Renaissance*. A remark I made a while ago suggests a thought—and a hope. Is it not possible that the reason I find such charms in this picture is because it is out of the crazy chaos of the galleries? If some of the others were set apart, might not they be beautiful? If this were set in the midst of the tempest of pictures one finds in the vast galleries of the Roman palaces, would I think it so handsome? If, up to this time, I had seen only one "old master" in each palace, instead of acres and acres of walls and ceilings fairly papered with them, might I not have a more civilized opinion of the old masters than I have now? I think so. When I was a school-boy and was to have a new knife, I could not make

up my mind as to which was the prettiest in the show-case, and I did not think any of them were particularly pretty; and so I chose with a heavy heart. But when I looked at my purchase, at home, where no glittering blades came into competition with it, I was astonished to see how handsome it was. To this day my new hats look better out of the shop than they did in it with other new hats. It begins to dawn upon me, now, that possibly, what I have been taking for uniform ugliness in the galleries may be uniform beauty af-

AT THE STORE.

ter all. I honestly hope it is, to others, but certainly it is not to me. Perhaps the reason I used to enjoy going to the Academy

of Fine Arts in New York was because there were but a few
hundred paintings in it, and it did not surfeit me to go through

AT HOME.

the list.   I suppose the Academy
was bacon and beans in the
Forty-Mile Desert, and a European gallery is a state dinner of
thirteen courses.   One leaves no
sign after him of the one dish,
but the thirteen frighten away
his appetite and give him no
satisfaction.

There is one thing I am certain of, though.   With all the
Michael Angelos, the Raphaels,
the Guidos and the other old
masters, the sublime history of
Rome remains unpainted! They
painted Virgins enough, and
popes enough and saintly scare-
crows enough, to people Paradise, almost, and these things are
all they did paint.   "Nero fiddling o'er burning Rome," the
assassination of Cæsar, the stirring spectacle of a hundred
thousand people bending forward with rapt interest, in the
Coliseum, to see two skillful gladiators hacking away each others' lives, a tiger springing upon a kneeling martyr—these and
a thousand other matters which we read of with a living interest, must be sought for only in books—not among the rubbish
left by the old masters—who are no more, I have the satisfaction of informing the public.

They did paint, and they did carve in marble, one historical
scene, and one only, (of any great historical consequence.)
And what was it and why did they choose it, particularly ?   It
was the Rape of the Sabines, and they chose it for the legs and
busts.

I like to look at statues, however, and I like to look at pictures, also—even of monks looking up in sacred ecstacy, and
monks looking down in meditation, and monks skirmishing for

something to eat—and therefore I drop ill nature to thank the papal government for so jealously guarding and so industriously gathering up these things; and for permitting me, a stranger and not an entirely friendly one, to roam at will and unmolested among them, charging me nothing, and only requiring that I shall behave myself simply as well as I ought to behave in any other man's house. I thank the Holy Father right heartily, and I wish him long life and plenty of happiness.

The Popes have long been the patrons and preservers of art, just as our new, practical Republic is the encourager and upholder of mechanics. In their Vatican is stored up all that is curious and beautiful in art; in our Patent Office is hoarded all that is curious or useful in mechanics. When a man invents a new style of horse-collar or discovers a new and superior method of telegraphing, our government issues a patent to him that is worth a fortune; when a man digs up an ancient statue in the Campagna, the Pope gives him a fortune in gold coin. We can make something of a guess at a man's character by the style of nose he carries on his face. The Vatican and the Patent Office are governmental noses, and they bear a deal of character about them.

The guide showed us a colossal statue of Jupiter, in the Vatican, which he said looked so damaged and rusty—so like the God of the Vagabonds—because it had but recently been dug up in the Campagna. He asked how much we supposed this Jupiter was worth? I replied, with intelligent promptness, that he was probably worth about four dollars—may be four and a half. "A hundred thousand dollars!" Ferguson said. Ferguson said, further, that the Pope permits no ancient work of this kind to leave his dominions. He appoints a commission to examine discoveries like this and report upon the value; then the Pope pays the discoverer one-half of that assessed value and takes the statue. He said this Jupiter was dug from a field which had just been bought for thirty-six thousand dollars, so the first crop was a good one for the new farmer. I do not know whether Ferguson always tells the truth or not, but I suppose he does. I know that an exorbitant export duty is

20

exacted upon all pictures painted by the old masters, in order to discourage the sale of those in the private collections. I am satisfied, also, that genuine old masters hardly exist at all, in America, because the cheapest and most insignificant of them are valued at the price of a fine farm. I proposed to buy a small trifle of a Raphael, myself, but the price of it was eighty thousand dollars, the export duty would have made it considerably over a hundred, and so I studied on it awhile and concluded not to take it.

I wish here to mention an inscription I have seen, before I forget it:

"Glory to God in the highest, peace on earth TO MEN OF GOOD WILL!" It is not good scripture, but it is sound Catholic and human nature.

This is in letters of gold around the apsis of a mosaic group at the side of the *scala santa*, church of St. John Lateran, the Mother and Mistress of all the Catholic churches of the world. The group represents the Saviour, St. Peter, Pope Leo, St. Silvester, Constantine and Charlemagne. Peter is giving the *pallium* to the Pope, and a standard to Charlemagne. The Saviour is giving the keys to St. Silvester, and a standard to Constantine. No prayer is offered to the Saviour, who seems to be of little importance any where in Rome; but an inscription below says, "*Blessed Peter, give life to Pope Leo and victory to King Charles.*" It does not say, "*Intercede for us*, through the Saviour, with the Father, for this boon," but "Blessed Peter, *give it* us."

In all seriousness—without meaning to be frivolous—without meaning to be irreverent, and more than all, without meaning to be blasphemous,—I state as my simple deduction from the things I have seen and the things I have heard, that the Holy Personages rank thus in Rome:

First—"The Mother of God"—otherwise the Virgin Mary.

Second—The Deity.

Third—Peter.

Fourth—Some twelve or fifteen canonized Popes and martyrs.

Fifth—Jesus Christ the Saviour—(but always as an infant in arms.)

I may be wrong in this—my judgment errs often, just as is the case with other men's—but it *is* my judgment, be it good or bad.

Just here I will mention something that seems curious to me. There are no "Christ's Churches" in Rome, and no "Churches of the Holy Ghost," that I can discover. There are some four hundred churches, but about a fourth of them seem to be named for the Madonna and St. Peter. There are so many named for Mary that they have to be distinguished by all sorts of affixes, if I understand the matter rightly. Then we have churches of St. Louis; St. Augustine; St. Agnes; St. Calixtus; St. Lorenzo in Lucina; St. Lorenzo in Damaso; St. Cecilia; St. Athanasius; St. Philip Neri; St. Catherine, St. Dominico, and a multitude of lesser saints whose names are not familiar in the world—and away down, clear out of the list of the churches, comes a couple of hospitals: one of them is named for the Saviour and the other for the Holy Ghost!

Day after day and night after night we have wandered among the crumbling wonders of Rome; day after day and night after night we have fed upon the dust and decay of five-and-twenty centuries—have brooded over them by day and dreampt of them by night till sometimes we seemed moldering away ourselves, and growing defaced and cornerless, and liable at any moment to fall a prey to some antiquary and be patched in the legs, and "restored" with an unseemly nose, and labeled wrong and dated wrong, and set up in the Vatican for poets to drivel about and vandals to scribble their names on forever and forevermore.

But the surest way to stop writing about Rome is to stop. I wished to write a real "guide-book" chapter on this fascinating city, but I could not do it, because I have felt all the time like a boy in a candy-shop—there was every thing to choose from, and yet no choice. I have drifted along hopelessly for a hundred pages of manuscript without knowing where to commence. I will not commence at all. Our passports have been examined. We will go to Naples.

CHAPTER XXIX.

THE ship is lying here in the harbor of Naples—quarantined. She has been here several days and will remain several more. We that came by rail from Rome have escaped this misfortune. Of course no one is allowed to go on board the ship, or come ashore from her. She is a prison, now. The passengers probably spend the long, blazing days looking out from under the awnings at Vesuvius and the beautiful city—and in swearing. Think of ten days of this sort of pastime!—We go out every day in a boat and request them to come ashore. It soothes them. We lie ten steps from the ship and tell them how splendid the city is; and how much better the hotel fare is here than any where else in Europe; and how cool it is; and what frozen continents of ice cream there are; and what a time we are having cavorting about the country and sailing to the islands in the Bay. This tranquilizes them.

ASCENT OF VESUVIUS.

I shall remember our trip to Vesuvius for many a day—partly because of its sight-seeing experiences, but chiefly on account of the fatigue of the journey. Two or three of us had been resting ourselves among the tranquil and beautiful scenery of the island of Ischia, eighteen miles out in the harbor, for two days; we called it " resting," but I do not remember now what the resting consisted of, for when we got back to Naples we had not slept for forty-eight hours. We were just about to go to bed early in the evening, and catch up on some of the sleep we had lost, when we heard of this Vesuvius expedition. There was to be eight of us in the party, and we were to leave Naples at midnight. We laid in some provisions for the trip, engaged carriages to take us to Annunciation, and then moved about the city, to keep awake, till twelve. We got away punctually, and in the course of an hour and a half arrived at the town of Annunciation. Annunciation is the very last place under the sun. In other towns in Italy the people lie around quietly and wait for you to ask them a question or do some overt act that can be charged for—but in Annunciation they have lost even that fragment of delicacy; they seize a lady's shawl from a chair and hand it to her and charge a penny; they open a carriage door,

SOOTHING THE PILGRIMS.

and charge for it—shut it when you get out, and charge for it; they help you to take off a duster—two cents; brush your clothes and make them worse than they were before—two cents; smile upon you—two cents; bow, with a lick-spittle smirk, hat in hand—two cents; they volunteer all information, such as that the mules will arrive presently—two cents—warm day, sir—two cents—take you four hours to make the ascent— two cents. And so they go. They crowd you—infest you— swarm about you, and sweat and smell offensively, and look sneaking and mean, and obsequious. There is no office too degrading for them to perform, for money. I have had no opportunity to find out any thing about the upper classes by my own observation, but from what I hear said about them I judge that what they lack in one or two of the bad traits the *canaille* have, they make up in one or two others that are worse. How the people beg!—many of them very well dressed, too.

I said I knew nothing against the upper classes by personal observation. I must recall it! I had forgotten. What I saw their bravest and their fairest do last night, the lowest multitude that could be scraped up out of the purlieus of Christendom would blush to do, I think. They assembled by hundreds, and even thousands, in the great Theatre of San Carlo, to do—what? Why, simply, to make fun of an old woman—to deride, to hiss, to jeer at an actress they once worshipped, but whose beauty is faded now and whose voice has lost its former richness. Every body spoke of the rare sport there was to be. They said the theatre would be crammed, because Frezzolini was going to sing. It was said she could not sing well, now, but then the people liked to see her, anyhow. And so we went. And every time the woman sang they hissed and laughed—the whole magnificent house—and as soon as she left the stage they called her on again with applause. Once or twice she was encored five and six times in succession, and received with hisses when she appeared, and discharged with hisses and laughter when she had finished—then instantly encored and insulted again! And how the high-born knaves enjoyed it! White-kidded gentlemen and ladies laughed till the tears came, and clapped their hands in very ecstacy when that unhappy old woman would come meekly out for the sixth time, with uncomplaining patience, to meet a storm of hisses! It was the cruelest exhibition—the most wanton, the most unfeeling. The singer would have conquered an audience of American rowdies by her brave, unflinching tranquillity (for she answered encore after encore, and smiled and bowed pleasantly, and sang the best she possibly could, and went bowing off, through all the jeers and hisses, without ever losing countenance or temper:) and surely in any other land than Italy her sex and her helplessness must have been an ample protection to her—she could have needed no other. Think what a multitude of small souls were crowded into that theatre last night. If the manager could have filled his theatre with Neapolitan souls alone, without the bodies, he could not have cleared less than ninety millions of dollars. What traits of character must a man have to enable him to help three thousand miscreants to hiss, and jeer, and laugh at one friendless old woman, and shamefully humiliate her? He must have *all* the vile, mean traits there are. My observation persuades me (I do not like to venture beyond my own personal observation,) that the upper classes of Naples possess those traits of character. Otherwise they may be very good people; I can not say.

ASCENT OF VESUVIUS—CONTINUED.

In this city of Naples, they believe in and support one of the wretchedest of all the religious impostures one can find in Italy—the miraculous liquefaction of the blood of St. Januarius. Twice a year the priests assemble all the people at the Cathedral, and get out this vial of clotted blood and let them see it slowly dissolve and become liquid—and every day for eight days, this dismal farce is repeated, while the priests go among the crowd and collect money for the exhibition. The first day, the blood liquefies in forty-seven minutes—the church is crammed, then, and time must be allowed the collectors to get around: after that it liquefies a little quicker and a little quicker, every day, as the houses grow smaller, till on the eighth day, with only a few dozens present to see the miracle, it liquefies in four minutes.

And here, also, they used to have a grand procession, of priests, citizens, soldiers, sailors, and the high dignitaries of the City Government, once a year, to shave the head of a made-up Madonna—a stuffed and painted image, like a milliner's dummy—whose hair miraculously grew and restored itself every twelve months. They still kept up this shaving procession as late as four or five years ago. It was a source of great profit to the church that possessed the remarkable effigy, and the ceremony of the public barbering of her was always carried out with the greatest possible eclat and display—the more the better, because the more excitement there was about it the larger the crowds it drew and the heavier the revenues it produced—but at last a day came when the Pope and his servants were unpopular in Naples, and the City Government stopped the Madonna's annual show.

There we have two specimens of these Neapolitans—two of the silliest possible frauds, which half the population religiously and faithfully believed, and the other half either believed also or else said nothing about, and thus lent themselves to the support of the imposture. I am very well satisfied to think the whole population believed in those poor, cheap miracles—a people who want two cents every time they bow to you, and who abuse a woman, are capable of it, I think.

ASCENT OF VESUVIUS—CONTINUED.

These Neapolitans always ask four times as much money as they intend to take, but if you give them what they first demand, they feel ashamed of themselves for aiming so low, and immediately ask more. When money is to be paid and received, there is always some vehement jawing and gesticulating about it. One can not buy and pay for two cents' worth of clams without trouble and a quarrel. One "course," in a two-horse carriage, costs a franc—that is law—but the hackman always demands more, on some pretence or other, and if he gets it he makes a new demand. It is said that a stranger took a one-horse carriage for a course—tariff, half a franc. He gave the man five francs, by way of experiment. He demanded more, and received another franc. Again he demanded more, and got a franc—demanded more, and it was refused. He grew vehement—was again refused, and became noisy. The stranger said, " Well, give me the seven francs again, and I will see what I can do "—and when he got them, he handed the hackman half a franc, and he immediately asked for two cents to buy a drink with. It may be thought that I am prejudiced. Perhaps I am. I would be ashamed of myself if I were not.

ASCENT OF VESUVIUS—CONTINUED.

Well, as I was saying, we got our mules and horses, after an hour and a half of bargaining with the population of Annunciation, and started sleepily up the mountain, with a vagrant at each mule's tail who pretended to be driving the brute along,

ASCENT OF VESUVIUS.

but was really holding on and getting himself dragged up instead. I made slow headway at first, but I began to get dissatisfied at the idea of paying my minion five francs to hold my mule back by the tail and keep him from going up the hill, and so I discharged him. I got along faster then.

We had one magnificent picture of Naples from a high point on the mountain side. We saw nothing but the gas lamps, of course—two-thirds of a circle, skirting the great Bay—a necklace of diamonds glinting up through the darkness from the remote distance—less brilliant than the stars overhead, but more softly, richly beautiful—and over all the great city the lights crossed and recrossed each other in many and many a sparkling line and curve. And back of the town, far around and abroad over the miles of level campagna, were scattered rows, and circles, and clusters of lights, all glowing like so many gems, and marking where a score of villages were sleeping. About this time, the fellow who was hanging on to the tail of the horse in front of me and practicing all sorts of unnecessary cruelty upon the animal, got kicked some fourteen rods, and this incident, together with the fairy spectacle of the lights far in the distance, made me serenely happy, and I was glad I started to Vesuvius.

ASCENT OF MOUNT VESUVIUS—CONTINUED.

This subject will be excellent matter for a chapter, and tomorrow or next day I will write it.

CHAPTER XXX.

"SEE Naples and die." Well, I do not know that one would necessarily die after merely seeing it, but 'to attempt to live there might turn out a little differently. To see Naples as we saw it in the early dawn from far up on the side of Vesuvius, is to see a picture of wonderful beauty. At that distance its dingy buildings looked white—and so, rank on rank of balconies, windows and roofs, they piled themselves up from the blue ocean till the colossal castle of St. Elmo topped the grand white pyramid and gave the picture symmetry, emphasis and completeness. And when its lilies turned to roses—when it blushed under the sun's first kiss—it was beautiful beyond all description. One might well say, then, "See Naples and die." The frame of the picture was charming, itself. In front, the smooth sea—a vast mosaic of many colors; the lofty islands swimming in a dreamy haze in the distance; at our end of the city the stately double peak of Vesuvius, and its strong black ribs and seams of lava stretching down to the limitless level campagna—a green carpet that enchants the eye and leads it on and on, past clusters of trees, and isolated houses, and snowy villages, until it shreds out in a fringe of mist and general vagueness far away. It is from the Hermitage, there on the side of Vesuvius, that one should "see Naples and die."

But do not go within the walls and look at it in detail. That takes away some of the romance of the thing. The people are filthy in their habits, and this makes filthy streets and breeds disagreeable sights and smells.   There never was a community so prejudiced against the cholera as these Neapolitans are.   But they have good reason to be.   The cholera generally vanquishes a Neapolitan when it seizes him, because, you understand, before the doctor can dig through the dirt and get at the disease the man dies.   The upper classes take a sea-bath every day, and are pretty decent.

BAY OF NAPLES.

The streets are generally about wide enough for one wagon, and how they do swarm with people!   It is Broadway repeated in every street, in every court, in every alley!   Such masses, such throngs, such multitudes of hurrying, bustling, struggling humanity!   We never saw the like of it, hardly even in New York, I think.   There are seldom any sidewalks, and when there are, they are not often wide enough to pass a man on without caroming on him.   So everybody walks in the street—and where the street is wide enough, carriages are forever dashing along.   Why a thousand people are not run over and crippled every day is a mystery that no man can solve.

But if there is an eighth wonder in the world, it must be the dwelling-houses of Naples.   I honestly believe a good majority

of them are a hundred feet high! And the solid brick walls
are seven feet through. You go up nine flights of stairs before you get to the "first" floor. No, not nine, but there or
thereabouts. There is a little bird-cage of an iron railing in
front of every window clear away up, up, up, among the eternal clouds, where the roof is, and there is always somebody looking out of every window—people of ordinary size looking out
from the first floor, people a shade smaller from the second,
people that look a little smaller yet from the third—and from
thence upward they grow smaller and smaller by a regularly
graduated diminution, till the folks in the topmost windows
seem more like birds in an uncommonly tall martin-box than
any thing else. The perspective of one of these narrow
cracks of streets, with its rows of tall houses stretching away
till they come together in the distance like railway tracks; its
clothes-lines crossing over at all altitudes and waving their
bannered raggedness over the swarms of people below; and
the white-dressed women perched in balcony railings all the
way from the pavement up to the heavens—a perspective like
that is really worth going into Neapolitan details to see.

ASCENT OF VESUVIUS—CONTINUED.

Naples, with its immediate suburbs, contains six hundred
and twenty-five thousand inhabitants, but I am satisfied it
covers no more ground than an American city of one hundred
and fifty thousand. It reaches up into the air infinitely higher
than three American cities, though, and there is where the
secret of it lies. I will observe here, in passing, that the contrasts between opulence and poverty, and magnificence and
misery, are more frequent and more striking in Naples than in
Paris even. One must go to the Bois de Boulogne to see
fashionable dressing, splendid equipages and stunning liveries,
and to the Faubourg St. Antoine to see vice, misery, hunger,
rags, dirt—but in the thoroughfares of Naples these things are
all mixed together. Naked boys of nine years and the fancy-
dressed children of luxury; shreds and tatters, and brilliant

uniforms; jackass-carts and state-carriages; beggars, Princes and Bishops, jostle each other in every street. At six o'clock every evening, all Naples turns out to drive on the *Riviere di Chiaja*, (whatever that may mean;) and for two hours one may stand there and see the motliest and the worst mixed procession go by that ever eyes beheld. Princes (there are more Princes than policemen in Naples—the city is infested with them)—Princes who live up seven flights of stairs and don't own any principalities, will keep a carriage and go hungry; and clerks, mechanics, milliners and strumpets will go without their dinners and squander the money on a hack-ride in the Chiaja; the rag-tag and rubbish of the city stack themselves up, to the number of twenty or thirty, on a rickety little go-cart hauled by a donkey not much bigger than a cat, and *they* drive in the Chiaja; Dukes and bankers, in sumptuous carriages and with gorgeous drivers and footmen, turn out, also, and so the furious procession goes. For two hours rank and wealth, and obscurity and poverty clatter along side by side in the wild procession, and then go home serene, happy, covered with glory!

I was looking at a magnificent marble staircase in the King's palace, the other day, which, it was said, cost five million francs, and I suppose it did cost half a million, may be. I felt as if it must be a fine thing to live in a country where there was such comfort and such luxury as this. And then I stepped out musing, and almost walked over a vagabond who was eating his dinner on the curbstone—a piece of bread and a bunch of grapes. When I found that this mustang was clerking in a fruit establishment (he had the establishment along with him in a basket,) at two cents a day, and that he had no palace at home where he lived, I lost some of my enthusiasm concerning the happiness of living in Italy.

This naturally suggests to me a thought about wages here. Lieutenants in the army get about a dollar a day, and common soldiers a couple of cents. I only know one clerk—he gets four dollars a month. Printers get six dollars and a half a month, but I have heard of a foreman who gets thirteen.

To be growing suddenly and violently rich, as this man is, naturally makes him a bloated aristocrat. The airs he puts on are insufferable.

And, speaking of wages, reminds me of prices of merchandise. In Paris you pay twelve dollars a dozen for Jouvin's best kid gloves; gloves of about as good quality sell here at three or four dollars a dozen. You pay five and six dollars apiece for fine linen shirts in Paris; here and in Leghorn you pay two and a half. In Marseilles you pay forty dollars for a first-class dress coat made by a good tailor, but in Leghorn you can get a full dress suit for the same money. Here you get handsome business suits at from ten to twenty dollars, and in Leghorn you can get an overcoat for fifteen dollars that would

MUSTANG.

cost you seventy in New York. Fine kid boots are worth eight dollars in Marseilles and four dollars here. Lyons velvets rank higher in America than those of Genoa. Yet the bulk of Lyons velvets you buy in the States are made in Genoa and imported into Lyons, where they receive the Lyons stamp and are then exported to America. You can buy enough velvet in Genoa for twenty-five dollars to make a five hundred dollar cloak in New York—so the ladies tell me. Of course these things bring me back, by a natural and easy transition, to the

ASCENT OF VESUVIUS—CONTINUED.

And thus the wonderful Blue Grotto is suggested to me.   It is situated on the Island of Capri, twenty-two miles from

ISLAND OF CAPRI.

Naples.   We chartered a little steamer and went out there. Of course, the police boarded us and put us through a health examination, and inquired into our politics, before they would let us land.   The airs these little insect Governments put on are in the last degree ridiculous.   They even put a policeman on board of our boat to keep an eye on us as long as we were in the Capri dominions.   They thought we wanted to steal the grotto, I suppose.   It was worth stealing.   The entrance to the cave is four feet high and four feet wide, and is in the face of a lofty perpendicular cliff—the sea-wall.   You enter in

small boats—and a tight squeeze it is, too. You can not go in
at all when the tide is up. Once within, you find yourself in
an arched cavern about one hundred and sixty feet long, one
hundred and twenty wide, and about seventy high. How
deep it is no man knows. It goes down to the bottom of the
ocean. The waters of this placid subterranean lake are the
brightest, loveliest blue that can be imagined. They are as
transparent as plate glass, and their coloring would shame the
richest sky that ever bent over Italy. No tint could be more
ravishing, no lustre more superb. Throw a stone into the

BLUE GROTTO.

water, and the myriad of tiny bubbles that are created flash out
a brilliant glare like blue theatrical fires. Dip an oar, and its
blade turns to splendid frosted silver, tinted with blue. Let a
man jump in, and instantly he is cased in an armor more gorgeous than ever kingly Crusader wore.

Then we went to Ischia, but I had already been to that

island and tired myself to death " resting " a couple of days and studying human villainy, with the landlord of the Grande Sentinelle for a model. So we went to Procida, and from thence to Pozzuoli, where St. Paul landed after he sailed from Samos. I landed at precisely the same spot where St. Paul landed, and so did Dan and the others. It was a remarkable coincidence. St. Paul preached to these people seven days before he started to Rome.

Nero's Baths, the ruins of Baiæ, the Temple of Serapis; Cumæ, where the Cumæn Sybil interpreted the oracles, the Lake Agnano, with its ancient submerged city still visible far down in its depths—these and a hundred other points of interest we examined with critical imbecility, but the Grotto of the Dog claimed our chief attention, because we had heard and read so much about it. Every body has written about the Grotto del Cane and its poisonous vapors, from Pliny down to Smith, and every tourist has held a dog over its floor by the legs to test the capabilities of the place. The dog dies in a minute and a half—a chicken instantly. As a general thing, strangers who crawl in there to sleep do not get up until they are called. And then they don't either. The stranger that ventures to sleep there takes a permanent contract. I longed to see this grotto. I resolved to take a dog and hold him myself; suffocate him a little, and time him; suffocate him some more and then finish him. We reached the grotto at about three in the afternoon, and proceeded at once to make the experiments. But now, an important difficulty presented itself. We had no dog.

ASCENT OF VESUVIUS—CONTINUED.

At the Hermitage we were about fifteen or eighteen hundred feet above the sea, and thus far a portion of the ascent had been pretty abrupt. For the next two miles the road was a mixture—sometimes the ascent was abrupt and sometimes it was not: but one characteristic it possessed all the time, without failure—without modification—it was all uncompromis-

VESUVIUS AND BAY OF NAPLES.

ingly and unspeakably infamous. It was a rough, narrow trail, and led over an old lava flow—a black ocean which was tumbled into a thousand fantastic shapes—a wild chaos of ruin, desolation, and barrenness—a wilderness of billowy upheavals, of furious whirlpools, of miniature mountains rent asunder—of gnarled and knotted, wrinkled and twisted masses of blackness that mimicked branching roots, great vines, trunks of trees, all interlaced and mingled together: and all these weird shapes, all this turbulent panorama, all this stormy, far-stretching waste of blackness, with its thrilling suggestiveness of life, of action, of boiling, surging, furious motion, was petrified !—all stricken dead and cold in the instant of its maddest rioting !—fettered, paralyzed, and left to glower at heaven in impotent rage for evermore !

Finally we stood in a level, narrow valley (a valley that had been created by the terrific march of some old time irruption) and on either hand towered the two steep peaks of Vesuvius. The one we had to climb—the one that contains the active volcano—seemed about eight hundred or one thousand feet high, and looked almost too straight-up-and-down for any man to climb, and certainly no mule could climb it with a man on his back. Four of these native pirates will carry you to the top in a sedan chair, if you wish it, but suppose they were to slip and let you fall,—is it likely that you would ever stop rolling ? Not this side of eternity, perhaps. We left the mules, sharpened our finger-nails, and began the ascent I have been writing about so long, at twenty minutes to six in the morning. The path led straight up a rugged sweep of loose chunks of pumice-stone, and for about every two steps forward we took, we slid back one. It was so excessively steep that we had to stop, every fifty or sixty steps, and rest a moment. To see our comrades, we had to look very nearly straight up at those above us, and very nearly straight down at those below. We stood on the summit at last—it had taken an hour and fifteen minutes to make the trip.

What we saw there was simply a circular crater—a circular ditch, if you please—about two hundred feet deep, and four or five hundred feet wide, whose inner wall was about half a mile in circumference. In the centre of the great circus ring thus formed, was a torn and ragged upheaval a hundred feet high, all snowed over with a sulphur crust of many and many a brilliant and beautiful color, and the ditch inclosed this like the moat of a castle, or surrounded it as a little river does a little island, if the simile is better. The sulphur coating of that island was gaudy in the extreme—all mingled together in the richest confusion were red, blue, brown, black, yellow, white—I do not know that there was a color, or shade of a color, or combination of colors, unrepresented—and when the sun burst through the morning mists and fired this tinted magnificence, it topped imperial Vesuvius like a jeweled crown!

The crater itself—the ditch—was not so variegated in coloring, but yet, in its softness, richness, and unpretentious elegance, it was more charming, more fascinating to the eye. There was nothing "loud" about its well-bred and well-dressed look. Beautiful? One could stand and look down upon it for a week without getting tired of it. It had the semblance of a pleasant meadow, whose slender grasses and whose velvety mosses were frosted with a shining dust, and tinted with palest green that deepened gradually to the darkest hue of the orange leaf, and deepened yet again into gravest brown, then faded into orange, then into brightest gold, and culminated in the delicate pink of a new-blown rose. Where portions of the meadow had sunk, and where other portions had been broken up like an ice-floe, the cavernous openings of the one, and the ragged upturned edges exposed by the other, were hung with a lace-work of soft-tinted crystals of sulphur that changed their deformities into quaint shapes and figures that were full of grace and beauty.

The walls of the ditch were brilliant with yellow banks of sulphur and with lava and pumice-stone of many colors. No fire was visible any where, but gusts of sulphurous steam issued silently and invisibly from a thousand little cracks and fissures in the crater, and were wafted to our noses with every breeze. But so long as we kept our nostrils buried in our handkerchiefs, there was small danger of suffocation.

Some of the boys thrust long slips of paper down into holes and set them on fire, and so achieved the glory of lighting their cigars by the flames of Vesuvius, and others cooked eggs over fissures in the rocks and were happy.

The view from the summit would have been superb but for the fact that the sun could only pierce the mists at long intervals. Thus the glimpses we had of the grand panorama below were only fitful and unsatisfactory.

THE DESCENT.

The descent of the mountain was a labor of only four minutes. Instead of stalking down the rugged path we ascended, we chose one which was bedded knee-deep in loose ashes, and ploughed our way with prodigious strides that would almost have shamed the performance of him of the seven-league boots.

THE DESCENT.

The Vesuvius of today is a very poor affair compared to the mighty volcano of Kilauea, in the Sandwich Islands, but I am glad I visited it. It was well worth it.

It is said that during one of the grand eruptions of Vesuvius it discharged massy rocks weighing many tons a thousand feet into the air, its vast jets of smoke and steam ascended thirty miles toward the firmament, and clouds of its ashes were wafted abroad and fell upon the decks of ships seven hundred and fifty miles at sea! I will take the ashes at a moderate discount, if any one will take the thirty miles of smoke, but I do not feel able to take a commanding interest in the whole story by myself.

CHAPTER XXXI.

THEY pronounce it Pom-*pay*-e. I always had an idea that you went down into Pompeii with torches, by the way of damp, dark stairways, just as you do in silver mines, and traversed gloomy tunnels with lava overhead and something on either hand like dilapidated prisons gouged out of the solid earth, that faintly resembled houses. But you do nothing of the kind. Fully one-half of the buried city, perhaps, is completely exhumed and thrown open freely to the light of day; and there stand the long rows of solidly-built brick houses (roofless) just as they stood eighteen hundred years ago, hot with the flaming sun; and there lie their floors, clean-swept, and not a bright fragment tarnished or wanting of the labored mosaics that pictured them with the beasts, and birds, and flowers which we copy in perishable carpets to-day; and there are the Venuses, and Bacchuses, and Adonises, making love and getting drunk in many-hued frescoes on the walls of saloon and bed-chamber; and there are the narrow streets and narrower sidewalks, paved with flags of good hard lava, the one deeply rutted with the chariot-wheels, and the other with the passing feet of the Pompeiians of by-gone centuries; and there are the bake-shops, the temples, the halls of justice, the baths, the theatres—all clean-scraped and neat, and suggesting nothing of the nature of a silver mine away down in the bowels of the earth. The broken pillars lying about, the door-less doorways and the crumbled tops of the wilderness of walls,

were wonderfully suggestive of the "burnt district" in one of
our cities, and if there had been any charred timbers, shattered
windows, heaps of debris, and general blackness and smokiness
about the place, the resemblance would have been perfect.

RUINS.—POMPEII.

But no—the sun shines as brightly down on old Pompeii
to-day as it did when Christ was born in Bethlehem, and its
streets are cleaner a hundred times than ever Pompeiian saw
them in her prime. I know whereof I speak—for in the great,
chief thoroughfares (Merchant street and the Street of Fortune) have I not seen with my own eyes how for two hundred
years at least the pavements were not repaired!—how ruts
five and even ten inches deep were worn into the thick flag-
stones by the chariot-wheels of generations of swindled tax-
payers? And do I not know by these signs that Street Commis-
sioners of Pompeii never attended to their business, and that
if they never mended the pavements they never cleaned them?
And, besides, is it not the inborn nature of Street Commis-

sioners to avoid their duty whenever they get a chance? I wish I knew the name of the last one that held office in Pompeii so that I could give him a blast. I speak with feeling on this subject, because I caught my foot in one of those ruts, and the sadness that came over me when I saw the first poor skeleton, with ashes and lava sticking to it, was tempered by the reflection that may be that party was the Street Commissioner.

No—Pompeii is no longer a buried city. It is a city of hundreds and hundreds of roofless houses, and a tangled maze of streets where one could easily get lost, without a guide, and have to sleep in some ghostly palace that had known no living tenant since that awful November night of eighteen centuries ago.

We passed through the gate which faces the Mediterranean, (called the "Marine Gate,") and by the rusty, broken image of Minerva, still keeping tireless watch and ward over the possessions it was powerless to save, and went up a long street and stood in the broad court of the Forum of Justice. The floor was level and clean, and up and down either side was a noble colonnade of broken pillars, with their beautiful Ionic and Corinthian columns scattered about them. At the upper end were the vacant seats of the Judges, and behind them we descended into a dungeon where the ashes and cinders had found two prisoners chained on that memorable November night, and tortured them to death. How they must have tugged at the pitiless fetters as the fierce fires surged around them!

Then we lounged through many and many a sumptuous private mansion which we could not have entered without a formal invitation in incomprehensible Latin, in the olden time, when the owners lived there—and we probably wouldn't have got it. These people built their houses a good deal alike. The floors were laid in fanciful figures wrought in mosaics of many-colored marbles. At the threshold your eyes fall upon a Latin sentence of welcome, sometimes, or a picture of a dog, with the legend "Beware of the Dog," and sometimes a picture of a bear or a faun with no inscription at all. Then you enter a sort of vestibule, where they used to keep the hat-rack, I suppose; next a room with a large marble basin in the midst and the pipes of a fountain; on either side are bed-rooms; beyond the fountain is a reception-room, then a little garden, dining-room, and so forth and so on. The floors were all mosaic, the walls were stuccoed, or frescoed, or ornamented with bas-reliefs, and here and there were statues, large and small, and little fish-pools, and cascades of sparkling water that sprang from secret places in the colonnade of handsome pillars that surrounded the court, and kept the flower-beds fresh and

FORUM OF JUSTICE.—POMPEII.

the air cool. Those Pompeiians were very luxurious in their tastes and habits. The most exquisite bronzes we have seen in Europe, came from the exhumed cities of Herculaneum and Pompeii, and also the finest cameos and the most delicate engravings on precious stones; their pictures, eighteen or nine-teen centuries old, are often much more pleasing than the celebrated rubbish of the old masters of three centuries ago. They were well up in art. 'From the creation of these works of the first, clear up to the eleventh century, art seems hardly to have existed at all—at least no remnants of it are left—and it was curious to see how far (in some things, at any rate,) these old time pagans excelled the remote generations of masters that came after them. The pride of the world in sculptures seem to be the Laocoon and the Dying Gladiator, in Rome. They are as old as Pompeii, were dug from the earth like Pompeii; but their exact age or who made them can only be conjectured. But worn, and cracked, without a history, and with the blemishing stains of numberless centuries upon them, they still mutely mock at all efforts to rival their perfections.

It was a quaint and curious pastime, wandering through this old silent city of the dead—lounging through utterly deserted streets where thousands and thousands of human beings once bought and sold, and walked and rode, and made the place resound with the noise and confusion of traffic and pleasure. They were not lazy. They hurried in those days. We had evidence of that. There was a temple on one corner, and it was a shorter cut to go between the columns of that temple from one street to the other than to go around—and behold that pathway had been worn deep into the heavy flag-stone floor of the building by generations of time-saving feet! They would not go around when it was quicker to go through. We do that way in our cities.

Every where, you see things that make you wonder how old these old houses were before the night of destruction came— things, too, which bring back those long dead inhabitants and place them living before your eyes. For instance: The steps (two feet thick—lava blocks) that lead up out of the school, and the same kind of steps that lead up into the dress circle of the principal theatre, are almost worn through! For ages the boys hurried out of that school, and for ages their parents hurried into that theatre, and the nervous feet that have been dust and ashes for eighteen centuries have left their record for

us to read to-day. I imagined I could see crowds of gentlemen and ladies thronging into the theatre, with tickets for
secured seats in their hands, and on the wall, I read the imaginary placard, in infamous grammar, "Positively No Free
List, Except Members of the Press!" Hanging about the
doorway (I fancied,) were slouchy Pompeiian street-boys utter-
ing slang and profanity, and keeping a wary eye out for checks.
I entered the theatre, and sat down in one of the long rows of
stone benches in the dress circle, and looked at the place for
the orchestra, and the ruined stage, and around at the wide
sweep of empty boxes, and thought to myself, "This house
won't pay." I tried to imagine the music in full blast, the
leader of the orchestra beating time, and the "versatile" So-
and-So (who had "just returned from a most successful tour
in the provinces to play his last and farewell engagement of
positively six nights only, in Pompeii, previous to his departure for Herculaneum,") charging around the stage and piling
the agony mountains high—but I could not do it with such a
"house" as that; those empty benches tied my fancy down to
dull reality. I said, these people that ought to be here have
been dead, and still, and moldering to dust for ages and ages,
and will never care for the trifles and follies of life any more
for ever—"Owing to circumstances, etc., etc., there will not
be any performance to-night." Close down the curtain. Put
out the lights.

And so I turned away and went through shop after shop and
store after store, far down the long street of the merchants,
and called for the wares of Rome and the East, but the trades-
men were gone, the marts were silent, and nothing was left
but the broken jars all set in cement of cinders and ashes: the
wine and the oil that once had filled them were gone with
their owners.

In a bake-shop was a mill for grinding the grain, and the
furnaces for baking the bread: and they say that here, in the
same furnaces, the exhumers of Pompeii found nice, well
baked loaves which the baker had not found time to remove
from the ovens the last time he left his shop, because circumstances compelled him to leave in such a hurry.

In one house (the only building in Pompeii which no woman is now allowed to enter,) were the small rooms and short beds of solid masonry, just as they were in the old times, and on the walls were pictures which looked almost as fresh as if they were painted yesterday, but which no pen could have the hardihood to describe; and here and there were Latin inscriptions—obscene scintillations of wit, scratched by hands that possibly were uplifted to Heaven for succor in the midst of a driving storm of fire before the night was done.

In one of the principal streets was a ponderous stone tank, and a water-spout that supplied it, and where the tired, heated toilers from the Campagna used to rest their right hands when they bent over to put their lips to the spout, the thick stone was worn down to a broad groove an inch or two deep. Think of the countless thousands of hands that had pressed that spot in the ages that are gone, to so reduce a stone that is as hard as iron!

They had a great public bulletin board in Pompeii—a place where announcements for gladiatorial combats, elections, and such things, were posted—not on perishable paper, but carved in enduring stone. One lady, who, I take it, was rich and well brought up, advertised a dwelling or so to rent, with baths and all the modern improvements, and several hundred shops, stipulating that the dwellings should not be put to immoral purposes. You can find out who lived in many a house in Pompeii by the carved stone door-plates affixed to them: and in the same way you can tell who they were that occupy the tombs. Every where around are things that reveal to you something of the customs and history of this forgotten people. But what would a volcano leave of an American city, if it once rained its cinders on it? Hardly a sign or a symbol to tell its story.

In one of these long Pompeiian halls the skeleton of a man was found, with ten pieces of gold in one hand and a large key in the other. He had seized his money and started toward the door, but the fiery tempest caught him at the very threshold, and he sank down and died. One more minute of precious time would have saved him. I saw the skeletons of a man, a woman, and two young girls. The woman had her hands spread wide apart, as if in mortal terror, and I imagined I could still trace upon her shapeless face something of the expression of wild despair that distorted it when the heavens rained fire in these streets, so many ages ago. The girls and the man lay with their faces upon their arms, as if they had tried to shield them from the enveloping cinders. In one apartment eighteen skeletons were found, all in sitting pos-

HOUSE.—POMPEII.

tures, and blackened places on the walls still mark their shapes and show their attitudes, like shadows. One of them, a woman, still wore upon her skeleton throat a necklace, with her name engraved upon it—JULIE DI DIOMEDE.

But perhaps the most poetical thing Pompeii has yielded to modern research, was that grand figure of a Roman soldier, clad in complete armor; who, true to his duty, true to his proud name of a soldier of Rome, and full of the stern courage which had given to that name its glory, stood to his post by the city gate, erect and unflinching, till the hell that raged around him *burned out* the dauntless spirit it could not conquer.

We never read of Pompeii but we think of that soldier; we can not write of Pompeii without the natural impulse to grant to him the mention he so well deserves. Let us remember that he was a soldier—not a policeman—and so, praise him. Being a soldier, he staid,—because the warrior instinct forbade him to fly. Had he been a policeman he would have staid, also—because he would have been asleep.

There are not half a dozen flights of stairs in Pompeii, and no other evidences that the houses were more than one story high. The people did not live in the clouds, as do the Venetians, the Genoese and Neapolitans of to-day.

We came out from under the solemn mysteries of this city of the Venerable Past—this city which perished, with all its old ways and its quaint old fashions about it, remote centuries ago, when the Disciples were preaching the new religion, which is as old as the hills to us now—and went dreaming among the trees that grow over acres and acres of its still buried streets and squares, till a shrill whistle and the cry of " *All aboard—last train for Naples!*" woke me up and reminded me that I belonged in the nineteenth century, and was not a dusty mummy, caked with ashes and cinders, eighteen hundred years old. The transition was startling. The idea of a railroad train actually running to old dead Pompeii, and whistling irreverently, and calling for passengers in the most bustling and business-like way, was as strange a thing as one could imagine, and as unpoetical and disagreeable as it was strange.

Compare the cheerful life and the sunshine of this day with the horrors the younger Pliny saw here, the 9th of November, A. D. 79, when he was so bravely striving to remove his mother out of reach of harm, while she begged him, with all a mother's unselfishness, to leave her to perish and save himself.

'By this time the murky darkness had so increased that one might have believed himself abroad in a black and moonless night, or in a chamber where all the lights had been extinguished. On every hand was heard the complaints of women, the wailing of children, and the cries of men. One called his father, another his son, and another his wife, and only by their voices could they know each other. Many in their despair begged that death would come and end their distress.

"Some implored the gods to succor them, and some believed that this night was the last, the eternal night which should engulf the universe!

"Even so it seemed to me—and I consoled myself for the coming death with the reflection: BEHOLD, THE WORLD IS PASSING AWAY!"

*   *   *   *   *   *   *

After browsing among the stately ruins of Rome, of Baiæ, of Pompeii, and after glancing down the long marble ranks of battered and nameless imperial heads that stretch down the corridors of the Vatican, one thing strikes me with a force it never had before: the unsubstantial, unlasting character of fame. Men lived long lives, in the olden time, and struggled feverishly through them, toiling like slaves, in oratory, in generalship, or in literature, and then laid them down and died, happy in the possession of an enduring history and a deathless name. Well, twenty little centuries flutter away, and what is left of these things? A crazy inscription on a block of stone, which snuffy antiquaries bother over and tangle up and make nothing out of but a bare name (which they spell wrong)—no history, no tradition, no poetry—nothing that can give it even a passing interest. What may be left of General Grant's great name forty centuries hence? This—in the Encyclopedia for A. D. 5868, possibly:

"URIAH S. (or Z.) GRAUNT—popular poet of ancient times in the Aztec provinces of the United States of British America. Some authors say flourished about A. D. 742; but the learned Ah-ah Foo-foo states that he was a cotemporary of Scharkspyre, the English poet, and flourished about A. D. 1328, some three centuries *after* the Trojan war instead of before it. He wrote 'Rock me to Sleep, Mother.'"

These thoughts sadden me. I will to bed.

CHAPTER XXXII.

HOME, again! For the first time, in many weeks, the ship's entire family met and shook hands on the quarter-deck. They had gathered from many points of the compass and from many lands, but not one was missing; there was no tale of sickness or death among the flock to dampen the pleasure of the reunion. Once more there was a full audience on deck to listen to the sailors' chorus as they got the anchor up, and to wave an adieu to the land as we sped away from Naples. The seats were full at dinner again, the domino parties were complete, and the life and bustle on the upper deck in the fine moonlight at night was like old times—old times that had been gone weeks only, but yet they were weeks so crowded with incident, adventure and excitement, that they seemed almost like years. There was no lack of cheerfulness on board the *Quaker City*. For once, her title was a misnomer.

At seven in the evening, with the western horizon all golden from the sunken sun, and specked with distant ships, the full moon sailing high over head, the dark blue of the sea under foot, and a strange sort of twilight affected by all these different lights and colors around us and about us, we sighted superb Stromboli. With what majesty the monarch held his lonely state above the level sea! Distance clothed him in a purple gloom, and added a veil of shimmering mist that so softened his rugged features that we seemed to see him through a web of silver gauze. His torch was out; his fires were smoldering; a tall column of smoke that rose up and lost

itself in the growing moonlight was all the sign he gave that
he was a living Autocrat of the Sea and not the spectre of a
dead one.

STROMBOLI.

At two in the morning we swept through the Straits of
Messina, and so bright was the moonlight that Italy on the
one hand and Sicily on the other seemed almost as distinctly
visible as though we looked at them from the middle of a
street we were traversing. The city of Messina, milk-white,
and starred and spangled all over with gaslights, was a fairy
spectacle. A great party of us were on deck smoking and
making a noise, and waiting to see famous Scylla and Charybdis. And presently the Oracle stepped out with his eternal
spy-glass and squared himself on the deck like another Colossus
of Rhodes. It was a surprise to see him abroad at such an
hour. Nobody supposed he cared any thing about an old fable
like that of Scylla and Charybdis. One of the boys said:

"Hello, doctor, what are you doing up here at this time of night?—What do you want to see this place for?"

"What do *I* want to see this place for? Young man, little do you know me, or you wouldn't ask such a question. I wish to see *all* the places that's mentioned in the Bible."

"Stuff—this place isn't mentioned in the Bible."

"It ain't mentioned in the Bible!—*this* place ain't—well now, what place *is* this, since you know so much about it?"

"Why it's Scylla and Charybdis."

"Scylla and Cha—confound it, I thought it was Sodom and Gomorrah!"

And he closed up his glass and went below. The above is the ship story. Its plausibility is marred a little by the fact that the Oracle was not a biblical student, and did not spend much of his time instructing himself about Scriptural localities. —They say the Oracle complains, in this hot weather, lately, that the only beverage in the ship that is passable, is the butter. He did not mean butter, of course, but inasmuch as that article remains in a melted state now since we are out of ice, it is fair to give him the credit of getting one long word in the right place, anyhow, for once in his life. He said, in Rome, that the Pope was a noble-looking old man, but he never *did* think much of his Iliad.

We spent one pleasant day skirting along the Isles of Greece. They are very mountainous. Their prevailing tints are gray and brown, approaching to red. Little white villages surrounded by trees, nestle in the valleys or roost upon the lofty perpendicular sea-walls.

We had one fine sunset—a rich carmine flush that suffused the western sky and cast a ruddy glow far over the sea.—Fine sunsets seem to be rare in this part of the world—or at least, striking ones. They are soft, sensuous, lovely—they are exquisite, refined, effeminate, but we have seen no sunsets here yet like the gorgeous conflagrations that flame in the track of the sinking sun in our high northern latitudes.

But what were sunsets to us, with the wild excitement upon us of approaching the most renowned of cities! What cared we for outward visions, when Agamemnon, Achilles, and a thousand other heroes of the great Past were marching in ghostly procession through our fancies? What were sunsets to us, who were about to live and breathe and walk in actual Athens; yea, and go far down into the dead centuries and bid in person for the slaves, Diogenes and Plato, in the public market-place, or gossip with the neighbors about the siege of Troy or the splendid deeds of Marathon? We scorned to consider sunsets.

We arrived, and entered the ancient harbor of the Piræus at last. We dropped anchor within half a mile of the village. Away off, across the undulating Plain of Attica, could be seen a little square-topped hill with a something on it, which our glasses soon discovered to be the ruined edifices of the citadel of the Athenians, and most prominent among them loomed the venerable Parthenon. So exquisitely clear and pure is this wonderful atmosphere that every column of the noble structure was discernible through the telescope, and even the smaller ruins about it assumed some semblance of shape. This at a distance of five or six miles. In the valley, near the Acropolis, (the square-topped hill before spoken of,) Athens itself could be vaguely made out with an ordinary lorgnette. Every body was anxious to get ashore and visit these classic localities as quickly as possible. No land we had yet seen had aroused such universal interest among the passengers.

But bad news came. The commandant of the Piræus came in his boat, and said we must either depart or else get outside the harbor and remain imprisoned in our ship, under rigid quarantine, for eleven days! So we took up the anchor and moved outside, to lie a dozen hours or so, taking in supplies, and then sail for Constantinople. It was the bitterest disappointment we had yet experienced. To lie a whole day in sight of the Acropolis, and yet be obliged to go away without visiting Athens! Disappointment was hardly a strong enough word to describe the circumstances.

All hands were on deck, all the afternoon, with books and maps and glasses, trying to determine which "narrow rocky

ridge " was the Areopagus, which sloping hill the Pnyx, which
elevation the Museum Hill, and so on. And we got things
confused. Discussion became heated, and party spirit ran
high. Church members were gazing with emotion upon a hill
which they
said was the
one St. Paul
p r e a c h e d
from, and an-
other faction
claimed that
that hill was
Hy m e t t u s,
and another
that it was
Pente li con!
After all the
trouble, we
could be cer-

VIEW OF THE ACROPOLIS, LOOKING WEST.

tain of only one thing—the square-topped hill was the Acropolis, and the grand ruin that crowned it was the Parthenon,
whose picture we knew in infancy in the school books.

We inquired of every body who came near the ship, whether
there were guards in the Piræus, whether they were strict,
what the chances were of capture should any of us slip ashore,
and in case any of us made the venture and were caught, what
would be probably done to us? The answers were discouraging: There was a strong guard or police force; the Piræus
was a small town, and any stranger seen in it would surely
attract attention—capture would be certain. The commandant
said the punishment would be "heavy;" when asked "how
heavy?" he said it would be "very severe"—that was all we
could get out of him.

At eleven o'clock at night, when most of the ship's company
were abed, four of us stole softly ashore in a small boat, a
clouded moon favoring the enterprise, and started two and two,
and far apart, over a low hill, intending to go clear around the

Piræus, out of the range of its police. Picking our way so
stealthily over that rocky, nettle-grown eminence, made me
feel a good deal as if I were on my way somewhere to steal
something. My immediate comrade and I talked in an under-
tone about quarantine laws and their penalties, but we found
nothing cheering in the subject. I was posted. Only a few
days before, I was talking with our captain, and he mentioned
the case of a man who swam ashore from a quarantined ship
somewhere, and got imprisoned six months for it; and when
he was in Genoa a few years ago, a captain of a quarantined
ship went in his boat to a departing ship, which was already
outside of the harbor, and put a letter on board to be taken to
his family, and the authorities imprisoned him three months
for it, and then conducted him and his ship fairly to sea, and
warned him never to show himself in that port again while he
lived. This kind of conversation did no good, further than to
give a sort of dismal interest to our quarantine-breaking expedition, and so we dropped it. We made the entire circuit of
the town without seeing any body but one man, who stared at
us curiously, but said nothing, and a dozen persons asleep on
the ground before their doors, whom we walked among and
never woke—but we woke up dogs enough, in all conscience—
we always had one or two barking at our heels, and several
times we had as many as ten and twelve at once. They made
such a preposterous din that persons aboard our ship said they
could tell how we were progressing for a long time, and where
we were, by the barking of the dogs. The clouded moon still
favored us. When we had made the whole circuit, and were
passing among the houses on the further side of the town, the
moon came out splendidly, but we no longer feared the light.
As we approached a well, near a house, to get a drink, the
owner merely glanced at us and went within. He left the
quiet, slumbering town at our mercy. I record it here proudly,
that we didn't do any thing to it.

Seeing no road, we took a tall hill to the left of the distant
Acropolis for a mark, and steered straight for it over all obstructions, and over a little rougher piece of country than

exists any where else outside of the State of Nevada, perhaps.
Part of the way it was covered with small, loose stones—we
trod on six at a time, and they all rolled.   Another part of it
was dry, loose, newly-ploughed ground.   Still another part of
it was a long stretch of low grape-vines, which were tangle-
some and troublesome, and which we took to be brambles.
The Attic Plain, barring the grape-vines, was a barren, desolate, unpoetical waste—I wonder what it was in Greece's Age
of Glory, five hundred years before Christ?

In the neighborhood of one o'clock in the morning, when
we were heated with fast walking and parched with thirst,
Denny exclaimed, " Why, these weeds are grape-vines!" and
in five minutes we had a score of bunches of large, white, delicious grapes, and were reaching down for more when a dark
shape rose mysteriously up out of the shadows beside us and
said " Ho!"   And so we left.

In ten minutes more we struck into a beautiful road, and
unlike some
others   we
had   stum-
bled upon at
intervals, it
led in the
right direc-
tion.   We
followed it.
It was broad,
and smooth,
and white—
h a n d·s o me
and in per-
fect   repair,
and   shaded
on both sides
for a mile or
so with sin-
gle ranks of

" HO!"

trees, and also with luxuriant vineyards.   Twice we entered and stole grapes, and the second time somebody shouted at us from some invisible place. Whereupon we left again. We speculated in grapes no more on that side of Athens.

Shortly we came upon an ancient stone aqueduct, built upon arches, and from that time forth we had ruins all about us— we were approaching our journey's end. We could not see the Acropolis now or the high hill, either, and I wanted to follow the road till we were abreast of them, but the others overruled me, and we toiled laboriously up the stony hill immediately in our front—and from its summit saw another— climbed it and saw another! It was an hour of exhausting work. Soon we came upon a row of open graves, cut in the

THE ASSAULT.

solid rock—(for a while one of them served Socrates for a prison)—we passed around the shoulder of the hill, and the citadel, in all its ruined magnificence, burst upon us! We hurried across the ravine and up a winding road, and stood on the old Acropolis, with the prodigious walls of the citadel towering above our heads. We did not stop to inspect their massive blocks of marble, or measure their height, or guess at their extraordinary thickness, but passed at once through a great arched passage like a railway tunnel, and went straight to the gate that leads to the ancient temples. It was locked! So, after all, it seemed that we were not to see the great Parthenon face to face. We sat down and held a council of war. Result: the gate was only a flimsy structure of wood—we would break it down. It seemed like desecration, but then we had traveled far, and our necessities were urgent. We could not hunt up guides and keepers—we must be on the ship before daylight. So we argued. This was all very fine, but when we came to break the gate, we could not do it. We moved around an angle of the wall and found a low bastion—eight feet high without—ten or twelve within. Denny prepared to scale it, and we got ready to follow. By dint of hard scrambling he finally straddled the top, but some loose stones crumbled away and fell with a crash into the court within. There was instantly a banging of doors and a shout. Denny dropped from the wall in a twinkling, and we retreated in disorder to the gate. Xerxes took that mighty citadel four hundred and eighty years before Christ, when his five millions of soldiers and camp-followers followed him to Greece, and if we four Americans could have remained unmolested five minutes longer, we would have taken it too.

The garrison had turned out—four Greeks. We clamored at the gate, and they admitted us. [Bribery and corruption.]

We crossed a large court, entered a great door, and stood upon a pavement of purest white marble, deeply worn by footprints. Before us, in the flooding moonlight, rose the noblest ruins we had ever looked upon—the Propylæ; a small Temple of Minerva; the Temple of Hercules, and the grand Parthenon. [We got these names from the Greek guide, who didn't seem to know more than seven men ought to know.] These edifices were all built of the whitest Pentelic marble, but have a pinkish stain upon them now. Where any part is broken, however, the fracture looks like fine loaf sugar. Six caryatides, or marble women, clad in flowing robes, support the portico of the Temple of Hercules, but the porticos and colonnades of the other structures are formed of massive Doric and Ionic pillars, whose flutings and capitals are still measurably perfect, notwithstanding the centuries that have gone over them and the sieges they have suffered. The Parthenon, originally, was two hundred and twenty-six feet long, one hundred wide, and seventy high, and had two rows of great columns, eight in each, at either end, and single rows of seventeen

CARYATIDES.

each down the sides, and was one of the most graceful and beautiful edifices ever erected.

Most of the Parthenon's imposing columns are still standing, but the roof is gone. It was a perfect building two hundred and fifty years ago, when a shell dropped into the Venetian magazine stored here, and the explosion which followed wrecked and unroofed it. I remember but little about the Parthenon, and I have put in one or two facts and figures for the use of other people with short memories. Got them from the guide-book.

As we wandered thoughtfully down the marble-paved length of this stately temple, the scene about us was strangely impressive. Here and there, in lavish profusion, were gleaming white statues of men and women, propped against blocks of marble, some of them armless, some without legs, others head-less—but all looking mournful in the moonlight, and start-lingly human! They rose up and confronted the midnight intruder on every side—they stared at him with stony eyes from unlooked-for nooks and recesces; they peered at him over fragmentary heaps far down the desolate corridors; they barred his way in the midst of the broad forum, and solemnly pointed with handless arms the way from the sacred fane; and through the roofless temple the moon looked down, and banded the floor and darkened the scattered fragments and broken statues with the slanting shadows of the columns.

What a world of ruined sculpture was about us! Set up in rows—stacked up in piles—scattered broadcast over the wide area of the Acropolis—were hundreds of crippled statues of all sizes and of the most exquisite workmanship; and vast frag-ments of marble that once belonged to the entablatures, cov-ered with bas-reliefs representing battles and sieges, ships of war with three and four tiers of oars, pageants and processions —every thing one could think of. History says that the tem-ples of the Acropolis were filled with the noblest works of Praxiteles and Phidias, and of many a great master in sculp-ture besides—and surely these elegant fragments attest it.

We walked out into the grass-grown, fragment-strewn court beyond the Parthenon. It startled us, every now and then, to see a stony white face stare suddenly up at us out of the grass with its dead eyes. The place seemed alive with ghosts. I half expected to see the Athenian heroes of twenty centuries ago glide out of the shadows and steal into the old temple they knew so well and regarded with such boundless pride.

The full moon was riding high in the cloudless heavens, now. We sauntered carelessly and unthinkingly to the edge of the lofty battlements of the citadel, and looked down—a vision! And such a vision! Athens by moonlight! The prophet that thought the splendors of the New Jerusalem were revealed to him, surely saw this instead! It lay in the level plain right under our feet—all spread abroad like a pic-ture—and we looked down upon it as we might have looked from a balloon. We saw no semblance of a street, but every house, every window, every clinging vine, every projection, was as distinct and sharply marked as if the time were noonday; and yet there was no glare, no glitter, nothing harsh or repulsive—the noiseless city was flooded with the mellowest light that ever streamed from the moon, and seemed like some living creature wrapped in peaceful slumber. On its further side was a little temple, whose delicate pillars and ornate front glowed with a rich lustre that chained the eye like a spell; and nearer by, the palace of the king reared its creamy walls out of the midst of a great garden of shrubbery that was flecked all over with a random shower of amber lights—a spray of golden sparks that lost their brightness in the glory of the moon, and glinted softly upon the sea of dark foliage like the pallid stars of the milky-way. Overhead the stately columns, majestic still in their ruin—under foot the dreaming city—in the distance the silver sea—not on the broad earth is there another picture half so beautiful!

As we turned and moved again through the temple, I wished that the illustrious men who had sat in it in the remote ages could visit it again and reveal themselves to our curious eyes —Plato, Aristotle, Demosthenes, Socrates, Phocion, Pythagoras, Euclid, Pindar, Xenophon, Herodotus, Praxiteles and Phidias, Zeuxis the painter. What a constellation of celebrated names! But more than all, I wished that old Diogenes, groping so patiently with his lantern, searching so zealously for one solitary honest man in all the world, might meander along and stumble on our party. I ought not to say it, may be, but still I suppose he would have put out his light.

We left the Parthenon to keep its watch over old Athens, as it had kept it for twenty-three hundred years, and went and stood outside the walls of the citadel. In the distance was the ancient, but still almost perfect Temple of Theseus, and close by, looking to the west, was the Bema, from whence Demosthenes thundered his philippics and fired the wavering patriotism of his countrymen. To the right was Mars Hill, where the Areopagus sat in ancient times, and where St. Paul defined

THE PARTHENON.

his position, and below was the market-place where he " disputed daily " with the gossip-loving Athenians. We climbed the stone steps St. Paul ascended, and stood in the square-cut place he stood in, and tried to recollect the Bible account of the matter—but for certain reasons, I could not recall the words. I have found them since :

"Now while Paul waited for them at Athens, his spirit was stirred in him, when he saw the city wholly given up to idolatry.

"Therefore disputed he in the synagogue with the Jews, and with the devout persons, and in the market daily with them that met with him.

* * * * * * * * *

"And they took him and brought him unto Areopagus, saying, May we know what this new doctrine whereof thou speakest is ?

* * * * * * * * *

"Then Paul stood in the midst of Mars hill, and said, Ye men of Athens, I perceive that in all things ye are too superstitious ;

"For as I passed by and beheld your devotions, I found an altar with this inscription : TO THE UNKNOWN GOD. Whom, therefore, ye ignorantly worship, him declare I unto you."—*Acts*, ch. xvii."

It occurred to us, after a while, that if we wanted to get home before daylight betrayed us, we had better be moving. So we hurried away. When far on our road, we had a parting view of the Parthenon, with the moonlight streaming through its open colonnades and touching its capitals with silver. As it looked then, solemn, grand, and beautiful it will always remain in our memories.

As we marched along, we began to get over our fears, and ceased to care much about quarantine scouts or any body else. We grew bold and reckless ; and once, in a sudden burst of courage, I even threw a stone at a dog. It was a pleasant reflection, though, that I did not hit him, because his master might just possibly have been a policeman. Inspired by this happy failure, my valor became utterly uncontrollable, and at intervals I absolutely whistled, though on a moderate key. But boldness breeds boldness, and shortly I plunged into a vineyard, in the full light of the moon, and captured a gallon of superb grapes, not even minding the presence of a peasant who rode by on a mule. Denny and Birch followed my example. Now I had grapes enough for a dozen, but then Jackson was all swollen up with courage, too, and he was obliged to enter a vineyard presently. The first bunch he seized brought trouble. A frowsy, bearded brigand sprang into the road with a shout, and flourished a musket in the light of the moon! We sidled toward the Piræus—not running, you understand, but only

WE SIDLED, NOT RAN.

advancing with celerity. The brigand shouted again, but still we advanced. It was getting late, and we had no time to fool away on every ass that wanted to drivel Greek platitudes to us. We would just as soon have talked with him as not if we had not been in a hurry. Presently Denny said, "Those fellows are following us!"

We turned, and, sure enough, there they were—three fantastic pirates armed with guns. We slackened our pace to let them come up, and in the meantime I got out my cargo of grapes and dropped them firmly but reluctantly into the shadows by the wayside. But I was not afraid. I only felt that it was not right to steal grapes. And all the more so when the owner was around—and not only around, but with his friends around also. The villains came up and searched a bundle Dr.

Birch had in his hand, and scowled upon him when they found it had nothing in it but some holy rocks from Mars Hill, and these were not contraband. They evidently suspected him of playing some wretched fraud upon them, and seemed half inclined to scalp the party. But finally they dismissed us with a warning, couched in excellent Greek, I suppose, and dropped tranquilly in our wake. When they had gone three hundred yards they stopped, and we went on rejoiced. But behold, another armed rascal came out of the shadows and took their place, and followed us two hundred yards. Then he delivered us over to another miscreant, who emerged from some mysterious place, and he in turn to another! For a mile and a half our rear was guarded all the while by armed men. I never traveled in so much state before in all my life.

It was a good while after that before we ventured to steal any more grapes, and when we did we stirred up another troublesome brigand, and then we ceased all further speculation in that line. I suppose that fellow that rode by on the mule posted all the sentinels, from Athens to the Piræus, about us.

Every field on that long route was watched by an armed sentinel, some of whom had fallen asleep, no doubt, but were on hand, nevertheless. This shows what sort of a country modern Attica is—a community of questionable characters. These men were not there to guard their possessions against strangers, but against each other; for strangers seldom visit Athens and the Piræus, and when they do, they go in daylight, and can buy all the grapes they want for a trifle. The modern inhabitants are confiscators and falsifiers of high repute, if gossip speaks truly concerning them, and I freely believe it does.

Just as the earliest tinges of the dawn flushed the eastern sky and turned the pillared Parthenon to a broken harp hung in the pearly horizon, we closed our thirteenth mile of weary, round-about marching, and emerged upon the sea-shore abreast the ships, with our usual escort of fifteen hundred Piræan dogs howling at our heels. We hailed a boat that was two or three hundred yards from shore, and discovered in a moment that it was a police-boat on the lookout for any quarantine-breakers that might chance to be abroad. So we dodged—we were used to that by this time—and when the scouts reached the spot we had so lately occupied, we were absent. They cruised along the shore, but in the wrong direction, and shortly our own boat issued from the gloom and took us aboard. They

had heard our signal on the ship. We rowed noiselessly away, and before the police-boat came in sight again, we were safe at home once more.

Four more of our passengers were anxious to visit Athens, and started half an hour after we returned; but

ANCIENT ACROPOLIS.

they had not been ashore five minutes till the police discovered and chased them so hotly that they barely escaped to their boat again, and that was all. They pursued the enterprise no further.

We set sail for Constantinople to-day, but some of us little care for that. We have seen all there was to see in the old city that had its birth sixteen hundred years before Christ was born, and was an old town before the foundations of Troy were laid—and saw it in its most attractive aspect. Wherefore, why should *we* worry?

Two other passengers ran the blockade successfully last night. So we learned this morning. They slipped away so quietly that they were not missed from the ship for several hours. They had the hardihood to march into the Piræus in the early dusk and hire a carriage. They ran some danger of adding two or three months' imprisonment to the other novelties of their Holy Land Pleasure Excursion. I admire "cheek." *   But they went and came safely, and never walked a step.

* Quotation from the Pilgrims.

23

CHAPTER XXXIII.

FROM Athens all through the islands of the Grecian Archipelago, we saw little but forbidding sea-walls and barren hills, sometimes surmounted by three or four graceful columns of some ancient temple, lonely and deserted—a fitting symbol of the desolation that has come upon all Greece in these latter ages. We saw no ploughed fields, very few villages, no trees or grass or vegetation of any kind, scarcely, and hardly ever an isolated house. Greece is a bleak, unsmiling desert, without agriculture, manufactures or commerce, apparently. What supports its poverty-stricken people or its Government, is a mystery.

I suppose that ancient Greece and modern Greece compared, furnish the most extravagant contrast to be found in history. George I., an infant of eighteen, and a scraggy nest of foreign office holders, sit in the places of Themistocles, Pericles, and the illustrious scholars and generals of the Golden Age of Greece. The fleets that were the wonder of the world when the Parthenon was new, are a beggarly handful of fishing-smacks now, and the manly people that performed such miracles of valor at Marathon are only a tribe of unconsidered slaves to-day. The classic Illyssus has gone dry, and so have all the sources of Grecian wealth and greatness. The nation numbers only eight hundred thousand souls, and there is poverty and misery and mendacity enough among them to furnish forty millions and be liberal about it. Under King Otho the revenues of the State were five millions of dollars—raised from a tax of *one-tenth* of all the agricultural products of the land (which tenth the farmer had to bring to the royal granaries on pack-mules any distance not exceeding six leagues)

QUEEN OF GREECE.

and from extravagant taxes on trade and commerce. Out of that five millions the small tyrant tried to keep an army of ten thousand men, pay all the hundreds of useless Grand Equerries in Waiting, First Grooms of the Bedchamber, Lord High Chancellors of the Exploded Exchequer, and all the other absurdities which these puppy-kingdoms indulge in, in imitation of the great monarchies; and in addition he set about building a white marble palace to cost about five millions itself. The result was, simply: ten into five goes no times and none over. All these things could not be done with five millions, and Otho fell into trouble.

The Greek throne, with its unpromising adjuncts of a ragged population of ingenious rascals who were out of employment eight months in the year because there was little for them to borrow and less to confiscate, and a waste of barren hills and weed-grown deserts, went begging for a good while. It was offered to one of Victoria's sons, and afterwards to various other younger sons of royalty who had no thrones and were out of business, but they all had the charity to decline the dreary honor, and veneration enough for Greece's ancient greatness to refuse to mock her sorrowful rags and dirt with a tinsel throne in this day of her humiliation—till they came to this young Danish George, and he took it. He has finished the splendid palace I saw in the radiant moonlight the other night, and is doing many other things for the salvation of Greece, they say.

PALACE OF GREECE.

We sailed through the barren Archipelago, and into the narrow channel they sometimes call the Dardanelles and sometimes the Hellespont. This part of the country is rich in historic reminiscences, and poor as Sahara in every thing else. For instance, as we approached the Dardanelles, we coasted along the Plains of Troy and past the mouth of the Scamander; we saw where Troy had stood (in the distance,) and where it does not stand now—a city that perished when the world was young. The poor Trojans are all dead, now. They were born too late to see Noah's ark, and died too soon to see our menagarie. We saw where Agamemnon's fleets rendezvoused, and away inland a mountain which the map said was Mount Ida. Within the

Hellespont we saw where the original first shoddy contract mentioned in history was carried out, and the " parties of the second part " gently rebuked by Xerxes.   I speak of the famous bridge of boats which Xerxes ordered to be built over the narrowest part of the Hellespont (where it is only two or three miles wide.)   A moderate gale destroyed the flimsy structure, and the King, thinking that to publicly rebuke the contractors might have a good effect on the next set, called them out before the army and had them beheaded.   In the next ten minutes he let a new contract for the bridge.   It has been observed by ancient writers that the second bridge was a very good bridge.   Xerxes crossed his host of five millions of men on it, and if it had not been purposely destroyed, it would probably have been there yet.   If our Government would rebuke some of our shoddy contractors occasionally, it might work much good.   In the Hellespont we saw where Leander and Lord Byron swam across, the one to see her upon whom his soul's affections were fixed with a devotion that only death could impair, and the other merely for a flyer, as Jack says. We had two noted tombs near us, too.   On one shore slept Ajax, and on the other Hecuba.

We had water batteries and forts on both sides of the Hellespont, flying the crimson flag of Turkey, with its white crescent, and occasionally a village, and sometimes a train of camels ; we had all these to look at till we entered the broad sea of Marmora, and then the land soon fading from view, we resumed euchre and whist once more.

We dropped anchor in the mouth of the Golden Horn at daylight in the morning.   Only three or four of us were up to see the great Ottoman capital.   The passengers do not turn out at unseasonable hours, as they used to, to get the earliest possible glimpse of strange foreign cities.   They are well over that.   If we were lying in sight of the Pyramids of Egypt, they would not come on deck until after breakfast, now-a-days.

The Golden Horn is a narrow arm of the sea, which branches from the Bosporus (a sort of broad river which connects the Marmora and Black Seas,) and, curving around, divides the

city in the middle. Galata and Pera are on one side of the
Bosporus, and the Golden Horn; Stamboul (ancient Byzan-
tium) is upon the other. On the other bank of the Bosporus
is Scutari and other suburbs of Constantinople. This great
city contains a million inhabitants, but so narrow are its streets,
and so crowded together are its houses, that it does not cover
much more than half as much ground as New York City.
Seen from the anchorage or from a mile or so up the Bosporus, it is by far the handsomest city we have seen. Its dense
array of houses swells upward from the water's edge, and
spreads over the domes of many hills; and the gardens that
peep out here and there, the great globes of the mosques, and
the countless minarets that meet the eye every where, invest
the metropolis with the quaint Oriental aspect one dreams of
when he reads books of eastern travel. Constantinople makes
a noble picture.

But its attractiveness begins and ends with its picturesque-
ness. From the time one starts ashore till he gets back again,
he execrates it. The boat he goes in is admirably miscalcula-
ted for the service it is built for. It is handsomely and neatly
fitted up, but no man could handle it well in the turbulent
currents that sweep down the Bosporus from the Black Sea,
and few men could row it satisfactorily even in still water. It
is a long, light canoe (caique,) large at one end and tapering
to a knife blade at the other. They make that long sharp end
the bow, and you can imagine how these boiling currents spin
it about. It has two oars, and sometimes four, and no rudder.
You start to go to a given point and you run in fifty different
directions before you get there. First one oar is backing water, and then the other; it is seldom that both are going ahead
at once. This kind of boating is calculated to drive an impatient man mad in a week. The boatmen are the awkwardest,
the stupidest, and the most unscientific on earth, without
question.

Ashore, it was—well, it was an eternal circus. People were
thicker than bees, in those narrow streets, and the men were
dressed in all the outrageous, outlandish, idolatrous, extrava-

STREET SCENE IN CONSTANTINOPLE.

gant, thunder-and-lightning costumes that ever a tailor with the delirium tremens and seven devils could conceive of. There was no freak in dress too crazy to be indulged in; no absurdity too absurd to be tolerated; no frenzy in ragged diabolism too fantastic to be attempted. No two men were dressed alike. It was a wild masquerade of all imaginable costumes—every struggling throng in every street was a dissolving view of stunning contrasts. Some patriarchs wore awful turbans, but the grand mass of the infidel horde wore the fiery red skull-cap they call a fez. All the remainder of the raiment they indulged in was utterly indescribable.

The shops here are mere coops, mere boxes, bath-rooms, closets—any thing you please to call them—on the first floor. The Turks sit cross-legged in them, and work and trade and smoke long pipes, and smell like—like Turks. That covers the ground. Crowding the narrow streets in front of them are beggars, who beg forever, yet never collect any thing; and wonderful cripples, distorted out of all semblance of humanity, almost; vagabonds driving laden asses; porters carrying dry-goods boxes as large as cottages on their backs; peddlers of grapes, hot corn, pumpkin seeds, and a hundred other things, yelling like fiends; and sleeping happily, comfortably, serenely, among the hurrying feet, are the famed dogs of Constantinople; drifting noiselessly about are squads of Turkish women, draped from chin to feet in flowing robes, and with snowy veils bound about their heads, that disclose only the eyes and a vague, shadowy notion of their features. Seen moving about, far away in the dim, arched aisles of the Great Bazaar, they look as the shrouded dead must have looked when they walked forth from their graves amid the storms and thunders and earth-quakes that burst upon Calvary that awful night of the Cruci-fixion. A street in Constantinople is a picture which one ought to see once—not oftener.

And then there was the goose-rancher—a fellow who drove a hundred geese before him about the city, and tried to sell them. He had a pole ten feet long, with a crook in the end of it, and occasionally a goose would branch out from the flock

and make a lively break around the corner, with wings half
lifted and neck stretched to its utmost. Did the goose-mer-
chant get excited? No. He took his pole and reached after
that goose with unspeakable *sang froid*—took a hitch round his
neck, and "yanked" him back to his place in the flock without an effort. He steered his geese with that stick as easily as

GOOSE-RANCHER.

another man would steer a yawl. A few hours afterward we
saw him sitting on a stone at a corner, in the midst of the tur-
moil, sound asleep in the sun, with his geese squatting around
him, or dodging out of the way of asses and men. We came

by again, within the hour, and he was taking account of stock, to see whether any of his flock had strayed or been stolen. The way he did it was unique. He put the end of his stick within six or eight inches of a stone wall, and made the geese march in single file between it and the wall. He counted them as they went by. There was no dodging that arrangement.

If you want dwarfs—I mean just a few dwarfs for a curiosity—go to Genoa. If you wish to buy them by the gross, for retail, go to Milan. There are plenty of dwarfs all over Italy, but it did seem to me that in Milan the crop was luxuriant. If you would see a fair average style of assorted cripples, go to Naples, or travel through the Roman States. But if you would see the very heart and home of cripples and human monsters, both, go straight to Constantinople. A beggar in Naples who can show a foot which has all run into one horrible toe, with one shapeless nail on it, has a fortune—but such an exhibition as that would not provoke any notice in Constantinople. The man would starve. Who would pay any attention to attractions like his among the rare monsters that throng the bridges of the Golden Horn and display their deformities in the gutters of Stamboul? O, wretched impostor! How could he stand against the three-legged woman, and the man with his eye in his cheek? How would he blush in presence of the man with fingers on his elbow? Where would he hide himself when the dwarf with seven fingers on each hand, no upper lip, and his under-jaw gone, came down in his majesty? Bismillah! The cripples of Europe are a delusion and a fraud. The truly gifted flourish only in the by-ways of Pera and Stamboul.

That three-legged woman lay on the bridge, with her stock in trade so disposed as to command the most striking effect— one natural leg, and two long, slender, twisted ones with feet on them like somebody else's fore-arm. Then there was a man further along who had no eyes, and whose face was the color of a fly-blown beefsteak, and wrinkled and twisted like a lava-flow—and verily so tumbled and distorted were his features that no man could tell the wart that served him for a nose from his cheek-bones. In Stamboul was a man with a prodigious head, an uncommonly long body, legs eight inches long and feet like snow-shoes. He traveled on those feet and his hand , and was as sway-backed as if the Colossus of Rhodes had been riding him. Ah, a beggar has to have exceedingly good points to make a living in Constantinople. A blue-faced man, who had nothing to offer except that he had been blown up in a mine, would be regarded as a rank impostor, and a mere damaged soldier on crutches would never make a cent. It would pay him to get a piece of his head taken off, and cultivate a wen like a carpet sack.

The Mosque of St. Sophia is the chief lion of Constantinople. You must get a firman and hurry there the first thing. We did that. We did not get a firman, but we took along four or five francs apiece, which is much the same thing.

I do not think much of the Mosque of St. Sophia. I suppose I lack appreciation. We will let it go at that. It is the rustiest old barn in heathendom. I believe all the interest that attaches to it comes from the fact that it was built for a Christian church and then turned into a mosque, without much alteration, by the Mohammedan conquerors of the land. They made me take off my boots and walk into the place in my stocking-feet. I caught cold, and got myself so stuck up with a complication of gums, slime and general corruption, that I wore out more than two thousand pair of boot-jacks getting my boots off that night, and even then some Christian hide peeled off with them. I abate not a single boot-jack.

St. Sophia is a colossal church, thirteen or fourteen hundred years old, and unsightly enough to be very, very much older. Its immense dome is said to be more wonderful than St. Peter's, but its dirt is much more wonderful than its dome, though they never mention it. The church has a hundred and seventy pillars in it, each a single piece, and all of costly marbles of various kinds, but they came from ancient temples at Baalbec, Heliopolis, Athens and Ephesus, and are battered, ugly and repulsive. They were a thousand years old when this

church was new, and then the contrast must have been ghastly—if Justinian's architects did not trim them any.   The
inside of the dome is figured all over with a monstrous inscription in Turkish characters, wrought in gold mosaic, that looks
as glaring as a circus bill; the pavements and the marble bal-

ST. SOPHIA.

ustrades are all battered and dirty; the perspective is marred
every where by a web of ropes that depend from the dizzy
height of the dome, and suspend countless dingy, coarse oil
lamps, and ostrich-eggs, six or seven feet above the floor.
Squatting and sitting in groups, here and there and far and
near, were ragged Turks reading books, hearing sermons, or
receiving lessons like children, and in fifty places were more

of the same sort bowing and straightening up, bowing again and getting down to kiss the earth, muttering prayers the while, and keeping up their gymnastics till they ought to have been tired, if they were not.

Every where was dirt, and dust, and dinginess, and gloom; every where were signs of a hoary antiquity, but with nothing touching or beautiful about it; every where were those groups of fantastic pagans; overhead the gaudy mosaics and the web of lamp-ropes—nowhere was there any thing to win one's love or challenge his admiration.

The people who go into ecstacies over St. Sophia must surely get them out of the guide-book (where every church is spoken of as being "considered by good judges to be the most marvelous structure, in many respects, that the world has ever seen.") Or else they are those old connoisseurs from the wilds of New Jersey who laboriously learn the difference between a fresco and a fire-plug and from that day forward feel privileged to void their critical bathos on painting, sculpture and architecture forever more.

We visited the Dancing Dervishes. There were twenty-one of them. They wore a long, light-colored loose robe that hung to their heels. Each in his turn went up to the priest (they were all within a large circular railing) and bowed profoundly and then went spinning away deliriously and took his appointed place in the circle, and continued to spin. When all had spun themselves to their places, they were about five or six feet apart—and so situated, the entire circle of spinning pagans spun itself three separate times around the room. It took twenty-five minutes to do it. They spun on the left foot, and kept themselves going by passing the right rapidly before it and digging it against the waxed floor. Some of them made incredible " time." Most of them spun around forty times in a minute, and one artist averaged about sixty-one times a minute, and kept it up during the whole twenty-five. His robe filled with air and stood out all around him like a balloon.

They made no noise of any kind, and most of them tilted their heads back and closed their eyes, entranced with a sort of

devotional ecstacy.   There was a rude kind of music, part of
the time, but the musicians were not visible.   None but spin-
ners were allowed within the circle.   A man had to either
spin or stay outside.   It was about as barbarous an exhibition
as we have witnessed yet.   Then sick persons came and lay
down, and beside them women laid their sick children (one a
babe at the breast,) and the patriarch of the Dervishes walked
upon their bodies.   He was supposed to cure their diseases by
trampling upon their breasts or backs or standing on the back
of their necks.   This is well enough for a people who think
all their affairs are made or marred by viewless spirits of
the air—by giants, gnomes, and genii—and who still believe,
to this day, all the wild tales in the Arabian Nights.   Even so
an intelligent missionary tells me.

We visited the Thousand and One Columns.   I do not know
what it was originally intended for, but they said it was built
for a reservoir.   It is situated in the centre of Constantinople.
You go down a flight of stone steps in the middle of a barren
place, and there you are.   You are forty feet under ground,
and in the midst of a perfect wilderness of tall, slender, granite columns, of Byzantine architecture.   Stand where you
would, or change your position as often as you pleased, you
were always a centre from which radiated a dozen long archways and colonnades that lost themselves in distance and the
sombre twilight of the place.   This old dried-up reservoir is
occupied by a few ghostly silk-spinners now, and one of them
showed me a cross cut high up in one of the pillars.   I suppose he meant me to understand that the institution was there
before the Turkish occupation, and I thought he made a remark to that effect; but he must have had an impediment in
his speech, for I did not understand him.

We took off our shoes and went into the marble mausoleum
of the Sultan Mahmoud, the neatest piece of architecture, inside, that I have seen lately.   Mahmoud's tomb was covered
with a black velvet pall, which was elaborately embroidered
with silver; it stood within a fancy silver railing; at the sides
and corners were silver candlesticks that would weigh more

than a hundred pounds, and they supported candles as large as a man's leg; on the top of the sarcophagus was a fez, with a handsome diamond ornament upon it, which an attendant said cost a hundred thousand pounds, and lied like a Turk when he said it. Mahmoud's whole family were comfortably planted around him.

TURKISH MAUSOLEUM.

We went to the great Bazaar in Stamboul, of course, and I shall not describe it further than to say it is a monstrous hive of little shops—thousands, I should say—all under one roof, and cut up into innumerable little blocks by narrow streets which are arched overhead. One street is devoted to a particular kind of merchandise, another to another, and so on.

When you wish to buy a pair of shoes you have the swing of the whole street—you do not have to walk yourself down hunting stores in different localities. It is the same with silks, antiquities, shawls, etc. The place is crowded with people all the time, and as the gay-colored Eastern fabrics are lavishly displayed before every shop, the great Bazaar of Stamboul is one of the sights that are worth seeing. It is full of life, and stir, and business, dirt, beggars, asses, yelling peddlers, porters, dervishes, high-born Turkish female shoppers, Greeks, and weird-looking and weirdly dressed Mohammedans from the mountains and the far provinces—and the only solitary thing one does not smell when he is in the Great Bazaar, is something which smells good.

CHAPTER XXXIV.

MOSQUES are plenty, churches are plenty, graveyards are plenty, but morals and whiskey are scarce. The Koran does not permit Mohammedans to drink. Their natural instincts do not permit them to be moral. They say the Sultan has eight hundred wives. This almost amounts to bigamy. It makes our cheeks burn with shame to see such a thing permitted here in Turkey. We do not mind it so much in Salt Lake, however.

Circassian and Georgian girls are still sold in Constantinople by their parents, but not publicly. The great slave marts we have all read so much about—where tender young girls were stripped for inspection, and criticised and discussed just as if they were horses at an agricultural fair—no longer exist. The exhibition and the sales are private now. Stocks are up, just at present, partly because of a brisk demand created by the recent return of the Sultan's suite from the courts of Europe; partly on account of an unusual abundance of breadstuffs, which leaves holders untortured by hunger and enables them to hold back for high prices; and partly because buyers are too weak to bear the market, while sellers are amply prepared to bull it. Under these circumstances, if the American metropolitan newspapers were published here in Constantinople, their next commercial report would read about as follows, I suppose :

SLAVE GIRL MARKET REPORT.

"Best brands Circassians, crop of 1850, £200; 1852, £250; 1854, £300. Best brands Georgian, none in market; second quality, 1851, £180. Nineteen fair to middling Wallachian girls offered at £130 @ 150, but no takers; sixteen prime A 1 sold in small lots to close out—terms private.

"Sales of one lot Circassians, prime to good, 1852 to 1854, at £240 @ 242½, buyer 30; one forty-niner—damaged—at £23, seller ten, no deposit. Several Georgians, fancy brands, 1852, changed hands to fill orders. The Georgians now on hand are mostly last year's crop, which was unusually poor. The new crop is a little backward, but will be coming in shortly. As regards its quantity and quality, the accounts are most encouraging. In this connection we can safely say, also, that the new crop of Circassians is looking extremely well. His Majesty the Sultan has already sent in large orders for his new harem, which will be finished within a fortnight, and this has naturally strengthened the market and given Circassian stock a strong upward tendency. Taking advantage of the inflated market, many of our shrewdest operators are selling short. There are hints of a "corner" on Wallachians.

"There is nothing new in Nubians. Slow sale.

"Eunuchs—None offering; however, large cargoes are expected from Egypt to-day."

I think the above would be about the style of the commercial report. Prices are pretty high now, and holders firm; but, two or three years ago, parents in a starving condition brought their young daughters down here and sold them for even twenty and thirty dollars, when they could do no better, simply to save themselves and the girls from dying of want. It is sad to think of so distressing a thing as this, and I for one am sincerely glad the prices are up again.

Commercial morals, especially, are bad. There is no gainsaying that. Greek, Turkish and Armenian morals consist only in attending church regularly on the appointed Sabbaths, and in breaking the ten commandments all the balance of the week. It comes natural to them to lie and cheat in the first place, and then they go on and improve on nature until they arrive at perfection. In recommending his son to a merchant as a valuable salesman, a father does not say he is a nice, moral, upright boy, and goes to Sunday School and is honest, but he says, " This boy is worth his weight in broad pieces of a hundred—for behold, he will cheat whomsoever hath dealings with him, and from the Euxine to the waters of Marmora there abideth not so gifted a liar!" How is that for a recommendation? The Missionaries tell me that they hear encomiums like that passed upon people every day. They say of a person they

24

admire, " Ah, he is a charming swindler, and a most exquisite liar !"

Every body lies and cheats—every body who is in business, at any rate. Even foreigners soon have to come down to the custom of the country, and they do not buy and sell long in Constantinople till they lie and cheat like a Greek. I say like a Greek, because the Greeks are called the worst transgressors in this line. Several Americans long resident in Constantinople contend that most Turks are pretty trustworthy, but few claim that the Greeks have any virtues that a man can discover—at least without a fire assay.

I am half willing to believe that the celebrated dogs of Constantinople have been misrepresented—slandered. I have always been led to suppose that they were so thick in the streets that they blocked the way; that they moved about in organized companies, platoons and regiments, and took what they wanted by determined and ferocious assault; and that at night they drowned all other sounds with their terrible howlings. The dogs I see here can not be those I have read of.

I find them every where, but not in strong force. The most I have found together has been about ten or twenty. And night or day a fair proportion of them were sound asleep. Those that were not asleep always looked as if they wanted to be. I never saw such utterly wretched, starving, sad-visaged, broken-hearted looking curs in my life. It seemed a grim satire to accuse such brutes as these of taking things by force of arms. They hardly seemed to have strength enough or ambition enough to walk across the street—I do not know that I have seen one walk that far yet. They are mangy and bruised and mutilated, and often you see one with the hair singed off him in such wide and well defined tracts that he looks like a map of the new Territories. They are the sorriest beasts that breathe—the most abject—the most pitiful. In their faces is a settled expression of melancholy, an air of hopeless despondency. The hairless patches on a scalded dog are preferred by the fleas of Constantinople to a wider range on a healthier dog; and the exposed places suit the fleas exactly. I saw a dog of this kind start to nibble at a flea—a fly attracted his attention, and he made a snatch at him; the flea called for him once more, and that forever unsettled him; he looked sadly at his flea-pasture, then sadly looked at his bald spot. Then he heaved a sigh and dropped his head resignedly upon his paws. He was not equal to the situation.

SLANDERED DOGS.

The dogs sleep in the streets, all over the city. From one end of the street to the other, I suppose they will average about eight or ten to a block. Sometimes, of course, there are fifteen or twenty to a block. They do not belong to any body, and they seem to have no close personal friendships among each other. But they district the city themselves, and the dogs of each district, whether it be half a block in extent, or ten blocks, have to remain within its bounds. Woe to a dog if he crosses the line! His neighbors would snatch the balance of his hair off in a second. So it is said. But they don't look it.

They sleep in the streets these days. They are my compass—my guide. When I see the dogs sleep placidly on, while men, sheep, geese, and all moving things turn out and go around them, I know I am not in the great street where the hotel is, and must go further. In the Grand Rue the dogs have a sort of air of being on the lookout—an air born of being obliged to get out of the way of many carriages every day—and that expression one recognizes in a moment. It does not exist upon the face of any dog without the confines of that street. All others sleep placidly and keep no watch. They would not move, though the Sultan himself passed by.

In one narrow street (but none of them are wide) I saw three dogs lying coiled up, about a foot or two apart. End to end they lay, and so they just bridged the street neatly, from gutter to gutter. A drove of a hundred sheep came along. They stepped right over the dogs, the rear crowding the front, impatient to get on. The dogs looked lazily up, flinched a little when the impatient feet of the sheep touched their raw backs—sighed, and lay peacefully down again. No talk could be plainer than that. So some of the sheep jumped over them and others scrambled between, occasionally chipping a leg with their sharp hoofs, and when the whole flock had made the trip, the dogs sneezed a little, in the cloud of dust, but never budged their bodies an inch. I thought I was lazy, but I am a steam-engine compared to a Constantinople dog. But was not that a singular scene for a city of a million inhabitants?

These dogs are the scavengers of the city. That is their official position, and a hard one it is. However, it is their protection. But for their usefulness in partially cleansing these terrible streets, they would not be tolerated long. They eat any thing and every thing that comes in their way, from melon rinds and spoiled grapes up through all the grades and species of dirt and refuse to their own dead friends and relatives—and yet they are always lean, always hungry, always despondent. The people are loath to kill them—do not kill them, in fact. The Turks have an innate antipathy to taking the life of any dumb animal, it is said. But they do worse. They hang and kick and stone and scald these wretched creatures to the very verge of death, and then leave them to live and suffer.

Once a Sultan proposed to kill off all the dogs here, and did begin the work—but the populace raised such a howl of horror about it that the massacre was stayed. After a while, he proposed to remove them all to an island in the Sea of Marmora. No objection was offered, and a ship-load or so was taken away. But when it came to be known that somehow or other the dogs never got to the island, but always fell overboard in the night and perished, another howl was raised and the transportation scheme was dropped.

So the dogs remain in peaceable possession of the streets. I do not say that they do not howl at night, nor that they do not attack people who have not a red fez on their heads. I only say that it would be mean for *me* to accuse them of these unseemly things who have not seen them do them with my own eyes or heard them with my own ears.

I was a little surprised to see Turks and Greeks playing newsboy right here in the mysterious land where the giants and genii of the Arabian Nights once dwelt—where winged horses and hydra-headed dragons guarded enchanted castles— where Princes and Princesses flew through the air on carpets that obeyed a mystic talisman—where cities whose houses were made of precious stones sprang up in a night under the hand of the magician, and where busy marts were suddenly stricken with a spell and each citizen lay or sat, or stood with weapon raised or foot advanced, just as he was, speechless and motionless, till time had told a hundred years!

It was curious to see newsboys selling papers in so dreamy a land as that. And, to say truly, it is comparatively a new thing here. The selling of newspapers had its birth in Constantinople about a year ago, and was a child of the Prussian and Austrian war.

There is one paper published here in the English language—*The Levant Herald*—and there are generally a number of Greek and a few French papers rising and falling, struggling up and falling again. Newspapers are not popular with the Sultan's Government. They do not understand journalism. The proverb says, "The unknown is always great." To the court, the newspaper is a mysterious and rascally institution. They know what a pestilence is, because they have one occasionally that thins the people out at the rate of two thousand a day, and they regard a newspaper as a mild form of pestilence. When it goes astray, they suppress it—pounce upon it without warning, and throttle it. When it don't go astray for a long time, they get suspicious and throttle it anyhow, because they think it is hatching deviltry. Imagine the Grand Vizier in solemn council with the magnates of the realm, spelling his way through the hated newspaper, and finally delivering his profound decision: "This thing means mischief—it is too darkly, too suspiciously inoffensive—suppress it! Warn the publisher that we can not have this sort of thing: put the editor in prison!"

THE CENSOR ON DUTY.

The newspaper business has its inconveniences in Constantinople. Two Greek papers and one French one were suppressed here within a few days of each other. No victories of the Cretans are allowed to be printed. From time to time the Grand Vizier sends a notice to the various editors that the Cretan insurrection is entirely suppressed, and although that editor knows better, he still has to print the notice. The *Levant Herald* is too fond of speaking praisefully of Americans to be popular with the Sultan, who does not relish our sympathy with the Cretans, and therefore that paper has to be particularly circumspect in order to keep out of trouble. Once the editor, forgetting the official notice in his paper that the Cretans were crushed out, printed a letter of a very different tenor, from the American Consul in Crete, and was fined two hundred and fifty dollars for it. Shortly he printed another from the same source and was imprisoned three months for his pains. I think I could get the assistant editorship of the *Levant Herald*, but I am going to try to worry along without it.

To suppress a paper here involves the ruin of the publisher, almost. But in Naples I think they speculate on misfortunes of that kind. Papers are suppressed there every day, and spring up the next day under a new name. During the ten days or a fortnight we staid there one paper was murdered and resurrected twice. The newsboys are smart there, just as they are elsewhere. They take advantage of popular weaknesses. When they find they are not likely to sell out, they approach a citizen mysteriously, and say in a low voice—"Last copy, sir: double price; paper just been suppressed!" The man buys it, of course, and finds nothing in it. They do say—I do not vouch for it—but they do say that men sometimes print a vast edition of a paper, with a ferociously seditious article in it, distribute it quickly among the newsboys, and clear out till the Government's indignation cools. It pays well. Confiscation don't amount to any thing. The type and presses are not worth taking care of.

There is only one English newspaper in Naples. It has seventy subscribers. The publisher is getting rich very deliberately—very deliberately indeed.

I never shall want another Turkish lunch. The cooking apparatus was in the little lunch room, near the bazaar, and it was all open to the street. The cook was slovenly, and so was the table, and it had no cloth on it. The fellow took a mass of sausage-meat and coated it round a wire and laid it on a charcoal fire to cook. When it was done, he laid it aside and a dog walked sadly in and nipped it. He smelt it first, and probably recognized the remains of a friend. The cook took it away from him and laid it before us. Jack said, " I pass "—he plays euchre sometimes—and we all passed in turn. Then the cook baked a broad, flat, wheaten cake, greased it well with the sausage, and started towards us with it. It dropped in the dirt, and he picked it up and polished it on his breeches, and laid it before us. Jack said, " I pass." We all passed. He put some eggs in a frying pan, and stood pensively prying slabs of meat from between his teeth with a fork. Then he used the fork to turn the eggs with—and brought them along. Jack said " Pass again." All followed suit. We did not know what to do, and so we ordered a new ration of sausage. The cook got out his wire, apportioned a proper amount of sausage-meat, spat it on his hands and fell to work! This time, with one accord, we all passed out. We paid and left. That is all I learned about Turkish lunches. A Turkish lunch is good, no doubt, but it has its little drawbacks.

When I think how I have been swindled by books of Oriental travel, I want a tourist for breakfast. For years and years I have dreamed of the wonders of the Turkish bath; for years and years I have promised myself that I would yet enjoy one. Many and many a time, in fancy, I have lain in the marble bath, and breathed the slumbrous fragrance of Eastern spices that filled the air; then passed through a weird and complicated system of pulling and hauling, and drenching and scrubbing, by a gang of naked savages who loomed vast and vaguely through the steaming mists, like demons; then rested for a while on a divan fit for a king; then passed through another complex ordeal, and one more fearful than the first; and, finally, swathed in soft fabrics, been conveyed to a princely saloon and laid on a bed of eider down, where eunuchs, gorgeous of costume, fanned me while I drowsed and dreamed, or contentedly gazed at the rich hangings of the apartment, the soft carpets, the sumptuous furniture, the pictures, and drank delicious coffee, smoked the soothing narghili, and dropped, at the last, into tranquil repose, lulled by sensuous odors from unseen censers, by the gentle influence of the narghili's Persian tobacco, and by the music of fountains that counterfeited the pattering of summer rain.

That was the picture, just as I got it from incendiary books of travel. It was a poor, miserable imposture. The reality is no more like it than the Five Points are like the Garden of Eden. They received me in a great court, paved with marble slabs; around it were broad galleries, one above another, carpeted with seedy matting, railed with unpainted balustrades, and furnished with huge rickety chairs, cushioned with rusty old mattresses, indented with impressions left by the forms of nine successive generations of men who had reposed upon them. The place was vast, naked, dreary; its court a barn, its galleries stalls for human horses. The cadaverous, half nude varlets that served in the establishment had nothing of poetry in their appearance, nothing of romance, nothing of Oriental splendor. They shed no entrancing odors—just the contrary. Their hungry eyes and their lank forms continually suggested one glaring, unsentimental fact—they wanted what they term in California "a square meal."

I went into one of the racks and undressed. An unclean starveling wrapped a gaudy table-cloth about his loins, and hung a white rag over my shoulders. If I had had a tub then, it would have come natural to me to take in washing. I was then conducted down stairs into the wet, slippery court, and the first things that attracted my attention were my heels. My fall excited no comment. They expected it, no doubt. It belonged in the list of softening, sensuous influences peculiar to this home of Eastern luxury. It was softening enough, certainly, but its application was not happy. They now gave me a pair of wooden clogs—benches in miniature, with leather straps over them to confine my feet (which they would have done, only I do not wear No. 13s.) These things dangled uncomfortably by the straps when I lifted up my feet, and came down in awkward and unexpected places when I put them on

the floor again, and sometimes turned sideways and wrenched
my ankles out of joint.   However, it was all Oriental luxury,
and I did what I could to enjoy it.

TURKISH BATH.

They put me in another part of the barn and laid me on a
stuffy sort of pallet, which was not made of cloth of gold, or
Persian shawls, but was merely the unpretending sort of thing
I have seen in the negro quarters of Arkansas.   There was
nothing whatever in this dim marble prison but five more of
these biers.   It was a very solemn place.   I expected that the
spiced odors of Araby were going to steal over my senses now,
but they did not.   A copper-colored skeleton, with a rag

around him, brought me a glass decanter of water, with a lighted tobacco pipe in the top of it, and a pliant stem a yard long, with a brass mouth-piece to it.

It was the famous "narghili" of the East—the thing the Grand Turk smokes in the pictures. This began to look like luxury. I took one blast at it, and it was sufficient; the smoke went in a great volume down into my stomach, my lungs, even into the uttermost parts of my frame. I exploded one mighty cough, and it was as if Vesuvius had let go. For the next five minutes I smoked at every pore, like a frame house that is on fire on the inside. Not any more narghili for me. The smoke had a vile taste, and the taste of a thousand infidel tongues that remained on that brass mouthpiece was viler still. I was getting discouraged. Whenever, hereafter, I see the cross-legged Grand Turk smoking his narghili, in pretended bliss, on the outside of a paper of Connecticut tobacco, I shall know him for the shameless humbug he is.

This prison was filled with hot air. When I had got warmed up sufficiently to prepare me for a still warmer temperature, they took me where it was—into a marble room, wet, slippery and steamy, and laid me out on a raised platform in the centre. It was very warm. Presently my man sat me down by a tank of hot water, drenched me well, gloved his hand with a coarse mitten, and began to polish me all over with it. I began to smell disgreeably. The more he polished the worse I smelt. It was alarming. I said to him:

"I perceive that I am pretty far gone. It is plain that I ought to be buried without any unnecessary delay. Perhaps you had better go after my friends at once, because the weather is warm, and I can not 'keep' long.'"

He went on scrubbing, and paid no attention. I soon saw that he was reducing my size. He bore hard on his mitten, and from under it rolled little cylinders, like maccaroni. It could not be dirt, for it was too white. He pared me down in this way for a long time. Finally I said:

"It is a tedious process. It will take hours to trim me to the size you want me; I will wait; go and borrow a jack-plane."

He paid no attention at all.

After a while he brought a basin, some soap, and something that seemed to be the tail of a horse. He made up a prodigious quantity of soap-suds, deluged me with them from head to foot, without warning me to shut my eyes, and then swabbed me viciously with the horse-tail. Then he left me there, a snowy statue of lather, and went away. When I got tired of waiting I went and hunted him up. He was propped against the wall, in another room, asleep. I woke him. He was not disconcerted. He took me back and flooded me with hot water, then turbaned my head, swathed me with dry table-cloths, and conducted me to a latticed chicken-coop in one of the galleries, and pointed to one of those Arkansas beds. I mounted it, and vaguely expected the odors of Araby again. They did not come.

The blank, unornamented coop had nothing about it of that oriental voluptuousness one reads of so much. It was more suggestive of the county hospital than any thing else. The skinny servitor brought a narghili, and I got him to take it out again without wasting any time about it. Then he brought the world-renowned Turkish coffee that poets have sung so rapturously for many generations, and I seized upon it as the last hope that was left of my old dreams of Eastern luxury. It was another fraud. Of all the unchristian beverages that ever passed my lips, Turkish coffee is the worst. The cup is small, it is smeared with grounds; the coffee is black, thick, unsavory of smell, and execrable in taste. The bottom of the cup has a muddy sediment in it half an inch deep. This goes down your throat, and portions of it lodge by the way, and produce a tickling aggravation that keeps you barking and coughing for an hour.

Here endeth my experience of the celebrated Turkish bath, and here also endeth my dream of the bliss the mortal revels in who passes through it. It is a malignant swindle. The man who enjoys it is qualified to enjoy any thing that is repulsive to sight or sense, and he that can invest it with a charm of poetry is able to do the same with any thing else in the world that is tedious, and wretched, and dismal, and nasty.

CHAPTER XXXV.

WE left a dozen passengers in Constantinople, and sailed through the beautiful Bosporus and far up into the Black Sea. We left them in the clutches of the celebrated Turkish guide, "FAR-AWAY MOSES," who will seduce them into buying a ship-load of ottar of roses, splendid Turkish vestments, and all manner of curious things they can never have any use for. Murray's invaluable guide-books have mentioned Far-away Moses' name, and he is a made man. He rejoices daily in the fact that he is a recognized celebrity. However, we can not alter our established customs to please the whims of guides; we can not show partialities this late in the day. Therefore, ignoring this fellow's brilliant fame, and ignoring the fanciful name he takes such pride in, we called him Ferguson, just as we had done with all other guides. It has kept him in a state of smothered exasperation all the time. Yet we meant him no harm. After he has gotten himself up regardless of expense, in showy, baggy trowsers, yellow, pointed slippers, fiery fez, silken jacket of blue, voluminous waist-sash of fancy Persian stuff filled with a battery of silver-mounted horse-pistols, and has strapped on his terrible scimetar, he considers it an unspeakable humiliation to be called Ferguson. It can not be helped. All guides are Fergusons to us. We can not master their dreadful foreign names.

Sebastopol is probably the worst battered town in Russia or any where else. But we ought to be pleased with it, nevertheless, for we have been in no country yet where we have been so kindly received, and where we felt that to be Americans was a sufficient *visé* for our passports. The moment the anchor was down, the Governor of the town immediately dispatched

an officer on board to inquire if he could be of any assistance to us, and to invite us to make ourselves at home in Sebastopol! If you know Russia, you know that this was a wild stretch of hospitality. They are usually so suspicious of strangers that they worry them excessively with the delays and aggravations incident to a complicated passport system. Had we come from any other country we could not have had permission to enter Sebastopol and leave again under three days—but as it was, we were at liberty to go and come when and where we pleased. Every body in Constantinople warned us to be very careful about our passports, see that they were strict-

FAR-AWAY MOSES.

ly *en regle*, and never to mislay them for a moment: and they told us of numerous instances of Englishmen and others who were delayed days, weeks, and even months, in Sebastopol, on account of trifling informalities in their passports, and for which they were not to blame. I had lost my passport, and was traveling under my room-mate's, who stayed behind in Constantinople to await our return. To read the description of him in that passport and then look at me, any man could see that I was no more like him than I am like Hercules. So I went into the harbor of Sebastopol with fear and trembling—full of a vague, horrible apprehension that I was going to be found out and hanged. But all that time my true passport had been floating gallantly overhead—and behold it was only our flag. They never asked us for any other.

We have had a great many Russian and English gentlemen and ladies on board to-day, and the time has passed cheerfully away. They were all happy-spirited people, and I never heard our mother tongue sound so pleasantly as it did when it fell from those English lips in this far-off land. I talked to the Russians a good deal, just to be friendly, and they talked to me from the same motive; I am sure that both enjoyed the conversation, but never a word of it either of us understood. I did most of my talking to those English people though, and I am sorry we can not carry some of them along with us.

We have gone whithersoever we chose, to-day, and have met with nothing but the kindest attentions. Nobody inquired whether we had any passports or not.

Several of the officers of the Government have suggested that we take the ship to a little watering-place thirty miles from here, and pay the Emperor of Russia a visit. He is rusticating there. These officers said they would take it upon themselves to insure us a cordial reception. They said if we would go, they would not only telegraph the Emperor, but send a special courier overland to announce our coming. Our time is so short, though, and more especially our coal is so nearly out, that we judged it best to forego the rare pleasure of holding social intercourse with an Emperor.

Ruined Pompeii is in good condition compared to Sebastopol. Here, you may look in whatsoever direction you please, and your eye encounters scarcely any thing but ruin, ruin, ruin!—fragments of houses, crumbled walls, torn and ragged hills, devastation every where! It is as if a mighty earthquake had spent all its terrible forces upon this one little spot. For eighteen long months the storms of war beat upon the helpless town, and left it at last the saddest wreck that ever the sun has looked upon. Not one solitary house escaped unscathed— not one remained habitable, even. Such utter and complete ruin one could hardly conceive of. The houses had all been solid, dressed stone structures; most of them were ploughed through and through by cannon balls—unroofed and sliced down from eaves to foundation—and now a row of them, half a mile long, looks merely like an endless procession of battered chimneys. No semblance of a house remains in such as these. Some of the larger buildings had corners knocked off; pillars cut in two; cornices smashed; hoies driven straight through the walls. Many of these holes are as round and as cleanly cut as if they had been made with an auger. Others are half pierced through, and the clean impression is there in the rock, as smooth and as shapely as if it were done in putty. Here and there a ball still sticks in a wall, and from it iron tears trickle down and discolor the stone.

The battle-fields were pretty close together. The Malakoff tower is on a hill which is right in the edge of the town. The Redan was within rifle-shot of the Malakoff; Inkerman was a mile away; and Balaklava removed but an hour's ride. The French trenches, by which they approached and invested the Malakoff were carried so close under its sloping sides that one might have stood by the Russian guns and tossed a stone into them. Repeatedly, during three terrible days, they swarmed up the little Malakoff hill, and were beaten back with terrible slaughter. Finally, they captured the place, and drove the Russians out, who then tried to retreat into the town, but the English had taken the Redan, and shut them off with a wall of flame; there was nothing for them to do but go back and retake the Malakoff or die under its guns. They did go back; they took the Malakoff and retook it two or three times, but their desperate valor could not avail, and they had to give up at last.

These fearful fields, where such tempests of death used to rage, are peaceful enough now; no sound is heard, hardly a living thing moves about them, they are lonely and silent— their desolation is complete.

There was nothing else to do, and so every body went to hunting relics. They have stocked the ship with them. They brought them from the Malakoff, from the Redan, Inkerman, Balaklava—every where. They have brought cannon balls,

broken ramrods, fragments of shell—iron enough to freight a
sloop. Some have even brought bones—brought them laboriously from great distances, and were grieved to hear the surgeon pronounce them only bones of mules and oxen. I knew
Blucher would not lose an opportunity like this. He brought
a sack full on board and was going for another. I prevailed
upon him not to go. He has already turned his state-room
into a museum of worthless trumpery, which he has gathered
up in his travels. He is labeling his trophies, now. I picked
up one a while ago, and found it marked "Fragment of a Russian General." I carried it out to get a better light upon it—
it was nothing but a couple of teeth and part of the jaw-bone
of a horse. I said with some asperity:

"Fragment of a Russian General! This
is absurd. Are you never going to learn
any sense?"

He only said: "Go slow—the old woman
won't know any different." [His aunt.]

This person gathers mementoes with a
perfect recklessness, now-a-days; mixes

A FRAGMENT.

them all up together, and then serenely labels them without
any regard to truth, propriety, or even plausibility. I have
found him breaking a stone in two, and labeling half of it
"Chunk busted from the pulpit of Demosthenes," and the
other half "Darnick from the Tomb of Abelard and Heloise."
I have known him to gather up a handful of pebbles by the
roadside, and bring them on board ship and label them as coming from twenty celebrated localities five hundred miles apart.
I remonstrate against these outrages upon reason and truth, of
course, but it does no good. I get the same tranquil, unan-
swerable reply every time:

"It don't signify—the old woman won't know any different."

Ever since we three or four fortunate ones made the midnight trip to Athens, it has afforded him genuine satisfaction
to give every body in the ship a pebble from the Mars-hill
where St. Paul preached. He got all those pebbles on the sea-
shore, abreast the ship, but professes to have gathered them

25.

from one of our party. However, it is not of any use for me
to expose the deception—it affords him pleasure, and does no
harm to any body. He says he never expects to run out of
mementoes of St. Paul as long as he is in reach of a sand-
bank. Well, he is no worse than others. I notice that all
travelers supply deficiencies in their collections in the same
way. I shall never have any confidence in such things again
while I live.

CHAPTER XXXVI.

WE have got so far east, now—a hundred and fifty-five degrees of longitude from San Francisco—that my watch can not "keep the hang" of the time any more. It has grown discouraged, and stopped. I think it did a wise thing. The difference in time between Sebastopol and the Pacific coast is enormous. When it is six o'clock in the morning here, it is somewhere about week before last in California. We are excusable for getting a little tangled as to time. These distractions and distresses about the time have worried me so much that I was afraid my mind was so much affected that I never would have any appreciation of time again; but when I noticed how handy I was yet about comprehending when it was dinner-time, a blessed tranquillity settled down upon me, and I am tortured with doubts and fears no more.

Odessa is about twenty hours' run from Sebastopol, and is the most northerly port in the Black Sea. We came here to get coal, principally. The city has a population of one hundred and thirty-three thousand, and is growing faster than any other small city out of America. It is a free port, and is the great grain mart of this particular part of the world. Its roadstead is full of ships. Engineers are at work, now, turning the open roadstead into a spacious artificial harbor. It is to be almost inclosed by massive stone piers, one of which will extend into the sea over three thousand feet in a straight line.

I have not felt so much at home for a long time as I did when I "raised the hill" and stood in Odessa for the first time. It looked just like an American city; fine, broad streets, and straight as well; low houses, (two or three stories,) wide, neat, and free from any quaintness of architectural ornamentation; locust trees bordering the sidewalks (they call them acacias ;) a stirring, business-look about the streets and the stores; fast walkers; a familiar *new* look about the houses and every thing; yea, and a driving and smothering cloud of dust that was so like a message from our own dear native land that we could hardly refrain from shedding a few grateful tears and execrations in the old time-honored American way. Look up the street or down the street, this way or that way, we saw only America! There was not one thing to remind us that we were in Russia. We walked for some little distance, reveling in this home vision, and then we came upon a church and a hack-driver, and presto! the illusion vanished! The church had a slender-spired dome that rounded inward at its base, and looked like a turnip turned upside down, and the hackman seemed to be dressed in a long petticoat without any hoops. These things were essentially foreign, and so were the carriages —but every body knows about these things, and there is no occasion for my describing them.

We were only to stay here a day and a night and take in coal; we consulted the guide-books and were rejoiced to know that there were no sights in Odessa to see; and so we had one good, untrammeled holyday on our hands, with nothing to do but idle about the city and enjoy ourselves. We sauntered through the markets and criticised the fearful and wonderful costumes from the back country; examined the populace as far as eyes could do it; and closed the entertainment with an ice-cream debauch. We do not get ice-cream every where, and so, when we do, we are apt to dissipate to excess. We never cared any thing about ice-cream at home, but we look upon it with a sort of idolatry now that it is so scarce in these red-hot climates of the East.

We only found two pieces of statuary, and this was another blessing. One was a bronze image of the Duc de Richelieu, grand-nephew of the splendid Cardinal. It stood in a spacious, handsome promenade, overlooking the sea, and from its base a vast flight of stone steps led down to the harbor—two hundred of them, fifty feet long, and a wide landing at the bottom of every twenty. It is a noble staircase, and from a distance the people toiling up it looked like insects. I mention this statue and this stairway because they have their story. Richelieu founded Odessa—watched over it with paternal care—labored with a fertile brain and a wise understanding for its best interests—spent his fortune freely to the same end—endowed it with a sound prosperity, and one which will yet make it one of the great cities of the Old World—built this noble stairway with money from his own private purse—and——. Well, the people for whom he had done so much, let him walk down these same steps, one day, unattended, old, poor, without a second coat to his back ; and when, years afterwards, he died in Sebastopol in poverty and neglect, they called a meeting, subscribed liberally, and immediately erected this tasteful monument to his memory, and named a great street after him. It reminds me of what Robert Burns' mother said when they erected a stately monument to his memory : "Ah, Robbie, ye asked them for bread and they hae gi'en ye a stane."

The people of Odessa have warmly recommended us to go and call on the Emperor, as did the Sebastopolians. They have telegraphed his Majesty, and he has signified his willingness to grant us an audience. So we are getting up the anchors and preparing to sail to his watering-place. What a scratching around there will be, now ! what a holding of important meetings and appointing of solemn committees !—and what a furbishing up of claw-hammer coats and white silk neck-ties ! As this fearful ordeal we are about to pass through pictures itself to my fancy in all its dread sublimity, I begin to feel my fierce desire to converse with a genuine Emperor cooling down and passing away. What am I to do with my hands ? What am I to do with my feet ? What in the world am I to do with myself ?

CHAPTER XXXVII.

WE anchored here at Yalta, Russia, two or three days ago. To me the place was a vision of the Sierras. The tall, gray mountains that back it, their sides bristling with pines—cloven with ravines—here and there a hoary rock towering into view—long, straight streaks sweeping down from the summit to the sea, marking the passage of some avalanche of former times—all these were as like what one sees in the Sierras as if the one were a portrait of the other. The little village of Yalta nestles at the foot of an amphitheatre which slopes backward and upward to the wall of hills, and looks as if it might have sunk quietly down to its present position from a higher elevation. This depression is covered with the great parks and gardens of noblemen, and through the mass of green foliage the bright colors of their palaces bud out here and there like flowers. It is a beautiful spot.

We had the United States Consul on board—the Odessa Consul. We assembled in the cabin and commanded him to tell us what we must do to be saved, and tell us quickly. He made a speech. The first thing he said fell like a blight on every hopeful spirit: he had never seen a court reception. (Three groans for the Consul.) But he said he had seen receptions at the Governor-General's in Odessa, and had often listened to people's experiences of receptions at the Russian and other courts, and believed he knew very well what sort of ordeal we were about to essay. (Hope budded again.) He said we were many; the summer-palace was small—a mere

mansion; doubtless we should be received in summer fashion
—in the garden; we would stand in a row, all the gentlemen
in swallow-tail coats, white kids, and white neck-ties, and the
ladies in light-colored silks, or something of that kind; at the
proper moment—12 meridian—the Emperor, attended by his
suite arrayed in splendid uniforms, would appear and walk
slowly along the line, bowing to some, and saying two or three
words to others. At the moment his Majesty appeared, a universal, delighted, enthusiastic smile ought to break out like a
rash among the passengers—a smile of love, of gratification,
of admiration—and with one accord, the party must begin to
bow—not obsequiously, but respectfully, and with dignity; at
the end of fifteen minutes the Emperor would go in the house,
and we could run along home again. We felt immensely relieved. It seemed, in a manner, easy. There was not a man
in the party but believed that with a little practice he could
stand in a row, especially if there were others along; there
was not a man but believed he could bow without tripping on
his coat tail and breaking his neck; in a word, we came to
believe we were equal to any item in the performance except
that complicated smile. The Consul also said we ought to
draft a little address to the Emperor, and present it to one of
his aides-de-camp, who would forward it to him at the proper
time. Therefore, five gentlemen were appointed to prepare
the document, and the fifty others went sadly smiling about
the ship—practicing. During the next twelve hours we had
the general appearance, somehow, of being at a funeral, where
every body was sorry the death had occurred, but glad it
was over—where every body was smiling, and yet broken-
hearted.

A committee went ashore to wait on his Excellency the Governor-General, and learn our fate. At the end of three hours
of boding suspense, they came back and said the Emperor
would receive us at noon the next day—would send carriages
for us—would hear the address in person. The Grand Duke
Michael had sent to invite us to his palace also. Any man
could see that there was an intention here to show that Russia's

friendship for America was so genuine as to render even her private citizens objects worthy of kindly attentions.

At the appointed hour we drove out three miles, and assembled in the handsome garden in front of the Emperor's palace.

YALTA, FROM THE EMPEROR'S PALACE.

We formed a circle under the trees before the door, for there was no one room in the house able to accommodate our three-score persons comfortably, and in a few minutes the imperial family came out bowing and smiling, and stood in our midst. A number of great dignitaries of the Empire, in undress uniforms, came with them. With every bow, his Majesty said a word of welcome. I copy these speeches. There is character in them—Russian character—which is politeness itself, and the genuine article. The French are polite, but it is often mere ceremonious politeness. A Russian imbues his polite things with a heartiness, both of phrase and expression, that compels belief in their sincerity. As I was saying, the Czar punctuated his speeches with bows :

" Good morning—I am glad to see you—I am gratified—I am delighted—I am happy to receive you !"

All took off their hats, and the Consul inflicted the address on him. He bore it with unflinching fortitude ; then took the rusty-looking document and handed it to some great officer or other, to be filed away among the archives of Russia—in the stove. He thanked us for the address, and said he was very much pleased to see us, especially as such friendly relations existed between Russia and the United States. The Empress said the Americans were favorites in Russia, and she hoped the Russians were similarly regarded in America. These were all the speeches that were made, and I

EMPEROR OF RUSSIA.

recommend them to parties who present policemen with gold watches, as models of brevity and point. After this the Empress went and talked sociably (for an Empress) with various ladies around the circle ; several gentlemen entered into a disjointed general conversation with the Emperor ; the Dukes and Princes, Admirals and Maids of Honor dropped into free-and-easy chat with first one and then another of our party, and whoever chose stepped forward and spoke with the modest little Grand Duchess Marie, the Czar's daughter. She is fourteen years old, light-haired, blue-eyed, unassuming and pretty. Every body talks English.

The Emperor wore a cap, frock coat and pantaloons, all of some kind of plain white drilling—cotton or linen—and sport-ed no jewelry or any insignia whatever of rank. No costume could be less ostentatious. He is very tall and spare, and a determined-looking man, though a very pleasant-looking one, nevertheless. It is easy to see that he is kind and affectionate. There is something very noble in his expression when his cap is off. There is none of that cunning in his eye that all of us noticed in Louis Napoleon's.

The Empress and the little Grand Duchess wore simple suits of foulard (or foulard silk, I don't know which is proper,) with a small blue spot in it; the dresses were trimmed with blue; both ladies wore broad blue sashes about their waists; linen collars and clerical ties of muslin; low-crowned straw-hats trimmed with blue velvet; parasols and flesh-colored gloves. The Grand Duchess had no heels on her shoes. I do not know this of my own knowledge, but one of our ladies told me so. I was not looking at her shoes. I was glad to observe that she wore her own hair, plaited in thick braids against the back of her head, instead of the uncomely thing they call a waterfall, which is about as much like a waterfall as a canvas-covered ham is like a cataract. Taking the kind expression that is in the Emperor's face and the gentleness that is in his young daughter's into consideration, I wondered if it would not tax the Czar's firmness to the utmost to condemn a supplicating wretch to misery in the wastes of Siberia if she pleaded for him. Every time their eyes met, I saw more and more what a tremendous power that weak, diffident school-girl could wield if she chose to do it. Many and many a time she might rule the Autocrat of Russia, whose lightest word is law to seventy millions of human beings! She was only a girl, and she looked like a thousand others I have seen, but never a girl provoked such a novel and peculiar interest in me before. A strange, new sensation is a rare thing in this hum-drum life, and I had it here. There was nothing stale or worn out about the thoughts and feelings the situation and the circumstances created. It seemed strange—stranger than I can tell—to think that the central figure in the cluster of men and women, chatting here under the trees like the most ordinary individual in the land, was a man who could open his lips and ships would fly through the waves, locomotives would speed over the plains, couriers would hurry from village to village, a hundred telegraphs would flash the word to the four corners of an Empire that stretches its vast proportions over a seventh part of the habitable globe, and a countless multitude of men would spring to do his bidding. I had a sort of vague desire to examine his hands and see if they were of flesh and blood, like other men's. Here was a man who could do this wonderful thing, and yet if I chose I could knock him down. The case was plain, but it seemed preposterous, nevertheless—as preposterous as trying to knock down a mountain or wipe out a continent. If this man sprained his ankle, a million miles of telegraph would carry the news over mountains—valleys— uninhabited deserts—under the trackless sea—and ten thousand newspapers would prate of it; if he were grievously ill, all the nations would know it before the sun rose again; if he dropped lifeless where he stood, his fall might shake the thrones of half a world! If I could have stolen his coat, I would have done it. When I meet a man like that, I want something to remember him by.

As a general thing, we have been shown through palaces by some plush-legged filagreed flunkey or other, who charged a franc for it; but after talking with the company half an hour, the Emperor of Russia and his family conducted us all through their mansion themselves. They made no charge. They seemed to take a real pleasure in it.

We spent half an hour idling through the palace, admiring the cosy apartments and the rich but eminently home-like appointments of the place, and then the Imperial family bade our party a kind good-bye, and proceeded to count the spoons.

An invitation was extended to us to visit the palace of the eldest son, the Crown Prince of Russia, which was near at hand. The young man was absent, but the Dukes and Countesses and Princes went over the premises with us as leisurely as was the case at the Emperor's, and conversation continued as lively as ever.

It was a little after one o'clock, now. We drove to the Grand Duke Michael's, a mile away, in response to his invitation, previously given.

We arrived in twenty minutes from the Emperor's. It is a lovely place. The beautiful palace nestles among the grand old groves of the park, the park sits in the lap of the picturesque crags and hills, and both look out upon the breezy ocean. In the park are rustic seats, here and there, in secluded nooks that are dark with shade; there are rivulets of crystal water; there are lakelets, with inviting, grassy banks; there are glimpses of sparkling cascades through openings in the wilderness of foliage; there are streams of clear water gushing from mimic knots on the trunks of forest trees; there are miniature marble temples perched upon gray old crags; there are airy lookouts whence one may gaze upon a broad expanse of landscape and ocean. The palace is modeled after the choicest forms of Grecian architecture, and its wide colonnades surround a central court that is banked with rare flowers that fill the place with their fragrance, and in their midst springs a fountain that cools the summer air, and may possibly breed mosquitoes, but I do not think it does.

The Grand Duke and his Duchess came out, and the presentation ceremonies were as simple as they had been at the Emperor's. In a few minutes, conversation was under way, as before. The Empress appeared in the verandah, and the little Grand Duchess came out into the crowd. They had beaten us there. In a few minutes, the Emperor came himself on horseback. It was very pleasant. You can appreciate it if you have ever visited royalty and felt occasionally that possibly you might be wearing out your welcome—though as a general thing, I believe, royalty is not scrupulous about discharging you when it is done with you.

The Grand Duke is the third brother of the Emperor, is about thirty-seven years old, perhaps, and is the princeliest figure in Russia. He is even taller than the Czar, as straight as an Indian, and bears himself like one of those gorgeous knights we read about in romances of the Crusades. He looks like a great-hearted fellow who would pitch an enemy into the river in a moment, and then jump in and risk his life fishing him out again. The stories they tell of him show him to be of a brave and generous nature. He must have been desirous of proving that Americans were welcome guests in the imperial palaces of Russia, because he rode all the way to Yalta and escorted our procession to the Emperor's himself, and kept his aids scurrying about, clearing the road and offering assistance wherever it could be needed. We were rather familiar with him then, because we did not know who he was. We recognized him now, and appreciated the friendly spirit that prompted him to do us a favor that any other Grand Duke in the world would have doubtless declined to do. He had plenty of servitors whom he could have sent, but he chose to attend to the matter himself.

The Grand Duke was dressed in the handsome and showy uniform of a Cossack officer. The Grand Duchess had on a white alpaca robe, with the seams and gores trimmed with black barb lace, and a little gray hat with a feather of the same color. She is young, rather pretty modest and unpretending, and full of winning politeness.

Our party walked all through the house, and then the nobility escorted them all over the grounds, and finally brought them back to the palace about half-past two o'clock to breakfast. They called it breakfast, but we would have called it luncheon. It consisted of two kinds of wine; tea, bread, cheese, and cold meats, and was served on the centre-tables in the reception room and the verandahs—any where that was convenient; there was no ceremony. It was a sort of picnic. I had heard before that we were to breakfast there, but Blucher said he believed Baker's boy had suggested it to his Imperial Highness. I think not—though it would be like him. Baker's boy is the famine-breeder of the ship. He is always hungry. They say he goes about the state-rooms when the passengers are out, and eats up all the soap. And they say he eats oakum. They say he will eat any thing he can get between meals, but he prefers oakum. He does not like oakum for dinner, but he likes it for a lunch, at odd hours, or any thing that way. It makes him very disagreeable, because it makes his breath bad, and keeps his teeth all stuck up with tar. Baker's boy may have suggested the breakfast, but I hope he did not. It went off well, anyhow. The illustrious host moved about from place to place, and helped to destroy the provisions and keep the conversation lively, and the Grand Duchess talked with the verandah parties and such as had satisfied their appetites and straggled out from the reception room.

The Grand Duke's tea was delicious. They give one a lemon to squeeze into it, or iced milk, if he prefers it. The former is best. This tea is brought overland from China. It injures the article to transport it by sea.

When it was time to go, we bade our distinguished hosts good-bye, and they retired happy and contented to their apartments to count *their* spoons.

We had spent the best part of half a day in the home of royalty, and had been as cheerful and comfortable all the time as we could have been in the ship. I would as soon have thought of being cheerful in Abraham's bosom as in the palace of an Emperor. I supposed that Emperors were terrible people. I thought they never did any thing but wear magnificent crowns and red velvet dressing-gowns with dabs of wool sewed on them in spots, and sit on thrones and scowl at the flunkies and the people in the parquette, and order Dukes and Duchesses off to execution. I find, however, that when one is so fortunate as to get behind the scenes and see them at home and in the privacy of their firesides, they are strangely like common mortals. They are pleasanter to look upon then than they are in their theatrical aspect. It seems to come as natural to them to dress and act like other people as it is to put a friend's cedar pencil in your pocket when you are done using it. But I can never have any confidence in the tinsel kings of the theatre after this. It will be a great loss. I used to take such a thrilling pleasure in them. But, hereafter, I will turn me sadly away and say;

"This does not answer—this isn't the style of king that *I* am acquainted with."

When they swagger around the stage in jeweled crowns and splendid robes, I shall feel bound to observe that all the Emperors that ever *I* was personally acquainted with wore the commonest sort of clothes, and did not swagger. And when they come on the stage attended by a vast body-guard of supes in helmets

TINSEL KING.

and tin breastplates, it will be my duty as well as my pleasure to inform the ignorant that no crowned head of my acquaintance has a soldier any where about his house or his person.

Possibly it may be thought that our party tarried too long, or did other improper things, but such was not the case. The company felt that they were occupying an unusually responsible position—they were representing the people of America, not the Government—and therefore they were careful to do their best to perform their high mission with credit.

On the other hand, the Imperial families, no doubt, consid-

ered that in entertaining us they were more especially entertaining the people of America than they could by showering
attentions on a whole platoon of ministers plenipotentiary;
and therefore they gave to the event its fullest significance, as
an expression of good will and friendly feeling toward the entire country. We took the kindnesses we received as attentions thus directed, of course, and not to ourselves as a party.
That we felt a personal pride in being received as the representatives of a nation, we do not deny; that we felt a national
pride in the warm cordiality of that reception, can not be
doubted.

Our poet has been rigidly suppressed, from the time we let
go the anchor. When it was announced that we were going
to visit the Emperor of Russia, the fountains of his great deep
were broken up, and he rained ineffable bosh for four-and-
twenty hours. Our original anxiety as to what we were going
to do with ourselves, was suddenly transformed into anxiety
about what we were going to do with our poet. The problem
was solved at last. Two alternatives were offered him—he
must either swear a dreadful oath that he would not issue a
line of his poetry while he was in the Czar's dominions, or else
remain under guard on board the ship until we were safe at
Constantinople again. He fought the dilemma long, but yielded
at last. It was a great deliverance. Perhaps the savage
reader would like a specimen of his style. I do not mean this
term to be offensive. I only use it because "the gentle reader"
has been used so often that any change from it can not but be
refreshing:

> "Save us and sanctify us, and finally, then,
> See good provisions we enjoy while we journey to Jerusalem.
> For so man proposes, which it is most true,
> And time will wait for none, nor for us too."

The sea has been unusually rough all day. However, we
have had a lively time of it, anyhow. We have had quite a
run of visitors. The Governor-General came, and we received
him with a salute of nine guns. He brought his family with
him. I observed that carpets were spread from the pier-head

to his carriage for him to walk on, though I have seen him walk there without any carpet when he was not on business. I thought may be he had what the accidental insurance people might call an extra-hazardous polish ("policy"—joke, but not above mediocrity,) on his boots, and wished to protect them, but I examined and could not see that they were blacked any better than usual. It may have been that he had forgotten his carpet, before, but he did not have it with him, anyhow. He was an exceedingly pleasant old gentleman; we all liked him, especially Blucher. When he went away, Blucher invited him to come again and fetch his carpet along.

Prince Dolgorouki and a Grand Admiral or two, whom we had seen yesterday at the reception, came on board also. I was a little distant with these parties, at first, because when I have been visiting Emperors I do not like to be too familiar with people I only know by reputation, and whose moral characters and standing in society I can not be thoroughly acquainted with. I judged it best to be a little offish, at first. I said to myself, Princes and Counts and Grand Admirals are very well, but they are not Emperors, and one can not be too particular about who he associates with.

Baron Wrangel came, also. He used to be Russian Ambassador at Washington. I told him I had an uncle who fell down a shaft and broke himself in two, as much as a year before that. That was a falsehood, but then I was not going to let any man eclipse me on surprising adventures, merely for the want of a little invention. The Baron is a fine man, and is said to stand high in the Emperor's confidence and esteem.

Baron Ungern-Sternberg, a boisterous, whole-souled old nobleman, came with the rest. He is a man of progress and enterprise—a representative man of the age. He is the Chief Director of the railway system of Russia—a sort of railroad king. In his line he is making things move along in this country. He has traveled extensively in America. He says he has tried convict labor on his railroads, and with perfect success. He says the convicts work well, and are quiet and peaceable. He observed that he employs nearly ten thousand of them now.

26

This appeared to be another call on my resources. I was equal to the emergency. I said we had eighty thousand convicts employed on the railways in America—all of them under sentence of death for murder in the first degree. That closed *him* out.

We had General Todtleben (the famous defender of Sebastopol, during the siege,) and many inferior army and also navy officers, and a number of unofficial Russian ladies and gentlemen. Naturally, a champagne luncheon was in order, and was accomplished without loss of life. Toasts and jokes were discharged freely, but no speeches were made save one thanking the Emperor and the Grand Duke, through the Governor-General, for our hospitable reception, and one by the Governor-General in reply, in which he returned the Emperor's thanks for the speech, etc., etc.

CHAPTER XXXVIII.

WE returned to Constantinople, and after a day or two spent in exhausting marches about the city and voyages up the Golden Horn in *caiques*, we steamed away again. We passed through the Sea of Marmora and the Dardanelles, and steered for a new land—a new one to us, at least—Asia. We had as yet only acquired a bowing acquaintance with it, through pleasure excursions to Scutari and the regions round about.

We passed between Lemnos and Mytilene, and saw them as we had seen Elba and the Balearic Isles—mere bulky shapes, with the softening mists of distance upon them—whales in a fog, as it were. Then we held our course southward, and began to "read up" celebrated Smyrna.

At all hours of the day and night the sailors in the forecastle amused themselves and aggravated us by burlesquing our visit to royalty. The opening paragraph of our Address to the Emperor was framed as follows:

"We are a handful of private citizens of America, traveling simply for recreation—and unostentatiously, as becomes our unofficial state—and, therefore, we have no excuse to tender for presenting ourselves before your Majesty, save the desire of offering our grateful acknowledgments to the lord of a realm, which, through good and through evil report, has been the steadfast friend of the land we love so well."

The third cook, crowned with a resplendent tin basin and

wrapped royally in a table-cloth mottled with grease-spots and
coffee stains, and bearing a sceptre that looked strangely like a
belaying-pin, walked upon a dilapidated carpet and perched
himself on the capstan, careless of the flying spray; his tarred
and weather-beaten Chamberlains, Dukes and Lord High Admirals surrounded him, arrayed in all the pomp that spare
tarpaulins and remnants of old sails could furnish.   Then the
visiting "watch below," transformed into graceless ladies and

SHIP EMPEROR.

uncouth pilgrims, by
rude travesties upon
waterfalls, hoopskirts,
white kid gloves and
swallow-tail coats, mov-
ed solemnly up the
companion way, and
bowing low, began a
system of complicated
and extraordinary smil-
ing which few monarchs
could look upon and
live.   Then the mock
consul, a slush-plastered
deck-sweep, drew out a
soiled fragment of paper
and proceeded to read,
laboriously

"To His Imperial
Majesty, Alexander II.,
Emperor of Russia:

"We are a handful of private citizens of America, traveling
simply for recreation,—and unostentatiously, as becomes our
unofficial state—and therefore, we have no excuse to tender for
presenting ourselves before your Majesty—"

The Emperor—"Then what the devil did you come for?"

—"Save the desire of offering our grateful acknowledgments
to the lord of a realm which—"

The Emperor—"Oh, d—n the Address!—read it to the

police. Chamberlain, take these people over to my brother, the Grand Duke's, and give them a square meal. Adieu! I am happy—I am gratified—I am delighted—I am bored. Adieu, adieu—vamos the ranch! The First Groom of the Palace will proceed to count the portable articles of value belonging to the premises."

The farce then closed, to be repeated again with every

THE RECEPTION.

change of the watches, and embellished with new and still more extravagant inventions of pomp and conversation.

At all times of the day and night the phraseology of that tiresome address fell upon our ears. Grimy sailors came down out of the foretop placidly announcing themselves as " a handful of private citizens of America, *traveling simply for recreation and unostentatiously*," etc.; the coal passers moved to their duties in the profound depths of the ship, explaining the blackness of their faces and their uncouthness of dress, with the reminder that *they* were " a handful of private citizens, traveling simply for recreation," etc., and when the cry rang through the vessel at midnight: " EIGHT BELLS!—LARBOARD WATCH, TURN OUT!" the larboard watch came gaping and stretching out of their den, with the everlasting formula: " Aye-

aye, sir! We are a handful of private citizens of America, traveling simply for recreation, and unostentatiously, as becomes our unofficial state!"

As I was a member of the committee, and helped to frame the Address, these sarcasms came home to me. I never heard a sailor proclaiming himself as a handful of American citizens traveling for recreation, but I wished he might trip and fall overboard, and so reduce his handful by one individual, at least. I never was so tired of any one phrase as the sailors made me of the opening sentence of the Address to the Emperor of Russia.

This seaport of Smyrna, our first notable acquaintance in Asia, is a closely packed city of one hundred and thirty thousand inhabitants, and, like Constantinople, it has no outskirts. It is as closely packed at its outer edges as it is in the centre, and then the habitations leave suddenly off and the plain beyond seems houseless. It is just like any other Oriental city. That is to say, its Moslem houses are heavy and dark, and as comfortless as so many tombs; its streets are crooked, rudely and roughly paved, and as narrow as an ordinary staircase; the streets uniformly carry a man to any other place than the one he wants to go to, and surprise him by landing him in the most unexpected localities; business is chiefly carried on in great covered bazaars, celled like a honeycomb with innumerable shops no larger than a common closet, and the whole hive cut up into a maze of alleys about wide enough to accommodate a laden camel, and well calculated to confuse a stranger and eventually lose him; every where there is dirt, every where there are fleas, every where there are lean, broken-hearted dogs; every alley is thronged with people; wherever you look, your eye rests upon a wild masquerade of extravagant costumes; the workshops are all open to the streets, and the workmen visible; all manner of sounds assail the ear, and over them all rings out the muezzin's cry from some tall minaret, calling the faithful vagabonds to prayer; and superior to the call to prayer, the noises in the streets, the interest of the costumes—superior to every thing, and claiming the bulk of at-

tention first, last, and all the time—is a combination of Mohammedan stenches, to which the smell of even a Chinese quarter
would be as pleasant as the roasting odors of the fatted calf to
the nostrils of the returning Prodigal.   Such is Oriental luxury—such is Oriental splendor! We read about it all our
days, but we comprehend it not until we see it.   Smyrna is a
very old city.   Its name occurs several times in the Bible, one
or two of the disciples of Christ visited it, and here was located
one of the original seven apocalyptic churches spoken of in
Revelations.   These churches were symbolized in the Scriptures as candlesticks, and on certain conditions there was a
sort of implied promise that Smyrna should be endowed
with a "crown of life." She was to "be faithful unto death"
—those were the terms.   She has not kept up her faith
straight along, but the pilgrims that wander hither consider that she has come near enough to it to save her, and so
they point to the fact that Smyrna to-day wears her crown of
life, and is a great city, with a great commerce and full of energy, while the cities wherein were located the other six
churches, and to which no crown of life was promised, have
vanished from the earth.   So Smyrna really still possesses her
crown of life, in a business point of view.   Her career, for
eighteen centuries, has been a chequered one, and she has been
under the rule of princes of many creeds, yet there has been
no season during all that time, as far as we know, (and during
such seasons as she was inhabited at all,) that she has been without her little community of Christians "faithful unto death."
Hers was the only church against which no threats were implied in the Revelations, and the only one which survived.

With Ephesus, forty miles from here, where was located another of the seven churches, the case was different.   The "candlestick" has been removed from Ephesus. Her light has been
put out. Pilgrims, always prone to find prophecies in the
Bible, and often where none exist, speak cheerfully and complacently of poor, ruined Ephesus as the victim of prophecy.
And yet there is no sentence that promises, without due quali-
fication, the destruction of the city.   The words are;

"Remember, therefore, from whence thou art fallen, and repent, and do the first works; or else I will come unto thee quickly, and will remove thy candlestick out of his place, except thou repent."

That is all; the other verses are singularly *complimentary* to Ephesus. The threat is qualified. There is no history to show that she did not repent. But the cruelest habit the modern prophecy-savans have, is that one of coolly and arbitrarily fitting the prophetic shirt on to the wrong man. They do it without regard to rhyme or reason. Both the cases I have just mentioned are instances in point. Those "prophecies" are distinctly leveled at the "*churches* of Ephesus, Smyrna," etc., and yet the pilgrims invariably make them refer to the *cities* instead. No crown of life is promised to the town of Smyrna and its commerce, but to the handful of Christians who formed its "church." If *they* were "faithful unto death," they have their crown now—but no amount of faithfulness and legal shrewdness combined could legitimately drag the *city* into a participation in the promises of the prophecy. The stately language of the Bible refers to a crown of life whose lustre will reflect the day-beams of the endless ages of eternity, not the butterfly existence of a city built by men's hands, which must pass to dust with the builders and be forgotten even in the mere handful of centuries vouchsafed to the solid world itself between its cradle and its grave.

The fashion of delving out fulfillments of prophecy where that prophecy consists of mere "ifs," trenches upon the absurd. Suppose, a thousand years from now, a malarious swamp builds itself up in the shallow harbor of Smyrna, or something else kills the town; and suppose, also, that within that time the swamp that has filled the renowned harbor of Ephesus and rendered her ancient site deadly and uninhabitable to-day, becomes hard and healthy ground; suppose the natural consequence ensues, to wit: that Smyrna becomes a melancholy ruin, and Ephesus is rebuilt. What would the prophecy-savans say? They would coolly skip over our age of the world, and say: "Smyrna was not faithful unto death, and so her crown of life was denied her; Ephesus repented, and lo! her candlestick was not removed. Behold these evidences! How wonderful is prophecy!"

Smyrna has been utterly destroyed six times. If her crown of life had been an insurance policy, she would have had an opportunity to collect on it the first time she fell. But she holds it on sufferance and by a complimentary construction of language which does not refer to her. Six different times, however, I suppose some infatuated prophecy-enthusiast blundered along and said, to the infinite disgust of Smyrna and the Smyrniotes: "In sooth, here is astounding fulfillment of prophecy! Smyrna hath not been faithful unto death, and behold her crown of life is vanished from her head. Verily, these things be astonishing!"

Such things have a bad influence. They provoke worldly men into using light conversation concerning sacred subjects. Thick-headed commentators upon the Bible, and stupid preachers and teachers, work more damage to religion than sensible, cool-brained clergymen can fight away again, toil as they may. It is not good judgment to fit a crown of life upon a city which has been destroyed six times. That other class of wiseacres who twist prophecy in such a manner as to make it promise the destruction and desolation of the same city, use judgment just as bad, since the city is in a very flourishing condition now, unhappily for them. These things put arguments into the mouth of infidelity.

A portion of the city is pretty exclusively Turkish; the Jews have a quarter to themselves; the Franks another quarter; so, also, with the Armenians. The Armenians, of course, are Christians. Their houses are large, clean, airy, handsomely paved with black and white squares of marble, and in the centre of many of them is a square court, which has in it a luxuriant flower-garden and a sparkling fountain; the doors of all the rooms open on this. A very wide hall leads to the street door, and in this the women sit, the most of the day. In the cool of the evening they dress up in their best raiment and show themselves at the door. They are all comely of countenance, and exceedingly neat and cleanly; they look as if they were just out of a band-box. Some of the young ladies—many of them, I may say—are even very beautiful; they average a shade better than American girls—which treasonable words I pray may be forgiven me. They are very sociable, and will smile back when a stranger smiles at them, bow back when he bows, and talk back if he speaks to them. No introduction is required. An hour's chat at the door with a pretty girl one never saw before, is easily obtained, and is very pleasant. I have tried it. I could not talk any thing but English, and the girl knew nothing but Greek, or Armenian, or some such barbarous tongue, but we got along very well. I find that in cases like these, the fact that you can not comprehend each other isn't much of a drawback. In that Russian town of Yalta I danced an astonishing sort of dance an hour long, and one I had not heard of before, with a very pretty girl, and we talked incessantly, and laughed exhaustingly, and neither one ever knew what the other was driving at. But it was splendid. There were twenty people in the set, and the dance was very lively and complicated. It was complicated enough without me—with me it was more so. I threw in a figure now and then that surprised those Russians. But I have never ceased to think of that girl. I have written to her, but I can not direct the epistle because her name is one of those nine-jointed Russian affairs, and there are not letters enough in our alphabet to hold out. I am not reckless enough to try to pronounce it when I am awake, but I make a stagger at it in my dreams, and get up with the lockjaw in the morning. I am fading. I do not take my meals now, with any sort of regularity. Her dear name haunts me still in my dreams. It is awful on teeth. It never comes out of my mouth but it fetches an old snag along with it. And then the lockjaw closes down and nips off a couple of the last syllables—but they taste good.

Coming through the Dardanelles, we saw camel trains on shore with the glasses, but we were never close to one till we got to Smyrna. These camels are very much larger than the scrawny specimens one sees in the menagerie. They stride along these streets, in single file, a dozen in a train, with heavy loads on their backs, and a fancy-looking negro in Turkish costume, or an Arab, preceding them on a little donkey and completely overshadowed and rendered insignificant by the huge beasts. To see a camel train laden with the spices of Arabia and the rare fabrics of Persia come marching through the narrow alleys of the bazaar, among porters with their burdens, money-changers, lamp-merchants, Alnaschars in the glassware business, portly cross-legged Turks smoking the famous narghili, and

STREET SCENE IN SMYRNA.

the crowds drifting to and fro in the fanciful costumes of the East, is a genuine revelation of the Orient. The picture lacks nothing. It casts you back at once into your forgotten boyhood, and again you dream over the wonders of the Arabian Nights; again your companions are princes, your lord is the Caliph Haroun Al Raschid, and your servants are terrific giants and genii that come with smoke and lightning and thunder, and go as a storm goes when they depart!

CHAPTER XXXIX.

WE inquired, and learned that the lions of Smyrna consisted of the ruins of the ancient citadel, whose broken and prodigious battlements frown upon the city from a lofty hill just in the edge of the town—the Mount Pagus of Scripture, they call it; the site of that one of the Seven Apocalyptic Churches of Asia which was located here in the first century of the Christian era; and the grave and the place of martyrdom of the venerable Polycarp, who suffered in Smyrna for his religion some eighteen hundred years ago.

We took little donkeys and started. We saw Polycarp's tomb, and then hurried on.

The "Seven Churches"—thus they abbreviate it—came next on the list. We rode there—about a mile and a half in the sweltering sun—and visited a little Greek church which they said was built upon the ancient site; and we paid a small fee, and the holy attendant gave each of us a little wax candle as a remembrancer of the place, and I put mine in my hat and the sun melted it and the grease all ran down the back of my neck; and so now I have not any thing left but the wick, and it is a sorry and a wilted-looking wick at that.

Several of us argued as well as we could that the " church" mentioned in the Bible meant a party of Christians, and not a building; that the Bible spoke of them as being very poor—so poor, I thought, and so subject to persecution (as per Polycarp's martyrdom) that in the first place they probably could

not have afforded a church edifice, and in the second would
not have dared to build it in the open light of day if they
could ; and finally, that if they had had the privilege of building it, common judgment would have suggested that they
build it somewhere near the town.   But the elders of the
ship's family ruled us down and scouted our evidences.   However, retribution came to them afterward.   They found that
they had been led astray and had gone to the wrong place ; they
discovered that the accepted site is in the city.

SMYRNA.

Riding through the town, we could see marks of the six
Smyrnas that have existed here and been burned up by fire or
knocked down by earthquakes.   The hills and the rocks are
rent asunder in places, excavations expose great blocks of
building-stone that have lain buried for ages, and all the mean
houses and walls of modern Smyrna along the way are spotted
white with broken pillars, capitals and fragments of sculptured
marble that once adorned the lordly palaces that were the
glory of the city in the olden time.

The ascent of the hill of the citadel is very steep, and we proceeded rather slowly. But there were matters of interest about us. In one place, five hundred feet above the sea, the perpendicular bank on the upper side of the road was ten or fifteen feet high, and the cut exposed three veins of oyster shells, just as we have seen quartz veins exposed in the cutting of a road in Nevada or Montana. The veins were about eighteen inches thick and two or three feet apart, and they slanted along downward for a distance of thirty feet or more, and then disappeared where the cut joined the road. Heaven only knows how far a man might trace them by " stripping." They were clean, nice oyster shells, large, and just like any other oyster shells. They were thickly massed together, and none were scattered above or below the veins. Each one was a well-defined lead by itself, and without a spur. My first instinct was to set up the usual—

NOTICE:

" We, the undersigned, claim five claims of two hundred feet each, (and one for discovery,) on this ledge or lode of oyster-shells, with all its dips, spurs, angles, variations and sinuosities, and fifty feet on each side of the same, to work it, etc., etc., according to the mining laws of Smyrna."

They were such perfectly natural-looking leads that I could hardly keep from " taking them up." Among the oyster-shells were mixed many fragments of ancient, broken crockery ware. Now how did those masses of oyster-shells get there? I can not determine. Broken crockery and oyster-shells are suggestive of restaurants—but then they could have had no such places away up there on that mountain side in our time, because nobody has lived up there. A restaurant would not pay in such a stony, forbidding, desolate place. And besides, there were no champagne corks among the shells. If there ever was a restaurant there, it must have been in Smyrna's palmy days, when the hills were covered with palaces. I could believe in one restaurant, on those terms; but then how about the three? Did they have restaurants there at three different periods of the world?—because there are two or three feet of solid earth between the oyster leads.   Evidently, the restaurant solution will not answer.

The hill might have been the bottom of the sea, once, and been lifted up, with its oyster-beds, by an earthquake—but, then, how about the crockery?   And moreover, how about *three* oyster beds, one above another, and thick strata of good honest earth between?

That theory will not do.   It is just possible that this hill is Mount Ararat, and that Noah's Ark rested here, and he ate oysters and threw the shells overboard.   But that will not do, either.   There are the three layers again and the solid earth between—and, besides, there were only eight in Noah's family, and they could not have eaten all these oysters in the two or three months they staid on top of that mountain.   The beasts—however, it is simply absurd to suppose he did not know any more than to feed the beasts on oyster suppers.

It is painful—it is even humiliating—but I am reduced at last to one slender theory: that the oysters climbed up there of their own accord.   But what object could they have had in view?—what did they want up there?   What could any oyster want to climb a hill for?   To climb a hill must necessarily be fatiguing and annoying exercise for an oyster.   The most natural conclusion would be that the oysters climbed up there to look at the scenery.   Yet when one comes to reflect upon the nature of an oyster, it seems plain that he does not care for scenery.   An oyster has no taste for such things; he cares nothing for the beautiful.   An oyster is of a retiring disposition, and not lively—not even cheerful above the average, and never enterprising.   But above all, an oyster does not take any interest in scenery—he scorns it.   What have I arrived at now?   Simply at the point I started from, namely, *those oyster shells are there*, in regular layers, five hundred feet above the sea, and no man knows how they got there.   I have hunted up the guide-books, and the gist of what they say is this: "They are there, but how they got there is a mystery."

Twenty-five years ago, a multitude of people in America put on their ascension robes, took a tearful leave of their friends, and made ready to fly up into heaven at the first blast of the trumpet. But the angel did not blow it. Miller's resurrection day was a failure. The Millerites were disgusted. I did not suspect that there were Millers in Asia Minor, but a gentleman tells me that they had it all set for the world to come to an end in Smyrna one day about three years ago. There was much buzzing and preparation for a long time pre-

AN APPARENT SUCCESS.

viously, and it culminated in a wild excitement at the appointed time. A vast number of the populace ascended the citadel hill early in the morning, to get out of the way of the general destruction, and many of the infatuated closed up their shops and retired from all earthly business. But the strange part of it was that about three in the afternoon, while this gentleman and his friends were at dinner in the hotel, a terrific storm of rain, accompanied by thunder and lightning, broke forth and continued with dire fury for two or three hours. It was a thing unprecedented in Smyrna at that time of the year, and scared some of the most skeptical. The streets ran rivers and the hotel floor was flooded with water. The dinner had to be suspended. When the storm finished and left every body drenched through and through, and melancholy and half-drowned, the ascensionists came down from the mountain as dry as so many charity-sermons! They had been looking down upon the fearful storm going on below, and really believed that their proposed destruction of the world was proving a grand success.

A railway here in Asia—in the dreamy realm of the Orient—in the fabled land of the Arabian Nights—is a strange thing to think of. And yet they have one already, and are building another. The present one is well built and well conducted, by an English Company, but is not doing an immense amount of business. The first year it carried a good many passengers, but its freight list only comprised eight hundred pounds of figs!

It runs almost to the very gates of Ephesus—a town great in all ages of the world—a city familiar to readers of the Bible, and one which was as old as the very hills when the disciples of Christ preached in its streets. It dates back to the shadowy ages of tradition, and was the birthplace of gods renowned in Grecian mythology. The idea of a locomotive tearing through such a place as this, and waking the phantoms of its old days of romance out of their dreams of dead and gone centuries, is curious enough.

We journey thither to-morrow to see the celebrated ruins.

27

CHAPTER XL.

THIS has been a stirring day. The Superintendent of the railway put a train at our disposal, and did us the further kindness of accompanying us to Ephesus and giving to us his watchful care. We brought sixty scarcely perceptible donkeys in the freight cars, for we had much ground to go over. We have seen some of the most grotesque costumes, along the line of the railroad, that can be imagined. I am glad that no possible combination of words could describe them, for I might then be foolish enough to attempt it.

At ancient Ayassalook, in the midst of a forbidding desert, we came upon long lines of ruined aqueducts, and other remnants of architectural grandeur, that told us plainly enough we were nearing what had been a metropolis, once. We left the train and mounted the donkeys, along with our invited guests—pleasant young gentlemen from the officers' list of an American man-of-war.

The little donkeys had saddles upon them which were made very high in order that the rider's feet might not drag the ground. The preventative did not work well in the cases of our tallest pilgrims, however. There were no bridles—nothing but a single rope, tied to the bit. It was purely ornamental, for the donkey cared nothing for it. If he were drifting to starboard, you might put your helm down hard the other way, if it were any satisfaction to you to do it, but he would continue to drift to starboard all the same. There was only one process which could be depended on, and that was to get down and lift his rear around until his head pointed in the right direction, or take him under your arm and carry him to a part of the road which he could not get out of without climbing. The sun flamed down as hot as a furnace, and neck-scarfs, veils and umbrellas seemed hardly any protection; they served only to make the long procession look more than ever fantastic—for be it known the ladies were all riding astride because they could not stay on the shapeless saddles

DRIFTING TO STARBOARD.

sidewise, the men were perspiring and out of temper, their feet were banging against the rocks, the donkeys were caper-ing in every direction but the right one and being belabored with clubs for it, and every now and then a broad umbrella would suddenly go down out of the cavalcade, announcing to all that one more pilgrim had bitten the dust. It was a wilder picture than those solitudes had seen for many a day. No donkeys ever existed that were as hard to navigate as these, I think, or that had so many vile, exasperating instincts. Occasionally we grew so tired and breathless with fighting them that we had to desist,—and immediately the donkey would come down to a deliberate walk. This, with the fatigue, and the sun, would put a man asleep; and as soon as the man was asleep, the donkey would lie down. My donkey shall never see his boyhood's home again. He has lain down once too often. He must die.

A SPOILED NAP.

We all stood in the vast theatre of ancient Ephesus,—the stone-benched amphitheatre I mean—and had our picture taken. We looked as proper there as we would look any where, I suppose. We do not embellish the general desolation of a desert much. We add what dignity we can to a stately ruin with our green umbrellas and jackasses, but it is little. However, we mean well.

I wish to say a brief word of the aspect of Ephesus.

On a high, steep hill, toward the sea, is a gray ruin of ponderous blocks of marble, wherein, tradition says, St. Paul was imprisoned eighteen centuries ago. From these old walls you have the finest view of the desolate scene where once stood Ephesus, the proudest city of ancient times, and whose Temple of Diana was so noble in design, and so exquisite of workmanship, that it ranked high in the list of the Seven Wonders of the World.

Behind you is the sea; in front is a level green valley, (a marsh, in fact,) extending far away among the mountains; to the right of the front view is the old citadel of Ayassalook, on a high hill; the ruined Mosque of the Sultan Selim stands near it in the plain, (this is built over the grave of St. John, and was formerly a Christian Church;) further toward you is the hill of Pion, around whose front is clustered all that remains of the ruins of Ephesus that still stand; divided from it by a narrow valley is the long, rocky, rugged mountain of Coressus. The scene is a pretty one, and yet desolate—for in that wide plain no man can live, and in it is no human habitation. But for the crumbling arches and monstrous piers and broken walls that rise from the foot of the hill of Pion, one could not believe that in this place once stood a city whose renown is older than tradition itself. It is incredible to reflect that things as familiar all over the world to-day as household words, belong in the history and in the shadowy legends of this silent, mournful solitude. We speak of Apollo and of Diana—they were born here; of the metamorphosis of Syrinx into a reed—it was done here; of the great god Pan—he dwelt in the caves of this hill of Coressus; of the Amazons—this was their best prized home; of Bacchus and Hercules—both fought the warlike women here; of the Cyclops—they laid the ponderous marble blocks of some of the ruins yonder; of Homer—this was one of his many birthplaces; of Cimon of Athens; of Alcibiades, Lysander, Agesilaus—they visited here; so did Alexander the Great; so did Hannibal and Antiochus, Scipio, Lucullus and Sylla; Brutus, Cassius, Pompey, Cicero, and Augustus; Antony was a judge in this place, and left his seat in the open court, while the advocates were speaking, to run after Cleopatra, who passed the door; from this city these two sailed on pleasure excursions, in galleys with silver oars and perfumed sails, and with companies of beautiful girls to serve them, and actors and musicians to amuse them; in days that seem almost modern, so remote are they from the early history of this city, Paul the Apostle preached the new religion here, and so did John, and here it is supposed the former was pitted against wild beasts, for in 1 Corinthians, xv. 32 he says:

"If after the manner of men I have fought with beasts at Ephesus," &c.,

when many men still lived who had seen the Christ; here

Mary Magdalen died, and here the Virgin Mary ended her days with John, albeit Rome has since judged it best to locate her grave elsewhere; six or seven hundred years ago—almost yesterday, as it were—troops of mail-clad Crusaders thronged the streets; and to come down to trifles, we speak of meandering streams, and find a new interest in a common word when we discover that the crooked river Meander, in yonder valley, gave it to our dictionary. It makes me feel as old as these

ANCIENT AMPHITHEATRE AT EPHESUS.

dreary hills to look down upon these moss-hung ruins, this historic desolation. One may read the Scriptures and believe, but he can not go and stand yonder in the ruined theatre and in imagination people it again with the vanished multitudes who mobbed Paul's comrades there and shouted, with one voice, "Great is Diana of the Ephesians!" The idea of a shout in such a solitude as this almost makes one shudder.

It was a wonderful city, this Ephesus. Go where you will about these broad plains, you find the most exquisitely sculptured marble fragments scattered thick among the dust and weeds; and protruding from the ground, or lying prone upon it, are beautiful fluted columns of porphyry and all precious marbles ; and at every step you find elegantly carved capitals and massive bases, and polished tablets engraved with Greek inscriptions. It is a world of precious relics, a wilderness of marred and mutilated gems. And yet what are these things to the wonders that lie buried here under the ground? At Constantinople, at Pisa, in the cities of Spain, are great mosques and cathedrals, whose grandest columns came from the temples and palaces of Ephesus, and yet one has only to scratch the ground here to match them. We shall never know what magnificence is, until this imperial city is laid bare to the sun.

The finest piece of sculpture we have yet seen and the one that impressed us most, (for we do not know much about art and can not easily work up ourselves into ecstacies over it,) is one that lies in this old theatre of Ephesus which St. Paul's riot has made so celebrated. It is only the headless body of a man, clad in a coat of mail, with a Medusa

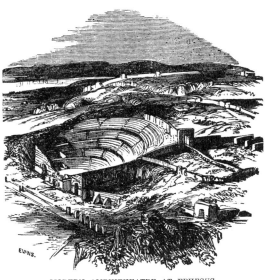

MODERN AMPHITHEATRE AT EPHESUS.

head upon the breast-plate, but we feel persuaded that such dignity and such majesty were never thrown into a form of stone before.

What builders they were, these men of antiquity! The massive arches of some of these ruins rest upon piers that are fifteen feet square and built entirely of solid blocks of marble, some of which are as large as a Saratoga trunk, and some the size of a boarding-house sofa. They are not shells or shafts of stone filled inside with rubbish, but the whole pier is a mass of solid masonry. Vast arches, that may have been the gates of the city, are built in the same way. They have braved the storms and sieges of three thousand years, and have been shaken by many an earthquake, but still they stand. When they

RUINS OF EPHESUS.

dig alongside of them, they find ranges of ponderous masonry that are as perfect in every detail as they were the day those old Cyclopian giants finished them. An English Company is going to excavate Ephesus—and then!

And now am I reminded of—

THE LEGEND OF THE SEVEN SLEEPERS.

In the Mount of Pion, yonder, is the Cave of the Seven Sleepers. Once upon a time, about fifteen hundred years ago, seven young men lived near each other in Ephesus, who belonged to the despised sect of the Christians. It came to pass that the good King Maximilianus, (I am telling this story for nice little boys and girls,) it came to pass, I say, that the good King Maximilianus fell to persecuting the Christians, and as time rolled on he made it very warm for them. So the seven young men said one to the other, let us get up and travel. And they got up and traveled. They tarried not to bid their fathers and mothers good-bye, or any friend they knew. They only took certain moneys which their parents had, and gar-

THE JOURNEY.

ments that belonged unto their friends, whereby they might remember them when far away; and they took also the dog Ketmehr, which was the property of their neighbor Malchus, because the beast did run his head into a noose which one of the young men was carrying carelessly, and they had not time to release him; and they took also certain chickens that seemed lonely in the neighboring coops, and likewise some bottles of curious liquors that stood near the grocer's window; and then they departed from the city. By-and-by they came to a marvelous cave in the Hill of Pion and entered into it and feasted, and presently they hurried on again. But they forgot the bottles of curious liquors, and left them behind. They traveled in many lands, and had many strange adventures. They were virtuous young men, and lost no opportunity that fell in their way to make their livelihood. Their motto was in these words, namely, " Procrastination is the thief of time." And so, whenever they did come upon a man who was alone, they said, Behold, this person hath the wherewithal—let us go through him. And they went through him. At the end of five years they had waxed tired of travel and adventure, and longed to revisit their old home again and hear the voices and see the faces that were dear unto their youth. Therefore they went through such parties as fell in their way where they sojourned at that time, and journeyed back toward Ephesus again. For the good King Maximilianus was become converted unto the new faith, and the Christians rejoiced because they were no longer persecuted. One day as the sun went down, they came to the cave in the Mount of Pion, and they said, each to his fellow, Let us sleep here, and go and feast and make merry with our friends when the morning cometh. And each of the seven lifted up his voice and said, It is a whiz. So they went in, and lo, where they had put them, there lay the bottles of strange liquors, and they judged that age had not impaired their excellence. Wherein the wanderers were right, and the heads of the same were level. So each of the young men drank six bottles, and behold they felt very tired, then, and lay down and slept soundly.

When they awoke, one of them, Johannes—surnamed Smithianus—said, We are naked. And it was so. Their raiment was all gone, and the money which they had gotten from a stranger whom they had proceeded through as they approached the city, was lying upon the ground, corroded and rusted and defaced. Likewise the dog Ketmehr was gone, and nothing save the brass that was upon his collar remained. They wondered much at these things. But they took the money, and they wrapped about their bodies some leaves, and came up to the top of the hill. Then were they perplexed. The wonderful temple of Diana was gone; many grand edifices they had never seen before stood in the city; men in strange garbs moved about the streets, and every thing was changed.

Johannes said, It hardly seems like Ephesus. Yet here is the great gymnasium; here is the mighty theatre, wherein I have seen seventy thousand men assembled; here is the Agora; there is the font where the sainted John the Baptist immersed the converts; yonder is the prison of the good St. Paul, where we all did use to go to touch the ancient chains that bound him and be cured of our distempers; I see the tomb of the disciple Luke, and afar off is the church wherein repose the ashes of the holy John, where the Christians of Ephesus go twice a year to gather the dust from the tomb, which is able to make bodies whole again that are corrupted by disease, and cleanse the soul from sin; but see how the wharves encroach upon the sea, and what multitudes of ships are anchored in the bay; see, also, how the city hath stretched abroad, far over the valley behind Pion, and even unto the walls of Ayassalook; and lo, all the hills are white with palaces and ribbed with colonnades of marble. How mighty is Ephesus become!

And wondering at what their eyes had seen, they went down into the city and purchased garments and clothed themselves. And when they would have passed on, the merchant bit the coins which they had given him, with his teeth, and turned them about and looked curiously upon them, and cast them upon his counter, and listened if they rang; and then he said, These be bogus. And they said, Depart thou to Hades, and went their way. When they were come to their houses, they recognized them, albeit they seemed old and mean; and they rejoiced, and were glad. They ran to the doors, and knocked, and strangers opened, and looked inquiringly upon them. And they said, with great excitement, while their hearts beat high, and the color in their faces came and went, Where is my father? Where is my mother? Where are Dionysius and

Serapion, and Pericles, and Decius? And the strangers that
opened said, We know not these. The Seven said, How, you
know them not? How long have ye dwelt here, and whither
are they gone that dwelt here before ye? And the strangers
said, Ye play upon us with a jest, young men; we and our
fathers have sojourned under these roofs these six generations;
the names ye utter rot upon the tombs, and they that bore
them have run their brief race, have laughed and sung, have
borne the sorrows and the weariness that were allotted them,
and are at rest; for nine-score years the summers have come
and gone, and the autumn leaves have fallen, since the roses
faded out of their cheeks and they laid them to sleep with the
dead.

Then the seven young men turned them away from their
homes, and the strangers shut the doors upon them. The
wanderers marveled greatly, and looked into the faces of all
they met, as hoping to find one that they knew; but all were
strange, and passed them by and spake no friendly word.
They were sore distressed and sad. Presently they spake unto
a citizen and said, Who is King in Ephesus? And the citizen
answered and said, Whence come ye that ye know not that
great Laertius reigns in Ephesus? They looked one at the
other, greatly perplexed, and presently asked again, Where,
then, is the good King Maximilianus? The citizen moved him
apart, as one who is afraid, and said, Verily these men be mad,
and dream dreams, else would they know that the King
whereof they speak is dead above two hundred years agone.

Then the scales fell from the eyes of the Seven, and one said,
Alas, that we drank of the curious liquors. They have made
us weary, and in dreamless sleep these two long centuries have
we lain. Our homes are desolate, our friends are dead. Behold, the jig is up—let us die. And that same day went they
forth and laid them down and died. And in that self-same
day, likewise, the Seven-up did cease in Ephesus, for that the
Seven that were up were down again, and departed and dead
withal. And the names that be upon their tombs, even unto
this time, are Johannes Smithianus, Trumps, Gift, High, and

Low, Jack, and The Game. And with the sleepers lie also the bottles wherein were once the curious liquors; and upon them is writ, in ancient letters, such words as these— names of heathen gods of olden time, perchance: Rumpunch, Jinsling, Egnog.

GRAVES OF THE SEVEN SLEEPERS.

Such is the story of the Seven Sleepers, (with slight variations,) and I know it is true, because I have seen the cave myself.

Really, so firm a faith had the ancients in this legend, that as late as eight or nine hundred years ago, learned travelers held it in superstitious fear. Two of them record that they ventured into it, but ran quickly out again, not daring to tarry lest they should fall asleep and outlive their great grand-children a century or so. Even at this day the ignorant denizens of the neighboring country prefer not to sleep in it.

CHAPTER XLI.

WHEN I last made a memorandum, we were at Ephesus. We are in Syria, now, encamped in the mountains of Lebanon. The interregnum has been long, both as to time and distance. We brought not a relic from Ephesus! After gathering up fragments of sculptured marbles and breaking ornaments from the interior work of the Mosques; and after bringing them at a cost of infinite trouble and fatigue, five miles on muleback to the railway depot, a government officer compelled all who had such things to disgorge! He had an order from Constantinople to *look out for our party*, and see that we carried nothing off. It was a wise, a just, and a well-deserved rebuke, but it created a sensation. I never resist a temptation to plunder a stranger's premises without feeling insufferably vain about it. This time I felt proud beyond expression. I was serene in the midst of the scoldings that were heaped upon the Ottoman government for its affront offered to a pleasuring party of entirely respectable gentlemen and ladies. I said, "We that have free souls, it touches us not." The shoe not only pinched our party, but it pinched hard; a principal sufferer discovered that the imperial order was inclosed in an envelop bearing the seal of the British Embassy at Constantinople, and therefore must have been inspired by the representative of the Queen. This was bad—very bad. Coming solely from the Ottomans, it might have signified only Ottoman hatred of Christians, and a vulgar ignorance as to genteel methods of expressing it; but coming from the Christianized, educated, politic British legation, it simply intimated that we were a sort of gentlemen and ladies who would bear watching! So the party regarded it, and were incensed accordingly. The truth doubtless was, that the same precautions would have been taken against *any* travelers, because the English Company who have acquired the right to excavate Ephesus, and have paid a great sum for that right, need to be protected, and deserve to be. They can not afford to run the risk of having their hospitality abused by travelers, especially since travelers are such notorious scorners of honest behavior.

We sailed from Smyrna, in the wildest spirit of expectancy, for the chief feature, the grand goal of the expedition, was near at hand—we were approaching the Holy Land! Such a burrowing into the hold for trunks that had lain buried for weeks, yes for months; such a hurrying to and fro above decks and below; such a riotous system of packing and unpacking; such a littering up of the cabins with shirts and skirts, and indescribable and unclassable odds and ends; such a making up of bundles, and setting apart of umbrellas, green spectacles and thick veils; such a critical inspection of saddles and bridles that had never yet touched horses; such a cleaning and loading of revolvers and examining of bowie-knives; such a half-soling of the seats of pantaloons with serviceable buckskin; then such a poring over ancient maps; such a reading up of Bibles and Palestine travels; such a marking out of routes; such exasperating efforts to divide up the company into little bands of congenial spirits who might make the long and arduous journey without quarreling; and morning, noon and night, such mass-meetings in the cabins, such speech-making, such sage suggesting, such worrying and quarreling, and such a general raising of the very mischief, was never seen in the ship before!

But it is all over now. We are cut up into parties of six or eight, and by this time are scattered far and wide. Ours is the only one, however, that is venturing on what is called " the long trip "—that is, out into Syria, by Baalbec to Damascus, and thence down through the full length of Palestine. It would be a tedious, and also a too risky journey, at this hot season of the year, for any but strong, healthy men, accustomed somewhat to fatigue and rough life in the open air. The other parties will take shorter journeys.

For the last two months we have been in a worry about one portion of this Holy Land pilgrimage. I refer to transportation service. We knew very well that Palestine was a country which did not do a large passenger business, and every man we came across who knew any thing about it gave us to understand that not half of our party would be able to get dragomen and animals. At Constantinople every body fell to telegraphing the American Consuls at Alexandria and Beirout to give notice that we wanted dragomen and transportation. We were desperate—would take horses, jackasses, cameleopards, kangaroos—any thing. At Smyrna, more telegraphing was done, to the same end. Also, fearing for the worst, we telegraphed for a large number of seats in the diligence for Damascus, and horses for the ruins of Baalbec.

As might have been expected, a notion got abroad in Syria and Egypt that the whole population of the Province of America (the Turks consider us a trifling little province in some unvisited corner of the world,) were coming to the Holy Land—and so, when we got to Beirout yesterday, we found the place full of dragomen and their outfits. We had all intended to go by diligence to Damascus, and switch off to Baalbec as we went along—because we expected to rejoin the ship, go to Mount Carmel, and take to the woods from there. However, when our own private party of eight found that it was possible, and proper enough, to make the "long trip," we adopted that programme. We have never been much trouble to a Consul before, but we have been a fearful nuisance to our Consul at Beirout. I mention this because I can not help admiring his patience, his industry, and his accommodating spirit. I mention it also, because I think some of our ship's company did not give him as full credit for his excellent services as he deserved.

Well, out of our eight, three were selected to attend to all business connected with the expedition. The rest of us had nothing to do but look at the beautiful city of Beirout, with its bright, new houses nestled among a wilderness of green shrubbery spread abroad over an upland that sloped gently down to the sea; and also at the mountains of Lebanon that environ it; and likewise to bathe in the transparent blue water that rolled its billows about the ship (we did not know there were sharks there.) We had also to range up and down through the town and look at the costumes. These are picturesque and fanciful, but not so varied as at Constantinople and Smyrna; the women of Beirout add an agony—in the two former cities the sex wear a thin veil which one can see through (and they often expose their ancles,) but at Beirout they cover their entire faces with dark-colored or black veils, so that they look like mummies, and then expose their breasts to the public. A young gentleman (I believe he was a Greek,) volunteered to show us around the city, and said it would afford him great pleasure, because he was studying English and wanted practice in that language. When we had finished the rounds, however, he called for remuneration—said he hoped the gentlemen would give him a trifle in the way of a few piastres (equivalent to a few five cent pieces.) We did so. The Consul was surprised when he heard it, and said he knew the young fellow's family very well, and that they were an old and highly respectable family and worth a hundred and fifty thousand dollars! Some people, so situated, would have been ashamed of the berth he had with us and his manner of crawling into it.

At the appointed time our business committee reported, and said all things were in readiness—that we were to start to-day, with horses, pack animals, and tents, and go to Baalbec, Damascus, the Sea of Tiberias, and thence southward by the way of the scene of Jacob's Dream and other notable Bible localities to Jerusalem—from thence probably to the Dead Sea, but possibly not—and then strike for the ocean and rejoin the ship three or four weeks hence at Joppa; terms, five dollars a day apiece, in gold, and every thing to be furnished by the dragoman. They said we would live as well as at a hotel. I had read something like that before, and did not shame my judgment by believing a word of it. I said nothing, however, but packed up a blanket and a shawl to sleep in, pipes and tobacco, two or three woollen shirts, a portfolio, a guide-book, and a Bible. I also took along a towel and a cake of soap, to inspire respect in the Arabs, who would take me for a king in disguise.

We were to select our horses at 3 P. M. At that hour Abraham, the dragoman, marshaled them before us. With all solemnity I set it down here, that those horses were the hardest lot I ever did come across, and their accoutrements were in exquisite keeping with their style.

THE SELECTION.

One brute had an eye out; another had his tail sawed off close, like a rabbit, and was proud of it; another had a bony ridge running from his neck to his tail, like one of those ruined aqueducts one sees about Rome, and had a neck on him like a bowsprit; they all limped, and had sore backs, and likewise raw places and old scales scattered about their persons like brass nails in a hair trunk; their gaits were marvelous to contemplate, and replete with variety—under way the procession looked like a fleet in a storm. It was fearful. Blucher shook his head and said:

"That dragon is going to get himself into trouble fetching these old crates out of the hospital the way they are, unless he has got a permit."

I said nothing. The display was exactly according to the guide-book, and were we not traveling by the guide-book? I selected a certain horse because I thought I saw him shy, and I thought that a horse that had spirit enough to shy was not to be despised.

At 6 o'clock P. M., we came to a halt here on the breezy summit of a shapely mountain overlooking the sea, and the handsome valley where dwelt some of those enterprising Phœnicians of ancient times we read so much about; all around us are what were once the dominions of Hiram, King of Tyre, who furnished timber from the cedars of these Labanon hills to build portions of King Solomon's Temple with.

Shortly after six, our pack train arrived. I had not seen it before, and a good right I had to be astonished. We had nineteen serving men and twenty-six pack mules! It was a perfect caravan. It looked like one, too, as it wound among the rocks. I wondered what in the very mischief we wanted with such a vast turn-out as that, for eight men. I wondered awhile, but soon I began to long for a tin plate, and some bacon and beans. I had camped out many and many a time before, and knew just what was coming. I went off, without waiting for serving men, and unsaddled my horse, and washed such portions of his ribs and his spine as projected through his hide, and when I came back, behold five stately circus tents were up— tents that were brilliant, within, with blue, and gold, and crimson, and all manner of splendid adornment! I was speechless. Then they brought eight little iron bedsteads, and set them up in the tents; they put a soft mattress and pillows and good blankets and two snow-white sheets on each bed. Next, they rigged a table about the centre-pole, and on it placed pewter pitchers, basins, soap, and the whitest of towels— one set for each man; they pointed to pockets in the tent, and said we could put our small trifles in them for convenience, and if we needed pins or such things, they were sticking every

where. Then came the finishing touch—they spread carpets
on the floor ! I simply said, " If you call this camping out,
all right—but it isn't the style *I* am used to ; my little baggage that I brought along is at a discount."

It grew dark, and they put candles on the tables—candles
set in bright, new, brazen candlesticks. And soon the bell—a

CAMPING OUT.

genuine, simon-pure bell—rang, and we were invited to " the
saloon." I had thought before that we had a tent or so too
many, but now here was one, at least, provided for ; it was to
be used for nothing but an eating-saloon. Like the others, it
was high enough for a family of giraffes to live in, and was
very handsome and clean and bright-colored within. It was a
gem of a place. A table for eight, and eight canvas chairs ; a
table-cloth and napkins whose whiteness and whose fineness
laughed to scorn the things we were used to in the great excursion steamer ; knives and forks, soup-plates, dinner-plates
—every thing, in the handsomest kind of style. It was wonderful ! And they call *this* camping out. Those stately fellows in baggy trowsers and turbaned fezzes brought in a dinner
which consisted of roast mutton, roast chicken, roast goose,

potatoes, bread, tea, pudding, apples, and delicious grapes; the viands were better cooked than any we had eaten for weeks, and the table made a finer appearance, with its large German silver candlesticks and other finery, than any table we had sat down to for a good while, and yet that polite drago-man, Abraham, came bowing in and apologizing for the whole affair, on account of the unavoidable confusion of getting under way for a very long trip, and promising to do a great deal better in future!

It is midnight, now, and we break camp at six in the morning.

They call this camping out. At this rate it is a glorious privilege to be a pilgrim to the Holy Land.

CHAPTER XLII.

WE are camped near *Temnin-el-Foka*—a name which the boys have simplified a good deal, for the sake of convenience in spelling. They call it Jacksonville. It sounds a little strangely, here in the Valley of Lebanon, but it has the merit of being easier to remember than the Arabic name.

"COME LIKE SPIRITS, SO DEPART."

"The night shall be filled with music,
And the cares that infest the day
Shall fold their tents like the Arabs,
And as silently steal away."

I slept very soundly last night, yet when the dragoman's bell rang at half-past five this morning and the cry went abroad of "Ten minutes to dress for breakfast!" I heard both. It surprised me, because I have not heard the breakfast gong in the ship for a month, and whenever we have had occasion to fire a salute at daylight, I have only found it out in the course of conversation afterward. However, camping out, even though it be in a gorgeous tent, makes one fresh and lively in the morning—especially if the air you are breathing is the cool, fresh air of the mountains.

I was dressed within the ten minutes, and came out. The saloon tent had been stripped of its sides, and had nothing left but its roof; so when we sat down to table we could look out over a noble panorama of mountain, sea and hazy valley. And sitting thus, the sun rose slowly up and suffused the picture with a world of rich coloring.

Hot mutton chops, fried chicken, omelettes, fried potatoes and coffee—all excellent. This was the bill of fare. It was sauced with a savage appetite purchased by hard riding the day before, and refreshing sleep in a pure atmosphere. As I called for a second cup of coffee, I glanced over my shoulder, and behold our white village was gone—the splendid tents had vanished like magic! It was wonderful how quickly those Arabs had "folded their tents;" and it was wonderful, also, how quickly they had gathered the thousand odds and ends of the camp together and disappeared with them.

By half-past six we were under way, and all the Syrian world seemed to be under way also. The road was filled with mule trains and long processions of camels. This reminds me that we have been trying for some time to think what a camel looks like, and now we have made it out. When he is down on all his knees, flat on his breast to receive his load, he looks something like a goose swimming; and when he is upright he looks like an ostrich with an extra set of legs. Camels are not beautiful, and their long under lip gives them an exceedingly "gallus"* expression. They have immense, flat, forked cushions of feet, that make a track in the dust like a pie with a slice cut out of it. They are not particular about their diet. They would eat a tombstone if they could bite it. A thistle grows about here which has needles on it that would pierce through leather, I think; if one touches you, you can find relief in nothing but profanity. The camels eat these. They show by their actions that they enjoy them. I suppose it would be a real treat to a camel to have a keg of nails for supper.

A GOOD FEEDER.

While I am speaking of animals, I will mention that I have a horse now by the name of "Jericho." He is a mare. I have seen remarkable horses before, but none so remarkable as this. I wanted a horse that could shy, and this one fills the bill. I

* Excuse the slang—no other word will describe it.

had an idea that shying indicated spirit. If I was correct, I have got the most spirited horse on earth. He shies at every thing he comes across, with the utmost impartiality. He appears to have a mortal dread of telegraph poles, especially; and it is fortunate that these are on both sides of the road, because as it is now, I never fall off twice in succession on the same side. If I fell on the same side always, it would get to be monotonous after a while. This creature has scared at every thing he has seen to-day, except a haystack. He walked up to that with an intrepidity and a recklessness that were astonishing. And it would fill any one with admiration to see how he preserves his self-possession in the presence of a barley sack. This dare-devil bravery will be the death of this horse some day.

He is not particularly fast, but I think he will get me through the Holy Land. He has only one fault. His tail has been chopped off or else he has sat down on it too hard, some time

INTERESTING FETE.

or other, and he has to fight the flies with his heels. This is all very well, but when he tries to kick a fly off the top of his head with his hind foot, it is too much variety. He is going to get himself into trouble that way some day. He reaches around and bites my legs too. I do not care particularly about that, only I do not like to see a horse too sociable.

I think the owner of this prize had a wrong opinion about him. He had an idea that he was one of those fiery, untamed steeds, but he is not of that character. I know the Arab had this idea, because when he brought the horse out for inspection in Beirout, he kept jerking at the bridle and shouting in Arabic, "Ho! will you? Do you want to run away, you ferocious beast, and break your neck?" when all the time the horse was not doing any thing in the world, and only looked like he wanted to lean up against something and think. Whenever he is not shying at things, or reaching after a fly, he wants to do that yet. How it would surprise his owner to know this.

We have been in a historical section of country all day. At noon we camped three hours and took luncheon at Mekseh, near the junction of the Lebanon Mountains and the Jebel el Kuneiyiseh, and looked down into the immense, level, garden-like Valley of Lebanon. To-night we are camping near the same valley, and have a very wide sweep of it in view. We can see the long, whale-backed ridge of Mount Hermon projecting above the eastern hills. The "dews of Hermon" are falling upon us now, and the tents are almost soaked with them.

Over the way from us, and higher up the valley, we can discern, through the glasses, the faint outlines of the wonderful ruins of Baalbec, the supposed Baal-Gad of Scripture. Joshua, and another person, were the two spies who were sent into this land of Canaan by the children of Israel to report upon its character—I mean they were the spies who reported favorably. They took back with them some specimens of the grapes of this country, and in the children's picture-books they are always represented as bearing one monstrous bunch swung to a pole between them, a respectable load for a pack-train. The Sunday-school books exaggerated it a little. The grapes are most excellent to this day, but the bunches are not as large as those in the pictures. I was surprised and hurt when I saw them, because those colossal bunches of grapes were one of my most cherished juvenile traditions.

Joshua reported favorably, and the children of Israel journeyed on, with Moses at the head of the general government, and Joshua in command of the army of six hundred thousand fighting men. Of women and children and civilians there was a countless swarm. Of all that mighty host, none but the two faithful spies ever lived to set their feet in the Promised Land. They and their descendants wandered forty years in the desert,

SUNDAY-SCHOOL GRAPES.

and then Moses, the gifted warrior, poet, statesman and philosopher, went up into Pisgah and met his mysterious fate. Where he was buried no man knows—for

> " * * * no man dug that sepulchre,
> And no man saw it e'er—
> For the Sons of God upturned the sod
> And laid the dead man there!"

Then Joshua began his terrible raid, and from Jericho clear to this Baal-Gad, he swept the land like the Genius of Destruction. He slaughtered the people, laid waste their soil, and razed their cities to the ground. He wasted thirty-one kings also. One may call it that, though really it can hardly be called wasting them, because there were always plenty of kings in those days, and to spare. At any rate, he destroyed thirty-one kings, and divided up their realms among his Israelites. He divided up this valley stretched out here before us, and so it was once Jewish territory. The Jews have long since disappeared from it, however.

Back yonder, an hour's journey from here, we passed through an Arab village of stone dry-goods boxes (they look like that,) where Noah's tomb lies under lock and key. [Noah built the ark.] Over these old hills and valleys the ark that contained all that was left of a vanished world once floated.

I make no apology for detailing the above information. It will be news to some of my readers, at any rate.

Noah's tomb is built of stone, and is covered with a long stone building. Bucksheesh let us in. The building had to be long, because the grave of the honored old navigator is two hundred and ten feet long itself! It is only about four feet high, though. He must have cast a shadow like a lightning-rod. The proof that this is the genuine spot where Noah was buried can only be doubted by uncommonly incredulous people. The evidence is pretty straight. Shem, the son of Noah, was present at the burial, and showed the place to his descendants, who transmitted the knowledge to their descendants, and the lineal descendants of these introduced themselves to us to-day. It was pleasant to make the acquaintance of members of so respectable a family. It was a thing to be proud of. It was the next thing to being acquainted with Noah himself.

Noah's memorable voyage will always possess a living interest for me, henceforward.

If ever an oppressed race existed, it is this one we see fettered around us under the inhuman tyranny of the Ottoman Empire. I wish Europe would let Russia annihilate Turkey a little—not much, but enough to make it difficult to find the place again without a divining-rod or a diving-bell. The Syrians are very poor, and yet they are ground down by a system of taxation that would drive any other nation frantic. Last year their taxes were heavy enough, in all conscience—but this year they have been increased by the addition of taxes that were forgiven them in times of famine in former years. On top of this the Government has levied a tax of *one-tenth* of the whole proceeds of the land. This is only half the story. The Pacha of a Pachalic does not trouble himself with appointing tax-collectors. He figures up what all these taxes ought to amount to in a certain district. Then he farms the collection out. He calls the rich men together, the highest bidder gets the speculation, pays the Pacha on the spot, and then sells out to smaller fry, who sell in turn to a piratical horde of still smaller fry. These latter compel the peasant to bring his little trifle of grain to the village, at his own cost. It must be weighed, the various taxes set apart, and the remainder returned to the producer. But the collector delays this duty day after day, while the producer's family are perishing for bread; at last the poor wretch, who can not but understand the game, says, " Take a quarter—take half—take two-thirds if you will, and let me go!" It is a most outrageous state of things.

These people are naturally good-hearted and intelligent, and with education and liberty, would be a happy and contented race. They often appeal to the stranger to know if the great world will not some day come to their relief and save them. The Sultan has been lavishing money like water in England and Paris, but his subjects are suffering for it now.

This fashion of camping out bewilders me. We have boot-jacks and a bath-tub, now, and yet all the mysteries the pack-mules carry are not revealed. What next?

CHAPTER XLIII.

WE had a tedious ride of about five hours, in the sun, across the Valley of Lebanon. It proved to be not quite so much of a garden as it had seemed from the hill-sides. It was a desert, weed-grown waste, littered thickly with stones the size of a man's fist. Here and there the natives had scratched the ground and reared a sickly crop of grain, but for the most part the valley was given up to a handful of shepherds, whose flocks were doing what they honestly could to get a living, but the chances were against them. We saw rude piles of stones standing near the roadside, at intervals, and recognized the custom of marking boundaries which obtained in Jacob's time. There were no walls, no fences, no hedges—nothing to secure a man's possessions but these random heaps of stones. The Israelites held them sacred in the old patriarchal times, and these other Arabs, their lineal descendants, do so likewise. An American, of ordinary intelligence, would soon widely extend his property, at an outlay of mere manual labor, performed at night, under so loose a system of fencing as this.

AN OLD FOGY.

The plows these people use are simply a sharpened stick, such as Abraham plowed with, and they still winnow their wheat as he did—they pile it on the house-top, and then toss it by shovel-fulls into the air until the wind has blown all the chaff away. They never invent any thing, never learn any thing.

We had a fine race, of a mile, with an Arab perched on a camel. Some of the horses were fast, and made very good time, but the camel scampered by them without any very great effort. The yelling and shouting, and whipping and

RACE WITH CAMEL.

galloping, of all parties interested, made it an exhilarating, exciting, and particularly boisterous race.

At eleven o'clock, our eyes fell upon the walls and columns of Baalbec, a noble ruin whose history is a sealed book. It has stood there for thousands of years, the wonder and admiration of travelers; but who built it, or when it was built, are questions that may never be answered. One thing is very sure, though. Such grandeur of design, and such grace of execution, as one sees in the temples of Baalbec, have not been equaled or even approached in any work of men's hands that has been built within twenty centuries past.

The great Temple of the Sun, the Temple of Jupiter, and several smaller temples, are clustered together in the midst of one of these miserable Syrian villages, and look strangely enough in such plebeian company. These temples are built upon massive substructions that might support a world, almost; the materials used are blocks of stone as large as an omnibus —very few, if any of them, are smaller than a carpenter's tool chest—and these substructions are traversed by tunnels of masonry through which a train of cars might pass. With such foundations as these, it is little wonder that Baalbec has lasted so long. The Temple of the Sun is nearly three hundred feet long and one hundred and sixty feet wide. It had fifty-four columns around it, but only six are standing now—the others lie broken at its base, a confused and picturesque heap. The six columns are perfect, as also are their bases, Corinthian capitals and entablature—and six more shapely columns do not exist. The columns and the entablature together are ninety feet high—a prodigious altitude for

TEMPLE OF THE SUN, BAALBEC.

shafts of stone to reach, truly—and yet one only thinks of their beauty and symmetry when looking at them; the pillars look slender and delicate, the entablature, with its elaborate sculpture, looks like rich stucco-work. But when you have gazed aloft till your eyes are weary, you glance at the great fragments of pillars among which you are standing, and find that they are eight feet through; and with them lie beautiful capitals apparently as large as a small cottage; and also single slabs of stone, superbly sculptured, that are four or five feet thick, and would completely cover the floor of any ordinary parlor. You wonder where these monstrous things came from, and it takes some little time to satisfy yourself that the airy and graceful fabric that towers above your head is made up of their mates. It seems too preposterous.

The Temple of Jupiter is a smaller ruin than the one I have been speaking of, and yet is immense. It is in a tolerable state of preservation. One row of nine columns stands almost uninjured. They are sixty-five feet high and support a sort of porch or roof, which connects them with the roof of the building. This porch-roof is composed of tremendous slabs of stone, which are so finely sculptured on the under side that the work looks like a fresco from below. One or two of these slabs had fallen, and again I wondered if the gigantic masses of carved stone that lay about me were no larger than those above my head. Within the temple, the ornamentation was elaborate and colossal. What a wonder of architectural beauty and grandeur this edifice must have been when it was new! And what a noble picture it and its statelier companion, with the chaos of mighty fragments scattered about them, yet makes in the moonlight!

I can not conceive how those immense blocks of stone were ever hauled from the quarries, or how they were ever raised to the dizzy heights they occupy in the temples. And yet these sculptured blocks are trifles in size compared with the rough-hewn blocks that form the wide verandah or platform which surrounds the Great Temple. One stretch of that platform, two hundred feet long, is composed of blocks of stone as large, and some of them larger, than a street-car. They surmount a wall about ten or twelve feet high. I thought those were large rocks, but they sank into insignificance compared with those which formed another section of the platform. These were three in number, and I thought that each of them was

RUINS OF BAALBEC.

about as long as three street cars placed end to end, though of course they are a third wider and a third higher than a street car.   Perhaps two railway freight cars of the largest pattern, placed end to end, might better represent their size.   In combined length these three stones stretch nearly two hundred feet; they are thirteen feet square; two of them are sixty-four feet long each, and the third is sixty-nine.   They are built into the massive wall some twenty feet above the ground. They are there, but how they got there is the question.   I have seen the hull of a steamboat that was smaller than one of those stones.   All these great walls are as exact and shapely as the flimsy things we build of bricks in these days.   A race

29

of gods or of giants must have inhabited Baalbec many a century ago. Men like the men of our day could hardly rear such temples as these.

We went to the quarry from whence the stones of Baalbec were taken. It was about a quarter of a mile off, and down hill. In a great pit lay the mate of the largest stone in the ruins. It lay there just as the giants of that old forgotten time had left it when they were called hence—just as they had left it, to remain for thousands of years, an eloquent rebuke unto such as are prone to think slightingly of the men who lived before them. This enormous block lies there, squared

HEWN STONES—IN QUARRY.

and ready for the builders' hands—a solid mass fourteen feet by seventeen, and but a few inches less than seventy feet long! Two buggies could be driven abreast of each other, on its surface, from one end of it to the other, and leave room enough for a man or two to walk on either side.

One might swear that all the John Smiths and George Wilkinsons, and all the other pitiful nobodies between Kingdom Come and Baalbec would inscribe their poor little names upon the walls of Baalbec's magnificent ruins, and would add the town, the county and the State they came from—and swearing thus, be infallibly correct. It is a pity some great ruin does not fall in and flatten out some of these reptiles, and scare their kind out of ever giving their names to fame upon any walls or monuments again, forever.

Properly, with the sorry relics we bestrode, it was a three days' journey to Damascus. It was necessary that we should do it in less than two. It was necessary because our three pilgrims would not travel on the Sabbath day. We were all perfectly willing to keep the Sabbath day, but there are times when to keep the *letter* of a sacred law whose spirit is righteous, becomes a sin, and this was a case in point. We pleaded for the tired, ill-treated horses, and tried to show that their faithful service deserved kindness in return, and their hard lot compassion. But when did ever self-righteousness know the sentiment of pity? What were a few long hours added to the hardships of some over-taxed brutes when weighed against the peril of those human souls? It was not the most promising party to travel with and hope to gain a higher veneration for religion through the example of its devotees. We said the Saviour who pitied dumb beasts and taught that the ox must be rescued from the mire even on the Sabbath day, would not have counseled a forced march like this. We said the "long trip" was exhausting and therefore dangerous in the blistering heats of summer, even when the ordinary days' stages were traversed, and if we persisted in this hard march, some of us might be stricken down with the fevers of the country in consequence of it. Nothing could move the pilgrims. They *must* press on. Men might die, horses might die, but they must enter upon holy soil next week, with no Sabbath-breaking stain upon them. Thus they were willing to commit a sin against the spirit of religious law, in order that they might preserve the letter of it. It was not worth while to tell them "the letter kills." I am talking now about personal friends; men whom I like; men who are good citizens; who are honorable, upright, conscientious; but whose idea of the Saviour's religion seems to me distorted. They lecture our shortcomings unsparingly, and every night they call us together and read to us chapters from the Testament that are full of gentleness, of

MERCY.

charity, and of tender mercy; and then all the next day they stick to their saddles clear up to the summits of these rugged mountains, and clear down again. Apply the Testament's gentleness, and charity, and tender mercy to a toiling, worn and weary horse?—Nonsense—these are for God's human creatures, not His dumb ones. What the pilgrims choose to do, respect for their almost sacred character demands that I should allow to pass—but I would so like to catch any other member of the party riding his horse up one of these exhausting hills once!

We have given the pilgrims a good many examples that might benefit them, but it is virtue thrown away. They have

never heard a cross word out of our lips toward each other—
but *they* have quarreled once or twice. We love to hear them
at it, after they have been lecturing us. The very first thing
they did, coming ashore at Beirout, was to quarrel in the boat.
I have said I like them, and I do like them—but every time
they read me a scorcher of a lecture I mean to talk back in print.

Not content with doubling the legitimate stages, they
switched off the main road
and went away out of the
way to visit an absurd
fountain called Figia, because Baalam's ass had
drank there once. So we
journeyed on, through the
terrible hills and deserts
and the roasting sun, and
then far into the night,
seeking the honored pool
of Baalam's ass, the patron

PATRON SAINT.

saint of all pilgrims like us. I find no entry but this in my
note-book:

"Rode to-day, altogether, thirteen hours, through deserts, partly, and partly over
barren, unsightly hills, and latterly through wild, rocky scenery, and camped at
about eleven o'clock at night on the banks of a limpid stream, near a Syrian village.
Do not know its name—do not wish to know it—want to go to bed. Two horses
lame (mine and Jack's) and the others worn out. Jack and I walked three or four
miles, over the hills, and led the horses. Fun—but of a mild type."

Twelve or thirteen hours in the saddle, even in a Christian
land and a Christian climate, and on a good horse, is a tiresome journey; but in an oven like Syria, in a ragged spoon of
a saddle that slips fore-and-aft, and "thort-ships," and every
way, and on a horse that is tired and lame, and yet must be
whipped and spurred with hardly a moment's cessation all day
long, till the blood comes from his side, and your conscience
hurts you every time you strike, if you are half a man,—it is a
journey to be remembered in bitterness of spirit and execrated
with emphasis for a liberal division of a man's lifetime.

CHAPTER XLIV.

THE next day was an outrage upon men and horses both. It was another thirteen-hour stretch (including an hour's "nooning.") It was over the barrenest chalk-hills that even Syria can show. The heat quivered in the air every where. In the canons we almost smothered in the baking atmosphere. On high ground, the reflection from the chalk-hills was blinding. It was cruel to urge the crippled horses, but it had to be done in order to make Damascus Saturday night. We saw ancient tombs and temples of fanciful architecture carved out of the solid rock high up in the face of precipices above our heads, but we had neither time nor strength to climb up there and examine them. The terse language of my note-book will answer for the rest of this day's experiences:

Broke camp at 7 A. M., and made a ghastly trip through the Zeb Dana valley and the rough mountains—horses limping and that Arab screech-owl that does most of the singing and carries the water-skins, always a thousand miles ahead, of course, and no water to drink—will he *never* die? Beautiful stream in a chasm, lined thick with pomegranate, fig, olive and quince orchards, and nooned an hour at the celebrated Baalam's Ass Fountain of Figia, second in size in Syria, and the coldest water out of Siberia—guide-books do not say Baalam's ass ever drank there —somebody been imposing on the pilgrims, may be. Bathed in it—Jack and I. Only a second—ice-water. It is the principal source of the Abana river—only one-half mile down to where it joins. Beautiful place—giant trees all around—*so* shady and cool, if one could keep awake—vast stream gushes straight out from under the mountain in a torrent. Over it is a very ancient ruin, with no known history— supposed to have been for the worship of the deity of the fountain or Baalam's ass or somebody. Wretched nest of human vermin about the fountain—rags, dirt, sunken cheeks, pallor of sickness, sores, projecting bones, dull, aching misery in their eyes and ravenous hunger speaking from every eloquent fibre and muscle from head to foot. How they sprang upon a bone, how they crunched the bread we gave them! Such as these to swarm about one and watch every bite he takes, with greedy looks, and swallow unconsciously every time he swallows, as if they half fancied the precious morsel went down their own throats—hurry up the caravan!—I never shall enjoy a meal in this distressful country. To think of eating three times every day under *such* circumstances for three weeks yet—it is worse punishment than riding all day in the sun. There are sixteen starving babies from one to six years old in the party, and their legs are no larger than broom handles. Left the fountain at 1 P. M. (the fountain took us at least two hours out of our way,) and reached Mahomet's lookout perch, over Damascus, in time to get a good long look before it was necessary to move on. Tired? Ask of the winds that far away with fragments strewed the sea."

WATER CARRIER.

As the glare of day mellowed into twilight, we looked down upon a picture which is celebrated all over the world. I think I have read about four hundred times that when Mahomet was a simple camel-driver he reached this point and looked down upon Damascus for the first time, and then made a certain renowned remark. He said man could enter only one paradise; he preferred to go to the one above. So he sat down there and feasted his eyes upon the earthly paradise of Damascus, and then went away without entering its gates. They have erected a tower on the hill to mark the spot where he stood.

Damascus *is* beautiful from the mountain. It is beautiful even to foreigners accustomed to luxuriant vegetation, and I can easily understand how unspeakably beautiful it must be to eyes that are only used to the God-forsaken barrenness and desolation of Syria. I should think a Syrian would go wild with ecstacy when such a picture bursts upon him for the first time.

From his high perch, one sees before him and below him, a wall of dreary mountains, shorn of vegetation, glaring fiercely in the sun; it fences in a level desert of yellow sand, smooth as velvet and threaded far away with fine lines that stand for roads, and dotted with creeping mites we know are camel-trains and journeying men; right in the midst of the desert is spread a billowy expanse of green foliage; and nestling in its heart sits the great white city, like an island of pearls and opals gleaming out of a sea of emeralds. This is the picture you see spread far below you, with distance to soften it, the sun to glorify it, strong contrasts to heighten the effects, and over it and about it a drowsing air of repose to spiritualize it and make it seem rather a beautiful estray from the mysterious worlds we visit in dreams than a substantial tenant of our coarse, dull globe. And when you think of the leagues of blighted, blasted, sandy, rocky, sun-burnt, ugly, dreary, infamous country you have ridden over to get here, you think it is the most beautiful, beautiful picture that ever human eyes rested upon in all the broad universe! If I were to go to Damascus again, I would camp on Mahomet's hill about a week, and then go away. There is no need to go inside the walls. The Prophet was wise without knowing it when he decided not to go down into the paradise of Damascus.

There is an honored old tradition that the immense garden which Damascus stands in was the Garden of Eden, and modern writers have gathered up many chapters of evidence tending to show that it really was the Garden of Eden, and that the rivers Pharpar and Abana are the "two rivers" that watered Adam's Paradise. It may be so, but it is not paradise now, and one would be as happy outside of it as he would be likely to be within. It is so crooked and cramped and dirty that one can not realize that he is in the splendid city he saw from the hill-top. The gardens are hidden by high mud-walls, and the paradise is become a very sink of pollution and un-comeliness. Damascus has plenty of clear, pure water in it, though, and this is enough, of itself, to make an Arab think it beautiful and blessed. Water is scarce in blistered Syria. We run railways by our large cities in America; in Syria they curve the roads so as to make them run by the meagre little

VIEW OF DAMASCUS

puddles they call "fountains," and which are not found oftener on a journey than every four hours. But the "rivers" of Pharpar and Abana of Scripture (mere creeks,) run through Damascus, and so every house and every garden have their sparkling fountains and rivulets of water. With her forest of foliage and her abundance of water, Damascus must be a wonder of wonders to the Bedouin from the deserts. Damascus is simply an oasis—that is what it is. For four thousand years its waters have not gone dry or its fertility failed. Now we can understand why the city has existed so long. It could not die. So long as its waters remain to it away out there in the midst of that howling desert, so long will Damascus live to bless the sight of the tired and thirsty wayfarer.

"Though old as history itself, thou art fresh as the breath of spring, blooming as thine own rose-bud, and fragrant as thine own orange flower, O Damascus, pearl of the East!"

Damascus dates back anterior to the days of Abraham, and is the oldest city in the world. It was founded by Uz, the grandson of Noah. "The early history of Damascus is shrouded in the mists of a hoary antiquity." Leave the matters written of in the first eleven chapters of the Old Testament out, and no recorded event has occurred in the world but Damascus was in existence to receive the news of it. Go back as far as you will into the vague past, there was always a Damascus. In the writings of every century for more than four thousand years, its name has been mentioned and its praises sung. To Damascus, years are only moments, decades are only flitting trifles of time. She measures time, not by days and months and years, but by the empires she has seen rise, and prosper and crumble to ruin. She is a type of immortality. She saw the foundations of Baalbec, and Thebes, and Ephesus laid; she saw these villages grow into mighty cities, and amaze the world with their grandeur—and she has lived to see them desolate, deserted, and given over to the owls and the bats. She saw the Israelitish empire exalted, and she saw it annihilated. She saw Greece rise, and flourish two thousand years, and die. In her old age she saw Rome built; she saw it overshadow the world with its power; she saw it perish. The few hundreds of years of Genoese and Venetian might and splendor were, to grave old Damascus, only a trifling scintillation hardly worth remembering. Damascus has seen all that has ever occurred on earth, and still she lives. She has looked upon the dry bones of a thousand empires, and will see the tombs of a thousand more before she dies. Though another claims the name, old Damascus is by right the Eternal City.

We reached the city gates just at sundown. They do say that one can get into any walled city of Syria, after night, for bucksheesh, except Damascus. But Damascus, with its four thousand years of respectability in the world, has many old fogy notions. There are no street lamps there, and the law compels all who go abroad at night to carry lanterns, just as was the case in old days, when heroes and heroines of the Arabian Nights walked the streets of Damascus, or flew away toward Bagdad on enchanted carpets.

It was fairly dark a few minutes after we got within the wall, and we rode long distances through wonderfully crooked streets, eight to ten feet wide, and shut in on either side by the high mud-walls of the gardens. At last we got to where lanterns could be seen flitting about here and there, and knew we were in the midst of the curious old city. In a little narrow street, crowded with our pack-mules and with a swarm of uncouth Arabs, we alighted, and through a kind of a hole in the wall entered the hotel. We stood in a great flagged court, with flowers and citron trees about us, and a huge tank in the centre that was receiving the waters of many pipes. We crossed the court and entered the rooms prepared to receive four of us. In a large marble-paved recess between the two rooms was a tank of clear, cool water, which was kept running over all the time by the streams that were pouring into it from half a dozen pipes. Nothing, in this scorching, desolate land could look so refreshing as this pure water flashing in the lamp-light; nothing could look so beautiful, nothing could sound so delicious as this mimic rain to ears long unaccustomed to sounds of such a nature. Our rooms were large, comfortably furnished, and even had their floors clothed with soft, cheerful-tinted carpets. It was a pleasant thing to see a carpet again, for if there is any thing drearier than the tomb-like, stone-paved parlors and bed-rooms of Europe and Asia, I do not know what it is. They make one think of the grave all the time. A very broad, gaily caparisoned divan, some twelve or fourteen feet long, extended across one side of each room, and opposite were single beds with spring mattrasses. There were great looking-glasses and marble-top tables. All this luxury was as grateful to systems and senses worn out with an exhausting day's travel, as it was unexpected—for one can not tell what to expect in a Turkish city of even a quarter of a million inhabitants.

I do not know, but I think they used that tank between the rooms to draw drinking water from ; that did not occur to me, however, until I had dipped my baking head far down into its cool depths. I thought of it then, and superb as the bath was, I was sorry I had taken it, and was about to go and explain to the landlord. But a finely curled and scented poodle dog frisked up and nipped the calf of my leg just then, and before I had time to think, I had soused him to the bottom of the tank, and when I saw a servant coming with a pitcher I went off and left the pup trying to climb out and not succeeding very well. Satisfied revenge was all I needed to make me perfectly happy, and when I walked in to supper that first night in Damascus I was in that condition. We lay on those divans a long time, after supper, smoking narghilies and long-stemmed chibouks, and talking about the dreadful ride of the day, and I knew then what I had sometimes known before—that it is worth while to get tired out, because one so enjoys resting afterward.

In the morning we sent for donkeys. It is worthy of note that we had to *send* for these things. I said Damascus was an old fossil, and she is. Any where else we would have been assailed by a clamorous army of donkey-drivers, guides, peddlers and beggars—but in Damascus they so hate the very sight of a foreign Christian that they want no intercourse whatever with him; only a year or two ago, his person was not always safe in Damascus streets. It is the most fanatical Mohammedan purgatory out of Arabia. Where you see one green turban of a Hadji elsewhere (the honored sign that my lord has made the pilgrimage to Mecca,) I think you will see a dozen in Damascus. The Damascenes are the ugliest, wickedest looking villains we have seen. All the veiled women we had seen yet, nearly, left their eyes exposed, but numbers of these in Damascus completely hid the face under a close-drawn black veil that made the woman look like a mummy. If ever we caught an eye exposed it was quickly hidden from our contaminating Christian vision; the beggars actually passed us by without demanding bucksheesh; the merchants in the bazaars did not hold up their goods and cry out eagerly, "Hey, John!" or "Look this, Howajji!" On the contrary, they only scowled at us and said never a word.

STREET CARS OF DAMASCUS.

The narrow streets swarmed like a hive with men and women in strange Oriental costumes, and our small donkeys knocked them right and left as we plowed through them, urged on by the merciless donkey-boys. These persecutors run after the animals, shouting and goading them for hours together; they keep the donkey in a gallop always, yet never get tired themselves or

fall behind. The donkeys fell down and spilt us over their
heads occasionally, but there was nothing for it but to mount
and hurry on again. We were banged against sharp corners,
loaded porters, camels, and citizens generally; and we were so
taken up with looking out for collisions and casualties that we
had no chance to look about us at all. We rode half through
the city and through the famous "street which is called
Straight" without seeing any thing, hardly. Our bones were
nearly knocked out of joint, we were wild with excitement,
and our sides ached with the jolting we had suffered. I do
not like riding in the Damascus street-cars

We were on our way to the reputed houses of Judas and
Ananias. About eighteen or nineteen hundred years ago,
Saul, a native of Tarsus, was particularly bitter against the
new sect called Christians, and he left Jerusalem and started
across the country on a furious crusade against them. He
went forth "breathing threatenings and slaughter against the
disciples of the Lord."

"And as he journeyed, he came near Damascus, and suddenly there shined round
about him a light from heaven:

"And he fell to the earth and heard a voice saying unto him, 'Saul, Saul, why
persecutest thou me?'

"And when he knew that it was Jesus that spoke to him he trembled, and was
astonished, and said, 'Lord, what wilt thou have me to do?' "

He was told to arise and go into the ancient city and one
would tell him what to do. In the meantime his soldiers
stood speechless and awe-stricken, for they heard the mysterious voice but saw no man. Saul rose up and found that that
fierce supernatural light had destroyed his sight, and he was
blind, so " they led him by the hand and brought him to Damascus." He was converted.

Paul lay three days, blind, in the house of Judas, and during
that time he neither ate nor drank.

There came a voice to a citizen of Damascus, named Ana-
nias, saying, "Arise, and go into the street which is called
Straight, and inquire at the house of Judas, for one called
Saul, of Tarsus; for behold, he prayeth."

Ananias did not wish to go at first, for he had heard of Saul before, and he had his doubts about that style of a "chosen vessel" to preach the gospel of peace. However, in obedience to orders, he went into the "street called Straight" (how he ever found his way into it, and after he did, how he ever found his way out of it again, are mysteries only to be accounted for by the fact that he was acting under Divine inspiration.) He found Paul and restored him, and ordained him a preacher; and from this old house we had hunted up in the street which is miscalled Straight, he had started out on that bold missionary career which he prosecuted till his death. It was not the house of the disciple who sold the Master for thirty pieces of silver. I make this explanation in justice to Judas, who was á far different sort of man from the person just referred to. A very different style of man, and lived in a very good house. It is a pity we do not know more about him.

I have given, in the above paragraphs, some more information for people who will not read Bible history until they are defrauded into it by some such method as this. I hope that no friend of progress and education will obstruct or interfere with my peculiar mission.

The street called Straight is straighter than a corkscrew, but not as straight as a rainbow. St. Luke is careful not to commit himself; he does not say it is the street which *is* straight, but the "street which is *called* Straight." It is a fine piece of irony; it is the only facetious remark in the Bible, I believe. We traversed the street called Straight a good way, and then turned off and called at the reputed house of Ananias. There is small question that a part of the original house is there still; it is an old room twelve or fifteen feet under ground, and its masonry is evidently ancient. If Ananias did not live there in St. Paul's time, somebody else did, which is just as well. I took a drink out of Ananias' well, and singularly enough, the water was just as fresh as if the well had been dug yesterday.

We went out toward the north end of·the city to see the place where the disciples let Paul down over the Damascus wall at dead of night—for he preached Christ so fearlessly in Damascus that the people sought to kill him, just as they would to-day for the same offense, and he had to escape and flee to Jerusalem.

Then we called at the tomb of Mahomet's children and at a tomb which purported to be that of St. George who killed the dragon, and so on out to the hollow place under a rock where Paul hid during his flight till his pursuers gave him up; and to the mausoleum of the five thousand Christians who were massacred in Damascus in 1861 by the Turks. They say those narrow streets ran blood for several days, and that men, women and children were butchered indiscriminately and left to rot by hundreds all through the Christian quarter; they say, further, that the stench was dreadful. All the Christians who could get away fled from the city, and the Mohammedans would not defile their hands by burying the "infidel dogs." The thirst for blood extended to the high lands of Hermon and Anti-Lebanon, and in a short time twenty-five thousand more Christians were massacred and their possessions laid waste. How they hate a Christian in Damascus!—and pretty much all over Turkeydom as well. And how they will pay for it when Russia turns her guns upon them again!

It is soothing to the heart to abuse England and France for interposing to save the Ottoman Empire from the destruction it has so richly deserved for a thousand years. It hurts my vanity to see these pagans refuse to eat of food that has been cooked for us; or to eat from a dish we have eaten from; or to drink from a goatskin which we have polluted with our Christian lips, except by filtering the water through a rag which they put over the mouth of it or through a sponge! I never disliked a Chinaman as I do these degraded Turks and Arabs, and when Russia is ready to war with them again, I hope England and France will not find it good breeding or good judgment to interfere.

In Damascus they think there are no such rivers in all the world as their little Abana and Pharpar. The Damascenes have always thought that way. In 2 Kings, chapter v., Naaman boasts extravagantly about them. That was three thousand years ago. He says: "Are not Abana and Pharpar, rivers of Damascus, better than all the waters of Israel? May I not wash in them and be clean?" But some of my readers have forgotten who Naaman was, long ago. Naaman was the commander of the Syrian armies. He was the favorite of the king and lived in great state. "He was a mighty man of valor, but he was a leper." Strangely enough, the house they point out to you now as his, has been turned into a leper hospital, and the inmates expose their horrid deformities and hold up their hands and beg for bucksheesh when a stranger enters.

One can not appreciate the horror of this disease until he looks upon it in all its ghastliness, in Naaman's ancient dwelling in Damascus. Bones all twisted out of shape, great knots protruding from face and body, joints decaying and dropping away—horrible!

CHAPTER XLV.

THE last twenty-four hours we staid in Damascus I lay prostrate with a violent attack of cholera, or cholera morbus, and therefore had a good chance and a good excuse to lie there on that wide divan and take an honest rest. I had nothing to do but listen to the pattering of the fountains and take medicine and throw it up again. It was dangerous recreation, but it was pleasanter than traveling in Syria. I had plenty of snow from Mount Hermon, and as it would not stay on my stomach, there was nothing to interfere with my eating it—there was always room for more. I enjoyed myself very well. Syrian travel has its interesting features, like travel in any other part of the world, and yet to break your leg or have the cholera adds a welcome variety to it.

We left Damascus at noon and rode across the plain a couple of hours, and then the party stopped a while in the shade of some fig-trees to give me a chance to rest. It was the hottest day we had seen yet—the sun-flames shot down like the shafts of fire that stream out before a blow-pipe; the rays seemed to fall in a steady deluge on the head and pass downward like rain from a roof. I imagined I could distinguish between the floods of rays—I thought I could tell when each flood struck my head, when it reached my shoulders, and when the next one came. It was terrible. All the desert glared so fiercely that my eyes were swimming in tears all the time. The boys had white umbrellas heavily lined with dark green. They were a priceless blessing. I thanked fortune that I had one, too, notwithstanding it was packed up with the baggage and was ten miles ahead. It is madness to travel in Syria without an umbrella. They told me in Beirout (these people who always gorge you with advice) that it was madness to travel in Syria without an umbrella. It was on this account that I got one.

But, honestly, I think an umbrella is a nuisance any where when its business is to keep the sun off. No Arab wears a brim to his fez, or uses an umbrella, or any thing to shade his eyes or his face, and he always looks comfortable and proper in the sun. But of all the ridiculous sights I ever have seen, our party of eight is the most so— they do cut such an outlandish figure. They travel single file; they all wear the endless white rag of Constantinople wrapped round and round their hats and dangling down their backs; they all wear thick green spectacles, with side-glasses to them; they all hold white umbrellas, lined with green, over their heads; without exception their stirrups are too short—they are the very worst gang of horsemen on

FULL-DRESSED TOURIST.

earth; their animals to a horse trot fearfully hard—and when they get strung out one after the other; glaring straight ahead and breathless; bouncing high and out of turn, all along the line; knees well up and stiff, elbows flapping like a rooster's that is going to crow, and the long file of umbrellas popping convulsively up and down—when one sees this outrageous picture exposed to the light of day, he is amazed that the gods don't get out their thunderbolts and destroy them off the face of the earth! I do—I wonder at it. I wouldn't let any such caravan go through a country of mine.

And when the sun drops below the horizon and the boys close their umbrellas and put them under their arms, it is only a variation of the picture, not a modification of its absurdity.

But may be you can not see the wild extravagance of my panorama. You could if you were here. Here, you feel all the time just as if you were living about the year 1200 before Christ—or back to the patriarchs—or forward to the New Era. The scenery of the Bible is about you—the customs of the patriarchs are around you—the same people, in the same flowing robes, and in sandals, cross your path—the same long trains of stately camels go and come—the same impressive religious solemnity and silence rest upon the desert and the mountains that were upon them in the remote ages of antiquity, and behold, intruding upon a scene like this, comes this fantastic mob of green-spectacled Yanks, with their flapping elbows and bobbing umbrellas! It is Daniel in the lion's den with a green cotton umbrella under his arm, all over again.

My umbrella is with the baggage, and so are my green spectacles—and there they shall stay. I will not use them. I will show some respect for the eternal fitness of things. It will be bad enough to get sun-struck, without looking ridiculous into the bargain. If I fall, let me fall bearing about me the semblance of a Christian, at least.

Three or four hours out from Damascus we passed the spot where Saul was so abruptly converted, and from this place we looked back over the scorching desert, and had our last glimpse of beautiful Damascus, decked in its robes of shining green. After nightfall we reached our tents, just outside of the nasty Arab village of Jonesborough. Of course the real name of the place is El something or other, but the boys still refuse to

recognize the Arab names or try to pronounce them. When
I say that that village is of the usual style, I mean to insin-
uate that all Syrian villages within fifty miles of Damascus are
alike—so much alike that it would require more than human
intelligence to tell wherein one differed from another. A Syrian village is a hive of huts one story high (the height of a
man,) and as square as a dry-goods box; it is mud-plastered
all over, flat roof and all, and generally whitewashed after a
fashion. The same roof often extends over half the town, covering many of the *streets*, which are generally about a yard
wide. When you ride through one of these villages at noonday, you first meet a melancholy dog, that looks up at you and
silently begs that you won't run over him, but he does not
offer to get out of the way; next you meet a young boy without any clothes on, and he holds out his hand and says " Bucksheesh !"—he don't really expect a cent, but then he learned to
say that before he learned to say mother, and now he can not
break himself of it; next you meet a woman with a black veil
drawn closely over her face, and her bust exposed; finally, you
come to several sore-eyed children and children in all stages of
mutilation and decay; and sitting humbly in the dust, and all
fringed with filthy rags, is a poor devil whose arms and legs
are gnarled and twisted like grape-vines. These are all the
people you are likely to see. The balance of the population
are asleep within doors, or abroad tending goats in the plains
and on the hill-sides. The village is built on some consumptive
little water-course, and about it is a little fresh-looking vegetation. Beyond this charmed circle, for miles on every side,
stretches a weary desert of sand and gravel, which produces a
gray bunchy shrub like sage-brush. A Syrian village is the
sorriest sight in the world, and its surroundings are eminently
in keeping with it.

I would not have gone into this dissertation upon Syrian
villages but for the fact that Nimrod, the Mighty Hunter of
Scriptural notoriety, is buried in Jonesborough, and I wished
the public to know about how he is located. Like Homer, he
is said to be buried in many other places, but this is the only
true and genuine place his ashes inhabit.

When the original tribes were dispersed, more than four thousand years ago, Nimrod and a large party traveled three or four hundred miles, and settled where the great city of Babylon afterwards stood. Nimrod built that city. He also began to build the famous Tower of Babel, but circumstances over which he had no control put it out of his power to finish it. He ran it up eight stories high, however, and two of them still stand, at this day—a colossal mass of brickwork, rent down the centre by earthquakes, and seared and vitrified by the lightnings of an angry God. But the vast ruin will still stand for ages, to shame the puny labors of these modern generations of men. Its huge compartments are tenanted by owls and lions, and old Nimrod lies neglected in this wretched village, far from the scene of his grand enterprise.

We left Jonesborough very early in the morning, and rode forever and forever and forever, it seemed to me, over parched deserts and rocky hills, hungry, and with no water to drink. We had drained the goat-skins dry in a little while. At noon we halted before the wretched Arab town of El Yuba Dam, perched on the side of a mountain, but the dragoman said if we applied there for water we would be attacked by the whole tribe, for they did not love Christians. We had to journey on. Two hours later we reached the foot of a tall isolated mountain, which is crowned by the crumbling castle of Banias, the stateliest ruin of that kind on earth, no doubt. It is a thousand feet long and two hundred wide, all of the most symmetrical, and at the same time the most ponderous masonry. The massive towers and bastions are more than thirty feet high, and have been sixty. From the mountain's peak its broken turrets rise above the groves of ancient oaks and olives, and look wonderfully picturesque. It is of such high antiquity that no man knows who built it or when it was built. It is utterly inaccessible, except in one place, where a bridle-path winds upward among the solid rocks to the old portcullis. The horses' hoofs have bored holes in these rocks to the depth of six inches during the hundreds and hundreds of years that the castle was garrisoned. We wandered for three hours among the chambers and crypts and dungeons of the fortress, and trod where the mailed heels of many a knightly Crusader had rang, and where Phenician heroes had walked ages before them.

We wondered how such a solid mass of masonry could be affected even by an earthquake, and could not understand what agency had made Banias a ruin; but we found the destroyer, after a while, and then our wonder was increased tenfold. Seeds had fallen in crevices in the vast walls; the seeds had sprouted; the tender, insignificant sprouts had hardened; they grew larger and larger, and by a steady, imperceptible pressure forced the great stones apart, and now are bringing sure destruction upon a giant work that has even mocked the earthquakes to scorn! Gnarled and twisted trees spring from the old walls every where, and beautify and overshadow the gray battlements with a wild luxuriance of foliage.

From these old towers we looked down upon a broad, far-reaching green plain, glittering with the pools and rivulets which are the sources of the sacred river Jordan. It was a grateful vision, after so much desert.

And as the evening drew near, we clambered down the mountain, through groves of the Biblical oaks of Bashan, (for we were just stepping over the border and entering the long-sought Holy Land,) and at its extreme foot, toward the wide valley, we entered this little execrable village of Banias and camped in a great grove of olive trees near a torrent of sparkling water whose banks are arrayed in fig-trees, pomegranates and oleanders in full leaf. Barring the proximity of the village, it is a sort of paradise.

The very first thing one feels like doing when he gets into camp, all burning up and dusty, is to hunt up a bath. We followed the stream up to where it gushes out of the mountain side, three hundred yards from the tents, and took a bath that was so icy that if I did not know this was the main source of the sacred river, I would expect harm to come of it. It was bathing at noonday in the chilly source of the Abana, "River of Damascus," that gave me the cholera, so Dr. B. said. However, it generally does give me the cholera to take a bath.

The incorrigible pilgrims have come in with their pockets full of specimens broken from the ruins. I wish this vandalism could be stopped. They broke off fragments from Noah's tomb; from the exquisite sculptures of the temples of Baalbec; from the houses of Judas and Ananias, in Damascus; from the tomb of Nimrod the Mighty Hunter in Jonesborough; from the worn Greek and Roman inscriptions set in the hoary walls of the Castle of Banias; and now they have been hacking and chipping these old arches here that Jesus looked upon in the flesh. Heaven protect the Sepulchre when this tribe invades Jerusalem!

The ruins here are not very interesting. There are the massive walls of a great square building that was once the citadel; there are many ponderous old arches that are so smothered with debris that they barely project above the ground; there are heavy-walled sewers through which the crystal brook of which Jordan is born still runs; in the hill-side are the substructions of a costly marble temple that Herod the Great built here—patches of its handsome mosaic floors still remain; there is a quaint old stone bridge that was here before Herod's time, may be; scattered everywhere, in the paths and in the woods, are Corinthian capitals, broken porphyry pillars, and little fragments of sculpture; and up yonder in the precipice where the fountain gushes out, are well-worn Greek inscriptions over niches in the rock where in ancient times the Greeks, and after them the Romans, worshipped the sylvan god Pan. But trees and bushes grow above many of these ruins now; the miserable huts of a little crew of filthy Arabs are perched upon the broken masonry of antiquity, the whole place has a sleepy, stupid, rural look about it, and one can hardly bring himself to believe that a busy, substantially built city once existed here, even two thousand years ago. The place was nevertheless the scene of an event whose effects have added page after page and volume after volume to the world's history. For in this place Christ stood when he said to Peter:

"Thou art Peter; and upon this rock will I build my church, and the gates of hell shall not prevail against it. And I will give unto thee the keys of the Kingdom of Heaven; and whatsoever thou shalt bind on earth shall be bound in heaven, and whatsoever thou shalt loose on earth shall be loosèd in heaven."

On those little sentences have been built up the mighty edifice of the Church of Rome; in them lie the authority for the imperial power of the Popes over temporal affairs, and their godlike power to curse a soul or wash it white from sin. To sustain the position of " the only true Church," which Rome claims was thus conferred upon her, she has fought and labored and struggled for many a century, and will continue to keep herself busy in the same work to the end of time. The memorable words I have quoted give to this ruined city about all the interest it possesses to people of the present day.

It seems curious enough to us to be standing on ground that was once actually pressed by the feet of the Saviour. The situation is suggestive of a reality and a tangibility that seem at variance with the vagueness and mystery and ghostliness that one naturally attaches to the character of a god. I can not comprehend yet that I am sitting where a god has stood, and looking upon the brook and the mountains which that god looked upon, and am surrounded by dusky men and women whose ancestors saw him, and even talked with him, face to face, and carelessly, just as they would have done with any other stranger. I can not comprehend this; the gods of my understanding have been always hidden in clouds and very far away.

This morning, during breakfast, the usual assemblage of squalid humanity sat patiently without the charmed circle of the camp and waited for such crumbs as pity might bestow upon their misery. There were old and young, brown-skinned and yellow. Some of the men were tall and stalwart, (for one hardly sees any where such splendid-looking men as here in the East,) but all the women and children looked worn and sad, and distressed with hunger. They reminded me much of Indians, did these people. They had but little clothing, but such as they had was fanciful in character and fantastic in its arrangement. Any little absurd gewgaw or gimcrack they had they disposed in such a way as to make it attract attention most readily. They sat in silence, and with tireless patience watched our every motion with that vile, uncomplaining impoliteness which is so truly Indian, and which makes a white man so nervous and uncomfortable and savage that he wants to exterminate the whole tribe.

These people about us had other peculiarities, which I have noticed in the noble red man, too: they were infested with vermin, and the dirt had caked on them till it amounted to bark.

The little children were in a pitiable condition—they all had sore eyes, and were otherwise afflicted in various ways. They say that hardly a native child in all the East is free from sore eyes, and that thousands of them go blind of one eye or both every year. I think this must be so, for I see plenty of blind people every day, and I do not remember seeing any children that hadn't sore eyes. And, would you suppose that an American mother could sit for an hour, with her child in her arms, and let a hundred flies roost upon its eyes all that time undisturbed? I see that every day. It makes my flesh creep. Yesterday we met a woman riding on a little jackass, and she had a little child in her arms; honestly, I thought the child had goggles on as we approached, and I wondered how its mother could afford so much style. But when we drew near, we saw that the goggles were nothing but a camp meeting of flies assembled around each of the child's eyes, and at the same time there was a detachment prospecting its nose. The flies were happy, the child was contented, and so the mother did not interfere.

As soon as the tribe found out that we had a doctor in our party, they began to flock in from all quarters. Dr. B., in the charity of his nature, had taken a child from a woman who sat near by, and put some sort of a wash upon its diseased eyes. That woman went off and started the whole nation, and it was a sight to see them swarm! The lame, the halt, the blind, the leprous—all the distempers that are bred of indolence, dirt, and iniquity—were represented in the Congress in ten minutes, and still they came! Every woman that had a

sick baby brought it along, and every woman that hadn't, borrowed one.   What reverent and what worshiping looks they
bent upon that dread, mysterious power, the Doctor !   They
watched him take his phials out ; they watched him measure
the particles of white powder ; they watched him add drops
of one precious liquid, and drops of another ; they lost not the
slightest movement ; their eyes were riveted upon him with a

IMPROMPTU HOSPITAL.

fascination that nothing could distract. I believe they thought
he was gifted like a god. When each individual got his portion of medicine, his eyes were radiant with joy—notwithstanding by nature they are a thankless and impassive race—
and upon his face was written the unquestioning faith that
nothing on earth could prevent the patient from getting well
now.

   Christ knew how to preach to these simple, superstitious,
disease-tortured creatures : He healed the sick. They flocked
to our poor human doctor this morning when the fame of what
he had done to the sick child went abroad in the land, and
they worshiped him with their eyes while they did not know

as yet whether there was virtue in his simples or not. The ancestors of these—people precisely like them in color, dress, manners, customs, simplicity—flocked in vast multitudes after Christ, and when they saw Him make the afflicted whole with a word, it is no wonder they worshiped Him. No wonder His deeds were the talk of the nation. No wonder the multitude that followed Him was so great that at one time—thirty miles from here—they had to let a sick man down through the roof because no approach could be made to the door; no wonder His audiences were so great at Galilee that He had to preach from a ship removed a little distance from the shore; no wonder that even in the desert places about Bethsaida, five thousand invaded His solitude, and He had to feed them by a miracle or else see them suffer for their confiding faith and devotion; no wonder when there was a great commotion in a city in those days, one neighbor explained it to another in words to this effect: "They say that Jesus of Nazareth is come!"

Well, as I was saying, the doctor distributed medicine as long as he had any to distribute, and his reputation is mighty in Galilee this day. Among his patients was the child of the Shiek's daughter—for even this poor, ragged handful of sores and sin has its royal Shiek—a poor old mummy that looked as if he would be more at home in a poor-house than in the Chief Magistracy of this tribe of hopeless, shirtless savages. The princess—I mean the Shiek's daughter—was only thirteen or fourteen years old, and had a very sweet face and a pretty one. She was the only Syrian female we have seen yet who was not so sinfully ugly that she couldn't smile after ten o'clock Saturday night without breaking the Sabbath. Her child was a hard specimen, though—there wasn't enough of it to make a pie, and the poor little thing looked so pleadingly up at all who came near it (as if it had an idea that now was its chance or never,) that we were filled with compassion which was genuine and not put on.

But this last new horse I have got is trying to break his neck over the tent-ropes, and I shall have to go out and anchor

him. Jericho and I have parted company. The new horse is
not much to boast of, I think. One of his hind legs bends the
wrong way, and the other one is as straight and stiff as a tent-

THE HORSE "BAALBEC."

pole. Most
of his teeth
are gone,
and he is as
blind as a
bat. His
nose has
been broken
at some time
or other, and
is arched
like a cul-
vert now.
His under
lip hangs
down like a camel's, and his ears are chopped off close to his
head. I had some trouble at first to find a name for him, but
I finally concluded to call him Baalbec, because he is such a
magnificent ruin. I can not keep from talking about my
horses, because I have a very long and tedious journey before
me, and they naturally occupy my thoughts about as much as
matters of apparently much greater importance.

We satisfied our pilgrims by making those hard rides from
Baalbec to Damascus, but Dan's horse and Jack's were so crippled we had to leave them behind and get fresh animals for
them. The dragoman says Jack's horse died. I swapped
horses with Mohammed, the kingly-looking Egyptian who is
our Ferguson's lieutenant. By Ferguson I mean our dragoman
Abraham, of course. I did not take this horse on account of
his personal appearance, but because I have not seen his back.
I do not wish to see it. I have seen the backs of all the other
horses, and found most of them covered with dreadful saddle-
boils which I know have not been washed or doctored for
years. The idea of riding all day long over such ghastly in-

quisitions of torture is sickening. My horse must be like the others, but I have at least the consolation of not knowing it to be so.

I hope that in future I may be spared any more sentimental praises of the Arab's idolatry of his horse. In boyhood I longed to be an Arab of the desert and have a beautiful mare, and call her Selim or Benjamin or Mohammed, and feed her with my own hands, and let her come into the tent, and teach her to caress me and look fondly upon me with her great tender eyes ; and I wished that a stranger might come at such a time and offer me a hundred thousand dollars for her, so that I could do like the other Arabs—hesitate, yearn for the money, but overcome by my love for my mare, at last say, "Part with thee, my beautiful one! Never with my life! Away, tempter, I scorn thy gold!" and then bound into the saddle and speed over the desert like the wind!

But I recall those aspirations. If these Arabs be like the other Arabs, their love for their beautiful mares is a fraud. These of my acquaintance have no love for their horses, no sentiment of pity for them, and no knowledge of how to treat them or care for them. The Syrian saddle-blanket is a quilted mattrass two or three inches thick. It is never removed from the horse, day or night. It gets full of dirt and hair, and becomes soaked with sweat. It is bound to breed sores. These pirates never think of washing a horse's back. They do not shelter the horses in the tents, either ; they must stay out and take the weather as it comes. Look at poor cropped and dilapidated "Baalbec," and weep for the sentiment that has been wasted upon the Selims of romance!

CHAPTER XLVI.

ABOUT an hour's ride over a rough, rocky road, half flooded with water, and through a forest of oaks of Bashan, brought us to Dan.

From a little mound here in the plain issues a broad stream of limpid water and forms a large shallow pool, and then rushes furiously onward, augmented in volume. This puddle is an important source of the Jordan. Its banks, and those of the brook are respectably adorned with blooming oleanders, but the unutterable beauty of the spot will not throw a well-balanced man into convulsions, as the Syrian books of travel would lead one to suppose.

From the spot I am speaking of, a cannon-ball would carry beyond the confines of Holy Land and light upon profane ground three miles away. We were only one little hour's travel within the borders of Holy Land—we had hardly begun to appreciate yet that we were standing upon any different sort of earth than that we had always been used to, and yet see how the historic names began already to cluster! Dan—Bashan—Lake Huleh—the Sources of Jordan—the Sea of Galilee. They were all in sight but the last, and it was not far away. The little township of Bashan was once the kingdom so famous in Scripture for its bulls and its oaks. Lake Huleh is the Biblical "Waters of Merom." Dan was the northern and Beersheba the southern limit of Palestine—hence the expression "from Dan to Beersheba." It is equivalent to our phrases "from Maine to Texas"—"from Baltimore to San Francisco." Our expression and that of the Israelites both mean the same—great distance. With their slow camels and asses, it was about a seven days' journey from Dan to Beer-sheba—say a hundred and fifty or sixty miles—it was the entire length of their country, and was not to be un- dertaken without great preparation and much cer-emony. When the Prodigal traveled to "a far country," it is not likely that he went more than

OAK OF BASHAN.

eighty or ninety miles. Palestine is only from forty to sixty miles wide. The State of Missouri could be split into three Palestines, and there would then be enough material left for part of another—possibly a whole one. From Baltimore to San Francisco is several thousand miles, but it will be only a seven days' journey in the cars when I am two or three years older.* If I live I shall necessarily have to go across the con-tinent every now and then in those cars, but one journey from Dan to Beersheba will be sufficient, no doubt. It must be the most trying of the two. Therefore, if we chance to discover that from Dan to Beersheba seemed a mighty stretch of coun-try to the Israelites, let us not be airy with them, but reflect that it *was* and *is* a mighty stretch when one can not traverse it by rail.

The small mound I have mentioned a while ago was once occupied by the Phenician city of Laish. A party of filibus-ters from Zorah and Eschol captured the place, and lived there

---

* The railroad has been completed, since the above was written.

480 REMINISCENCE OF LOT.

in a free and easy way, worshiping gods of their own manufacture and stealing idols from their neighbors whenever they wore their own out. Jeroboam set up a golden calf here to fascinate his people and keep them from making dangerous trips to Jerusalem to worship, which might result in a return to their rightful allegiance. With all respect for those ancient Israelites, I can not overlook the fact that they were not always virtuous enough to withstand the seductions of a golden calf. Human nature has not changed much since then.

Some forty centuries ago the city of Sodom was pillaged by the Arab princes of Mesopotamia, and among other prisoners they seized upon the patriarch Lot and brought him here on their way to their own possessions. They brought him to Dan, and father Abraham, who was pursuing them, crept softly in at dead of night, among the whispering oleanders and under the shadows of the stately oaks, and fell upon the slumbering victors and startled them from their dreams with the clash of steel. He recaptured Lot and all the other plunder.

We moved on. We were now in a green valley, five or six miles wide and fifteen long. The streams which are called the sources of the Jordan flow through it to Lake Huleh, a shallow pond three miles in diameter, and from the southern extremity of the Lake the concentrated Jordan flows out. The Lake is surrounded by a broad marsh, grown with reeds. Between the marsh and the mountains which wall the valley is a respectable strip of fertile land; at the end of the valley, toward Dan, as much as half the land is solid and fertile, and watered by Jordan's sources. There is enough of it to make a farm. It almost warrants the enthusiasm of the spies of that rabble of adventurers who captured Dan. They said: "We have seen the land, and behold it is very good. * * * A place where there is no want of any thing that is in the earth."

Their enthusiasm was at least warranted by the fact that they had never seen a country as good as this. There was enough of it for the ample support of their six hundred men and their families, too.

When we got fairly down on the level part of the Danite farm, we came to places where we could actually run our horses. It was a notable circumstance.

We had been painfully clambering over interminable hills and rocks for days together, and when we suddenly came upon this astonishing piece of rockless plain, every man drove the spurs into his horse and sped away with a velocity he could surely enjoy to the utmost, but could never hope to comprehend in Syria.

Here were evidences of cultivation—a rare sight in this country—an acre or two of rich soil studded with last season's dead corn-stalks of the thickness of your thumb and very wide apart. But in such a land it was a thrilling spectacle. Close to it was a stream, and on its banks a great herd of curious-looking Syrian goats and sheep were gratefully eating gravel. I do not state this as a petrified fact—I only *suppose* they were eating gravel, because there did not appear to be any thing else for them to eat. The shepherds that tended them were the very pictures of Joseph and his brethren I have no doubt in the world. They were tall, muscular, and very dark-skinned Bedouins, with inky black beards. They had firm lips, unquailing eyes, and a kingly stateliness of bearing. They wore the parti-colored half bonnet, half hood, with fringed ends falling upon their shoulders, and the full, flowing robe barred with broad black stripes—the dress one sees in all pictures of the swarthy sons of the desert. These chaps would sell their younger brothers if they had a chance, I think. They have the manners, the customs, the dress, the occupation and the loose principles of the ancient stock. [They attacked our camp last night, and I bear them no good will.] They had with them the pigmy jackasses one sees all over Syria and remembers in all pictures of the " Flight into Egypt," where Mary and the Young Child are riding and Joseph is walking alongside, towering high above the little donkey's shoulders.

But really, here the man rides and carries the child, as a

31

general thing, and the woman walks. The customs have not changed since Joseph's time. We would not have in our houses a picture representing Joseph riding and Mary walking; we would see profanation in it, but a Syrian Christian would not. I know that hereafter the picture I first spoke of will look odd to me.

We could not stop to rest two or three hours out from our camp, of course, albeit the brook was beside us. So we went on an hour longer. We saw water, then, but nowhere in all the waste around was there a foot of shade, and we were scorching to death. "Like unto the shadow of a great rock in a weary land." Nothing in the Bible is more beautiful than that, and surely there is no place we have wandered to that is able to give it such touching expression as this blistering, naked, treeless land.

Here you do not stop just when you please, but when you

DANGEROUS ARAB.

can. We found water, but no shade. We traveled on and found a tree at last, but no water. We rested and lunched, and came on to this place, Ain Mellahah (the boys call it Baldwinsville.) It was a very short day's run, but the dragoman does not want to go further, and has invented a plausible lie about the country beyond this being infested by ferocious Arabs, who would make sleeping in their midst a dangerous pastime. Well, they ought to be dangerous. They carry a rusty old weather-beaten flint-lock gun, with a barrel that is longer than themselves; it has no sights on it; it will not carry farther than a brickbat, and is not half so certain. And the great sash they wear in many a fold around their waists has two or three absurd old horse-pistols in it that are rusty from eternal disuse—weapons that would hang fire just about long enough for you to walk out of range, and then burst and blow the Arab's head off. Exceedingly dangerous these sons of the desert are.

It used to make my blood run cold to read Wm. C. Grimes' hairbreadth escapes from Bedouins, but I think I could read them now without a tremor. He never said he was attacked by Bedouins, I believe, or was ever treated uncivilly, but then in about every other chapter he discovered them approaching, any how, and he had a blood-curdling fashion of working up the peril; and of wondering how his relations far away would feel could they see their poor wandering boy, with his weary feet and his dim eyes, in such fearful danger; and of thinking for the last time of the old homestead, and the dear old church, and the cow, and those things; and of finally straightening his

GRIMES ON THE WAR PATH.

form to its utmost height in the saddle, drawing his trusty revolver, and then dashing the spurs into "Mohammed" and sweeping down upon the ferocious enemy determined to sell his life as dearly as possible. True the Bedouins never did any thing to him when he arrived, and never had any intention of doing any thing to him in the first place, and wondered what in the mischief he was making all that to-do about ; but still I could not divest myself of the idea, somehow, that a frightful peril had been escaped through that man's dare-devil bravery, and so I never could read about Wm. C. Grimes' Bedouins and sleep comfortably afterward. But I believe the Bedouins to be a fraud, now. I have seen the monster, and I can outrun him. I shall never be afraid of his daring to stand behind his own gun and discharge it.

About fifteen hundred years before Christ, this camp-ground of ours by the Waters of Merom was the scene of one of Joshua's exterminating battles. Jabin, King of Hazor, (up yonder above Dan,) called all the shieks about him together, with their hosts, to make ready for Israel's terrible General who was approaching.

"And when all these Kings were met together, they came and pitched together by the Waters of Merom, to fight against Israel.

"And they went out, they and all their hosts with them, much people, even as the sand that is upon the sea-shore for multitude," etc.

But Joshua fell upon them and utterly destroyed them, root and branch. That was his usual policy in war. He never left any chance for newspaper controversies about who won the battle. He made this valley, so quiet now, a reeking slaughter-pen.

Somewhere in this part of the country—I do not know exactly where—Israel fought another bloody battle a hundred years later. Deborah, the prophetess, told Barak to take ten thousand men and sally forth against another King Jabin who had been doing something. Barak came down from Mount Tabor, twenty or twenty-five miles from here, and gave battle to Jabin's forces, who were in command of Sisera. Barak won the fight, and while he was making the victory complete by the usual method of exterminating the remnant of the defeated host, Sisera fled away on foot, and when he was nearly exhausted by fatigue and thirst, one Jael, a woman he seems to have been acquainted with, invited him to come into her tent and rest himself. The weary soldier acceded readily enough, and Jael put him to bed. He said he was very thirsty, and asked his generous preserver to get him a cup of water. She brought him some milk, and he drank of it gratefully and lay down again, to forget in pleasant dreams his lost battle and his humbled pride. Presently when he was asleep she came softly in with a hammer and drove a hideous tent-pen down through his brain !

"For he was fast asleep and weary. So he died." Such is the touching language of the Bible. "The Song of Deborah and Barak" praises Jael for the memorable service she had rendered, in an exultant strain:

"Blessed above women shall Jael the wife of Heber the Kenite be, blessed shall she be above women in the tent.

"He asked for water, and she gave him milk; she brought forth butter in a lordly dish.

"She put her hand to the nail, and her right hand to the workman's hammer; and with the hammer she smote Sisera, she smote off his head when she had pierced and stricken through his temples.

"At her feet he bowed, he fell, he lay down: at her feet he bowed, he fell: where he bowed, there he fell down dead."

Stirring scenes like these occur in this valley no more. There is not a solitary village throughout its whole extent— not for thirty miles in either direction. There are two or three small clusters of Bedouin tents, but not a single permanent habitation. One may ride ten miles, hereabouts, and not see ten human beings.

To this region one of the prophecies is applied:

I will bring the land into desolation; and your enemies which dwell therein shall be astonished at it. And I will scatter you among the heathen, and I will draw out a sword after you; and your land shall be desolate and your cities waste."

No man can stand here by deserted Ain Mellahah and say the prophecy has not been fulfilled.

In a verse from the Bible which I have quoted above, occurs the phrase " all these kings." It attracted my attention in a moment, because it carries to my mind such a vastly different significance from what it always did at home. I can see easily enough that if I wish to profit by this tour and come to a correct understanding of the matters of interest connected with it, I must studiously and faithfully unlearn a great many things I have somehow absorbed concerning Palestine. I must begin a system of reduction. Like my grapes which the spies bore out of the Promised Land, I have got every thing in Palestine on too large a scale. Some of my ideas were wild enough. The word Palestine always brought to my mind a vague suggestion of a country as large as the United States. I do not know why, but such was the case. I suppose it was because I could not conceive of a small country having so large a history. I think I was a little surprised to find that the grand Sultan of Turkey was a man of only ordinary size. I must try to reduce my ideas of Palestine to a more reasonable shape. One gets large impressions in boyhood, sometimes, which he has to fight against all his life. " All these kings." When I used to read that in Sunday School, it suggested to me the several kings of such countries as England, France, Spain, Germany, Russia, etc., arrayed in splendid robes ablaze with jewels, marching in grave procession, with sceptres of gold in their hands and flashing crowns upon their heads. But here in Ain Mellahah, after coming through Syria, and after giving serious study to the character and customs of the country, the phrase " all these kings " loses its grandeur. It suggests only a parcel of petty chiefs—ill-clad and ill-conditioned savages much like our Indians, who lived in full sight of each other and whose " kingdoms " were large when they were five miles square and contained two thousand souls. The combined monarchies of the thirty "kings" destroyed by Joshua on one of his famous campaigns, only covered an area about equal to four of our counties of ordinary size. The poor old sheik we saw at Cesarea Philippi with his ragged band of a hundred followers, would have been called a "king" in those ancient times.

It is seven in the morning, and as we are in the country, the grass ought to be sparkling with dew, the flowers enrich-

ing the air with their fragrance, and the birds singing in the
trees.   But alas, there is no dew here, nor flowers, nor birds,
nor trees.   There is a plain and an unshaded lake, and beyond
them some barren mountains.   The tents are tumbling, the
Arabs are quarreling like dogs and cats, as usual, the camp-
ground is strewn with packages and bundles, the labor of
packing them upon the backs of the mules is progressing with
great activity, the horses are saddled, the umbrellas are out,
and in ten minutes we shall mount and the long procession
will move again.   The white city of the Mellahah, resurrected
for a moment out of the dead centuries, will have disappeared
again and left no sign.

CHAPTER XLVII.

WE traversed some miles of desolate country whose soil is rich enough, but is given over wholly to weeds—a silent, mournful expanse, wherein we saw only three persons —Arabs, with nothing on but a long coarse shirt like the " tow-linen " shirts which used to form the only summer garment of little negro boys on Southern plantations. Shepherds they were, and they charmed their flocks with the traditional shepherd's pipe—a reed instrument that made music as exquisitely infernal as these same Arabs create when they sing.

In their pipes lingered no echo of the wonderful music the shepherd forefathers heard in the Plains of Bethlehem what time the angels sang " Peace on earth, good will to men."

Part of the ground we came over was not ground at all, but rocks—cream-colored rocks, worn smooth, as if by water; with seldom an edge or a corner on them, but scooped out, honeycombed, bored out with eye-holes, and thus wrought into all manner of quaint shapes, among which the uncouth imitation of skulls was frequent. Over this part of the route were occasional remains of an old Roman road like the Appian Way, whose paving-stones still clung to their places with Roman tenacity.

Gray lizards, those heirs of ruin, of sepulchres and desolation, glided in and out among the rocks or lay still and sunned themselves. Where prosperity has reigned, and fallen; where glory has flamed, and gone out; where beauty has dwelt, and passed away; where gladness was, and sorrow is; where the pomp of life has been, and silence and death brood in its high places, there this reptile makes his home, and mocks at human vanity. His coat is the color of ashes: and ashes are the symbol of hopes that have perished, of aspirations that came to nought, of loves that are buried. If he could speak, he would say, Build temples: I will lord it in their ruins; build palaces: I will inhabit them; erect empires: I will inherit

HOUSE OF ANCIENT POMP.

them; bury your beautiful: I will watch the worms at their work; and you, who stand here and moralize over me: I will crawl over *your* corpse at the last.

A few ants were in this desert place, but merely to spend the summer. They brought their provisions from Ain Mellahah—eleven miles.

Jack is not very well to-day, it is easy to see; but boy as he is, he is too much of a man to speak of it. He exposed himself to the sun too much yesterday, but since it came of his earnest desire to learn, and to make this journey as useful as the opportunities will allow, no one seeks to discourage him by fault-finding. We missed him an hour from the camp, and then found him some distance away, by the edge of a brook, and with no umbrella to protect him from the fierce sun. If he had been used to going without his umbrella, it would have been well enough, of course ; but he was not. He was just in

JACK.

the act of throwing a clod at a mud-turtle which was sunning itself on a small log in the brook. We said:

"Don't do that, Jack. What do you want to harm him for? What has he done?"

"Well, then, I won't kill him, but I ought to, because he is a fraud."

We asked him why, but he said it was no matter. We asked him why, once or twice, as we walked back to the camp, but he still said

it was no matter. But late at night, when he was sitting in a thoughtful mood on the bed, we asked him again and he said :

"Well, it don't matter ; I don't mind it now, but I did not like it to-day, you know, because *I* don't tell any thing that isn't so, and I don't think the Colonel ought to, either. But he did ; he told us at prayers in the Pilgrims' tent, last night, and he seemed as if he was reading it out of the Bible, too, about this country flowing with milk and honey, and about the voice of the turtle being heard in the land. I thought that was drawing it a little strong, about the turtles, any how, but I asked Mr. Church if it was so, and he said it was, and what Mr. Church tells me, I believe. But I sat there and watched that turtle nearly an hour to-day, and I almost burned up in the sun ; but I never heard him sing. I believe I sweated a double handful of sweat—I *know* I did—because it got in my eyes, and it was running down over my nose all the time ; and you know my pants are tighter than any body else's—Paris foolishness—and the buckskin seat of them got wet with sweat, and then got dry again and began to draw up and pinch and tear loose—it was awful—but I never heard him sing. Finally I said, This is a fraud—that is what it is, it is a fraud—and if I had had any sense I might have known a cursed mud-turtle couldn't sing. And then I said, I don't wish to be hard on this fellow, and I will just give him ten minutes to commence; ten minutes—and then if he don't, down goes his building. But he *didn't* commence, you know. I had staid

A DISAPPOINTED AUDIENCE.

there all that time, thinking may be he might, pretty soon, because he kept on raising his head up and letting it down, and drawing the skin over his eyes for a minute and then opening them out again, as if he was trying to study up something to sing, but just as the ten minutes were up and I was all beat out and blistered, he laid his blamed head down on a knot and went fast asleep."

"It *was* a little hard, after you had waited so long."

"I should think so. I said, Well, if you won't sing, you

shan't sleep, any way; and if you fellows had let me alone I would have made him shin out of Galilee quicker than any turtle ever did yet. But it isn't any matter now—let it go. The skin is all off the back of my neck."

About ten in the morning we halted at Joseph's Pit. This is a ruined Khan of the Middle Ages, in one of whose side courts is a great walled and arched pit with water in it, and this pit, one tradition says, is the one Joseph's brethren cast him into. A more authentic tradition, aided by the geography of the country, places the pit in Dothan, some two days' journey from here. However, since there are many who believe in this present pit as the true one, it has its interest.

It is hard to make a choice of the most beautiful passage in a book which is so gemmed with beautiful passages as the Bible; but it is certain that not many things within its lids may take rank above the exquisite story of Joseph. Who taught those ancient writers their simplicity of language, their felicity of expression, their pathos, and above all, their faculty of sinking themselves entirely out of sight of the reader and making the narrative stand out alone and seem to tell itself? Shakspeare is always present when one reads his book; Macaulay is present when we follow the march of his stately sentences; but the Old Testament writers are hidden from view.

If the pit I have been speaking of is the right one, a scene transpired there, long ages ago, which is familiar to us all in pictures. The sons of Jacob had been pasturing their flocks near there. Their father grew uneasy at their long absence, and sent Joseph, his favorite, to see if any thing had gone wrong with them. He traveled six or seven days' journey; he was only seventeen years old, and, boy like, he toiled through that long stretch of the vilest, rockiest, dustiest country in Asia, arrayed in the pride of his heart, his beautiful clawhammer coat of many colors. Joseph was the favorite, and that was one crime in the eyes of his brethren; he had dreamed dreams, and interpreted them to foreshadow his elevation far above all his family in the far future, and that was another; he was dressed well and had doubtless displayed the harmless vanity of youth in keeping the fact prominently before his brothers. These were crimes his elders fretted over among themselves and proposed to punish when the opportunity should offer. When they saw him coming up from the Sea of Galilee, they recognized him and were glad. They said, "Lo, here is this dreamer—let us kill him." But Reuben pleaded for his life, and they spared it. But they seized the boy, and stripped the hated coat from his back and pushed him into the pit. *They* intended to let him die there, but Reuben intended to liberate him secretly. However, while Reuben was away for a little while, the brethren sold Joseph to some Ishmaelitish merchants who were journeying towards Egypt. Such is the history of the pit. And the self-same pit is there in that place, even to this day; and there it will remain until the next detachment of image-breakers and tomb-desecraters arrives from the *Quaker City* excursion, and they will infallibly dig it up and carry it away with them. For behold in them is no reverence for the solemn monuments of the past, and whithersoever they go they destroy and spare. not.

Joseph became rich, distinguished, powerful—as the Bible expresses it, "lord over all the land of Egypt." Joseph was the real king, the strength, the brain of the monarchy, though Pharaoh held the title. Joseph is one of the truly great men of the Old Testament. And he was the noblest and the manliest, save Esau. Why shall we not say a good word for the princely Bedouin? The only crime that can be brought against him is that he was unfortunate. Why must every body praise Joseph's great-hearted generosity to his cruel brethren, without stint of fervent language, and fling only a reluctant bone of praise to Esau for his still sublimer generosity to the brother who had wronged him? Jacob took advantage of Esau's consuming hunger to rob him of his birthright and the great honor and consideration that belonged to the position; by treachery and falsehood he robbed him of his father's blessing; he made of him a stranger in his home, and a wanderer. Yet after twenty years had passed away and Jacob met Esau and fell at his feet quaking with fear and begging piteously to be spared the punishment he knew he deserved, what did that magnificent savage do? He fell upon his neck and embraced him! When Jacob—who was incapable of comprehending nobility of character—still doubting, still fearing, insisted upon "finding grace with my lord" by the bribe of a present of cattle, what did the gorgeous son of the desert say?

"Nay, I have enough, my brother; keep that thou hast unto thyself!"

Esau found Jacob rich, beloved by wives and children, and traveling in state, with servants, herds of cattle and trains of camels—but he himself was still the uncourted outcast this brother had made him. After thirteen years of romantic mystery, the brethren who had wronged Joseph, came, strangers in a strange land, hungry and humble, to buy "a little food;" and being summoned to a palace, charged with crime, they beheld in its owner their wronged brother; they were trembling beggars—he, the lord of a mighty empire! What Joseph that ever lived would have thrown away such a chance to "show off?" Who stands first—outcast Esau forgiving Jacob in prosperity, or Joseph on a king's throne forgiving the ragged tremblers whose happy rascality placed him there?

Just before we came to Joseph's Pit, we had "raised" a hill, and there, a few miles before us, with not a tree or a shrub to interrupt the view, lay a vision which millions of worshipers in the far lands of the earth would give half their possessions to see—the sacred Sea of Galilee!

Therefore we tarried only a short time at the pit. We rested the horses and ourselves, and felt for a few minutes the blessed shade of the ancient buildings. We were out of water, but the two or three scowling Arabs, with their long guns, who were idling about the place, said they had none and that there was none in the vicinity. They knew there was a little brackish water in the pit, but they venerated a place made sacred by their ancestor's imprisonment too much to be willing to see Christian dogs drink from it. But Ferguson tied rags and handkerchiefs together till he made a rope long enough to lower a vessel to the bottom, and we drank and then rode on ; and in a short time we dismounted on those shores which the feet of the Saviour have made holy ground.

At noon we took a swim in the Sea of Galilee—a blessed privilege in this roasting climate—and then lunched under a neglected old fig-tree at the fountain they call Ain-et-Tin, a hundred yards from ruined Capernaum. Every rivulet that gurgles out of the rocks and sands of this part of the world is dubbed with the title of "fountain," and people familiar with the Hudson, the great lakes and the Mississippi fall into transports of admiration over them, and exhaust their powers of composition in writing their praises. If all the poetry and nonsense that have been discharged upon the fountains and the bland scenery of this region were collected in a book, it would make a most valuable volume to burn.

During luncheon, the pilgrim enthusiasts of our party, who had been so light-hearted and

FIG TREE.

happy ever since they touched holy ground that they did little but mutter incoherent rhapsodies, could scarcely eat, so anxious were they to "take shipping" and sail in very person upon the waters that had borne the vessels of the Apostles. Their anxiety grew and their excitement augmented with every fleeting moment, until my fears were aroused and I began to have misgivings that in their present condition they might break recklessly loose from all considerations of prudence and buy a whole fleet of ships to sail in instead of hiring a single one for an hour, as quiet folk are wont to do. I trembled to think of the ruined purses this day's performances might result in. I could not help reflecting bodingly upon the intemperate zeal with which middle-aged men are apt to surfeit themselves upon a seductive folly which they have tasted for the first time. And yet I did not feel that I had a right to be surprised at the state of things which was giving me so much concern. These men had been taught from infancy to revere, almost to worship, the holy places whereon their happy eyes were resting now. For many and many a year this very picture had visited their thoughts by day and floated through their dreams by night. To stand before it in the flesh—to see it as they saw it now—to sail upon the hallowed sea, and kiss the holy soil that compassed it about: these were aspirations they had cherished while a generation dragged its lagging seasons by and left its furrows in their faces and its frosts upon their hair. To look upon this picture, and sail upon this sea, they had forsaken home and its idols and journeyed thousands and thousands of miles, in weariness and tribulation. What wonder that the sordid lights of work-day prudence should pale before the glory of a hope like theirs in the full splendor of its fruition? Let them squander millions! I said—who speaks of money at a time like this?

In this frame of mind I followed, as fast as I could, the eager footsteps of the pilgrims, and stood upon the shore of the lake, and swelled, with hat and voice, the frantic hail they sent after the "ship" that was speeding by. It was a success. The toilers of the sea ran in and beached their barque. Joy sat upon every countenance.

"How much?—ask him how much, Ferguson!—how much to take us all—eight of us, and you—to Bethsaida, yonder, and to the mouth of Jordan, and to the place where the swine ran down into the sea—quick !—and we want to coast around every where—every where !—all day long !—*I* could sail a year in these waters !—and tell him we'll stop at Magdala and finish at Tiberias !—ask him how much ?—any thing—any thing whatever !—tell him we don't care what the expense is !"   [I said to myself, I knew how it would be.]

Ferguson—(interpreting)—"He says two Napoleons—eight dollars."

One or two countenances fell.   Then a pause.

"Too much !—we'll give him one !"

I never shall know how it was—I shudder yet when I think how the place is given to miracles—but in a single instant of

FARE TOO HIGH.

time, as it seemed to me, that ship was twenty paces from the shore, and speeding away like a frightened thing !   Eight crestfallen creatures stood upon the shore, and O, to think of it ! this—this—after all that overmastering ecstacy !   Oh, shameful, shameful ending, after such unseemly boasting !   It was

32

too much like "Ho! let me at him!" followed by a prudent "Two of you hold him—one can hold me!"

Instantly there was wailing and gnashing of teeth in the camp. The two Napoleons were offered—more if necessary—and pilgrims and dragoman shouted themselves hoarse with pleadings to the retreating boatmen to come back. But they sailed serenely away and paid no further heed to pilgrims who had dreamed all their lives of some day skimming over the sacred waters of Galilee and listening to its hallowed story in the whisperings of its waves, and had journeyed countless leagues to do it, and—and then concluded that the fare was too high. Impertinent Mohammedan Arabs, to think such things of gentlemen of another faith!

Well, there was nothing to do but just submit and forego the privilege of voyaging on Genessaret, after coming half around the globe to taste that pleasure. There was a time, when the Saviour taught here, that boats were plenty among the fishermen of the coasts—but boats and fishermen both are gone, now; and old Josephus had a fleet of men-of-war in these waters eighteen centuries ago—a hundred and thirty bold canoes—but they, also, have passed away and left no sign. They battle here no more by sea, and the commercial marine of Galilee numbers only two small ships, just of a pattern with the little skiffs the disciples knew. One was lost to us for good—the other was miles away and far out of hail. So we mounted the horses and rode grimly on toward Magdala, cantering along in the edge of the water for want of the means of passing over it

How the pilgrims abused each other! Each said it was the other's fault, and each in turn denied it. No word was spoken by the sinners—even the mildest sarcasm might have been dangerous at such a time. Sinners that have been kept down and had examples held up to them, and suffered frequent lectures, and been so put upon in a moral way and in the matter of going slow and being serious and bottling up slang, and so crowded in regard to the matter of being proper and always and forever behaving, that their lives have become a burden to them, would not lag behind pilgrims at such a time as this, and wink furtively, and be joyful, and commit other such crimes—because it would not occur to them to do it. Otherwise they would. But they did do it, though—and it did them a world of good to hear the pilgrims abuse each other, too. We took an unworthy satisfaction in seeing them fall out, now and then, because it showed that they were only poor human people like us, after all.

So we all rode down to Magdala, while the gnashing of teeth waxed and waned by turns, and harsh words troubled the holy calm of Galilee.

Lest any man think I mean to be ill-natured when I talk about our pilgrims as I have been talking, I wish to say in all sincerity that I do not. I would not listen to lectures from men I did not like and could not respect; and none of these can say I ever took their lectures unkindly, or was restive under the infliction, or failed to try to profit by what they said to me. They are better men than I am; I can say that honestly; they are good friends of mine, too—and besides, if they did not wish to be stirred up occasionally in print, why in the mischief did they travel with me? They knew me. They knew my liberal way—that I like to give and take—when it is for me to give and other people to take. When one of them threatened to leave me in Damascus when I had the cholera, he had no real idea of doing it—I know his passionate nature and the good impulses that underlie it. And did I not overhear Church, another pilgrim, say he did not care who went or who staid, *he* would stand by me till I walked out of Damascus on my own feet or was carried out in a coffin, if it was a year? And do I not include Church every time I abuse the pilgrims—and would I be likely to speak ill-naturedly of him? I wish to stir them up and make them healthy; that is all.

We had left Capernaum behind us. It was only a shapeless ruin. It bore no semblance to a town, and had nothing about it to suggest that it had ever been a town. But all desolate and unpeopled as it was, it was illustrious ground. From it sprang that tree of Christianity whose broad arms overshadow so many distant lands to-day. After Christ was tempted of the devil in the desert, he came here and began his teachings; and during the three or four years he lived afterward, this place was his home almost altogether. He began to heal the sick, and his fame soon spread so widely that sufferers came from Syria and beyond Jordan, and even from Jerusalem, several days' journey away, to be cured of their diseases. Here he healed the centurion's servant and Peter's mother-in-law, and multitudes of the lame and the blind and persons possessed of devils; and here, also, he raised Jairus's daughter from the dead. He went into a ship with his disciples, and when they roused him from sleep in the midst of a storm, he quieted the winds and lulled the troubled sea to rest with his voice. He passed over to the other side, a few miles away, and relieved two men of devils, which passed into some swine. After his return he called Matthew from the receipt of customs, performed some cures, and created scandal by eating with publicans and sinners. Then he went healing and teaching through Galilee, and even journeyed to Tyre and Sidon. He chose the twelve disciples, and sent them abroad to preach the new gospel. He worked miracles in Bethsaida and Chorazin—villages two or three miles from Capernaum. It was near one of them that the miraculous draft of fishes is supposed to have been taken, and it was in the desert places near the other that he fed the thousands by the miracles of the loaves and fishes. He cursed them both, and Capernaum also, for not repenting, after all the great works he had done in their midst, and prophesied against them. They are all in ruins, now—which is gratifying to the pilgrims, for, as usual, they fit the eternal words of gods to the evanescent things of this earth; Christ, it is more probable, referred to the *people*, not their shabby villages of wigwams: he said it would be sad for them at "the day of judgment"—and what business have mud-hovels at the Day of Judgment? it would not affect the prophecy in the least—it would neither prove it or disprove it —if these towns were splendid cities now instead of the almost vanished ruins they are. Christ visited Magdala, which is near by Capernaum, and he also visited Cesarea Philippi. He went up to his old home at Nazareth, and saw his brothers Joses, and Judas, and James, and Simon—those persons who, being own brothers to Jesus Christ, one would expect to hear mentioned sometimes, yet who ever saw their names in a newspaper or heard them from a pulpit? Who ever inquires what manner of youths they were; and whether they slept with Jesus, played with him and romped about him; quarreled with him concerning toys and trifles; struck him in anger, not suspecting what he was? Who ever wonders what they thought when they saw him come back to Nazareth a celebrity, and looked long at his unfamiliar face to make sure, and then said, " It *is* Jesus?" Who wonders what passed in their minds when they saw this brother, (who was *only* a brother to them, however much he might be to others a mysterious stranger who was a god and had stood face to face with God above the clouds,) doing strange miracles with crowds of astonished people for witnesses? Who wonders if the brothers of Jesus asked him to come home with them, and said his mother and his sisters were grieved at his long absence, and would be wild with delight to see his face again? Who ever gives a thought to the sisters of Jesus at all?—yet he had sisters; and memories of them must have stolen into his mind often when he was ill-treated among strangers; when he was homeless and said he had not where to lay his head; when all deserted him, even Peter, and he stood alone among his enemies.

Christ did few miracles in Nazareth, and staid but a little while. The people said, " *This* the Son of God! Why, his father is nothing but a carpenter. We know the family. We see them every day. Are not his brothers named so and so, and his sisters so and so, and is not his mother the person they call Mary? This is absurd." He did not curse his home, but he shook its dust from his feet and went away.

Capernaum lies close to the edge of the little sea, in a small plain some five miles long and a mile or two wide, which is mildly adorned with oleanders which look all the better contrasted with the bald hills and the howling deserts which surround them, but they are not as deliriously beautiful as the books paint them. If one be calm and resolute he can look upon their comeliness and live.

One of the most astonishing things that have yet fallen under our observation is the exceedingly small portion of the earth from which sprang the now flourishing plant of Christianity. The longest journey our Saviour ever performed was from here to Jerusalem—about one hundred to one hundred and twenty miles. The next longest was from here to Sidon —say about sixty or seventy miles. Instead of being wide apart—as American appreciation of distances would naturally suggest—the places made most particularly celebrated by the presence of Christ are nearly all right here in full view, and within cannon-shot of Capernaum. Leaving out two or three short journeys of the Saviour, he spent his life, preached his gospel, and performed his miracles within a compass no larger than an ordinary county in the United States. It is as much as I can do to comprehend this stupefying fact. How it wears a man out to have to read up a hundred pages of history every two or three miles—for verily the celebrated localities of Palestine occur that close together. How wearily, how bewilderingly they swarm about your path !

In due time we reached the ancient village of Magdala.

CHAPTER XLVIII.

MAGDALA is not a beautiful place. It is thoroughly Syrian, and that is to say that it is thoroughly ugly, and cramped, squalid, uncomfortable, and filthy—just the style of cities that have adorned the country since Adam's time, as all writers have labored hard to prove, and have succeeded. The streets of Magdala are any where from three to six feet wide, and reeking with uncleanliness. The houses are from five to seven feet high, and all built upon one arbitrary plan— the ungraceful form of a dry-goods box. The sides are daubed with a smooth white plaster, and tastefully frescoed aloft and alow with disks of camel-dung placed there to dry. This gives the edifice the romantic appearance of having been riddled with cannon-balls, and imparts to it a very warlike aspect. When the artist has arranged his materials with an eye to just proportion—the small and the large flakes in alternate rows, and separated by carefully-considered intervals—I know of nothing more cheerful to look upon than a spirited Syrian fresco. The flat, plastered roof is garnished by picturesque stacks of fresco materials, which, having become thoroughly dried and cured, are placed there where it will be convenient. It is used for fuel. There is no timber of any consequence in Palestine—none at all to waste upon fires—and neither are there any mines of coal. If my description has been intelligible, you will perceive, now, that a square, flat-roofed hovel, neatly frescoed, with its wall-tops gallantly bastioned and turreted with dried camel-refuse, gives to a landscape a feature that is exceedingly festive and picturesque, especially if one is careful to remember to stick in a cat wherever, about the premises, there is room for a cat to sit. There are no windows to a Syrian hut, and no chimneys. When I used to read that they let a bed-ridden man down through the roof of a house in Capernaum to get him into the presence of the Saviour, I generally had a three-story brick in my mind, and marveled

SYRIAN HOUSE.

that they did not break his neck with the strange experiment. I perceive now, however, that they might have taken him by the heels and thrown him clear over the house without discommoding him very much. Palestine is not changed any since those days, in manners, customs, architecture, or people.

As we rode into Magdala not a soul was visible. But the ring of the horses' hoofs roused the stupid population, and they all came trooping out—old men and old women, boys and girls, the blind, the crazy, and the crippled, all in ragged, soiled and scanty raiment, and all abject beggars by nature, instinct and education. How the vermin-tortured vagabonds did swarm! How they showed their scars and sores, and piteously pointed to their maimed and crooked limbs, and begged with their pleading eyes for charity! We had invoked a spirit we could not lay. They hung to the horses's tails, clung to their manes and the stirrups, closed in on every side in scorn of dangerous hoofs—and out of their infidel throats, with one accord, burst an agonizing and most infernal chorus: "Howajji, bucksheesh! howajji, bucksheesh! howajji, bucksheesh! bucksheesh! bucksheesh!" I never was in a storm like that before.

As we paid the bucksheesh out to sore-eyed children and brown, buxom girls with repulsively tattooed lips and chins, we filed through the town and by many an exquisite fresco, till we came to a bramble-infested inclosure and a Roman-looking ruin which had been the veritable dwelling of St. Mary Magdalene, the friend and follower of Jesus. The guide believed it, and so did I. I could not well do otherwise, with the house right there before my eyes as plain as day. The pilgrims took down portions of the front wall for specimens, as is their honored custom, and then we departed.

We are camped in this place, now, just within the city walls of Tiberias. We went into the town before nightfall and looked at its people—we cared nothing about its houses. Its people are best examined at a distance. They are particularly uncomely Jews, Arabs, and negroes. Squalor and poverty are the pride of Tiberias. The young women wear their dower strung upon a strong wire that curves downward from the top of the head to the jaw—Turkish silver coins which they have raked together or inherited. Most of these maidens were not wealthy, but some few had been very kindly dealt with by fortune. I saw heiresses there worth, in their own right—worth, well, I suppose I might venture to say, as much as nine dollars and a half. But such cases are rare. When you come across one of these, she naturally puts on airs. She will not ask for bucksheesh. She will not even permit of undue familiarity. She assumes a crushing dignity and goes on serenely practicing with her fine-tooth comb and quoting poetry just the same as if you were not present at all. Some people can not stand prosperity.

They say that the long-nosed, lanky, dyspeptic-looking body-snatchers, with the indescribable hats on, and a long curl dangling down in front of each ear, are the old, familiar, self-righteous Pharisees we read of in the Scriptures. Verily, they look it. Judging merely by their general style, and without other evidence, one might easily suspect that self-righteousness was their specialty.

From various authorities I have culled information concerning Tiberias. It was built by Herod Antipas, the murderer of John the Baptist, and named after the Emperor Tiberius. It is believed that it stands upon the site of what must have been, ages ago, a city of considerable architectural pretensions, judging by the fine porphyry pillars that are scattered through Tiberias and down the lake shore southward. These were fluted, once, and yet, although the stone is about as hard as iron, the flutings are almost worn away. These pillars are

TIBERIAS, AND SEA OF GALILEE.

small, and doubtless the edifices they adorned were distinguished more for elegance than grandeur. This modern town —Tiberias—is only mentioned in the New Testament; never in the Old.

The Sanhedrim met here last, and for three hundred years

Tiberias was the metropolis of the Jews in Palestine. It is one of the four holy cities of the Israelites, and is to them what Mecca is to the Mohammedan and Jerusalem to the Christian. It has been the abiding place of many learned and famous Jewish rabbins. They lie buried here, and near them lie also twenty-five thousand of their faith who traveled far to be near them while they lived and lie with them when they died. The great Rabbi Ben Israel spent three years here in the early part of the third century. He is dead, now.

The celebrated Sea of Galilee is not so large a sea as Lake Tahoe* by a good deal—it is just about two-thirds as large. And when we come to speak of beauty, this sea is no more to be compared to Tahoe than a meridian of longitude is to a rainbow. The dim waters of this pool can not suggest the limpid brilliancy of Tahoe; these low, shaven, yellow hillocks of rocks and sand, so devoid of perspective, can not suggest the grand peaks that compass Tahoe like a wall, and whose ribbed and chasmed fronts are clad with stately pines that seem to grow small and smaller as they climb, till one might fancy them reduced to weeds and shrubs far upward, where they join the everlasting snows. Silence and solitude brood over Tahoe; and silence and solitude brood also over this lake of Genessaret. But the solitude of the one is as cheerful and fascinating as the solitude of the other is dismal and repellant.

In the early morning one watches the silent battle of dawn and darkness upon the waters of Tahoe with a placid interest; but when the shadows sulk away and one by one the hidden beauties of the shore unfold themselves in the full splendor of noon; when the still surface is belted like a rainbow with broad bars of blue and green and white, half the distance from circumference to centre; when, in the lazy summer afternoon, he lies in a boat, far out to where the dead blue of the deep water begins, and smokes the pipe of peace and idly winks at the

* I measure all lakes by Tahoe, partly because I am far more familiar with it than with any other, and partly because I have such a high admiration for it and such a world of pleasant recollections of it, that it is very nearly impossible for me to speak of lakes and not mention it.

distant crags and patches of snow from under his cap-brim;
when the boat drifts shoreward to the white water, and he lolls
over the gunwale and gazes by the hour down through the
crystal depths and notes the colors of the pebbles and reviews
the finny armies gliding in procession a hundred feet below;
when at night he sees moon and stars, mountain ridges feath-
ered with pines, jutting white capes, bold promontories, grand
sweeps of rugged scenery topped with bald, glimmering peaks,
all magnificently pictured in the polished mirror of the lake,
in richest, softest detail, the tranquil interest that was born
with the morning deepens and deepens, by sure degrees, till it
culminates at last in resistless fascination!

It is solitude, for birds and squirrels on the shore and fishes
in the water are all the creatures that are near to make it otherwise, but it is not the sort of solitude to make one dreary.
Come to Galilee for that. If these unpeopled deserts, these
rusty mounds of barrenness, that never, never, never do shake
the glare from their harsh outlines, and fade and faint into
vague perspective; that melancholy ruin of Capernaum; this
stupid village of Tiberias, slumbering under its six funereal
plumes of palms; yonder desolate declivity where the swine
of the miracle ran down into the sea, and doubtless thought it
was better to swallow a devil or two and get drowned into the
bargain than have to live longer in such a place; this cloudless, blistering sky; this solemn, sailless, tintless lake, reposing
within its rim of yellow hills and low, steep banks, and looking just as expressionless and unpoetical (when we leave its
sublime history out of the question,) as any metropolitan reservoir in Christendom—if these things are not food for rock
me to sleep, mother, none exist, I think.

But I should not offer the evidence for the prosecution and
leave the defense unheard. Wm. C. Grimes deposes as follows :—

"We had taken ship to go over to the other side. The sea was not more than
six miles wide. Of the beauty of the scene, however, I can not say enough, nor
can I imagine where those travelers carried their eyes who have described the
scenery of the lake as tame or uninteresting. The first great characteristic of it is

the deep basin in which it lies. This is from three to four hundred feet deep on all sides except at the lower end, and the sharp slope of the banks, which are all of the richest green, is broken and diversified by the wâdys and water-courses which work their way down through the sides of the basin, forming dark chasms or light sunny valleys. Near Tiberias these banks are rocky, and ancient sepulchres open in them, with their doors toward the water. They selected grand spots, as did the Egyptians of old, for burial places, as if they designed that when the voice of God should reach the sleepers, they should walk forth and open their eyes on scenes of glorious beauty. On the east, the wild and desolate mountains contrast finely with the deep blue lake; and toward the north, sublime and majestic, Hermon looks down on the sea, lifting his white crown to heaven with the pride of a hill that has seen the departing footsteps of a hundred generations. On the north-east shore of the sea was a single tree, and this is the only tree of any size visible from the water of the lake, except a few lonely palms in the city of Tiberias, and by its solitary position attracts more attention than would a forest. The whole appearance of the scene is precisely what we would expect and desire the scenery of Genessaret to be, grand beauty, but quiet calm. The very mountains are calm."

It is an ingeniously written description, and well calculated to deceive. But if the paint and the ribbons and the flowers be stripped from it, a skeleton will be found beneath.

So stripped, there remains a lake six miles wide and neutral in color ; with steep green banks, unrelieved by shrubbery ; at one end bare, unsightly rocks, with (almost invisible) holes in them of no consequence to the picture ; eastward, "wild and desolate mountains ;" (low, desolate hills, he should have said ;) in the north, a mountain called Hermon, with snow on it ; peculiarity of the picture, " calmness ;" its prominent feature, one tree.

No ingenuity could make such a picture beautiful—to one's actual vision.

I claim the right to correct misstatements, and have so corrected the color of the water in the above recapitulation. The waters of Genessaret are of an exceedingly mild blue, even from a high elevation and a distance of five miles. Close at hand (the witness was sailing on the lake,) it is hardly proper to call them blue at all, much less " deep" blue. I wish to state, also, not as a correction, but as matter of opinion, that Mount Hermon is not a striking or picturesque mountain by any means, being too near the height of its immediate neighbors to be so. That is all. I do not object to the witness dragging a mountain forty-five miles to help the scenery under consideration, because it is entirely proper to do it, and besides, the picture needs it.

"C. W. E.," (of "Life in the Holy Land,") deposes as follows :—

> "A beautiful sea lies unbosomed among the Galilean hills, in the midst of that land once possessed by Zebulon and Naphtali, Asher and Dan. The azure of the sky penetrates the depths of the lake, and the waters are sweet and cool. On the west, stretch broad fertile plains; on the north the rocky shores rise step by step until in the far distance tower the snowy heights of Hermon; on the east through a misty veil are seen the high plains of Perea, which stretch away in rugged mountains leading the mind by varied paths toward Jerusalem the Holy. Flowers bloom in this terrestrial paradise, once beautiful and verdant with waving trees; singing birds enchant the ear; the turtle-dove soothes with its soft note; the crested lark sends up its song toward heaven, and the grave and stately stork inspires the mind with thought, and leads it on to meditation and repose. Life here was once idyllic, charming; here were once no rich, no poor, no high, no low. It was a world of ease, simplicity, and beauty; now it is a scene of desolation and misery."

This is not an ingenious picture. It is the worst I ever saw. It describes in elaborate detail what it terms a "terrestrial paradise," and closes with the startling information that this paradise is "a scene of *desolation and misery.*"

I have given two fair, average specimens of the character of the testimony offered by the majority of the writers who visit this region. One says, "Of the beauty of the scene I can not say enough," and then proceeds to cover up with a woof of glittering sentences a thing which, when stripped for inspection, proves to be only an unobtrusive basin of water, some mountainous desolation, and one tree. The other, after a conscientious effort to build a terrestrial paradise out of the same materials, with the addition of a "grave and stately stork," spoils it all by blundering upon the ghastly truth at the last.

Nearly every book concerning Galilee and its lake describes the scenery as beautiful. No—not always so straightforward as that. Sometimes the *impression* intentionally conveyed is that it is beautiful, at the same time that the author is careful not to *say* that it is, in plain Saxon. But a careful analysis of these descriptions will show that the materials of which they are formed are not individually beautiful and can not be wrought into combinations that are beautiful. The veneration and the affection which some of these men felt for the scenes they were speaking of, heated their fancies and biased their judgment; but the pleasant falsities they wrote were full of honest sincerity, at any rate. Others wrote as they did, because they feared it would be unpopular to write otherwise. Others were hypocrites and deliberately meant to deceive. Any of them would say in a moment, if asked, that it was *always* right and always *best* to tell the truth. They would say that, at any rate, if they did not perceive the drift of the question.

But why should not the truth be spoken of this region? Is the truth harmful? Has it ever needed to hide its face? God made the Sea of Galilee and its surroundings as they are. Is it the province of Mr. Grimes to improve upon the work?

I am sure, from the tenor of books I have read, that many who have visited this land in years gone by, were Presbyterians, and came seeking evidences in support of their particular creed; they found a Presbyterian Palestine, and they had already made up their minds to find no other, though possibly they did not know it, being blinded by their zeal. Others were Baptists, seeking Baptist evidences and a Baptist Palestine. Others were Catholics, Methodists, Episcopalians, seeking evidences indorsing their several creeds, and a Catholic, a Methodist, an Episcopalian Palestine. Honest as these men's intentions may have been, they were full of partialities and prejudices, they entered the country with their verdicts already prepared, and they could no more write dispassionately and impartially about it than they could about their own wives and children. Our pilgrims have brought *their* verdicts with them. They have shown it in their conversation ever since we left Beirout. I can almost tell, in set phrase, what they will say when they see Tabor, Nazareth, Jericho and Jerusalem—*because I have the books they will* " *smouch* " *their ideas from*. These authors write pictures and frame rhapsodies, and lesser men follow and see with the author's eyes instead of their own, and speak with his tongue. What the pilgrims said at Cesarea Philippi surprised me with its wisdom. I found it afterwards in Robinson. What they said when Genessaret burst upon their vision, charmed me with its grace. I find it in Mr. Thompson's "Land and the Book." They have spoken often, in happily worded language which never varied, of how they mean to lay their weary heads upon a stone at Bethel, as Jacob did, and close their dim eyes, and dream, perchance, of angels descending out of heaven on a ladder. It was very pretty. But I have recognized the weary head and the dim eyes, finally. They borrowed the idea—and the words—and the construction—and the punctuation—from Grimes. The pilgrims will tell of Palestine, when they get home, not as it appeared to *them*, but as it appeared to Thompson and Robinson and Grimes—with the tints varied to suit each pilgrim's creed.

Pilgrims, sinners and Arabs are all abed, now, and the camp is still. Labor in loneliness is irksome. Since I made my last few notes, I have been sitting outside the tent for half an hour. Night is the time to see Galilee. Genessaret under these lustrous stars, has nothing repulsive about it. Genessaret with the glittering reflections of the constellations flecking its surface, almost makes me regret that I ever saw the rude glare of the day upon it. Its history and its associations are its chiefest charm, in any eyes, and the spells they weave are feeble in the searching light of the sun. *Then*, we scarcely feel the fetters. Our thoughts wander constantly to the practical concerns of life, and refuse to dwell upon things that seem vague and unreal. But when the day is done, even the most unimpressible must yield to the dreamy influences of this tranquil starlight. The old traditions of the place steal upon his memory and haunt his reveries, and then his fancy clothes all sights and sounds with the supernatural. In the lapping of the waves upon the beach, he hears the dip of ghostly oars; in the secret noises of the night he hears spirit voices; in the soft sweep of the breeze, the rush of invisible wings. Phantom ships are on the sea, the dead of twenty centuries come forth from the tombs, and in the dirges of the night wind the songs of old forgotten ages find utterance again.

In the starlight, Galilee has no boundaries but the broad compass of the heavens, and is a theatre meet for great events; meet for the birth of a religion able to save a world; and meet for the stately Figure appointed to stand upon its stage and proclaim its high decrees. But in the sunlight, one says: Is it for the deeds which were done and the words which were spoken in this little acre of rocks and sand eighteen centuries gone, that the bells are ringing to-day in the remote islands of the sea and far and wide over continents that clasp the circumference of the huge globe?

One can comprehend it only when night has hidden all incongruities and created a theatre proper for so grand a drama.

33

CHAPTER XLIX.

WE took another swim in the Sea of Galilee at twilight yesterday, and another at sunrise this morning. We have not sailed, but three swims are equal to a sail, are they not? There were plenty of fish visible in the water, but we have no outside aids in this pilgrimage but " Tent Life in the Holy Land," " The Land and the Book," and other literature of like description—no fishing-tackle. There were no fish to be had in the village of Tiberias. True, we saw two or three vagabonds mending their nets, but never trying to catch any thing with them.

We did not go to the ancient warm baths two miles below Tiberias. I had no desire in the world to go there. This seemed a little strange, and prompted me to try to discover what the cause of this unreasonable indifference was. It turned out to be simply because Pliny mentions them. I have conceived a sort of unwarrantable unfriendliness toward Pliny and St. Paul, because it seems as if I can never ferret out a place that I can have to myself. It always and eternally transpires that St. Paul has been to that place, and Pliny has " mentioned " it.

In the early morning we mounted and started. And then a weird apparition marched forth at the head of the procession— a pirate, I thought, if ever a pirate dwelt upon land. It was a tall Arab, as swarthy as an Indian ; young—say thirty years of age. On his head he had closely bound a gorgeous yellow and red striped silk scarf, whose ends, lavishly fringed with tassels, hung down between his shoulders and dallied with the wind. From his neck to his knees, in ample folds, a robe swept down that was a very star-spangled banner of curved and sinuous bars of black and white. Out of his back, some-where, apparently, the long stem of a chibouk projected, and reached far above his right shoulder. Athwart his back, diag-onally, and extending high above his left shoulder, was an Arab gun of Saladin's time, that was splendid with silver pla-ting from stock clear up to the end of its measureless stretch of barrel. About his waist was bound many and many a yard of elaborately figured but sadly tarnished stuff that came from sumptuous Persia, and among the baggy folds in front the sun-beams glinted from a formidable battery of old brass-mounted horse-pistols and the gilded hilts of blood-thirsty knives. There were holsters for more pistols appended to the wonder-ful stack of long-haired goat-skins and Persian carpets, which the man had been taught to regard in the light of a saddle ; and down among the pendulous rank of vast tassels that swung from that saddle, and clanging against the iron shovel of a stirrup that propped the warrior's knees up toward his chin, was a crooked, silver-clad scimetar of such awful dimen-sions and such implacable expression that no man might hope to look upon it and not shudder. The fringed and bedizened prince whose privilege it is to ride the pony and lead the ele-phant into a country village is poor and naked compared to this chaos of paraphernalia, and the happy vanity of the one is the very poverty of satisfaction compared to the majestic serenity, the overwhelming complacency of the other.

"*Who* is this ? *What* is this?" That was the trembling in-quiry all down the line.

"Our guard ! From Galilee to the birthplace of the Saviour, the country is infested with fierce Bedouins, whose sole happi-ness it is, in this life, to cut and stab and mangle and murder unoffending Christians. Allah be with us !"

"Then hire a regiment ! Would you send us out among these desperate hordes, with no salvation in our utmost need but this old turret ?"

The dragoman laughed—not at the facetiousness of the simile, for verily, that guide or that courier or that dragoman never yet lived upon earth who had in him the faintest appreciation of a joke, even though that joke were so broad and so ponderous that if it fell on him it would flatten him out like a postage stamp—the dragoman laughed, and then, emboldened

THE GUARD.

by some thought that was in his brain, no doubt, proceeded to extremities and winked.

In straits like these, when a man laughs, it is encouraging; when he winks, it is positively reassuring. He finally intimated that one guard would be sufficient to protect us, but that that one was an absolute necessity. It was because of the moral weight his awful panoply would have with the Bedouins. Then I said we didn't want any guard at all. If one fantastic vagabond could protect eight armed Christians and a pack of Arab servants from all harm, surely that detachment could protect themselves. He shook his head doubtfully. Then I said, just think of how it looks—think of now it would read, to self-reliant Americans, that we went sneaking through this deserted wilderness under the protection of this masquerading Arab, who would break his neck getting out of the country if a man that *was* a man ever started after him. It was a mean, low, degrading position. Why were we ever told to bring navy revolvers with us if we had to be protected at last by this infamous star-spangled scum of the desert? These appeals were vain—the dragoman only smiled and shook his head.

I rode to the front and struck up an acquaintance with King Solomon-in-all-his-glory, and got him to show me his lingering eternity of a gun. It had a rusty flint lock; it was ringed and barred and plated with silver from end to end, but it was as desperately out of the perpendicular as are the billiard cues of '49 that one finds yet in service in the ancient mining camps of California. The muzzle was eaten by the rust of centuries into a ragged filagree-work, like the end of a burnt-out stove-pipe. I shut one eye and peered within—it was flaked with iron rust like an old steamboat boiler. I borrowed the ponderous pistols and snapped them. They were rusty inside, too—had not been loaded for a generation. I went back, full of encouragement, and reported to the guide, and asked him to discharge this dismantled fortress. It came out, then. This fellow was a retainer of the Sheik of Tiberias. He was a source of Government revenue. He was to the Empire of Tiberias what the customs are to America. The Sheik imposed guards upon travelers and charged them for it. It is a lucrative source of emolument, and sometimes brings into the national treasury as much as thirty-five or forty dollars a year.

I knew the warrior's secret now; I knew the hollow vanity of his rusty trumpery, and despised his asinine complacency.

I told on him, and with reckless daring the cavalcade rode straight ahead into the perilous solitudes of the desert, and scorned his frantic warnings of the mutilation and death that hovered about them on every side.

Arrived at an elevation of twelve hundred feet above the lake, (I ought to mention that the lake lies six hundred feet below the level of the Mediterranean—no traveler ever neglects to flourish that fragment of news in his letters,) as bald and unthrilling a panorama as any land can afford, perhaps, was spread out before us. Yet it was so crowded with historical interest, that if all the pages that have been written about it were spread upon its surface, they would flag it from horizon to horizon like a pavement. Among the localities comprised in this view, were Mount Hermon; the hills that border Cesarea Philippi, Dan, the Sources of the Jordan and the Waters of Merom; Tiberias; the Sea of Galilee; Joseph's Pit; Capernaum; Bethsaida; the supposed scenes of the Sermon on the Mount, the feeding of the multitudes and the miraculous draught of fishes; the declivity down which the swine ran to the sea; the entrance and the exit of the Jordan; Safed, "the city set upon a hill," one of the four holy cities of the Jews, and the place where they believe the real Messiah will appear when he comes to redeem the world; part of the battle-field of Hattin, where the knightly Crusaders fought their last fight, and in a blaze of glory passed from the stage and ended their splendid career forever; Mount Tabor, the traditional scene of the Lord's Transfiguration. And down toward the southeast lay a landscape that suggested to my mind a quotation (imperfectly remembered, no doubt :)

"The Ephraimites, not being called upon to share in the rich spoils of the Am- monitish war, assembled a mighty host to fight against Jeptha, Judge of Israel; who, being apprised of their approach, gathered together the men of Israel and gave them battle and put them to flight. To make his victory the more secure, he stationed guards at the different fords and passages of the Jordan, with instructions to let none pass who could not say Shibboleth. The Ephraimites, being of a dif- ferent tribe, could not frame to pronounce the word aright, but called it Sibboleth, which proved them enemies and cost them their lives; wherefore, forty and two thousand fell at the different fords and passages of the Jordan that day."

We jogged along peacefully over the great caravan route
from Damascus to Jerusalem and Egypt, past Lubia and other
Syrian hamlets, perched, in the unvarying style, upon the summit of steep mounds and hills, and fenced round about with
giant cactuses, (the sign of worthless land,) with prickly pears
upon them like hams, and came at last to the battle-field of
Hattin.

It is a grand, irregular plateau, and looks as if it might have
been created for a battle-field. Here the peerless Saladin met
the Christian host some seven hundred years ago, and broke
their power in Palestine for all time to come. There had long
been a truce between the opposing forces, but according to the
Guide-Book, Raynauld of Chatillon, Lord of Kerak, broke it
by plundering a Damascus caravan, and refusing to give up
either the merchants or their goods when Saladin demanded
them. This conduct of an insolent petty chieftain stung the
Sultan to the quick, and he swore that he would slaughter
Raynauld with his own hand, no matter how, or when, or
where he found him. Both armies prepared for war. Under
the weak King of Jerusalem was the very flower of the Christian chivalry. He foolishly compelled them to undergo a long,
exhausting march, in the scorching sun, and then, without
water or other refreshment, ordered them to encamp in this
open plain. The splendidly mounted masses of Moslem soldiers
swept round the north end of Genessaret, burning and destroying as they came, and pitched their camp in front of the opposing lines. At dawn the terrific fight began. Surrounded on
all sides by the Sultan's swarming battalions, the Christian
Knights fought on without a hope for their lives. They fought
with desperate valor, but to no purpose; the odds of heat and
numbers, and consuming thirst, were too great against them.
Towards the middle of the day the bravest of their band cut
their way through the Moslem ranks and gained the summit
of a little hill, and there, hour after hour, they closed around
the banner of the Cross, and beat back the charging squadrons
of the enemy.

But the doom of the Christian power was sealed. Sunset

found Saladin Lord of Palestine, the Christian chivalry strewn in heaps upon the field, and the King of Jerusalem, the Grand Master of the Templars, and Raynauld of Chatillon, captives in the Sultan's tent. Saladin treated two of the prisoners with princely courtesy, and ordered refreshments to be set before them. When the King handed an iced Sherbet to Chatillon, the Sultan said, "It is thou that givest it to him, not I." He remembered his oath, and slaughtered the hapless Knight of Chatillon with his own hand.

It was hard to realize that this silent plain had once resounded with martial music and trembled to the tramp of armed men. It was hard to people this solitude with rushing columns of cavalry, and stir its torpid pulses with the shouts of victors, the shrieks of the wounded, and the flash of banner and steel above the surging billows of war. A desolation is here that not even imagination can grace with the pomp of life and action.

We reached Tabor safely, and considerably in advance of that old iron-clad swindle of a guard. We never saw a human being on the whole route, much less lawless hordes of Bedouins. Tabor stands solitary and alone, a giant sentinel above the Plain of Esdraelon. It rises some fourteen hundred feet above the surrounding level, a green, wooden cone, symmetrical and full of grace—a prominent landmark, and one that is exceedingly pleasant to eyes surfeited with the repulsive monotony of desert Syria. We climbed the steep path to its summit, through breezy glades of thorn and oak. The view presented from its highest peak was almost beautiful. Below, was the broad, level plain of Esdraelon, checkered with fields like a chess-board, and full as smooth and level, seemingly; dotted about its borders with white, compact villages, and faintly penciled, far and near, with the curving lines of roads and trails. When it is robed in the fresh verdure of spring, it must form a charming picture, even by itself. Skirting its southern border rises "Little Hermon," over whose summit a glimpse of Gilboa is caught. Nain, famous for the raising of the widow's son, and Endor, as famous for the performances of her witch, are in view. To the eastward lies the Valley of the Jordan and beyond it the mountains of Gilead. Westward is Mount Carmel. Hermon in the north—the table-lands of Bashan—Safed, the holy city, gleaming white upon a tall spur of the mountains of Lebanon—a steel-blue corner of the Sea of Galilee—saddle-peaked Hattin, traditional "Mount of Beatitudes" and mute witness of the last brave fight of the Crusading host for Holy Cross— these fill up the picture.

To glance at the salient features of this landscape through the picturesque

MOUNT TABOR.

framework of a ragged and ruined stone window-arch of the time of Christ, thus hiding from sight all that is unattractive, is to secure to yourself a pleasure worth climbing the mountain to enjoy. One must stand on his head to get the best effect in a fine sunset, and set a landscape in a bold, strong framework that is very close at hand, to bring out all its beauty. One learns this latter truth never more to forget it, in that mimic land of enchantment, the wonderful garden of my lord the Count Pallavicini, near Genoa. You go wandering for hours among hills and wooded glens, artfully contrived to leave the impression that Nature shaped them and not man; following winding paths and coming suddenly upon leaping cascades and rustic bridges; finding sylvan lakes where you expected them not; loitering through battered mediæval castles in miniature that seem hoary with age and yet were built a dozen years ago; meditating over ancient crumbling tombs, whose marble columns were marred and broken purposely by the modern artist that made them ; stumbling unawares upon toy palaces, wrought of rare and costly materials, and again upon a peasant's hut, whose dilapidated furniture would never suggest that it was made so to order ; sweeping round and round in the midst of a forest on an enchanted wooden horse that is moved by some invisible agency ; traversing Roman roads and passing under majestic triumphal arches; resting in quaint bowers where unseen spirits discharge jets of water on you from every possible direction, and where even the flowers you touch assail you with a shower; boating on a subterranean lake among caverns and arches royally draped with clustering stalactites, and passing out into open day upon another lake, which is bordered with sloping banks of grass and gay with patrician barges that swim at anchor in the shadow of a miniature marble temple that rises out of the clear water and glasses its white statues, its rich capitals and fluted columns in the tranquil depths. So, from marvel to marvel you have drifted on, thinking all the time that the one last seen must be the chiefest. And, verily, the chiefest wonder *is* reserved until the last, but you do not see it until you step ashore, and passing through a wilderness of rare flowers, collected from every corner of the earth, you stand at the door of one more mimic temple. Right in this place the artist taxed his genius to the utmost, and fairly opened the gates of fairy land. You look through an unpretending pane of glass, stained yellow ; the first thing you see is a mass of quivering foliage, ten short steps before you, in the midst of which is a ragged opening like a gateway—a thing that is common enough in nature, and not apt to excite suspicions of a deep human design—and above the bottom of the gateway, project, in the most careless way, a few broad tropic leaves and brilliant flowers. All of a sudden, through this bright, bold gateway, you catch a glimpse of the faintest, softest, richest picture that ever graced the dream of a dying Saint, since John saw the New Jerusalem glimmering above the clouds of Heaven. A broad sweep of sea, flecked with careening sails ; a sharp, jutting cape, and a lofty lighthouse on it; a sloping lawn behind it; beyond, a portion of the old "city of palaces," with its parks and hills and stately mansions; beyond these, a prodigious mountain, with its strong outlines sharply cut against ocean and sky; and over all, vagrant shreds and flakes of cloud, floating in a sea of gold. The ocean is gold, the city is gold, the meadow, the mountain, the sky—every thing is golden—rich, and mellow, and dreamy as a vision of Paradise. No artist could put upon canvas its entrancing beauty, and yet, without the yellow glass, and the carefully contrived accident of a framework that cast it into enchanted distance and shut out from it all unattractive features, it was not a picture to fall into ecstacies over. Such is life, and the trail of the serpent is over us all.

There is nothing for it now but to come back to old Tabor, though the subject is tiresome enough, and I can not stick to it for wandering off to scenes that are pleasanter to remember. I think I will skip, any how. There is nothing about Tabor (except we concede that it was the scene of the Transfiguration,) but some gray old ruins, stacked up there in all ages of the world from the days of stout Gideon and parties that flourished thirty centuries ago to the fresh yesterday of Crusading times. It has its Greek Convent, and the coffee there is good, but never a splinter of the true cross or bone of a hallowed saint to arrest the idle thoughts of worldlings and turn them into graver channels. A Catholic church is nothing to me that has no relics.

The plain of Esdraelon—"the battle-field of the nations"—only sets one to dreaming of Joshua, and Benhadad, and Saul, and Gideon; Tamerlane, Tancred, Cœur de Lion, and Saladin; the warrior Kings of Persia, Egypt's heroes, and Napoleon—for they all fought here. If the magic of the moonlight could summon from the graves of forgotten centuries and many lands the countless myriads that have battled on this wide, far-reaching floor, and array them in the thousand strange costumes of their hundred nationalities, and send the vast host sweeping down the plain, splendid with plumes and banners and glittering lances, I could stay here an age to see the phan-

tom pageant. But the magic of the moonlight is a vanity and
a fraud; and whoso putteth his trust in it shall suffer sorrow
and disappointment.

Down at the foot of Tabor, and just at the edge of the storied Plain of Esdraelon, is the insignificant village of Deburieh,
where Deborah, prophetess of Israel, lived. It is just like
Magdala.

CHAPTER L.

WE descended from Mount Tabor, crossed a deep ravine, and followed a hilly, rocky road to Nazareth—distant two hours. All distances in the East are measured by hours, not miles. A good horse will walk three miles an hour over nearly any kind of a road; therefore, an hour, here, always stands for three miles. This method of computation is bothersome and annoying; and until one gets thoroughly accustomed to it, it carries no intelligence to his mind until he has stopped and translated the pagan hours into Christian miles, just as people do with the spoken words of a foreign language they are acquainted with, but not familiarly enough to catch the meaning in a moment. Distances traveled by human feet are also estimated by hours and minutes, though I do not know what the base of the calculation is. In Constantinople you ask, "How far is it to the Consulate?" and they answer, "About ten minutes." "How far is it to the Lloyds' Agency?" "Quarter of an hour." "How far is it to the lower bridge?" "Four minutes." I can not be positive about it, but I think that there, when a man orders a pair of pantaloons, he says he wants them a quarter of a minute in the legs and nine seconds around the waist.

Two hours from Tabor to Nazareth—and as it was an uncommonly narrow, crooked trail, we necessarily met all the camel trains and jackass caravans between Jericho and Jacksonville in that particular place and nowhere else. The donkeys do not matter so much, because they are so small that you can jump your horse over them if he is an animal of spirit, but a camel is not jumpable. A camel is as tall as any ordinary dwelling-house in Syria—which is to say a camel is from one to two, and sometimes nearly three feet taller than a good-sized man. In this part of the country his load is oftenest in the shape of colossal sacks—one on each side. He and his cargo take up as much room as a carriage. Think of meeting this style of obstruction in a narrow trail. The camel would not turn out for a king. He stalks serenely along, bringing his cushioned stilts forward with the long, regular swing of a pendulum, and whatever is in the way must get out of the way peaceably, or be wiped out forcibly by the bulky sacks. It was a tiresome ride to us, and perfectly exhausting to the horses. We were compelled to jump over upwards of eighteen hundred donkeys, and only one person in the party was unseated less than sixty times by the camels. This seems like a powerful statement, but the poet has said, "Things are not what they seem." I can not think of any thing, now, more certain to make one shudder, than to have a soft-footed camel sneak up behind him and touch him on the ear with its cold, flabby under-lip. A camel did this for one of the boys, who was drooping over his saddle in a brown study. He glanced up and saw the majestic apparition hovering above him, and made frantic efforts to get out of the way, but the camel reached out and bit him on the shoulder before he accomplished it. This was the only pleasant incident of the journey.

At Nazareth we camped in an olive grove near the Virgin Mary's fountain, and that wonderful Arab "guard" came to collect some bucksheesh for his "services" in following us from Tiberias and warding off invisible dangers with the terrors of his armament. The dragoman had paid his master, but that counted as nothing—if you hire a man to sneeze for you, here, and another man chooses to help him, you have got to pay both. They do nothing whatever without pay. How it must have surprised these people to hear the way of salvation offered to them "*without money and without price.*" If the manners, the people or the customs of this country have changed since the Saviour's time, the figures and metaphors of the Bible are not the evidences to prove it by.

We entered the great Latin Convent which is built over the traditional dwelling-place of the Holy Family. We went down a flight of fifteen steps below the ground level, and stood in a small chapel tricked out with tapestry hangings, silver lamps, and oil paintings. A spot marked by a cross, in the marble floor, under the altar, was exhibited as the place made forever holy by the feet of the Virgin when she stood up to receive the message of the angel. So simple, so unpretending a locality, to be the scene of so mighty an event! The very scene of the Annunciation—an event which has been commemorated by splendid shrines and august temples all over the civilized world, and one which the princes of art have made it their loftiest ambition to picture worthily on their canvas; a spot whose history is familiar to the very children of every house, and city, and obscure hamlet of the furthest lands of Christendom; a spot which myriads of men would toil across the breadth of a world to see, would consider it a priceless privilege to look upon. It was easy to think these thoughts. But it was not easy to bring myself up to the magnitude of the situation. I could sit off several thousand miles and imagine the angel appearing, with shadowy wings and lustrous countenance, and note the glory that streamed downward upon the Virgin's head while the message from the Throne of God fell upon her ears—any one can do that, beyond the ocean, but few can do it here. I saw the little recess from which the angel stepped, but could not fill its void. The angels that I know are creatures of unstable fancy—they will not fit in niches of substantial stone. Imagination labors best in distant fields. I doubt if any man can stand in the Grotto of the Annunciation and people with the phantom images of his mind its too tangible walls of stone.

They showed us a broken granite pillar, depending from the roof, which they said was hacked in two by the Moslem conquerors of Nazareth, in the vain hope of pulling down the sanctuary. But the pillar remained miraculously suspended in the air, and, unsupported itself, supported then and still supports the roof. By dividing this statement up among eight, it was found not difficult to believe it.

These gifted Latin monks never do any thing by halves. If they were to show you the Brazen Serpent that was elevated in the wilderness, you could depend upon it that they had on hand the pole it was elevated on also, and even the hole it stood in. They have got the "Grotto" of the Annunciation here; and just as convenient to it as one's throat is to his mouth, they have also the Virgin's Kitchen, and even her sitting-room, where she and Joseph watched the infant Saviour play with Hebrew toys eighteen hundred years ago. All under one roof, and all clean, spacious, comfortable "grottoes." It seems curious that personages intimately connected with the Holy Family always lived in grottoes—in Nazareth, in Bethlehem, in imperial Ephesus—and yet nobody else in their day and generation thought of doing any thing of the kind. If they ever did, their grottoes are all gone, and I suppose we ought to wonder at the peculiar marvel of the preservation of these I speak of. When the Virgin fled from Herod's wrath, she hid in a grotto in Bethlehem, and the same is there to this day. The slaughter of the innocents in Bethlehem was done in a grotto; the Saviour was born in a grotto—both are shown to pilgrims yet. It is exceedingly strange that these tremendous events all happened in grottoes—and exceedingly fortunate, likewise, because the strongest houses must crumble to ruin in time, but a grotto in the living rock will last forever. It is an imposture—this grotto stuff—but it is one that all men ought to thank the Catholics for. Wherever they ferret out a lost locality made holy by some Scriptural event, they straightway build a massive—almost imperishable—church there, and preserve the memory of that locality for the gratification of future generations. If it had been left to Protestants to do this most worthy work, we would not even know where Jerusalem is to-day, and the man who could go and put his finger on Nazareth would be too wise for this world. The world owes the Catholics its good will even for the happy rascality of hewing out these bogus grottoes in the rock ; for it is infinitely more satisfactory to look at a grotto, where people have faithfully believed for centuries that the Virgin once lived, than to have to imagine a dwelling-place for her somewhere, any where, nowhere, loose and at large all over this town of Nazareth. There is too large a scope of country. The imagination can not work. There is no one particular spot to chain your eye, rivet your interest, and make you think. The memory of the Pilgrims can not perish while Plymouth Rock remains to us. The old monks are wise. They know how to drive a stake through a pleasant tradition that will hold it to its place forever.

We visited the places where Jesus worked for fifteen years as a carpenter, and where he attempted to teach in the synagogue and was driven out by a mob. Catholic chapels stand upon these sites and protect the little fragments of the ancient walls which remain. Our pilgrims broke off specimens. We visited, also, a new chapel, in the midst of the town, which is built around a boulder some twelve feet long by four feet thick ; the priests discovered, a few years ago, that the disciples had sat upon this rock to rest, once, when they had walked up from Capernaum. They hastened to preserve the relic. Relics are very good property. Travelers are expected to pay for seeing them, and they do it cheerfully. We like the idea. One's conscience can never be the worse for the knowledge that he has paid his way like a man. Our pilgrims would have liked very well to get out their lampblack and stencil-plates and paint their names on that rock, together with the names of the villages they hail from in America, but the priests permit nothing of that kind. To speak the strict truth, however, our party seldom offend in that way, though we have men in the ship who never lose an opportunity to do it. Our pilgrims' chief sin is their lust for " specimens." I suppose that by this time they know the dimensions of that rock to an inch, and its weight to a ton ; and I do not hesitate to charge that they will go back there to-night and try to carry it off.

This " Fountain of the Virgin " is the one which tradition

34

says Mary used to get water from, twenty times a day, when she was a girl, and bear it away in a jar upon her head. The water streams through faucets in the face of a wall of ancient masonry which stands removed from the houses of the village. The young girls of Nazareth still collect about it by the dozen and keep up a riotous laughter and sky-larking. The Nazarene

FOUNTAIN OF THE VIRGIN.

girls are homely. Some of them have large, lustrous eyes, but none of them have pretty faces. These girls wear a single garment, usually, and it is loose, shapeless, of undecided color; it is generally out of repair, too. They wear, from crown to jaw, curious strings of old coins, after the manner of the belles of Tiberias, and brass jewelry upon their wrists and in their ears. They wear no shoes and stockings. They are the most human girls we have found in the country yet, and the best natured. But there is no question that these picturesque maidens sadly lack comeliness.

A pilgrim—the "Enthusiast"—said: "See that tall, graceful girl! look at the Madonna-like beauty of her countenance!"

Another pilgrim came along presently and said: "Observe that tall, graceful girl; what queenly Madonna-like gracefulness of beauty is in her countenance."

I said: "She is not tall, she is short; she is not beautiful, she is homely; she is graceful enough, I grant, but she is rather boisterous."

The third and last pilgrim moved by, before long, and he said: "Ah, what a tall, graceful girl! what Madonna-like gracefulness of queenly beauty!"

The verdicts were all in. It was time, now, to look

"WHAT MADONNA-LIKE BEAUTY!"

up the authorities for all these opinions. I found this paragraph, which follows. Written by whom? Wm. C. Grimes:

"After we were in the saddle, we rode down to the spring to have a last look at the women of Nazareth, who were, as a class, much the prettiest that we had seen in the East. As we approached the crowd a tall girl of nineteen advanced toward

Miriam and offered her a cup of water. Her movement was graceful and queenly.
We exclaimed on the spot at the Madonna-like beauty of her countenance. Whitely was suddenly thirsty, and begged for water, and drank it slowly, with his eyes
over the top of the cup, fixed on her large black eyes, which gazed on him quite
as curiously as he on her. Then Moreright wanted water. She gave it to him and
he managed to spill it so as to ask for another cup, and by the time she came to me
she saw through the operation; her eyes were full of fun as she looked at me. I
laughed outright, and she joined me in as gay a shout as ever country maiden in
old Orange county. I wished for a picture of her. A Madonna, whose face was a
portrait of that beautiful Nazareth girl, would be a 'thing of beauty' and 'a joy
forever.' "

That is the kind of gruel which has been served out from
Palestine for ages.   Commend me to Fennimore Cooper to find
beauty in the Indians, and to Grimes to find it in the Arabs.
Arab men are often fine looking, but Arab women are not.
We can all believe that the Virgin Mary was beautiful; it is
not natural to think otherwise; but does it follow that it is
our duty to find beauty in these present women of Nazareth?

I love to quote from Grimes, because he is so dramatic. And
because he is so romantic.   And because he seems to care but
little whether he tells the truth or not, so he scares the reader
or excites his envy or his admiration.

He went through this peaceful land with one hand forever
on his revolver, and the other on his pocket-handkerchief. Always, when he was not on the point of crying over a holy
place, he was on the point of killing an Arab. More surprising things happened to him in Palestine than ever happened
to any traveler here or elsewhere since Munchausen died.

At Beit Jin, where nobody had interfered with him, he
crept out of his tent at dead of night and shot at what he
took to be an Arab lying on a rock, some distance away, plan-
ning evil. The ball killed a wolf. Just before he fired, he
makes a dramatic picture of himself—as usual, to scare the
reader:

" Was it imagination, or did I see a moving object on the surface of the rock ?
If it were a man, why did he not now drop me? He had a beautiful shot as I
stood out in my black boornoose against the white tent. I had the sensation of an
entering bullet in my throat, breast, brain."

Reckless creature !

Riding toward Genessaret, they saw two Bedouins, and "we looked to our pistols and loosened them quietly in our shawls," etc. Always cool.

In Samaria, he charged up a hill, in the face of a volley of stones; he fired into the crowd of men who threw them. He says:

"*I never lost an opportunity* of impressing the Arabs with the perfection of American and English weapons, and the danger of attacking any one of the armed Franks. I think the lesson of that ball not lost."

At Beitin he gave his whole band of Arab muleteers a piece of his mind, and then—

" I contented myself with a solemn assurance that if there occurred another instance of disobedience to o r d e r s, I would thrash the responsible party as h e n e v e r dreamed of being thrashed, and if I could not find who was responsible, I would whip them all, from first to last, whether there was a governor at hand to do it or I had to do it myself."

PUTNAM OUTDONE.

Perfectly fearless, this man.

He rode down the perpendicular path in the rocks, from the

Castle of Banias to the oak grove, at a flying gallop, his horse striding "thirty feet" at every bound. I stand prepared to bring thirty reliable witnesses to prove that Putnam's famous feat at Horseneck was insignificant compared to this.

Behold him—always theatrical—looking at Jerusalem—this time, by an oversight, with his hand off his pistol for once.

"I stood in the road, my hand on my horse's neck, and with my dim eyes sought to trace the outlines of the holy places which I had long before fixed in my mind, but the fast-flowing tears forbade my succeeding. There were our Mohammedan servants, a Latin monk, two Armenians and a Jew in our cortege, and all alike gazed with overflowing eyes."

If Latin monks and Arabs cried, I know to a moral certainty that the horses cried also, and so the picture is complete.

But when necessity demanded, he could be firm as adamant. In the Lebanon Valley an Arab youth—a Christian; he is particular to explain that Mohammedans do not steal—robbed him of a paltry ten dollars' worth of powder and shot. He convicted him before a sheik and looked on while he was punished by the terrible bastinado. Hear him:

"He (Mousa) was on his back in a twinkling, howling, shouting, screaming, but he was carried out to the piazza before the door, where we could see the operation, and laid face down. One man sat on his back and one on his legs, the latter holding up his feet, while a third laid on the bare soles a rhinoceros-hide koorbash* that whizzed through the air at every stroke. Poor Moreright was in agony, and Nama and Nama the Second (mother and sister of Mousa,) were on their faces begging and wailing, now embracing my knees and now Whitely's, while the brother, outside, made the air ring with cries louder than Mousa's. Even Yusef came and asked me on his knees to relent, and last of all, Betuni—the rascal had lost a feed-bag in their house and had been loudest in his denunciations that morning—besought the Howajji to have mercy on the fellow."

But not he! The punishment was "suspended," at the *fifteenth blow*, to hear the confession. Then Grimes and his party rode away, and left the entire Christian family to be fined and as severely punished as the *Mohammedan sheik* should deem proper.

---

* "A Koorbash is Arabic for cowhide, the cow being a rhinoceros. It is the most cruel whip known to fame. Heavy as lead, and flexible as India-rubber, usually about forty inches long and tapering gradually from an inch in diameter to a point, it administers a blow which *leaves its mark for time.*"—*Scow Life in Egypt,* by the same author.

"As I mounted, Yusef once more begged me to interfere and have mercy on them, but I looked around at the dark faces of the crowd, and I couldn't find one drop of pity in my heart for them."

He closes his picture with a rollicking burst of humor which contrasts finely with the grief of the mother and her children.

THE BASTINADO.

One more paragraph:

"Then once more I bowed my head. It is no shame to have wept in Palestine. I wept, when I saw Jerusalem, I wept when I lay in the starlight at Bethlehem. I wept on the blessed shores of Galilee. My hand was no less firm on the rein, my finger did not tremble on the trigger of my pistol when I rode with it in my right hand along the shore of the blue sea" (weeping.) "My eye was not dimmed by those tears nor my heart in aught weakened. Let him who would sneer at my emotion close this volume here, for he will find little to his taste in my journeyings through Holy Land."

He never bored but he struck water.

I am aware that this is a pretty voluminous notice of Mr. Grimes' book. However, it is proper and legitimate to speak of it, for "Nomadic Life in Palestine" is a representative book —the representative of a *class* of Palestine books—and a criti-

"I WEPT."

cism upon it will serve for a criticism upon them all. And since I am treating it in the comprehensive capacity of a representative book, I have taken the liberty of giving to both book and author fictitious names. Perhaps it is in better taste, any how, to do this.

CHAPTER LI.

NAZARETH is wonderfully interesting because the town has an air about it of being precisely as Jesus left it, and one finds himself saying, all the time, "The boy Jesus has stood in this doorway—has played in that street—has touched these stones with his hands—has rambled over these chalky hills." Whoever shall write the Boyhood of Jesus ingeniously, will make a book which will possess a vivid interest for young and old alike. I judge so from the greater interest we found in Nazareth than any of our speculations upon Capernaum and the Sea of Galilee gave rise to. It was not possible, standing by the Sea of Galilee, to frame more than a vague, far-away idea of the majestic Personage who walked upon the crested waves as if they had been solid earth, and who touched the dead and they rose up and spoke. I read among my notes, now, with a new interest, some sentences from an edition of 1621 of the Apocryphal New Testament. [Extract.]

"Christ, kissed by a bride made dumb by sorcerers, cures her. A leprous girl cured by the water in which the infant Christ was washed, and becomes the servant of Joseph and Mary. The leprous son of a Prince cured in like manner.

"A young man who had been bewitched and turned into a mule, miraculously cured by the infant Saviour being put on his back, and is married to the girl who had been cured of leprosy. Whereupon the bystanders praise God.

"Chapter 16. Christ miraculously widens or contracts gates, milk-pails, sieves or boxes, not properly made by Joseph, he not being skillful at his carpenter's trade. The King of Jerusalem gives Joseph an order for a throne. Joseph works on it for two years and makes it two spans too short. The King being angry with him, Jesus comforts him—commands him to pull one side of the throne while he pulls the other, and brings it to its proper dimensions.

"Chapter 19. Jesus, charged with throwing a boy from the roof of a house, miraculously causes the dead boy to speak and acquit him; fetches water for his mother, breaks the pitcher and miraculously gathers the water in his mantle and brings it home.

"Sent to a schoolmaster, refuses to tell his letters, and the schoolmaster going to whip him, his hand withers."

Further on in this quaint volume of rejected gospels is an epistle of St. Clement to the Corinthians, which was used in the churches and considered genuine fourteen or fifteen hundred years ago. In it this account of the fabled phœnix occurs:

"1. Let us consider that wonderful type of the resurrection, which is seen in the Eastern countries, that is to say, in Arabia.

"2. There is a certain bird called a phœnix. Of this there is never but one at a time, and that lives five hundred years. And when the time of its dissolution draws near, that it must die, it makes itself a nest of frankincense, and myrrh, and other spices, into which, when its time is fulfilled, it enters and dies.

"3. But its flesh, putrefying, breeds a certain worm, which, being nourished by the juice of the dead bird, brings forth feathers; and when it is grown to a perfect state, it takes up the nest in which the bones of its parent lie, and carries it from Arabia into Egypt, to a city called Heliopolis:

"4. And flying in open day in the sight of all men, lays it upon the altar of the sun, and so returns from whence it came.

"5. The priests then search into the records of the time, and find that it returned precisely at the end of five hundred years."

Business is business, and there is nothing like punctuality, especially in a phœnix.

The few chapters relating to the infancy of the Saviour contain many things which seem frivolous and not worth preserving. A large part of the remaining portions of the book read like good Scripture, however. There is one verse that ought not to have been rejected, because it so evidently prophetically refers to the general run of Congresses of the United States:

"199. They carry themselves high, and as prudent men; and though they are fools, yet would seem to be teachers."

I have set these extracts down, as I found them. Every where, among the cathedrals of France and Italy, one finds traditions of personages that do not figure in the Bible, and of miracles that are not mentioned in its pages. But they are all in this Apocryphal New Testament, and though they have been ruled out of our modern Bible, it is claimed that they were accepted gospel twelve or fifteen centuries ago, and ranked as high in credit as any. One needs to read this book before he visits those venerable cathedrals, with their treasures of tabooed and forgotten tradition.

They imposed another pirate upon us at Nazareth—another invincible Arab guard. We took our last look at the city, clinging like a whitewashed wasp's nest to the hill-side, and at eight o'clock in the morning, departed. We dismounted and drove the horses down a bridle-path which I think was fully as crooked as a corkscrew; which I know to be as steep as the downward sweep of a rainbow, and which I believe to be the worst piece of

WANT OF DIGNITY.

road in the geography, except one in the Sandwich Islands, which I remember painfully, and possibly one or two mountain trails in the Sierra Nevadas. Often, in this narrow path, the horse had to poise himself nicely on a rude stone step and then drop his fore-feet over the edge and down something more than half his own height. This brought his nose near the ground, while his tail pointed up toward the sky somewhere, and gave him the appearance of preparing to stand on his head. A horse can not look dignified in this position. We accomplished the long descent at last, and trotted across the great Plain of Esdraelon.

Some of us will be shot before we finish this pilgrimage. The pilgrims read " Nomadic Life " and keep themselves in a constant state of Quixotic heroism. They have their hands on their pistols all the time, and every now and then, when you least expect it, they snatch them out and take aim at Bedouins who are not visible, and draw their knives and make savage passes at other Bedouins who do not exist. I am in deadly peril always, for these spasms are sudden and irregular, and of course I can not tell when to be getting out of the way. If I am accidentally murdered, some time, during one of these romantic frenzies of the pilgrims, Mr. Grimes must be rigidly held to answer as an accessory before the fact. If the pilgrims would take deliberate aim and shoot at a man, it would be all right and proper—because that man would not be in any danger; but these random assaults are what I object to. I do not wish to see any more places like Esdraelon, where the ground is level and people can gallop. It puts melodramatic nonsense into the pilgrims' heads. All at once, when one is jogging along stupidly in the sun, and thinking about something ever so far away, here they come, at a stormy gallop, spurring and whooping at those ridgy old sore-backed plugs till their heels fly higher than their heads, and as they whiz by, out comes a little potato-gun of a revolver, there is a startling little pop, and a small pellet goes singing through the air. Now that I have begun this pilgrimage, I intend to go through with it, though sooth to say, nothing but the most desperate valor has kept me to my purpose up to the present time. I do not mind Bedouins,—I am not afraid of them ; because neither Bedouins nor ordinary Arabs have shown any disposition to harm us, but I *do* feel afraid of my own comrades.

Arriving at the furthest verge of the Plain, we rode a little way up a hill and found ourselves at Endor, famous for its witch. Her descendants are there yet. They were the wildest horde of half-naked savages we have found thus far. They swarmed out of mud bee-hives; out of hovels of the dry-goods box pattern; out of gaping caves under shelving rocks; out of crevices in the earth. In five minutes the dead solitude and silence of the place were no more, and a begging, screeching, shouting mob were struggling about the horses' feet and block-ing the way. "Bucksheesh! bucksheesh! bucksheesh! how-ajji, bucksheesh!" It was Magdala over again, only here the glare from the infidel eyes was fierce and full of hate. The population numbers two hundred and fifty, and more than half the citizens live in caves in the rock. Dirt, degradation and savagery are Endor's specialty. We say no more about Magdala and Deburieh now. Endor heads the list. It is worse than any Indian *campoodie*. The hill is barren, rocky, and for-bidding. No sprig of grass is visible, and only one tree. This is a fig-tree, which maintains a precarious footing among the rocks at the mouth of the dismal cavern once occupied by the veritable Witch of Endor. In this cavern, tradition says, Saul, the King, sat at midnight, and stared and trembled, while the earth shook, the thunders crashed among the hills, and out of the midst of fire and smoke the spirit of the dead prophet rose up and confronted him. Saul had crept to this place in the darkness, while his army slept, to learn what fate awaited him in the morrow's battle. He went away a sad man, to meet disgrace and death.

A spring trickles out of the rock in the gloomy recesses of the cavern, and we were thirsty. The citizens of Endor ob-jected to our going in there. They do not mind dirt; they do not mind rags; they do not mind vermin; they do not mind barbarous ignorance and savagery; they do not mind a reason-able degree of starvation, but they *do* like to be pure and holy before their god, whoever he may be, and therefore they shud-der and grow almost pale at the idea of Christian lips pollu-ting a spring whose waters must descend into their sanctified gulliets. We had no wanton desire to wound even *their* feelings or trample upon their prejudices, but we were out of water, thus early in the day, and were burning up with thirst. It was at this time, and under these circumstances, that I framed an aphorism which has already become celebrated. I said : "Necessity knows no law." We went in and drank.

We got away from the noisy wretches, finally, dropping them in squads and couples as we filed over the hills—the aged first, the infants next, the young girls further on ; the strong men ran beside us a mile, and only left when they had secured the last possible piastre in the way of bucksheesh.

In an hour, we reached Nain, where Christ raised the widow's son to life. Nain is Magdala on a small scale. It has no population of any consequence. Within a hundred yards of it is the original graveyard, for aught I know ; the tombstones lie flat on the ground, which is Jewish fashion in Syria. I believe the Moslems do not allow them to have upright tombstones. A Moslem grave is usually roughly plastered over and whitewashed, and has at one end an upright projection which is shaped into exceedingly rude attempts at ornamentation. In the cities, there is often no appearance of a grave at all ; a tall, slender marble tombstone, elaborately lettred, gilded and painted, marks the burial place, and this is surmounted by a turban, so carved and shaped as to signify the dead man's rank in life.

They showed a fragment of ancient wall which they said was one side of the gate out of which the widow's dead son was being brought so many centuries ago when Jesus met the procession :

"Now when he came nigh to the gate of the city, behold there was a dead man carried out, the only son of his mother, and she was a widow: and much people of the city was with her.

"And when the Lord saw her, he had compassion on her, and said, Weep not.

"And he came and touched the bier : and they that bare him stood still. And he said, Young man, I say unto thee, arise.

"And he that was dead sat up, and began to speak. And he delivered him to his mother.

"And there came a fear on all. And they glorified God, saying, That a great prophet is risen up among us; and That God hath visited his people."

A little mosque stands upon the spot which tradition says was occupied by the widow's dwelling. Two or three aged Arabs sat about its door. We entered, and the pilgrims broke specimens from the foundation walls, though they had to touch, and even step, upon the "praying carpets" to do it. It was almost the same as breaking pieces from the hearts of those old Arabs. To step rudely upon the sacred praying mats, with booted feet—a thing not done by any Arab—was to inflict pain upon men who had not offended us in any way. Suppose a party of armed foreigners were to enter a village church in America and break ornaments from the altar railings for curiosities, and climb up and walk upon the Bible and the pulpit cushions? However, the cases are different. One is the profanation of a temple of our faith—the other only the profanation of a pagan one.

We descended to the Plain again, and halted a moment at a well—of Abraham's time, no doubt. It was in a desert place. It was walled three feet above ground with squared and heavy blocks of stone, after the manner of Bible pictures. Around it some camels stood, and others knelt. There was a group of sober little donkeys with naked, dusky children clambering about them, or sitting astride their rumps, or pulling their tails. Tawny, black-eyed, barefooted maids, arrayed in rags and adorned with brazen armlets and pinchbeck ear-rings, were poising water-jars upon their heads, or drawing water from the well. A flock of sheep stood by, waiting for the shepherds to fill the hollowed stones with water, so that they might drink—stones which, like those that walled the well, were worn smooth and deeply creased by the chafing chins of a hundred generations of thirsty animals. Picturesque Arabs sat upon the ground, in groups, and solemnly smoked their long-stemmed chibouks. Other Arabs were filling black hog-skins with water—skins which, well filled, and distended with water till the short legs projected painfully out of the proper line, looked like the corpses of hogs bloated by drowning. Here was a grand Oriental picture which I had worshiped a thousand times in soft, rich steel engravings! But in the engra-

ving there was no desolation; no dirt; no rags; no fleas; no
ugly features; no sore eyes; no feasting flies; no besotted ignorance in the countenances; no raw places on the donkeys'
backs; no disagreeable jabbering in unknown tongues; no
stench of camels; no suggestion that a couple of tons of pow-

AN ORIENTAL WELL.

der placed under the party and touched off would heighten the
effect and give to the scene a genuine interest and a charm
which it would always be pleasant to recall, even though a
man lived a thousand years.

Oriental scenes look best in steel engravings. I can not be
imposed upon any more by that picture of the Queen of Sheba
visiting Solomon. I shall say to myself, You look fine, Mad-
am, but your feet are not clean, and you smell like a camel.

Presently a wild Arab in charge of a camel train recognized an old friend in Ferguson, and they ran and fell upon each other's necks and kissed each other's grimy, bearded faces upon both cheeks. It explained instantly a something which had always seemed to me only a far-fetched Oriental figure of speech. I refer to the circumstance of Christ's rebuking a Pharisee, or some such character, and reminding him that from

ARABS SALUTING.

him he had received no "kiss of welcome." It did not seem reasonable to me that men should kiss each other, but I am aware, now, that they did. There was reason in it, too. The custom was natural and proper; because people must kiss, and a man would not be likely to kiss one of the women of this country of his own free will and accord. One must travel, to learn. Every day, now, old Scriptural phrases that never possessed any significance for me before, take to themselves a meaning.

We journeyed around the base of the mountain—"Little Hermon,"—past the old Crusaders' castle of El Fuleh, and arrived at Shunem. This was another Magdala, to a fraction, frescoes and all. Here, tradition says, the prophet Samuel was born, and here the Shunamite woman built a little house upon the city wall for the accommodation of the prophet Elisha. Elisha asked her what she expected in return. It was a perfectly natural question, for these people are and were in the habit of proffering favors and services and then expecting and begging for pay. Elisha knew them well. He could not comprehend that any body should build for him that humble little chamber for the mere sake of old friendship, and with no selfish motive whatever. It used to seem a very impolite, not to say

35

a rude question, for Elisha to ask the woman, but it does not seem so to me now. The woman said she expected nothing. Then for her goodness and her unselfishness, he rejoiced her heart with the news that she should bear a son. It was a high reward—but she would not have thanked him for a daughter —daughters have always been unpopular here. The son was born, grew, waxed strong, died. Elisha restored him to life in Shunem.

We found here a grove of lemon trees—cool, shady, hung with fruit. One is apt to overestimate beauty when it is rare, but to me this grove seemed very beautiful. It *was* beautiful. I do not overestimate it. I must always remember Shunem gratefully, as a place which gave to us this leafy shelter after our long, hot ride. We lunched, rested, chatted, smoked our pipes an hour, and then mounted and moved on.

"FREE SONS OF THE DESERT."

As we trotted across the Plain of Jezreel, we met half a dozen Digger Indians (Bedouins) with very long spears in their hands, cavorting around on old crowbait horses, and spearing imaginary enemies; whooping, and fluttering their rags in the wind, and carrying on in every respect like a pack of hopeless lunatics. At last, here were the "wild, free sons of the desert, speeding over the plain like the wind, on their beautiful Arabian mares" we had read so much about and longed so much to see! Here were the "picturesque costumes!" This was the "gallant spectacle!" Tatterdemalion vagrants—cheap braggadocio—"Arabian mares" spined and necked like the ichthyosaurus in the museum, and humped and cornered like a dromedary! To glance at the genuine son of the desert is to take the romance out of him forever—to behold his steed is to long in charity to strip his harness off and let him fall to pieces.

Presently we came to a ruinous old town on a hill, the same being the ancient Jezreel.

Ahab, King of Samaria, (this was a very vast kingdom, for those days, and was very nearly half as large as Rhode Island) dwelt in the city of Jezreel, which was his capital. Near him lived a man by the name of Naboth, who had a vineyard. The King asked him for it, and when he would not give it, offered to buy it. But Naboth refused to sell it. In those days it was considered a sort of crime to part with one's inheritance at any price—and even if a man did part with it, it reverted to himself or his heirs again at the next jubilee year. So this spoiled child of a King went and lay down on the bed with his face to the wall, and grieved sorely. The Queen, a notorious character in those days, and whose name is a by-word and a reproach even in these, came in and asked him wherefore he sorrowed, and he told her. Jezebel said she could secure the vineyard; and she went forth and forged letters to the nobles and wise men, in the King's name, and ordered them to proclaim a fast and set Naboth on high before the people, and suborn two witnesses to swear that he had blasphemed. They did it, and the people stoned the accused by the city wall, and he died. Then Jezebel came and told the King, and said, Behold, Naboth is no more—rise up and seize the vineyard. So Ahab seized the vineyard, and went into it to possess it.   But the Prophet Elijah came to him there and read his fate to him, and the fate of Jezebel ; and said that in the place where dogs licked the blood of Naboth, dogs should also lick his blood—and he said, likewise, the dogs should eat Jezebel by the wall of Jezreel. In the course of time, the King was killed in battle, and when his chariot wheels were washed in the pool of Samaria, the dogs licked the blood.   In after years, Jehu, who was King of Israel, marched down against Jezreel, by order of one of the Prophets, and administered one of those convincing rebukes so common among the people of those days : he killed many kings and their subjects, and as he came along he saw Jezebel, painted and finely dressed, looking out of a window, and ordered that she be thrown down to him.   A servant did it, and Jehu's horse trampled her under foot.   Then Jehu went in and sat down to dinner ; and presently he said, Go and bury this cursed woman, for she is a King's daughter.   The spirit of charity came upon him too late, however, for the prophecy had already been fulfilled—the dogs had eaten her, and they " found no more of her than the skull, and the feet, and the palms of her hands."

Ahab, the late King, had left a helpless family behind him, and Jehu killed seventy of the orphan sons.   Then he killed all the relatives, and teachers, and servants and friends of the family, and rested from his labors, until he was come near to Samaria, where he met forty-two persons and asked them who they were ; they said they were brothers of the King of Judah. He killed them.   When he got to Samaria, he said he would show his zeal for the Lord ; so he gathered all the priests and people together that worshiped Baal, pretending that he was going to adopt that worship and offer up a great sacrifice ; and when they were all shut up where they could not defend themselves, he caused every person of them to be killed.   Then Jehu, the good missionary, rested from his labors once more.

We went back to the valley, and rode to the Fountain of Ain Jelûd.   They call it the Fountain of Jezreel, usually.   It is a pond about one hundred feet square and four feet deep, with a stream of water trickling into it from under an over-hanging ledge of rocks. It is in the midst of a great solitude. Here Gideon pitched his camp in the old times; behind Shu-nem lay the "Midianites, the Amalekites, and the Children of the East," who were "as grasshoppers for multitude; both they and their camels were without number, as the sand by the sea-side for multitude." Which means that there were one hundred and thirty-five thousand men, and that they had transportation service accordingly.

Gideon, with only three hundred men, surprised them in the night, and stood by and looked on while they butchered each other until a hundred and twenty thousand lay dead on the field.

We camped at Jenin before night, and got up and started again at one o'clock in the morning. Somewhere towards daylight we passed the locality where the best authenticated tradition locates the pit into which Joseph's brethren threw him, and about noon, after passing over a succession of moun-tain tops, clad with groves of fig and olive trees, with the Med-iterranean in sight some forty miles away, and going by many ancient Biblical cities whose inhabitants glowered savagely upon our Christian procession, and were seemingly inclined to practice on it with stones, we came to the singularly terraced and unlovely hills that betrayed that we were out of Galilee and into Samaria at last.

We climbed a high hill to visit the city of Samaria, where the woman may have hailed from who conversed with Christ at Jacob's Well, and from whence, no doubt, came also the cel-ebrated Good Samaritan. Herod the Great is said to have made a magnificent city of this place, and a great number of coarse limestone columns, twenty feet high and two feet through, that are almost guiltless of architectural grace of shape and ornament, are pointed out by many authors as evi-dence of the fact. They would not have been considered handsome in ancient Greece, however.

The inhabitants of this camp are particularly vicious, and stoned two parties of our pilgrims a day or two ago who brought about the difficulty by showing their revolvers when they did not intend to use them—a thing which is deemed bad judgment in the Far West, and ought certainly to be so considered any where. In the new Territories, when a man puts his hand on a weapon, he knows that he must use it; he must use it instantly or expect to be shot down where he stands. Those pilgrims had been reading Grimes.

There was nothing for us to do in Samaria but buy handfuls of old Roman coins at a franc a dozen, and look at a dilapidated church of the Crusaders and a vault in it which once contained the body of John the Baptist. This relic was long ago carried away to Genoa.

Samaria stood a disastrous siege, once, in the days of Elisha, at the hands of the King of Syria. Provisions reached such a figure that " an ass' head was sold for eighty pieces of silver and the fourth part of a cab of dove's dung for five pieces of silver."

An incident recorded of that heavy time will give one a very good idea of the distress that prevailed within these crumbling walls. As the King was walking upon the battlements one day, " a woman cried out, saying, Help, my lord, O King! And the King said, What aileth thee? and she answered, This woman said unto me, Give thy son, that we may eat him to-day, and we will eat my son to-morrow. So we boiled my son, and did eat him; and I said unto her on the next day, Give thy son that we may eat him; and she hath hid her son."

The prophet Elisha declared that within four and twenty hours the prices of food should go down to nothing, almost, and it was so. The Syrian army broke camp and fled, for some cause or other, the famine was relieved from without, and many a shoddy speculator in dove's dung and ass's meat was ruined.

We were glad to leave this hot and dusty old village and hurry on. At two o'clock we stopped to lunch and rest at ancient Shechem, between the historic Mounts of Gerizim and Ebal where in the old times the books of the law, the curses and the blessings, were read from the heights to the Jewish multitudes below.

CHAPTER LII.

THE narrow canon in which Nablous, or Shechem, is situated, is under high cultivation, and the soil is exceedingly black and fertile. It is well watered, and its affluent vegetation gains effect by contrast with the barren hills that tower on either side. One of these hills is the ancient Mount of Blessings and the other the Mount of Curses; and wise men who seek for fulfillments of prophecy think they find here a wonder of this kind—to wit, that the Mount of Blessings is strangely fertile and its mate as strangely unproductive. We could not see that there was really much difference between them in this respect, however.

Shechem is distinguished as one of the residences of the patriarch Jacob, and as the seat of those tribes that cut themselves loose from their brethren of Israel and propagated doctrines not in conformity with those of the original Jewish creed. For thousands of years this clan have dwelt in Shechem under strict *tabu*, and having little commerce or fellowship with their fellow men of any religion or nationality. For generations they have not numbered more than one or two hundred, but they still adhere to their ancient faith and maintain their ancient rites and ceremonies. Talk of family and old descent! Princes and nobles pride themselves upon lineages they can trace back some hundreds of years. What is this trifle to this handful of old first families of Shechem, who can name their fathers straight back without a flaw for thousands —straight back to a period so remote that men reared in a country where the days of two hundred years ago are called

" ancient " times grow dazed and bewildered when they try to comprehend it! Here is respectability for you—here is "family"—here is high descent worth talking about. This sad, proud remnant of a once mighty community still hold themselves aloof from all the world ; they still live as their fathers lived, labor as their fathers labored, think as they did, feel as they did, worship in the same place, in sight of the same landmarks, and in the same quaint, patriarchal way their ancestors did more than thirty centuries ago. I found myself gazing at any straggling scion of this strange race with a riveted fascination, just as one would stare at a living mastodon, or a megatherium that had moved in the grey dawn of creation and seen the wonders of that mysterious world that was before the flood.

Carefully preserved among the sacred archives of this curious community is a MSS. copy of the ancient Jewish law, which is said to be the oldest document on earth. It is written on vellum, and is some four or five thousand years old. Nothing but bucksheesh

SHECHEM.

can purchase a sight. Its fame is somewhat dimmed in these latter days, because of the doubts so many authors of Palestine travels have felt themselves privileged to cast upon it. Speaking of this MSS. reminds me that I procured from the high-priest of this ancient Samaritan community, at great expense, a secret document of still higher antiquity and far more extraordinary interest, which I propose to publish as soon as I have finished translating it.

Joshua gave his dying injunction to the children of Israel at Shechem, and buried a valuable treasure secretly under an oak tree there about the same time.   The superstitious Samaritans have always been afraid to hunt for it.   They believe it is guarded by fierce spirits invisible to men.

About a mile and a half from Shechem we halted at the base of Mount Ebal, before a little square area, inclosed by a high stone wall, neatly whitewashed.   Across one end of this inclosure is a tomb built after the manner of the Moslems.   It is the tomb of Joseph.   No truth is better authenticated than this.

When Joseph was dying he prophesied that exodus of the Israelites from Egypt which occurred four hundred years afterwards.   At the same time he exacted of his people an oath that when they journeyed to the land of Canaan, they would bear his bones with them and bury them in the ancient inheritance of his fathers.   The oath was kept.

"And the bones of Joseph, which the children of Israel brought up out of Egypt, buried they in Shechem, in a parcel of ground which Jacob bought of the sons of Hamor the father of Shechem, for a hundred pieces of silver."

Few tombs on earth command the veneration of so many races and men of divers creeds as this of Joseph.   "Samaritan and Jew, Moslem and Christian alike, revere it, and honor it with their visits.   The tomb of Joseph, the dutiful son, the affectionate, forgiving brother, the virtuous man, the wise Prince and ruler.   Egypt felt his influence—the world knows his history."

In this same "parcel of ground" which Jacob bought of the sons of Hamor for a hundred pieces of silver, is Jacob's celebrated well.   It is cut in the solid rock, and is nine feet square and ninety feet deep.   The name of this unpretending hole in the ground, which one might pass by and take no notice of, is as familiar as household words to even the children and the peasants of many a far-off country.   It is more famous than the Parthenon; it is older than the Pyramids.

It was by this well that Jesus sat and talked with a woman

of that strange, antiquated Samaritan community I have been speaking of, and told her of the mysterious water of life. As descendants of old English nobles still cherish in the traditions of their houses how that this king or that king tarried a day with some favored ancestor three hundred years ago, no doubt the descendants of the woman of Samaria, living there in Shechem, still refer with pardonable vanity to this conversation of their ancestor, held some little time gone by, with the Messiah of the Christians. It is not likely that they undervalue a distinction such as this. Samaritan nature is human nature, and human nature remembers contact with the illustrious, always.

For an offense done to the family honor, the sons of Jacob exterminated all Shechem once.

We left Jacob's Well and traveled till eight in the evening, but rather slowly, for we had been in the saddle nineteen hours, and the horses were cruelly tired. We got so far ahead of the tents that we had to camp in an Arab village, and sleep on the ground. We could have slept in the largest of the houses; but there were some little drawbacks: it was populous with vermin, it had a dirt floor, it was in no respect cleanly, and there was a family of goats in the only bedroom, and two donkeys in the parlor. Outside there were no inconveniences, except that the dusky, ragged, earnest-eyed villagers of both sexes and all ages grouped themselves on their haunches all around us, and discussed us and criticised us with noisy tongues till midnight. We did not mind the noise, being tired, but, doubtless, the reader is aware that it is almost an impossible thing to go to sleep when you know that people are looking at you. We went to bed at ten, and got up again at two and started once more. Thus are people persecuted by dragomen, whose sole ambition in life is to get ahead of each other.

About daylight we passed Shiloh, where the Ark of the Covenant rested three hundred years, and at whose gates good old Eli fell down and "brake his neck" when the messenger, riding hard from the battle, told him of the defeat of his people, the death of his sons, and, more than all, the capture of Israel's pride, her hope, her refuge, the ancient Ark her fore-

fathers brought with them out of Egypt. It is little wonder
that under circumstances like these he fell down and brake his
neck. But Shiloh had no charms for us. We were so cold
that there was no comfort but in motion, and so drowsy
we could hardly sit upon the horses.

After a while we came to a shapeless mass of ruins, which
still bears the name of Beth-el. It was here that Jacob lay
down and had that superb vision of angels flitting up and
down a ladder that reached from the clouds to earth, and
caught glimpses of their blessed home through the open gates
of Heaven.

The pilgrims took what was left of the hallowed ruin, and
we pressed on toward the goal of our crusade, renowned Jerusalem.

The further we went the hotter the sun got, and the more
rocky and bare, repulsive and dreary the landscape became.
There could not have been more fragments of stone strewn
broadcast over this part of the world, if every ten square feet
of the land had been occupied by a separate and distinct stone-
cutter's establishment for an age. There was hardly a tree or
a shrub any where. Even the olive and the cactus, those fast
friends of a worthless soil, had almost deserted the country.
No landscape exists that is more tiresome to the eye than that
which bounds the approaches to Jerusalem. The only difference between the roads and the surrounding country, perhaps,
is that there are rather more rocks in the roads than in the
surrounding country.

We passed Ramah, and Beroth, and on the right saw the
tomb of the prophet Samuel, perched high upon a commanding eminence. Still no Jerusalem came in sight. We hurried
on impatiently. We halted a moment at the ancient Fountain
of Beira, but its stones, worn deeply by the chins of thirsty
animals that are dead and gone centuries ago, had no interest
for us—we longed to see Jerusalem. We spurred up hill after
hill, and usually began to stretch our necks minutes before we
got to the top—but disappointment always followed:—more
stupid hills beyond—more unsightly landscape—no Holy City.

At last, away in the middle of the day, ancient bits of wall and crumbling arches began to line the way—we toiled up one more hill, and every pilgrim and every sinner swung his hat on high! Jerusalem!

Perched on its eternal hills, white and domed and solid, massed together and hooped with high gray walls, the venerable city gleamed in the sun. So small! Why, it was no larger than an American village of four thousand inhabitants, and no larger than an ordinary Syrian city of thirty thousand. Jerusalem numbers only fourteen thousand people.

We dismounted and looked, without speaking a dozen sentences, across the wide intervening valley for an hour or more; and noted those prominent features of the city that pictures make familiar to all men from their school days till their death. We could recognize the Tower of Hippicus, the Mosque of Omar, the Damascus Gate, the Mount of Olives,

GATE OF JERUSALEM.

the Valley of Jehoshaphat, the Tower of David, and the Garden of Gethsemane—and dating from these landmarks could tell very nearly the localities of many others we were not able to distinguish.

I record it here as a notable but not discreditable fact that not even our pilgrims wept. I think there was no individual in the party whose brain was not teeming with thoughts and images and memories invoked by the grand history of the venerable city that lay before us, but still among them all was no " voice of them that wept."

There was no call for tears. Tears would have been out of place. The thoughts Jerusalem suggests are full of poetry, sublimity, and more than all, dignity. Such thoughts do not find their appropriate expression in the emotions of the nursery.

Just after noon we entered these narrow, crooked streets, by the ancient and the famed Damascus Gate, and now for several hours I have been trying to comprehend that I am actually in the illustrious old city where Solomon dwelt, where Abraham held converse with the Deity, and where walls still stand that witnessed the spectacle of the Crucifixion.

CHAPTER LIII.

A FAST walker could go outside the walls of Jerusalem and walk entirely around the city in an hour. I do not know how else to make one understand how small it is. The appearance of the city is peculiar. It is as knobby with countless little domes as a prison door is with bolt-heads. Every house has from one to half a dozen of these white plastered domes of stone, broad and low, sitting in the centre of, or in a cluster upon, the flat roof. Wherefore, when one looks down from an eminence, upon the compact mass of houses (so closely crowded together, in fact, that there is no appearance of streets at all, and so the city looks solid,) he sees the knobbiest town in the world, except Constantinople. It looks as if it might be roofed, from centre to circumference, with inverted saucers. The monotony of the view is interrupted only by the great Mosque of Omar, the Tower of Hippicus, and one or two other buildings that rise into commanding prominence.

The houses are generally two stories high, built strongly of masonry, whitewashed or plastered outside, and have a cage of wooden lattice-work projecting in front of every window. To reproduce a Jerusalem street, it would only be necessary to up-end a chicken-coop and hang it before each window in an alley of American houses.

The streets are roughly and badly paved with stone, and are tolerably crooked—enough so to make each street appear to close together constantly and come to an end about a hundred yards ahead of a pilgrim as long as he chooses to walk in it. Projecting from the top of the lower story of many of the

houses is a very narrow porch-roof or shed, without supports
from below ; and I have several times seen cats jump across
the street from one shed to the other when they were out calling. The cats could have jumped double the distance without
extraordinary exertion. I mention these things to give an idea
of how narrow the streets are. Since a cat can jump across
them without the least inconvenience, it is hardly necessary to
state that such streets are too narrow for carriages. These
vehicles can not navigate the Holy City.

The population of Jerusalem is compose of Moslems, Jews,
Greeks, Latins, Armenians, Syrians, Copts, Abyssinians, Greek
Catholics, and a handful of Protestants. One hundred of the
latter sect are all that dwell now in this birthplace of Christianity. The nice shades of nationality comprised in the above
list, and the languages spoken by them, are altogether too
numerous to
mention. It
seems to me
that all the
races and
colors and
tongues of the
earth must be
represented
among the
fourteen thou-
sand souls
that dwell in
Jerusalem.
Rags, wretch-
edness, pover-

BEGGARS IN JERUSALEM.

ty and dirt, those signs and symbols that indicate the presence
of Moslem rule more surely than the crescent-flag itself,
abound. Lepers, cripples, the blind, and the idiotic, assail you
on every hand, and they know but one word of but one language apparently—the eternal " bucksheesh." To see the
numbers of maimed, malformed and diseased humanity that

throng the holy places and obstruct the gates, one might suppose that the ancient days had come again, and that the angel of the Lord was expected to descend at any moment to stir the waters of Bethesda. Jerusalem is mournful, and dreary, and lifeless. I would not desire to live here.

One naturally goes first to the Holy Sepulchre. It is right in the city, near the western gate; it and the place of the Crucifixion, and, in fact, every other place intimately connected with that tremendous event, are ingeniously massed together and covered by one roof—the dome of the Church of the Holy Sepulchre.

Entering the building, through the midst of the usual assemblage of beggars, one sees on his left a few Turkish guards—for Christians of different sects will not only quarrel, but fight, also, in this sacred place, if allowed to do it. Before you is a marble slab, which covers the Stone of Unction, whereon the Saviour's body was laid to prepare it for burial. It was found necessary to conceal the real stone in this way in order to save it from destruction. Pilgrims were too much given to chipping off pieces of it to carry home. Near by is a circular railing which marks the spot where the Virgin stood when the Lord's body was anointed.

Entering the great Rotunda, we stand before the most sacred locality in Christendom—the grave of Jesus. It is in the centre of the church, and immediately under the great dome. It is inclosed in a sort of little temple of yellow and white stone, of fanciful design. Within the little temple is a portion of the very stone which was rolled away from the door of the Sepulchre, and on which the angel was sitting when Mary came thither "at early dawn." Stooping low, we enter the vault—the Sepulchre itself. It is only about six feet by seven, and the stone couch on which the dead Saviour lay extends from end to end of the apartment and occupies half its width. It is covered with a marble slab which has been much worn by the lips of pilgrims. This slab serves as an altar, now. Over it hang some fifty gold and silver lamps, which are kept always burning, and the place is otherwise scandalized by trumpery gewgaws and tawdry ornamentation.

All sects of Christians (except Protestants,) have chapels under the roof of the Church of the Holy Sepulchre, and each must keep to itself and not venture upon another's ground. It has been proven conclusively that they can not worship together around the grave of the Saviour of the World in peace. The chapel of the Syrians is not handsome; that of the Copts is the humblest of them all. It is nothing but a dismal cavern, roughly hewn in the living rock of the Hill of Calvary. In one side of it two ancient tombs are hewn, which are claimed to be those in which Nicodemus and Joseph of Aramathea were buried.

As we moved among the great piers and pillars of another part of the church, we came upon a party of black-robed, animal-looking Italian monks, with candles in their hands, who were chanting something in Latin, and going through some kind of religious performance around a disk of white marble let into the floor. It was there that the risen Saviour appeared to Mary Magdalen in the likeness of a gardener. Near by was a similar stone, shaped like a star—here the Magdalen herself stood, at the same time. Monks were performing in this place also. They perform every where—all over the vast building, and at all hours. Their candles are always flitting about in the gloom, and making the dim old church more dismal than there is any necessity that it should be, even though it is a tomb.

We were shown the place where our Lord appeared to His mother after the Resurrection. Here, also, a marble slab marks the place where St. Helena, the mother of the Emperor Constantine, found the crosses about three hundred years after the Crucifixion. According to the legend, this great discovery elicited extravagant demonstrations of joy. But they were of short duration. The question intruded itself: "Which bore the blessed Saviour, and which the thieves?" To be in doubt, in so mighty a matter as this—to be uncertain which one to adore—was a grievous misfortune. It turned the public joy to sorrow. But when lived there a holy priest who could not set so simple a trouble as this at rest? One of these soon hit

36

upon a plan that would be a certain test. A noble lady lay very ill in Jerusalem. The wise priests ordered that the three crosses be taken to her bedside one at a time. It was done. When her eyes fell upon the first one, she uttered a scream that was heard beyond the Damascus Gate, and even upon the Mount of Olives, it was said, and then fell back in a deadly swoon. They recovered her and brought the second cross. Instantly she went into fearful convulsions, and it was with the greatest difficulty that six strong men could hold her. They were afraid, now, to bring in the third cross. They began to fear that possibly they had fallen upon the wrong crosses, and that the true cross was not with this number at all. However, as the woman seemed likely to die with the convulsions that were tearing her, they concluded that the third could do no more than put her out of her misery with a happy dispatch. So they brought it, and behold, a miracle! The woman sprang from her bed, smiling and joyful, and perfectly restored to health. When we listen to evidence like this, we can not but believe. We would be ashamed to doubt, and properly, too. Even the very part of Jerusalem where this all occurred is there yet. So there is really no room for doubt.

The priests tried to show us, through a small screen, a fragment of the genuine Pillar of Flagellation, to which Christ was bound when they scourged him. But we could not see it, because it was dark inside the screen. However, a baton is kept here, which the pilgrim thrusts through a hole in the screen, and then he no longer doubts that the true Pillar of Flagellation is in there. He can not have any excuse to doubt it, for he can feel it with the stick. He can feel it as distinctly as he could feel any thing.

Not far from here was a niche where they used to preserve a piece of the True Cross, but it is gone, now. This piece of the cross was discovered in the sixteenth century. The Latin priests say it was stolen away, long ago, by priests of another sect. That seems like a hard statement to make, but we know very well that it *was* stolen, because we have seen it ourselves in several of the cathedrals of Italy and France.

But the relic that touched us most was the plain old sword of that stout Crusader, Godfrey of Bulloigne—King Godfrey of Jerusalem. No blade in Christendom wields such enchantment as this—no blade of all that rust in the ancestral halls of Europe is able to invoke such visions of romance in the brain of him who looks upon it—none that can prate of such chivalric deeds or tell such brave tales of the warrior days of old. It stirs within a man every memory of the Holy Wars that has been sleeping in his brain for years, and peoples his thoughts with mail-clad images, with marching armies, with battles and with sieges. It speaks to him of Baldwin, and Tancred, the princely Saladin, and great Richard of the Lion Heart. It was with just such blades as these that these splendid heroes of romance used to segregate a man, so to speak, and leave the half of him to fall one way and the other half the other. This very sword has cloven hundreds of Saracen Knights from crown to chin in those old times when Godfrey wielded it. It was enchanted, then, by a genius that was under the command of King Solomon. When danger approached its master's tent it always struck the shield and clanged out a fierce alarm upon the startled ear of night. In times of doubt, or in fog or darkness, if it were drawn from its sheath it would point instantly toward the foe, and thus reveal the way —and it would also attempt to start after them of its own accord. A Christian could not be so disguised that it would not know him and refuse to hurt him—nor a Moslem so disguised that it would not leap from its scabbard and take his life. These statements are all well authenticated in many legends that are among the most trustworthy legends the good old Catholic monks preserve. I can never forget old Godfrey's sword, now. I tried it on a Moslem, and clove him in twain like a doughnut. The spirit of Grimes was upon me, and if I had had a graveyard I would have destroyed all the infidels in Jerusalem. I wiped the blood off the old sword and handed it back to the priest—I did not want the fresh gore to obliterate those sacred spots that crimsoned its brightness one day six hundred years ago and thus gave Godfrey warning that before the sun went down his journey of life would end.

Still moving through the gloom of the Church of the Holy Sepulchre we came to a small chapel, hewn out of the rock—

CHURCH OF THE HOLY SEPULCHRE.

a place which has been known as " The Prison of Our Lord " for many centuries. Tradition says that here the Saviour was confined just previously to the crucifixion. Under an altar by the door was a pair of stone stocks for human legs. These things are called the " Bonds of Christ," and the use they were once put to has given them the name they now bear.

The Greek Chapel is the most roomy, the richest and the showiest chapel in the Church of the Holy Sepulchre. Its altar, like that of all the Greek churches, is a lofty screen that extends clear across the chapel, and is gorgeous with gilding and pictures. The numerous lamps that hang before it are of gold and silver, and cost great sums.

But the feature of the place is a short column that rises from the middle of the marble pavement of the chapel, and marks the exact *centre of the earth*. The most reliable traditions tell us that this was known to be the earth's centre, ages ago, and that when Christ was upon earth he set all doubts upon the subject at rest forever, by stating with his own lips that the tradition was correct. Remember, He said that that particular column stood upon the centre of the world. If the centre of the world changes, the column changes its position accordingly. This column has moved three different times, of its own accord. This is because, in great convulsions of nature, at three different times, masses of the earth—whole ranges of mountains, probably—have flown off into space, thus lessening the diameter of the earth, and changing the exact locality of its centre by a point or two. This is a very curious and interesting circumstance, and is a withering rebuke to those philosophers who would make us believe that it is not possible for any portion of the earth to fly off into space.

To satisfy himself that this spot was really the centre of the earth, a sceptic once paid well for the privilege of ascending to the dome of the church to see if the sun gave him a shadow at noon. He came down perfectly convinced. The day was very cloudy and the sun threw no shadows at all; but the man was satisfied that if the sun had come out and made shadows it could not have made any for him. Proofs like these are not to be set aside by the idle tongues of cavilers. To such as are not bigoted, and are willing to be convinced, they carry a conviction that nothing can ever shake.

If even greater proofs than those I have mentioned are
wanted, to satisfy the headstrong and the foolish that this is
the genuine centre of the earth, they are here. The greatest
of them lies in the fact that from under this very column was
taken the *dust from which Adam was made*. This can surely
be regarded in the light of a settler. It is not likely that the
original first man would have been made from an inferior
quality of earth when it was entirely convenient to get first
quality from the world's centre. This will strike any reflecting mind forcibly. That Adam was formed of dirt procured
in this very spot is amply proven by the fact that in six thou-

THE GRAVE OF ADAM.

sand years
no man has
ever been
a b l e t o
prove that
the dirt was
not procured
here where-
of he was
made.

It is a
singular cir-
c u m s tance
that right
under the
roof of this
same great
church, and
not far away
from that
illus trious
c o l u m n,
Adam him-
self, the fa-
ther of the
human race,

lies buried. There is no question that he is actually buried in the grave which is pointed out as his—there can be none—because it has never yet been proven that that grave is not the grave in which he is buried.

The tomb of Adam! How touching it was, here in a land of strangers, far away from home, and friends, and all who cared for me, thus to discover the grave of a blood relation. True, a distant one, but still a relation. The unerring instinct of nature thrilled its recognition. The fountain of my filial affection was stirred to its profoundest depths, and I gave way to tumultuous emotion. I leaned upon a pillar and burst into tears. I deem it no shame to have wept over the grave of my poor dead relative. Let him who would sneer at my emotion close this volume here, for he will find little to his taste in my journeyings through Holy Land. Noble old man —he did not live to see me—he did not live to see his child. And I—I—alas, I did not live to see *him*. Weighed down by sorrow and disappointment, he died before I was born—six thousand brief summers before I was born. But let us try to bear it with fortitude. Let us trust that he is better off, where he is. Let us take comfort in the thought that his loss is our eternal gain.

The next place the guide took us to in the holy church was an altar dedicated to the Roman soldier who was of the military guard that attended at the crucifixion to keep order, and who—when the vail of the Temple was rent in the awful darkness that followed ; when the rock of Golgotha was split asunder by an earthquake ; when the artillery of heaven thundered, and in the baleful glare of the lightnings the shrouded dead flitted about the streets of Jerusalem—shook with fear and said, " Surely this was the Son of God !" Where this altar stands now, that Roman soldier stood then, in full view of the crucified Saviour—in full sight and hearing of all the marvels that were transpiring far and wide about the circumference of the Hill of Calvary. And in this self-same spot the priests of the Temple beheaded him for those blasphemous words he had spoken.

In this altar they used to keep one of the most curious relics

that human eyes ever looked upon—a thing that had power to
fascinate the beholder in some mysterious way and keep him
gazing for hours together. It was nothing less than the copper
plate Pilate put upon the Saviour's cross, and upon which he
wrote, "THIS IS THE KING OF THE JEWS." I think St. Helena,
the mother of Constantine, found this wonderful memento
when she was here in the third century. She traveled all over
Palestine, and was always fortunate. Whenever the good old
enthusiast found a thing mentioned in her Bible, Old or New,
she would go and search for that thing, and never stop until
she found it. If it was Adam, she would find Adam ; if it was
the Ark, she would find the Ark ; if it was Goliah, or Joshua,
she would find *them*. She found the inscription here that I
was speaking of, I think. She found it in this very spot, close
to where the martyred Roman soldier stood. That copper
plate is in one of the churches in Rome, now. Any one can
see it there. The inscription is very distinct.

We passed along a few steps and saw the altar built over
the very spot where the good Catholic priests say the soldiers
divided the raiment of the Saviour.

Then we went down into a cavern which cavilers say was
once a cistern. It is a chapel, now, however—the Chapel of
St. Helena. It is fifty-one feet long by forty-three wide. In
it is a marble chair which Helena used to sit in while she su-
perintended her workmen when they were digging and delving
for the True Cross. In this place is an altar dedicated to St.
Dimas, the penitent thief. A new bronze statue is here—a
statue of St. Helena. It reminded us of poor Maximilian, so
lately shot. He presented it to this chapel when he was about
to leave for his throne in Mexico.

From the cistern we descended twelve steps into a large
roughly-shaped grotto, carved wholly out of the living rock.
Helena blasted it out when she was searching for the true
cross. She had a laborious piece of work, here, but it was
richly rewarded. Out of this place she got the crown of
thorns, the nails of the cross, the true cross itself, and the cross
of the penitent thief. When she thought she had found every

thing and was about to stop, she was told in a dream to continue a day longer. It was very fortunate. She did so, and found the cross of the other thief.

The walls and roof of this grotto still weep bitter tears in memory of the event that transpired on Calvary, and devout pilgrims groan and sob when these sad tears fall upon them from the dripping rock. The monks call this apartment the "Chapel of the Invention of the Cross"—a name which is unfortunate, because it leads the ignorant to imagine that a tacit acknowledgment is thus made that the tradition that Helena found the true cross here is a fiction—an invention. It is a happiness to know, however, that intelligent people do not doubt the story in any of its particulars.

Priests of any of the chapels and denominations in the Church of the Holy Sepulchre can visit this sacred grotto to weep and pray and worship the gentle Redeemer. Two different congregations are not allowed to enter at the same time, however, because they always fight.

Still marching through the venerable Church of the Holy Sepulchre, among chanting priests in coarse long robes and sandals; pilgrims of all colors and many nationalities, in all sorts of strange costumes; under dusky arches and by dingy piers and columns; through a sombre cathedral gloom freighted with smoke and incense, and faintly starred with scores of candles that appeared suddenly and as suddenly disappeared, or drifted mysteriously hither and thither about the distant aisles like ghostly jack-o'-lanterns—we came at last to a small chapel which is called the "Chapel of the Mocking." Under the altar was a fragment of a marble column; this was the seat Christ sat on when he was reviled, and mockingly made King, crowned with a crown of thorns and sceptred with a reed. It was here that they blindfolded him and struck him, and said in derision, "Prophesy who it is that smote thee." The tradition that this is the identical spot of the mocking is a very ancient one. The guide said that Saewulf was the first to mention it. I do not know Saewulf, but still, I can not well refuse to receive his evidence—none of us can.

They showed us where the great Godfrey and his brother Baldwin, the first Christian Kings of Jerusalem, once lay buried by that sacred sepulchre they had fought so long and so valiantly to wrest from the hands of the infidel. But the niches that had contained the ashes of these renowned crusaders were empty. Even the coverings of their tombs were gone—destroyed by devout members of the Greek Church, because Godfrey and Baldwin were Latin princes, and had been reared in a Christian faith whose creed differed in some unimportant respects from theirs.

We passed on, and halted before the tomb of Melchisedek! You will remember Melchisedek, no doubt; he was the King who came out and levied a tribute on Abraham the time that he pursued Lot's captors to Dan, and took all their property from them. That was about four thousand years ago, and Melchisedek died shortly afterward. However, his tomb is in a good state of preservation.

When one enters the Church of the Holy Sepulchre, the Sepulchre itself is the first thing he desires to see, and really is almost the first thing he does see. The next thing he has a strong yearning to see is the spot where the Saviour was crucified. But this they exhibit last. It is the crowning glory of the place. One is grave and thoughtful when he stands in the little Tomb of the Saviour—he could not well be otherwise in such a place—but he has not the slightest possible belief that ever the Lord lay there, and so the interest he feels in the spot is very, very greatly marred by that reflection. He looks at the place where Mary stood, in another part of the church, and where John stood, and Mary Magdalen; where the mob derided the Lord; where the angel sat; where the crown of thorns was found, and the true cross; where the risen Saviour appeared—he looks at all these places with interest, but with the same conviction he felt in the case of the Sepulchre, that there is nothing genuine about them, and that they are imaginary holy places created by the monks. But the place of the Crucifixion affects him differently. He fully believes that he is looking upon the very spot where the Saviour gave up his life. He remembers that Christ was very celebrated, long before he came to Jerusalem; he knows that his fame was so great that crowds followed him all the time; he is aware that his entry into the city produced a stirring sensation, and that his reception was a kind of ovation; he can not overlook the fact that when he was crucified there were very many in Jerusalem who believed that he was the true Son of God. To publicly execute such a personage was sufficient in itself to make the locality of the execution a memorable place for ages; added to this, the storm, the darkness, the earthquake, the rending of the vail of the Temple, and the untimely waking of the dead, were events calculated to fix the execution and the scene of it in the memory of even the most thoughtless witness. Fathers would tell their sons about the strange affair, and point out the spot; the sons would transmit the story to their children, and thus a period of three hundred years would easily be spanned*—at which time Helena came and built a church upon Calvary to commemorate the death and burial of the Lord and preserve the sacred place in the memories of men; since that time there has always been a church there. It is not possible that there can be any mistake about the locality of the Crucifixion. Not half a dozen persons knew where they buried the Saviour, perhaps, and a burial is not a startling event, any how; therefore, we can be pardoned for unbelief in the Sepulchre, but not in the place of the Crucifixion. Five hundred years hence there will be no vestige of Bunker Hill Monument left, but America will still know where the battle was fought and where Warren fell. The crucifixion of Christ was too notable an event in Jerusalem, and the Hill of Calvary made too celebrated by it, to be forgotten in the short space of three hundred years. I climbed the stairway in the church which brings one to the top of the small inclosed pinnacle of rock, and looked upon the place where the true cross once stood, with a far more absorbing interest than I had ever felt in any thing earthly before. I could not believe that the

---

* The thought is Mr. Prime's, not mine, and is full of good sense. I borrowed it from his "Tent Life."—M. T.

three holes in the top of the rock were the actual ones the crosses stood in, but I felt satisfied that those crosses had stood so near the place now occupied by them, that the few feet of possible difference were a matter of no consequence.

When one stands where the Saviour was crucified, he finds it all he can do to keep it strictly before his mind that Christ was not crucified in a Catholic Church. He must remind himself every now and then that the great event transpired in the open air, and not in a gloomy, candle-lighted cell in a little corner of a vast church, up-stairs—a small cell all bejeweled and bespangled with flashy ornamentation, in execrable taste.

Under a marble altar like a table, is a circular hole in the marble floor, corresponding with the one just under it in which the true cross stood. The first thing every one does is to kneel down and take a candle and examine this hole. He does this strange prospecting with an amount of gravity that can never be estimated or appreciated by a man who has not seen the operation. Then he holds his candle before a richly engraved picture of the Saviour, done on a massy slab of gold, and wonderfully rayed and starred with diamonds, which hangs above the hole within the altar, and his solemnity changes to lively admiration. He rises and faces the finely wrought figures of the Saviour and the malefactors uplifted upon their crosses behind the altar, and bright with a metallic lustre of many colors. He turns next to the figures close to them of the Virgin and Mary Magdalen; next to the rift in the living rock made by the earthquake at the time of the Crucifixion, and an extension of which he had seen before in the wall of one of the grottoes below; he looks next at the show-case with a figure of the Virgin in it, and is amazed at the princely fortune in precious gems and jewelry that hangs so thickly about the form as to hide it like a garment almost. All about the apartment the gaudy trappings of the Greek Church offend the eye and keep the mind on the rack to remember that this is the Place of the Crucifixion—Golgotha—the Mount of Calvary. And the last thing he looks at is that which was also the first—the place where the true cross stood. That will chain him to the spot and compel him to look once more, and once again, after he has satisfied all curiosity and lost all interest concerning the other matters pertaining to the locality.

And so I close my chapter on the Church of the Holy Sepulchre—the most sacred locality on earth to millions and millions of men, and women, and children, the noble and the humble, bond and free. In its history from the first, and in its tremendous associations, it is the most illustrious edifice in Christendom. With all its clap-trap side-shows and unseemly impostures of every kind, it is still grand, reverend, venerable —for a god died there ; for fifteen hundred years its shrines have been wet with the tears of pilgrims from the earth's remotest confines ; for more than two hundred, the most gallant knights that ever wielded sword wasted their lives away in a struggle to seize it and hold it sacred from infidel pollution. Even in our own day a war, that cost millions of treasure and rivers of blood, was fought because two rival nations claimed the sole right to put a new dome upon it. History is full of this old Church of the Holy Sepulchre—full of blood that was shed because of the respect and the veneration in which men held the last resting-place of the meek and lowly, the mild and gentle, Prince of Peace!

CHAPTER LIV.

WE were standing in a narrow street, by the Tower of Antonio. "On these stones that are crumbling away," the guide said, "the Saviour sat and rested before taking up the cross. This is the beginning of the Sorrowful Way, or the Way of Grief." The party took note of the sacred spot, and moved on. We passed under the "Ecce Homo Arch," and saw the very window from which Pilate's wife warned her husband to have nothing to do with the persecution of the Just Man. This window is in an excellent state of preservation, considering its great age. They showed us where Jesus rested the second time, and where the mob refused to give him up, and said, "Let his blood be upon our heads, and upon our children's children forever." The French Catholics are building a church on this spot, and with their usual veneration for historical relics, are incorporating into the new such scraps of ancient walls as they have found there. Further on, we saw the spot where the fainting Saviour fell under the weight of his cross. A great granite column of some ancient temple lay there at the time, and the heavy cross struck it such a blow that it broke in two in the middle. Such was the guide's story when he halted us before the broken column.

We crossed a street, and came presently to the former residence of St. Veronica. When the Saviour passed there, she came out, full of womanly compassion, and spoke pitying words to him, undaunted by the hootings and the threatenings of the mob, and wiped the perspiration from his face with her handkerchief. We had heard so much of St. Veronica, and seen

VIEW OF JERUSALEM FROM THE NORTH EAST.

her picture by so many masters, that it was like meeting an old friend unexpectedly to come upon her ancient home in Jerusalem. The strangest thing about the incident that has made her name so famous, is, that when she wiped the perspiration away, the print of the Saviour's face remained upon the handkerchief, a perfect portrait, and so remains unto this day. We knew this, because we saw this handkerchief in a cathedral in Paris, in another in Spain, and in two others in Italy. In the Milan cathedral it costs five francs to see it, and at St. Peter's, at Rome, it is almost impossible to see it at any price. No tradition is so amply verified as this of St. Veronica and her handkerchief.

At the next corner we saw a deep indention in the hard stone masonry of the corner of a house, but might have gone heedlessly by it but that the guide said it was made by the elbow of the Saviour, who stumbled here and fell. Presently we came to just such another indention in a stone wall. The guide said the Saviour fell here, also, and made this depression with his elbow.

There were other places where the Lord fell, and others where he rested; but one of the most curious landmarks of ancient history we found on this morning walk through the crooked lanes that lead toward Calvary, was a certain stone built into a house—a stone that was so seamed and scarred that it bore a sort of grotesque resemblance to the human face. The projections that answered for cheeks were worn smooth by the passionate kisses of generations of pilgrims from distant lands. We asked "Why?" The guide said it was because this was one of "the very stones of Jerusalem" that Christ mentioned when he was reproved for permitting the people to cry "Hosannah!" when he made his memorable entry into the city upon an ass. One of the pilgrims said, "But there is no evidence that the stones *did* cry out—Christ said that if the people stopped from shouting Hosannah, the very stones *would* do it." The guide was perfectly serene. He said, calmly, "This is one of the stones that *would* have cried out." It was of little use to try to shake this fellow's simple faith—it was easy to see that.

And so we came at last to another wonder, of deep and abiding interest—the veritable house where the unhappy wretch once lived who has been celebrated in song and story for more than eighteen hundred years as the Wandering Jew. On the memorable day of the Crucifixion he stood in this old doorway with his arms akimbo, looking out upon the struggling mob that was approaching, and when the weary Saviour would have sat down and rested him a moment, pushed him rudely away and said, "Move on!" The Lord said, "Move on, thou, likewise," and the command has never been revoked from that day to this. All men know how that the miscreant upon whose head that just curse fell has roamed up and down the wide world, for ages and ages, seeking rest and never finding it—courting death but always in vain—longing to stop, in city, in wilderness, in desert solitudes, yet hearing always that relentless warning to march—march on! They say—do these hoary traditions—that when Titus sacked Jerusalem and slaughtered eleven hundred thousand Jews in her streets and by-ways, the Wandering Jew was seen always in the thickest of the fight, and that when battle-axes gleamed in the air, he bowed his head beneath them; when swords flashed their deadly lightnings, he sprang in their way; he bared his breast to whizzing javelins, to hissing arrows, to any and to every weapon that promised death and forgetfulness, and rest. But it was useless—he walked forth out of the carnage without a wound. And it is said that five hundred years afterward he followed Mahomet when he carried destruction to the cities of Arabia, and then turned against him, hoping in this way to win the death of a traitor. His calculations were wrong again. No quarter was given to any living creature but one, and that was the only one of all the host that did not want it. He sought death five hundred years later, in the wars of the Crusades, and offered himself to famine and pestilence at Ascalon. He escaped again—he could not die. These repeated annoyances could have at last but one effect—they shook his confidence. Since then the Wandering Jew has carried on a kind of desultory toying with the most promising of the aids and implements of destruction, but with small hope, as a general thing. He has speculated some in cholera and railroads, and has taken almost a lively interest in infernal machines and patent medicines. He is old, now, and grave, as becomes an age like his; he indulges in no light amusements save that he goes sometimes to executions, and is fond of funerals.

There is one thing he can not avoid; go where he will about the world, he must never fail to report in Jerusalem every fiftieth year. Only a year or two ago he was here for the thirty-seventh time since Jesus was crucified on Calvary. They say that many old people, who are here now, saw him then, and

THE WANDERING JEW.

had seen him before. He looks always the same—old, and withered, and hollow-eyed, and listless, save that there is about him something which seems to suggest that he is looking for some one, expecting some one—the friends of his youth, perhaps. But the most of them are dead, now. He always pokes about the

37

old streets looking lonesome, making his mark on a wall here and there, and eyeing the oldest buildings with a sort of friendly half interest; and he sheds a few tears at the threshold of his ancient dwelling, and bitter, bitter tears they are. Then he collects his rent and leaves again. He has been seen standing near the Church of the Holy Sepulchre on many a starlight night, for he has cherished an idea for many centuries that if he could only enter there, he could rest. But when he approaches, the doors slam to with a crash, the earth trembles, and all the lights in Jerusalem burn a ghastly blue! He does this every fifty years, just the same. It is hopeless, but then it is hard to break habits one has been eighteen hundred years accustomed to. The old tourist is far away on his wanderings, now. How he must smile to see a pack of blockheads like us, galloping about the world, and looking wise, and imagining we are finding out a good deal about it! He must have a consuming contempt for the ignorant, complacent asses that go skurrying about the world in these railroading days and call it traveling.

When the guide pointed out where the Wandering Jew had left his familiar mark upon a wall, I was filled with astonishment. It read:

"S. T.—1860—X."

All I have revealed about the Wandering Jew can be amply proven by reference to our guide.

The mighty Mosque of Omar, and the paved court around it, occupy *a fourth part* of Jerusalem. They are upon Mount Moriah, where King Solomon's Temple stood. This Mosque is the holiest place the Mohammedan knows, outside of Mecca. Up to within a year or two past, no Christian could gain admission to it or its court for love or money. But the prohibition has been removed, and we entered freely for bucksheesh.

I need not speak of the wonderful beauty and the exquisite grace and symmetry that have made this Mosque so celebrated —because I did not see them. One can not see such things at an instant glance—one frequently only finds out how really beautiful a really beautiful woman is after considerable acquaintance with her; and the rule applies to Niagara Falls, to majestic mountains and to mosques—especially to mosques.

The great feature of the Mosque of Omar is the prodigious rock in the centre of its rotunda. It was upon this rock that Abraham came so near offering up his son Isaac—this, at least, is authentic—it is very much more to be relied on than most of the traditions, at any rate. On this rock, also, the angel stood and threatened Jerusalem, and David persuaded him to spare the city. Mahomet was well acquainted with this stone. From it he ascended to heaven. The stone tried to follow him, and if the angel Gabriel had not happened by the merest good luck to be there to seize it, it would have done it. Very few people have a grip like Gabriel—the prints of his monstrous fingers, two inches deep, are to be seen in that rock to-day.

This rock, large as it is, is suspended in the air. It does not touch any thing at all. The guide said so. This is very wonderful. In the place on it where Mahomet stood, he left his foot-prints in the solid stone. I should judge that he wore about eighteens. But what I was going to say, when I spoke of the rock being suspended, was, that in the floor of the cavern under it they showed us a slab which they said covered a hole which was a thing of extraordinary interest to all Mohammedans, because that hole leads down to perdition, and every soul that is transferred from thence to Heaven must pass up through this orifice. Mahomet stands there and lifts them out by the hair. All Mohammedans shave their heads, but they are careful to leave a lock of hair for the Prophet to take hold of. Our guide observed that a good Mohammedan would consider himself doomed to stay with the damned for- ever if he were to lose his scalp-lock and die before it grew again. The most of them that I have seen ought to stay with the damned, any how, without reference to how they were barbered.

For several ages no woman has been allowed to enter the cavern where that important hole is. The reason is that one of the sex was once caught there blabbing every thing she knew about what was going on above ground, to the rapscallions in the infernal regions down below. She carried her gossiping to such an extreme that nothing could be kept private —nothing could be done or said on earth but every body in perdition knew all about it before the sun went down. It was about time to suppress this woman's telegraph, and it was promptly done. Her breath subsided about the same time.

The inside of the great mosque is very showy with variegated marble walls and with windows and inscriptions of elaborate mosaic. The Turks have their sacred relics, like the Catholics. The guide showed us the veritable armor worn by the great son-in-law and successor of Mahomet, and also the buckler of Mahomet's uncle. The great iron railing which surrounds the rock was ornamented in one place with a thousand rags tied to its open work. These are to remind Mahomet not to forget the worshipers who placed them there. It is considered the next best thing to tying threads around his finger by way of reminders.

Just outside the mosque is a miniature temple, which marks the spot where David and Goliah used to sit and judge the people.*

Every where about the Mosque of Omar are portions of pillars, curiously wrought altars, and fragments of elegantly carved marble—precious remains of Solomon's Temple. These have been dug from all depths in the soil and rubbish of Mount Moriah, and the Moslems have always shown a disposition to preserve them with the utmost care. At that portion of the ancient wall of Solomon's Temple which is called the Jew's Place of Wailing, and where the Hebrews assemble every Friday to kiss the venerated stones and weep over the fallen greatness of Zion, any one can see a part of the unquestioned and undisputed Temple of Solomon, the same consisting of three or four stones lying one upon the other, each of which is about twice as long as a seven-octave piano, and about as thick as such a piano is high. But, as I have remarked before, it is

---

* A pilgrim informs me that it was not David and Goliah, but David and Saul. I stick to my own statement—the guide told me, and he ought to know.

only a year or two ago that the ancient edict prohibiting
Christian rubbish like ourselves to *enter* the Mosque of Omar
and see the costly marbles that once adorned the inner Temple
was annulled. The designs wrought upon these fragments are
all quaint and peculiar, and so the charm of novelty is added
to the deep interest they naturally inspire. One meets with
these venerable scraps at every turn, especially in the neighboring Mosque el Aksa, into whose inner walls a very large number of them are carefully built for preservation. These pieces
of stone, stained and dusty with age, dimly hint at a grandeur
we have all been taught to regard as the princeliest ever seen
on earth; and they call up pictures of a pageant that is familiar

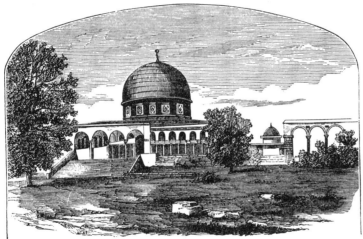

MOSQUE OF OMAR.

to all imaginations—camels laden with spices and treasure—
beautiful slaves, presents for Solomon's harem—a long cavalcade
of richly caparisoned beasts and warriors—and Sheba's Queen in
the van of this vision of "Oriental magnificence." These elegant fragments bear a richer interest than the solemn vastness
of the stones the Jews kiss in the Place of Wailing can ever
have for the heedless sinner.

Down in the hollow ground, underneath the olives and the

orange-trees that flourish in the court of the great Mosque, is a wilderness of pillars—remains of the ancient Temple; they supported it. There are ponderous archways down there, also, over which the destroying "plough" of prophecy passed harmless. It is pleasant to know we are disappointed, in that we never dreamed we might see portions of the actual Temple of Solomon, and yet experience no shadow of suspicion that they were a monkish humbug and a fraud.

We are surfeited with sights. Nothing has any fascination for us, now, but the Church of the Holy Sepulchre. We have been there every day, and have not grown tired of it; but we are weary of every thing else. The sights are too many. They swarm about you at every step; no single foot of ground in all Jerusalem or within its neighborhood seems to be without a stirring and important history of its own. It is a very relief to steal a walk of a hundred yards without a guide along to talk unceasingly about every stone you step upon and drag you back ages and ages to the day when it achieved celebrity.

It seems hardly real when I find myself leaning for a moment on a ruined wall and looking *listlessly* down into the historic pool of Bethesda. I did not think such things *could* be so crowded together as to diminish their interest. But in serious truth, we have been drifting about, for several days, using our eyes and our ears more from a sense of duty than any higher and worthier reason. And too often we have been glad when it was time to go home and be distressed no more about illustrious localities.

Our pilgrims compress too much into one day. One can gorge sights to repletion as well as sweetmeats. Since we breakfasted, this morning, we have seen enough to have furnished us food for a year's reflection if we could have seen the various objects in comfort and looked upon them deliberately. We visited the pool of Hezekiah, where David saw Uriah's wife coming from the bath and fell in love with her.

We went out of the city by the Jaffa gate, and of course were told many things about its Tower of Hippicus.

We rode across the Valley of Hinnom, between two of the

Pools of Gihon, and by an aqueduct built by Solomon, which still conveys water to the city. We ascended the Hill of Evil Counsel, where Judas received his thirty pieces of silver, and we also lingered a moment under the tree a venerable tradition says he hanged himself on.

We descended to the canon again, and then the guide began to give name and history to every bank and boulder we came to: "This was the Field of Blood; these cuttings in the rocks were shrines and temples of Moloch; here they sacrificed children; yonder is the Zion Gate; the Tyropean Valley; the Hill of Ophel; here is the junction of the Valley of Jehoshaphat—on your right is the Well of Job." We turned up Jehoshaphat. The recital went on. "This is the Mount of Olives; this is the Hill of Offense; the nest of huts is the Village of Siloam; here, yonder, every where, is the King's Garden; under this great tree Zacharias, the high priest, was murdered; yonder is Mount Moriah and the Temple wall; the tomb of Absalom; the tomb of St. James; the tomb of Zacharias; beyond, are the Garden of Gethsemane and the tomb of the Virgin Mary; here is the Pool of Siloam, and—"

We said we would dismount, and quench our thirst, and rest. We were burning up with the heat. We were failing under the accumulated fatigue of days and days of ceaseless marching. All were willing.

The Pool is a deep, walled ditch, through which a clear stream of water runs, that comes from under Jerusalem somewhere, and passing through the Fountain of the Virgin, or being supplied from it, reaches this place by way of a tunnel of heavy masonry. The famous pool looked exactly as it looked in Solomon's time, no doubt, and the same dusky, Oriental women, came down in their old Oriental way, and carried off jars of the water on their heads, just as they did three thousand years ago, and just as they will do fifty thousand years hence if any of them are still left on earth.

We went away from there and stopped at the Fountain of the Virgin. But the water was not good, and there was no comfort or peace any where, on account of the regiment of boys

and girls and beggars that persecuted us all the time for bucksheesh. The guide wanted us to give them some money, and
we did it; but when he went on to say that they were starving
to death we could not but feel that we had done a great sin in
throwing obstacles in the way of such a desirable consummation, and so we tried to collect it back, but it could not be
done.

We entered the Garden of Gethsemane, and we visited the
Tomb of the Virgin, both of which we had seen before. It is
not meet that I should speak of them now. A more fitting
time will come.

I can not speak now of the Mount of Olives or its view of
Jerusalem, the Dead Sea and the mountains of Moab; nor of
the Damascus Gate or the tree that was planted by King Godfrey of Jerusalem. One ought to feel pleasantly when he talks
of these things. I can not say any thing about the stone column that projects over Jehoshaphat from the Temple wall like
a cannon, except that the Moslems believe Mahomet will sit
astride of it when he comes to judge the world. It is a pity
he could not judge it from some roost of his own in Mecca,
without trespassing on *our* holy ground. Close by is the Golden
Gate, in the Temple wall—a gate that was an elegant piece of
sculpture in the time of the Temple, and is even so yet. From
it, in ancient times, the Jewish High Priest turned loose the
scapegoat and let him flee to the wilderness and bear away his
twelve-month load of the sins of the people. If they were to
turn one loose now, he would not get as far as the Garden of
Gethsemane, till these miserable vagabonds here would gobble
him up,* sins and all. *They* wouldn't care. Mutton-chops and
sin is good enough living for them. The Moslems watch the
Golden Gate with a jealous eye, and an anxious one, for they
have an honored tradition that when it falls, Islamism will fall,
and with it the Ottoman Empire. It did not grieve me any to
notice that the old gate was getting a little shaky.

We are at home again. We are exhausted. The sun has
roasted us, almost.

* Favorite pilgrim expression.

We have full comfort in one reflection, however. Our experiences in Europe have taught us that in time this fatigue will be forgotten; the heat will be forgotten; the thirst, the tiresome volubility of the guide, the persecutions of the beggars —and then, all that will be left will be pleasant memories of Jerusalem, memories we shall call up with always increasing interest as the years go by, memories which some day will become all beautiful when the last annoyance that incumbers them shall have faded out of our minds never again to return. School-boy days are no happier than the days of after life, but we look back upon them regretfully because we have forgotten our punishments at school, and how we grieved when our marbles were lost and our kites destroyed—because we have forgotten all the sorrows and privations of that canonized epoch and remember only its orchard robberies, its wooden sword pageants and its fishing holydays. We are satisfied. We can wait. Our reward will come. To us, Jerusalem and to-day's experiences will be an enchanted memory a year hence—a memory which money could not buy from us.

CHAPTER LV.

WE cast up the account. It footed up pretty fairly. There was nothing more at Jerusalem to be seen, except the traditional houses of Dives and Lazarus of the parable, the Tombs of the Kings, and those of the Judges; the spot where they stoned one of the disciples to death, and beheaded another; the room and the table made celebrated by the Last Supper; the fig-tree that Jesus withered; a number of historical places about Gethsemane and the Mount of Olives, and fifteen or twenty others in different portions of the city itself.

We were approaching the end. Human nature asserted itself, now. Overwork and consequent exhaustion began to have their natural effect. They began to master the energies and dull the ardor of the party. Perfectly secure now, against failing to accomplish any detail of the pilgrimage, they felt like drawing in advance upon the holyday soon to be placed to their credit. They grew a little lazy. They were late to breakfast and sat long at dinner. Thirty or forty pilgrims had arrived from the ship, by the short routes, and much swapping of gossip had to be indulged in. And in hot afternoons, they showed a strong disposition to lie on the cool divans in the hotel and smoke and talk about pleasant experiences of a month or so gone by—for even thus early do episodes of travel which were sometimes annoying, sometimes exasperating and full as often of no consequence at all when they transpired, begin to rise above the dead level of monotonous reminiscences and become shapely landmarks in one's memory. The fog-whistle, smothered among a million of trifling sounds, is not noticed a block away, in the city, but the sailor hears it far at sea, whither none of those thousands of trifling sounds can reach. When one is in Rome, all the domes are alike; but when he has gone away twelve miles, the city fades utterly from sight and leaves St. Peter's swelling above the level plain like an anchored balloon. When one is traveling in Europe, the daily incidents seem all alike; but when he has placed them all two months and two thousand miles behind him, those that were worthy of being remembered are prominent, and those that were really insignificant have vanished. This disposition to smoke, and idle and talk, was not well. It was plain that it must not be allowed to gain ground. A diversion must be tried, or demoralization would ensue. The Jordan, Jericho and the Dead Sea were suggested. The remainder of Jerusalem must be left unvisited, for a little while. The journey was approved at once. New life stirred in every pulse. In the saddle—abroad on the plains—sleeping in beds bounded only by the horizon: fancy was at work with these things in a moment.—It was painful to note how readily these town-bred men had taken to the free life of the camp and the desert. The nomadic instinct is a human instinct; it was born with Adam and transmitted through the patriarchs, and after thirty centuries of steady effort, civilization has not educated it entirely out of us yet. It has a charm which, once tasted, a man will yearn to taste again. The nomadic instinct can not be educated out of an Indian at all.

The Jordan journey being approved, our dragoman was notified.

At nine in the morning the caravan was before the hotel door and we were at breakfast. There was a commotion about the place. Rumors of war and bloodshed were flying every where. The lawless Bedouins in the Valley of the Jordan and the deserts down by the Dead Sea were up in arms, and were going to destroy all comers. They had had a battle with a troop of Turkish cavalry and defeated them; several men killed. They had shut up the inhabitants of a village and a

Turkish garrison in an old fort near Jericho, and were besieging them. They had marched upon a camp of our excursionists by the Jordan, and the pilgrims only saved their lives by stealing away and flying to Jerusalem under whip and spur in the darkness of the night. Another of our parties had been fired on from an ambush and then attacked in the open day. Shots were fired on both sides. Fortunately there was no bloodshed. We spoke with the very pilgrim who had fired one of the shots, and learned from his own lips how, in this imminent deadly peril, only the cool courage of the pilgrims, their strength of numbers and imposing display of war material, had saved them from utter destruction. It was reported that the Consul had requested that no more of our pilgrims should go to the Jordan while this state of things lasted; and further, that he was unwilling that any more should go, at least without an unusually strong military guard. Here was trouble. But with the horses at the door and every body aware of what they were there for, what would *you* have done? Acknowledged that you were afraid, and backed shamefully out? Hardly. It would not be human nature, where there were so many women. You would have done as we did: said you were not afraid of a million Bedouins—and made your will and proposed quietly to yourself to take up an unostentatious position in the rear of the procession.

I think we must all have determined upon the same line of tactics, for it did seem as if we never would get to Jericho. I had a notoriously slow horse, but somehow I could not keep him in the rear, to save my neck. He was forever turning up in the lead. In such cases I trembled a little, and got down to fix my saddle. But it was not of any use. The others all got down to fix their saddles, too. I never saw such a time with saddles. It was the first time any of them had got out of order in three weeks, and now they had all broken down at once. I tried walking, for exercise—I had not had enough in Jerusalem searching for holy places. But it was a failure. The whole mob were suffering for exercise, and it was not fifteen

minutes till they were all on foot and I had the lead again. It
was very discouraging.

AN EPIDEMIC.

This was all after we got beyond Bethany. We stopped at
the village of Bethany, an hour out from Jerusalem. They
showed us the tomb of Lazarus. I had rather live in it than
in any house in the town. And they showed us also a large
" Fountain of Lazarus," and in the centre of the village the
ancient dwelling of Lazarus. Lazarus appears to have been a
man of property. The legends of the Sunday Schools do him
great injustice; they give one the impression that he was poor.
It is because they get him confused with that Lazarus who had
no merit but his virtue, and virtue never has been as respectable as money. The house of Lazarus is a three-story edifice,
of stone masonry, but the accumulated rubbish of ages has
buried all of it but the upper story. We took candles and descended to the dismal cell-like chambers where Jesus sat at
meat with Martha and Mary, and conversed with them about
their brother. We could not but look upon these old dingy
apartments with a more than common interest.

We had had a glimpse, from a mountain top, of the Dead Sea, lying like a blue shield in the plain of the Jordan, and now we were marching down a close, flaming, rugged, desolate defile, where no living creature could enjoy life, except, perhaps, a salamander. It was such a dreary, repulsive, horrible solitude! It was the "wilderness" where John preached, with camel's hair about his loins—raiment enough—but he never could have got his locusts and wild honey here. We were moping along down through this dreadful place, every man in the rear. Our guards—two gorgeous young Arab sheiks, with cargoes of swords, guns, pistols and daggers on board—were loafing ahead.

"Bedouins!"

Every man shrunk up and disappeared in his clothes like a

CHARGE ON BEDOUINS.

mud-turtle. My first impulse was to dash forward and destroy the Bedouins. My second was to dash to the rear to see if there were any coming in that direction. I acted on the latter impulse. So did all the others. If any Bedouins had approached us, then, from that point of the compass, they would have paid dearly for their rashness. We all remarked that, afterwards. There would have been scenes of riot and bloodshed there that no pen could describe. I know that, because each man told what he would have done, individually; and such a medley of strange and unheard-of inventions of cruelty you could not conceive of. One man said he had calmly made up his mind to perish where he stood, if need be, but never yield an inch; he was going to wait, with deadly patience, till he could count the stripes upon the first Bedouin's jacket, and then count them and let him have it. Another was going to sit still till the first lance reached within an inch of his breast, and then dodge it and seize it. I forbear to tell what he was going to do to that Bedouin that owned it. It makes my blood run cold to think of it. Another was going to scalp such Bedouins as fell to his share, and take his bald-headed sons of the desert home with him alive for trophies. But the wild-eyed pilgrim rhapsodist was silent. His orbs gleamed with a deadly light, but his lips moved not. Anxiety grew, and he was questioned. If he had got a Bedouin, what would he have done with him—shot him? He smiled a smile of grim contempt and shook his head. Would he have stabbed him? Another shake. Would he have quartered him—flayed him? More shakes. Oh! horror, what *would* he have done?

"Eat him!"

Such was the awful sentence that thundered from his lips. What was grammar to a desperado like that? I was glad in my heart that I had been spared these scenes of malignant carnage. No Bedouins attacked our terrible rear. And none attacked the front. The new-comers were only a reinforcement of cadaverous Arabs, in shirts and bare legs, sent far ahead of us to brandish rusty guns, and shout and brag, and carry on like lunatics, and thus scare away all bands of marauding Bedouins that might lurk about our path. What a shame it is that armed white Christians must travel under guard of vermin like this as a protection against the prowling vagabonds of the desert—those sanguinary outlaws who are always going to do something desperate, but never do it. I may as well mention here that on our whole trip we saw no

Bedouins, and had no more use for an Arab guard than we could have had for patent leather boots and white kid gloves. The Bedouins that attacked the other parties of pilgrims so fiercely were provided for the occasion by the Arab guards of those parties, and shipped from Jerusalem for temporary service as Bedouins. They met together in full view of the pilgrims, after the battle, and took lunch, divided the bucksheesh extorted in the season of danger, and then accompanied the cavalcade home to the city! The nuisance of an Arab guard is one which is created by the Sheiks and the Bedouins together, for mutual profit, it is said, and no doubt there is a good deal of truth in it.

We visited the fountain the prophet Elisha sweetened (it is sweet yet;) where he remained some time and was fed by the ravens.

Ancient Jericho is not very picturesque as a ruin. When Joshua marched around it seven times, some three thousand years ago, and blew it down with his trumpet, he did the work so well and so completely that he hardly left enough of the city to cast a shadow. The curse pronounced against the rebuilding of it, has never been removed. One King, holding the curse in light estimation, made the attempt, but was stricken sorely for his presumption. Its site will always remain unoccupied; and yet it is one of the very best locations for a town we have seen in all Palestine.

At two in the morning they routed us out of bed—another piece of unwarranted cruelty—another stupid effort of our dragoman to get ahead of a rival. It was not two hours to the Jordan. However, we were dressed and under way before any one thought of looking to see what time it was, and so we drowsed on through the chill night air and dreamed of camp fires, warm beds, and other comfortable things.

There was no conversation. People do not talk when they are cold, and wretched, and sleepy. We nodded in the saddle, at times, and woke up with a start to find that the procession had disappeared in the gloom. Then there was energy and attention to business until its dusky outlines came in sight again. Occasionally the order was passed in a low voice down the line: "Close up—close up! Bedouins lurk here, every where!" What an exquisite shudder it sent shivering along one's spine!

We reached the famous river before four o'clock, and the night was so black that we could have ridden into it without seeing it. Some of us were in an unhappy frame of mind. We waited and waited for daylight, but it did not come. Finally we went away in the dark and slept an hour on the ground, in the bushes, and caught cold. It was a costly nap, on that account, but otherwise it was a paying investment because it brought unconsciousness of the dreary minutes and put us in a somewhat fitter mood for a first glimpse of the sacred river.

With the first suspicion of dawn, every pilgrim took off his clothes and waded into the dark torrent, singing:

> " On Jordan's stormy banks I stand,
>   And cast a wistful eye
> To Canaan's fair and happy land,
>   Where my possessions lie."

But they did not sing long. The water was so fearfully cold that they were obliged to stop singing and scamper out again. Then they stood on the bank shivering, and so chagrined and so grieved, that they merited honest compassion. Because another dream, another cherished hope, had failed. They had promised themselves all along that they would cross the Jordan where the Israelites crossed it when they entered Canaan from their long pilgrimage in the desert. They would cross where the twelve stones were placed in memory of that great event. While they did it they would picture to themselves that vast army of pilgrims marching through the cloven waters, bearing the hallowed ark of the covenant and shouting hosannahs, and singing songs of thanksgiving and praise. Each had promised himself that he would be the first to cross. They were at the goal of their hopes at last, but the current was too swift, the water was too cold!

It was then that Jack did them a service. With that engaging recklessness of consequences which is natural to youth, and so proper and so seemly, as well, he went and led the way across the Jordan, and all was happiness again. Every individual waded over, then, and stood upon the further bank. The water was not quite breast deep, any where. If it had been more, we could hardly have accomplished the feat, for the strong current would have swept us down the stream, and we would have been exhausted and drowned before reaching a place where we could make a landing. The main object compassed, the drooping, miserable party sat down to wait for the sun again, for all wanted to see the water as well as feel it. But it was too cold a pastime. Some cans were filled from the holy river, some canes cut from its banks, and then we mounted and rode reluctantly away to keep from freezing to death. So we saw the Jordan very dimly. The thickets of bushes that bordered its banks threw their shadows across its shallow, turbulent waters ("stormy," the hymn makes them, which is rather a complimentary stretch of fancy,) and we could not judge of the width of the stream by the eye. We knew by our wading experience, however, that many streets in America are double as wide as the Jordan.

Daylight came, soon after we got under way, and in the course of an hour or two we reached the Dead Sea. Nothing grows in the flat, burning desert around it but weeds and the Dead Sea apple the poets say is beautiful to the eye, but crumbles to ashes and dust when you break it. Such as we found were not

THE DEAD SEA.

handsome, but they were bitter to the taste. They yielded no dust. It was because they were not ripe, perhaps.

The desert and the barren hills gleam painfully in the sun, around the Dead Sea, and there is no pleasant thing or living creature upon it or about its borders to cheer the eye. It is a scorching, arid, repulsive solitude. A silence broods over the scene that is depressing to the spirits. It makes one think of funerals and death.

The Dead Sea is small. Its waters are very clear, and it has a pebbly bottom and is shallow for some distance out from the shores. It yields quantities of asphaltum; fragments of it lie all about its banks; this stuff gives the place something of an unpleasant smell.

All our reading had taught us to expect that the first plunge into the Dead Sea would be attended with distressing results —our bodies would feel as if they were suddenly pierced by millions of red-hot needles; the dreadful smarting would continue for hours; we might even look to be blistered from head to foot, and suffer miserably for many days. We were disappointed. Our eight sprang in at the same time that another party of pilgrims did, and nobody screamed once. None of them ever did complain of any thing more than a slight pricking sensation in places where their skin was abraded, and then only for a short time. My face smarted for a couple of hours, but it was partly because I got it badly sun-burned while I was bathing, and staid in so long that it became plastered over with salt.

No, the water did not blister us; it did not cover us with a slimy ooze and confer upon us an atrocious fragrance; it was not very slimy; and I could not discover that we smelt really any worse than we have always smelt since we have been in Palestine. It was only a different kind of smell, but not conspicuous on that account, because we have a great deal of variety in that respect. We didn't smell, there on the Jordan, the same as we do in Jerusalem; and we don't smell in Jerusalem just as we did in Nazareth, or Tiberias, or Cesarea Philippi, or any of those other ruinous ancient towns in Galilee. No, we change all the time, and generally for the worse. We do our own washing.

It was a funny bath. We could not sink. One could stretch himself at full length on his back, with his arms on his breast, and all of his body above a line drawn from the corner of his jaw past the middle of his side, the middle of his leg and through his ancle bone, would remain out of water. He could lift his head clear out, if he chose. No position can be retained long; you lose your balance and whirl over, first on your back and then on your face, and so on. You can lie comfortably, on your back, with your head out, and your legs out from your knees down, by steadying yourself with your hands. You can sit, with your knees drawn up to your chin and your arms clasped around them, but you are bound to turn over presently, because you are top-heavy in that position. You can stand up straight in water that is over your head, and from the middle of your breast upward you will not be wet. But you can not remain so. The water will soon float your feet to the surface. You can not swim on your back and make any progress of any consequence, because your feet stick away above the surface, and there is nothing to propel yourself with but your heels. If you swim on your face, you kick up the water like a stern-wheel boat. You make no headway. A horse is so top-heavy that he can neither swim nor stand up in the Dead Sea. He turns over on his side at once. Some of us bathed for more than an hour, and then came out coated with salt till we shone like icicles. We scrubbed it off with a coarse towel and rode off with a splendid brand-new smell, though it was one which was not any more disagreeable than those we have been for several weeks enjoying. It was the variegated villainy and novelty of it that charmed us. Salt crystals glitter in the sun about the shores of the lake. In places they coat the ground like a brilliant crust of ice.

When I was a boy I somehow got the impression that the river Jordan was four thousand miles long and thirty-five miles wide. It is only ninety miles long, and so crooked that a man does not know which side of it he is on half the time. In going ninety miles it does not get over more than fifty miles of ground. It is not any wider than Broadway in New York.

There is the Sea of Galilee and this Dead Sea—neither of them twenty miles long or thirteen wide. And yet when I was in Sunday School I thought they were sixty thousand miles in diameter.

Travel and experience mar the grandest pictures and rob us of the most cherished traditions of our boyhood. Well, let them go. I have already seen the Empire of King Solomon diminish to the size of the State of Pennsylvania; I suppose I can bear the reduction of the seas and the river.

We looked every where, as we passed along, but never saw grain or crystal of Lot's wife. It was a great disappointment. For many and many a year we had known her sad story, and taken that interest in her which misfortune always inspires. But she was gone. Her picturesque form no longer looms above the desert of the Dead Sea to remind the tourist of the doom that fell upon the lost cities.

I can not describe the hideous afternoon's ride from the Dead Sea to Mars Saba. It oppresses me yet, to think of it. The sun so pelted us that the tears ran down our cheeks once or twice. The ghastly, treeless, grassless, breathless canons smothered us as if we had been in an oven. The sun had positive *weight* to it, I think. Not a man could sit erect under it. All drooped low in the saddles. John preached in this "Wilderness!" It must have been exhausting work. What a very heaven the massy towers and ramparts of vast Mars Saba looked to us when we caught a first glimpse of them!

We staid at this great convent all night, guests of the hospitable priests. Mars Saba, perched upon a crag, a human nest stuck high up against a perpendicular mountain wall, is a world of grand masonry that rises, terrace upon terrace away above your head, like the terraced and retreating colonnades one sees in fanciful pictures of Belshazzar's Feast and the palaces of the ancient Pharaohs. No other human dwelling is near. It was founded many ages ago by a holy recluse who lived at first in a cave in the rock—a cave which is inclosed in the convent walls, now, and was reverently shown to us by the priests. This recluse, by his rigorous torturing of his flesh,

his diet of bread and water, his utter withdrawal from all society and from the vanities of the world, and his constant
prayer and saintly contemplation of a skull, inspired an emu-
lation that brought about him many disciples. The precipice
on the opposite side of the canon is well perforated with the
small holes they dug in the rock to live in. The present occupants of Mars Saba, about seventy in number, are all hermits.
They wear a coarse robe, an ugly, brimless stove-pipe of a hat,
and go without shoes. They eat nothing whatever but bread
and salt; they drink nothing but water. As long as they live
they can never go outside the walls, or look upon a woman—
for no woman is permitted to enter Mars Saba, upon any pretext whatsoever.

Some of those men have been shut up there for thirty years.
In all that dreary time they have not heard the laughter of a
child or the blessed voice of a woman; they have seen no
human tears, no human smiles; they have known no human
joys, no wholesome human sorrows. In their hearts are no
memories of the past, in their brains no dreams of the future.
All that is lovable, beautiful, worthy, they have put far away
from them; against all things that are pleasant to look upon,
and all sounds that are music to the ear, they have barred
their massive doors and reared their relentless walls of stone
forever. They have banished the tender grace of life and left
only the sapped and skinny mockery. Their lips are lips that
never kiss and never sing; their hearts are hearts that never
hate and never love; their breasts are breasts that never swell
with the sentiment, "I have a country and a flag." They are
dead men who walk.

I set down these first thoughts because they are natural—
not because they are just or because it is right to set them
down. It is easy for book-makers to say "I thought so and so
as I looked upon such and such a scene"—when the truth
is, they thought all those fine things afterwards. One's first
thought is not likely to be strictly accurate, yet it is no crime
to think it and none to write it down, subject to modification
by later experience. These hermits *are* dead men, in several

respects, but not in all; and it is not proper, that, thinking ill of them at first, I should go on doing so, or, speaking ill of them I should reiterate the words and stick to them. No, they treated us too kindly for that. There is something human about them somewhere. They knew we were foreigners and Protestants, and not likely to feel admiration or much friendliness toward them. But their large charity was above considering such things. They simply saw in us men who were hungry, and thirsty, and tired, and that was sufficient. They opened their doors and gave us welcome. They asked no questions, and they made no self-righteous display of their hospitality. They fished for no compliments. They moved quietly about, setting the table for us, making the beds, and bringing water to wash in, and paid no heed when we said it was wrong for them to do that when we had men whose business it was to perform such offices. We fared most comfortably, and sat late at dinner. We walked all over the building with the hermits afterward, and then sat on the lofty battlements and smoked while we enjoyed the cool air, the wild scenery and the sunset. One or two chose cosy bed-rooms to sleep in, but the nomadic instinct prompted the rest to sleep on the broad divan that extended around the great hall, because it seemed like sleeping out of doors, and so was more cheery and inviting. It was a royal rest we had.

When we got up to breakfast in the morning, we were new men. For all this hospitality no strict charge was made. We could give something if we chose; we need give nothing, if we were poor or if we were stingy. The pauper and the miser are as free as any in the Catholic Convents of Palestine. I have been educated to enmity toward every thing that is Catholic, and sometimes, in consequence of this, I find it much easier to discover Catholic faults than Catholic merits. But there is one thing I feel no disposition to overlook, and no disposition to forget: and that is, the honest gratitude I and all pilgrims owe, to the Convent Fathers in Palestine. Their doors are always open, and there is always a welcome for any worthy man who comes, whether he comes in rags or clad in purple. The Catholic Convents are a priceless blessing to the poor. A pilgrim without money, whether he be a Protestant or a Catholic, can travel the length and breadth of Palestine, and in the midst of her desert wastes find wholesome food and a clean bed every night, in these buildings. Pilgrims in better circumstances are often stricken down by the sun and the fevers of the country, and then their saving refuge is the Convent. Without these hospitable retreats, travel in Palestine would be a pleasure which none but the strongest men could dare to undertake. Our party, pilgrims and all, will always be ready and always willing, to touch glasses and drink health, prosperity and long life to the Convent Fathers of Palestine.

So, rested and refreshed, we fell into line and filed away over the barren mountains of Judea, and along rocky ridges and through sterile gorges, where eternal silence and solitude reigned. Even the scattering groups of armed shepherds we met the afternoon before, tending their flocks of long-haired goats, were wanting here. We saw but two living creatures. They were gazelles, of "soft-eyed" notoriety. They looked like very young kids, but they annihilated distance like an express train. I have not seen animals that moved faster, unless I might say it of the antelopes of our own great plains.

At nine or ten in the morning we reached the Plain of the Shepherds, and stood in a walled garden of olives where the shepherds were watching their flocks by night, eighteen centuries ago, when the multitude of angels brought them the tidings that the Saviour was born. A quarter of a mile away was Bethlehem of Judea, and the pilgrims took some of the stone wall and hurried on.

The Plain of the Shepherds is a desert, paved with loose stones, void of vegetation, glaring in the fierce sun. Only the music of the angels it knew once could charm its shrubs and flowers to life again and restore its vanished beauty. No less potent enchantment could avail to work this miracle.

In the huge Church of the Nativity, in Bethlehem, built fifteen hundred years ago by the inveterate St. Helena, they took us below ground, and into a grotto cut in the living rock. This was

GROTTO OF THE NATIVITY.

the "manger" where Christ was born. A silver star set in the floor bears a Latin inscription to that effect. It is polished with the kisses of many generations of worshiping pilgrims. The grotto was tricked out in the usual tasteless style observable in all the holy places of Palestine. As in the Church of the Holy Sepulchre, envy and uncharitableness were apparent here. The priests and the members of the Greek and Latin Churches can not come by the same corridor to kneel in the sacred birthplace of the Redeemer, but are compelled to approach and retire by different avenues, lest they quarrel and fight on this holiest ground on earth.

I have no "meditations," suggested by this spot where the very first "Merry Christmas!" was uttered in all the world, and from whence the friend of my childhood, Santa Claus, departed on his first journey, to gladden and continue to gladden roaring firesides on wintry mornings in many a distant land forever and forever. I touch, with reverent finger, the actual spot where the infant Jesus lay, but I think—nothing.

You *can not* think in this place any more than you can in any other in Palestine that would be likely to inspire reflection. Beggars, cripples and monks compass you about, and make you think only of bucksheesh when you would rather think of something more in keeping with the character of the spot.

I was glad to get away, and glad when we had walked through the grottoes where Eusebius wrote, and Jerome fasted, and Joseph prepared for the flight into Egypt, and the dozen other distinguished grottoes, and knew we were done. The Church of the Nativity is almost as well packed with exceeding holy places as the Church of the Holy Sepulchre itself. They even have in it a grotto wherein twenty thousand children were slaughtered by Herod when he was seeking the life of the infant Saviour.

We went to the Milk Grotto, of course—a cavern where Mary hid herself for a while before the flight into Egypt. Its walls were black before she entered, but in suckling the Child, a drop of her milk fell upon the floor and instantly changed the darkness of the walls to its own snowy hue. We took many little fragments of stone from here, because it is well known in all the East that a barren woman hath need only to touch her lips to one of these and her failing will depart from her. We took many specimens, to the end that we might confer happiness upon certain households that we wot of.

We got away from Bethlehem and its troops of beggars and relic-peddlers in the afternoon, and after spending some little time at Rachel's tomb, hurried to Jerusalem as fast as possible. I never was *so* glad to get home again before. I never have enjoyed rest as I have enjoyed it during these last few hours. The journey to the Dead Sea, the Jordan and Bethlehem was short, but it was an exhausting one. Such roasting heat, such oppressive solitude, and such dismal desolation can not surely exist elsewhere on earth. And *such* fatigue !

The commonest sagacity warns me that I ought to tell the customary pleasant lie, and say I tore myself reluctantly away from every noted place in Palestine. Every body tells that, but with as little ostentation as I may, I doubt the word of every he who tells it. I could take a dreadful oath that I have never heard any one of our forty pilgrims say any thing of the sort, and they are as worthy and as sincerely devout as any that come here. They will say it when they get home, fast enough, but why should they not ? They do not wish to array themselves against all the Lamartines and Grimeses in the world. It does not stand to reason that men are reluctant to leave places where the very life is almost badgered out of them by importunate swarms of beggars and peddlers who hang in strings to one's sleeves and coat-tails and shriek and shout in his ears and horrify his vision with the ghastly sores and malformations they exhibit. One is *glad* to get away. I have heard shameless people say they were glad to get away from Ladies' Festivals where they were importuned to buy by bevies of lovely young ladies. Transform those houris into dusky hags and ragged savages, and replace their rounded forms with shrunken and knotted distortions, their soft hands with scarred and hideous deformities, and the persuasive music of their voices with the discordant din of a hated language, and *then* see how much lingering reluctance to leave could be mustered. No, it is the neat thing to say you were reluctant, and then append the profound thoughts that " struggled for utterance," in your brain; but it is the true thing to say you were not reluctant, and found it impossible to think at all—though in good sooth it is not respectable to say it, and not poetical, either.

We do not think, in the holy places; we think in bed, afterwards, when the glare, and the noise, and the confusion are gone, and in fancy we revisit alone, the solemn monuments of the past, and summon the phantom pageants of an age that has passed away.

CHAPTER LVI.

W E visited all the holy places about Jerusalem which we had left unvisited when we journeyed to the Jordan, and then, about three o'clock one afternoon, we fell into procession and marched out at the stately Damascus gate, and the walls of Jerusalem shut us out forever. We paused on the summit of a distant hill and took a final look and made a final farewell to the venerable city which had been such a good home to us.

For about four hours we traveled down hill constantly. We followed a narrow bridle-path which traversed the beds of the mountain gorges, and when we could we got out of the way of the long trains of laden camels and asses, and when we could not we suffered the misery of being mashed up against perpendicular walls of rock and having our legs bruised by the passing freight. Jack was caught two or three times, and Dan and Moult as often. One horse had a heavy fall on the slippery rocks, and the others had narrow escapes. However, this was as good a road as we had found in Palestine, and possibly even the best, and so there was not much grumbling.

Sometimes, in the glens, we came upon luxuriant orchards of figs, apricots, pomegranates, and such things, but oftener the scenery was rugged, mountainous, verdureless and forbidding. Here and there, towers were perched high up on acclivities which seemed almost inaccessible. This fashion is as old as Palestine itself and was adopted in ancient times for security against enemies.

We crossed the brook which furnished David the stone that

killed Goliah, and no doubt we looked upon the very ground whereon that noted battle was fought. We passed by a picturesque old gothic ruin whose stone pavements had rung to the armed heels of many a valorous Crusader, and we rode through a piece of country which we were told once knew Samson as a citizen.

We staid all night with the good monks at the convent of Ramleh, and in the morning got up and galloped the horses a good part of the distance from there to Jaffa, or Joppa, for the plain was as level as a floor and free from stones, and besides this was our last march in Holy Land. These two or three hours finished, we and the tired horses could have rest and sleep as long as we wanted it. This was the plain of which Joshua spoke when he said, "Sun, stand thou still on Gibeon, and thou moon in the valley of Ajalon." As we drew near to Jaffa, the boys spurred up the horses and indulged in the excitement of an actual race—an experience we had hardly had since we raced on donkeys in the Azores islands.

We came finally to the noble grove of orange-trees in which the Oriental city of Jaffa lies buried; we passed through the walls, and rode again down narrow streets and among swarms of animated rags, and saw other sights and had other experiences we had long been familiar with. We dismounted, for the last time, and out in the offing, riding at anchor, we saw the ship! I put an exclamation point there because we felt one when we saw the vessel. The long pilgrimage was ended, and somehow we seemed to feel glad of it.

[For description of Jaffa, see Universal Gazetteer.] Simon the Tanner formerly lived here. We went to his house. All the pilgrims visit Simon the Tanner's house. Peter saw the vision of the beasts let down in a sheet when he lay upon the roof of Simon the Tanner's house. It was from Jaffa that Jonah sailed when he was told to go and prophesy against Nineveh, and no doubt it was not far from the town that the whale threw him up when he discovered that he had no ticket. Jonah was disobedient, and of a fault-finding, complaining disposition, and deserves to be lightly spoken of, almost. The timbers used in the construction of Solomon's temple were floated to Jaffa in rafts, and the narrow opening in the reef through which they passed to the shore is not an inch wider or a shade less dangerous to navigate than it was then. Such is the sleepy nature of the population Palestine's only good seaport has now and always had. Jaffa has a history and a stirring one. It will not be discovered any where in this book. If the reader will call at the circulating library and mention my name, he will be furnished with books which will afford him the fullest information concerning Jaffa.

So ends the pilgrimage. We ought to be glad that we did not make it for the purpose of feasting our eyes upon fascinating aspects of nature, for we should have been disappointed— at least at this season of the year. A writer in "Life in the Holy Land" observes :

"Monotonous and uninviting as much of the Holy Land will appear to persons accustomed to the almost constant verdure of flowers, ample streams and varied surface of our own country, we must remember that its aspect to the Israelites after the weary march of forty years through the desert must have been very different."

Which all of us will freely grant. But it truly *is* "monotonous and uninviting," and there is no sufficient reason for describing it as being otherwise.

Of all the lands there are for dismal scenery, I think Palestine must be the prince. The hills are barren, they are dull of color, they are unpicturesque in shape. The valleys are unsightly deserts fringed with a feeble vegetation that has an expression about it of being sorrowful and despondent. The Dead Sea and the Sea of Galilee sleep in the midst of a vast stretch of hill and plain wherein the eye rests upon no pleasant tint, no striking object, no soft picture dreaming in a purple haze or mottled with the shadows of the clouds. Every outline is harsh, every feature is distinct, there is no perspective—distance works no enchantment here. It is a hopeless, dreary, heart-broken land.

Small shreds and patches of it must be very beautiful in the full flush of spring, however, and all the more beautiful by

JAFFA.

contrast with the far-reaching desolation that surrounds them on every side. I would like much to see the fringes of the Jordan in spring-time, and Shechem, Esdraelon, Ajalon and the borders of Galilee—but even then these spots would seem mere toy gardens set at wide intervals in the waste of a limitless desolation.

Palestine sits in sackcloth and ashes. Over it broods the spell of a curse that has withered its fields and fettered its energies. Where Sodom and Gomorrah reared their domes and towers, that solemn sea now floods the plain, in whose bitter waters no living thing exists—over whose waveless surface the blistering air hangs motionless and dead—about whose borders nothing grows but weeds, and scattering tufts of cane, and that treacherous fruit that promises refreshment to parching lips, but turns to ashes at the touch. Nazareth is forlorn; about that ford of Jordan where the hosts of Israel entered the Promised Land with songs of rejoicing, one finds only a squalid camp of fantastic Bedouins of the desert; Jericho the accursed, lies a moldering ruin, to-day, even as Joshua's miracle left it more than three thousand years ago; Bethlehem and Bethany, in their poverty and their humiliation, have nothing about them now to remind one that they once knew the high honor of the Saviour's presence; the hallowed spot where the shepherds watched their flocks by night, and where the angels sang Peace on earth, good will to men, is untenanted by any living creature, and unblessed by any feature that is pleasant to the eye. Renowned Jerusalem itself, the stateliest name in history, has lost all its ancient grandeur, and is become a pauper village; the riches of Solomon are no longer there to compel the admiration of visiting Oriental queens; the wonderful temple which was the pride and the glory of Israel, is gone, and the Ottoman crescent is lifted above the spot where, on that most memorable day in the annals of the world, they reared the Holy Cross. The noted Sea of Galilee, where Roman fleets once rode at anchor and the disciples of the Saviour sailed in their ships, was long ago deserted by the devotees of war and commerce, and its borders are a silent wilderness; Capernaum is a shapeless ruin; Magdala is the home of beggared Arabs; Bethsaida and Chorazin have vanished from the earth, and the " desert places" round about them where thousands of men once listened to the Saviour's voice and ate the miraculous bread, sleep in the hush of a solitude that is inhabited only by birds of prey and skulking foxes.

Palestine is desolate and unlovely. And why should it be otherwise? Can the *curse* of the Deity beautify a land?

Palestine is no more of this work-day world. It is sacred to poetry and tradition—it is dream-land.

CHAPTER LVII.

IT was worth a kingdom to be at sea again. It was a relief to drop all anxiety whatsoever—all questions as to where we should go; how long we should stay; whether it were worth while to go or not; all anxieties about the condition of the horses; all such questions as "Shall we *ever* get to water?" "Shall we *ever* lunch?" "Ferguson, how many *more* million miles have we got to creep under this awful sun before we camp?" It was a relief to cast all these torturing little anxieties far away—ropes of steel they were, and every one with a separate and distinct strain on it—and feel the temporary contentment that is born of the banishment of all care and responsibility. We did not look at the compass: we did not care, now, where the ship went to, so that she went out of sight of land as quickly as possible. When I travel again, I wish to go in a pleasure ship. No amount of money could have purchased for us, in a strange vessel and among unfamiliar faces, the perfect satisfaction and the sense of being *at home* again which we experienced when we stepped on board the "Quaker City,"—*our own ship*—after this wearisome pilgrimage. It is a something we have felt always when we returned to her, and a something we had no desire to sell.

We took off our blue woollen shirts, our spurs, and heavy boots, our sanguinary revolvers and our buckskin-seated pantaloons, and got shaved and came out in Christian costume once more. All but Jack, who changed all other articles of his dress, but clung to his traveling pantaloons. They still preserved their ample buckskin seat intact; and so his short peajacket and his long, thin legs assisted to make him a pictu-

39

resque object whenever he stood on the forecastle looking abroad upon the ocean over the bows. At such times his father's last injunction suggested itself to me. He said:

" Jack, my boy, you are about to go among a brilliant company of gentlemen and ladies, who are refined and cultivated, and thoroughly accomplished in the manners and customs of good society. Listen to their conversation, study their habits of life, and learn. Be polite and obliging to all, and considerate towards every one's opinions, failings and prejudices. Command the just respect of all your fellow-voyagers, even though you fail to win their friendly regard. And Jack—don't you ever dare, while you live, appear in public on those decks in fair weather, in a costume unbecoming your mother's drawing-room !"

REAR ELEVATION OF JACK.

It would have been worth any price if the father of this hopeful youth could have stepped on board some time, and seen him standing high on the fore-castle, pea-jacket, tasseled red fez, buckskin patch and all, — placidly contemplating the ocean—a rare spectacle for any body's drawing-room.

After a pleasant voyage and a good rest, we drew near to Egypt and out of the mellowest of sunsets we saw the domes and minarets of Alexandria rise into view. As soon as the anchor was down, Jack and I got a boat and went ashore. It was night by this time, and the other passengers were content to remain at home and visit ancient Egypt after breakfast. It was the way they did at Constantinople. They took a lively interest in new countries, but their school-boy impatience had worn off, and they had learned that it was wisdom to take things easy and go along comfortably—these old countries do not go away in the night; they stay till after breakfast.

When we reached the pier we found an army of Egyptian boys with donkeys no larger than themselves, waiting for passengers—for donkeys are the omnibuses of Egypt. We preferred to walk, but we could not have our own way. The boys crowded about us, clamored around us, and slewed their donkeys exactly across our path, no matter which way we turned. They were good-natured rascals, and so were the donkeys. We mounted, and the boys ran behind us and kept the donkeys in a furious gallop, as is the fashion at Damascus.

STREET IN ALEXANDRIA.

I believe I would rather ride a donkey than any beast in the world. He goes briskly, he puts on no airs, he is docile, though

opinionated. Satan himself could not scare him, and he is convenient—very convenient. When you are tired riding you can
rest your feet on the ground and let him gallop from under you.

We found the hotel and secured rooms, and were happy to
know that the Prince of Wales had stopped there once. They
had it every where on signs. No other princes had stopped
there since, till Jack and I came. We went abroad through
the town, then, and found it a city of huge commercial buildings, and broad, handsome streets brilliant with gas-light. By
night it was a sort of reminiscence of Paris. But finally Jack
found an ice-cream saloon, and that closed investigations for
that evening. The weather was very hot, it had been many a
day since Jack had seen ice-cream, and so it was useless to
talk of leaving the saloon till it shut up.

In the morning the lost tribes of America came ashore and
infested the hotels and took possession of all the donkeys and
other open barouches that offered. They went in picturesque
procession to the American Consul's; to the great gardens; to
Cleopatra's Needles; to
Pompey's Pillar; to the
palace of the Viceroy of
Egypt; to the Nile; to
the superb groves of date-
palms. One of our most
inveterate relic-hunters
had his hammer with
him, and tried to break a
fragment off the upright
Needle and could not do
it; he tried the prostrate
one and failed; he bor-
rowed a heavy sledge
hammer from a mason
and failed again. He
tried Pompey's Pillar, and

VICEROY OF EGYPT.

this baffled him. Scattered all about the mighty monolith were
sphinxes of noble countenance, carved out of Egyptian granite as

hard as blue steel, and whose shapely features the wear of five thousand years had failed to mark or mar. The relic-hunter battered at these persistently, and sweated profusely over his work. He might as well have attempted to deface the moon. They regarded him serenely with the stately smile they had worn so long, and which seemed to say, "Peck away, poor insect; we were not made to fear such as you; in ten-score dragging ages we have seen more of your kind than there are sands at your feet: have they left a blemish upon us?"

But I am forgetting the Jaffa Colonists. At Jaffa we had taken on board some forty members of a very celebrated community. They were male and female; babies, young boys and young girls; young married people, and some who had passed a shade beyond the prime of life. I refer to the "Adams Jaffa Colony." Others had deserted before. We left in Jaffa Mr. Adams, his wife, and fifteen unfortunates who not only had no money but did not know where to turn or whither to go. Such was the statement made to us. Our forty were miserable enough in the first place, and they lay about the decks seasick all the voyage, which about completed their misery, I take it. However, one or two young men remained upright, and by constant persecution we wormed out of them some little information. They gave it reluctantly and in a very fragmentary condition, for, having been shamefully humbugged by their prophet, they felt humiliated and unhappy. In such circumstances people do not like to talk.

The colony was a complete *fiasco*. I have already said that such as could get away did so, from time to time. The prophet Adams—once an actor, then several other things, afterward a Mormon and a missionary, always an adventurer—remains at Jaffa with his handful of sorrowful subjects. The forty we brought away with us were chiefly destitute, though not all of them. They wished to get to Egypt. What might become of them then they did not know and probably did not care—any thing to get away from hated Jaffa. They had little to hope for. Because after many appeals to the sympathies of

New England, made by strangers of Boston, through the news-papers, and after the establishment of an office there for the reception of moneyed contributions for the Jaffa colonists,

EASTERN MONARCH.

One Dollar was sub-scribed. The consul-general for Egypt showed me the news-paper paragraph which mentioned the circumstance and men-tioned also the discon-tinuance of the effort and the closing of the office. It was evident that practical New England was not sorry to be rid of such vis-ionaries and was not in the least inclined to hire any body to bring them back to her. Still, to get to Egypt, was something, in the eyes of the unfortunate colonists, hopeless as the prospect seemed of ever getting further.

Thus circumstanced, they landed at Alexandria from our ship. One of our passengers, Mr. Moses S. Beach, of the New York *Sun*, inquired of the consul-general what it would cost to send these people to their home in Maine by the way of Liverpool, and he said fifteen hundred dollars in gold would do it. Mr. Beach gave his check for the money and so the troubles of the Jaffa colonists were at an end.*

Alexandria was too much like a European city to be novel, and we soon tired of it. We took the cars and came up here

---

* It was an unselfish act of benevolence; it was done without any ostentation, and has never been mentioned in any newspaper, I think. Therefore it is refresh-ing to learn now, several months after the above narrative was written, that another man received all the credit of this rescue of the colonists. Such is life.

to ancient Cairo, which *is* an Oriental city and of the completest pattern. There is little about it to disabuse one's mind

of the error if he should take it into his head that he was in the heart of Arabia. Stately camels and dromedaries, swarthy Egyptians, and likewise Turks and black Ethiopians, turbaned, sashed, and blazing in a rich variety of Oriental costumes of all shades of flashy colors, are what one sees on every hand crowding the narrow streets and the honeycombed bazaars. We are stopping at Shepherd's Hotel,

MOSES S. BEACH.

which is the worst on earth except the one I stopped at once in a small town in the United States. It is pleasant to read this sketch in my note-book, now, and know that I can stand Shepherd's Hotel, sure, because I have been in one just like it in America and survived:

I stopped at the Benton House. It used to be a good hotel, but that proves nothing—I used to be a good boy, for that matter. Both of us have lost character of late years. The Benton is not a good hotel. The Benton lacks a very great deal of being a good hotel. Perdition is full of better hotels than the Benton.

It was late at night when I got there, and I told the clerk I would like plenty of lights, because I wanted to read an hour or two. When I reached No. 15 with the porter (we came along a dim hall that was clad in ancient carpeting, faded, worn out in many places, and patched with old scraps of oil cloth—a hall that sank under one's feet, and creaked dismally to every footstep,) he struck a light—two inches of sallow, sorrowful, consumptive tallow candle, that burned blue, and sputtered, and got discouraged and went out. The porter lit it again, and I asked if that was all the light the clerk sent. He said, "Oh no, I've got another one here," and he produced another couple of inches of tallow candle. I said, "Light them both —I'll have to have one to see the other by." He did it, but the result was drearier than darkness itself. He was a cheery, accommodating rascal. He said he would go "somewheres" and steal a lamp. I abetted and encouraged him in his criminal design. I heard the landlord get after him in the hall ten minutes afterward.

"Where are you going with that lamp?"

"Fifteen wants it, sir."

"Fifteen! why he's got a double lot of candles—does the man want to illuminate the house?—does he want to get up a torch-light procession?—what *is* he up to, any how?"

"He don't like them candles—says he wants a lamp."

"Why what in the nation does—why I never heard of such a thing? What on earth can he want with that lamp?"

"Well, he only wants to read—that's what he says."

"Wants to read, does he?—ain't satisfied with a thousand candles, but has to have a lamp!—I do wonder what the devil that fellow wants that lamp for? Take him another candle, and then if——"

"But he wants the lamp—says he'll burn the d—d old house down if he don't get a lamp!" (a remark which I never made.)

"I'd like to see him at it once. Well, you take it along—but I swear it beats *my* time, though—and see if you can't find out what in the very nation he *wants* with that lamp."

And he went off growling to himself and still wondering and wondering over the unaccountable conduct of No. 15. The lamp was a good one, but it revealed some disagreeable things—a bed in the suburbs of a desert of room—a bed that had hills and valleys in it, and you'd have to accommodate your body to the impression left in it by the man that slept there last, before you could lie comfortably; a carpet that had seen better days; a melancholy washstand in a remote corner, and a dejected pitcher on it sorrowing over a broken nose; a looking-glass split across the centre, which chopped your head off at the chin and made you look like some dreadful unfinished monster or other; the paper peeling in shreds from the walls.

I sighed and said: "This is charming; and now don't you think you could get me something to read?"

The porter said, "Oh, certainly; the old man's got dead loads of books;" and he was gone before I could tell him what sort of literature I would rather have. And yet his countenance expressed the utmost confidence in his ability to execute the commission with credit to himself. The old man made a descent on him.

"What are you going to do with that pile of books?"

"Fifteen wants 'em, sir."

"Fifteen, is it? He'll want a warming-pan, next—he'll want a nurse! Take him every thing there is in the house—take him the bar-keeper—take him the baggage-wagon—take him a chamber-maid! Confound me, I never saw any thing like it. What did he say he wants with those books?"

"Wants to read 'em, like enough; it ain't likely he wants to eat 'em, I don't reckon."

"Wants to read 'em—wants to read 'em this time of night, the infernal lunatic! Well, he can't have them."

"But he says he's mor'ly bound to have 'em; he says he'll just go a-rairin' and a-chargin' through this house and raise more——well, there's no tellin' what he won't do if he don't get 'em; because he's drunk and crazy and desperate, and nothing'll soothe him down but them cussed books." [I had not made any threats,

and was not in the condition ascribed to me by the porter.]

"Well, go on; but I will be around when he goes to rairing and charging, and the first rair he makes I'll make him rair out of the window." And then the old gentleman went off, growling as before.

The genius of that porter was something wonderful. He put an armful of books on the bed and said "Good night" as confidently as if he knew perfectly well that those books were exactly my style of reading matter. And well

ROOM NO. 15.

he might. His selection covered the whole range of legitimate literature. It comprised "The Great Consummation," by Rev. Dr. Cummings—theology; "Revised Statutes of the State of Missouri"—law; "The Complete Horse-Doctor"—medicine; "The Toilers of the Sea," by Victor Hugo—romance; "The works of William Shakspeare"—poetry. I shall never cease to admire the tact and the intelligence of that gifted porter.

But all the donkeys in Christendom, and most of the Egyptian boys, I think, are at the door, and there is some noise going on, not to put it in stronger language.—We are about starting to the illustrious Pyramids of Egypt, and the donkeys for the voyage are under inspection. I will go and select one before the choice animals are all taken.

CHAPTER LVIII.

THE donkeys were all good, all handsome, all strong and in good condition, all fast and all willing to prove it. They were the best we had found any where, and the most *recherche*. I do not know what *recherche* is, but that is what these donkeys were, anyhow. Some were of a soft mouse-color, and the others were white, black, and vari-colored. Some were close-shaven, all over, except that a tuft like a paint-brush was left on the end of the tail. Others were so shaven in fanciful landscape garden patterns, as to mark their bodies with curving lines, which were bounded on one side by hair and on the other by the close plush left by the shears. They had all been newly barbered, and were exceedingly stylish. Several of the white ones were barred like zebras with rainbow stripes of blue and red and yellow paint. These were indescribably gorgeous. Dan and Jack selected from this lot because they brought back Italian reminiscences of the "old masters." The saddles were the high, stuffy, frog-shaped things we had known in Ephesus and Smyrna. The donkey-boys were lively young Egyptian rascals who could follow a donkey and keep him in a canter half a day without tiring. We had plenty of spectators when we mounted, for the hotel was full of English people bound overland to India and officers getting ready for the African campaign against the Abyssinian King Theodorus. We were not a very large party, but as we charged through the streets of the great metropolis, we made noise for five hundred, and displayed activity and created excitement in proportion. Nobody can steer a donkey, and some collided with camels, dervishes, effendis, asses, beggars and every thing else that offered to the donkeys a reasonable chance for a collision. When we turned into the broad avenue that leads out of the city toward Old Cairo, there was plenty of room. The walls of stately date-palms that fenced the gardens and bordered the way, threw their shadows down and made the air cool and bracing. We rose to the spirit of the time and the race became a wild rout, a stampede, a terrific panic. I wish to live to enjoy it again.

Somewhere along this route we had a few startling exhibitions of Oriental simplicity. A girl apparently thirteen years of age came along the great thoroughfare dressed like Eve before the fall. We would have called her thirteen at home ; but here girls who look thirteen are often not more than nine, in reality. Occasionally we saw stark-naked men of superb build, bathing, and making no attempt at concealment. However, an hour's acquaintance with this cheerful custom reconciled the pilgrims to it, and then it ceased to occasion remark. Thus easily do even the most startling novelties grow tame and spiritless to these sight-surfeited wanderers.

Arrived at Old Cairo, the camp-followers took up the donkeys and tumbled them bodily aboard a small boat with a lateen sail, and we followed and got under way. The deck was closely packed with donkeys and men ; the two sailors had to climb over and under and through the wedged mass to work the sails, and the steersman had to crowd four or five donkeys out of the way when he wished to swing his tiller and put his helm hard-down. But what were their troubles to us? We had nothing to do ; nothing to do but enjoy the trip ; nothing to do but shove the donkeys off our corns and look at the charming scenery of the Nile.

On the island at our right was the machine they call the Nilometer, a stone-column whose business it is to mark the rise of the river and prophecy whether it will reach only thirty-two feet and produce a famine, or whether it will properly flood the land at forty and produce plenty, or whether it will rise to forty-three and bring death and destruction to flocks and crops—but how it does all this they could not explain to us so that we could understand. On the same island is still shown the spot where Pharaoh's daughter found Moses in the bul-

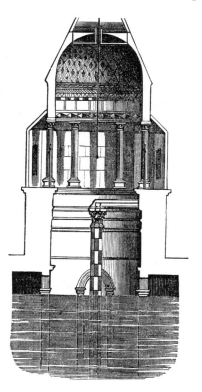

NILOMETER.

rushes. Near the spot we sailed from, the Holy Family dwelt when they sojourned in Egypt till Herod should complete his slaughter of the innocents. The same tree they rested under when they first arrived, was there a short time ago, but the Viceroy of Egypt sent it to the Empress Eugenie lately. He was just in time, otherwise our pilgrims would have had it.

The Nile at this point is muddy, swift and turbid, and does not lack a great deal of being as wide as the Mississippi.

We scrambled up the steep bank at the shabby town of Ghizeh, mounted the donkeys again, and scampered away. For four or five miles the route lay along a high embankment which they say is to be the bed of a railway the Sultan means to build for no other reason than that when the Empress of the French comes to visit him she can go to the Pyramids in comfort. This is true Oriental hospitality. I am very glad it is our privilege to have donkeys instead of cars.

At the distance of a few miles the Pyramids rising above the palms, looked very clean-cut, very grand and imposing, and very soft and filmy, as well. They swam in a rich haze that took from them all suggestions of unfeeling stone, and made them seem only the airy nothings of a dream—structures which might blossom into tiers of vague arches, or ornate colonnades, may be, and change and change again, into all graceful forms of architecture, while we looked, and then melt deliciously away and blend with the tremulous atmosphere.

At the end of the levee we left the mules and went in a sailboat across an arm of the Nile or an overflow, and landed where the sands of the Great Sahara left their embankment, as straight as a wall, along the verge of the alluvial plain of the river. A laborious walk in the flaming sun brought us to the foot of the great Pyramid of Cheops. It was a fairy vision no longer. It was a corrugated, unsightly mountain of stone. Each of its monstrous sides was a wide stairway which rose upward, step above step, narrowing as it went, till it tapered to a point far aloft in the air. Insect men and women—pilgrims from the *Quaker City*—were creeping about its dizzy perches, and one little black swarm were waving postage stamps from the airy summit—handkerchiefs will be understood.

Of course we were besieged by a rabble of muscular Egyptians and Arabs who wanted the contract of dragging us to the top—all tourists are. Of course you could not hear your own voice for the din that was around you. Of course the Sheiks said *they* were the only responsible parties; that all contracts must be made with them, all moneys paid over to them, and none exacted from us by any but themselves alone. Of course they contracted that the varlets who dragged us up should not mention bucksheesh once. For such is the usual routine. Of course we contracted with them, paid them, were delivered into the hands of the draggers, dragged up the Pyramids, and harried and be-deviled for bucksheesh from the foundation clear to the summit. We paid it, too, for we were purposely spread very far apart over the vast side of the Pyramid. There was no help near if we called, and the Herculeses who dragged us had a way of asking sweetly and flatteringly for bucksheesh, which was seductive, and of looking fierce and threatening to throw us down the precipice, which was persuasive and convincing.

Each step being full as high as a dinner-table; there being very, very many of the steps; an Arab having hold of each of our arms and springing upward from step to step and snatching us with them, forcing us to lift our feet as high as our breasts every time, and do it rapidly and keep it up till we were ready to faint, who shall say it is not lively, exhilarating, lacerating, muscle-straining, bone-wrenching and perfectly excruciating and exhausting pastime, climbing the Pyramids? I beseeched the varlets not to twist *all* my joints asunder; I iterated, reiterated, even *swore* to them that I did not wish to beat any body to the top; did all I could to convince them that if I got there

the last of all I would feel blessed above men and grateful to them forever; I begged them, prayed them, pleaded with them to let me stop and rest a moment—only one little moment: and they only

ASCENT OF THE PYRAMID.

answered with some more frightful springs, and an unenlisted volunteer behind opened a bombardment of determined boosts with his head which threatened to batter my whole political economy to wreck and ruin.

Twice, for one minute, they let me rest while they extorted bucksheesh, and then continued their maniac flight up the Pyramid. They wished to beat the other parties. It was nothing to them that I, a stranger, must be sacrificed upon the altar of their unholy ambition. But in the midst of sorrow, joy blooms. Even in this dark hour I had a sweet consolation. For I knew that except these Mohammedans repented they would go straight to perdition some day. And *they* never repent—they never forsake their paganism. This thought calmed me, cheered me, and I sank down, limp and exhausted, upon the summit, but happy, *so* happy and serene within.

On the one hand, a mighty sea of yellow sand stretched away toward the ends of the earth, solemn, silent, shorn of vegetation, its solitude uncheered by any forms of creature life ; on the other, the Eden of Egypt was spread below us—a broad green floor, cloven by the sinuous river, dotted with villages, its vast distances measured and marked by the diminishing stature of receding clusters of palms. It lay asleep in an enchanted atmosphere. There was no sound, no motion. Above the date-plumes in the middle distance, swelled a domed and pinnacled mass, glimmering through a tinted, exquisite mist ; away toward the horizon a dozen shapely pyramids watched over ruined Memphis : and at our feet the bland impassible Sphynx looked out upon the picture from her throne in the sands as placidly and pensively as she had looked upon its like full fifty lagging centuries ago.

We suffered torture no pen can describe from the hungry appeals for bucksheesh that gleamed from Arab eyes and poured incessantly from Arab lips. Why try to call up the traditions of vanished Egyptian grandeur ; why try to fancy Egypt following dead Rameses to his tomb in the Pyramid, or the long multitude of Israel departing over the desert yonder? Why try to think at all? The thing was impossible. One must bring his meditations cut and dried, or else cut and dry them afterward.

The traditional Arab proposed, in the traditional way, to run down Cheops, cross the eighth of a mile of sand intervening between it and the tall pyramid of Cephron, ascend to Cephron's summit and return to us on the top of Cheops—all in nine minutes by the watch, and the whole service to be rendered for a single dollar. In the first flush of irritation, I said let the Arab and his exploits go to the mischief. But stay. The upper third of Cephron was coated with dressed marble, smooth as glass. A blessed thought entered my brain. He must infallibly break his neck. Close the contract with dispatch, I said, and let him go. He started. We watched. He went bounding down the vast broadside, spring after spring, like an ibex. He grew small and smaller till he became a bobbing pigmy, away down toward the bottom—then disappeared. We turned and peered over the other side—forty seconds—eighty seconds—a hundred—happiness, he is dead already!—two minutes—and a quarter—" There he goes!" Too true—it was too true. He was very small, now. Gradually, but surely, he overcame the level ground. He began to spring and climb again. Up, up, up—at last he reached the smooth coating—now for it. But he clung to it with toes and fingers, like a fly. He crawled this way and that—away to the right, slanting upward—away to the left, still slanting upward—and stood at last, a black peg on the summit, and waved his pigmy scarf! Then he crept downward to the raw steps again, then picked up his agile heels and flew. We lost him presently. But presently again we saw him under us, mounting with undiminished energy. Shortly he bounded into our midst with a gallant war-whoop. Time, eight minutes, forty-one seconds. He had won. His bones were intact. It was a failure. I reflected. I said to myself, he is tired, and must grow dizzy. I will risk another dollar on him.

He started again. Made the trip again. Slipped on the smooth coating—I almost had him. But an infamous crevice saved him. He was with us once more—perfectly sound. Time, eight minutes, forty-six seconds.

I said to Dan, " Lend me a dollar—I can beat this game, yet."
Worse and worse. He won again. Time, eight minutes,
forty-eight seconds. I was out of all patience, now. I was

HIGH HOPES FRUSTRATED.

desperate.—M o n e y
was no longer of any
consequence. I said,
" Sirrah, I will give
you a hundred dol-
lars to jump off this
pyramid head first.
If you do not like the terms, name your bet. I scorn to stand
on expenses now. I will stay right here and risk money on
you as long as Dan has got a cent."

I was in a fair way to win, now, for it was a dazzling opportunity for an Arab. He pondered a moment, and would have
done it, I think, but his mother arrived, then, and interfered.
Her tears moved me—I never can look upon the tears of
woman with indifference—and I said I would give her a hundred to jump off, too.

But it was a failure. The Arabs are too high-priced in
Egypt. They put on airs unbecoming to such savages.

40

We descended, hot and out of humor. The dragoman lit candles, and we all entered a hole near the base of the pyramid, attended by a crazy rabble of Arabs who thrust their services upon us uninvited. They dragged us up a long inclined chute, and dripped candle-grease all over us. This chute was not more than twice as wide and high as a Saratoga trunk, and was walled, roofed and floored with solid blocks of Egyptian granite as wide as a wardrobe, twice as thick and three times as long. We kept on climbing, through the oppressive gloom, till I thought we ought to be nearing the top of the pyramid again, and then came to the " Queen's Chamber," and shortly to the Chamber of the King. These large apartments were tombs. The walls were built of monstrous masses of smoothed granite, neatly joined together. Some of them were nearly as large square as an ordinary parlor. A great stone sarcophagus like a bath-tub stood in the centre of the King's Chamber. Around it were gathered a picturesque group of Arab savages and soiled and tattered pilgrims, who held their candles aloft in the gloom while they chattered, and the winking blurs of light shed a dim glory down upon one of the irrepressible memento-seekers who was pecking at the venerable sarcophagus with his sacrilegious hammer.

We struggled out to the open air and the bright sunshine, and for the space of thirty minutes received ragged Arabs by couples, dozens and platoons, and paid them bucksheesh for services they swore and proved by each other that they had rendered, but which we had not been aware of before—and as each party was paid, they dropped into the rear of the procession and in due time arrived again with a newly-invented delinquent list for liquidation.

We lunched in the shade of the pyramid, and in the midst of this encroaching and unwelcome company, and then Dan and Jack and I started away for a walk. A howling swarm of beggars followed us—surrounded us—almost headed us off. A sheik, in flowing white bournous and gaudy head-gear, was with them. He wanted more bucksheesh. But we had adopted a new code—it was millions for defense, but not a cent for

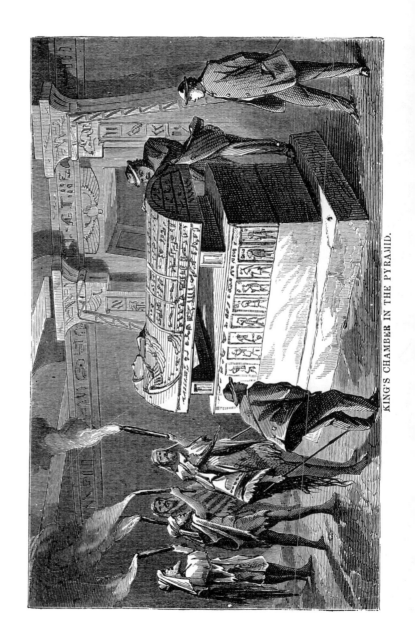

KING'S CHAMBER IN THE PYRAMID.

bucksheesh. I asked him if he could persuade the others to depart if we paid him. He said yes—for ten francs. We accepted the contract, and said—

" Now persuade your vassals to fall back."

He swung his long staff round his head and three Arabs
bit the dust. He capered among the mob like a very maniac.
His blows fell like hail, and wherever one fell a subject
went down. We had to hurry to the rescue and tell him
it was only
necessary to
damage them a
little, he need
not kill them.—
In two minutes
we were alone
with the sheik,
and remained
so. The per-
suasive powers
of this illiter-
ate savage
were remark-
able.

A POWERFUL ARGUMENT.

Each side of the Pyramid of Cheops is about as long as the
Capitol at Washington, or the Sultan's new palace on the Bosporus, and is longer than the greatest depth of St. Peter's at
Rome—which is to say that each side of Cheops extends seven
hundred and some odd feet. It is about seventy-five feet
higher than the cross on St. Peter's. The first time I ever
went down the Mississippi, I thought the highest bluff on the
river between St. Louis and New Orleans—it was near Selma,
Missouri—was probably the highest mountain in the world.
It is four hundred and thirteen feet high. It still looms in my
memory with undiminished grandeur. I can still see the trees
and bushes growing smaller and smaller as I followed them up
its huge slant with my eye, till they became a feathery fringe
on the distant summit. This symmetrical Pyramid of Cheops

—this solid mountain of stone reared by the patient hands of men—this mighty tomb of a forgotten monarch—dwarfs my cherished mountain. For it is four hundred and eighty feet high. In still earlier years than those I have been recalling, Holliday's Hill, in our town, was to me the noblest work of God. It appeared to pierce the skies. It was nearly three hundred feet high. In those days I pondered the subject much, but I never could understand why it did not swathe its summit with never-failing clouds, and crown its majestic brow with everlasting snows. I had heard that such was the custom of great mountains in other parts of the world. I remembered how I worked with another boy, at odd afternoons stolen from study and paid for with stripes, to undermine and start from its bed an immense boulder that rested upon the edge of that hill-top; I remembered how, one Saturday afternoon, we gave three hours of honest effort to the task, and saw at last that our reward was at hand; I remembered how we sat down, then, and wiped the perspiration away, and waited to let a picnic party get out of the way in the road below—and then we started the boulder. It was splendid. It went crashing down the hill-side, tearing up saplings, mowing bushes down like grass, ripping and crushing and smashing every thing in its path— eternally splintered and scattered a wood pile at the foot of the hill, and then sprang from the high bank clear over a dray in the road—the negro glanced up once and dodged—and the next second it made infinitesimal mince-meat of a frame cooper-shop, and the coopers swarmed out like bees. Then we said it was perfectly magnificent, and left. Because the coopers were starting up the hill to inquire.

Still, that mountain, prodigious as it was, was nothing to the Pyramid of Cheops. I could conjure up no comparison that would convey to my mind a satisfactory comprehension of the magnitude of a pile of monstrous stones that covered thirteen acres of ground and stretched upward four hundred and eighty tiresome feet, and so I gave it up and walked down to the Sphynx.

After years of waiting, it was before me at last. The great

PYRAMIDS AND SPHYNX.

face was so sad, so earnest, so longing, so patient. There was
a dignity not of earth in its mien, and in its countenance a be-
nignity such as never any thing human wore. It was stone,
but it seemed sentient. If ever image of stone thought, it was
thinking. It was looking toward the verge of the landscape,
yet looking *at* nothing—nothing but distance and vacancy. It
was looking over and beyond every thing of the present, and
far into the past. It was gazing out over the ocean of Time—
over lines of century-waves which, further and further receding, closed nearer and nearer together, and blended at last into
one unbroken tide, away toward the horizon of remote antiquity. It was thinking of the wars of departed ages; of the
empires it had seen created and destroyed; of the nations
whose birth it had witnessed, whose progress it had watched,
whose annihilation it had noted; of the joy and sorrow, the
life and death, the grandeur and decay, of five thousand slow
revolving years. It was the type of an attribute of man—of a
faculty of his heart and brain. It was MEMORY—RETROSPEC-
TION—wrought into visible, tangible form. All who know
what pathos there is in memories of days that are accomplished
and faces that have vanished—albeit only a trifling score of
years gone by—will have some appreciation of the pathos that
dwells in these grave eyes that look so steadfastly back upon
the things they knew before History was born—before Tradition had being—things that were, and forms that moved, in a
vague era which even Poetry and Romance scarce know of—and
passed one by one away and left the stony dreamer solitary in
the midst of a strange new age, and uncomprehended scenes.

The Sphynx is grand in its loneliness; it is imposing in its
magnitude; it is impressive in the mystery that hangs over its
story. And there is that in the overshadowing majesty of this
eternal figure of stone, with its accusing memory of the deeds
of all ages, which reveals to one something of what he shall
feel when he shall stand at last in the awful presence of God.

There are some things which, for the credit of America,
should be left unsaid, perhaps; but these very things happen
sometimes to be the very things which, for the real benefit of

Americans, ought to have prominent notice. While we stood looking, a wart, or an excrescence of some kind, appeared on the jaw of the Sphynx. We heard the familiar clink of a hammer, and understood the case at once. One of our well-meaning reptiles —I mean relic-hunters—had crawled up there and was trying to break a "specimen" from the face of this the most majestic creation the hand of man has wrought. But the great image contemplated the dead ages as calmly as ever, unconscious of

THE RELIC-HUNTER.

the small insect that was fretting at its jaw. Egyptian granite that has defied the storms and earthquakes of all time has nothing to fear from the tack-hammers of ignorant excursionists—highwaymen like this specimen. He failed in his enterprise. We sent a sheik to arrest him if he had the authority, or to warn him, if he had not, that by the laws of Egypt the crime he was attempting to commit was punishable with imprisonment or the bastinado. Then he desisted and went away.

The Sphynx: a hundred and twenty-five feet long, sixty feet high, and a hundred and two feet around the head, if I remember rightly—carved out of one solid block of stone harder than any iron. The block must have been as large as the Fifth Avenue Hotel before the usual waste (by the necessities of sculpture) of a fourth or a half of the original mass was begun. I only set down these figures and these remarks to suggest the prodigious labor the carving of it so elegantly, so symmetrically, so faultlessly, must have cost. This species of stone is so hard that figures cut in it remain sharp and unmarred after exposure to the weather for two or three thousand years. Now did it take a hundred years of patient toil to carve the Sphynx? It seems probable.

Something interfered, and we did not visit the Red Sea and walk upon the sands of Arabia. I shall not describe the great mosque of Mehemet Ali, whose entire inner walls are built of polished and glistening alabaster; I shall not tell how the little birds have built their nests in the globes of the great chandeliers that hang in the mosque, and how they fill the whole place with their music and are not afraid of any body because their audacity is pardoned, their rights are respected, and nobody is allowed to interfere with them, even though the mosque be thus doomed to go unlighted; I certainly shall not tell the hackneyed story of the massacre of the Mamelukes, because I am glad the lawless rascals were massacred, and I do not wish to get up any sympathy in their behalf; I shall not tell how that one solitary

THE MAMELUKE'S LEAP.

tary Mameluke jumped his horse a hundred feet down from the battlements of the citadel and escaped, because I do not think much of that—I could have done it myself; I shall not tell of Joseph's well which he dug in the solid rock of the citadel hill and which is still as good as new, nor how the same mules he bought to draw up the water (with an endless chain) are still at it yet and are getting tired of it, too ; I shall not tell about Joseph's granaries which he built to store the grain in, what time the Egyptian brokers were "selling short," unwitting that there would be no corn in all the land when it should be time for them to deliver ; I shall not tell any thing about the strange, strange city of Cairo, because it is only a repetition, a good deal intensified and exaggerated, of the Oriental cities I have already spoken of ; I shall not tell of the Great Caravan which leaves for Mecca every year, for I did not see it ; nor of the fashion the people have of prostrating themselves and so forming a long human pavement to be ridden over by the chief of the expedition on its return, to the end that their salvation may be thus secured, for I did not see that either ; I shall not speak of the railway, for it is like any other railway—I shall only say that the fuel they use for the locomotive is composed of mummies three thousand years old, purchased by the ton or by the graveyard for that purpose, and that sometimes one hears the profane engineer call out pettishly, "D—n these plebeians, they don't burn worth a cent—pass out a King;"* I shall not tell of the groups of mud cones stuck like wasps' nests upon a thousand mounds above high water-mark the length and breadth of Egypt—villages of the lower classes ; I shall not speak of the boundless sweep of level plain, green with luxuriant grain, that gladdens the eye as far as it can pierce through the soft, rich atmosphere of Egypt ; I shall not speak of the vision of the Pyramids seen at a distance of five and twenty miles, for the picture is too ethereal to be limned by an uninspired pen ; I shall not tell of the crowds of dusky women who flocked to the cars when they stopped a moment at a station, to sell us a drink of water or a ruddy, juicy pomegranate ; I shall not tell of the motley multitudes and wild costumes that graced a fair we found in full blast at another barbarous station ; I shall not tell how we feasted on fresh dates and enjoyed the pleasant landscape all through the

* Stated to me for a fact.   I only tell it as I got it.   I am willing to believe it. I can believe any thing.

flying journey; nor how we thundered into Alexandria, at last, swarmed out of the cars, rowed aboard the ship, left a comrade behind, (who was to return to Europe, thence home,) raised the anchor, and turned our bows homeward finally and forever from the long voyage; nor how, as the mellow sun went down upon the oldest land on earth, Jack and Moult assembled in solemn state in the smoking-room and mourned over the lost comrade the whole night long, and would not be comforted. I shall not speak a word of any of these things, or write a line. They shall be as a sealed book. I do not know what a sealed book is, because I never saw one, but a sealed book is the expression to use in this connection, because it is popular.

We were glad to have seen the land which was the mother of civilization—which taught Greece her letters, and through Greece Rome, and through Rome the world; the land which could have humanized and civilized the hapless children of Israel, but allowed them to depart out of her borders little better than savages. We were glad to have seen that land which had an enlightened religion with future eternal rewards and punishment in it, while even Israel's religion contained no promise of a hereafter. We were glad to have seen that land which had glass three thousand years before England had it, and could paint upon it as none of us can paint now; that land which knew, three thousand years ago, well nigh all of medicine and surgery which science has *discovered* lately; which had all those curious surgical instruments which science has *invented*

WOULD NOT BE COMFORTED.

recently; which had in high excellence a thousand luxuries and necessities of an advanced civilization which we have gradually contrived and accumulated in modern times and claimed as things that were new under the sun; that had paper untold centuries before we dreampt of it—and waterfalls before our women thought of them; that had a perfect system of common schools so long before we boasted of our achievements in that direction that it seems forever and forever ago; that so embalmed the dead that flesh was made almost immortal—which we can not do; that built temples which mock at destroying time and smile grimly upon our lauded little prodigies of architecture; that old land that knew all which we know now, perchance, and more; that walked in the broad highway of civilization in the gray dawn of creation, ages and ages before we were born; that left the impress of exalted, cultivated Mind upon the eternal front of the Sphynx to confound all scoffers who, when all her other proofs had passed away, might seek to persuade the world that imperial Egypt, in the days of her high renown, had groped in darkness.

CHAPTER LIX.

WE were at sea now, for a very long voyage—we were to pass through the entire length of the Levant; through the entire length of the Mediterranean proper, also, and then cross the full width of the Atlantic—a voyage of several weeks.

HOMEWARD BOUND.

We naturally settled down into a very slow, stay-at-home manner of life, and resolved to be quiet, exemplary people, and roam no more for twenty or thirty days. No more, at least, than from stem to stern of the ship. It was a very comfortable prospect, though, for we were tired and needed a long rest.

We were all lazy and satisfied, now, as the meager entries in my note-book (that sure index, to me, of my condition,) prove. What a stupid thing a note-book gets to be at sea, any way. Please observe the style:

"*Sunday*—Services, as usual, at four bells. Services at night, also. No cards.

"*Monday*—Beautiful day, but rained hard. The cattle purchased at Alexandria for beef ought to be shingled. Or else fattened. The water stands in deep puddles in the depressions forward of their after shoulders. Also here and there all over their backs. It is well they are not cows—it would soak in and ruin the milk. The poor devil eagle* from Syria looks miserable and droopy in the rain, perched on the forward capstan. He appears to have his own opinion of a sea voyage, and if it were put into language and the language solidified, it would probably essentially dam the widest river in the world.

"*Tuesday*—Somewhere in the neighborhood of the island of Malta. Can not stop there. Cholera. Weather very stormy. Many passengers seasick and invisible.

"*Wednesday*—Weather still very savage. Storm blew two land birds to sea, and they came on board. A hawk was blown off, also. He circled round and round the ship, wanting to light, but afraid of the people. He was so tired, though, that he had to light, at last, or perish. He stopped in the foretop, repeatedly, and was as often blown away by the wind. At last Harry caught him. Sea full of flying-fish. They rise in flocks of three hundred and flash along above the tops of the waves a distance of two or three hundred feet, then fall and disappear.

"*Thursday*—Anchored off Algiers, Africa. Beautiful city, beautiful green hilly landscape behind it. Staid half a day and left. Not permitted to land, though we showed a clean bill of health. They were afraid of Egyptian plague and cholera.

"*Friday*—Morning, dominoes. Afternoon, dominoes. Evening, promenading the deck. Afterwards, charades.

"*Saturday*—Morning, dominoes. Afternoon, dominoes. Evening, promenading the decks. Afterwards, dominoes.

"*Sunday*—Morning service, four bells. Evening service, eight bells. Monotony till midnight.—Whereupon, dominoes.

"*Monday*—Morning, dominoes. Afternoon, dominoes. Evening, promenading the decks. Afterward, charades and a lecture from Dr. C. Dominoes.

"*No date*—Anchored off the picturesque city of Cagliari, Sardinia. Staid till midnight, but not permitted to land by these infamous foreigners. They smell inodorously—they do not wash—they dare not risk cholera.

"*Thursday*—Anchored off the beautiful cathedral city of Malaga, Spain.—Went ashore in the captain's boat—not ashore, either, for they would not let us land. Quarantine. Shipped my newspaper correspondence, which they took with tongs, dipped it in sea water, clipped it full of holes, and then fumigated it with villainous vapors till it smelt like a Spaniard. Inquired about chances to run the blockade and visit the Alhambra at Granada. Too risky—they might hang a body. Set sail—middle of afternoon.

* Afterwards presented to the Central Park.

"And so on, and so on, and so forth, for several days. Finally, anchored off
Gibraltar, which looks familiar and home-like."

It reminds me of the journal I opened with the New Year,
once, when I was a boy and a confiding and a willing prey to
those impossible schemes of reform which well-meaning old
maids and grandmothers set for the feet of unwary youths at
that season of the year—setting oversized tasks for them,
which, necessarily failing, as infallibly weaken the boy's
strength of will, diminish his confidence in himself and injure
his chances of success in life. Please accept of an extract:

" *Monday*—Got up, washed, went to bed.
" *Tuesday*—Got up, washed, went to bed.
" *Wednesday*—Got up, washed, went to bed.
" *Thursday*—Got up, washed, went to bed.
" *Friday*—Got up, washed, went to bed.
" *Next Friday*—Got up, washed, went to bed.
" *Friday fortnight*—Got up, washed, went to bed.
" *Following month*—Got up, washed, went to bed."

I stopped, then, discouraged. Startling events appeared to
be too rare, in my career, to render a diary necessary. I still
reflect with pride, however, that even at that early age I
washed when I got up. That journal finished me. I never
have had the nerve to keep one since. My loss of confidence
in myself in that line was permanent.

The ship had to stay a week or more at Gibraltar to take in
coal for the home voyage.

It would be very tiresome staying here, and so four of us
ran the quarantine blockade and spent seven delightful days
in Seville, Cordova, Cadiz, and wandering through the pleasant rural scenery of Andalusia, the garden of Old Spain.
The experiences of that cheery week were too varied and numerous for a short chapter and I have not room for a long one.
Therefore I shall leave them all out.

CHAPTER LX.

TEN or eleven o'clock found us coming down to breakfast one morning in Cadiz. They told us the ship had been lying at anchor in the harbor two or three hours. It was time for us to bestir ourselves. The ship could wait only a little while because of the quarantine. We were soon on board, and within the hour the white city and the pleasant shores of Spain sank down behind the waves and passed out of sight. We had seen no land fade from view so regretfully.

It had long ago been decided in a noisy public meeting in the main cabin that we could not go to Lisbon, because we must surely be quarantined there. We did every thing by mass-meeting, in the good old national way, from swapping off one empire for another on the programme of the voyage down to complaining of the cookery and the scarcity of napkins. I am reminded, now, of one of these complaints of the cookery made by a passenger. The coffee had been steadily growing more and more execrable for the space of three weeks, till at last it had ceased to be coffee altogether and had assumed the nature of mere discolored water—so this person said. He said it was so weak that it was transparent an inch in depth around the edge of the cup. As he approached the table one morning he saw the transparent edge—by means of his extraordinary vision—long before he got to his seat. He went back and complained in a high-handed way to Capt. Duncan. He said the coffee was disgraceful. The Captain showed his. It seemed tolerably good. The incipient mutineer was more outraged than ever, then, at what he denounced as the partiality shown the captain's table over the other tables in the ship. He flourished back and got his cup and set it down triumphantly, and said :

"Just try that mixture once, Captain Duncan."

He smelt it—tasted it—smiled benignantly—then said :

"It *is* inferior—for *coffee*—but it is pretty fair *tea*."

The humbled mutineer smelt it, tasted it, and returned to his seat. He had made an egregious ass of himself before the whole ship. He did it no more. After that he took things as they came. That was me.

The old-fashioned ship-life

COFFEE.

had returned, now that we were no longer in sight of land. For days and days it continued just the same, one day being exactly like another, and, to me, every one of them pleasant. At last we anchored in the open roadstead of Funchal, in the beautiful islands we call the Madeiras.

The mountains looked surpassingly lovely, clad as they were in living green ; ribbed with lava ridges ; flecked with white cottages ; riven by deep chasms purple with shade ; the great slopes dashed with sunshine and mottled with shadows flung from the drifting squadrons of the sky, and the superb picture fitly crowned by towering peaks whose fronts were swept by the trailing fringes of the clouds.

But we could not land. We staid all day and looked, we abused the man who invented quarantine, we held half a dozen mass-meetings and crammed them full of interrupted speeches, motions that fell still-born, amendments that came to nought and resolutions that died from sheer exhaustion in trying to get before the house.   At night we set sail.

We averaged four mass-meetings a week for the voyage— we seemed always in labor in this way, and yet so often fallaciously that whenever at long intervals we were safely delivered of a resolution, it was cause for public rejoicing, and we hoisted the flag and fired a salute.

Days passed—and nights ; and then the beautiful Bermudas

"OUR FRIENDS, THE BERMUDIANS."

rose out of the sea, we entered the tortuous channel, steamed hither and thither among the bright summer islands, and rested at last under the flag of England and were welcome.   We were not a nightmare here, where were civilization and intelligence in place of Spanish and Italian superstition, dirt and dread of cholera.   A few days among the breezy groves, the flower gardens, the coral caves, and the lovely vistas of blue water that went curving in and out, disappearing and anon again appearing through jungle walls of brilliant foliage, restored the energies dulled by long drowsing on the ocean, and fitted us for our final cruise—our little run of a thousand miles to New York —America—HOME.

We bade good-bye to "our friends the Bermudians," as our programme hath it—the majority of those we were most intimate with were negroes—and courted the great deep again. I said the majority. We knew more negroes than white people, because we had a deal of washing to be done, but we made some most excellent friends among the whites, whom it will be a pleasant duty to hold long in grateful remembrance.

We sailed, and from that hour all idling ceased. Such another system of overhauling, general littering of cabins and packing of trunks we had not seen since we let go the anchor in the harbor of Beirout. Every body was busy. Lists of all purchases had to be made out, and values attached, to facilitate matters at the customhouse. Purchases bought by bulk in partnership had to be equitably divided, outstanding debts canceled, accounts compared, and trunks, boxes and packages labeled. All day long the bustle and confusion continued.

CAPT. DUNCAN.

And now came our first accident. A passenger was running through a gangway, between decks, one stormy night, when he caught his foot in the iron staple of a door that had been heedlessly left off a hatchway, and the bones of his leg broke

41

at the ancle. It was our first serious misfortune. We had traveled much more than twenty thousand miles, by land and sea, in many trying climates, without a single hurt, without a serious case of sickness and without a death among five and sixty passengers. Our good fortune had been wonderful. A sailor had jumped overboard at Constantinople one night, and was seen no more, but it was suspected that his object was to desert, and there was a slim chance, at least, that he reached the shore. But the passenger list was complete. There was no name missing from the register.

At last, one pleasant morning, we steamed up the harbor of New York, all on deck, all dressed in Christian garb—by special order, for there was a latent disposition in some quarters to come out as Turks—and amid a waving of handkerchiefs from welcoming friends, the glad pilgrims noted the shiver of the decks that told that ship and pier had joined hands again and the long, strange cruise was over. Amen.

CHAPTER LXI.

IN this place I will print an article which I wrote for the New York *Herald* the night we arrived. I do it partly because my contract with my publishers makes it compulsory; partly because it is a proper, tolerably accurate, and exhaustive summing up of the cruise of the ship and the performances of the pilgrims in foreign lands; and partly because some of the passengers have abused me for writing it, and I wish the public to see how thankless a task it is to put one's self to trouble to glorify unappreciative people. I was charged with "rushing into print" with these compliments. I did not rush. I had written news letters to the *Herald* sometimes, but yet when I visited the office that day I did not say any thing about writing a valedictory. I did go to the *Tribune* office to see if such an article was wanted, because I belonged on the regular staff of that paper and it was simply a duty to do it. The managing editor was absent, and so I thought no more about it. At night when the *Herald's* request came for an article, I did not "rush." In fact, I demurred for a while, because I did not feel like writing compliments then, and therefore was afraid to speak of the cruise lest I might be betrayed into using other than complimentary language. However, I reflected that it would be a just and righteous thing to go down and write a kind word for the Hadjis—Hadjis are people who have made the pilgrimage—because parties not interested could not do it so feelingly as I, a fellow-Hadji, and so I penned the valedictory. I have read it, and read it again; and if there is a sentence in it that is not fulsomely complimentary to captain, ship and passengers, *I* can not find it. If it is not a chapter that any company might be proud to have a body write about them, my judgment is fit for nothing. With these remarks I confidently submit it to the unprejudiced judgment of the reader:

RETURN OF THE HOLY LAND EXCURSIONISTS—THE STORY OF THE CRUISE.

To the Editor of the Herald:

The steamer Quaker City has accomplished at last her extraordinary voyage and returned to her old pier at the foot of Wall street. The expedition was a success in some respects, in some it was not. Originally it was advertised as a "pleasure excursion." Well, perhaps, it was a pleasure excursion, but certainly it did not look like one; certainly it did not act like one. Any body's and every body's notion of a pleasure excursion is that the parties to it will of a necessity be young and giddy and somewhat boisterous. They will dance a good deal, sing a good deal, make love, but sermonize very little. Any body's and every body's notion of a well conducted funeral is that there must be a hearse and a corpse, and chief mourners and mourners by courtesy, many old people, much solemnity, no levity, and a prayer and a sermon withal. Three-fourths of the Quaker City's passengers were between forty and seventy years of age! There was a picnic crowd for you! It may be supposed that the other fourth was composed of young girls. But it was not. It was chiefly composed of rusty old bachelors and a child of six years. Let us average the ages of the Quaker City's pilgrims and set the figure down as fifty years. Is any man insane enough to imagine that this picnic of patriarchs sang, made love, danced, laughed, told anecdotes, dealt in ungodly levity? In my experience they sinned little in these matters. No doubt it was presumed here at home that these frolicsome veterans laughed and sang and romped all day, and day after day, and kept up a noisy excitement from one end of the ship to the other; and that they played blind-man's buff or danced quadrilles and waltzes on moonlight evenings on the quarter-deck; and that at odd moments of unoccupied time they jotted a laconic item or two in the journals they opened on such an elaborate plan when they left home, and then skurried off to their whist and euchre labors under the cabin lamps. If these things were presumed, the presumption was at fault. The venerable excursionists were not gay and frisky. They played no blind-man's buff; they dealt not in whist; they shirked not the irksome journal, for alas! most of them were even writing books. They never romped, they talked but little, they never sang, save in the nightly prayer-meeting. The pleasure ship was a synagogue, and the pleasure trip was a funeral excursion without a corpse. (There is nothing exhilarating about a funeral excursion without a corpse.) A free, hearty laugh was a sound that was not heard oftener than once in seven days about those decks or in those cabins, and when it was heard it met with precious little sympathy. The excursionists danced, on three separate evenings, long, long ago, (it seems an age.) quadrilles, of a single set, made up of three ladies and five gentlemen, (the latter with handkerchiefs around their arms to signify their sex,) who timed their feet to the solemn wheezing of a melodeon; but even this melancholy orgie was voted to be sinful, and dancing was discontinued.

The pilgrims played dominoes when too much Josephus or Robinson's Holy Land Researches, or book-writing, made recreation necessary—for dominoes is about as mild and sinless a game as any in the world, perhaps, excepting always the ineffably insipid diversion they call croquet, which is a game where you don't pocket any balls and don't carom on any thing of any consequence, and when you are done nobody has to pay, and there are no refreshments to saw off, and, consequently, there isn't any satisfaction whatever about it—they played dominoes till they were rested, and then they blackguarded each other privately till prayer-time. When they were not seasick they were uncommonly prompt when the dinner-gong sounded. Such was our daily life on board the ship—solemnity, decorum, dinner, dominoes, devotions, slander. It was not lively enough for a pleasure trip; but if we had only had a corpse it would have made a noble funeral excursion. It is all over now; but when I look back, the idea of these venerable fossils skipping forth on a six months' picnic, seems exquisitely refreshing. The advertised title of the expedition—"The Grand Holy Land Pleasure Excursion"—was a misnomer. "The Grand Holy Land Funeral Procession" would have been better—much better.

Wherever we went, in Europe, Asia, or Africa, we made a sensation, and, I suppose I may add, created a famine. None of us had ever been any where before; we all hailed from the interior; travel was a wild novelty to us, and we conducted ourselves in accordance with the natural instincts that were in us, and trammeled ourselves with no ceremonies, no conventionalities. We always took care to make it understood that we were Americans—Americans! When we found that a good many foreigners had hardly ever heard of America, and that a good many more knew it only as a barbarous province away off somewhere, that had lately been at war with somebody, we pitied the ignorance of the Old World, but abated no jot of our importance. Many and many a simple community in the Eastern hemisphere will remember for years the incursion of the strange horde in the year of our Lord 1867, that called themselves Americans, and seemed to imagine in some unaccountable way that they had a right to be proud of it. We generally created a famine, partly because the coffee on the Quaker City was unendurable, and sometimes the more substantial fare was not strictly first class; and partly because one naturally tires of sitting long at the same board and eating from the same dishes.

The people of those foreign countries are very, very ignorant. They looked curiously at the costumes we had brought from the wilds of America. They observed that we talked loudly at table sometimes. They noticed that we looked out for expenses, and got what we conveniently could out of a franc, and wondered where in the mischief we came from. In Paris they just simply opened their eyes and stared when we spoke to them in French! We never did succeed in making those idiots understand their own language. One of our passengers said to a shopkeeper, in reference to a proposed return to buy a pair of gloves, "*Allong restay trankeel—may be ve coom Moonday ;*" and would you believe it, that shopkeeper, a born

Frenchman, had to ask what it was that had been said. Sometimes it seems to me, somehow, that there must be a difference between Parisian French and Quaker City French.

The people stared at us every where, and we stared at them. We generally made them feel rather small, too, before we got done with them, because we bore down on them with America's greatness until we crushed them. And yet we took kindly to the manners and customs, and especially to the fashions of the various people we visited. When we left the Azores, we wore awful capotes and used fine tooth combs—successfully. When we came back from Tangier, in Africa, we were topped with fezzes of the bloodiest hue, hung with tassels like an Indian's scalp-lock. In France and Spain we attracted some attention in these costumes. In Italy they naturally took us for distempered Garibaldians, and set a gunboat to look for any thing significant in our changes of uniform. We made Rome howl. We could have made any place howl when we had all our clothes on. We got no fresh raiment in Greece—they had but little there of any kind. But at Constantinople, how we turned out! Turbans, scimetars, fezzes, horse-pistols, tunics, sashes, baggy trowsers, yellow slippers—Oh, we were gorgeous! The illustrious dogs of Constantinople barked their under jaws off, and even then failed to do us justice. They are all dead by this time. They could not go through such a run of business as we gave them and survive.

And then we went to see the Emperor of Russia. We just called on him as comfortably as if we had known him a century or so, and when we had finished our visit we variegated ourselves with selections from Russian costumes and sailed away again more picturesque than ever. In Smyrna we picked up camel's hair shawls and other dressy things from Persia; but in Palestine—ah, in Palestine— our splendid career ended. They didn't wear any clothes there to speak of. We were satisfied, and stopped. We made no experiments. We did not try their costume. But we astonished the natives of that country. We astonished them with such eccentricities of dress as we could muster. We prowled through the Holy Land, from Cesarea Philippi to Jerusalem and the Dead Sea, a weird procession of pilgrims, gotten up regardless of expense, solemn, gorgeous, green-spectacled, drowsing under blue umbrellas, and astride of a sorrier lot of horses, camels and asses than those that came out of Noah's ark, after eleven months of seasickness and short rations. If ever those children of Israel in Palestine forget when Gideon's Band went through there from America, they ought to be cursed once more and finished. It was the rarest spectacle that ever astounded mortal eyes, perhaps.

Well, we were at home in Palestine. It was easy to see that that was the grand feature of the expedition. We had cared nothing much about Europe. We galloped through the Louvre, the Pitti, the Ufizzi, the Vatican—all the galleries—and through the pictured and frescoed churches of Venice, Naples, and the cathedrals of Spain; some of us said that certain of the great works of the old masters were glorious creations of genius, (we found it out in the guide-book, though we got hold of the wrong picture sometimes,) and the others said they were disgraceful old daubs. We examined modern and ancient statuary with a critical eye in Florence, Rome, or any where we found it, and praised it if we saw fit, and if we didn't we said we preferred the wooden Indians in front of the cigar stores of America. But the Holy Land brought out all our enthusiasm. We fell into raptures by the barren shores of Galilee; we pondered at Tabor and at Nazareth; we exploded into poetry over the questionable loveliness of Esdraelon; we meditated at Jezreel and Samaria over the missionary zeal of Jehu; we rioted—fairly rioted among the holy places of Jerusalem; we bathed in Jordan and the Dead Sea, reckless whether our accident-insurance policies were extra-hazardous or not, and brought away so many jugs of precious water from both places that all the country from Jericho to the mountains of Moab will suffer from drouth this year, I think. Yet, the pilgrimage part of the excursion was its pet feature—there is no question about that. After dismal, smileless Palestine, beautiful Egypt had few charms for us. We merely glanced at it and were ready for home.

They wouldn't let us land at Malta—quarantine; they would not let us land in Sardinia; nor at Algiers, Africa; nor at Malaga, Spain, nor Cadiz, nor at the Madeira islands. So we got offended at all foreigners and turned our backs upon them and came home. I suppose we only stopped at the Bermudas because they were in the programme. We did not care any thing about any place at all. We wanted to go home. Homesickness was abroad in the ship—it was epidemic. If the authorities of New York had known how badly we had it, they would have quarantined us here.

The grand pilgrimage is over. Good-bye to it, and a pleasant memory to it, I am able to say in all kindness. I bear no malice, no ill-will toward any individual that was connected with it, either as passenger or officer. Things I did not like at all yesterday I like very well to-day, now that I am at home, and always hereafter I shall be able to poke fun at the whole gang if the spirit so moves me to do, without ever saying a malicious word. The expedition accomplished all that its programme promised that it should accomplish, and we ought all to be satisfied with the management of the matter, certainly. Bye-bye!

MARK TWAIN.

I call that complimentary. It *is* complimentary; and yet I never have received a word of thanks for it from the Hadjis; on the contrary I speak nothing but the serious truth when I say that many of them even took exceptions to the article. In endeavoring to please them I slaved over that sketch for two hours, and had my labor for my pains. I never will do a generous deed again.

CONCLUSION.

NEARLY one year has flown since this notable pilgrimage was ended; and as I sit here at home in San Francisco thinking, I am moved to confess that day by day the mass of my memories of the excursion have grown more and more pleasant as the disagreeable incidents of travel which encumbered them flitted one by one out of my mind—and now, if the *Quaker City* were weighing her anchor to sail away on the very same cruise again, nothing could gratify me more than to be a passenger. With the same captain and even the same pilgrims, the same sinners. I was on excellent terms with eight or nine of the excursionists (they are my staunch friends yet,) and was even on speaking terms with the rest of the sixty-five. I have been at sea quite enough to know that that was a very good average. Because a long sea-voyage not only brings out all the mean traits one has, and exaggerates them, but raises up others which he never suspected he possessed, and even creates new ones. A twelve months' voyage at sea would make of an ordinary man a very miracle of meanness. On the other hand, if a man has good qualities, the spirit seldom moves him to exhibit them on shipboard, at least with any sort of emphasis. Now I am satisfied that our pilgrims are pleasant old people on shore; I am also satisfied that at sea on a second voyage they would be pleasanter, somewhat, than they were on our grand excursion, and so I say without hesitation that I would be glad enough to sail with them again. I could at least enjoy life with my handful of old friends. They could enjoy life with *their* cliques as well—passengers invariably divide up into cliques, on *all* ships.

And I will say, here, that I would rather travel with an excursion party of Methuselahs than have to be changing ships and comrades constantly, as people do who travel in the ordinary way. Those latter are always grieving over some *other* ship they have known and lost, and over *other* comrades whom diverging routes have separated from them. They learn to love a ship just in time to change it for another, and they become attached to a pleasant traveling companion only to lose him. They have that most dismal experience of being in a strange vessel, among strange people who care nothing about them, and of undergoing the customary bullying by strange officers and the insolence of strange servants, repeated over and over again within the compass of every month. They have also that other misery of packing and unpacking trunks —of running the distressing gauntlet of custom-houses—of the anxieties attendant upon getting a mass of baggage from point to point on land in safety. I had rather sail with a whole brigade of patriarchs than suffer so. We never packed our trunks but twice—when we sailed from New York, and when we returned to it. Whenever we made a land journey, we estimated how many days we should be gone and what amount of clothing we should need, figured it down to a mathematical nicety, packed a valise or two accordingly, and left the trunks on board. We chose our comrades from among our old, tried friends, and started. We were never dependent upon strangers for companionship. We often had occasion to pity Americans whom we found traveling drearily among strangers with no friends to exchange pains and pleasures with. Whenever we were coming back from a land journey, our eyes sought one thing in the distance first—the ship—and when we saw it riding at anchor with the flag apeak, we felt as a returning wanderer feels when he sees his home. When we stepped on board, our cares vanished, our troubles were at an end—for the ship was home to us. We always had the same familiar old state-room to go to, and feel safe and at peace and comfortable again.

I have no fault to find with the manner in which our excursion was conducted. Its programme was faithfully carried out —a thing which surprised me, for great enterprises usually promise vastly more than they perform. It would be well if such an excursion could be gotten up every year and the system regularly inaugurated. Travel is fatal to prejudice, bigotry and narrow-mindedness, and many of our people need it sorely on these accounts. Broad, wholesome, charitable views of men and things can not be acquired by vegetating in one little corner of the earth all one's lifetime.

The Excursion is ended, and has passed to its place among the things that were. But its varied scenes and its manifold incidents will linger pleasantly in our memories for many a year to come. Always on the wing, as we were, and merely pausing a moment to catch fitful glimpses of the wonders of half a world, we could not hope to receive or retain vivid impressions of all it was our fortune to see. Yet our holyday flight has not been in vain—for above the confusion of vague recollections, certain of its best prized pictures lift themselves and will still continue perfect in tint and outline after their surroundings shall have faded away.

We shall remember something of pleasant France; and something also of Paris, though it flashed upon us a splendid meteor, and was gone again, we hardly knew how or where. We shall remember, always, how we saw majestic Gibraltar glorified with the rich coloring of a Spanish sunset and swimming in a sea of rainbows. In fancy we shall see Milan again, and her stately Cathedral with its marble wilderness of graceful spires. And Padua—Verona—Como, jeweled with stars; and patrician Venice, afloat on her stagnant flood—silent, desolate, haughty—scornful of her humbled state—wrapping herself in memories of her lost fleets, of battle and triumph, and all the pageantry of a glory that is departed.

We can not forget Florence—Naples—nor the foretaste of heaven that is in the delicious atmosphere of Greece—and surely not Athens and the broken temples of the Acropolis. Surely not venerable Rome—nor the green plain that compasses her round about, contrasting its brightness with her gray decay—nor the ruined arches that stand apart in the plain and clothe their looped and windowed raggedness with vines. We shall remember St. Peter's : not as one sees it when he walks the streets of Rome and fancies all her domes are just alike, but as he sees it leagues away, when every meaner edifice has faded out of sight and that one dome looms superbly up in the flush of sunset, full of dignity and grace, strongly outlined as a mountain.

We shall remember Constantinople and the Bosporus—the colossal magnificence of Baalbec—the Pyramids of Egypt— the prodigious form, the benignant countenance of the Sphynx —Oriental Smyrna—sacred Jerusalem—Damascus, the " Pearl of the East," the pride of Syria, the fabled Garden of Eden, the home of princes and genii of the Arabian Nights, the oldest metropolis on earth, the one city in all the world that has kept its name and held its place and looked serenely on while the Kingdoms and Empires of four thousand years have risen to life, enjoyed their little season of pride and pomp, and then vanished and been forgotten !

PERSONAL HISTORY OF
ULYSSES S. GRANT,

ILLUSTRATED WITH

Twenty-five New and Elegant Full Page Engravings,

In Steel and Wood, among which are two of General Grant, by the best Artists in the country. Also, Fac-similes of Rare Documents, Public and Private, the famous Unconditional-Surrender, and other equally interesting and important Letters, from Originals intrusted to the author by General Grant and his friends.

THE MOST POPULAR BOOK OF THE SEASON.

This volume contains many Documents and Letters of the Highest Importance, relating to Civil and Military Matters, SINCE THE WAR, which have never before been made public.

By ALBERT D. RICHARDSON,

AUTHOR OF "FIELD, DUNGEON, AND ESCAPE," AND "BEYOND THE MISSISSIPPI."

AUTHENTIC, AUTHORIZED AND APPROVED.

Written with the knowledge, consent, and full concurrence of the illustrious General.

In view of the prominent position now occupied by General Grant, it must be conceded by all that a full and truthful history of him, should find its way into the hands of every reader.

No American citizen should live under any President with whose character and antecedents, both public and private, he is not perfectly familiar.

This work differs very essentially from the many "LIVES OF GRANT," now before the public, and should by no means be classified with them. While recording his illustrious achievements both in the Field and in the Cabinet, it is yet personal, rather than martial, or political, free from military technicalities or partisan coloring, depicting not merely the exploits of Grant, the soldier, but the entire life of Grant the man, his daily habits and conversation, his thoughts, and his motives, as evinced by his acts and his words, under all of the many different circumstances of his eventful career, giving, in fact, a full and clear *exhibit of the inner, as well as the outer man.* It has not been prepared for a campaign document, but for the library, and it has been admitted by all to be a great acquisition to the biographical literature of the country. It contains 560 pages, and in mechanical execution is fully up to our well known style. Its sub-scription price is,

Beautifully Bound in Fine Cloth, Sprinkled Edge, - - - -	$3.00
" " Gilt Edge, - - - - -	3.50
" Leather, Library Style, - - - - -	4.00
Elegantly Bound in Extra Half Calf, or Half Turkey, - - -	5.00

Agents Wanted. Apply to AMERICAN PUBLISHING CO., Hartford, Conn

---

THE GREAT METROPOLIS,
A Mirror of
NEW YORK,

By JUNIUS HENRI BROWNE.

The author of this work needs no endorsement. His well known signature, as a leading and popular correspondent of the press, is welcomed at thousands of firesides in the land. His habits of close observation, his long experience as a journalist, and his acknowledged talents as a writer have all been drawn upon and concentrated for months upon this work.

Reflecting every phase of Metropolitan life and society, giving life-like pictures of the interesting localities and peculiar institutions of New York, the manners and customs of every class of its people; their modes and habits of life; how and where they live; the great contest for wealth existing among them, and how it is gained and how lost; revealing scenes of wickedness and of misery; exposing the tricks of the dishonest, and the traps laid for the unwary; in fact, showing up the whole inner life of the great heart of our country, in a manner and with a fullness never equalled. This volume is respectfully offered by the publishers, with implicit faith in its great value as a book of profit and amusement.

This work is embellished by

Over Twenty Appropriate and Spirited Engravings.

and is a most beautiful and attractive octavo volume of 700 pages,

It is sold exclusively by Agents and can be obtained from no other source, and is delivered to subscribers,

Elegantly Bound in Fancy Cloth, Gilt Back and Sides, Sprinkled Edge, -	$3.00
" " " " Gilt Edge, - -	3.50
" " Leather, (Library Style,) Sprinkled Edge, - - -	4.00
" " Extra Half Calf, or Half Turkey, . - -	5.00

☞ *Payment to be made upon receipt of the work.*

Agents Wanted. Apply to AMERICAN PUBLISHING CO., Hartford, Conn

AFTERWORD

David E. E. Sloane

The *Innocents Abroad, or The New Pilgrims' Progress* (1869) bid for a place on the drawing room reading table beside its notable predecessor by John Bunyan. The book's binding — ornate gold letters marked on the spine by oak and laurel and on the cover by icons of Egypt and Greece — certainly justified such a placement, and so did the provenance, for the book was a product of Elisha Bliss's American Publishing Company, one of the fourteen major publishers in Hartford, Connecticut, a center for publishing religiously oriented literature and serious books. If not Bunyanesque in intent, the book at least appeared to have some educational content: Bliss was also the publisher of A. D. Richardson's travelogue *Beyond the Mississippi*, still a hot seller as *The Innocents Abroad* was being prepared for print. American book buyers, however, well knew they were ordering a humor book by subscription only, and not for sale in the book-stores, when the book agent stood at the front door, sample in hand; for Mark Twain's reputation as a newspaper humorist and Western storyteller had been established through a variety of pieces on the Saturday humor pages and through his "Celebrated Jumping Frog of Calaveras County" story, widely recognized as a truly "American" piece of humor. "Mark Twain" might be depended upon to combine morality, educational reportage, the humor of the West, and an American viewpoint in a new and pleasurable way. The sales of *Innocents Abroad* show that readers felt that he did.

Partly, the persona of Mark Twain himself sold the book. Even as early as his first flamboyant national success with "Jumping Frog," Mark Twain represented something truly new in the quality of the stories he told and the colloquial language in which they were presented. As a reportorial writer, storyteller, and traveler, he was a fusion of previously rather staid genres practiced by other popular writers. The letters from which *Innocents Abroad* was made had already appeared in the *San Francisco Daily Alta California*, and some in the *New York Tribune* and *New York Herald*. In fact, a lot more letters than Twain cared to reprint had appeared, and he had pruned and revised extensively in his bid for an upscale but still middle-class audience. Yet he showed none of the literary cleverness of the Boston Brahmin Oliver Wendell Holmes in *The Autocrat of the Breakfast-Table* or of G. W. Curtis's light comedy of social manners in *The Potiphar Papers*, satirizing New York society of the 1850s. (Curtis had taken his crack at the Holy Land in 1851–52 with a pair of books on his travels in the Near East, but they were too coy in tone to sell well.) Twain's characters were realistic, his voice impudent and unregenerate, but his spirit humane. Where the earlier writers were stilted and constrained, he was garishly pictorial or harshly ironic.

A humorous travelogue tradition of sorts also existed, not only in European satires like Swifts *Gulliver's Travels*, but also in the work of such American humorists as James Kirke Paulding, who sent his Yankee to China in the 1830s in "Jonathan's Visit to the Celestial Empire," Q. K. Philander Doesticks (Mortimer Thomson), who burlesqued the sentimental trip to Niagara Falls in the 1850s, and P. T. Barnum, whose *Life* in 1855 chronicled his doings in Europe as a showman. Most recently, Artemus Ward (Charles Farrar Browne) had chronicled his travels among the Mormons (during which he met Twain and subsequently solicited the "Jumping Frog" story) and in London in the 1860s, in the persona of an outspoken vulgarian whose pragmatic skepticism was tempered by the half-educated awe of the Yankee democrat. Twain gathered much from Ward, Barnum, and the other literary comedians, who were often criticized as "phunny fellows" for their pretense to uneducated misspellings. Twain's newspaper humor, shorn of the misspellings, was still plainly stated, vulgar and vernacular, and usually downright colloquial in voice, and democratic in language and attitude; he was more comic than the serious travel writers, more ambitious and socially critical than the light satirists and literary comedians with whom he was associated.

Many of Twain's fellow comedians, such as Orpheus C. Kerr (Robert Henry Newell), Petroleum Vesuvius Nasby (David Ross Locke), and others less notable, would try to write longer works, both comic and serious, with mixed success. Among the literary comedians of the period, only Twain was able to write comic *literature* which took on broader importance. He was the voice of democracy broken loose and intending to rise to the highest level of consideration. The rampant humor, irony, sarcasm, and burlesque were amalgamated in a new voice with a strong moral overtone, an indignation at sham and inhumanity, and a democratic distaste for hypocrisy and self-importance.

American technology and industry had attracted British attention as early as 1817, when an English commission came to study the "American" system of manufacture, and it had leapt forward during the Civil War. Feeling this new economic power, Americans were ready to assert their claim to cultural supremacy as well. Twain's references in *Innocents Abroad* to farming tools and working inventions such as the wheelbarrow, the plow, and the threshing machine when he is in the Azores were intended to be boldly critical of non-technological and therefore non-American ways of doing things. He may have praised in passing the smooth roads of the Azores or the railroads of Italy, but his flamboyant attack on Roman ignorance, fostered by the church and the nobility (ch. 26), touted our highest virtues: universal education, religious toleration, freedom of dress (which dress Twain burlesques), and other advantages. He concludes thunderously by having his mock Roman narrator identify with astonishment the reaping machines, threshers, and agricultural methods which were transforming America into the world's breadbasket, or so we were coming to believe. Americans agreed enthusiastically: *Innocents Abroad* remained among Twain's best-selling books to the end of his life. It was reprinted in edition after edition with its illustrations intact, and later in the uniform Harper and Brothers editions, without pictures, as an American classic among other American classics by Twain.

I first read *The Innocents Abroad* in the Harper "Uniform Trade Edition," setting out naively to use it for a monthly book report during my senior year in high school. I realized a week later that page 407 at the end of the volume was actually the last page of the *second* volume of my two-in-one edition and that I would have to read at the rate of 50 pages a day for the rest of the term to finish the book. But as readers in 1869 must have discovered as well, Twain's fluid English, written as if spoken, and the mixture of grotesque comedy and serious ideas made the pages fly by. The "Is he dead?" question the "boys" (in real life, Twain's friends Dan Slote, Jack Van Nostrand, and Charley Langdon) ask of the Egyptian mummy and of Christopher Columbus delighted me — it *was* me, as far as I was concerned, with its gorgeously false innocence, and it must also have been seen as a benchmark by the Harper editors, who chose the illustration and caption of that moment as the frontispiece for volume 1 of my edition. Only later did I learn that the "Is he dead?" joke was an undisguised borrowing from Artemus Ward, Twain's most widely known comic predecessor, who had put the question in the mouth of a vulgar Cockney landlord in his *Artemus Ward in London* (1867), in reference to Oliver Cromwell's appearing at a spiritualist's séance, and had thus established it as a showman's joke on pretentious manipulation of historical dignity by charlatans. Twain presented the mood as a new American tradition: the Vandal Abroad (as he titled his popular lecture on the Holy Land journey), Barnum, who brought home Jenny Lind and almost captured Shakespeare's birthplace, and Ward, who claimed in a London *Punch* letter to want to buy the place on the Avon where Shakespeare fell down on the ice, had blazed a trail which Twain widened and deepened in the much longer and more ambitious *Innocents Abroad*.

Bernard DeVoto, in *Mark Twain at Work*, tried to wish such borrowings away in his quest to prove Twain a unique offspring of the muddy Mississippi riverbank, but contemporary readers all knew the source, and recognized, as I felt without knowing specifically, that an American tradition of pragmatic common sense was being projected, that a new skepticism was infusing the way Americans looked at things European. The frontispiece to my volume 2 pictured Twain weeping at the tomb of his first ancestor, Adam. The burlesque of the exploitation of Holy Land relics in sentimental travel narratives was not lost on Americans, or on William Dean Howells, who became a life-long friend of Twain's after his enthusiastic review of *Innocents Abroad* in the prestigious *Atlantic Monthly*. Howells cited the Adam episode as one of the outstanding parts of the book, one destined to rock America with laughter.

Twain's travelogue did indeed have much of the breezy air of literary comedy and social irreverence. To me, based on my initiating experience with *The Innocents Abroad*, Twain was a working comedian with an American message; and as I learned about Artemus Ward and P. T. Barnum, Doesticks, and some of his other forebears, I understood Twain as a genius who rose above a grand tradition of American comic skepticism, taking his social idealism to a truly visionary level of discourse which illuminates our time as well as his. In yet another of the "uniform editions" I acquired, the "corner in the Capuchin convent" — a grisly monument of skeletons and bone structures — is reproduced photographically as the volume 2 frontispiece: the picture of the bone sculptures accompanied by a mummy transforms the book into a documentary of humankind's failings. Contemporary readers were certainly engaged by *Innocents Abroad*, and Twain's lectures on the *Quaker City* trip helped to publicize it even more. While he spoke of the "vandal abroad" as a cultureless boor, his "innocent" is a hero, too, and he appealed to Americans' idealism as well as to their need to assert their own importance in the face of the old world. Wealthy souvenir hunters and religious poseurs were the true vandals, along with the shameless promoters who exploited art, culture, history, and humanity; Europeans and Bedouins alike shared failings with the American travelers.

Previous treatments of the Holy Land had been frequent enough to allow or force Twain to take a new tack along satiric lines. Franklin Walker, in *Irreverent Pilgrims*, finds comparisons between Herman Melville's verse drama *Clarel*, J. Ross Browne's *Yusef*, and Twain's *Innocents Abroad*.[1] *Yusef* focuses on Browne's guide as the comic central figure, whereas Twain stayed with his own viewpoint and that of the "boys." Like Twain, Browne, in a slapstick passage, burlesqued the "confusion of agonies" making up the Turkish baths in Damascus; Twain provided a lasting portrait of romance run afoul of reality in the five pages of chapter 34 (376–80) he lavished on the "malignant swindle" in Constantinople, where his bath followed the equally repulsive

"Turkish lunch."[2] Like Twain, but with less of the gaudy exaggeration of mood that makes Twain the traveler a boon companion, Browne described fleas and Arabs as far more present and unpleasant than had the earlier generation of sentimental writers represented by Englishman Eliot Warburton (*The Crescent and the Cross*), G. W. Curtis (*Nile Notes of a Howadji, The Howadji in Syria*, both 1851), and William C. Prime (*Tent Life in the Holy Land*, 1857). Browne foreshadowed the post–Civil War pragmatic skepticism which helped make Twain's book a departure from its sentimental ancestors. Twain hated the Prime book and mercilessly ridiculed Prime under the name of William C. Grimes in *The Innocents Abroad*.

Curtis's *Nile Notes of a Howadji*, given a discreet reference in the preface to Nathanial Hawthorne's *Blithedale Romance*, blazed a lightly ironic trail into the Holy Land with a comedy that suggested possibilities for a writer like Mark Twain, but without developing them. For Curtis, flatly, "The sole hope of the East is Western inoculation" to accomplish economic and social growth.[3] Whether viewing slavers — "human crocodiles," he calls them — or ravaged tombs of kings, he is predominantly serious in carrying his American attitude abroad, and his humor is banal, as in the following passage on the theme of the fragility of greatness, an obligatory exercise from Shelley's "Ozymandias" onward (the speaker is not the author but the hot desert sun):

> "Kings!" scoffed the sun, "Here's a royal shin-bone — the shin of a real Theban king. You may buy it for a pound to-day, if it were not sold for a shilling yesterday, and for a farthing if you'll give no more. The ring in his slave's ear in the plebeian tombs is worth a hundred of it." . . .
>
> "Ho, ho! Kings' shins, going, going! Kings' hands and feet, who bids? Not a para [small coin] from any of the crowd who sell their souls every day to kiss the hands and feet of some sort of royalty, the world over. Ho, ho, ho, kings!"[4]

The theme was an American favorite in such works as *The Life of P. T. Barnum, Written by Himself*.[5] Before Barnum, Albert Smith, the English comic travel writer and lecturer, also wrote of his adventures in the Holy Land and at notable sites like Mont Blanc; in 1845 Smith threatened to get a duplicate set of Napoleon's bones and bust up a balky sexton's Waterloo show. Twain outshone them all at the Capuchin Convent in Rome, where he dramatized the vanity of one complacent monk's fancying his thighbone to be just the right thing to finish off a skeletal arch. Comparing the brief sequence by Curtis in 1851 with Twain's ch. 28 on the "picturesque horrors" of the Capuchin Convent shows how much more able Twain was in 1869 to mix irony and sentiment while at the same time dramatizing his own persona — a gift not given to lesser writers like Curtis. With some perspective on travelers who tirelessly hunt antiquity, Curtis congratulates himself that he is seeing many of the sights before they have been excavated and commercialized;[6] Twain would see them after, and his view, consequently, could be and needed to be stronger, for the romance Curtis depended upon had worn off. Clearly, *Innocents Abroad* was a different kind of book than Curtis could have written, and owed far more to the tradition of *Artemus Ward in London* or Barnum's *Life*, humorous American books narrated by colloquial reporters progressing through a pretentious history that they could mock.

P. T. Barnum, of New York, Bridgeport, and the world, and his burlesque literary counterpart Artemus Ward, of Baldinsville, Indiana, provided motifs of chicanery, American brag, and colloquial language which were part of an American tradition of skepticism and opportunism. As wary showmen, insiders to the art of humbugging the public for ready cash, both Barnum and Ward readily detected the fraud, insincerity, and hypocrisy of other "shows." Twain's travel narratives continued in this mode. His burlesque scenarios are directed at the insincerity of money-driven and ego-driven cultures, which subordinated what is really sublime and important to their own self-aggrandizement. So the guides touting Christopher Columbus signatures, the Church of Santa Sophia, and the central sites of the Holy Land and Jerusalem get comic treatment. When Twain's "boys" asked, "Is he dead?" about the mummy and Columbus, Americans saw their green innocence as a weapon of resistance and a boast rather than a shame. As a literary comedian, Twain thrust himself into areas of the world where Americans wished to experience a sublimity presumably not to be obtained in their own "go-ahead" culture. His colloquial language was emblematic of his "Western" slant on the world, originally appealing to his California readers as their own, later modified to appeal to all Americans.

Barnum, Ward, and Twain ultimately saw the demands of history and custom as repugnant; they asserted the values of honesty and plain dealing, and — most obviously in Ward and Twain — the importance of basic virtues. Posing as vandals, they reconfirmed the true significance of historical sites, a significance which needed to be excavated from under the layers of souvenir sellers, both physical and literary. Thus, Twain could write at his angriest on entering the Holy Land that the pilgrims pushed their horses to the limit to avoid riding on a Sunday, keeping the letter of the law but violating its "spirit." Twain hated such a mixture of inhumanity and cant, nor would he apologize for native or local customs when they violated his sense of simple kindness to people and animals. If uncultured Americans were emotionally threatened by the cultural pretensions of older civilizations, *The Innocents Abroad* was the voice of a cultural counterattack; neither the nouveaux riches nor the ancien régime would abash the critic.

The Innocents Abroad was a product of the first of the major organized expeditions of middle-class Americans to Europe and the Holy Land. The wealthy and the adventurous had been outside the United States, but they had scarcely communicated with the American heartland. The organized troop of self-proclaimed "pilgrims" was a new departure for American culture, far different from Washington Irving's reports from the Continent or the later travels of writers like Melville, Browne, and Curtis. In the same year as *The Innocents Abroad*, Charles Carleton Coffin published *Our New Way Round the World*, which compared the Atlantic and Pacific railway union with the Suez Canal, connecting the Red Sea and the Mediterranean.[7] Thus, Coffin provided himself with the subject matter of Egypt, India, Malacca (then the dominant commercial city of the Malay Peninsula), China, Japan, and California — in other words, everything *not* covered by Twain's book. (Twain would write about those regions in *Roughing It* and *Following the Equator*.) Coffin in Egypt, like Twain in the Azores, observes the universal use of donkeys for transportation (and small boys to goad them) and the primitive cultivation of fields with a sharpened stick pulled by a camel and cow yoked together.[8] Coffin, like Twain in Greece, has an adventure getting ashore (in this case bribery merely) and finds the Greeks degraded — "descended" — from their ancestors of old. The circumstances of the moment, he recounts dryly, were not favorable for inspiring a thrill of enthusiasm or an elevation of the soul.[9] The viewpoint is markedly similar to Twain's; the vision and presentation fall profoundly below the mix of braggadocio and sublimity Twain created in describing his and the "boys'" raid on the Parthenon in chapter 32 of *Innocents*.

For Twain, issues of culture, technology, and faith were intermingled. He wanted faith so much that he once got down on his knees and prayed for it.[10] But the pilgrims he saw aboard the *Quaker City*, and the churches he saw in Europe and the Holy Lad, and the Roman Catholicism he saw, were as unpromising as he expected them to be, and he borrows "humbuggery" from the Barnum lexicon as soon as he arrives in the Azores (ch. 6) to describe Jesuits and the ignorant population they control. American technology is contrasted with the sloth and ignorance of the Portuguese of the Azores. The pragmatism of the machine shop is symbolized for readers in a list of inventions — the American steam press, the fire engine, the steel plow, and the telegraph — which are set against intellectual laziness, a "devout refusal to learn more than his father knew before him" (56). Will Carleton, one of America's most popular reformist poets of the period from 1870 to 1890 (it was Carleton who wrote "Over the Hill to the Poorhouse," calling into question the treatment of the elderly) found this same theme compelling in "The Clang of the Yankee Reaper" (1873), where the reaper heard moving on Salisbury Plain in England is equated with the American flag.[11] In this period, American national identity and technology seem to have merged into a new kind of chauvinism. The Americanism which Twain, Carleton, and others put forward was wedded to the improvement of physical life. If money was gathered and no value was rendered in palpable, measurable terms — or even in emotional terms which they could accept as consistent with their own values — a fraud was being perpetrated.

The sale of religious relics, the showing off of curiosities, the boasting about pieces of the true cross, and the fighting over the use of certain sanctified spots were evidence of chicanery, delusion, and uncivilized behavior that Twain lambasted in episode after episode of *Innocents Abroad*. The book found its coherence in the sarcasm and irony of the protests. Twain adopted Barnum's penchant for gaudy advertising to describe the ornamentation of churches and mosques in the original *Alta* letters, though his comparison of shrines to circuses was significantly toned down in the book.[12] Faith, surrounded by such trumpery, was easy for an irascible visionary to burlesque. Yet Twain was not merely taking cheap shots, for he also wrote ambivalently against technology as panacea in *A Connecticut Yankee in King Arthur's Court* (1889) and *The American Claimant* (1892), for the same reasons he caricatured the pilgrims and the Holy Land: their beliefs brought no benefits; they were as frequently gulled by themselves as by others. Religion could be bad or good, and in the Europe and Holy Land that Twain saw, it was bad. He had planned from the outset to expose the badness. And he knew what he would find, pessimist that he was, because the same was to be found virtually everywhere a dollar was to be hustled. One of the great virtues of Dewey Ganzel's *Mark Twain Abroad* lies in its demonstration that much of Twain's prose was predesigned to fit what he anticipated seeing. His artlessly uncontrived "responses" were actually an American viewpoint in place before the journey had begun, blunt, Western in both language and exaggerated attitude, and superpatriotic to the point of caricature.

Twain criticizes the *Quaker City* pilgrims as well as European guides and cultural sacred cows, portraying them as stuffed shirts falsely inflated with their own importance. Henry Nash Smith, analyzing Twain's irreverent lampoons in *Mark Twain: The Development of a Writer*, finds that they helped free him to fictionalize his narrator and tell more of the story he wanted to tell. Twain satirizes his fellow travelers as ungainly birds, and their actions as hypocritical or misguided by turns, most notably when they lose their chance to sail on the Sea of Galilee because they are so cheap as to haggle over the price of the boat ride. His caricatures of Captain Duncan so rankled the man that he was still attacking Twain a decade later in the newspapers; of course, the continuing popularity of the book kept the burlesque of his insufficiency as captain alive to rankle.[13]

Twain was not the only correspondent — there were at least nine, as named offhandedly in a shipboard letter by Mrs. Solon Severance, which claimed a dozen total — but Twain was the most critical, and by virtue of his exaggerated comic tone, the most notorious.[14] (It is no wonder that those he pilloried were angry.) Another set of letters to find its way into print, but not until two years after *Innocents Abroad*, in 1871, was Louisa Griswold's *A Woman's Pilgrimage to the Holy Land; or Pleasant Days Abroad*.[15] The prevailing dullness of Griswold's account is in stark contrast to what Twain accomplished; where he was biting or funny, she says of her visit to the tomb of Lazarus, "I may here remark that there is more or less skepticism among travelers regarding the identity of many of the places pointed out in Palestine."[16] That Mark Twain could dramatize such skepticism as comedy is testimony to his skill both as a "realistic" writer and as a humorist. Where Mrs. Griswold merely notes the low status of women, who rank beneath horses to a Bedouin, Twain sarcastically describes them, and treats their status as part of the general degradation of life rather than an isolated component. Mrs. Griswold is a literalist, a reporter. In the Mosque of Omar, she tells us, all but the fat "venerable Major" squeeze between two pillars that are supposed by Moslems to cleanse one of sin: the major is then teased as the only "sinner" remaining in the party.[17] Such trivialization of the religious encounter is bland and unappealing; when Twain enters a mosque, we can anticipate delicious particularizations of overwrought architectural details, caustic asides about the sincerity of the attending clerics, and an engaged, role-playing narrator. Twain will involve us.

American reformers had looked abroad well before Twain's adventure, and Twain intended to find cultures needing reform on American principles. Examples of the precedents Twain translated into comedy can be found as early as the 1840s and 1850s — for instance, *Dr. Scudder's Appeal to the Children and Youth of the United States of America, in Behalf of the Heathen World* (1867), which describes child mutilation and slavery. Americans were ready to criticize the world, and not just accept the world's criticism. Twain takes up the issue of human backwardness at the very outset of his narrative, as soon as he reaches the Azores (ch. 6), and then in Constantinople (ch. 34, where he covers not only female slavery but also the famous dogs of Constantinople, the Turkish bath, and the Turkish lunch in some of the funniest sequences in the book) and in the Holy Land (chs. 44, 45, 47, and other passages). His angry sarcasm is a notable element of *The Innocents Abroad*. The comment "a beggar has to have exceedingly good points to make a living in Constantinople" (362) is the ironic language of the stranger in "Jumping Frog" who dupes Jim Smiley by claiming he "don't see no p'ints about that frog that's any better'n any other frog." Twain's democratic values are oriented around individual welfare, and evil lies in the perpetuation of human suffering. Twain's antagonism to suffering and cruelty reappears in Pap Finn's mistreatment of Huck and presages his antagonism to the violence perpetrated by white imperialists in the third world, a subject he would address in "To the Person Sitting in Darkness" and "King Leopold's Soliloquy."

Although critics for the last hundred years and more have prized *Innocents Abroad* not for the string of jokes it contains but for the wider humorous perspective it projects so successfully, it is also a book of great comic moments. Mark Twain's tongue-in-cheek introduction of himself into the pleasure voyage establishes his irreverent tone, yet it still makes the point that this sort of excursion to the Holy Land is indeed unlike other excursions before it. Twain also positions himself as a working newspaperman and skeptic, thereby representing the practical viewpoint of the American middle class, better off financially following the Civil War — at least in the North — but still concrete in their view of life, as Twain himself implies when he remarks in the Holy Land that physically standing where Jesus has stood alters his perspective and gives it substance. Beginning in the Azores, Mark Twain's attack on ignorance and his assertion of the importance of technology sets an aggressive comic tone which boosts American ways of thinking.[18] The play between Europeans and Americans goes back and forth. He burlesques himself in the glove-buying episode in Paris and in his comments on the Louvre, where the old world's icons confront the unabashed greenness of the American naif; then the "Is he dead?" sequences dramatize how the "boys" dismiss grotesque European historical pretension with frontier Western disrespect, the mood which Artemus Ward had pioneered.

Moments, of course, become motifs. The behavior of the pilgrims them-selves on the *Quaker City* weaves in and out of the narrative, travestied at Yalta with the visit to the czar and displayed as meanness in the Holy Land. Twain's response to Leonardo da Vinci's *Last Supper* — part vandalism abroad and part realism — and his pretense of spoon and overcoat stealing at Yalta leave him both inside and outside these critiques. These sequences have remained among the best examples of the literary comedian's art. The Roman Coliseum burlesque, juvenile though it seems on early readings, is yet anoth-er translation of hallowed antiquity into the language of small-town America: sheer fantastic Barnum rises out of the pages in the form of a seventeen-hun-dred-year-old "playbill" for a Christian sacrifice in the Coliseum, followed by the review in the *Roman Daily Battle-Ax*. Vulgar American reality intrudes its unsentimental viewpoint — a special Twain perspective which binds the book's various episodes together brilliantly and seemingly effortlessly. The monks' bones in the Capuchin Convent in Rome, where the "Is he dead?" joke reemerges joyously and appropriately, and Twain's expansion of his treatment of vanity as a target of his irony add substantial comic power to the middle of the book. The illicit visit to the Acropolis (seemingly a staple of travel literature about Greece) shows American vandals in action, converting their lawlessness into an innocent search for the true feeling of history. We are engaged by the day-to-day adventures in a real-world setting, conflicting with their historical aura, and made fresh by the comedian's slapstick portrayal.

The approach to Jerusalem and the Holy Land via the Sea of Galilee reaches its burlesque crescendo in the Tomb of Adam sequence and at the Church of the Holy Sepulcher. Humor, travesty, and serious commentary are merged as fully in the Holy Land as in any other part of the book. It is hard to imagine a reader grasping the essence of *Innocents Abroad* without respond-ing to Twain's intrusions into the various holy shrines, churches, and gar-dens. The Tomb of Adam was particularly beloved by contemporaries and was often reprinted in anthologies with its illustration. In Egypt the intensity diminishes, but humor counterpoints sentiment in treating the Sphinx and the pyramids. The Sphinx draws somewhat artificial respect, consciously marred when Twain sees despised relic hunters climbing its face — although, as Franklin Walker notes in *Irreverent Pilgrims*, Twain himself toted home broken cornices and tree branches ripped from holy gardens, like any other American vandal.[19]

With so many components to manage, Twain achieved a substantial transformation of a series of newspaper travel letters into a book. D. M. McKeithan, in *Traveling with the Innocents Abroad*, allows us to see how Twain altered the letters, substituting serious sentiment for the more sophomoric sections, as he wrote to Mary Mason Fairbanks, a fellow passenger who became his friend and adviser. Passages like the one on the Sphinx were intended to woo more conventional Victorian readers. He had written Elisha Bliss on 2 December 1867 that he would take the letters and "weed them of their chief faults of construction and inelegancies of expression" to make them more acceptable, and he promised Mrs. Fairbanks to take out the slang, except in mild dialogue.[20] He raced to San Francisco when the *Alta California* projected an edition of the original letters, agonizing, "If the *Alta*'s book were to come out with those wretched, slangy letters unrevised, I should be utterly ruined."[21] Twain well knew that he had a valuable literary property and that he must manage it, despite the frequent claims that he was either a natural or a jackleg writer unable to exercise control over his own compositions. He knew that the breezy Western slang, for example, would appeal to California newspaper readers far more than it would to a national audience familiar with Eastern periodicals and willing to buy books.

Some things were lost that remain delicious. McKeithan reprints a letter from the *Alta California* series containing Twain's description of Prime's entrance into Jerusalem: "He wept, and his party all wept, and the dragoman wept, and so did the muleteers, and even a Latin priest, and a Jew that came straggling along. It would have been just as cheap to believe that the camels and asses wept also, and fully as likely. . . . he went through Palestine and irrigated it from one end to the other."[22] The comparable passage in the revised chapter 52 ends colorlessly, merely denying that tears which belonged to the nursery had any place in the emotional first sighting of Jerusalem (557). On the other hand, chapter 50 blossomed with invective against "Grimes" and his view of the Holy Land, including descriptions of his weeping, and ending with the double sarcasm "He never bored but he struck water" (535). Twain made many such tradeoffs in transmuting newspaper letters to a sustained narrative. Episodes were made more consistent, themes sharpened, and transitions established.

The letters were edited stylistically as well. Twain eliminated slang and rough diction in what some critics see as an attempt to lessen offense to the religiously conservative, and others as a capitulation to the emasculating genteel influence of the Northeast and a corruption of Twain's "natural" American voice. Some expressions would have been good to keep, such as the idea of the golden calf "as pleasantly suggestive of a free lunch" to the Israelites.[23] He changed "hanker" to "long for," "bother" to "trouble," "we dusted" to "we travelled": a good analyst has to conclude that some of this slang would merely have dated and lowered the effect of the book and that other alterations may have made a stronger "voice," but no flat assessment can be proven either way. Although later in his career he was glad to pretend to be a writer whose books happened by chance rather than by design (as he would present himself in *Pudd'nhead Wilson* and *Those Extraordinary Twins*), at this point he was eager to identify himself as an educated writer communicating above the level of newspaper humor to modern Americans not afraid to mix seriousness and comedy. He had staked out the higher ground of literary comedy: his subject was elevated, and his tone had to rise to a compatible level, and it did. But he was still offensive to many. Franklin Walker reports in *Irreverent Pilgrims* that "he, who had written that Christ would never come to Palestine a second time as he had been there once, was called by one minister 'this son of the devil' and by another 'this person, Mark Twain, who visits the Holy Land and ridicules sacred scenes and things.' "[24]

William Dean Howells, in the *Atlantic Monthly* in December 1869, praised Twain's stance because it took on sham and maintained its own "good humor," and he argued on behalf of Twain's vandal, "Yet the man who can be honest enough to let himself see the realities of human life everywhere, or who has only seen Americans as they are abroad, has not traveled in vain and is far from a useless guide." The unregenerate irony throughout, as well as the "delicious impudence" of the comedy, caught Howells' attention, and seemed to him to ensure that Twain's book "would secure him something better than the uncertain standing of a popular favorite."[25] Twain himself, after the first reviews, told Elisha Bliss that the "irreverence of the volume appears to be a tip-top good feature of it, . . . though I wish with all my heart there wasn't an irreverent passage in it."[26] For Twain, the achievement of the book was to raise him above the level of other "phunny fellows" to the ranks of writers of serious literature. That *Innocents Abroad* achieved this goal is attested by the status it still enjoys as one of the major books in the Twain canon.

Later, lesser imitators kept the irreverence but lacked the humanitarian breadth of vision. *Innocents from Abroad*, published in 1877 by G. W. Carleton, the firm that had originally rejected *The Celebrated Jumping Frog of Calaveras County*, reversed Twain's attacks on Europe by showing what a farce foreign expectations of American economy and efficiency were in light of the thievery of customs officials, the municipal corruption manifest in New York City's unusable streets, and other such instances of American "progressiveness." Walter T. Gray's *The Bad Boy Abroad* delivered the basic traveler jokes in yokel dialect. The bad boy's "Pa" does indeed buy a nail from the true cross, although the boy soon discovers under the rust the inscription "O Bros. & P. Pgh, Pa." True to form, "The galleries where they keep the paintins' is boss."[27] The rest of the humor is cacography of the "Prince of Whales" variety, showing how low a line of humor *could* devolve from American vandals, and suggesting how great, really, was Twain's capacity to make his materials universal and visionary.

The Innocents Abroad still speaks to us today despite its roots in a fading, well-heeled, travel-oriented, pietistic nineteenth-century American culture, and despite its length. The innocent's detestation of willful cruelty, self-important vanity, and fanaticism still applies, and the book presages Twain's later attacks on imperialism and international inhumanity. Its greatest strength, however, lies in the rambunctious Americanness of its humor, an egregious vandalism with a serious core — a specialty of our greatest national writer.

NOTES

1. Franklin Walker, *Irreverent Pilgrims: Melville, Browne, and Mark Twain in the Holy Land* (Seattle: University of Washington Press, 1974).

2. Walker, p. 86. The Turkish bath continues to be a comic subject; see Gerard Hoffnung, "A Turkish Bath Night," reprinted in *Essays in Arts and Sciences* 21 (October 1992): 86–90.

3. G. W. Curtis, *Nile Notes of a Howadji* (New York: Harper and Brothers, 1851), p. 50.

4. Curtis, p. 263.

5. P. T. Barnum, *The Life of P. T. Barnum, Written by Himself* (New York: Redfield, 1855). On his visit to Europe with Tom Thumb, Barnum bought bones and relics at Waterloo that turned out to be regularly imported and planted, and he identified other relics as fraudulent products for tourists. Twain's treatment of pieces of the "true cross" in *The Innocents Abroad* echoes Barnum's skeptical attitude.

6. Curtis, p. 289.

7. Charles Carleton Coffin, *Our New Way Round the World* (Boston: Fields, Osgood 1869).

8. Coffin, p. 37.

9. Coffin, p. 21.

10. This is according to a handwritten reminiscence of his life, now in the Beinecke Library at Yale University, by Twain's pastor and friend the Reverend Joseph Twichell.

11. Will Carleton, "The Clang of the Yankee Reaper," in *Farm Ballads* (New York: Harper and Brothers, 1873), pp. 101–2.

12. An agent of P. T. Barnum's was along on the *Quaker City* trip looking for curiosities, so Twain had another reason for thinking of Barnum. Artemus Ward, in the 1866 travel letters which became *Artemus Ward in London*, had also leaned heavily on Barnum's showmanship as a comic mode for making fun of falsely inflated historical artifacts.

13. Captain Charles C. Duncan tried to sue Twain twice for slander and claimed in lectures in 1877 that he smelled of cheap whiskey and was often drunk. Twain wrote in his own defense against Duncan's attacks that his "moral scaffolding" was only partly constructed in the 1860s; the 1870s, he comments sarcastically, find him with a much better article, so he bequeaths the old scaffolding to Duncan. The letter is reprinted from the *New York World* of 17 February 1877 in *The Literary Humor of the Urban Northeast: 1830–1890*, (pp. 241–43); the clipping is preserved in the Mark Twain scrapbooks at the University of California, Berkeley.

14. *Mark Twain to Mrs. Fairbanks*, ed. Dixon Wecter (San Marino, Calif.: Huntington Library, 1949), p. xix. I am indebted to Jeffrey A. Melton's paper, "Same Trip, Different Holy Lands: Aboard the *Quaker City* with Mark Twain and Mrs. Stephen M. Griswold" (American Literature Association Convention, 4 June 1994), for information on Mrs. Severance. Melton's paper significantly expands Wecter's work.

15. Louisa Griswold, *A Woman's Pilgrimage to the Holy Land; or Pleasant Days Abroad*

(Hartford: J. B. Burr and Hyde, 1871). Jeffrey Melton (see n. 14) deserves credit for his discovery and thoughtful analysis of this work.

16. Griswold, p. 278.

17. Griswold, p. 260.

18. Chapter 43 gives the ultimate critique of the Arabs of Lebanon in terms of Americanism: "An American, of ordinary intelligence, would soon widely extend his property, at an outlay of mere manual labor, performed at night, under so loose a system of fencing. . . . They never invent anything, never learn anything" (445–46). Invention and learning take primary place in the value scheme, but midnight acquisition reflects ironically on the American go-getter entrepreneur as well.

19. Walker, p. 192.

20. Daniel Morley McKeithan, *Traveling with the Innocents Abroad* (Norman: University of Oklahoma Press, 1958), p. x; *Mark Twain to Mrs. Fairbanks*, p. 22.

21. *Mark Twain to Mrs. Fairbanks*, p. 24.

22. McKeithan, p. 265.

23. Walker, pp. 206–8.

24. Walker, p. 198.

25. Howells included his essay from the December 1869 *Atlantic Monthly* in *My Mark Twain* (New York: Harper and Brothers, 1910); it can most easily be found in the reprinted *My Mark Twain* (Baton Rouge: Louisiana State University Press, 1967), pp. 89–94.

26. *Mark Twain's Letters, Volume 3 (1869)*, ed. Victor Fischer and Michael B. Frank (Berkeley: University of California Press, 1992), p. 329.

27. Walter T. Gray, *The Bad Boy Abroad* (New York: J. S. Ogilvie, 1883), pp. 61–63.

FOR FURTHER READING

David E. E. Sloane

The Innocents Abroad has continued to draw respectful attention from scholars, but without becoming a lightning rod for racial issues, as in the case of *Huckleberry Finn* and *Pudd'nhead Wilson*. Three valuable book-length scholarly studies are devoted to its composition and construction: Daniel Morley McKeithan's reprinting of the original reports from Europe and the Holy Land as they appeared in contemporary newspapers, in *Traveling with the Innocents Abroad* (Norman: University of Oklahoma Press, 1958); Franklin Walker and G. Ezra Dane's *Mark Twain's Travels with Mr. Brown* (New York: Knopf, 1940; New York: Russell and Russell, 1971), which reprints the twenty-six weekly letters to the *Alta California* preceding the *Quaker City* letters; and Dewey Ganzel's *Mark Twain Abroad* (Chicago: University of Chicago Press, 1968), analyzing Twain's intentions and delivery of the skeptical American comic viewpoint before, during, and after the trip. Richard Bridgman, *Traveling in Mark Twain* (Berkeley: University of California Press, 1987), is also worth consulting. Dixon Wecter's *Mark Twain and Mrs. Fairbanks* (San Marino, Calif.: Huntington Library, 1949) reprints illuminating letters to her as his critic and adviser about his stylistic and intellectual concerns. They offer a fascinating window into the personal aspirations of a Victorian-American of his time and place. The tightly focused biographical study by Jeffrey Steinbrink in *Getting to be Mark Twain* (Berkeley: University of California Press, 1991) provides a richness of detail and analysis covering the period around Twain's first major book that is seldom attempted.

More general books have also given careful attention to *Innocents Abroad*. Franklin Walker's *Irreverent Pilgrims: Melville, Browne, and Mark Twain in the Holy Land* (Seattle: University of Washington Press, 1974) relates Twain's work to that of other American writers who tried to reinterpret the cultural-religious experience of the Holy Land for American readers. David E. E. Sloane's "Toward the Novel" in *Mark Twain as a Literary Comedian* (Baton

Rouge: Louisiana State University Press, 1979), reprinted in *Mark Twain's Humor: Critical Essays* (New York: Garland, 1993), pp. 109–31, argues that Twain's growth as a literary comedian proceeded naturally through this semifictional work to extended fiction. Henry Nash Smith's chapter on *The Innocents Abroad* in *Mark Twain: The Development of a Writer* (Cambridge: Harvard University Press, 1962) analyzes Twain's treatment of the pilgrims deftly, and is consistently insightful about the generic construction of the book. A very helpful group of nine reviews, including William Dean Howells' and Bret Harte's, is reprinted in Frederick Anderson's *Mark Twain: The Critical Heritage* (New York: Barnes and Noble, 1971). Tony Tanner's *The Reign of Wonder* (London: Cambridge University Press, 1965) succinctly identifies how Clemens evaded the "conspiracy of prevailing taste" in developing his voice in the book. Shelly Fisher Fishkin's *From Fact to Fiction: Journalism and Imaginative Writing in America* (New York: Oxford University Press, 1988) adds further valuable remarks in a thoughtful chapter on Twain with references to *The Innocents Abroad*.

Articles are best found through *American Literary Scholarship: Annual*, published by Duke University Press, which reviews scholarship on Mark Twain each year in a separate article under his name, or through bibliographies in the *Mark Twain Circular*, the newsletter of the Mark Twain Circle, published from The Citadel in Charleston, South Carolina. Leon T. Dickenson's "Marketing a Best Seller: Mark Twain's *Innocents Abroad*," *Papers of the Bibliographical Society of America* 41, no. 2 (1947): 102–22, provides further background. To compare travelogue comedy from Twain's immediate predecessor, see Charles Farrar Browne's *Artemus Ward in London* (New York: G. W. Carleton, 1867), most easily available in *The Compete Works of Artemus Ward*, from various publishers between 1869 and 1922; *The Life of P. T. Barnum, Written by Himself* (New York: Redfield, 1855) is also relevant. *Mark Twain's Letters, Volume 3 (1869)*, edited by Victor Fischer and Michael B. Frank (Berkeley: University of California Press, 1992), offers many letters with detailed notes bearing on *Innocents Abroad*. Hamlin Hill's *Mark Twain and Elisha Bliss* (Columbia: University of Missouri Press, 1964) thoroughly explores the significance of Twain's relationship with his publisher during what Hill sees as a formative decade; *Mark Twain's Letters to his Publishers, 1867–1894* (Berkeley: University of California Press, 1967), edited by Hill, also applies to this period.

ILLUSTRATORS AND ILLUSTRATIONS

IN MARK TWAIN'S FIRST AMERICAN EDITIONS

Beverly R. David & Ray Sapirstein

From the "gorgeous gold frog" stamped into the cover of *The Celebrated Jumping Frog of Calaveras County* in 1867 to the comet-riding captain on the frontispiece of *Extract from Captain Stormfield's Visit to Heaven* in 1909, illustrators and illustrations were an integral part of Mark Twain's first editions.

Twain marketed most of his major works by subscription, and illustration functioned as an important sales tool. Subscription books were packed with pictures of every type and size and were bound in brassy gold-stamped covers. The books were sold by agents who flipped through a prospectus filled with lively illustrations, selected text, and binding samples. Illustrations quickly conveyed a sense of the story, condensing the proverbial "thousand words" and outlining the scope and tone of the work, making an impression on the potential purchaser even before the full text had been printed. Book canvassers were rewarded with up to 50 percent of the selling price, which started at $3.50 and ranged as high as $7.00 for more ornate bindings. The books themselves were seldom produced until a substantial number of customers had placed orders. To justify the relatively high price and to reassure buyers that they were getting their money's worth, books published by subscription had to offer sensational volume and apparent substance. As Frank Bliss of the American Publishing Company observed, these consumers "would not pay for blank paper and wide margins. They wanted everything filled up with type or pictures." While authors of trade books generally tolerated lighter sales, gratified by attracting a "better class of readers," as Hamlin Hill put it, authors of subscription books sacrificed literary respectability for popular appeal and considerable profit.[1]

The humorist George Ade remembered Twain's books vividly, offering us a child's-eye view of the nineteenth-century subscription book market.

Just when front-room literature seemed at its lowest ebb, so far as the American boy was concerned, along came Mark Twain. His books looked at a distance, just like the other distended, diluted, and altogether tasteless volumes that had been used for several decades to balance the ends of the center table . . . so thick and heavy and emblazoned with gold that [they] could keep company with the bulky and high-priced Bible. . . . The publisher knew his public, so he gave a pound of book for every fifty cents, and crowded in plenty of wood-cuts and stamped the outside with golden bouquets and put in a steel engraving of the author, with a tissue paper veil over it, and "sicked" his multitude of broken-down clergymen, maiden ladies, grass widows, and college students on the great American public.

Can you see the boy, Sunday morning prisoner, approach the book with a dull sense of foreboding, expecting a dose of Tupper's *Proverbial Philosophy?* Can you see him a few minutes later when he finds himself linked arm-in-arm with Mulberry Sellers or Buck Fanshaw or the convulsing idiot who wanted to know if Christopher Columbus was sure-enough dead? No wonder he curled up on the hair-cloth sofa and hugged the thing to his bosom and lost all interest in Sunday school. *Innocents Abroad* was the most enthralling book ever printed until *Roughing It* appeared. Then along came *The Gilded Age, Life on the Mississippi,* and *Tom Sawyer.* . . . While waiting for a new one we read the old ones all over again.[2]

Publishers, editors, and Twain himself spent a good deal of time on design — choosing the most talented artists, directing their interpretations of text, selecting from the final prints, and at times removing material they deemed unfit for illustration.[3]

With the exception of *Following the Equator* (1897), books released in the twilight of Twain's career were not sold by subscription. Twain's later books, published for the trade market by Harper and Brothers, seldom contained more than a frontispiece and a dozen or so tasteful illustrations, rather than the hundreds of illustrations per volume that subscription publishing demanded. Illustration, however, remained a major component of Twain's later work in two important cases: *Extracts from Adam's Diary,* illustrated by Fred

Strothmann in 1904, and *Eve's Diary*, illustrated by Lester Ralph in 1906.

The stories behind the illustrators and illustrations of Mark Twain's first editions abound in back-room intrigue. The besotted or negligent lapses of some of the artists and the procrastinations of the engravers are legendary. The consequent production delays, mistimed releases, and copyright infringements all implied a lack of competent supervision that frequently infuriated Twain and ultimately encouraged him to launch his own publishing company.

In many cases, Twain took illustrations into account as he wrote and edited his text, using them as counterpoint and accompaniment to his words, often allowing them to inform his general narrative strategy and to influence the amount of detail he felt necessary to include in his written descriptions. In the most artful and carefully considered illustrated works, an analysis of the relationships between author and illustrator and between text and pictures illuminates key dimensions of Twain's writings and the responses they have elicited from readers. Examinations of even the most straightforward examples of decorative imagery yield insights into the publishing history of Twain's books and his attitudes toward the production process.

The original illustrations in Twain's works have often been replaced in the twentieth century by subsequent visual interpretations. But while Norman Rockwell's well-known nostalgic renderings of *Tom Sawyer* and *Huckleberry Finn* may tell us much about 1930s sensibilities, we would do well to reacquaint ourselves with the first American editions and the artwork they contained if we want to understand the books Twain wrote and the world they affected.

Illustrated books, like the illustrated weekly magazines that first appeared in the 1860s, were a significant source of visual images entering nineteenth-century homes. Because of their widespread popularity and the relative paucity of other sources of visual information, Twain's books helped to define America's perceptions of remote people, exotic scenes, and historic events. In addition to being an essential element of Mark Twain's body of work, illustrations are a documentary source in their own right, a window into Twain's world and our own.

NOTES

1. For background on subscription book publishing, see Hamlin Hill, *Mark Twain and Elisha Bliss* (Columbia: University of Missouri Press, 1964), chapter 1. See also R. Kent Rasmussen, "Subscription-book publishing" entry, *Mark Twain A to Z: The Essential Reference to His Life and Writings* (New York: Facts on File, 1995), p. 448.

2. George Ade, "Mark Twain and the Old-Time Subscription Book," *Review of Reviews* 61 (June 10, 1910): 703–4; reprinted in Frederick Anderson, ed., *Mark Twain: The Critical Heritage* (London: Routledge and Kegan Paul, 1971), pp. 337–39.

3. Beverly R. David, *Mark Twain and His Illustrators, Volume 1 (1869–1875)* (Troy, N.Y.: Whitston Publishing Company, 1986), discusses in detail Twain's involvement in the production of his early books.

READING THE ILLUSTRATIONS IN

THE INNOCENTS ABROAD

Beverly R. David & Ray Sapirstein

Mark Twain entered the subscription book market when he contracted with Elisha Bliss of the American Publishing Company for *The Innocents Abroad, or The New Pilgrims' Progress* (1869). Among Twain's first questions to his publisher was "whether [the book] should have pictures in it or not."[1] Bliss assured him it should. The team of illustrators for *The Innocents Abroad* included True Williams (1839–1897), a well-known graphic artist with considerable talent but little formal training.[2] Williams worked on each of Twain's books for the American Publishing Company, through *A Tramp Abroad* in 1880. Roswell Morse Shurtleff (1838–1915), a magazine illustrator and later a landscape painter and member of the National Academy of Design, contributed most of the detailed scenes of Genoa, Pisa, and Pompeii, and probably many other images. He would later provide similar prints for *Roughing It*.

Twain was actively involved in the production of the prints for his book, gathering extensive reference materials for the artists' use. He contributed photographs and cartes de visite that he and a fellow passenger, Moses Beach, had collected from foreign dignitaries on the trip. Twain also supplied photographic portraits of fellow pilgrims, many of whom he and the illustrators burlesqued ruthlessly. Several of the *Quaker City* passengers parade through the pages, including the supposedly abstemious captain of the ship, Charles C. Duncan, and Twain's "wine-drinking, godless" cabin mate Dan Slote. There is even a print allegedly depicting Bloodgood Haviland Cutter, the fool immortalized by Twain as the "Poet Lariat." Oddly, the figure captioned "Poet Lariat" is not a likeness of Cutter but a caricature of a frazzled, pen-wielding Mark Twain — a self-deprecating joke perpetrated either by Twain or by the illustrators. The artists also had at their disposal numerous stereopticon slides taken by William E. James, the photographer who documented the voyage.

They used several of his slides as studies, transforming them into impressive views of the Sea of Galilee, the ruins of Baalbec, and Mount Tabor.[3]

With the publishing deadline approaching, the frontispiece Twain suggested, an engraving of the *Quaker City*, had not been completed. Elisha Bliss reached into his handy stock of "electros" already engraved for a work previously published by his company, Thomas Knox's *Overland Through Asia*, and produced a full-page print of the steamship *Wright* instead of the stately side-wheeler on which the "innocents" had sailed.[4]

Reviewers generally thought highly of the illustrations, despite the haphazard production and assemblage. An anonymous reviewer in *Packard's Monthly* found *The Innocents Abroad* "splendidly illustrated, and produced in the best style of art."[5] William Dean Howells, the taste maker of American letters and later a close friend of Twain's, wrote a glowing review in the *Atlantic* of "Mr. Clements' [sic] very amusing" and "insolent" book, delivering the somewhat backhanded praise that

> the artist who has so copiously illustrated the volume has nearly always helped the author in the portraiture of his fellow-passengers, instead of hurting him, which is saying a good deal for an artist; in fact, we may go further and apply the commendation to all the illustrations; and this in spite of the variety of figures in which the same persons are represented, and the artist's tendency to show the characters on mules where the author says they rode horseback.[6]

Albert Bigelow Paine, Twain's friend and biographer, and an authority on illustration, was also the biographer of the famed editorial cartoonist Thomas Nast. In his 1912 biography of Twain, Paine discussed the illustrations in *The Innocents Abroad*, concluding,

> Williams was not a great draftsman, but no artist ever caught more perfectly the light and spirit of the author's text. Crude some of the pictures are, no doubt, but they convey the very essence of the story; they belong to it, they are a part of it, and they ought never to perish .... The public, which in the long run makes no mistakes, has rendered that verdict.[7]

Late in his career, Twain looked back at Williams' work sympathetically.

That publisher of mine in Hartford had an eye for the pennies, and he saved them. He did not waste any on the illustrations. He had a very good artist — Williams — who had never taken a lesson in drawing. Everything he did was original. The publisher hired the cheapest wood engraver he could find, and in my early books you can see a trace of that. You can see that if Williams had a chance he would have made some very good pictures. He had a good heart and good intentions.[8]

Despite the penurious habits of the publisher, *The Innocents Abroad* proved itself a best-seller in the subscription market, and it served as a model for many of Twain's later books. An enthusiastic Mark Twain claimed in a letter to a friend that his book "had the largest sale of a *four-dollar book* . . . ever achieved in America in so short a time."[9]

Reflecting Twain's frank journalistic prose and the crass extravagance of subscription books, the illustrations in *The Innocents Abroad* represent an American popular art largely free of aesthetic pretension and technical detail, a tradition with deep roots in humor, irreverence, and practicality. Cartooning and caricature, the dominant styles of illustration in Twain's early books, shared the same journalistic heritage that forged Twain's concise writing style and probing cynicism. Pressed by deadlines and limited staff, artists for illustrated weeklies and monthly comic reviews relied upon minimal detail, a quickly drawn symbolic vocabulary, and ironic captions to make their meaning clear. Under the guise of social satire, they expressed often damning criticism explicitly, imparting sharp insight and social commentary rather than trifling with aesthetic subtlety.

If Twain parodied the genre of the travel narrative in *The Innocents Abroad*, he likewise played the role of contrarian art critic on his own Grand Tour of the Continent. In the spirit of Twain's critique of the Old Masters, many of the illustrations refused to offer sentimental paeans to the genius and aestheticism of the monumental icons of the Old World (238–39). Presumably, the simple, straightforward drawings were meant to convey unadorned truths rather than distracting readers with technical virtuosity.

In Twain's facetiously genteel description of his fellow passengers' seasickness, he employs the accompanying illustration to make the truth plain, mocking the propriety to which he pretends; the pilgrims were not mildly out of sorts, they were bolting for the side of the ship (34). Similarly, Twain records that he and his fellow quarantine-breakers calmly "sidled" away from the Athens shore patrol, but the illustration shows what *really* happened (350). By presenting illustrations that undercut his text, Twain demonstrates to the reader the tendency of all firsthand narrators to recount their actions in self-aggrandizing and embellished terms. As part of his satire of genteel propriety, Twain feigns innocence, often playing straight man while the illustrators deliver the punch line.

The illustrations in *The Innocents Abroad* signaled that the book would be an entertaining and comic adventure, with the cynical humor and popular accessibility of a political cartoon. On the cover, stamped in gold on black cloth, the title appears emblazoned across a small vignette of various monuments of the Old World: the dome of St. Peter's in Rome, Vesuvius in eruption, minarets and a mosque, the Parthenon, the Sphinx, and an Egyptian pyramid. Several spindly figures appear in the image. A tourist-toting camel lopes atop the word "Abroad," an elephant tramps across "Progress," and a small figure slides down the edge of the pyramid. Two antlike pilgrims are in the process of carving Mark Twain's name into the pyramid's face, foreshadowing the assault upon the icons of the Old World that issued from Twain's pen. The evocative and symbolic frontispiece, "The Quaker City in a Storm" (actually the storm-tossed *Wright*), promised thrilling adventure. Yet in light of the text, the image may also suggest that Twain brought the wrath of the Almighty down upon the ship, in divine retribution for his Holy Land blasphemies. Similarly, the "Illuminated Title-Page — The Pilgrim's Vision" offered buyers a glimpse of the exotic and mythic, depicting the romantic daydreams that informed America's idyllic vision of the Old World, the very target Twain took aim at, the very image he sought to puncture.

Despite Twain's best efforts to undermine the awe in which many Americans held Europe, *The Innocents Abroad* presents several historic sites and landscapes deferentially, suggesting Twain's profound attraction to

European civilization — as well as his fatigue as he faced the challenge of padding the book until it had a heft equal to its hype. Actually lifted, in several cases, from the travel guides he parodied, many of the scenic views were allotted full-page monumentality.

Although Twain may originally have intended to ridicule the Grand Tour, he was increasingly caught up in its attractions. Noticeably impressed with Lake Como, Pompeii, Versailles, and the Acropolis, he lapsed into an uncharacteristically reverential stance in spots. Twain's vision of European civilization was contradictory; appropriately, the illustrations reflect his ambivalence, split almost evenly between majestic adulation and parodic cartoon.

NOTES

1. SLC to Elisha Bliss, December 2, 1867, in *Mark Twain's Letters to His Publishers, 1867–1894* Hamlin Hill, ed. (Berkeley: University of California Press, 1967), p. 12.

2. Nathan M. Wood, "True Williams, Pen Drew Literary Giant of Old," *Watertown [N.Y.] Daily Times*, August 30, 1938, p. 11. Until recently, very little biographical information on Williams has been available. Unearthed by Barbara Schmidt, instructional media coordinator at Tarleton State University in Stephenville, Texas, and a regular contributor to the Mark Twain Forum on the Internet, this article provides significant biographical information, including his dates and publishing history. We are indebted to Barbara Schmidt for generously sharing this reference and her pioneering research on Williams' later career, which she is working on for a forthcoming article. Biographical information on Williams is presented in greater detail in this series in "Reading the Illustrations in Tom Sawyer," in *The Adventures of Tom Sawyer*, The Oxford Mark Twain (New York: Oxford University Press, 1996).

3. Robert Hirst and Brandt Rowles, "William E. James' Stereoscopic Views of the *Quaker City* Excursion," *Mark Twain Journal* 22 (Spring 1984): 20–25.

4. A detailed account of the genesis of the illustrations in *The Innocents Abroad* constitutes a chapter in Beverly R. David, *Mark Twain and His Illustrators, Volume 1 (1869–1875)* (Troy, N.Y.: Whitston Publishing Company 1986).

5. Unsigned review, *Packard's Monthly*, October 1869, ii, pp. 318–19; reprinted in Frederick Anderson, ed., *Mark Twain: The Critical Heritage* (London: Routledge and Kegan Paul, 1971), p. 23.

6. William Dean Howells, unsigned review, *Atlantic*, December 1869, xxiv, pp. 764–66; reprinted in Anderson, *Mark Twain: The Critical Heritage*, pp. 27–28.

7. Albert Bigelow Paine, *Mark Twain: A Biography*, 3 vols. (New York: Harper and Brothers, 1912), 1:384.

8. Mark Twain, Society of Illustrators speech, New York, December 21, 1905; reprinted in *Mark Twain Speaking*, Paul Fatout, ed. (Iowa City: University of Iowa Press, 1976), p. 474.

9. Cited in Leon T. Dickinson, "Innocents Abroad" entry, *The Mark Twain Encyclopedia*, J. R. LeMaster and James D. Wilson, eds. (New York: Garland Publishing Company, 1993), p. 400.

A NOTE ON THE TEXT

Robert H. Hirst

This text of *The Innocents Abroad, or The New Pilgrims' Progress* is a photographic facsimile of a copy of the first American edition dated 1869 on the title page. Although books printed from the first edition plates were manufactured until at least 1901, the earliest copies of the first edition came from the bindery on July 20, 1869. The copyright was registered on July 28, the same day the first review of the book was published. The copy reproduced here is an example of Jacob Blanck's "third issue" (*BAL* 3316). Unlike the very earliest copies ("first issue"), the second and third issues incorporated several necessary corrections: page numbers previously omitted from the table of contents were supplied (xvii–xviii) and a correction was made to the wording of the last entry (xviii); a previously missing portrait of Napoleon III was supplied (129) and the correct chapter number was used for chapter 61 (643). In all likelihood, this copy was among the 31,680 that were printed and bound by the end of December 1869. The original volume is in the collection of the Mark Twain House in Hartford, Connecticut (810/C625in/1869b/c. 8).

THE MARK TWAIN HOUSE

The Mark Twain House is a museum and research center dedicated to the study of Mark Twain, his works, and his times. The museum is located in the nineteen-room mansion in Hartford, Connecticut, built for and lived in by Samuel L. Clemens, his wife, and their three children, from 1874 to 1891. The Picturesque Gothic-style residence, with interior design by the firm of Louis Comfort Tiffany and Associated Artists, is one of the premier examples of domestic Victorian architecture in America. Clemens wrote *Adventures of Huckleberry Finn*, *The Adventures of Tom Sawyer*, *A Connecticut Yankee in King Arthur's Court*, *The Prince and the Pauper*, and *Life on the Mississippi* while living in Hartford.

The Mark Twain House is open year-round. In addition to tours of the house, the educational programs of the Mark Twain House include symposia, lectures, and teacher training seminars that focus on the contemporary relevance of Twain's legacy. Past programs have featured discussions of literary censorship with playwright Arthur Miller and writer William Styron; of the power of language with journalist Clarence Page, comedian Dick Gregory, and writer Gloria Naylor; and of the challenges of teaching *Adventures of Huckleberry Finn* amidst charges of racism.

Beverly R. David is professor emerita of humanities and theater at Western Michigan University in Kalamazoo. She is currently working on volume 2 of *Mark Twain and His Illustrators*, and on a Mark Twain mystery entitled *Murder at the Matterhorn*. She has written a number of sections on illustration for the *Mark Twain Encyclopedia* and her *Mark Twain and His Illustrators, Volume 1 (1869–1875)* was published in 1989. Dr. David resides in Allegan, Michigan, in the summer and Green Valley, Arizona, in the winter.

Shelley Fisher Fishkin, professor of American Studies and English at the University of Texas at Austin, is the author of the award-winning books *Was Huck Black? Mark Twain and African-American Voices* (1993) and *From Fact to Fiction: Journalism and Imaginative Writing in America* (1985). Her most recent book is *Lighting Out for the Territory: Reflections on Mark Twain and American Culture* (1996). She holds a Ph.D. in American Studies from Yale University, has lectured on Mark Twain in Belgium, England, France, Israel, Italy, Mexico, the Netherlands, and Turkey, as well as throughout the United States, and is president-elect of the Mark Twain Circle of America.

Robert H. Hirst is the General Editor of the Mark Twain Project at The Bancroft Library, University of California at Berkeley. Apart from that, he has no other known eccentricities.

Mordecai Richler is the author of the novels *A Choice of Enemies* (1955), *Son of a Smaller Hero* (1957), *The Apprenticeship of Duddy Kravitz* (1959), which was made into a feature film nominated for an Academy Award in 1974, *The Incomparable Atuk* (1963), *Cocksure* (1968), *St. Urbain's Horseman* (1971), *Joshua Then and Now* (1980), and *Solomon Gursky Was Here* (1990). His nonfiction includes *Oh Canada! Oh Quebec! Lament for a*

Divided Country (1992), the autobiographical *The Street* (1972), and a memoir, *This Year in Jerusalem* (1994). He divides his time between London and Quebec's Eastern Townships.

Ray Sapirstein is a doctoral student in the American Civilization Program at the University of Texas at Austin. He curated the 1993 exhibition *Another Side of Huckleberry Finn: Mark Twain and Images of African Americans* at the Harry Ransom Humanities Research Center at the University of Texas at Austin. He is currently completing a dissertation on the photographic illustrations in several volumes of Paul Laurence Dunbar's poetry.

David E. E. Sloane, professor of English at the University of New Haven in West Haven, Connecticut, is past president of the Mark Twain Circle and the American Humor Studies Association. He earned his doctorate at Duke University in 1970. His books on Mark Twain and American humor include *Mark Twain as a Literary Comedian* (1979), *The Literary Humor of the Urban Northeast, 1830-1890* (1982), *American Humor Magazines and Comic Periodicals* (1987), *Adventures of Huckleberry Finn: American Comic Vision* (1987), and *Mark Twain's Humor: Critical Essays* (1993). He is also the author of *Sister Carrie: Theodore Dreiser's Sociological Tragedy* (1992), and is working on a biographical study entitled *Edison's Daughter*, which examines issues in the life of his grandmother, Madeleine Edison Sloane. He is a member of the Board of Trustees and of the Education Committee of the Mark Twain Memorial in Hartford.

ACKNOWLEDGMENTS

There are a number of people without whom The Oxford Mark Twain would not have happened. I am indebted to Laura Brown, senior vice president and trade publisher, Oxford University Press, for suggesting that I edit an "Oxford Mark Twain," and for being so enthusiastic when I proposed that it take the present form. Her guidance and vision have informed the entire undertaking.

Crucial as well, from the earliest to the final stages, was the help of John Boyer, executive director of the Mark Twain House, who recognized the importance of the project and gave it his wholehearted support.

My father, Milton Fisher, believed in this project from the start and helped nurture it every step of the way, as did my stepmother, Carol Plaine Fisher. Their encouragement and support made it all possible. The memory of my mother, Renée B. Fisher, sustained me throughout.

I am enormously grateful to all the contributors to The Oxford Mark Twain for the effort they put into their essays, and for having been such fine, collegial collaborators. Each came through, just as I'd hoped, with fresh insights and lively prose. It was a privilege and a pleasure to work with them, and I value the friendships that we forged in the process.

In addition to writing his fine afterword, Louis J. Budd provided invaluable advice and support, even going so far as to read each of the essays for accuracy. All of us involved in this project are greatly in his debt. Both his knowledge of Mark Twain's work and his generosity as a colleague are legendary and unsurpassed.

Elizabeth Maguire's commitment to The Oxford Mark Twain during her time as senior editor at Oxford was exemplary. When the project proved to be more ambitious and complicated than any of us had expected, Liz helped make it not only manageable, but fun. Assistant editor Elda Rotor's wonderful help in coordinating all aspects of The Oxford Mark Twain, along with literature editor T. Susan Chang's enthusiastic involvement with the project in its final stages, helped bring it all to fruition.

I am extremely grateful to Joy Johannessen for her astute and sensitive copyediting, and for having been such a pleasure to work with. And I appreciate the conscientiousness and good humor with which Kathy Kuhtz Campbell heroically supervised all aspects of the set's production. Oxford president Edward Barry, vice president and editorial director Helen McInnis, marketing director Amy Roberts, publicity director Susan Rotermund, art director David Tran, trade editorial, design and production manager Adam Bohannon, trade advertising and promotion manager Woody Gilmartin, director of manufacturing Benjamin Lee, and the entire staff at Oxford were as supportive a team as any editor could desire.

The staff of the Mark Twain House provided superb assistance as well. I would like to thank Marianne Curling, curator, Debra Petke, education director, Beverly Zell, curator of photography, Britt Gustafson, assistant director of education, Beth Ann McPherson, assistant curator, and Pam Collins, administrative assistant, for all their generous help, and for allowing us to reproduce books and photographs from the Mark Twain House collection. One could not ask for more congenial or helpful partners in publishing.

G. Thomas Tanselle, vice president of the John Simon Guggenheim Memorial Foundation, and an expert on the history of the book, offered essential advice about how to create as responsible a facsimile edition as possible. I appreciate his very knowledgeable counsel.

I am deeply indebted to Robert H. Hirst, general editor of the Mark Twain Project at The Bancroft Library in Berkeley, for bringing his outstanding knowledge of Twain editions to bear on the selection of the books photographed for the facsimiles, for giving generous assistance all along the way, and for providing his meticulous notes on the text. The set is the richer for his advice. I would also like to express my gratitude to the Mark Twain Project, not only for making texts and photographs from their collection available to us, but also for nurturing Mark Twain studies with a steady infusion of matchless, important publications.

I would like to thank Jeffrey Kaimowitz, curator of the Watkinson Library at Trinity College, Hartford (where the Mark Twain House collection is kept), along with his colleagues Peter Knapp and Alesandra M. Schmidt, for having been instrumental in Robert Hirst's search for first editions that could be safely reproduced. Victor Fischer, Harriet Elinor Smith, and especially Kenneth M. Sanderson, associate editors with the Mark Twain Project, reviewed the note on the text in each volume with cheerful vigilance. Thanks are also due to Mark Twain Project associate editor Michael Frank and administrative assistant Brenda J. Bailey for their help at various stages.

I am grateful to Helen K. Copley for granting permission to publish photographs in the Mark Twain Collection of the James S. Copley Library in La Jolla, California, and to Carol Beales and Ron Vanderhye of the Copley Library for making my research trip to their institution so productive and enjoyable.

Several contributors — David Bradley, Louis J. Budd, Beverly R. David, Robert Hirst, Fred Kaplan, James S. Leonard, Toni Morrison, Lillian S. Robinson, Jeffrey Rubin-Dorsky, Ray Sapirstein, and David L. Smith — were particularly helpful in the early stages of the project, brainstorming about the cast of writers and scholars who could make it work. Others who participated in that process were John Boyer, James Cox, Robert Crunden, Joel Dinerstein, William Goetzmann, Calvin and Maria Johnson, Jim Magnuson, Arnold Rampersad, Siva Vaidhyanathan, Steve and Louise Weinberg, and Richard Yarborough.

Kevin Bochynski, famous among Twain scholars as an "angel" who is gifted at finding methods of making their research run more smoothly, was helpful in more ways than I can count. He did an outstanding job in his official capacity as production consultant to The Oxford Mark Twain, supervising the photography of the facsimiles. I am also grateful to him for having put me in touch via e-mail with Kent Rasmussen, author of the magisterial *Mark Twain A to Z*, who was tremendously helpful as the project proceeded, sharing insights on obscure illustrators and other points, and generously being "on call" for all sorts of unforeseen contingencies.

I am indebted to Siva Vaidhyanathan of the American Studies Program of the University of Texas at Austin for having been such a superb research assistant. It would be hard to imagine The Oxford Mark Twain without the benefit of his insights and energy. A fine scholar and writer in his own right, he was crucial to making this project happen.

Georgia Barnhill, the Andrew W. Mellon Curator of Graphic Arts at the American Antiquarian Society in Worcester, Massachusetts, Tom Staley, director of the Harry Ransom Humanities Research Center at the University of Texas at Austin, and Joan Grant, director of collection services at the Elmer Holmes Bobst Library of New York University, granted us access to their collections and assisted us in the reproduction of several volumes of The Oxford Mark Twain. I would also like to thank Kenneth Craven, Sally Leach, and Richard Oram of the Harry Ransom Humanities Research Center for their help in making HRC materials available, and Jay and John Crowley, of Jay's Publishers Services in Rockland, Massachusetts, for their efforts to photograph the books carefully and attentively.

I would like to express my gratitude for the grant I was awarded by the University Research Institute of the University of Texas at Austin to defray some of the costs of researching The Oxford Mark Twain. I am also grateful to American Studies director Robert Abzug and the University of Texas for the computer that facilitated my work on this project (and to UT systems analyst Steve Alemán, who tried his best to repair the damage when it crashed). Thanks also to American Studies administrative assistant Janice Bradley and graduate coordinator Melanie Livingston for their always generous and thoughtful help.

The Oxford Mark Twain would not have happened without the unstinting, wholehearted support of my husband, Jim Fishkin, who went way beyond the proverbial call of duty more times than I'm sure he cares to remember as he shared me unselfishly with that other man in my life, Mark Twain. I am also grateful to my family — to my sons Joey and Bobby, who cheered me on all along the way, as did Fannie Fishkin, David Fishkin, Gennie Gordon, Mildred Hope Witkin, and Leonard, Gillis, and Moss

Plaine — and to honorary family member Margaret Osborne, who did the same.

My greatest debt is to the man who set all this in motion. Only a figure as rich and complicated as Mark Twain could have sustained such energy and interest on the part of so many people for so long. Never boring, never dull, Mark Twain repays our attention again and again and again. It is a privilege to be able to honor his memory with The Oxford Mark Twain.

Shelley Fisher Fishkin
Austin, Texas
April 1996